THE CONCISE DICTIONARY OF
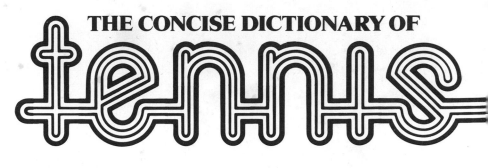
tennis

MARTIN HEDGES

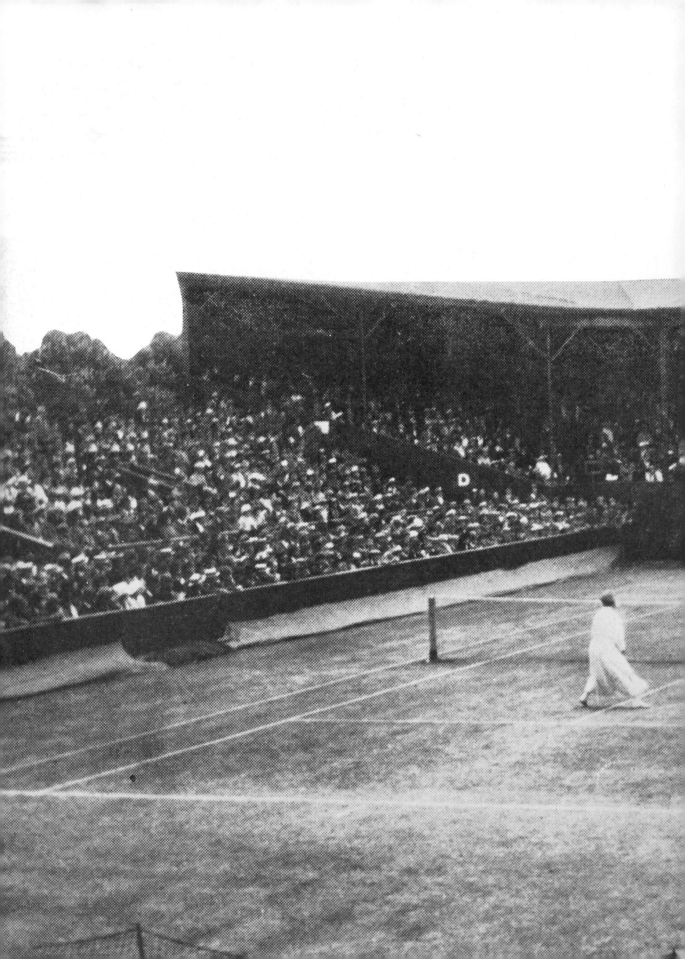

THE CONCISE DICTIONARY OF

tennis

MARTIN HEDGES

MAYFLOWER BOOKS
MAYFLOWER BOOKS INC
575 Lexington Avenue
New York NY10022
A Bison Book

First published 1978 by
Mayflower Books Inc
575 Lexington Avenue
New York NY 10022

Copyright © 1978 by Bison Books, London

Printed in Hong Kong
ISBN 0-86124-012X

contents

players and venues

ADAMSON, Nelly *see* **Landry Mrs N**

AKHURST, Daphne (Mrs R Cozens), Australia Born April 1903, Ashfield, NSW, died January 1933. Her record of five Australian women's singles titles gained in 1925–6, 1928–30, was not beaten until Nancye Bolton achieved her sixth title in 1951. (Later Margaret Smith Court gained 11 titles.) She also gained the Australian women's doubles title four times and the mixed doubles twice yet she never achieved similar success at Wimbledon.

Australian women's singles won 1925 (beat Miss E F Boyd, 1-6, 8-6, 6-4), 1926 (beat Miss Boyd 6-1, 6-3), 1928 (beat Miss Boyd, 7-5, 6-2), 1929 (beat Miss L Bickerton, 6-1, 5-7, 6-2), 1930 (beat Mrs S Harper, 10-8, 2-6, 7-5).

Australian women's doubles won 1924 with Miss S Lance (beat Mrs P O'Hara Wood/Miss K Le Messurier, 7-5, 6-2), 1925 with Mrs S Harper (beat Miss Boyd/Miss Le Messurier, 6-4, 6-3), r/u 1926 with Miss M Cox (Mrs O'Hara Wood/Miss L M Bickerton won, 6-3, 6-3), won 1928 with Miss Boyd (beat Miss Le Messurier/Miss D Weston, 6-3, 6-1), 1929 with Miss Bickerton (beat Mrs O'Hara Wood/Mrs Harper, 6-2, 3-6, 6-2).

Australian mixed doubles won 1924 (beat G Hone/Miss Boyd, 6-3, 6-4), 1925 (beat R Schlesinger/Mrs Harper, 6-4, 6-4), r/u 1926 (J Hawkes/Miss Boyd won, 6-2, 6-4), all with J Willard.

Wimbledon mixed doubles r/u 1928 with J H Crawford (P D B Spence/Miss E Ryan won, 7-5, 6-4).

Albert Hall, London
Though world-renowned as a concert hall, the circular Royal Albert Hall has also been used for indoor tennis since 1970. In that year the Rothmans' international tournament was first held there after the floor had been raised by ten feet (three metres) and the playing area covered with a synthetic compound. With excellent viewing facilities, the hall was an instant success as a tennis venue. The finals of the Dewar Cup were also staged there in the autumn of 1970 and are still held there.

Below: The Rothmans' International Tournament was held at the Royal Albert Hall between 1970 and 1973 before it became too large. The preliminary matches are now played at the Deeside Leisure Centre in North Wales.
Preceding page: Australia's Tony Roche has been plagued by back injuries in the past few years.

ALEXANDER, Frederick, USA

Born August 1880, died 1969. The first American to win the Australian singles in 1908, beating A W Dunlop. He also won the doubles with Dunlop in the same year. His greatest successes came as a doubles player in his native America, where he won the men's doubles five times (1907–10, 1917) and was four times runner-up.

US men's singles r/u 1908 (beat B C Wright, 6-3, 6-3, 6-3).

US men's doubles r/u 1905 with H H Hackett (H Ward/Wright won, 6-3, 6-1, 6-2), r/u 1906 (Ward/Wright won, 6-3, 3-6, 6-3, 6-3), won 1907–10, r/u 1911 (R D Little/G F Touchard won, 7-5, 13-15, 6-2, 6-4), all with Hackett, won 1917 with H A Throckmorton (beat H Johnson/I C Wright, 11-9, 6-4, 6-4), r/u 1918 with I C Wright (W Tilden/V Richards won, 6-3, 6-4, 3-6, 2-6, 6-2).

US mixed doubles r/u 1918 with Miss M Bjurstedt (I C Wright/Mrs G W Wightman won, 6-2, 6-4).

ALEXANDER, John, Australia

Born July 1951, Sydney. In 1968 he played in the Davis Cup Challenge Round against the United States at age 17 years 5 months – believed to be the youngest player to reach this stage of the Davis Cup. (Australia lost 4-1 and Alexander lost his doubles with R Ruffles to R Lutz and S Smith, 6-4, 6-4, 6-2). The same year he won the Wimbledon boys' junior invitation event. He joined World Professional Tennis (WCT) in 1970 and was seen as one of its most promising recruits. He reached the WCT singles finals in 1973–5, the doubles final with Phil Dent in 1974 and finished sixth in WCT doubles in 1976. He married the daughter of a Canadian judge in 1973. In 1977 he was r/u with Phil Dent in both the Australian and Wimbledon doubles.

Australia men's doubles r/u 1970 (R Lutz/ S Smith won, 8-6, 6-3, 6-4) and 1973 (J Newcombe/M Anderson won, 6-3, 6-4, 7-6), won 1975 (beat A Stone/R Carmichael, 6-3, 7-6),

Right: John G Alexander is one of the top Australian players on today's circuit.

r/u 1977–8 (A Stone/R Ruffels won, 7-6, 7-6), all with Dent.

West German doubles won 1971 with A Gimeno (beat R Crealy/A Stone, 6-4, 7-5, 7-9, 6-4).

French doubles r/u 1975 with Dent (R Ramirez/B Gottfried won, 6-4, 2-6, 6-2, 6-4).

Wimbledon doubles r/u 1977 with Dent (R Case/G Masters won, 6-3, 6-4, 3-6, 8-9, 6-4).

All England Club

Founded in July 1868, before the modern game of tennis had even been invented, the All England Croquet Club did not secure a ground until the following year, when four acres were leased in Worple Road, Wimbledon. In 1872 Major Harry Gem, Clerk to Birmingham Magistrates, founded the Leamington Lawn Tennis Club after trying out his version of the game on the lawns of the home of J B Perera in Edgbaston, Birmingham. Then in 1874, Major Walter Clopton Wingfield applied to patent 'A new and improved portable court for playing the ancient game of tennis', which he proceeded to market as 'Sphairistiké'. By the time the patent application lapsed in March 1877 Wingfield had succeeded in selling the game across the country and it was rapidly replacing croquet as the popular game of the middle classes. Indeed the All England Croquet Club had noted the trend and in 1875 admitted tennis players and set aside one ground for tennis and badminton. Four more courts – in those days they were hour-glass shaped – were brought into use the following year and in

April 1877 a change of name to the All England Croquet and Lawn Tennis Club was approved.

Only three months later the first lawn tennis meeting, open to all amateurs was held. The entrance fee was one guinea and two prizes were offered – 'one gold championship prize to the winner, one silver to the second player'. The announcement of this first championship was inserted in *The Field* sporting magazine and was signed by the club's tennis sub-committee secretary, Henry Jones, who was to play an outstanding role in regularising the playing and rules of lawn tennis and who acted as referee during that first tournament. There were 22 entrants for the event, which was won by Spencer Gore, a strong volleyer, who beat Julian Marshall, a base liner, 6-1, 6-2, 6-4. From 1878 until 1921 the previous year's champion only defended his title in the Challenge Round, playing against the winner of the All-Comers rounds.

The first championship made a profit of £500 for the All England Club, which imposed a spectators' entry fee of 1s (5p). The fee remained unchanged until 1880, when it was raised to 2s 6d (12½p). In the intervening years the club saw an increase in entrants, spectators and profits: in 1878 there were 34 entrants and the final, in which Gore was beaten in the Challenge Round 7-5, 6-1, 9-7, by Frank Hadow, was watched by 700 people. In 1879 there were 44 contestants in the men's singles (women's singles and mixed doubles were introduced in the Irish championships in Dublin that year but

Below: Enthusiasts wait at the gates at Worple Road to enter Wimbledon in 1913.

not at Wimbledon) and the final was watched by 1100 spectators. The club made £116 and the title was taken by the Rev John Thorneycroft Hartley, who beat the pseudonymous 'St Leger' (in fact Vere Thomas St Leger Goold) 6-2, 6-4, 6-2 in the final and had a walkover in the Challenge Round. In 1880 (after the admission fee had been increased) the profit was £306 14s (£306.70), the entries numbered 60 – the highest until 1904 – and all 12 courts at Worple Road were used during the meeting. The championship was again won by Hartley who, watched by 1300 people, beat Herbert Lawford 6-3, 6-2, 2-6, 6-3.

The club's name was changed in 1882 to the All England Lawn Tennis and Croquet Club. In 1884 the All England Club introduced women's singles and men's doubles events to the programme and Wimbledon saw its first overseas entrants, R Sears and J Dwight of America. Women's doubles were allowed as a non-championship event from 1899 (becoming 'full championship' in 1913) and mixed doubles did not appear on the Wimbledon programme until 1900. Until 1885 byes had been distributed in the draw through all rounds but in this year the Bagnall-Wild system (still used today) was introduced, restricting all byes to the first round.

During the 1880s the All England Club's early supremacy in the game as its pioneer and legislative body (a duty it had carried out in consultation first with the Marylebone Cricket Club and later with a conference of clubs) was suffering a temporary decline; entries too had dropped to below 30 and in fact did not reach 31 until 1896. In 1895 the club had its first and only loss on the Wimbledon championships – £33. In 1888 the Lawn Tennis Association was inaugurated with William Renshaw, of the famous Wimbledon Renshaw twins, as its first president. Between 1881 and 1889 Willie Renshaw won the Wimbledon Challenge Round seven times and Ernest Renshaw once, though the latter also won the All-Comers three times. They were followed by the Baddeley twins, Wilfred and Herbert, who dominated from 1891 to 1896 and then by the Doherty brothers, Reggie and Laurie. It was these two, known respectively as 'Big Do' and 'Little Do', who not only revived the flagging interest in the Wimbledon events at Worple Road over which they ruled from 1897 to 1906, but also could be said to have attracted so much interest to the game that the All England Club had eventually to find a new home, which it did at Church Road, Wimbledon. The move was made in 1922, the year in which the Challenge Round was abolished and holders played through.

Improvements were made at Worple Road before World War I, when it became evident that the game's popularity was assured. The stands were enlarged to take 3200 spectators instead of 2000 but demand for seats for the 1919 championships was such that a ballot had to be held. This same year applications for entry in the men's singles reached exactly the agreed limit of 128 set by the club and the following year selection was introduced. The decision to move to Church Road was also taken in 1919; Stanley Peach was commissioned to design the new club and in a joint venture by the All England Club and the LTA the cost of £140,000 was raised by issuing £50 debenture shares which secured Centre Court seats for their purchasers.

In 1921 a poll by the club among players

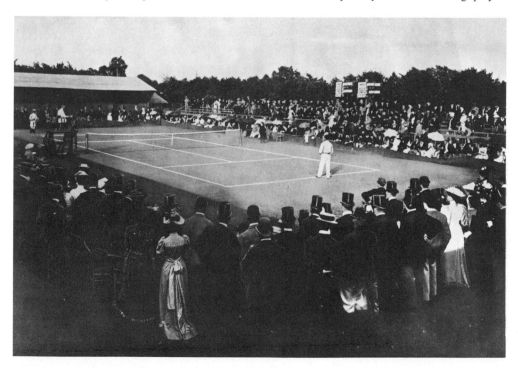

Right: The 1892 All-Comers' men's singles final at Wimbledon between E W Lewis and J Pim.

resulted in 91 voting for the 'play through' system for the championships and only 27 for the retention of the Challenge Round. When the All England Club moved to Church Road next year the Challenge Round was dropped. The new club retained the traditional Centre Court with a capacity of around 10,000. Not all went smoothly in the move. The new concrete buildings, not then covered by today's prolific greenery, seemed to many to lack the friendliness of the old Worple Road 'home' and the soft Cumberland turf chosen for the Centre Court proved unequal to the wear and tear of a game which was already considerably faster than in its early days. In addition bad weather stretched the championships to the middle of the third week.

From 1913, when the ILTF was formed, until 1923, the Wimbledon meeting had borne the somewhat ponderous title of 'The Championships of the World on Grass Courts'. However when the United States joined the international governing body it was sensitive to the standing of America's own national championships and their price for joining was the abandonment by the club of that title. No major changes took place in the All England Club for more than a decade, while their championships continued to attract the cream of the world's players and increasing numbers of spectators. In 1932, 24,000 people attended on the first Thursday, a record which was broken the next year with 30,000.

The All England Club and the LTA formalised their joint agreement over control of the championships in 1934. Twelve of the 18 members of the championships committee were appointed by the club, which also filled the posts of chairman and secretary. The LTA has the greater financial interest since to it belongs the surplus from the championships. The grounds and buildings are jointly owned by the club and LTA through the All England Ground Company Ltd. During World War II the club was virtually dormant, the committee being concerned with the care and maintenance of the Church Road ground and premises. Bombs caused damage in October 1941, when a corner of the competitors' stand on the Centre Court was hit. Repairs could not be made until 1947. Lt Col Duncan Macaulay was appointed club secretary in 1946 and the Committee of Management met for the first time after the war on 18 January 1946 under the chairmanship of Group Captain Sir Louis Greig. The meeting decided to revive the Wimbledon championships that year and though it was a time of acute shortage of all kinds there was no lack of applicants for seats and a ballot for tickets, now usual, had to be held. The quality of competitors was also well up to standard. Wimbledon was reborn.

The next major change involving the championships and the All England Club came in 1968 when, after more than a decade of political wrangling and lobbying, open lawn tennis came to Wimbledon and many of the post-war amateur champions who had since turned professional were again able to play at Church Road. For years the status of 'amateur' had been questionable when applied to many leading players and the term 'shamateur' grew in credence. In October 1959 came the All England Club's first attempt to bring about reforms which would end the anomalous situation and restore the status of the championships from which so many leading players who turned

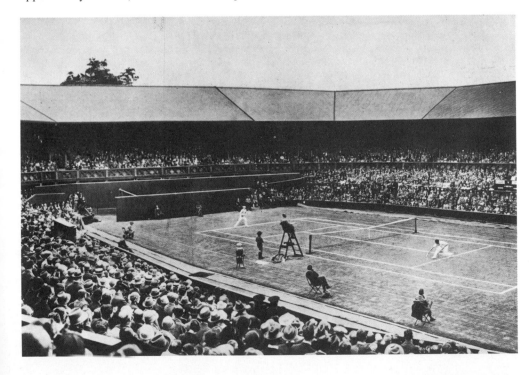

Left: Wimbledon's centre court in 1925 as R Lacoste (far side) defeats J Borotra in the men's singles final.

Right: The layout of the courts at the grounds of the All England Club at Church Road, Wimbledon.

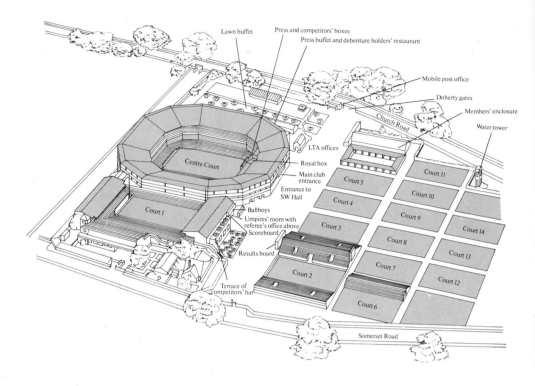

professional were barred. A special general meeting of the club called on the LTA to recommend the ILTF to allow the Wimbledon championships to be open to all players. However, at the next meeting of the ILTF in July 1960 the proposal failed by five votes, despite the support of Australia, France and the USA. Pressure by the club was maintained with Herman David, its chairman, as a leading proponent of open tennis. Eventually in 1967 the LTA rebelled against the ILTF and gave permission to the Committee of Management for the 1968 championships to be open. Prize money at the first open Wimbledon was £26,150. Today it is over £155,000. The ILFT capitulated in March 1968 and changed its rules to allow each nation to choose its own legislation on admission of amateurs and professionals. Even before that first open meeting the All England Club broke from its history of amateurism by staging the Wimbledon world professional lawn tennis championships in August 1967. Profits from Wimbledon are still passed to the LTA after the club has covered expenses (including prize money). The club has 16 grass courts and ten hard courts.

Barring the occasions when bad weather forces the postponement of matches, the championships last two weeks. For the rest of the year the All England Club is an ordinary tennis club, though its staff and committee spend a large part of their time planning the next year's championships. The club has a membership of 375, excluding honorary members. There are also 90 temporary members elected annually. Debenture holders are allowed two daily free Centre court seats during the Championships.

ALLERDICE, Mrs E *see* **Hansell, Ellen**

ALVAREZ, Lili de (Comtesse de la Valdene), Spain
Born May 1905, in Rome. Adored by the crowds at Wimbledon, where she seemed about to gain the women's title in the finals of 1926, 1927 and 1928, Miss de Alvarez was on each occasion let down by her greatest weakness – a tendency to commit serious errors at vital moments. Even so, she had a capacity to drive volley and half volley which had not been seen in a woman player at Wimbledon before. Despite her mercurial brilliance and skill she won only one major international title – the French women's doubles of 1929 with Miss Kea Bouman.

Wimbledon women's single r/u 1926 (Mrs L A Godfree won, 6-2, 4-6, 6-3), r/u 1927 (Miss H N Wills won, 6-2, 6-4), r/u 1928 (Miss Wills won, 6-2, 6-3).

French women's doubles won in 1929 with Miss Bouman (beat Miss E L Heine/Mrs Neave, 7-5, 6-3); French mixed doubles r/u 1927 with W Tilden (J Borotra/Mrs M Bordes won, 6-4, 2-6, 6-2).

AMAYA, Victor, USA
Born July 1954, Holland, Michigan. A good clay court player, this left-hander makes good use of his height (6 ft 5½ in, 1.96 metres). He was a member of the USA's BP under-21 Cup team which lost the 1974 final to Britain and a member of the team which won the cup in 1975, defeating France. In the same year he beat J Fassbender in US clay court championships. Won US Amateur grass court championship doubles in 1973.

American Tennis Association
Founded in 1916 as the governing body for black American players, the association held its first men's and women's singles championships in 1917, when Tally Holmes won the men's and Lucy Stowe the women's titles. Doubles and events for juniors and veterans were added later. Althea Gibson (former US and Wimbledon women's champion) and Arthur Ashe (US and Wimbledon men's champion) are among previous association title holders.

AMRITRAJ, Anand, India
Born March 1952, Madras. Eldest of tennis-playing trio which includes his brothers, Vijay and Ashok. He and Vijay have made a good doubles pair, though not always fulfilling their potential. In 1974 they took India to the Davis Cup final against South Africa but the Indian team was instructed to withdraw in protest against the other country's race policies. In 1975 they were runners-up in WCT tournaments at Toronto, Washington and Atlanta and in 1976 the pair won WCT Memphis doubles and reached s/f of Wimbledon.

Anand and Ilie Năstase, r/u Hong Kong doubles; Anand and Corrado Barazzutti, r/u Manila doubles.

AMRITRAJ, Vijay, India
Born December 1953, Madras. An excellent and attractive touch player with charming court manners which have won him many friends. He reached the q/f of the US Open, Forest Hills, 1973–4 and q/f of Wimbledon in 1973. Ranked No 1 in India in 1975 and in 1976 finished eighth in WCT doubles with his brother Anand. He won the 1977 India GP (beat T Moor, 7-6, 6-4).

ANDERSON, James Outram, Australia
Born September 1895, Enfield, NSW, died December 1973. One of the outstanding Australian players of the early 1920s, he was three times Australian men's singles champion (1922, 1924–5) and won the Wimbledon doubles with R Lycett in 1922, a year of male Australian dominance. He also won the Australian doubles in 1924 with Norman Brookes. With a powerful forehand and firm, defensive backhand, the tall and lean Anderson was the only Australian player to beat the famous American, W M 'Little Bill' Johnston. His victory of 4-6, 6-2, 2-6, 7-5, 6-2 was in the first match of the Challenge Round between the US and Australia at Forest Hills in 1923 and it gave Australia the only win of the match.

Australian men's singles won 1922 (beat G Patterson, 6-0, 3-6, 3-6, 6-3, 6-2), won 1924 (beat R Schlesinger, 6-3, 6-4, 3-6, 5-7, 6-3), won 1925 (beat Patterson, 11-9, 2-6, 6-2, 6-3).

Australian men's doubles won 1924 with N Brookes (beat Patterson/P O'Hara Wood, 6-2, 6-4, 6-3), r/u 1925 with F Kalms (Patterson/O'Hara Wood won, 6-4, 8-6, 7-5), r/u 1926 with

Left: Anand Amritraj, the eldest of the three tennis-playing brothers, has often teamed up with his brother Vijay with some success.

Left: Vijay Amritraj is perhaps the best known and popular of the Amritraj brothers. He is ranked No 1 in India.

O'Hara Wood (Patterson/J Hawkes won, 6-1, 6-4, 6-2).

Wimbledon doubles won 1922 with Lycett (beat Patterson/O'Hara Wood, 3-6, 7-9, 6-4, 6-3, 11-9).

ANDERSON, Malcolm, Australia

Born March 1935, Rockhampton, Queensland. Winner of the US singles title in 1957, 'Mal' Anderson's playing career continued with good results in 1974 and he is justly rated among the most consistent of Australian players even though his successes have been overshadowed by those of Ken Rosewall, Roy Emerson, Lew Hoad, Neale Fraser and Ashley Cooper. He turned professional in 1959 and joined WCT as a contract professional in 1968–69. Married Roy Emerson's sister, Daphne.

Australian men's singles r/u 1958 (Cooper won, 7-5, 6-3, 6-4), r/u 1972 (Rosewall won, 7-6, 6-3, 7-5); men's doubles r/u 1957 with Cooper (Hoad/Fraser won, 6-3, 8-6, 6-1), won 1973 with J Newcombe (beat J Alexander/P Dent, 6-3, 6-4, 7-6). Australian Davis Cup team 1954, 1957–8, 1972–3.

US men's singles won 1957 (beat A Cooper, 10-8, 7-5, 6-4), r/u 1958 (Cooper won, 6-2, 3-6, 4-6, 10-8, 8-6).

ANDREWS, John, USA

Born May 1952, Fullerton, California. A promising young player who rose rapidly in US rankings, from 47 in 1975 to 22 in 1976. In 1975 he reached q/f of French Open singles; in 1976 reached q/f of Barcelona ATP and won Majorca

ATP doubles with C Dibley.

ANLIOT, Helena, Sweden

Born September 1956, Falun, near Stockholm. Swedish junior champion in 1974, when she also won Australian Hard Courts and played mixed doubles with Björn Borg at Wimbledon. Qualified for Wimbledon 1974 women's singles but lost in first round. She won the Swedish 1975 national singles and mixed doubles championships, the latter with Kjell Johansson. Beaten 6-3, 6-2 by Renata Tomanova in Swedish Open women's singles, 1976, she won Austrian Open doubles with Mimmi Wikstedt.

ANTHONY, Julie, USA

Born January 1948, Santa Monica, California. A PhD graduate in clinical psychology, she attracted attention as an up-and-coming young player when she was runner-up in the US Under-18s in 1965, beating Rosie Casals on the way to the final, and again in 1969 when, on her first trip to Europe, she beat Françoise Durr 6-4 final set at Wimbledon. In 1975 she had doubles wins with Olga Morozova against Miss Casals and Billie Jean King, Evonne Cawley and Peggy Michel, and defeated Margaret Court to win Canadian Open singles. In 1976 she became a TV tennis commentator for US networks, but continued to play a reduced circuit.

ARAUJO, Beatriz, Argentina

Born 1955. Unbeaten in South American team championships, she has been regarded as possibly the best girl player in South America next

Right: Australian Malcolm Anderson won his last major event in 1973 when he teamed up with John Newcombe to win the Australian men's doubles. He was also part of the Australian Davis Cup team of that year.

to Maria Bueno. She won the South American Open singles in 1975, beating Kristien Shaw, and was runner-up in 1976. Has yet to fulfil potential.

ARTH, Jeanne Marie, USA

Born July 1935, St Paul, Minnesota. A school teacher from Minnesota, Miss Arth achieved rapid but brief fame in tennis when she won the US championship doubles in 1958 and 1959 with Miss Darlene Hard and with the same partner won the Wimbledon doubles in 1959. She was a member of the winning US Wightman Cup team in 1959, but then left the international tennis scene.

US championship women's doubles won 1958 (beat Miss A Gibson/Miss M Bueno, 2-6, 6-3, 6-4), won 1959 (beat Miss Bueno/Miss S Moore, 6-2, 6-3).

Wimbledon doubles won 1959 (beat Miss J Fleitz/Miss C Truman, 2-6, 6-2, 6-3), all with Miss Hard.

ASBÓTH, Jozsef, Hungary

Born September 1927, Szombathely. Considered his country's outstanding international player, Asbóth was at his best on clay courts. A player of great finesse, he won the French championships in 1947 and reached the Wimbledon men's

Left: Swedish champion Helena Anliot won the 1975 Swedish national singles as well as many other championships.
Below: Julie Anthony, winner of many singles and doubles championships, is now a TV tennis commentator for US television.

semi-finals in 1948. He was a member of the Hungarian Davis Cup team in 1938–9, 1948–9, 1952–5 and 1957 and turned professional in 1958.

French men's singles won 1947 (beat E W Sturgess, 8-6, 7-5, 6-4).

ASHE, Arthur Robert, USA

Born July 1943, Richmond, Virginia. The son of a policeman, Ashe's career has been a succession of triumph and disaster, of unpredictability and determination and a series of notable 'firsts'. He was the first black American to play in the US Davis Cup team (1963), the first to be US Open champion (1968), the first to be president of the Association of Tennis Professionals (ATP), and the first black American male to win the Wimbledon title when, in 1975, aged 32, he beat the fancied Jimmy Connors 6-1, 6-1, 5-7, 6-4.

Denied an entry visa to South Africa in 1970 because of that country's policy on blacks in sport, he defeated apartheid in 1973 when he was South African men's doubles winner with Tom Okker and also runner-up for the singles title. In 1970 he won the longest singles match ever played in the Davis Cup when he was representing the US in the Challenge Round against West Germany at Cleveland Heights, Ohio. In the fifth rubber he beat C Kuhnke after 84 games, 6-8, 10-12, 9-7, 13-11, 6-4. His first Davis Cup appearance in 1963 was followed by regular team inclusion from 1965 to 1970, during which he had 25 wins and only four defeats in 15 rubbers. Ashe, who married early in 1977, has become increasingly involved in the administrative side of the game as far as securing better terms and conditions for professional circuit players is concerned.

Above: Hungarian born, Jozsef Asbóth turned professional in 1958.

Right: Arthur Ashe is one of the most successful of American tennis players. In recent years he has begun to become involved in the administration of the game although he was still ranked No 3 in the US for 1977.

Ashe's playing technique has been one of brain rather than brawn and his 1975 Wimbledon triumph was, perhaps, the best illustration of this. In his earlier playing days he used his mercurial abilities combined with strategy but by the time he won Wimbledon, within a few days of his 32nd birthday, he was able to make intelligent play the dominant factor against the aggression of Connors. Rather than attempting to match the pace and power of the younger man, shot for shot, he deliberately slowed down, backed off and used wide angled shots to reduce the chance of 'cannon-ball' returns by Connors.

Despite his brilliance, unpredictability has not infrequently been his downfall, as it was when he had been a popular Wimbledon semi-finalist in 1968 and 1969, only to disappoint his supporters, and again in 1972 when he seemed poised to win his second US Open. With a lead of two sets to one and 4-2 in the fourth against Năstase he lost that set 6-4 and the fifth 6-3.

US Open singles won 1968 (beat T Okker, 14-12, 5-7, 6-3, 3-6, 6-3), r/u 1972 (Năstase won, 3-6, 6-3, 6-7, 6-4, 6-3); men's doubles r/u 1968 with A Gimeno (R Lutz/S Smith won, 11-9, 6-1, 7-5).

WCT Finals r/u 1973, won 1974; US hard courts won 1963; US clay courts won 1967; US amateur championships won 1968.

Australian men's singles r/u 1966 (R Emerson won, 6-4, 6-8, 6-2, 6-3), r/u 1967 (Emerson won, 6-4, 6-1, 6-4), won 1970 (beat R Crealy, 6-4, 9-7, 6-2), r/u 1971 (K Rosewall won, 6-1, 7-5, 6-3).

French men's doubles r/u 1970 with C Pasarell (Năstase/I Tiriac won, 6-2, 6-4, 6-3), won 1971 with M Riessen (beat T Gorman/S Smith, 6-8, 4-6, 6-3, 6 4, 11-9).

Wimbledon men's singles won 1975 (beat Connors, 6-1, 6-1, 5-7, 6-4); men's doubles r/u 1971 with R Ralston (Emerson/R Laver won, 4-6, 9-7, 6-8, 6-4, 6-4).

Joined WCT in 1971, singles champion, Dallas, 1975. Ranked world No 1 in 1976, won first five tournaments and was heading WCT points table when heel injury hampered him for rest of season. Ranked No 3 in US for 1977.

Association of Tennis Professionals

The association was formed in 1972 to watch over the interests of professionals and regularise matters such as prize money, conditions, standards of behaviour, tournament qualifications and the welfare of players. It had over 60 founder members and Jack Kramer, the great American player-turned-promoter, was appointed director and Cliff Drysdale, of South Africa, president. Most leading tennis internationals were members. 1973 saw the withdrawal of almost every top male player from Wimbledon when the ATP supported the Yugoslavian Nikki Pilić in a protest against his suspension for failing to represent his country in a Davis Cup tie. The suspension by the Yugoslavian Federation was for nine months; this was reduced to one month by the ILTF but the ATP still claimed this was unjust and 79 members withdrew their Wimbledon entries. (Three who did not were Jan Kodeš of Czechoslovakia, who was not an ATP member, and Ilie Năstase of Rumania and Roger Taylor of Britain, who were members.) Since its foundation the ATP has grown in strength and influence and has brought about an improvement in the running of many tournaments. One of its successes was to ensure that professionals would be eligible for the Davis Cup. *See also* **Women's International Lawn Tennis Federation.**

ATKINSON, Juliette P, USA

Three times winner of the US women's singles title, Juliette Atkinson was one of the pioneers of women's tennis in America and a leading doubles player. She won the women's singles title in 1895, 1897, 1898 and was runner up 1896 and 1899. She won the women's doubles championship seven times, twice with Helen Helwig (1894–5), once with Elisabeth Moore (1896), twice with her sister Kathleen (1897–8), twice with Myrtle McAteer (1899, 1901) and once with Marion Jones (1902). She also won the mixed doubles three times (1894–6) with E P Fischer.

AUSSEM, Cilly, (Contessa F M Della Corta Brae), Germany

Born January 1909, Cologne, died March 1963, Genoa, Italy. A graceful and charming player, Cilly Aussem was lacking in the physical strength necessary to compete for many years in the tough international field. In 1931, having already won the French women's title, she was top seed at Wimbledon and took part in the all-German final with Hilda Krahwinkel to become the only German to win the women's championship at Wimbledon. Appendicitis prevented her from defending her title in 1932 but she succeeded in reaching the quarter finals in 1934 on her last Wimbledon appearance. In 1936 the fragile player, then aged 27, married an Italian Count and retired from tennis. During her brief playing career she had also won the German singles three times and the mixed doubles twice.

German singles won 1927, 1930, 1931; mixed doubles won 1928, 1935.

French women's singles won 1931 (beat Miss B Nuthall, 8-6, 6-1); women's doubles r/u 1931 with Miss E Ryan (Mrs E Whittingstall/Miss B Nuthall won, 9-7, 6-2); mixed doubles won 1930 with W T Tilden (beat H Cochet/Mrs Whittingstall, 6-4, 6-4).

Wimbledon women's singles won 1931 (beat Miss H Krahwinkel, 6-2, 7-5).

AUSTIN, Henry Wilfred (Bunny), GB

Born August 1906. Twice Wimbledon runner-up (1932 and 1938), three times a semi-finalist and ten times a quarter finalist, Austin was one of Britain's most consistent players of the 1930s. He and Fred Perry formed the backbone of Britain's run of Davis Cup successes from 1933 to 1936. In 1937 Austin was Britain's only

pionship tournament was held in 1880 at Melbourne. The first state championship was staged by the Sydney Lawn Tennis Club, New South Wales, in 1885. The LTA of Australasia was formed in 1904 on a resolution by the NSW Lawn Tennis Association that Australia and New Zealand should combine as one tennis 'nation'. The first singles championship of the new association was held in the following year. Australasia was a founder member of the ILTF in 1913.

The Wimbledon men's singles have been won by 20 Australians since 1905, when N E Brookes became the first non-British champion. R G (Rod) Laver gained the men's singles four times, J D Newcombe and N E Brookes three, L A Hoad, G L Patterson and R S Emerson twice each. The men's strongest period was between 1956 and 1971 when the Wimbledon title went to Australia 13 times. Mrs B M Smith (Miss Margaret Court) won the Wimbledon women's singles three times and the Australian women's singles on 11 occasions. Australasia first competed in the Davis Cup in 1905 and first won in 1907, followed by wins in 1908, 1909, 1911, 1914 and 1919. Since 1939 Australia on its own has won the cup on 17 occasions. (The Australasian LTA changed its name to the LTA of Australia in 1926, New Zealand's own LTA having been recognised by the ILTF in 1923.)

Among other Australian all-time greats are Jack Crawford whose Wimbledon victory over Ellsworth Vines in 1933 was regarded as 'perfect tennis'; John Bromwich and Adrian Quist who together won the Australian men's doubles on eight occasions from 1938 to 1950, Quist also winning – partnered by Don Turnbull – in 1936 and 1937. Tony Roche won the Australian doubles on four occasions with Newcombe (1965, 1967, 1971, 1976); Gerald Patterson won four times (three times with J B Hawkes and once with James Anderson), Lew Hoad won three times (twice with Fraser and once with Rosewall). First president of the Australian LTA was Norman E Brookes, who was knighted in 1939. The first Australian to win the US National singles title was Frank Sedgman in 1951 and again in 1952. Since then Neale Fraser, Ken Rosewall, Roy Emerson, Rod Laver and John Newcombe have each won that title twice. Laver (1969) Rosewall (1970) and Newcombe (1973) have also each won the US Open men's singles once and Miss Court won the US Open women's singles three times (1969–70, 1973). Though Australia had some of its finest players during the 1950s and 1960s, interest in tennis actually declined both in playing and watching, though the Davis Cup continued to draw good spectator support.

Australian women have also been prominent in the game in their own country and internationally. The Federation Cup, started in 1963 and first held in Australia in 1965, has been won by Australian women's teams on seven occasions (1964–5, 1968, 1970–1, 1973–4). Leading women

winner in the Challenge Round against the US, beating Frank Parker 6-3, 6-2, 7-5 before losing to the great Donald Budge 8-6, 3-6, 6-4, 6-3.

'Bunny' Austin's style was in fact a complete contrast to the fiery approach of Perry. He was an immaculate stroke player with a gentle touch and beautifully symmetrical ground strokes, but his overhead shots and his service were almost totally lacking in power. His first challenge at Wimbledon was in 1926 and his last in 1939. In the 1932 final against the tremendously powerful American, Ellsworth Vines, Austin was at the receiving end of one of the most extraordinary serves ever seen – or not seen – at Wimbledon. With Vines leading two sets to love and preparing to serve at 5-0, 40-15 in the third, he was seen to throw the ball in the air and swing at it. There was a cloud of dust by Austin's service line and behind him the noise of ball hitting canvas backcloth. The service had been so fast that the ball disappeared in flight, leaving Austin no chance even to shape a return shot. Contemporary writers described it as the fastest service ever hit and it gave Vines the championship.

Wimbledon men's singles r/u 1932 (Vines won, 6-4, 6-2, 6-0), r/u 1938 (Budge won, 6-1, 6-0, 6-3); mixed doubles r/u 1934 with Mrs D C Shepherd-Barron (R Miki/Miss D Round won, 3-6, 6-4, 6-0). British Davis Cup team 1929–37.

US mixed doubles r/u 1929 with Mrs B Covell (G Lott/Miss B Nuthall won, 6-3, 6-3).

French men's singles r/u 1937 (H Henkel won, 6-1, 6-4, 6-3); mixed doubles r/u 1931 with Mrs Shepherd-Barron (B D P Spence/Miss Nuthall won, 6-3, 5-7, 6-3).

Australia

Lawn Tennis appears to have been introduced in Australia in the late 1800s and the first cham-

players have included: Daphne Akhurst, five times Australian women's singles champion; Nancye Bolton (*née* Wynne), six times champion, and four times Australian women's doubles winner with Thelma Long; Evonne Goolagong Cawley, three times Australian women's champion (1974–6), four times Australian women's doubles (1971, 1974–6), and Wimbledon and French women's singles champion (1971).

Tennis coaching and facilities in Australia receive strong backing not only from state and national associations but also sports goods manufacturers and various industries. There are state and interstate championships and youngsters are given every encouragement to play their best. Junior trophies include the Linton Cup for interstate competition by boys, started in 1924 and the Wilson Cup for girls, first presented in 1931. The majority of tennis is on hard courts. The Australian LTA has no playing centre of its own but its constituent State associations each have their own grounds.

Auteuil, France

When France won the Davis Cup for the first time in 1927 the country had no major tennis stadium which could be a venue for the Challenge Round. The city of Paris presented the *Fédération Française de Lawn-Tennis* with a site of some seven acres (three hectares) at the Auteuil gate on the south-west edge of Paris and here two large Parisian sports clubs, the *Stade Français* and the Racing Club of Paris, built a large concrete arena with a centre court surrounded by spectators' benches. This was named the *Stade Roland Garros* after the French trans-Mediterranean aviator who had been a member of the *Stade Français* athletics team.

Left: Luis Ayala enjoyed most of his successes in the late 1950s.

AYALA, Luis Alberto, Chile

Born September 1932, Santiago. A keen footballer as a youngster, Ayala is reputed to have been persuaded by his family to turn to tennis at the age of 12 when they decided he was wearing out too many pairs of shoes. He joined Santiago Lawn Tennis Club in 1944 and gave up football entirely at the age of 16. He won the junior championships of Chile in 1949 and that year represented his country against Peru in the Mitre Cup. The following year he won the South American championships. His best year was 1959, when he won the Italian championship after beating Nicola Pietrangeli and Neale

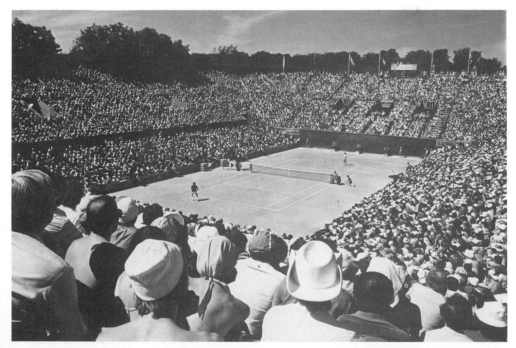

Left: Centre Court of Stade Roland Garros, Auteuil, Paris.

Fraser. He married the Chilean women's No 2 seed Maria Tort in 1958 and toured with her in 1959, when he was also quarter-finalist in the Wimbledon men's singles, the US singles, and French semi-finalist. In 1960 he was runner-up in the Italian and French championships and in 1961 he turned professional.

French men's singles r/u 1958 (M G Rose won, 6-3, 6-4, 6-4), r/u 1960 (Pietrangeli won, 3-6, 6-3, 6-4, 4-6, 6-3), mixed doubles r/u 1955 with Miss J Staley (G L Forbes/Miss D Hard won, 5-7, 6-1, 6-2), won 1956 with Mrs T D Long (beat R Howe/Miss Hard, 4-6, 6-4, 6-1), r/u 1957 with Miss E Buding (J Javorsky/Miss V Pužejová won, 6-3, 6-4).

BADDELEY, Herbert and Wilfred, GB

Identical twins born January 1872, Bromley, Kent. The Baddeleys dominated Wimbledon between 1890 and 1899. Wilfred, the elder twin, was, in 1891, the youngest man to win the men's title at the age of 19 years 5 months 23 days. He won again in 1892 and 1895. Together Herbert and Wilfred won the doubles Challenge Rounds in 1891, 1894-7 and were runners-up in 1892-3. In 1895, when Wilfred won the singles title for the third time, there were only 18 entries and he played only two matches, thanks to three retirements. Even so, he came within one point of losing the final to the Australian W V Eaves. Herbert was the less dominant of the two players and did not achieve singles success, though he reached the semi-finals in 1894-6. The brothers also won the Irish championship doubles in 1896-7. Herbert died in July 1931 in Cannes, France, and Wilfred in 1929 in Mentone, France.

Herbert: Wimbledon men's doubles won 1891 (beat J Pim/F Stoker, 6-1, 6-3, 1-6, 6-2), r/u 1892 (H S Barlow/E W Lewis won, 4-6, 6-2, 8-6, 6-4), r/u 1893 (Pim/Stoker won, 6-2, 4-6, 6-3, 5-7, 6-2), won 1894 (Pim/Stoker, wo), won 1895 (beat W V Eaves/Lewis, 8-6, 5-7, 6-4, 6-3), won 1896 (beat R F Doherty/H Nisbet, 1-6, 3-6, 6-4, 6-2, 6-1), won 1897 (beat H L Doherty/R F Doherty, 6-4, 4-6, 8-6, 6-4), all with Wilfred.

Wilfred: Wimbledon men's singles, won 1891 Challenge Round (beat W J Hamilton, wo), won 1892 (beat J Pim, 4-6, 6-3, 6-3, 6-2), r/u 1893 (Pim won, 3-6, 6-1, 6-3, 6-2), r/u 1894 (Pim won, 10-8, 6-2, 8-6), won 1895 (beat Pim, wo), r/u 1896 (H S Mahoney won, 6-2, 6-8, 5-7, 8-6, 6-3).

Bagnall-Wild System

The system of seeding players, named after its 19th century inventor. Under it, all byes were placed randomly in the first round, the number being calculated by subtracting the number of players in the draw from the next power of two. Wimbledon adopted this system in 1887. Previously, until 1884, byes were distributed through all rounds until the final and in 1885-86 byes all fell in the first round but were evenly distributed throughout the draw.

BAKER, Beverley *see* Fleitz, Mrs Beverley

BARANYI, Szabolcs, Hungary

Born January 1944, Nagyvarad. A computer technician now living in Budapest, Baranyi won the European Amateur championships in 1969, when he was also Hungary's national champion, after ending the dominance of Istvan Gulyás. He won the European Amateur again in 1972, and also won the Hungarian International. His career was interrupted in 1974 by an operation for tennis elbow but in 1975 he returned to the Hungarian Davis Cup team for the eighth time.

BARAZZUTTI, Corrado, Italy

Born February 1953. Son of a lorry driver, he won the French Roland Garros junior title at the age of 18 in 1971 and in the same year became the first Italian to win the US Orange Bowl for under-18s. In 1973 he beat Jan Kodeš in the European zone Davis Cup semi-final and he was one of the heroes of the Italian team which went through to win the 1976 Davis Cup against Chile in Santiago. Politics had played a disruptive role in the competition that year after Russia refused to play their inter-zone match against Chile in protest against that country's policies. There were riots in Rome by those wanting a similar withdrawal by Italy. Barazzutti, who beat Newcombe (Australia) in the inter-zone semi-finals, went on to defeat Chile's

Right: Corrado Barazzutti is ranked No 2 in Italy having shown great prowess in many international events.

Jaime Fillol in the opening rubber of the final, 7-5, 4-6, 7-5, 6-1, and Italy won decisively, 4-1. He joined WCT in 1975 and was r/u in the Munich doubles with Antoni Zugarelli, r/u in the Manila singles, and came within two points of defeating Arthur Ashe at Bologna WCT. In 1976 he was r/u in the Japanese Open singles to Roscoe Tanner and r/u with Anand Amritraj in the Manila doubles.

BARKER, Susan, GB

Born April 1956, Paignton, Devon. In 1972 at the age of 15 Sue Barker was already marked down as one of Britain's up-and-coming junior players, having been runner-up in the junior championships of 1970, winner of the South-western junior indoors in 1971 and winner of the Green Shield British junior titles on grass and wood in 1972. A pupil of Arthur Roberts in Torquay, Devon (he coached leading players such as Angela Mortimer and Mike Sangster among others), Sue Barker was voted most improved player of the year in 1976 by the Women's Tennis Association. Her chief attributes in play are her athleticism, spirited determination and her winning and powerful forehand, plus a much improved backhand; her weakness is possibly inflexibility in play. In 1975 she was a member of Britain's first successful Wightman Cup team since 1925. In 1976 she became the first British woman player since Ann Haydon Jones (1966) to win the French women's championship, beating Renata Tomanova, whom she defeated again later in the year to win the German championship. She was runner-up to Chris Evert in the 1977 Virginia Slims championship finals and r/u to Evonne Cawley in the NSW Open after an enforced lay-off through illness during the summer.

French women's singles, won 1976 (beat Mrs Tomanova, 6-2, 0-6, 6-2).

German women's singles, won 1976 (beat Mrs Tomanova, 6-3, 6-1).

Italian doubles r/u 1975 with Miss G Coles (Miss C Evert/Miss M Navratilova won, 6-1, 6-2).

Canadian doubles r/u 1976.

World Invitation doubles won 1976 with Mrs E Cawley.

Gunze Open, Japan, singles r/u 1976.

Colgate Melbourne singles r/u 1976.

Virginia Slims Championship singles r/u 1977 (Miss Evert won, 2-6, 6-1, 6-1). NSW Open singles r/u 1977 (Mrs E Cawley won, 6-2, 6-3).

BARLOW, Harold S, GB

Born April 1860. Took part in a classic Wimbledon men's All-Comers final in 1889 against Willie Renshaw, one of the Renshaw twins who ruled Wimbledon for a decade. The 29-year-old Barlow took the first two sets 6-3, 7-5, from the 28-year-old Renshaw (who was in poor health) and was within two sets of winning the match until his rival won the third 8-6. Then, in the fourth, Barlow led 5-2 and six times came within a point of victory. In the 14th game Renshaw followed his service to the net only to drop his racket at 6-7, 30-40. But Barlow returned such a simple shot that Renshaw was able to retrieve his racket and win the point and then the set! In the final set Barlow again went ahead to 5-0. Renshaw drew level and Barlow then went to 6-5 only to lose service in the 13th game. Renshaw went on to take the set 8-6 and win the match. Next year Barlow again figured in a game of swinging fortunes when he met Wil-

Left: Sue Barker is one of Britain's up-and-coming stars of the court.

loughby Hamilton in the final. This time Hamilton had been leading 2-6, 6-4, 6-4, 4-6 when he lost six successive games to trail 2-4 in the fifth set. Apparently poised for his long-sought title, Barlow let it slip, Hamilton winning 7-5 with love victories in the last two games.

Wimbledon men's singles r/u All-Comers 1889 (Renshaw won, 3-6, 5-7, 8-6, 10-8, 8-6), r/u 1890 (Hamilton won, 2-6, 6-4, 6-4, 4-6, 7-5); men's doubles r/u All-Comers 1891 with E Renshaw (H Baddeley/W Baddeley won, 4-6, 6-4, 7-5, 0-6, 6-2), won All-Comers 1892 with E Lewis (beat H Mahony/J Pim, wo), r/u Challenge Round 1893 with Lewis (Pim/F Stoker won, 4-6, 6-3, 6-1, 2-6, 6-0), r/u All-Comers 1894 with C Martin (H Baddeley/W Baddeley won, 5-7, 7-5, 4-6, 6-3, 8-6).

BARRETT, Herbert Roper, GB

Born November 1873, Upton, Essex. A skilful and energetic player who was active on the British tennis scene for some 40 years, Roper Barrett was a member of the first British Davis Cup team in 1900, was in the team until 1919 and was its non-playing captain from 1924 to 1939. He did consistently well at his Wimbledon appearances both in singles and doubles, was twice runner-up in the men's All-Comers and once in the Challenge Round. In doubles he gained the Wimbledon title with Arthur Gore in 1909 by a walk-over and in 1912–13 with C P Dixon and was four times Challenge Round runner-up. Barrett, who was noted as something of a joker, had the habit of entering events under pseudonyms. In 1897 he called himself 'A L Gydear', in 1899 it was as 'Mr Player' that he reached the semi-finals; in 1900 his 'Verne' was a quarter-finalist and in 1901 'Dagger' was the name that cloaked his entry! In 1910 he and Gore had the dubious distinction of being beaten 6-1, 6-1, 6-2 by M Ritchie and A Wilding – the shortest Wimbledon doubles ever.

Wimbledon men's singles r/u All-Comers 1908 (A W Gore won, 6-3, 6-2, 4-6, 3-6, 6-4), r/u 1909 (M J G Ritchie won, 6-2, 6-3, 4-6, 6-4), r/u 1911 Challenge Round (A F Wilding won, 6-4, 4-6, 2-6, 6-2, retired); men's doubles r/u 1899 All-Comers with Gore (C Hobart/H Nisbet won, 6-4, 6-1, 8-6), r/u Challenge Round 1900 with Nisbet (H L Doherty/R F Doherty won, 9-7, 7-5, 4-6, 3-6, 6-3), r/u 1901 All-Comers with G M Simond (Dwight Davis/H Ward won, 7-5, 6-4, 6-4), r/u 1908 All-Comers (M Ritchie/A Wilding won, 6-1, 6-2, 1-6, 1-6, 9-7), won Challenge Round 1909 with Gore (wo), r/u 1910 Challenge Round with Gore (Ritchie/Wilding won, 6-1, 6-1, 6-2), won 1912 Challenge Round (beat M Decugis/A Gobert, 3-6, 6-3, 6-4, 7-5), won 1913 (beat A Kleinschroth/F Rahe, 6-2, 6-4, 4-6, 6-2), r/u 1914 (N Brookes/Wilding won, 6-1, 6-1, 5-7, 8-6), all with Dixon.

Olympic gold medallist 1908. Won Saxmundham men's single 17 times between 1898 and 1921.

BARRETT, Mrs J *see* Mortimer, Angela

BARTKOWICZ, Jean (Peaches), USA

Born April 1949, Detroit. Armed with a double-handed backhand, she had a remarkable record as a junior player, winning the US National Girls' 18 singles and doubles for three successive years (1965–7). By the end of 1967, at age 18, she had never been beaten in any age group. She won the Wimbledon junior invitation at age 16 in 1964 and made her Wightman Cup debut in 1968 at Wimbledon, beating Winnie Shaw (GB). The following year she was a member of the Federation Cup team which beat Australia 2-1; she and Nancy Richey beat Margaret Court and Judy Tegart 6-4, 6-4. She turned professional in 1971.

BATTRICK, Gerald, GB

Born May 1947, Bridgend, Glamorgan. At age 17 Battrick won the British junior championship, British Junior covered court championship, the French junior title and qualified to play at Wimbledon. He followed this by becoming British under-21 champion in 1967 and with David Lloyd reached the final of the Galea Cup, which France won. He won the Wimbledon Plate in 1968 and was selected for the first time for the Davis Cup team but did not play. During that year he had wins against Mark Cox, Owen Davidson, Tom Okker, Arthur Ashe and Stan Smith on the Dewar Cup circuit. He had an excellent season in 1971, winning the Rothmans' Spectacular at Kingston, the Rothmans' British hard courts championship, the Dutch championships, the Lebanon international and beating Bob Hewitt in the Albert Hall Dewar Cup final.

However, in 1972, after signing for WCT he failed to defend the BHC title and was dropped from the Davis Cup team and has since shown inconsistent form. In play he uses the full court and has a strong backhand, drive and volley.

BEATTY, Mary Ann, USA
Born November 1946, St Louis. Formerly Mary Ann Eisel and previously married to Peter Curtis. In 1963 she was runner-up in the US indoor championship at age 17 and the following year won the American junior championship and national indoors. She made her Wightman Cup debut in 1966, losing her singles to Winnie Shaw (GB) but winning the doubles with Nancy Richey. In 1967 she was r/u in US national doubles and the following year won a 60-game Dewar Cup singles match against Patricia Walkden (South Africa), 7-9, 7-5, 17-15. The match was a British women's singles record and two games short of the world record. In 1969 she again won the US indoors and gained her third title in this event in 1970. With Françoise Durr she won the Rothmans' British hard court championship doubles of 1971 and with Valerie Ziegenfuss, her Wightman Cup doubles.

BEAVEN, Lindsey, GB
Born January 1950, Friern Barnet. Became a Bachelor of Divinity in 1973, when she also made her Wightman Cup debut and had her most successful year, winning the Rothmans' hard court, Sutton, the Athens international and the Greek Filothei. In 1974 she won the North of England women's singles and was r/u in the Wimbledon Plate and the following year spent some months coaching in America. In 1976 she again spent a large part of her time coaching but also played World Team Tennis for the then-champion team the New York Sets (now named the Apples).

BENGSTON, Ove, Sweden
Born April 1945, Stockholm, the son of a First Chairman of the Swedish Parliament. This 6 ft 6 in (1.98 m) physical education teacher wrote a thesis on the behaviour patterns of the top tennis players of the world for his qualifying examinations. His strong serve and powerful physique make him a particularly effective player on fast courts. Four times Swedish junior champion, he first played in the Swedish Davis Cup team in 1966.

Left: Swedish Ove Bengston's height and strength make him a powerful player on fast courts.

Above: Lennart Bergelin is best known today as the mentor of Björn Borg although he was a top player himself in the 1940s and 1950s.

BERGELIN, Lennart, Sweden

Born June 1925, Alingsas. Though best known today as the mentor of the brilliant Björn Borg, Bergelin was himself a fine touch player of the 1940s, won the French men's doubles of 1948 with Jaroslav Drobný (beat H Hopman/F Sedgman, 8-6, 6-1, 12-10), and was in the Swedish Davis Cup team 1946–51, 1953–5. In 1948 he dramatically beat the Wimbledon No 1 seed, American Frank Parker in the fourth round, 5-7, 7-5, 9-7, 0-6, 10-8, despite an attack of cramp in the fifth set when he was 3-5 down.

BERNARD, Marcel, France

Born May 1914, Lille. A left-hander, Bernard has been rated the best French player after the 'Four Musketeers' (Borotra, Brugnon, Cochet and Lacoste) and had an international playing career which stretched from the early 1930s to 1956. His relaxed style of play and good sense of anticipation brought him early successes as a junior player and by the age of 16 he was already classified as a 'first series' player (see 'France'). He was at times capable of inspired play, as when, at the age of 35 in 1946, he defeated Drobný to take the French title after being two sets down. He repeated his victory against the Czech in 1949 when they met in the Davis Cup. After the 'Musketeers' had retired Bernard became the backbone of the French Davis Cup team which he had first joined in 1935. He was a Davis Cup player in 1935–7, 1946–8, 1950, 1953, 1955–6. In 1968 he was elected president of the FFLT.

French men's singles won 1946 (beat Drobný, 3-6, 2-6, 6-1, 6-4, 6-3); men's doubles r/u 1932 with C Boussus (H Cochet/J Brugnon won, 6-4, 3-6, 7-5, 6-3), won 1936 with J Borotra (beat C Tuckey/G Hughes, 6-2, 3-6, 9-7, 6-1), won 1946 with Y Petra (beat E Morea/F Segura, 7-5, 6-3, 0-6, 1-6, 10-8); mixed doubles won 1935 with Miss L Payot (beat R Legeay/Miss S Henrotin, 4-6, 6-2, 6-4), won 1936 with Miss A M Yorke (beat Legeay/Miss Henrotin 7-5, 6-8, 6-3).

BERTOLUCCI, Paulo, Italy

Born August 1951 in Tuscany. This tough, friendly player who can sometimes appear irresolute was one of the heroes of Italy's 1976 Davis Cup victory against Chile – a final which was marred beforehand by political protest against the Chilean government's policies. Bertolucci and Adriano Panatta beat Patricio Cornejo and Jaime Fillol 3-6, 6-2, 9-7, 6-3 in the doubles. He was r/u in the Italian national championships in 1972–3 and r/u with Corrado Barazzutti in the British hard courts championship of 1974, when he also won the Swedish championship, beating Panatta. Davis Cup team 1974–

BETZ, Pauline M (Mrs R Addie), USA

Born August 1919, Dayton, Ohio. One of the great women players of all time, winning the women's singles in the USA four times, Wimbledon once and the French doubles and mixed doubles once each. She exhibited the grace of a dancer and bounding agility, combined with strict self-discipline. A tall, striking blonde, her gracefulness was a deceptive cover for her stroke power. She did not lose a single set in beating her compatriot Louise Brough to take the Wimbledon title in 1946, 6-2, 6-4. She had previously beaten Miss Brough in the 1942 US finals 4-6, 6-1, 6-4, and in 1943, 6-3, 5-7, 6-3. These two Americans and Margaret Osborne (later duPont) and Doris Hart, dominated women's tennis for some years and proved that *some* women could play like men. In 1947 Miss Betz was deprived of her amateur status by the US LTA for discussing the terms of a professional contract. That year she turned professional and signed to play tour tennis for promoter Bobby Riggs against 'Gorgeous Gussy' Moran, who had broken Wimbledon tradition by daring to play on the Centre Court in lace panties. Not to be outdone, Miss Betz appeared at the opening tour match at Madison Square Garden wearing leopard skin shorts! Miss Betz won.

US women's singles r/u 1941 (Mrs E T Cooke won, 6-1, 6-4), won 1942 (beat Miss Brough, 4-6, 6-1, 6-4), won 1943 (beat Miss Brough 6-3, 5-7, 6-3), won 1944 (beat Miss Osborne, 6-3, 8-6), r/u 1945 (Mrs Cooke won, 3-6, 8-6, 6-4), won 1946 (beat Miss Hart, 11-9, 6-3).

Wimbledon singles won 1946 (beat Miss Brough, 6-2, 6-4); women's doubles r/u 1946 with Miss Hart (Miss Brough/Miss Osborne won, 6-3, 2-6, 6-3).

French singles r/u 1946 (Miss Osborne won, 1-6, 8-6, 7-5), women's doubles r/u 1946 with Miss Hart (Miss Brough/Miss Osborne won, 6-4, 0-6, 6-1); mixed doubles won 1946 with J E Patty (beat T Brown/Miss D Bundy, 7-5, 9-7).

BINGLEY, Blanche *see* Hillyard, Mrs G W

Right: Paulo Bertolucci was a member of Italy's Davis Cup team from 1974 to 1976.

Arthur Ashe – United States of America

Sue Barker – Great Britain

Björn Borg – Sweden

Maria Bueno – Brazil

Evonne Cawley – Australia

Jimmy Connors – United States of America

Margaret Court – Australia

33

BLAKSTAD, Mrs W L *see* **Watson, Phoebe**

BLOOMER, Shirley (Mrs C Brasher), GB
Born June 1934, Grimsby. A hard-working but unspectacular player who was at her best on hard courts, where she was rated world No 3 in 1957, when she was ranked No 1 in Britain. That year she won the French championships, beating Mrs D P Knode but failed to retain the title in 1958, losing to Zuzi Körmöczy in the final. Also in 1957 she won the singles and doubles in the British hard court championships, the Italian championship singles and the Swedish international hard court championship. In 1958 she won the singles and mixed doubles of the British hard courts championship; the latter success with Billy Knight was repeated in 1959 to achieve a record in that the pair had a walk-over in both finals. In 1959 she married Chris Brasher, British Olympic gold medallist athlete who took part in the successful record attempt on a sub-four-minute mile by Roger Bannister in 1954. She was a former British junior squash rackets player, a fine horsewoman and good table tennis player.

French women's singles won 1957 (beat Mrs Knode, 6-1, 6-3), r/u 1958 (Mrs Körmöczy won, 6-4, 1-6, 6-2), women's doubles r/u 1955 with Miss P Ward (Mrs J Fleitz/Miss D Hard won, 7-5, 6-8, 13-11), won 1957 with Miss Hard (beat Miss Y Ramirez/Miss R M Reyes, 7-5, 4-6, 7-5), mixed doubles won 1958 with N

Pietrangeli (beat R Howe/Miss L Coghlan, 9-7, 6-8, 6-2).
Wightman Cup 1955–60.

BOLTON, Nancye (*née* Wynne), Australia
Born June 1917, Melbourne. Ten times winner of the Australian women's doubles and six times of the singles, her style combined power with grace and fluent stroke work, though her timing was sometimes suspect. Her career began in the mid 1930s and she won her last major title (her tenth Australian doubles) in 1952, the year in which she became a professional. In the 1946–7 season she established a record by winning the Australian singles and doubles and the championships of all the Australian states. The power and speed of her play left little room for error and she has been ranked as a player almost in the class of Margaret Court, who won the Australian title eleven times. Though Mrs Bolton was several times ranked among the top ten women players in the world, she might have been among the top three or four had she not restricted her play to Australia for several seasons. She reached the finals of the US singles in 1938 (her best result in America), but was beaten 6-0, 6-3 by Alice Marble in only 22 minutes.

Australian women's singles r/u 1936 (Miss J Hartigan won, 6-4, 6-4), won 1937 (beat Mrs V Westacott, 6-3, 5-7, 6-4), won 1940 (wo), won 1946 (beat Miss J Fitch, 6-4, 6-4), won 1947

Left: Shirley Bloomer (Mrs Brasher) was one of England's top players in the 1950s. In 1957 she was ranked as world No 3.

(beat Mrs H C Hopman, 6-3, 6-2), won 1948 (beat Miss M Toomey, 6-3, 6-1), r/u 1949 (Miss D Hart won 6-3, 6-4), won 1951 (beat Mrs T D Long, 6-1, 7-5); women's doubles won 1936 (beat Miss M Blick/Miss K Woodward, 6-2, 6-4), won 1937 (beat Mrs Hopman/Mrs Westacott, 6-2, 6-2), won 1938 (beat Miss D M Bundy/Miss D E Workman, 9-7, 6-4), won 1939 (beat Mrs Westacott/Miss M Hardcastle, 7-5, 6-4), won 1940 (wo), all with Miss T D Coyne, won 1947 (beat Miss J Fitch/Miss M Bevis, 6-3, 6-3), won 1949 (beat Miss Bevis/Miss N Jones, 6-3, 6-3), won 1949 (beat Miss D Toomey/Miss M Toomey, 6-0, 6-1), r/u 1950 (Miss Hart/Miss Brough won, 6-2, 2-6, 6-3), won 1951 (beat Mrs M Hawton/Miss Fitch, 6-2, 6-1), won 1952 (beat Mrs R Baker/Mrs Hawton, 6-1, 6-1), all with Mrs Long; mixed doubles r/u 1938 (J Bromwich/Miss J Wilson won, 6-3, 6-2), won 1940 (wo), won 1946, won 1947 (beat Bromwich/Miss Fitch, 6-3, 6-3), won 1948 (beat O Sidwell/Mrs T C Long, 7-5, 4-6, 8-6), all with C F Long.

Wimbledon mixed doubles r/u 1947 with C F Long (J Bromwich/Miss Brough won, 1-6, 6-4, 6-2), r/u 1951 with M G Rose (F Sedgman/Miss Hart won, 7-5, 6-2).

BOOTHBY, Penelope Dora Harvey (Mrs A C Geen), GB

Born August 1888, Finchley, Middlesex, died February 1970. Dora Boothby won the Wimbledon women's title in 1909 from Mrs Charlotte Sterry, 6-4, 4-6, 8-6 after the longest championship match since 1889. A report of the time stated that the match was 'remarkable for its tension and protracted rallies. There have been more scientific, more stroke-varied ladies' finals at Wimbledon but none in which the result hung so long in the balance or in which the combatants showed such hardihood and such resolution.' However, a year later Miss Boothby lost her title quickly to Mrs Lambert Chambers, 6-2, 6-2, and in 1911 had to suffer the ignominy of being beaten by her in the Challenge Round, 6-0, 6-0, in just 22 minutes – the shortest final of all time and the only one consisting of two love games. In 1913 with Mrs R J McNair, she gained some revenge by winning the doubles from Mrs Lambert Chambers and Mrs Sterry, 4-6, 2-4, retired.

BORG, Björn, Sweden

Born June 1956 at Sodertalje, near Stockholm. The arrival of Borg, a handsome blond Swede, on the international tennis scene in 1972, when he won the Wimbledon junior invitation event and made a striking Davis Cup debut, aged 15, passed almost unnoticed. But in 1973, when the ATP dispute with the ILTF resulted in the withdrawal of professionals from Wimbledon, Borg found himself promoted in the seedings to No 6, and he and the Rumanian Ilie Năstase (No 1) suddenly became the focus of a new phenomenon – mass hysteria and mobbing on the part of thousands of teenage fans. Such was the frenzy that both players had to be provided with police escorts. Apparently unflurried by the fuss Borg, then aged 17, made an impressive debut in the championships and played with extraordinary maturity to reach the quarterfinals before losing to Britain's Roger Taylor. He had, however, served notice of things to come and in 1974 he became the youngest player (just 18) to win the US professional title, which he retained in 1975 and 1976. In 1974 and 1975 he also won the French title and in 1975 led Sweden to a dramatic 3-2 Davis Cup victory against Czechoslovakia.

By 1976, when he became the third youngest to win the Wimbledon title, aged 20 years 27 days, he was firmly established as a player of quite exceptional ability, concentration and determination. His Wimbledon challenge that year was an illustration of his overall talent. On his way to the Wimbledon title he overcame the Australian Roscoe Tanner, whose power many thought would be too much for Borg. Instead it was the Swede who dominated, using fast, accurate services (he did not lose service once in the match) and superb passing shots to make him the first man from his country to reach a Wimbledon final. Now he met the other idol, Năstase and the match was played in an atmosphere more like that of a 'pop' concert, with rival fans screaming their encouragements. Borg had pulled a stomach muscle early in the week and had to have pain killing injections before each round; it seemed likely that the more experienced but stormy Năstase would take the title. Yet again Borg produced brilliance when it was most needed and after being 3-0 down, twice saved the fourth game and then took the first set 6-4. Năstase visibly wilted and lost the next set 6-2 before regaining some confidence in the third against his inspired opponent. Though the Rumanian broke service, Borg broke back and took the title at 9-7. He had not lost a set in any round and he had showed conclusively that he had adapted his heavily topspun forehand and two-handed backhand to the demands of fast grass. In 1976, too, Borg won the WCT Finals in Dallas but lost his French title and was runner-up to Jim Connors in the US Open.

In 1977 Borg was again in scintillating form which took him through 25 matches without a loss and brought him the Wimbledon title for the second time, beating Connors in a superb display of power tennis by both men. He was later runner-up to Connors in the Masters' but meantime had his long series of wins and gained titles at Wembley, Madrid, Barcelona, Basle and Cologne amongst other venues. He ended the year clearly rated world No 1, pressed only by Guillermo Vilas of Argentina, whom he played twice, in Nice and Monte Carlo, winning each time.

Swedish Open men's singles won 1972–4; men's doubles won 1975 with O Bengsten; Scandinavian Open singles won 1973; Scandinavian Open Indoors won 1974; Stockholm Open singles r/u 1973.

French men's singles won 1974 (beat M Orantes, 2-6, 6-7, 6-0, 6-1, 6-1), won 1975 (beat G Vilas, 6-2, 6-3, 6-4).

US professional championship singles won 1974–6; US Clay Courts r/u 1974; US professional Indoor r/u 1976; US Open r/u 1976 (Connors won, 6-4, 3-6, 7-6, 6-4); US Orange Bowl won 1971–2; WCT finals r/u 1974, r/u 1975, won 1976 (beat Vilas, 1-6, 6-1, 7-5, 6-1); doubles r/u 1974 with Bengsten.

Italian Open singles won 1974 (beat Năstase, 6-3, 6-4, 6-2).

World invitation doubles won 1975.

Commercial Union Masters' r/u 1975 (Năs-tase won, 6-2, 6-2, 6-1), r/u 1977 (Connors won, 6-4, 6-1, 6-4).

Wimbledon singles won 1976 (beat Năstase, 6-4, 6-2, 9-7), won 1977 (beat Connors, 3-6, 6-2, 6-1, 5-7, 6-4), won 1978 (beat Connors, 6-2, 6-2, 6-3).

Benson & Hedges Wembley won 1977 (beat J Lloyd, 6-4, 6-4, 6-3).

BOROTRA, Jean, France
Born August 1898, Arbonne, Basses-Pyrenees. Known as the 'Bounding Basque' because of his boundless energy and athleticism, Borotra was one of France's 'Four Musketeers' of tennis, along with Jacques Brugnon, Henri Cochet and Rene Lacoste. Born in Pelote, he un-

Left: Handsome and versatile, Sweden's Björn Borg has brought a new dimension to tennis – hero worship on the part of a large number of teenage fans. He is perhaps the most brilliant tennis player of the seventies.

doubtedly gained his exceptionally fast reactions from playing pelota, which may also have been responsible for a strange tennis style and unorthodox ground strokes which were far from aesthetically pure. Nonetheless, he possessed a fine service, excellent overhead strokes and volleys and enormous determination which sent him hurling after every ball. He was an early exponent of the serve-volley technique and his strange backhand volley was a uniquely great stroke. He was always extremely fit and continued playing into his seventies.

Borotra particularly delighted British crowds, who gave him the 'Bounding Basque' nickname and who were captivated not just by his enthusiasm but by the succession of berets which he wore through his matches. The Basque would come on to court with an armful of berets which he laid neatly in a row beside the umpire's chair. As, one after another, they became sweat-soaked by his exertions, they were laid on the other side of the chair and a fresh one was snatched up. There was considerable friendly rivalry among the 'Musketeers', each of whom won and lost regularly against the others. In 1924 Wimbledon saw its first all-French final when Borotra met Lacoste. The match went

to five sets at break-neck speed, each set lasting only about 15 minutes. Borotra won 6-1, 3-6, 6-1, 3-6, 6-4 and the Frenchmen then delighted the crowd by leaving the court arm in arm. In 1925 Cochet, Lacoste and Borotra were all in the quarter-finals, and unusually, Borotra defeated Cochet and again faced Lacoste in the final. This time the match was longer and fortunes see-sawed, Lacoste winning the first two sets and then seeing his lead reducing. Eventually Lacoste won three sets to one.

In his remarkable career Borotra won the French singles title twice, the doubles five times and mixed doubles twice, the Wimbledon singles twice, doubles three times and mixed doubles once, the Australian singles, doubles and mixed doubles once each and the US mixed doubles once. He was also French covered court champion 12 times between 1922 and 1947 and 11 times British covered court champion between 1926 and 1949. Of 235 games he played at Wimbledon, he won 154 and lost 81 – a record unequalled. He last entered the championships in 1964 aged 66! He and the other Musketeers formed the backbone of France's Davis Cup successes in the 1920s and early 1930s and Borotra was in the team in 1922, 1924–37 and

1947. He played in the Wimbledon veterans event in 1977. From 1940–2 he was France's Minister of Sport and was later imprisoned by the Gestapo.

French men's singles won 1924 (beat Lacoste), r/u 1925 (Lacoste won, 7-5, 6-1, 6-4), r/u 1929 (Lacoste won, 6-3, 2-6, 6-0, 2-6, 8-6), won 1931 (beat C Boussus, 2-6, 6-4, 7-5, 6-4); men's doubles won 1924 with Lacoste (closed event), won 1925 with Lacoste (beat Cochet/Brugnon, 7-5, 4-6, 6-3, 2-6, 6-3), r/u 1927 (Cochet/Brugnon won, 2-6, 6-2, 6-0, 1-6, 6-4), won 1928 (beat Cochet/R de Buzelet, 6-4, 3-6, 6-2, 3-6, 6-4), won 1929 (beat Cochet/Brugnon, 6-3, 3-6, 6-3, 3-6, 8-6), all with Lacoste, won 1934 with Brugnon (beat J Crawford/V B McGrath, 11-9, 6-3, 2-6, 4-6, 9-7), won 1936 with M Bernard (beat C R D Tuckey/G P Hughes, 6-2, 3-6, 9-7, 6-1); mixed doubles won 1924, r/u 1926 with Mrs Le Besnerais (Brugnon/Miss S Lenglen won, 6-4, 6-3), won 1927 with Mrs M Bordes (beat W Tilden/Miss L de Alvarez, 6-4, 2-6, 6-2), won 1934 with Miss C Rosambert (beat A Quist/Miss E Ryan, 6-2, 6-4).

Wimbledon men's singles won 1924 (beat Lacoste, 6-1, 3-6, 6-1, 3-6, 6-4), r/u 1925 (Lacoste won, 6-3, 6-3, 4-6, 8-6), won 1926 (beat H Kinsey, 8-6, 6-1, 6-3), r/u 1927 (Cochet won, 4-6, 4-6, 6-3, 6-4, 7-5), r/u 1929 (Cochet won, 6-4, 6-3, 6-4); men's doubles won 1925 with Lacoste (beat R Casey/J Hennessey, 6-4, 11-9, 4-6, 1-6, 6-3), won 1932 (beat G Hughes/F Perry, 6-0, 4-6, 3-6, 7-5, 7-5), won 1933 (beat R Nunoi/J Satoh, 4-6, 6-3, 6-3, 7-5), r/u 1934 (G Lott/L Stocfen won, 6-2, 6-3, 6-4), all with Brugnon; mixed doubles won 1925 with Miss Lenglen (beat H de Morpurgo/Miss Ryan, 6-3, 6-3).

US singles r/u 1926 (Lacoste won, 6-4, 6-0, 6-4); mixed doubles won 1926 with Miss Ryan (beat Lacoste/Mrs G Wightman, 6-4, 7-5).

Australian men's singles won 1928 (beat R Cummings, 6-4, 6-1, 4-6, 5-7, 6-3); doubles won 1928 with Brugnon (beat J Willard/E Moon, 6-2, 4-6, 6-4, 6-4); mixed doubles won 1928 with Miss D Akhurst (J B Hawkes/Miss E Boyd retired).

BOROWIAK, Jeff, USA

Born September 1949, Lafayette. At 6 ft 4 in and around 182 lb Borowiak is a fine all-round athlete who was coached by Glenn Bassett and Paul Cohen. Outside tennis his keen interest is in music and he plays piano, clarinet, flute and saxophone. He joined WCT in 1971 and was r/u in the WCT Cologne singles. He was US national 18 champion in 1967 and the following year was r/u in the Orange Bowl and helped the US win the Sunshine Cup for boys under 18. As an adult player, now married, he has had some good wins, including those over John Newcombe, Stan Smith, Ken Rosewall, Jim Connors, Charles Pasarell, Harry Solomon and Colin Dibley, and in 1977 won the Swedish Open.

US national amateur indoor singles r/u 1971;

Left: Linky Boshoff is one of South Africa's newest successful tennis stars.

Osaka Open doubles won 1973 with T Gorman; Oslo Open won 1974; men's doubles won 1974 with V Gerulaitis; WCT Atlanta singles r/u 1976. Swedish Open singles won 1977 (beat J Caujolle, 2-6, 6-1, 6-3).

BOSHOFF, Linda (Linky), South Africa

Born 1955, Uitenhage. Daughter of an international hockey player and long distance runner, 'Linky' Boshoff fulfilled a schoolgirl's dream when she beat Sue Barker, Michele Gurdal, Helen Gourlay and Rosie Casals to reach the 1974 Wimbledon quarter-finals before losing to Virginia Wade. In the previous season she had won the South African doubles with Ilana Kloss, beating Chris Evert and Miss Wade and she has since gone on to establish a reputation as one of the world's leading doubles players – a reputation helped by winning the US Open doubles in 1976 with Miss Kloss, beating Olga Morozova and Miss Wade decisively.

South African women's doubles won 1973 with Miss Kloss (beat Miss Evert/Miss Wade, 7-6, 2-6, 6-1).

German championship doubles won 1976, (beat Miss L Dupont/Miss W Turnbull, 4-6, 7-5, 6-1).

Bournemouth doubles won 1976.

US Open doubles won 1976 (beat Miss Morozova/Miss Wade, 6-1, 6-4); US clay court doubles won 1976 (beat Miss Dupont/Miss Turnbull, 6-2, 6-3), US clay court doubles won 1977 with Miss Kloss (beat Miss Carillo/Miss W Overton, 5-7, 7-5, 6-3).

Italian Open doubles won 1976 (beat Miss V Ruzici/Miss M Simionescu, 6-1, 6-2).

Bournemouth, GB

Home of the West Hampshire Club, Bournemouth is the second most important tennis venue in Britain, after Wimbledon, and made history in 1968 when the first Open tournament was held there. The British hard court championships, which started at Torquay in 1924, have been held at Bournemouth since 1927 and have consistently attracted the world's leading players. Winners have included Jacques Brugnon and René Lacoste (two of the French 'Four Musketeers'), Fred Perry (five times champion), Jaroslav Drobný (four times), Billy Knight

38

Right: Virginia Wade (forecourt) wins one of her four titles at the Rothmans' Bournemouth Championships.

(three times), 'Buster' Mottram, Ken Rosewall, John Newcombe, Adriano Panatta, Manuel Orantes and Wojtek Fibak in the men's singles; Elizabeth Ryan (twice), Kay Stammers and Margaret Court (three times each), Doris Hart, Ann Jones, Angela Mortimer and Virginia Wade (four times each) in the women's singles. When the event became Open it was sponsored by W D & H O Wills, Rothmans' and Coca-Cola but it was not held in 1977, when sponsorship was withdrawn. Inchcape took on men's sponsorship for 1978. The British inter-counties hard court championships have been held there annually since 1965 and the Bournemouth tournament is an annual fixture each August.

BOWREY, Lesley (*née* Turner), Australia
Born August 1942 in Sydney. Though she was one of Australia's best women players, her prowess was overshadowed by the brilliance of her contemporary, Margaret Smith Court, whom she in fact beat on several occasions. She was most successful as a doubles player, winning the Australian women's doubles three times (1964–5, 1967) and mixed doubles twice (1962, 1967) and gaining 16 doubles and mixed doubles international titles. Even so, she could be a powerful singles opponent and twice won the French title (1963, 1965) and twice the Italian (1967–8). After America had won the first Federation Cup in 1963, Darlene Hard and Billie Jean Moffitt defeating Miss Smith and Miss Turner, the two Australians gained the trophy the following year, Miss Turner beating Nancy Richey in straight sets and Miss Smith

losing only five games against Billie Jean. The two, who had surprised the tennis world by their success against the Americans, repeated their victory again in 1965. In 1968 Miss Turner married that year's Australian men's champion, Bill Bowrey, with whom she had played in mixed doubles.

Australian women's doubles won 1964 with Miss J Tegart (beat Miss Smith/Miss R Ebbern, 6-4, 6-4), won 1965 with Miss Smith (beat Miss Moffitt/Miss Ebbern, 1-6, 6-2, 6-3), won

Right centre: Lesley Bowrey (née Turner) was one of Australia's most competent women players.

1967 with Miss Tegart (beat Miss Terras/Miss L Robinson, 6-0, 6-2), r/u 1975 with Miss R Tomanova (Miss Goolagong/Miss Michel won, 8-1, one set); mixed doubles won 1962 with F Stolle (beat R Taylor/Miss D Hard, 6-3, 9-7), won 1967 with O Davidson (beat A Roche/Miss Tegart, 9-7, 6-4).

US women's doubles won 1961 with Miss Hard (beat Miss E Buding/Miss Y Ramirez, 6-4, 5-7, 6-0).

French women's singles won 1963 (beat Mrs A Jones, 2-6, 6-3, 7-5), won 1965 (beat Miss Smith, 6-3, 6-4); women's doubles won 1964 (beat Miss N Baylon/Miss H Schultze, 6-3, 6-0), won 1965 (beat Miss F Durr/Miss J Lieffrig, 6-3, 6-1), both with Miss Smith.

Wimbledon women's doubles won 1964 with Miss Smith (beat Miss Moffitt/Mrs J Susman, 7-5, 6-2); mixed doubles won 1961 (beat R Howe/Miss Buding, 11-9, 6-2), won 1964 (beat K Fletcher/Miss Smith, 6-4, 6-4), both with Stolle.

Italian women's singles won 1967, 1968; doubles won 1961 with Miss J Lehane, 1964 with Miss Smith, 1967 with Miss R Casals; mixed doubles won 1962 with Stolle, 1967 with W W Bowrey.

BOWREY, William W (Tex), Australia

Born December 1943, Sydney. This tall, rangy Australian with a somewhat flashy style of play, was a sound all round player and popular with crowds. His greatest success, in winning the Australian title in 1968, came in a lean year when established stars such as Emerson, Newcombe and Roche had 'emigrated' to the professional circuit. Their departure brought Bowrey from the 'reserve' ranks to No 1 seeding and leader of the Australian Davis Cup attack. After winning the title he joined WCT in 1970 and was r/u with Owen Davidson in the Italian Open and British hard court doubles. In 1971 he and Davidson again won the British hard court title. However, he gained no other major victories and the following year retired to teach in Texas.

Australian men's singles won 1968 (beat J M Gisbert, 7-5, 2-6, 9-7, 6-4); men's doubles r/u 1967 with Davidson (J Newcombe/A Roche won, 3-6, 6-3, 7-5, 6-8, 8-6); mixed doubles r/u 1966 with Miss R Ebbern (Roche/Miss Tegart won, 6-1, 6-3).

US men's doubles r/u 1967 with Davidson (Newcombe/Roche won, 6-8, 9-7, 6-3, 6-3).

Wimbledon men's doubles r/u 1966 with Davidson (K Fletcher/Newcombe won, 6-3, 6-4, 3-6, 6-3). First British under-21 champion 1962; Welsh champion 1968.

BRASHER, Mrs S see Bloomer, Shirley

BRINKER, Mrs N see Connolly, Maureen

Bristol, GB

Founded in 1912, the Bristol Lawn Tennis Club staged one of Britain's most important tourna-

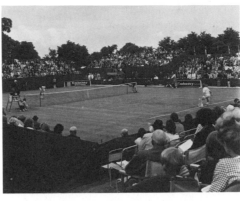

Left: Contestants strive for victory at the W D & H O Wills Open which is played on grass courts.

ments, the West of England championships, from 1920. In 1968 when it became Open and sponsored by the Bristol-based tobacco company, W D & H O Wills, the event was renamed the W D & H O Wills Open tennis championships. The grass court event offers the highest prize money in Britain apart from Wimbledon. It attracts leading international players and is held two weeks before Wimbledon. In 1971 the club made British tennis history by staging a men-only WCT event for the Dallas-based team of professionals and broke the national record for spectator receipts. Because of torrential rain (five inches fell in one night) only 13 minutes' play was possible in three days and the event was never finished, but the next year a protective inflatable plastic dome was constructed over the club's Centre Court.

British Covered Court Championships

Though first held in 1885 in the Hyde Park Court, London, the home of these championships was for 70 years the Queen's Club, London. Despite sponsorship late in the 1960s they declined in the strength of entry and as a major tennis attraction. They were last held at Queen's in 1968 as part of the Dewar Cup circuit for that year only. Next, they were taken over by W D & H O Wills and incorporated in their Embassy championships held at Wembley. However, in 1972, after WCT players had been barred, sponsorship was withdrawn and the event lapsed.

British Hard Court Championships see Bournemouth

British Junior Championships

National junior singles and doubles championships are held annually on hard courts, covered courts and grass for boys and girls under 18. The first hard court championships were held at Ventnor, Isle of Wight, in 1908, when C G Eames Jr and Miss L E Bull were the winners. After various other venues had been used, Wimbledon became the permanent home in 1924 and the event is known as 'junior Wimbledon'. Surprisingly, it does not usually produce future Wimbledon champions and Ann Haydon (now Mrs Ann Haydon Jones), who won in

1954–5, is the only junior champion to go on to win the Wimbledon women's singles title. The junior covered court event was first held in 1955 at Queen's Club, London, and the grass court championships, which started in 1970, are held at Eastbourne's Devonshire Park.

British Under-21 Championships

First held in 1962 and always at the Northern Club, Manchester, these championships, which are international, are for men and women under 21. Though usually played on grass, the tournament can, at the referee's discretion, be held on any surface in the event of bad weather. The championships are considered a good stepping stone for those too young or inexperienced for top-class senior tournaments but too old for junior events.

BROMWICH, John Edward, Australia

Born November 1918, Kogarah, NSW. Bromwich, who won no fewer than 13 men's doubles titles and was defeated only once in 21 Davis Cup rubbers, was considered a superb craftsman of the game. Basically left-handed, he was double-handed on his right hand side and used his right hand to serve. He used a very loosely-strung racket to give him more 'feel' of the ball and had a delicacy of touch rare in a male player. This, combined with superb ball control and a degree of wiliness, enabled him to rely on placing rather than speed. Like many others, Bromwich's career was interrupted in 1939 by World War II, in which he served in the RAF, at a time when he might have been expected to be at his playing peak. Yet he returned to the court after the war and gained some of his

Right: John Bromwich is considered to be one of the best doubles players ever born. (The other is the Frenchman Brugnon.)

greatest triumphs in the next five years, notably in doubles with Adrian Quist.

He was a great favourite with the crowds and spectators at Wimbledon were disappointed for him when he lost the 1948 men's finals to Bob Falkenburg when apparently poised for success. Not for the first time, Falkenburg annoyed the crowd by his apparent delaying tactics. When the match stood at one set all the American frequently broke Bromwich's rhythm by crouching ostensibly to tie his laces. Bromwich's habit of shaking his head slowly and ruefully, when things went wrong, became more noticeable when the match was square at two all and Falkenburg kept sinking to his knees. Even though visibly upset, Bromwich led 5-3 and 40-15 in the final set. Then Falkenburg struck, saving three match points and carrying on to win the title. Bromwich was a stalwart of the Australian Davis Cup team from 1937 to 1939, in 1946-7 and again in 1949-50. On his last Davis Cup appearance, in 1950, captained by non-playing Harry Hopman with whom he had played in the competition in the 1930s, Bromwich came in virtually as a reserve. But he and Frank Sedgman beat Americans Schroeder and Mulloy to seal Australia's victory.

Australian men's singles r/u 1937 (V B McGrath won, 6-3, 1-6, 6-0, 2-6, 6-1), r/u 1938 (J D Budge won, 6-4, 6-2, 6-1), won 1939 (beat Quist, 6-4, 6-1, 6-3), won 1946 (beat D Pails, 5-7, 6-3, 7-5, 3-6, 6-2), r/u 1947 (Pails won 4-6, 6-4, 3-6, 7-5, 8-6), r/u 1948 (Quist won, 6-4, 3-6, 6-3, 2-6, 6-3), r/u 1949 (Sedgman, 6-3, 6-3, 6-2); men's doubles r/u 1937 with J Harper (Quist/D P Turnbull won, 6-2, 9-7, 1-6, 6-8, 6-4), won 1939 (beat Turnbull/C F Long, 6-4, 7-5, 6-2), won 1940 (wo), won 1946 (wo), won 1947 (beat Sedgman/G Worthington, 6-1, 6-3, 6-1), won 1948 (beat Sedgman/Long, 1-6, 6-8, 9-7, 6-3, 8-6), won 1949 (beat G E Brown/D W Sidwell, 1-6, 7-5, 6-2, 6-3), won 1950 (beat E Sturgess/J Drobný, 6-3, 5-7, 4-6, 6-3, 8-6), r/u 1951 (Sedgman/K McGregor won, 11-9, 2-6, 6-3, 4-6, 6-3), all with Quist; mixed doubles won 1938 with Miss J Wilson (beat Long/Miss N Wynne, 6-3, 6-2), r/u 1939 with Miss M Wilson (H Hopman/Mrs Hopman won, 6-8 6-2, 6-3), r/u 1947 with Miss J Fitch (Long/Mrs N Bolton won, 6-3, 6-3), r/u 1949 with Miss Fitch (Sedgman/Miss Hart won, 6-1, 5-7, 12-10), r/u 1954 with Miss B Penrose (R Hartwig/Mrs T Long won, 4-6, 6-1, 6-2).

US men's doubles r/u 1938 (Budge/C G Mako won, 6-3, 6-2, 6-1), won 1939 (beat J Crawford/Hopman, 8-6, 6-1, 6-4), both with Quist, won 1949 with D Sidwell (beat Sedgman/Worthington, 6-4, 6-0, 6-1), won 1950 with Sedgman (beat Mulloy/W Talbert, 7-5, 8-6, 3-6, 6-1); mixed doubles r/u 1938 with Miss T Coyne (Budge/Miss A Marble won, 6-1, 6-2), won 1947 with Miss A L Brough (beat F Segura/Miss G Moran, 6-3, 6-1).

Wimbledon men's singles r/u 1948 (Falkenburg won, 7-5, 0-6, 6-2, 3-6, 7-5); men's doubles won 1948 with Sedgman (beat T Brown/Mulloy, 5-7, 7-5, 7-5, 9-7), won 1950 with Quist (beat G Brown/Sidwell, 7-5, 3-6, 6-3, 3-6, 6-2); mixed doubles won 1947 (beat C Long/Mrs Bolton, 1-6, 6-4, 6-2), won 1948 (beat Sedgman/Miss Hart, 6-2, 3-6, 6-3), r/u 1949 (Sturgess/Mrs S Summers won, 9-7, 9-11, 7-5), all with Miss Brough.

BROOKES, Sir Norman Everard, Australia
Born November 1877, Melbourne, died September 1968. The first of the great Australian players, Norman Brookes, a left-hander, was also the first overseas player to win the Wimbledon championship (1907). Slender and thin-faced, he was, nonetheless, tough and self-reliant. He had a devastating volley, superb footwork and a variety of disguised services which earned him the nickname 'The Wizard'. With his friend and Davis Cup colleague of many years, New Zealander Tony Wilding, Brookes had been instrumental in the formation of the Australasian LTA in 1904 and these two players helped turn the game from a social entertainment to a recognised sport in Australia and New Zealand. In 1905 Brookes won the Wimbledon All-Comers final on his first entry but lost the Challenge Round to Laurie Doherty, younger of the famous Doherty brothers.

Brookes first played in the Davis Cup in 1905 and from 1907 to 1914 Australasia, led by Brookes and Wilding, won the cup five times, and won it again in 1919 before losing to America in 1920, the 'Wizard's' last year in the team. He took part in 22 Davis Cup Challenge Round rubbers, winning 15. In 1914 Brookes took his second Wimbledon title, beating his friend Wilding, who had held the title for the four preceding years. Most critics of the time thought Wilding, who had twice recently beaten Brookes, would win again but Brookes took the championship in straight sets. He lost it the following year to fellow Australian Gerald Patterson.

In 1926 Brookes was elected president of the Australian LTA (New Zealand having formed its own association in 1922). He held office until 1955 and was knighted in 1939. Throughout those years he continued to be a force in the game in Australia and was a Davis Cup selector in post-war years.

Australian men's singles won 1911 (beat H M Rice); men's doubles r/u 1911 with J Addison (R Heath/R Lycett won), won 1924 with J O Anderson (beat G Patterson/P O'Hara Wood, 6-2, 6-4, 6-3).

US men's doubles won 1919 with Patterson (beat W Tilden/V Richards, 8-6, 6-3, 4-6, 4-6, 6-2).

Wimbledon men's singles Challenge Round r/u 1905 (H L Doherty won, 8-6, 6-2, 6-4, 7-5), won 1907 (wo), won 1914 (beat Wilding, 6-4, 6-4, 7-5), r/u 1919 (Patterson won, 6-3, 7-5, 6-2); men's doubles All-Comers r/u 1905 with A W Dunlop (F Riseley/S Smith won, 6-2, 1-6, 6-2,

6-3), won 1907 (beat K Behr/B C Wright, 6-4, 6-4, 6-2), won 1914 (beat C P Dixon/H Roper Barrett, 6-1, 6-1, 5-7, 8-6), both with Wilding.

BROUGH, Althea Louise (Mrs A T Clapp), USA Born March 1923, Oklahoma City. Triple Wimbledon champion (singles, doubles and mixed doubles) in 1948 and 1950, Miss Brough won the US doubles title 12 times, won the Wimbledon women's singles title four times, including three in succession, and was never beaten in 22 Wightman Cup rubbers between 1946–57. Undoubtedly one of the greatest women players of all time, she played a major part in establishing the American domination of women's tennis after World War II. She was aided in this by, among others, Mrs Margaret duPont (then Miss Osborne), Doris Hart and Pauline Betz, who were all with her as members

of the US team which won the Wightman Cup in 1946 and who dominated world tennis for over a decade. The Brough–duPont doubles partnership was probably the most devastating of all time in women's tennis.

The tall, blonde Miss Brough was one of the greatest of women servers and also had a winning sidespin drive. She was an aggressive volleyer and always favoured the attacking game. In 1948, when she won her first Wimbledon singles title, there were four other American women quarter-finalists: Mrs duPont, Miss Hart, Mrs Pat Todd and Miss Shirley Fry. It was Miss Hart who won through to be the other finalist, losing 6-3, 8-6. The following year, with Miss Hart and Miss Fry out and Mrs H Rihbany among the four US quarter-finalists, it was Mrs duPont who went into a 43-game final which Miss Brough won two sets to one. And in 1950, when there were no fewer than seven American quarter-finalists, Miss Brough repeated her two sets to one victory over Mrs duPont in 23 games. She did not win that title again until 1955, after Maureen 'Little Mo' Connolly had been forced into retiring from her brief but glorious three-year reign.

Miss Brough's 1948 triple crown came with the help of Mrs duPont in the doubles and John Bromwich in the mixed doubles. In 1950 Mrs duPont again shared her doubles victory and Eric Sturgess was her mixed doubles partner. One of her most dramatic matches, though not the greatest, was in 1950 when she faced Althea Gibson, the first black player to play on the Center Court at Forest Hills. The majority of the crowd were rooting for Miss Brough and Miss Gibson was extremely tense at the start of the second round match, held under densely piled thunder clouds. Miss Brough took the first set comfortably but then the black girl began to fight back. Four times she came close to beating the greatest woman player in the world: then the storm broke and the match was abandoned until next day, when it took Miss Brough just eleven minutes to secure the US title. The two met again seven years later in the US finals at Forest Hills and this time Miss Gibson won in two straight sets.

US singles r/u 1942 (Miss Betz won, 4-6, 6-1, 6-4), r/u 1943 (Miss Betz won, 6-3, 7-5, 6-3), won 1947 (beat Miss Osborne 8-6, 4-6, 6-1), r/u 1948 (Miss duPont won, 4-6, 6-4, 15-13), r/u 1954 (Miss Hart won, 6-8, 6-1, 8-6), r/u 1957 (Miss Gibson won, 6-3, 6-2); doubles won 1942–3 with Miss Osborne, won 1944 (beat Miss Betz/Miss Hart, 4-6, 6-4, 6-3), won 1945 (beat Miss Betz/Miss Hart, 6-4, 6-4), won 1946 (beat Miss D A Prentiss/Mrs Todd, 6-2, 6-0), won 1947 (beat Miss Hart/Mrs Todd, 5-7, 6-3, 7-5), all with Miss Osborne, won 1948 (beat Miss Hart/Mrs Todd, 6-4, 8-10, 6-1), won 1949 (beat Miss Hart/Miss Fry, 6-4, 8-6), won 1950 (beat Miss Hart/Miss Fry, 6-2, 6-2), all with Mrs duPont, r/u 1952 with Miss Connolly (Miss Fry/Miss Hart won, 10-8, 6-4), r/u 1953 (Miss Fry/Miss Hart won, 6-3, 7-9, 9-7), r/u 1954 (Miss Fry/Miss Hart won, 6-4, 6-4), won 1955 (beat Miss Hart/Miss Fry, 6-3, 1-6, 6-3), won 1956 (beat Miss Fry/Mrs B Pratt, 6-3, 6-0), won 1957 (beat Miss Gibson/Miss D R Hard, 6-2, 7-5), all with Mrs duPont; mixed doubles won 1942 with F Schroeder, r/u 1946 with R Kimbell (W Talbert/Miss Osborne won, 6-3, 6-4), won 1947 with Bromwich (beat Segura/Miss G Moran, 6-3, 6-1), won 1948 with T Brown (beat Talbert/Mrs duPont, 6-4, 6-4), won 1949 with Sturgess (beat Talbert/Mrs duPont, 4-6, 6-3, 7-5). US Wightman Cup team 1946–8, 1950, 1952–7.

Australian singles won 1950 (beat Miss Hart, 6-4, 3-6, 6-4), doubles won 1950 with Miss Hart (beat Mrs N Bolton/Mrs T Long, 6-2, 2-6, 6-3).

French women's doubles won 1946 (beat Miss Betz/Miss Hart, 6-4, 0-6, 6-1), won 1947 (beat Miss Hart/Mrs Todd, 7-5, 6-2), both with Miss Osborne, won 1949 (beat Mrs E Hilton/Miss J Gannon, 7-5, 6-1), r/u 1950 (Miss Hart/Miss Fry won, 1-6, 7-5, 6-2), both with Mrs duPont.

Wimbledon women's singles r/u 1946 (Miss Betz won, 6-2, 6-4), won 1948 (beat Miss Hart, 6-3, 8-6), won 1949 (beat Mrs duPont, 10-8, 1-6, 10-8), won 1950 (beat Mrs duPont, 6-1, 3-6, 6-1), r/u 1952 (Miss Connolly won, 7-5, 6-3), r/u 1954 (Miss Connolly won, 6-2, 7-5), won 1955 (beat Mrs J Fleitz, 7-5, 8-6); doubles won 1946 (beat Miss Betz/Miss Hart, 6-3, 6-2), r/u 1947 (Miss Hart/Mrs Todd won, 3-6, 6-4, 7-5), both with Miss Osborne, won 1948 (beat Miss Hart/Mrs Todd, 6-3, 3-6, 6-3), won 1949 (beat Miss Moran/Mrs Todd, 8-6, 7-5), won 1950 (beat Miss Fry/Miss Hart, 6-4, 5-7, 6-1), r/u 1951 (Miss Fry/Miss Hart won, 6-3, 13-11), all with Mrs duPont; r/u 1952 with Miss Connolly (Miss Fry/Miss Hart won, 8-6, 6-3), won 1954 with Mrs duPont (beat Miss Fry/Mrs Hart, 4-6, 9-7, 6-3); mixed doubles won 1946 with T Brown (beat G Brown/Miss D Bundy, 6-4, 6-4), won 1947 (beat C Long/Mrs Bolton, 1-6, 6-4, 6-2), won 1948 (beat Sedgman/Miss Hart, 6-2, 3-6, 6-3), r/u 1949 (E Sturgess/Mrs P Summers won, 9-7, 9-11, 7-5), all with Bromwich; won 1950 with Sturgess (beat G Brown/Mrs Todd, 11-9, 6-1, 6-4), r/u 1955 with E Morea (E Seixas/Miss Hart won, 8-6, 2-6, 6-3).

BROWN, Geoffrey, Australia
Born April 1924, Murrundi, NSW. Though small in stature, Brown made up for his lack of height with an explosive service and was probably the fastest returner of the ball of his day. He used a very short 'wind-up' swing for his service but then delivered the ball so fast and with such accuracy at a low trajectory that it gained him many aces. He had a left-handed forehand and a two-fisted power-punch backhand. Despite this he was never to achieve a major international title, coming closest in 1946 when he met Yvon Petra of France in the men's final at Wimbledon. Both had been rated as relative 'outsiders' and had surprised critics with their successes in a field which included Jack Kramer, Jaroslav Drobný, Lennart Bergelin, Tom Brown and Dinny Pails. Petra was some eight inches taller than Brown and their final was a David and Goliath affair with Petra, also a powerful server and thunderous forehand player, taking an early lead. Brown had apparently been advised to slow down his usual whirlwind game but the advice was wrong and he had to fight to draw level at two sets each, using all his reserves. Then he lost his opening service in the fifth set and Petra took it 6-4 for the title.

Australian men's doubles r/u 1949 with O W Sidwell (A Quist/J Bromwich won, 1-6, 7-5, 6-2, 6-3).

Wimbledon men's singles r/u 1946 (Petra won, 6-2, 6-4, 7-9, 5-7, 6-4); men's doubles r/u 1946 with D Pails (T Brown/Kramer won, 6-4, 6-4,

6-2), r/u 1950 with Sidwell (Bromwich/Quist won, 7-5, 3-6, 6-3, 3-6, 6-2); mixed doubles r/u 1946 with Miss D Bundy (T Brown/Miss L Brough won, 6-4, 6-4), r/u 1950 with Mrs P Todd (E Sturgess/Miss Brough won, 11-9, 6-1, 6-4). Australian Davis Cup team 1947–8.

BROWN, Thomas Pollock, USA

Born November 1922, San Francisco. Tom Brown was destined to be overshadowed in his career by his fellow-countryman Jack Kramer who not only robbed him of title chances on several occasions but also proved the dominant player in their doubles pairings. Because he always fought hard not to show any emotion, Brown gained the nickname 'Mr Poker Face'. The 1946 Wimbledon champion, Yvon Petra, described his semi-final match against Brown that year as 'my hardest match at Wimbledon' and he had to fight back from being two sets down to draw level and then take the final set 8-6. 'I shall never forget the fight in the last two sets,' said Petra, a close friend of Brown's. But for that unexpected loss Brown might have taken the Wimbledon 'Triple Crown' in 1946 for he won the doubles with Kramer and the mixed doubles with Louise Brough. Like many of his American contemporaries, Brown was a power player armed with extremely accurate ground shots. In autumn 1946 Brown faced Kramer in the US finals and lost in straight sets. Even so he had played brilliantly in preceding rounds to beat Frank Parker, the title holder, in a gruelling match and put out Gardnar Mulloy in a sensational semi-final. In the 1947 Wimbledon final Brown again met Kramer, who won in a record 48 minutes, dropping only six games.

US men's singles r/u 1946 (Kramer won, 9-7, 6-3, 6-0), mixed doubles won 1948 with Miss Brough (beat W Talbert/Mrs M duPont, 6-4, 6-4). US Davis Cup team 1950, 1953.

French men's doubles r/u 1947 with O W Sidwell (E Fannin/E Sturgess won, 6-4, 4-6, 6-4, 6-3), mixed doubles r/u 1946 with Miss D Bundy (J E Patty/Miss P Betz won, 7-5, 9-7).

Wimbledon men's singles r/u 1947 (Kramer won, 6-1, 6-3, 6-2), doubles won 1946 with Kramer (beat G Brown/D Pails, 6-4, 6-4, 6-2), r/u 1948 with Mulloy (J Bromwich/F Sedgman won, 5-7, 7-5, 7-5, 9-7), mixed doubles won 1946 with Miss Brough (beat G Brown/Miss Bundy, 6-4, 6-4).

BROWNE, Mary Kendall, USA

Born June 1891, Santa Monica, California, died August 1971. Regarded as one of the strongest American women players of her day, Mary Browne's successes spanned World War I and included winning the US singles title three years running and the US doubles three years running and five times in all. In 1912, when she was already champion for the first time, she spotted the then unknown Bill Tilden, whose interest in tennis was in those days casual. She suggested that they should team up for the National pairs, which they then won two years running. Though slender, Miss Browne had a lethal forehand drive and probably the best all-round command of the game of that time.

In 1926 she was indirectly involved in the famous Wimbledon outburst of the legendary Suzanne Lenglen (by whom she had been beaten in the first round of the singles). Miss Lenglen had earned the disfavour of the crowd, which usually worshipped her, when she was reported to have stormed out of the All England Club in anger for not being escorted to the court, leaving Queen Mary in the Royal Box waiting to watch her second round singles match. In fact, Miss Lenglen had arrived at the ground to find that she was down to play her singles and her doubles with Didi Vlasto against Mary Browne and 'Bunny' Ryan. A message from her to the referee asking to play only the doubles had not reached him. Hurt and angered by what she believed to be a deliberate insult, the Frenchwoman refused to play either match that day. The doubles was played the next day in front of a hostile crowd which had read garbled versions of the incident in the newspapers. Lenglen and Vlasto lost 3-6, 9-7, 6-2 and Browne and Ryan went on to win the final. Shortly afterwards both Miss Lenglen and Miss Browne signed professional contracts with Charles C Pyle and played not very successful exhibition matches on tour.

US women's singles won 1912 (beat Miss H V Hotchkiss by default), won 1913 (beat Miss D Green, 6-2, 7-5), won 1914 (beat Miss M Wagner, 6-2, 1-6, 6-1), r/u 1921 (Mrs M Mallory won, 4-6, 6-4, 6-2); women's doubles won 1912 with Miss Green (beat M Barger-Wallach/Mrs F Schmitz, 6-2, 5-7, 6-0), won 1913 (beat Miss E Wildey/Miss Green, 12-10, 2-6, 6-3), won 1914

(beat Mrs E Raymond/Miss Wildey, 8-6, 6-2),
both with Mrs R H Williams; won 1921 with
Mrs Williams, won 1925 with Mrs H Wills
(beat Mrs H Bundy/Miss Ryan, 6-4, 6-3), r/u
1926 with Mrs A Chaplin (Miss Ryan/Miss E
Goss won, 3-6, 6-4, 12-10); mixed doubles won
1912 with R N Williams (beat W Clothier/
Miss E Sears, 6-4, 2-6, 11-9), won 1913 (beat
C S Rogers/Miss Green, 7-5, 7-5), won 1914
(beat J R Rowland/Miss M Myers, 6-1, 6-4),
both with Tilden, won 1921 with W M Johnston.

French singles r/u 1926 (Miss Lenglen won,
6-1, 6-0).

Wimbledon women's doubles won 1926 with
Miss Ryan (beat Mrs L A Godfree/Miss E L
Colyer, 6-1, 6-1); mixed doubles r/u 1926 with
H Kinsey (L A Godfree/Mrs Godfree won, 6-3,
6-4).

BROWNING, Mrs B J *see* **Durr, Françoise**

BRUGNON, Jacques (Toto), France
Born May 1895, Paris, died March 1978. One of
the 'Four Musketeers' with Borotra, Cochet
and Lacoste, 'Toto' Brugnon, although a good
singles player, was generally outshone by the
three younger men. Instead he became probably
one of the greatest doubles players the world
has seen. He had shown promise before World
War I and in 1919 reached the Challenge Round
of the *Coupe de Nöel* and then, in 1920, the
French covered courts singles and doubles finals.
His game was steady and classic and, without
advantage of powerful strokes, he relied upon
superb ball placement and an attacking lob
which has seldom if ever been surpassed. The
'Musketeers' came together as a team when they
were selected to represent France in the 1924
Davis Cup competition. Then began a ten-year
reign during which, between them, they won
ten French singles titles, six consecutive Wimbledon championships, three US titles and retained
the Davis Cup for six years. Brugnon himself
took eleven doubles and five mixed doubles
titles. He was awarded the *Légion d'honneur*.

French men's singles r/u 1921 (J Samazeuilh
won); men's doubles won 1922 with Cochet
(the French championships were 'closed' until
1924), r/u 1925 (Lacoste/Borotra won, 7-5, 4-6,
6-3, 2-6, 6-3), r/u 1926 (V Richards/H Kinsey
won, 6-4, 6-1, 4-6, 6-4), won 1927 (beat Borotra/
Lacoste, 2-6, 6-2, 6-0, 1-6, 6-4), all with Cochet;
won 1928 with Borotra (beat Cochet/R de
Buzelet, 6-4, 3-6, 6-2, 3-6, 6-4), r/u 1929 (Lacoste/
Borotra won, 6-3, 3-6, 6-3, 3-6, 8-6), won 1930
(beat H Hopman/J Willard, 6-3, 9-7, 6-3), won
1932 (beat C Bossus/M Bernard, 6-4, 3-6, 7-5,
6-3), all with Cochet; won 1934 with Borotra
(beat J Crawford/V B McGrath, 11-9, 6-3, 2-6,
4-6, 9-7); mixed doubles won 1921-3, won 1925
(beat Cochet/Miss D Vlasto, 6-2, 6-2), won 1926
(beat Borotra/Mrs Le Besnerais, 6-4, 6-3), both
with Miss S Lenglen.

Australian men's doubles won 1928 with
Borotra (beat J Willard/E Moon, 6-2, 4-6, 6-4,

*Left: Jacques Brugnon, one of
the renowned French 'Four
Musketeers', was one of the
greatest doubles players the
world has ever seen. He is
seen here in 1933.*

6-4).

Wimbledon men's doubles won 1926 (beat Kinsey/Richards, 7-5, 4-6, 6-3, 6-2), r/u 1927 (F Hunter/W Tilden won, 1-6, 4-6, 8-6, 6-3, 6-4), won 1928 (beat J Hawkes/G Patterson, 13-11, 6-4, 6-4), r/u 1931 /G Lott/J Van Ryn won 6-2, 10-8, 9-11, 3-6, 6-3), all with Cochet, won 1932 (beat G Hughes/F Perry, 6-0, 4-6, 3-6, 7-5, 7-5), won 1933 (beat R Nunoi/J Satoh, 4-6, 6-3, 6-3, 7-5), r/u 1934 (Lott/L Stoefen won, 6-2, 6-3, 6-4), all with Borotra.

BUDGE, John Donald, USA

Born June 1916, Oakland, California. A fiery redhead, Don Budge's temperament did not match the colour of his hair and in his early days, on the way to becoming possibly the greatest tennis player the world has yet known, he was apparently shy and retiring, though with the essential streak of determination needed by all champions. He was slow to take up tennis, preferring basketball, neighbourhood football and baseball. But when he was about 15 Budge was taunted by his older brother, Hugh, into entering the 1930 California State Boy's Tennis Tournament. He practised secretly, got through to the finals and won 6-0, 6-4. Having achieved that first success he was fired to seek more and trained arduously to master every stroke. Later it was to be said of him that he was the complete player, with a powerful service, ferocious backhand, blistering forehand, strong groundstrokes, grace of movement, even-temperament and high concentration and a dedicated application to each game.

Son of a former footballer for Glasgow Rangers in Scotland, the gaunt young Budge won the Pacific Coast junior tournament in 1932 and in the following year gained both the junior and senior singles titles for California. His first national title was the junior championship, in the finals of which he beat Gene Mako. They became friends and later doubles partners and were both in the Davis Cup team which regained the trophy from Great Britain in 1937. Aged 19 he was spotted in 1934 by Walter Pate, who was soon to become Davis Cup captain and who picked Budge in his new team for 1935. In a preliminary Davis Cup round Budge astounded the tennis world for the first time by beating the great Jack Crawford, the world No 2, in a marathon match of four hours ten minutes. As the match finished Budge was attacked by cramps and, leaving the court,

Right: Donald Budge won the Wimbledon men's singles in 1937 as well as the Wimbledon men's doubles and mixed doubles.

turned to see his opponent pass out.

All the time Budge was practising and experimenting to improve his game: he changed from his early eastern 'shake-hands' grip to the western grip in which the palm grips the back of the racket; then, because that was not effective on soft turf, he switched back to and remained with the eastern grip. By watching Fred Perry he picked up the tip of moving in quickly to the net to follow up a forcing shot. When Perry turned professional in 1936 it was left to Budge and von Cramm to fight for position as the world's leading amateur. Budge won the rating in 1937 with wins over Crawford, Bromwich, Parker and von Cramm himself. The two met again that year in what has been rated the greatest Davis Cup match ever. Before it von Cramm, an anti-Nazi, received a telephone call from Adolf Hitler exhorting him to win for the fatherland. Von Cramm won the first two sets; Budge levelled but fell back to 1-4 in the fifth, then drew back to 4-4, 5-5 and 6-6. In the next game he came to match point five times and then on the sixth he miraculously scrambled to a speeding cross-court forehand from the German and returned a winning shot as he fell, gaining the game, the match and the Davis Cup series.

In 1938 Budge turned professional and made his debut in a cross-country series against Ellsworth Vines which he won 21 to 18. Then he beat Perry 18-11 and Tilden 51-7 before joining the Air Force in World War II. He returned to tennis after the war but, out of training and over-weight, lost his series against Bobby Riggs, 23-21 and retired. On his way to greatness and the record books Budge had become the first winner of the 'Grand Slam' (the US, French, Australian and Wimbledon titles in one year) and triple champion of Wimbledon (singles, doubles and mixed) in two successive years.

US men's singles r/u 1936 (Perry won, 2-6, 6-2, 8-6, 1-6, 10-8), won 1937 (beat von Cramm, 6-1, 7-9, 6-1, 3-6, 6-1), won 1938 (beat Mako, 6-3, 6-8, 6-2, 6-1); doubles r/u 1935 (W Allison/J Van Ryn won, 6-4, 6-2, 3-6, 2-6, 6-1), won 1936 (beat Allison/Van Ryn, 6-4, 6-2, 6-4), r/u 1937 (von Cramm/H Henkel won, 6-4, 7-5, 6-4), won 1938 (beat A Quist/J Bromwich, 6-3, 6-2, 6-1), all with Mako; mixed doubles r/u 1936 (Mako/Miss A Marble won, 6-3, 6-2), won 1937 (beat Y Petra/Mrs S Henrotin, 6-2, 8-10, 6-0), both with Mrs M Fabyan, won 1938 with Miss Marble (beat Bromwich/Miss T Coyne, 6-1, 6-2). US Davis Cup team 1935–8.

Australian men's singles won 1938 (beat Bromwich, 6-4, 6-2, 6-1).

French men's singles won 1938 (beat R Menzel, 6-3, 6-2, 6-4); doubles r/u 1938 with Mako (B Destremau/Petra won, 3-6, 6-3, 9-7, 6-1).

Wimbledon men's singles won 1937 (beat von Cramm, 6-3, 6-4, 6-2), won 1938 (beat H W Austin, 6-1, 6-0, 6-3); doubles won 1937 (beat G Hughes/C Tuckey, 6-0, 6-4, 6-8, 6-1), won 1938 (beat Henkel/G Von Metaxa, 6-4, 3-6, 6-3, 8-6), both with Mako; mixed doubles r/u 1936 with Mrs Fabyan (Perry/Miss D Round won, 7-9, 7-5, 6-4), won 1937 (beat Petra/Miss A Mathieu, 6-4, 6-1), won 1938 (Henkel/Mrs Fabyan, 6-1, 6-4), both with Miss Marble.

BUDING, Edda, Germany

Born November 1936, Lovrin, Rumania, of German parents. Taught to play tennis by her father, a professional, Edda Buding was a qualified beautician and was voted the most beautiful girl in tennis by players in Europe. She won the Argentine junior championships in 1952 aged 16, when she also won the Bavarian international championships, and first played at Wimbledon in 1954. Reaching the third round of the singles, she gave Maureen Connolly her toughest match and took five games off the reigning champion before losing. She won the German singles title in 1959, the doubles in 1960 and mixed doubles in 1957, when she also won the Egypt international championships women's doubles, playing with her sister, Ilse.

BUENO, Maria Esther, Brazil

Born October 1939, São Paulo. Though she never received any formal tennis coaching, Maria Bueno grew up in the game's atmosphere. Her well-to-do parents had an apartment opposite the São Paulo tennis club grounds and here she was put out in her pram to air. After she had taken up tennis as a youngster she qualified as a school teacher and before her first world tour her schedule for one month was: rise at 2 AM and study, 5.30 AM to 7.15 AM tennis practice; 7.30 AM bath, breakfast and study; 9 AM to 4 PM school; 4.30 PM more study, meal and bed at 11 PM. On her way to becoming the world's No 1 woman player in 1959 at the age of 20, she carefully studied the styles of her opponents. Her own game was one of supreme grace and majestically classic strokes, of intense concentration and efficiency and one of the greatest serves ever seen in a woman player. Her timing was usually superb but when it was not, her game became remarkably poor.

Miss Bueno won the first of her four US and three Wimbledon singles titles in 1959 and became a Brazilian heroine. When she retained the Wimbledon title in 1960 Brazil issued a stamp bearing her picture and São Paulo erected her statue. Together with Margaret Smith Court she dominated world women's tennis until the emergence of Billie Jean King (then Moffitt) in 1966. She did not lose a single set at Wimbledon until 1965 and in all played 135 championship games there, winning three singles and five doubles titles and a total of 114 games. Some of her greatest matches were against Margaret Court, from whom she regained the US title in 1963 and the Wimbledon title in 1964 and by whom she was beaten for the French championship in 1964 and the Australian and Wimbledon championships in 1965. Her domin-

ance is all the more remarkable when seen in the light of the poor health she suffered during her career, notably in 1961–2 when she had jaundice, and again in 1969 when tennis elbow prevented her competing in any major events and virtually forced her retirement in 1971, though she had been ranked No 1 in 1970 and did not play.

US women's singles won 1959 (beat Miss C Truman, 6-1, 6-4), r/u 1960 (Miss D Hard won, 6-4, 10-12, 6-4), won 1963 (beat Miss Smith, 7-5, 6-4), won 1964 (beat Miss C Graebner, 6-1, 6-0), won 1966 (beat Miss N Richey, 6-3, 6-1); doubles r/u 1958 with Miss A Gibson (Miss J Arth/Miss Hard won, 2-6, 6-3, 6-4), r/u 1959 with Miss S Moore (Miss Arth/Miss Hard won, 6-2, 6-3), won 1960 (beat Miss A Haydon/Miss D Catt, 6-1, 6-1), won 1962 (beat Miss Moffitt/Mrs J Susman, 4-6, 6-3, 6-2), r/u 1963 (Miss R Ebbern/Miss Smith won, 4-6, 10-8, 6-3), all with Miss Hard; won 1966 with Miss Richey (beat Mrs L W King/Miss R Casals, 6-3, 6-4), won 1968 with Mrs Court (beat Miss Casals/Mrs King, 4-6, 9-7, 8-6).

Australian women's singles r/u 1965 (Miss Smith won, 5-7, 6-4, 5-2 retired); doubles won 1960 with Miss Truman (beat Miss Smith/Miss L Robinson, 6-2, 5-7, 6-2).

French women's singles r/u 1964 (Miss Smith won, 5-7, 6-1, 6-2); doubles won 1960 (beat Mrs R Hales/Miss Haydon, 6-2, 7-5), r/u 1961 (scratched against Miss Reynolds/Miss R Schuurman), both with Miss Hard; mixed doubles won 1960 with R N Howe (beat R Emerson/Miss Haydon, 1-6, 6-1, 6-2), r/u 1965 with J Newcombe (K Fletcher/Miss Smith won, 6-4, 6-4).

Wimbledon women's singles won 1959 (beat Miss Hard, 6-4, 6-3), won 1960 (beat Miss Reynolds, 8-6, 6-0), won 1964 (beat Miss Smith, 6-4, 7-9, 6-3), r/u 1965 (Miss Smith won 6-4, 7-5), r/u 1966 (Mrs King won, 6-3, 3-6, 6-1); doubles won 1958 with Miss Gibson (beat Mrs W duPont/Miss M Varner, 6-3, 7-5), won 1960 (beat Miss Reynolds/Miss Schuurman, 6-4, 6-0), won 1963 (beat Miss Ebbern/Miss Smith, 8-6, 9-7), both with Miss Hard, won 1965 with Miss Moffitt (beat Miss F Durr/Miss J Liefrig, 6-2, 7-5), won 1966 (Miss Smith/Miss J Tegart, 6-3, 4-6, 6-4), r/u 1967 (Miss Casals/Mrs King won, 9-11, 6-4, 6-2), both with Miss Richey; mixed doubles r/u 1959 with N Fraser (R Laver/Miss Hard won, 6-4, 6-3), r/u 1960 with R Howe (Laver/Miss Hard won, 13-11, 3-6, 8-6), r/u 1967 K Fletcher (O Davidson/Mrs King won, 7-5, 6-2).

Phil Dent – Australia

Jaroslav Drobný – Czechoslovakia/Egypt/Great Britain

Françoise Durr – France

Roy Emerson – Australia

Chrissie Evert – United States of America

Vitas Gerulaitis – United States of America

Althea Gibson – United States of America

ship tournament was staged in Toronto in 1890 (won by E E Tanner of the US) and also in that notable year the Province of Quebec LTA Inter-Club Series was launched.

A women's singles championship event was included in the national championships for the first time in 1892 and the first final, won by a Miss Osborne against a Mrs Smith, was a four set match. Canada first entered the Davis Cup in 1913 and succeeded in reaching the final but was defeated 0-3 by the US in the final at Wimbledon. Canada has taken part regularly since then and also enters the Federation Cup and other major international events.

Canada joined the ILTF in 1923. The annual national championships were divided in 1968 into open and closed sections. Ten provincial championships played during July and August lead up to the national event. Each provincial LTA operates as a separate entity and the Canadian LTA directs the holding of a variety of veteran, adult and junior open and closed events under the auspices of the PLTAs. Canadian tennis receives backing not only from members of tennis clubs but also from the government, commercial sponsors and the National Advisory Council on Fitness and Amateur Sports. Considerable attention is paid to the coaching of jurnior players and the country has a dynamic, government-backed sports support programme administered through the Sports Administrative Centre, Ottawa.

CANNING, Miss M *see* **Todd, Margaret**

CARMICHAEL, Robert J (Nails), Australia
Born July 1940, Melbourne. A former carpenter, nicknamed 'Nails', Carmichael is a rugged player who has been a regular on the international tennis circuit for some years. He lived for a time in Paris and qualified by residence to play for France. In 1970 he joined WCT.

Australian Open men's doubles r/u 1975 with A Stone (J Alexander/P Dent won, 6-3, 7-6); Tasmanian championships r/u 1970; New Zealand Open singles won 1971 (beat Stone, 7-6, 7-6, 6-3); doubles won 1971 (beat B Fairlie/R Moore, 6-3, 6-7, 6-4, 4-6, 6-3), won 1975 (beat Fairlie/O Parun, 7-6, retired), both with R Ruffels; Perth doubles r/u 1976 with El Shafei.

US clay courts doubles won 1973 with F McMillan (beat M Orantes/I Tirias, 6-3, 6-4); Kansas singles r/u 1975; Las Vegas doubles r/u 1975 with C Drysdale; Sacramento singles r/u 1976.

Hong Kong doubles r/u 1975 with A Mayer.
Dusseldorf doubles r/u 1976 with Moore.
Japan Open doubles won 1976 with K Rosewall (beat El Shafei/Fairlie, 6-4, 6-4).

CARTER, Mary *see* **Reitans, Mrs S T**

CASALS, Rosemary, USA
Born September 1948, San Francisco. Though minute in physique, Miss Casals is a powerhouse

Rosie Casals (left) and Billie Jean King (picture page 139) are the only women to win US doubles titles on grass, clay, hard court and wood.

of energy on court and has proved herself one of the greatest women's doubles players of recent years, winning five Wimbledon women's doubles, all with Billie Jean King, and three US, including two with Mrs King. She turned professional in 1968 when George MacCall of Los Angeles added her, together with Mrs King, Mrs Ann Jones and Françoise Durr, to his new National Tennis League. She and Mrs King are the only women to win US doubles titles on grass, clay, hard court and wood. Miss Casals has yet to win a major international singles title, though she has won many junior and senior singles events within the US. In 1967 she won all seven of her Federation Cup matches. In 1972 she was 3rd in the ILTF Grand Prix.

US Championship r/u 1970 (Mrs B M Court won, 6-2, 2-6, 6-1), r/u 1971 (Mrs King won, 6-4, 7-6); women's doubles r/u 1966 (Miss M Bueno/Miss N Richey won, 6-3, 6-4), won 1967 (beat Miss M Eisel/Mrs D Fales, 4-6, 6-3, 6-4), r/u 1968 (Miss Bueno/Mrs Court won, 4-6, 9-7, 8-6), all with Mrs King; r/u 1970 with Miss V Wade (Mrs Court/Mrs R D Dalton won, 6-4, 6-3), won 1971 with Mrs Dalton (beat Mrs G Chanfreau/Miss F Durr, 6-3, 6-3), r/u 1973 (Mrs Court/Miss Wade won, 3-6, 6-3, 7-5), won 1974 (beat Mrs Court/Miss Wade, 7-6, 6-7, 6-4), r/u 1975 (Mrs Court/Miss Wade won, 7-5, 2-6, 7-6), all with Mrs King; mixed doubles r/u 1967 with S R Smith (O Davidson/Mrs King won), r/u 1972 with I Năstase (M Riessen/Mrs Court won, 6-3, 7-5).

Australian women's doubles r/u 1969 with Mrs King (Mrs Court/Miss J Tegart won, 6-4, 6-4).

French women's doubles r/u 1968 (Miss Durr/Mrs P F Jones won, 7-5, 4-6, 6-4), r/u 1970 (Mrs Chanfreau/Miss Durr won, 6-3, 1-6, 6-3), both with Mrs King.

Wimbledon women's doubles won 1967 (beat Miss Bueno/Miss Richey, 9-11, 6-4, 6-2), won 1968 (beat Miss Durr/Mrs Jones, 3-6, 6-4, 7-5), won 1970 (beat Miss Durr/Miss Wade, 6-2, 6-3), won 1971 (beat Mrs Court/Miss Goolagong, 6-3, 6-2), won 1973 (Miss Durr/Miss B Stöve, 6-1, 4-6, 7-5), all with Mrs King; mixed doubles won 1970 (beat A Metreveli/Miss O Morozova, 6-3, 4-6, 9-7), won 1972 (beat K Warwick/Miss Goolagong, 6-4, 6-4), both with Năstase.

CAWLEY, Evonne Fay (_née_ **Goolagong),** Australia

Born July 1951, Barellan, NSW. An outstandingly gifted player and crowd puller, Evonne Cawley plays with vivacity and charm, though sometimes erratically. Part-aboriginal – her maiden name means 'tall trees by still water' – she was born in the Australian wheat country and has four brothers and three sisters. She was spotted as a 'natural' tennis player by the famous Australian coach Vic Edwards, who trained her and brought her up from the age of 11 as her legal guardian. As a youngster Evonne

won 43 junior state and inter-state titles and won the national under-19 singles and doubles championships on grass and twice on hard courts. She first toured outside Australia in 1970 and immediately captivated spectators with her enthusiasm and sheer enjoyment of the game. That year, making her debut at Wimbledon, she had the unusual experience of playing in the first round on the Centre Court because of her popularity. Though she lost to 'Peaches' Bartkowicz, Vic Edwards then said that she might well be champion by 1973. In fact, she made it two years earlier and in an astonishing series of championship matches in 1971 gained the French singles title, the Wimbledon singles, the Dutch title, the Australian hard court (for the second year), the New Zealand and was runner-up in Australia, South Africa, Canada, and the British hard courts. In doubles she was r/u at Wimbledon and the British hard courts, both with Margaret Court, the singles champion she deposed at Wimbledon, and won the South African doubles with Helen Gourlay. She was awarded the MBE in 1972.

In that first great year of her tennis career she generally exhibited grace, alertness and an

Right: Evonne Cawley (née Goolagong) is one of modern tennis' most formidable women players.

instinctive 'feel' for the game, pulling off some outrageously daring shots. At the same time she showed a suspect forehand, weak second service and a tendency sometimes to lose concentration and become almost dreamy – or, as reporters put it, to go 'walkabout'. She has since worked on these weaknesses to become a formidable all-round player, winning some 20 international titles on all surfaces. In 1975 she split from Vic Edwards after marrying English businessman Roger Cawley and in 1976 she left the circuit early to prepare for the birth of her first child in May 1977. Within weeks of her return she was showing that she was as good as ever and served notice of her challenge to Evert and King with a brilliant run of singles and doubles wins, including both the Australian singles and doubles, the latter shared with Mona Guerrant and Kerry Reid when the match was rained off.

Australian singles r/u 1971 (Mrs B M Court won, 2-6, 7-6, 7-5), r/u 1972 (Miss V Wade won, 6-4, 6-4), r/u 1973 (Mrs Court won, 6-4, 7-5), won 1974 (beat Miss C Evert, 7-6, 4-6, 6-0), won 1975 (beat Miss M Navratilova, 6-3, 6-2), won 1976 (beat Miss R Tomanova, 6-2, 6-2), won 1977-8 (beat Mrs H Gourlay Cawley, 6-3, 6-0); doubles won 1971 with Mrs Court (beat Miss L Hunt/Miss J Emerson, 6-0, 6-0), won 1974 (beat Miss K Harris/Miss K Melville, 7-5, 6-3), won 1975 (beat Mrs W W Bowrey/Miss Tomanova, 8-1, one set only), both with Miss M Michel, won 1976 with Miss H Gourlay (beat Mrs Bowrey/Miss Tomanova, 8-1, one set only), shared 1977-8 with Mrs Gourlay Cawley (Mrs Guerrant/Mrs Reid, rained off). NSW Open won 1977 (beat Miss S Barker, 6-2, 6-3); doubles won 1977 with Mrs Gourlay Cawley (beat Mrs Reid/Mrs Guerrant, 6-0, 6-0). Member Australian Federation Cup team 1971– .

French singles won 1971 (beat Miss Gourlay, 6-3, 7-5), r/u 1972 (Mrs L W King, won 6-3, 6-3); mixed doubles won 1972 with K Warwick (beat J Barclay/Miss F Durr, 6-2, 6-4).

US singles r/u 1973 (Mrs Court won, 7-6, 5-7, 6-2), r/u 1974 (Mrs King won, 3-6, 6-3, 7-5), r/u 1975 (Miss Evert won, 5-7, 6-4, 6-2), r/u 1976 (Miss Evert won, 6-3, 6-0).

Smash 77 won 1977 (beat Miss Navratilova, 6-1, 6-4).

Toyota Classic won 1977 (beat Miss W Turnbull, 6-4, 6-1).

Wimbledon singles won 1971 (beat Mrs Court, 6-4, 6-1), r/u 1972 Mrs King won, 6-3, 6-3), r/u 1975 (Mrs King won, 6-0, 6-1), r/u 1976 (Miss Evert won, 6-3, 4-6, 8-6); women's doubles r/u 1971 with Mrs Court (Miss R Casals/Mrs King won, 6-3, 6-2), won unseeded 1974 with Miss Michel (beat Miss Gourlay/Miss K Krantzcke, 2-6, 6-4, 6-3); mixed doubles r/u 1972 with Warwick (I Năstase/Miss Casals won, 6-4, 6-4).

World invitation singles won 1976 (beat Miss Wade, 6-3, 6-4); won doubles 1976 with Miss Barker (beat Miss Navratilova/Miss Wade, 6-4, 4-6, 6-3).

Won Virginia Slims Championship 1976 (beat Miss Evert, 6-3, 5-7, 6-3).

Colgate International won 1977 (beat Mrs Reid, 6-1, 6-3); doubles shared with Miss Stöve (Mrs Reid/Miss Stevens abandoned).

CAWLEY, Mrs Helen Gourlay *see* **Gourlay, Helen**

Centre Court, Wimbledon, GB

The most famous Centre Court in the world is that at Wimbledon. There was a Centre Court at the original All England Club Wimbledon home in Worple Road and a larger one was built – and has since been extended – at the 'new' premises in Church Road. The court is never used between championships, a tradition established after the Davis Cup Challenge Round was last staged there in 1936 but broken once, in 1967, for the World Professional Tournament. It is traditionally the scene of all Wimbledon finals.

CHAMBERS, Dorothea Katherine Lambert (*née* **Douglass),** GB

Born September 1878, Ealing, died January 1960. The daughter of a parson, 'Dolly' Douglass, better known under her married name of Lambert Chambers, was a late developer on the tennis court and was 21 before she began to show the talent that was to make her the greatest woman player before World War I and one of those who laid the foundations for today's tough, fast women's game. She first appeared at Wimbledon in 1902 and played through to the semi-finals before losing to Muriel Robb. Next year she won the first of her seven women's titles, four of which she gained by playing through all rounds rather than playing only the

Below: A wide-angle view of the centre court at Wimbledon.

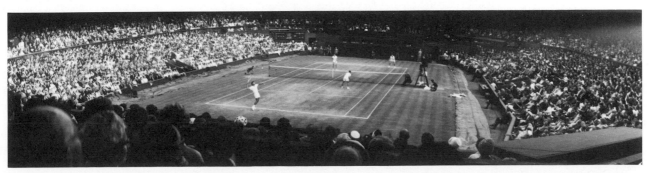

Right: Dorothea Lambert Chambers (née Douglass) was the greatest pre-World War I player in the world. She first appeared at Wimbledon in 1902.

Mrs Lambert Chambers' record of seven Wimbledon titles was broken only by Helen Moody (eight titles). In addition to being an Olympic gold medallist in 1908, she was an outstanding all-round athlete, All-England badminton doubles champion in 1903, mixed doubles champion in 1904 and played hockey for Middlesex county.

Wimbledon women's singles won Challenge Round 1903 (wo), won 1904 (beat Mrs A Sterry, 6-0, 6-3), r/u 1905 (Miss M Sutton won, 6-3, 6-4), won 1906 (beat Miss Sutton, 6-3, 9-7), r/u 1907 (Miss Sutton won, 6-1, 6-4), won 1910 (beat Miss D P Boothby, 6-2, 6-2), won 1911 (beat Miss Boothby, 6-0, 6-0), won 1913 (wo), won 1914 (beat Mrs D R Larcombe, 7-5, 6-4), r/u 1919 (Miss S Lenglen won, 10-8, 4-6, 9-7), r/u 1920 (Miss Lenglen won, 6-3, 6-0); women's doubles r/u 1913 with Mrs A Sterry (Mrs R McNair/Miss Boothby won, 4-6, 2-4, retired), r/u 1919 (Miss Lenglen/Miss E Ryan won, 4-6, 7-5, 6-3), r/u 1920 (Miss Lenglen/Miss Ryan won, 6-4, 6-0), both with Mrs Larcombe; mixed doubles r/u 1919 with A Prebble (R Lycett/Miss Ryan won, 6-0, 6-0). Wightman Cup in 1925–6.

CHANFREAU, Gail *see* **Lovera, Gail**

CHEYNEY, Mrs D M *see* **Bundy, Dorothy May**

CHYMRIOVA, Natasha, USSR
Born 1958, Moscow. In 1974, aged 16, she emerged as the chief challenger in Russia to Olga Morozova and by the end of 1975 she was making her mark on world tennis. She won the Australian junior title in 1974 and the Wimbledon junior invitation event for girls in both 1975 and 1976. She also won US Open Pepsi junior 1975. Her potential as an international star was recognised in 1976–7 as she threatened many of the world's leading women players and had wins against Rosie Casals, Sue Barker, Helen Gourlay and Renata Tomanova.

CLAPP, Mrs A T *see* **Brough, Althea**

CLERC, Jose Luis, Argentina
Born August 1958, Buenos Aires. Coached by Pat Rodrigues, this six-footer first attracted international attention as an up-and-coming junior in 1976. He reached the final of the Paris junior singles but lost to H Guenthardt after having match point; won Canadian junior singles; r/u in Pepsi junior international, Forest Hills, to R Ycaza.

CLOTHIER, William J, USA
Born September 1881, Philadelphia, died 1962. Winner of the US men's singles title in 1906, Clothier was also runner-up in the Challenge Round in 1909 and runner-up in the All-Comers of 1903 and 1904. He was among the first 'mass invasion' of Wimbledon by overseas players in 1905, when other Americans to enter were Beals Wright, Holcombe Ward and Wil-

Challenge Round as champion. In 1914 she played six matches to win the title and had 72 games to her credit and only 16 against. Her last challenge for the singles title was in 1920 (she did not play in 1909 or 1912) and her last Wimbledon appearance was in 1927 in the doubles – her twentieth Wimbledon at the age of 48. A slender, determined player who made every stroke count and was a superb tactician, she was at her peak from age 31 to 35.

In 1905 she lost the title she had held for the two previous years to the American, May Sutton, but gained it back from her in 1906. Twenty years later the two met again in the Wightman Cup of 1925. May Bundy and Molla Mallory lost to Dorothea Lambert Chambers and Ermyntrude Harvey, 10-8, 6-1 at Forest Hills. Dolly was then 46 and May 38.

As holder of the title when World War I broke out in 1914, Mrs Lambert Chambers, then 40, was back in 1919 to defend it against the precocious and already brilliant Frenchwoman, Suzanne Lenglen, aged 20. Unbeaten on the Riviera, Miss Lenglen had not then played on grass but won the All-Comers comfortably. Mrs Lambert Chambers had decided that if an English girl won the All-Comers she would not defend her title but if the French girl came through 'it was up to me to give her the chance to beat the reigning champion'. In front of King George V, Queen Mary and Princess Mary and a Centre Court packed by some 8000 other spectators, there followed a final of 44 games – a record not beaten for over 50 years – in which Miss Lenglen beat Mrs Lambert Chambers 10-8, 4-6, 9-7 after the Englishwoman had twice been at match point. A tougher, faster women's match had not been seen before at Wimbledon.

Left (centre): Russian-born Natasha Chymriova began to make herself known in world tennis in 1975 and has not looked back.
Left: Henri Cochet was one of the famous French 'Four Musketeers'. (The others were Borotra, Brugnon and Lacoste.)

liam Larned, and entries also came from Australasia, Belgium, Denmark, South Africa and Sweden.

US men's singles All-Comers r/u 1903 (H L Doherty won, 6-3, 6-2, 6-3), r/u 1904 (Doherty won, 10-8, 6-4, 9-7). US Davis Cup team 1905, 1909.

Challenge Round won 1906 (beat B C Wright, 6-3, 6-0, 6-4), Challenge Round r/u 1909 (W A Larned won, 6-1, 6-2, 5-7, 1-6, 6-1); men's doubles r/u 1907 with Larned (H Hackett/F B Alexander won, 6-3, 6-1, 6-4); mixed doubles r/u 1912 with Miss E Sears (R Williams/Miss M K Browne won, 6-4, 2-6, 11-9).

COCHET, Henri, France

Born December 1901, Villeurbanne, Lyons. One of the 'Four Musketeers' of France (with Borotra, Brugnon and Lacoste), Cochet was the son of the secretary of the Lyons tennis club and as a youngster spent much of his spare time acting as ball boy at the club's indoor courts. Here, too, he learned to play, often using a heavy adult racket to play against his sister and friends. He is reputed to have been inspired to take up serious tournament tennis after seeing the famous New Zealand player, Tony Wilding, in an exhibition match at Lyons before World War I and after the war he began entering tournaments. In 1920 he won five of six events at Aix-les-Bains and in 1921 he and another unknown player, Jean Borotra, met at the Racing Club of France in Paris in the final of the Criterium covered court championships. Cochet won in the fifth set. Next year the two made their debuts in the Davis Cup and defeated Denmark. By 1923 the Four Musketeers were together in the team to beat Ireland 4-1 and were at the start of a decade which has been called the golden age of tennis, when they gained international successes

that have never been equalled. Among them they won ten French singles titles, six consecutive Wimbledon titles, three US titles and numerous doubles and mixed doubles. Cochet, who had set up in a sports goods business after serving in the army, won five French titles, one US singles championship and two Wimbledon singles; three French doubles and two mixed doubles, one US mixed doubles and two Wimbledon doubles.

A small man, he lacked the power of many of his opponents but he was supple, calm and had marvellous anticipation. Though his service was weak and he had no particularly powerful shots, he possessed a remarkable half-volley and volley, exceptional footwork and reflexes and excellent forehand and smash. He taught himself to strike the ball as he advanced to the net, a tactic which gave him a fast return and a deceptive speed. Cochet's most remarkable win was probably that of the 1927 Wimbledon title against Borotra. In the quarter-final Cochet met Francis Hunter and won after being two sets down. In the semi-final he met 'Big Bill' Tilden, who towered above him both in actual height and in strength. Tilden led two sets to none and 5-1 in the third when Cochet broke service and won 17 consecutive points. Though Tilden led again in the fourth and fifth sets he had lost his grip on the match and Cochet went on to win 2-6, 4-6, 7-5, 6-4, 6-3. Then in the final Cochet was again two sets down to Borotra before saving six match points and winning the title, 4-6, 4-6, 6-3, 6-4, 7-5. He is the only man to have recovered from being two sets down in the quarter-final, semi-final and final and still win the championship.

Cochet turned professional in 1938 and was one of the first to join the US Professional Tennis Association. However, he was reinstated as an amateur in 1945 and in 1949 at the age of 47 reached the final of the British hard court championship.

French men's singles won 1922 (closed championship), won 1926 (beat R Lacoste, 6-2, 6-4, 6-3), won 1928 (beat Lacoste, 5-7, 6-3, 6-1, 6-3), won 1930 (beat W Tilden, 3-6, 8-6, 6-3, 6-1), won 1932 (beat G de Stefani, 6-0, 6-4, 4-6, 6-3), r/u 1933 (J Crawford won, 8-6, 6-1, 6-3); men's doubles r/u 1923–4 (closed), r/u 1925 (Lacoste/Borotra won, 7-5, 4-6, 6-3, 2-6, 6-3), r/u 1926 (V Richards/H Kinsey won, 6-4, 6-1, 4-6, 6-4), won 1927 (beat Borotra/Lacoste, 2-6, 6-2, 6-0, 1-6, 6-4), all with Brugnon, r/u 1928 with R de Buzelet (Borotra/Brugnon won, 6-4, 3-6, 6-2, 3-6, 6-4), r/u 1929 (Lacoste/Borotra won, 6-3, 3-6, 6-3, 3-6, 8-6), won 1930 (beat H Hopman/J Willard, 6-3, 9-7, 6-3), won 1932 (beat C Boussus/M Bernard, 6-4, 3-6, 7-5, 6-3), both with Brugnon; mixed doubles r/u 1923 (closed), r/u 1925 with Miss D Vlasto (Brugnon/Miss S Lenglen won, 6-2, 6-2), won 1928 (beat F T Hunter/Miss H Wills, 3-6, 6-3, 6-3), won 1929 (beat Hunter/Miss Wills, 6-3, 6-2), both with Miss E Bennett, r/u 1930 with Mrs F Whitingstall (Tilden/Miss C Aussem won, 6-4, 6-4). French Davis Cup team 1922–33.

US men's singles won 1928 (beat F T Hunter, 4-6, 6-4, 3-6, 7-5, 6-3), r/u 1932 (H Vines won, 6-4, 6-4, 6-4); mixed doubles won 1927 with Miss Bennett (beat Lacoste/Mrs G Wightman, 2-6, 6-0, 6-2).

Wimbledon men's singles won 1927 (beat Borotra, 4-6, 4-6, 6-3, 6-4, 7-5), r/u 1928 (Lacoste won, 6-1, 4-6, 6-4, 6-2), won 1929 (beat Borotra, 6-4, 6-3, 6-4); men's doubles won 1926 (beat H Kinsey/V Richards, 7-5, 4-6, 6-3, 6-2), r/u 1927 (Hunter/Tilden won, 1-6, 4-6, 8-6, 6-3, 6-4), won 1928 (beat J B Hawkes/G Patterson, 13-11, 6-4, 6-4), r/u 1931 (G M Lott/J Van Ryn won, 6-2, 10-8, 9-11, 3-6, 6-3), all with Brugnon.

Right: Glynis Coles is a new member of the international tennis world and has won several titles in both singles and doubles competitions.

COLES, Glynis, GB
Born February 1954, Middlesex. After an outstanding junior career Miss Coles has begun to make her mark in international competition. In 1971 aged just 17 she was the youngest ever winner of the British under-21 title and also won the British junior championship, British junior hard court and British junior covered court, creating a national record by winning junior titles on grass, clay and wood. The following year she was runner-up in the Wimbledon junior invitation to Ilana Kloss, British junior grass court, British junior covered court but retained the under-21 and junior titles and won the BP Shield. She has since had wins over Martina Navratilova, Ann Kiyomura, Marina Kroshina, and Linda Boshoff.

Italian Open women's doubles r/u 1975 with Miss S Barker (Miss C Evert/Miss M Navratilova won, 6-1, 6-2).

Swiss Open women's singles won 1975, (beat Miss L Boshoff, 9-7, 2-6, 8-6), r/u doubles with Miss D R Thompson.

Virginia Slims Akron doubles r/u 1976 with Miss F Mihai.

COLLIER, Mrs B see **Penrose, Beryl**

Commercial Union
The Commercial Union Life Assurance Company took over sponsorship of the ILTF's Grand Prix in 1972, announcing that it would contribute £100,000 for two years, including £20,000 for the Masters' Tournament. It was the first occasion on which a British finance house had offered such a large sports sponsorship. In fact the sponsorship continued for five years, during which time Ilie Năstase won the Masters' five times (he also won in 1971) and the Grand Prix twice (1972–3). Pepsi-Cola originally sponsored both the Grand Prix and the Masters' in 1970.

Commonwealth Caribbean LTA
The association was formed in 1947 by the LTAs of the Bahamas, Barbados, Guyana, Jamaica, St Lucia, St Vincent, and Trinidad and Tobago, with the name of the British Caribbean LTA. It changed its name in 1970. In addition to sponsoring the annual inter-Caribbean tournament, the Brandon Trophy, the Caribbean LTA provides teams for the Davis Cup.

CONNOLLY, Maureen (Mrs N Brinker), USA
Born September 1934, San Diego, California, died Dallas, Texas, June 1969. Affectionately known as 'Little Mo', Maureen Connolly was an extraordinarily brilliant young tennis player whose successes might well have eclipsed those of the all-time greats such as Suzanne Lenglen, Helen Wills Moody, Alice Marble and Margaret Court, had not a riding accident ended her career in 1954 and cancer ended her life tragically at the age of 34. As an 11-year-old she was spotted by children's tennis coach Wilbur Folson who was watching training sessions

through the fence of the Balboa municipal courts. He invited her in to try her hand and was impressed by a natural talent. Folson persuaded Maureen's widowed mother to let him coach her and in a few months had changed her from a left- to a right-hander. She began competing in junior tournaments and then came under the guidance of the famous coach Eleanor 'Teach' Tennant, whose protégé she became. Under her tuition Maureen made phenomenal progress and at 14 in 1949 became the youngest girl to win the national junior championships. By 15 she was already at No 10 in the national rankings and in 1951, when 16, she became the youngest US Wightman Cup team member, beating Britain's Kay Tuckey in her first match. Representing America again in 1953–4, she played nine rubbers and won them all.

Maureen also entered the 1951 US championships and reached the final against Shirley Fry after defeating Doris Hart 6-4, 6-4 on the way. She went on to win the US title after dropping the second set 1-6. Not quite 17, she was the youngest player for nearly 50 years to take the

Below: Maureen 'Little Mo' Connolly was a brilliant player whose career ended abruptly when she was involved in a riding accident.

ladies' title and she won it again in 1952 and 1953. Maureen, nicknamed 'Little Mo' after her 1951 triumph, first entered Wimbledon in 1952 and amazingly won the title, beating Louise Brough in straight sets. In the fourth round she dropped one set and in the quarter-final another. These were the only two sets she was ever to lose at Wimbledon.

Primarily a baseliner with unerring accuracy, she had fierce drives on both left- and right-hand side and could flash a winning cross court shot to within a fraction of the line. As she won a point she would turn and nod vigorously – a gesture which some took for arrogance but which was, in fact, an unconscious sign of determination.

In 1953 'Little Mo' became the first woman to win the Grand Slam (the Australian, French, US and Wimbledon titles), when she added the French and Australian championships to her other successes. Then in the mid-summer of 1954, after winning the French and Italian titles, Maureen, who had taken a few days rest, was riding her favourite horse, Colonel Merryboy, which had been presented to her by the people of San Diego, when he bolted and ran into a truck, smashing Maureen's right leg. The injury never healed and 'Little Mo' said 'If I can't play like I used to there is no point in playing at all.' The following year she became a professional, married Norman Brinker, a naval officer and Olympic equestrian and resisted all offers from tennis promoters.

US women's singles won 1951 (beat Miss S Fry, 6-3, 1-6, 6-4), won 1952 (beat Miss D Hart, 6-3, 7-5), won 1953 (beat Miss Hart, 6-2, 6-4); women's doubles r/u 1952 with Miss A L Brough (Miss Fry/Miss Hart won, 10-8, 6-4). US Wightman Cup, 1951–4.

Australian women's singles won 1953 (beat Miss J Sampson, 6-3, 6-2); women's doubles won 1953 with Miss Sampson (beat Mrs M Hawton/Miss B Penrose, 6-4, 6-2); mixed doubles r/u 1953 with H Richardson (R Hartwig/Miss Sampson won, 6-4, 6-3).

French singles won 1953 (beat Miss Hart, 6-2, 6-4), won 1954 (beat Mrs G Bucaille, 6-4, 6-1); women's doubles r/u 1953 with Miss Sampson (Miss Hart/Miss Fry won, 6-4, 6-3); mixed doubles r/u 1953 with M G Rose (E V Seixas/Miss Hart won, 4-6, 6-4, 6-0), won 1954 with L Hoad (beat Hartwig/Mrs J Patorni, 6-4, 6-3).

Wimbledon singles won 1952 (beat Miss Brough, 7-5, 6-3), won 1953 (beat Miss Hart, 8-6, 7-5), won 1954 (beat Miss Brough, 6-2, 7-5); women's doubles r/u 1952 with Miss Brough (Miss Fry/Miss Hart won, 8-6, 6-3), r/u 1953 with Miss Sampson (Miss Fry/Miss Hart won, 6-0, 6-0).

CONNORS, James Scott (Jimmy), USA
Born September 1952, East St Louis, Illinois. One of the new breed of 1970s 'power professionals', Jimmy Connors first came to inter-national prominence in 1972 when, aged 19 he reached the quarter-finals of the Wimbledon singles. His merit had already been·recognised in America, where he had gained seven national junior titles and was ranked No 4 in the under-21 world rankings after a sensational 1971 season which included wins against Graebner, Smith and Froehling and becoming US national inter-collegiate champion. He joined WCT in 1972 and won the John Player Round Robin, Roth-mans' London, Buckeye, Western, Ocean Pines, and Pacific Coast Championships and earned $90,000 in prize money.

A left-hander with a two-fisted backhand, he hits every time for a winner and fighting every point with usually devastating accuracy. Connors is naturally aggressive and can be an abrasive influence on court. He hits the ball early on return of service and dashes to the net to deliver savage volleys. When his opponent is also a powerful hitter he turns this to his advantage by feeding off the power to increase his speed of return still further; when the opponent is weaker he simply overwhelms with his own cannonball attacks. In 1973, seeded No 5 at Wimbledon after the ATP, in dispute with the ILTF, had withdrawn 70 of its professional players from the championship, he was beaten by Alex Metreveli in the singles but at his first attempt won the doubles with Ilie Năstase. The next year was to see his greatest triumph and his justifiable rating as the leading player in the world. He won the Wimbledon title from Aus-tralian Ken Rosewall, who had last appeared in a Wimbledon final in 1954; he took the US championship by beating Rosewall again at Forest Hills and he beat Phil Dent for the Australian title. In the same season he also took the South African title for the second year running, the US clay courts singles and doubles championships and the indoor championship. For a time he was engaged to Chris Evert, who won the Wimbledon women's title and was also making world headlines.

The successes of 1974, however, were fol-lowed by disappointment in 1975 when Con-nors, despite earning a reputed record sum of $600,273, lost his Wimbledon title to Arthur Ashe, the Australian title to John Newcombe and the US one to Manuel Orantes. He won only two Grand Prix tournaments and lost a crucial Davis Cup match to Raul Ramirez in the deciding rubber against Mexico. His Wimbledon loss to Ashe was against all pre-dictions and all odds as he had reached the final without losing a set. But Ashe, a wily tactician, deliberately slowed his own game to disorientate Connors. In 1976 despite the setbacks of the previous season, Connors regained his No 1 world ranking by winning 13 of 23 tournaments and beating Wimbledon champion Björn Borg in the final of the US Open and in the US Pro-fessional indoor championships. He finished third in the Commercial Union Grand Prix but as in the two previous years, declined to play in the Commercial Union Masters. However, in 1977–8 he played and beat Borg 6-4, 6-1, 6-4 in the Masters. His 1976 earnings of $687,335 broke all previous records. Not always the most popular player with crowds, perhaps because he makes his champion's killer instinct too obvious and also indulges in occasional fits of anger and shouted abuse, Connors nonetheless earns the admiration of watchers and players alike for the sheer gutsy determination of his fightback. He imposes himself on every match, on his opponents and on spectators.

US Open singles won 1974 (beat K Rosewall, 6-1, 6-0, 6-1), r/u 1975 (M Orantes won, 6-4, 6-3, 6-3), won 1976 (beat B Borg, 6-4, 3-6, 7-6, 6-4), r/u 1977 (G Vilas won, 2-6, 6-3, 7-6, 6-0); US Open men's doubles won 1975 with Năstase; US Open mixed doubles r/u 1974 with C Evert; US clay courts r/u 1972 (R Hewitt won, 7-6, 6-1, 6-2), won 1974–5, r/u 1977; US clay courts doubles won 1974 with Năstase (beat J Fassbender/H Pohmann, 6-7, 6-3, 6-4); US National indoors singles championship won 1973–5, r/u 1976; US indoor doubles won 1975 with Năstase; US Professional won 1975, won 1977; WCT Challenge Cup won 1977 (beat R Tanner, 6-2, 5-6, 3-6, 6-3, 6-5).

Australian singles won 1974 (beat P Dent, 7-6, 6-4, 4-6, 6-3), r/u 1975 (J Newcombe won, 6-7, 6-3, 7-6, 6-1), won 1977 (beat K Rosewall, 7-5, 6-4, 6-2).

French men's doubles r/u 1973 with Năstase (Newcombe/T Okker won, 6-1, 3-6, 6-3, 5-7, 6-4).

Italian Open men's doubles r/u 1974 with Năstase (B Gottfried/R Ramirez won, 6-4, 7-6, 2-6, 6-1).

Wimbledon men's singles won 1974 (beat Rosewall, 6-1, 6-1, 6-4), r/u 1975 (A Ashe won, 6-1, 6-1, 5-7, 6-4), r/u 1977 (Borg won, 3-6, 6-2, 6-1, 5-7, 6-4); Wimbledon men's doubles won 1973 with Năstase (beat J Cooper/N Fraser, 3-6, 6-3, 6-4, 8-9, 6-1); r/u men's singles 1978 (Borg won).

COOKE, Mrs E T *see* **Palfrey, Sarah Hammond**

COOPER, Ashley John, Australia
Born September 1936, Melbourne. Twice champion of Australia and once each of US and Wimbledon, Ashley Cooper came within one title (the French) of the coveted 'Grand Slam' in 1958. He started playing tennis at the age of ten and, coached by his father, took part in his

Below: Jimmy Connors was the first of the modern players to expound and practise 'power tennis'. In many championships it has proved itself invaluable although it has not always made him over-popular with fans.

Anderson (Hoad/Fraser won, 6-3, 8-6, 6-1), won 1958 with Fraser (beat R Emerson/R Mark, 7-5, 6-8, 3-6, 6-3, 7-5).

French men's doubles r/u 1956 with Hoad (D Candy/R Perry won, 7-5, 6-3, 6-3), won 1957 with Anderson (beat Candy/M G Rose, 6-3, 6-0, 6-3), won 1958 with Fraser (beat R Howe/A Segal, 3-6, 8-6, 6-3, 7-5).

US men's singles r/u 1957 (Anderson won, 10-8, 7-5, 6-4), won 1958 (beat Anderson, 6-2, 3-6, 4-6, 10-8. 8-6); men's doubles won 1957 with Fraser (beat G Mulloy/J Patty, 4-6, 6-3, 9-7, 6-3).

Wimbledon men's singles r/u 1957 (L Hoad won 6-2, 6-1, 6-2), won 1958 (beat Fraser, 3-6, 6-3, 6-4, 13-11); men's doubles r/u 1958 (S Davidson/U Schmidt won, 6-4, 6-4, 8-6).

COOPER, Miss C *see* **Sterry, Charlotte**

COURT, Margaret (*née* **Smith),** Australia
Born July 1942 Albury, NSW. A unique player not only in the number of major titles she has won but also for her athleticism and power, Margaret Court has a playing record which is unsurpassed by man or woman. She has won over 60 titles among the 'Big Four' tennis countries (Australia, France, United States and Great Britain), gained the mixed doubles 'Grand Slam' with Ken Fletcher in 1963 and the coveted women's singles 'Grand Slam' in 1970 after three times coming within one title of that achievement. Daughter of a foreman in the local dairy factory at Albury, Margaret started playing tennis on public clay courts across from her home when she was a spindly ten-year-old. As a teenager she showed none of the signs of the formidable athlete she was to become but nevertheless she won more than 50 junior tennis trophies.

At the age of 15 she came under the influence of Frank Sedgman, the famous Australian player of the 1950s, who set her to strenuous physical training sessions. At 5 ft 8¾ in (1.75 m) tall, she appears leggy but moves gracefully. A physical study of her in 1970 showed that she was well above average in body size, hand size and strength, and standing jump ability. Her height gives her an advantage in service against opponents which is increased by her sheer power. Opponents have described being overpowered by her presence, frightened of her and being unable to get the ball out of her reach. She has flawless ground strokes, relentless net attack, shattering smashes and drives and a determination to win every point.

In 1960, aged 17, she won the Australian championship for the first time, beating Maria Bueno, the only other woman to dominate women's tennis until Billie Jean King reached her peak. She went on to win the title 11 times in all and seven years in succession, the doubles eight times and mixed doubles twice. In 1962 came the first of her five French singles titles, to be accompanied by four doubles and four

first tournament at age 13. Despite a brilliant scholastic career he settled for a life of tennis after winning the Victoria hard court junior championship in 1953. The following year he toured Europe for the first time as a member of the Australian tennis invasion and reached the last 16 at Wimbledon. Picked for the Australian Davis Cup team in 1955 and 1956 he did not, in fact, make his debut until 1957, when he beat Vic Seixas in five sets in a vital Challenge Round singles match which enabled Australia to retain the cup. That year, he won the Australian title for the first time, the French and US doubles and, at his third attempt, reached the Wimbledon final. However, he was beaten 6-2, 6-1, 6-2 by fellow Australian Lew Hoad in just 57 minutes.

A ruggedly handsome player, Cooper had dogged determination and a powerful service-volley game in which, though he favoured rapid net follow-up, he tended to appear somewhat mechanical. He is remembered more for the solid persistence and consistency of his career than for all-round brilliance. In 1958 he retained his Australian title, won the French doubles and also won the US and Wimbledon singles and Australian doubles. After the 1958 Davis Cup Challenge Round in which Australia lost 3-2 to the US, Cooper turned professional and joined Jack Kramer's team to tour with Pancho Gonzales, Lew Hoad and Mal Anderson. He married Helen Wood, 'Miss Australia' beauty queen, in 1958. In 1959 he beat Hoad to win the final of the Slazenger professional tournament.

His younger brother, John, also took up a tennis career and in 1973 was runner-up with Neale Fraser for the Wimbledon men's doubles title, losing to Jim Connors and Ilie Năstase, 3-6, 6-3, 6-4, 8-9, 6-1. His career was ended by injury in 1973.

Australian singles won 1957 (beat N Fraser, 6-3, 9-11, 6-4, 6-2), won 1958 (beat M Anderson, 7-5, 6-3, 6-4); men's doubles r/u 1957 with

mixed doubles; the first of her US singles championships, which became a total of five, plus five doubles and eight mixed doubles.

Margaret Smith's first Wimbledon title in 1963 was won against Billie Jean Moffitt (later Mrs King), 6-3, 6-4, whom she was to meet on many other courts across the world in some classic confrontations. In 1966, with 35 'Big Four' titles already to her name, she announced her retirement but in 1967 she married wool broker Barry Court, who persuaded her back to the tennis circuit. On the way to winning the Grand Slam by taking the US title for the fourth time in 1970, she again met Mrs King and, though winning in two sets, took part in a record breaking match: the two sets consisted of a record 46 games and the first set went to a record 26 games.

In the Federation Cup, which Australia won for the first time in 1964, she gained a record 34 victories. The birth of her first baby in 1972 kept her out of the circuit until later in 1973 but she was immediately back among the titles in Australia, France and America. In 1974 she had her second child, again returned to the circuit and turned in consistently good performances though without ousting Chris Evert or Martina Navratilova on tour. After a miscarriage in 1976 she announced her retirement but changed her mind in time to play World Team Tennis in the second half of the season, and take part in three tournaments.

Australian women's singles won 1960 (beat Miss J Lehane, 7-5, 6-2), won 1961 (beat Miss Lehane, 6-1, 6-4), won 1962 (beat Miss Lehane, 6-0, 6-2), won 1963 (beat Miss Lehane, 6-2, 6-3), won 1964 (beat Miss L R Turner, 6-3, 6-2), won 1965 (beat Miss M Bueno, 5-7, 6-4, 5-2 default), won 1966 (beat Miss N Richey, default), r/u 1968 (Mrs L W King won, 6-1, 6-2), won 1969 (beat Mrs King, 6-4, 6-1), won 1970 (beat Miss K Melville, 6-1, 6-3), won 1971 (beat Miss E Goolagong, 2-6, 7-6, 7-5), won 1973 (beat Miss Goolagong, 6-4, 7-5); women's doubles r/u 1960 with Miss L Robinson (Miss Bueno/Miss C Truman won, 6-2, 5-7, 6-2), won 1961, with Miss S Reitano (beat Mrs M Hawton/Miss Lehane, 6-4, 3-6, 7-5), won 1962 (beat Miss Hard/Miss Reitano, 6-4, 6-4), won 1963 (beat Miss Lehane/Miss Turner, 6-1, 6-3), r/u 1964 (Miss Tegart/Miss Turner won, 6-4, 6-4), all with Miss R Ebbern, won 1965 with Miss Turner (beat Miss B Moffitt/Miss Ebbern, 1-6, 6-2, 6-3), r/u 1966 (Miss Richey/Mrs C Graebner won, 6-4, 7-5), won 1969 with Miss Tegart (beat Miss Casals/Mrs King, 6-4, 6-4), won 1970 with Miss J Dalton (beat Miss Melville/Miss K Krantczke, 6-3, 6-1), won 1971 with Miss Goolagong (beat Miss L Hunt/Miss J Emerson, 6-0, 6-0), won 1973 with Miss V Wade (beat Miss Melville/Miss K Harris, 6-4, 6-4); mixed doubles won 1963 with K Fletcher (beat Stolle/Miss Turner, 7-5, 5-7, 6-4), won 1964 with Fletcher (beat M Sangster/Miss Lehane, 6-3, 6-2), won 1965 with J Newcombe (beat O Davidson/Miss Ebbern, 6-1, 6-3), r/u 1968 with A Stone (R Crealy/Mrs King won, wo).

French women's singles won 1962 (beat Miss Turner, 6-3, 3-6, 7-5), won 1964 (beat Miss Bueno, 5-7, 6-1, 6-2), r/u 1965 (Miss Turner won, 6-3, 6-4), won 1968 (beat Mrs A Jones, 5-7, 6-4, 6-1), won 1969 (beat Mrs Jones, 6-1, 4-6, 6-3), won 1970 (beat Miss H Niessen, 6-2, 6-4), won 1973 (beat Miss Evert, 6-7, 7-6, 6-4); women's doubles r/u 1962 with Miss J Bricka (Mrs S Price/Miss R Schuurman won, 6-4, 6-4), r/u 1963 with Miss Ebbern (Mrs Jones/Miss Schuurman won, 7-5, 6-4), won 1964 (beat Miss N Baylon/Miss H Schultze, 6-3, 6-0), won 1965 (beat Miss F Durr/Miss J Lieffrig, 6-3, 6-1), both with Miss Turner, won 1966 with Miss Tegart (beat Miss J Blackman/Miss Toyne, 4-6, 6-1, 6-1), r/u 1969 with Miss Richey (Miss Durr/Mrs Jones won, 6-0, 4-6, 7-5), won 1973 with Miss Wade (beat Miss B Stöve/Miss Durr, 6-2, 6-3); mixed doubles won 1963 (beat Stolle/Miss Turner, 6-1, 6-2), won 1964 (beat Stolle/Miss Turner, 6-3, 6-4), won 1965 (beat Newcombe/Miss Bueno, 6-4, 6-4), all with Fletcher, won 1969 with M Riessen (beat J C Barclay/Miss Durr, 7-5, 6-4).

US women's singles, won 1962 (beat Miss D Hard, 9-7, 6-4), r/u 1963 (Miss Bueno won, 7-5, 6-4), won 1965 (beat Miss Moffitt, 8-6, 7-5), won 1969 (beat Miss Richey, 6-2, 6-2), won 1970 (beat Miss R Casals, 6-2, 2-6, 6-1), won 1973 (beat Miss Goolagong, 7-6, 5-7, 6-2); women's

doubles won 1963 with Miss Ebbern (beat Miss Hard/Miss Bueno, 4-6, 10-8, 6-3), r/u 1964 with Miss Turner (Miss Moffitt/Mrs J Susman won, 3-6, 6-2, 6-4), won 1968 with Miss Bueno (beat Miss Casals/Mrs King, 4-6, 9-7, 8-6), r/u 1969 with Miss Wade (Miss Durr/Miss Hard won, 0-6, 6-3, 6-4), won 1970 with Mrs R Dalton (beat Miss Casals/Miss Wade, 6-4, 6-3), r/u 1972 (Miss Durr/Miss Stöve won, 6-3, 1-6, 6-3), won 1973 (beat Mrs King/Miss Casals, 3-6, 6-3, 7-5), r/u 1974 (Miss Casals/Mrs King won 7-6, 6-7, 6-4), won 1975 (beat Mrs King/Miss Casals, 7-5, 2-6, 7-6), all with Miss Wade; mixed doubles won 1961 with R Mark (beat Ralston/Miss Hard, wo), won 1962 with Stolle (beat F Froehling/Miss Turner, 7-5, 6-2), won 1963 with Fletcher (beat E Rubinoff/Miss Tegart, 3-6, 8-6, 6-2), won 1964 with Newcombe (beat Rubinoff/Miss Tegart, 10-8, 4-6, 6-3), won 1965 with Stolle (beat Froehling/Miss Tegart, 6-2, 6-2), won 1969 (beat Ralston/Miss Durr, 7-5, 6-3), won 1970 (beat F McMillan/Mrs Dalton, 6-4, 6-4), won 1972 (beat Năstase/Miss Casals, 6-3, 7-5), r/u 1973 (Davidson/Mrs King won, 6-4, 3-6, 7-5), all with Riessen.

Wimbledon women's singles won 1963 (beat Miss Moffitt, 6-3, 6-4), r/u 1964 (Miss Bueno won, 6-4, 7-9, 6-3), won 1965 (beat Miss Bueno, 6-4, 7-5), won 1970 (beat Mrs King, 14-12, 11-9); women's doubles r/u 1961 with Miss Lehane (Miss K Hantze/Miss Moffitt won, 6-3, 6-4), r/u 1963 with Miss Ebbern (Miss Bueno/Miss Hard won, 8-6, 9-7), won 1964 (beat Miss Moffitt/Miss Susman, 7-5, 6-2), r/u 1966 (Miss Bueno/Miss Richey won, 6-3, 4-6, 6-4), won 1969 (beat Miss P Hogan/Miss M Michel, 9-7, 6-2), both with Miss Tegart, r/u 1971 with Miss Goolagong (Miss Casals/Mrs King won, 6-3, 6-2); mixed doubles won 1963 (beat Hewitt/Miss Hard, 11-9, 6-4), r/u 1964 (Stolle/Miss Turner won, 6-4, 6-4), won 1965 (beat A Roche/Miss Tegart, 12-10, 6-3), won 1966 (beat Ralston/Mrs King, 4-6, 6-3, 6-3), won 1968 (beat A Metreveli/Miss O Morozova, 6-1, 14-12), all with Fletcher, r/u 1971 (Davidson/Mrs King won, 3-6, 6-2, 15-13), won 1975 (beat Stone/Miss Stöve, 6-4, 7-5), both with Riessen.

Also Italian women's singles champion 1962–4, Italian doubles 1963–4, 1968, mixed 1961, 1964, 1968. German champion 1964–6, doubles 1964–6, mixed 1965–6, South African champion 1968, 1970–1, doubles 1966, 1971, mixed 1966, 1970–1, 1974. Member of Australian Federation Cup team 1963–5 and 1968–71.

COX, Mark, GB
Born July 1943, Leicester. A left-hander, Cox, who has a Cambridge University Economics degree, made tennis history in the first Open tournament at Bournemouth in 1968 when he became the first amateur to beat a professional in Open tennis with wins over Gonzales and Emerson. He joined WCT in 1969 but did not achieve his first tournament success with them until 1972, when he won Cleveland. During that

year he had wins over Rosewall and Laver (twice). In the US indoor championship doubles of 1968 with Bobby Wilson, he played a match lasting 6 hours 23 minutes against Holmberg and Pasarell and in 1969 with Peter Curtis he was on the losing end of a Davis Cup record-breaking 95-game doubles against Bungert and Kuhnke of Germany. However, Cox beat Bungert in the singles to assure a 3-2 British victory. That year he won the Dewar Cup singles finals at Crystal Palace, beating Bob Hewitt 4-6, 9-7, 6-2. In 1970 his major win was the Rothmans' British hard court championship. Other successes are: Cologne doubles won 1973 with Stilwell, Denver WCT won 1973, Irish Open won 1973, Dewar Cup Aberavon singles won 1973, London WCT won 1975, Washington WCT won 1975, Atlanta WCT won 1975, WCT finals Dallas doubles r/u with Drysdale; member of WCT title-winning Pittsburgh Triangles. In 1976, after living for two years in Canada, he returned to England and displayed brilliant form late in the season, beating Connors and Orantes and winning the Stockholm indoor.

COYNE, Thelma *see* **Long, Mrs Thelma**

CRAMM, Baron Gottfried von, Germany
Born July 1909, Nettlingen, Hanover, died November 1976 in car crash in Cairo. One of the most classically fluent stylists the game has ever seen, von Cramm was also one of its most gentlemanly exponents and it was said of him that the only line calls he ever questioned were in favour of his opponents. Though he won the German title six times – the first in 1932 and the last in 1949 – he is perhaps best remembered as the loser in some classic matches against the American Don Budge and the British champion Fred Perry. When Perry turned professional in 1937 it was left to Budge and the Baron to fight for the place as the World's No 1 amateur. Budge gained it, beating the German at Wimble-

don and Forest Hills and in a 1937 match which has been described as the greatest Davis Cup match ever (*see* Budge).

Von Cramm lost the 1935 Wimbledon final to Perry 6-2, 6-4, 6-4 and went down 6-1, 6-1, 6-0 to him in the 1936 final after pulling a leg muscle in the second game. It was typical of him that he disguised the injury successfully for several sets. In 1938 he was imprisoned by the German Gestapo. He would have been at the peak of his performance in the years covered by World War II but nevertheless came back in the late 1940s, still a fine player, fluent and supremely poised, with copybook strokes. He won his last title, the German international men's doubles, at Hamburg in 1956 and remained active in the administration of German tennis. He became President of the Rot-Weiss tennis club and an honorary committee member of the German controlling body, the *Deutscher Tennis Bund* until his death. During his career he did in fact number both Budge and Perry among his victims, as well as players such as Allison, Jack Crawford and Drobný. Of 102 Davis Cup rubbers between 1932 and 1953 he won 82.

German championships won 1932–5, 1948–9; doubles 1948–9; mixed doubles 1932–4.

French championships singles won 1934 (beat J H Crawford, 6-4, 7-9, 3-6, 7-5, 6-3), r/u 1935 (F Perry won, 6-3, 3-6, 6-1, 6-3), won 1936 (beat Perry, 6-0, 2-6, 6-2, 2-6, 6-0); doubles won 1937 with H Henkel (beat N Farquharson/V Kirby, 6-4, 7-5, 3-6, 6-1).

US championships singles r/u 1937 (Budge, 6-1, 7-9, 6-1, 3-6, 6-1); doubles won 1937 with Henkel (Budge/C G Mako, 6-4, 7-5, 6-4).

Australian men's doubles r/u 1938 with Henkel (A Quist/J Bromwich won, 7-5, 6-4, 6-0).

Wimbledon singles r/u 1935 (Perry won, 6-2, 6-4, 6-4), r/u 1936 (Perry won, 6-1, 6-1, 6-0), r/u 1937 (Budge won, 6-3, 6-4, 6-2); mixed doubles won 1933 with Miss H Krahwinkel (beat Farquharson/Miss M Heeley, 7-5, 8-6).

Top left: Left-handed Mark Cox continues to acquire international tennis titles. Above: Baron Gottfried von Cramm at Wimbledon in 1937. He eventually lost to American Don Budge.

CRAWFORD, John Herbert, Australia
Born March 1908, Albury, NSW. Four times winner of the Australian singles (1931–5) and doubles titles (1929–30, 1932, 1935). Crawford was in 1933 the first overseas player to take the French singles title in its 41-year history. That same year he took the Wimbledon title from the American Ellsworth Vines in a match described as the best the Centre Court had ever seen. Crawford presented a strangely old-fashioned figure on court with a long-sleeved white shirt buttoned at the wrists and using a square-topped racket. It was said that when, as occasionally happened, he rolled up his right sleeve he was facing a real crisis. For refreshment he kept hot, sweet, milky tea under the umpire's chair. His style was purely classic and his great strength was in his ground strokes, his persistent accuracy and concentration. By contrast Vines relied heavily on his power of service. In the 1933 Wimbledon final Vines took the first set in the tenth game after Crawford had pulled back from 2-5 down. The second set went to 20 games and only one service break, whereupon Crawford took it 11-9. He took the next against an apparently tiring Vines but in the fourth he tired himself, so that after 100 minutes they were two sets all. In the final set, at 4-4, the Australian suddenly followed his own serve to the net – something he rarely did – and won the point. Repeating the ploy, he took the set 6-4 and the title.

The following year saw spectators and players alike struck by a mysterious virus, 'Wimbledon throat', believed to have been caused by crystals which had formed on the grass courts after their treatment for weeds. In all 63 players scratched and Crawford, playing against doctor's orders, fought through to the final despite being a vic-

tim of the bug. However, the classic player was no match for Britain's Fred Perry, who was in devastating form and Crawford lost in three sets, 6-3, 6-0, 7-5. Later in the year Crawford lost again to Perry in the US finals, though he took the match to five sets and won the second 13-11 and third 6-4.

Australian men's singles won 1931 (beat H Hopman, 6-4, 6-2, 2-6, 6-1), won 1932 (beat Hopman, 4-6, 6-3, 3-6, 6-3, 6-1), won 1933 (beat K Gledhill, 2-6, 7-5, 6-3, 6-2), r/u 1934 (F Perry won, 6-3, 7-5, 6-1), won 1935 (beat Perry, 2-6, 6-4, 6-4, 6-4), r/u 1936 (A Quist won, 6-2, 6-3, 4-6, 3-6, 9-7); men's doubles won 1929 (beat R Cummings/F Moon, 6-1, 6-8, 4-6, 6-1, 6-3), won 1930 (beat J Hawkes/Fitchett, 8-6, 6-1, 2-6, 6-3), r/u 1931 (C Donohoe/R Dunlop won, 8-6, 6-2, 5-7, 7-9, 6-4), all with Hopman, won 1932 (beat Hopman/G Patterson, 12-10, 6-3, 4-6, 6-4), r/u 1933 (H Vines/K Gledhill won, 6-4, 10-8, 6-2), both with E F Moon, won 1935 (beat Perry/G Hughes, 6-4, 8-6, 6-2), r/u 1936 (Quist/D Turnbull won, 6-8, 6-2, 6-1, 3-6, 6-2), both with V McGrath; mixed doubles r/u 1929 (Moon/Miss D Akhurst won, 6-0, 7-5), r/u 1930 (Hopman/Miss N Hall won, 11-9, 3-6, 6-3), both with Miss M Cox; won 1931 (beat A Willard/Mrs V Westacott), won 1932 (beat J Sato/Mrs P O'Hara Wood, 6-8, 8-6, 6-3), won 1933 (beat Vines/Mrs J Van Ryn, 3-6, 7-5, 13-11), all with Mrs J H Crawford.

Davis Cup 1928, 1930, 1932–7.

French men's singles won 1933 (beat H Cochet, 8-6, 6-1, 6-3), r/u 1934 (G von Cramm won, 6-4, 7-9, 3-6, 7-5, 6-3); men's doubles r/u 1934 with McGrath (J Borotra/J Brugnon won, 11-9, 6-3, 2-6, 4-6, 9-7), won 1935 with Quist (beat McGrath/Turnbull, 6-1, 6-4, 6-2); mixed doubles won 1933 with Miss M C Scriven (beat Perry/Miss B Nuthall, 6-2, 6-3).

US men's singles r/u 1933 (Perry won, 6-3, 11-13, 4-6, 6-0, 6-1).

Wimbledon men's singles won 1933 (beat Vines, 4-6, 11-9, 6-2, 2-6, 6-4), r/u 1934 (Perry won, 6-3, 6-0, 7-5); men's doubles won 1935 with Quist (beat W Allison/J Van Ryn, 6-3, 5-7, 6-2, 5-7, 7-5); mixed doubles r/u 1928 with Miss Akhurst (P Spence/Miss E Ryan won, 7-5, 6-4), won 1930 with Miss Ryan (beat D Prenn/Miss Krahwinkel, 6-1, 6-3).

CREALY, Richard, Australia
Born September 1944, Sydney. Studied science at University of New South Wales. At 6 ft 4½ in (1.94 m) Crealy is a strong performer with powerful service and smash. He has turned in consistently good performances on the WCT circuit which he joined in 1970, though he has not gained any major titles since winning the French championship doubles with Allan Stone in 1974.

Australian men's singles r/u 1970 (A Ashe won, 6-4, 9-7, 6-2); doubles won 1968 with A Stone (beat T Addison/R Keldie, 10-6, 6-4, 6-3); mixed doubles won 1968 with Mrs L W

King (beat Stone/Mrs B M Court, wo). French championship doubles won 1974 with O Parun (beat R Lutz/S Smith, 6-3, 6-2, 3-6, 5-7, 6-1).

US National doubles won 1969 with Stone (beat W Bowrey/C Pasarell, 9-11, 6-3, 7-5); US clay court doubles r/u 1977 with C Letcher (J Fillol/P Cornejo won, 6-7, 6-4, 6-3).

West German doubles r/u 1971 with A Stone (J Alexander/A Gimeno won, 6-4, 7-5, 7-9, 6-4).

Wimbledon, won Plate 1971. Swedish Open singles won 1970; Danish Open won 1971; Nice ATP won 1975; Hamburg doubles r/u 1976 with K Warwick; Bermuda doubles r/u 1975 with R Ruffels.

CRISP, Hope, GB
Born February 1884, Highgate, London, died March 1950. A Cambridge University tennis player in 1911–13, Crisp, also played soccer for the University. In 1913 he won the Wimbledon mixed doubles with Mrs C O Tuckey (beat J Parke/Mrs D Larcombe, 3-6, 5-3). Despite losing a leg in World War I, he continued to play good tennis on an artificial leg in 1919 and 1920.

CUYPERS, Brigitte, South Africa
Born December 1955, Cape Town. Coached by Dennis Ralston, the US Davis Cup coach from 1971–6, Miss Cuypers has shown steadily improving form on the international circuit since winning the Rhodesian Open women's singles in 1974 and the singles and doubles in 1975. On the Virginia Slims circuit she has had wins against Chris Evert, Betty Stöve, Lesley Hunt, Carrie Meyer, Renata Tomanova, 'Linky' Boshoff, Virginia Wade, Olga Morozova, Glynis Coles, Greer Stevens and Laura Dupont.

South Africa Open women's singles r/u 1975 (Mrs A du Plooy won), won 1976 (beat Miss L Dupont). Rhodesia Open singles won 1974–5, doubles won 1975, mixed doubles won 1975. US clay courts singles r/u 1976 (Miss K May won, 6-4, 4-6, 6-2). Virginia Slims Akron doubles won 1976 with Mrs M Guerrant (beat Miss C Evert/Miss B Stöve). Italian Open doubles won 1977 with Miss M Kruger (beat Miss B Bruning/Miss S Walsh, 3-6, 7-5, 6-2).

Czechoslovakia
The history of lawn tennis in Czechoslovakia falls into three sections: the tennis of Bohemia, of Slovakia and of Czechoslovakia as a whole. The first lawn tennis competition was held in Bohemia at Choceň in 1879, by which time there were nearly 480 tennis courts, mostly of wood, concrete or brick, in various places in the country. This tournament is believed to have been the first in central Europe. From 1890 the game was played increasingly as a competitive sport as well as a social pastime and in 1894 the English rules were translated and the first official Czech lawn tennis club was established in Bohemia, the IČLTK of Prague. The first lawn tennis courts in Slovakia were built in 1880 in Bratislava and Piešťány and the earliest clubs founded at Banská Bystrica, Bratislava, and Komárno in 1899. It was another nine years before Slovakia's first championships were held. In 1906 the Czech LTA was founded and it was recognised by the ILTF in 1921. Though Czech players began playing in international competitions early in the century, the game's spread through the country was halted by World War I. In December 1918 the Czechoslovak Tennis Association was established and the popularity of the game spread over the new republic of Czechoslovakia. The most famous of the country's international players are J Drobný, J Kodeš, K Koželuh and Věra Suková-Pužejová.

Czechoslovakia first played in the Davis Cup in 1921 and reached the European zone finals in 1924. Up to World War II it reached these finals a further five times and after the war achieved its greatest successes in 1947 and 1948 by reaching the Inter-zone finals, losing on each occasion to Australia. Yet again it reached the finals in 1971 but lost to Brazil. After the Challenge Round system was abolished in 1971, Czechoslovakia was runner-up to Sweden in the final at Stockholm in 1975. The country has competed in the Federation Cup since 1963, the King's Cup, which it won in 1969, and the Galea Cup, which it won in 1963, 1965–6, 1970 and 1974–5. The Annie Soisbault Cup went to Czechoslovakia in 1974 and 1976; its women's team won the BP Cup women's section in 1973. The country has good tennis organisation and planning and pays particular attention to training young players. There are competitions for the under-12s, under-14s and under-18s and school clubs have padder tennis training for six-year-olds, using light wooden paddles instead of strung rackets on courts which are smaller than the normal (20 ft by 40 ft; 6 m × 12 m) and with the net at 2 ft 8 in (80 cm).

Above: Richard Crealy is a consistent and powerful player, known for his smash and service.

Dallas, Texas, USA

The Moody Coliseum, the gymnasium of the Southern Methodist University at Dallas, Texas, was constructed in 1956. It became famous in 1971 when it became the forum for the then richest tournament in the history of tennis – the 'World Championships of Tennis', with a first prize of $50,000. A synthetic green 'carpet' surface was laid and seating installed for 8500 people, together with facilities for the television cameras which were essential to the success of the venture. The event was watched by the largest television audience in the history of tennis and was an indication of the new turn that the big business of professional tennis was taking.

DALTON, Judith (*née* Tegart), Australia

Born December 1937, Melbourne. Daughter of a Scottish mother and a father who was a former Irish soccer international, Judy Tegart married an English doctor, David Dalton, of Sheffield in 1969, when she was ranked No 7 in the world. She was a popular runner-up to Billie Jean King in the Wimbledon final of 1968, beating Margaret Court and Nancy Richey in earlier rounds with a remarkable display of virtuosity. Always a fighter, her good humour made her a favourite with crowds. Her greatest successes were in doubles in which she won nine international titles.

Australian women's doubles won 1964 with Miss L Turner (beat Miss M Smith/Miss R Ebbern, 6-4, 6-4), won 1967 (beat Miss E Terras/Miss L Robinson, 6-0, 6-2), r/u 1968 (Miss K Krantzcke/Miss K Melville won, 6-4, 3-6, 6-2), both with Miss Turner, won 1969 (beat Mrs L W King/Miss R Casals, 6-4, 6-4), won 1970 (beat Miss Melville/Miss Krantzcke, 6-3, 6-1), both with Mrs B M Court; mixed doubles won 1966 (W Bowrey/Miss Ebbern, 6-1, 6-3), r/u 1967 (O Davidson/Miss Turner won, 9-7, 6-4), both with A Roche. Australian Federation Cup team 1965–7, 1969–70.

French doubles won 1966 with Miss Smith (beat Miss J Blackman/Miss Toyne, 4-6, 6-1, 6-1).

US women's doubles won 1970 with Mrs Court (beat Miss Casals/Miss Wade, 6-4, 6-3), won 1971 with Miss Casals (beat Mrs G Chanfreau/Miss F Durr, 6-3, 6-3); mixed doubles r/u 1963 (K Fletcher/Miss Smith won, 3-6, 8-6, 6-2), r/u 1964 (Newcombe/Miss Smith won, 10-8, 4-6, 6-3), both with E Rubinoff, r/u 1965 with F Froehling (F Stolle/Miss Smith won, 6-2, 6-2), r/u 1970 with F D McMillan (M Riessen/Mrs Court won, 6-4, 6-4).

Wimbledon women's singles r/u 1968 (Mrs King won, 9-7, 7-5); doubles r/u 1966 with Miss Smith (Miss M Bueno/Miss N Richey won, 6-3, 4-6, 6-4), won 1969 with Mrs Court (beat Miss P Hogan/Miss M Michel, 9-7, 6-2), r/u 1972 with Miss Durr (Mrs King/Miss Stöve won, 6-2, 4-6, 6-3); mixed doubles r/u 1965 (Fletcher/Miss Smith won, 12-10, 6-3), r/u 1969 (Stolle/Mrs A Jones won, 6-3, 6-2), both with Roche.

DANIELL, Agnes *see* Tuckey, Agnes

DANZIG, Mrs J *see* Palfrey, Sarah

DARBON, Mrs W A *see* Gibson, Althea

DAVID, Herman Francis, GB

Born June 1905, died 1974. A member of the Davis Cup team in 1932 and Britain's non-playing captain for the cup from 1953–8, he will be best known for his championship of the All England Club, for 15 years from 1959, and his determined advocacy of Open tennis.

DAVIDSON, Owen Keir, Australia

Born October 1943, Melbourne. A left-hander whose great prowess was the doubles game, Davidson will probably be best remembered for his mixed pairing with Billie Jean King which brought them eight 'Big Four' titles, including four at Wimbledon, the first of which

Right: The Moody Coliseum in Dallas Texas.
Centre right: Australian born Judy Dalton (née Tegart) was ranked No 7 in the world in 1969.

in 1967 gave Mrs King the 'Triple Crown' (singles, doubles and mixed championships). In all Davidson won 12 major international doubles titles. He moved to England in 1967 as professional for the All England Club at Wimbledon and he coached the British Davis Cup team until 1970, when he joined WCT. He married an American girl and signed for World Team Tennis in 1973. The following year he returned to Wimbledon and with Mrs King won their fourth mixed doubles title. With John Newcombe he won the 1974 WCT doubles final and retired from the circuit in 1975.

Australian men's doubles r/u 1967 with W W Bowrey (J Newcombe/A Roche won, 3-6, 6-3, 7-5, 6-8, 8-6), won 1972 with K Rosewall (beat G Masters/R Case, 3-6, 7-6, 6-2); mixed doubles r/u 1965 with Miss R Ebbern (Newcombe/Miss M Smith won), won 1967 with Miss L Turner (beat Roche/Miss Tegart, 9-7, 6-4).

French mixed doubles won 1967 (beat I Tiriac/Mrs A Jones, 6-3, 6-1), r/u 1968 (J C Barclay/Miss F Durr won, 6-1, 6-4), both with Mrs L W King.

US men's doubles r/u 1967 with Bowrey (Newcombe/Roche won, 6-8, 9-7, 6-3, 6-3), r/u 1972 (C Drysdale/R Taylor won, 6-4, 7-6, 6-3), won 1973 (beat R Laver/K Rosewall, 7-5, 2-6, 7-5, 7-5), both with Newcombe; mixed doubles won 1966 with Mrs D Fales (beat E Rubinoff/Miss C Aucamp, 6-3, 6-1), won 1967 (beat S R Smith/Miss R Casals), won 1971 (beat R Maud/Miss B Stövc, 6-3, 7-5), won 1973 (beat M Riessen/Mrs B M Court, 6-4, 3-6, 7-5), all with Mrs King.

Wimbledon plate won 1965; men's doubles r/u 1966 with Bowrey (K Fletcher/Newcombe won, 6-3, 6-4, 3-6, 6-3); mixed doubles won 1967 (beat Fletcher/Miss M Bueno, 7-5, 6-2), won 1971 (beat Riessen/Mrs Court, 3-6, 6-2, 15-13), won 1973 (R Ramirez/Miss J Newberry, 6-3, 6-2), won 1974 (beat M Farrell/Miss L Charles, 6-3, 9-7), all with Mrs King.

DAVIDSON, Sven Viktor, Sweden

Born July 1928, Boras. In a brief international career which lasted from 1950 until 1958, Davidson consistently ranked among the world's top players and in 1957, when he won the French singles title in his third successive final, he was ranked world No 3. The following year, in a season in which he was hampered by a serious leg injury, he won the Wimbledon doubles but retired at the end of the season to concentrate on university studies. He played again in 1959 for the Swedish Davis Cup team of which he had been a member since 1949. In 1960 he won the Swedish national singles title and though he had played very little tennis, he was the architect of Sweden's Davis Cup European zone victory against France. He won 18 Swedish and Scandinavian singles and doubles titles on grass, hard and indoor courts.

Wimbledon men's doubles won 1958 with U Schmidt (beat A Cooper/N Fraser, 6-4, 6-4, 8-6).

French men's singles r/u 1955 (M Trabert won, 2-6, 6-1, 6-4, 6-2), r/u 1956 (L Hoad won, 6-4, 8-6, 6-3), won 1957 (beat H Flam, 6-3, 6-4, 6-4)

Davis Cup

Donated by American Dwight F Davis, the Davis Cup was first played for in 1900, though moves to promote a competition arising out of the already traditional rivalry between the US and England had begun in 1897. The official title of the competition since the formation of the ILTF in 1913 has been the International Lawn Tennis Championship. From the outset the cup was open for international competition and the original regulations stated that for this purpose 'Australia with New Zealand, Austria, Belgium, the British Isles, British South Africa, Canada, France, Germany, Holland, India, Sweden and Norway, Switzerland, and the United States of America shall be regarded as separate nations.'

The British Isles was the only country to take up the American challenge and sent a team consisting of A W Gore, E D Black and H Roper Barrett to the first tie in Longwood, Boston. Playing in a temperature of 136°F (57.8°C), on grass described by Roper Barrett as twice as long as the worst in England and with a net which sagged two or three inches, the British team was unhappy and the Americans M D Whitman, Dwight Davis and H Ward had things much their own way. However, on the third day the weather broke and the tie was abandoned, America winning 3-0 with one game not played and one abandoned. There was no competition in 1901 because Britain withdrew when it was found impossible to raise a team with any likelihood of success. In 1902 the contest was resumed, again in America, and the US won 3-2. Britain had its revenge the following year – the last in which there were only two competing nations – and won 4-1 with the Doherty brothers Laurie and Reggie and Dr Joshua Pim making up the team. In 1904 with the tie at Wimbledon, Belgium and France entered for the first time but the US did not send a team and Austria, having entered, had to withdraw. For the first time a finals round preceded the Challenge Round and in this Belgium beat France 3-2 and in the Challenge Round went down 5-0 to Britain.

Australasia first entered in 1905 and Austria was able to support its entry, the United States returned, as did France, while Belgium had to withdraw. In the semi-finals the US beat France, Australasia beat Austria and the final went 5-0 to the US. However, the British Isles won the Challenge Round comfortably, with the US failing to take a match. Britain won the Challenge Round again in 1906 and by the same margin against the US but then began a run of four successive wins for Australasia (1907–11 with no competition in 1910), who took the title 3-2 at Wimbledon in 1907 and staged the next three competitions in Melbourne, Sydney and Christchurch (New Zealand). No competition was held between 1915 and 1918 but up to then Britain and Australasia had taken the Cup five times each and the US three. Though Australasia won again in 1919, it was the United States which then began a long series of successes as the number of competitors increased annually. From 1920 to 1926 competing countries rose from six to 24 and the US won in all seven years – still the longest winning run in the history of the Cup. These were the triumphant years of Tilden and Johnston, Tilden winning 16 Challenge Round matches and losing only twice, Johnston winning 13 and losing only once.

With 17 countries entering in 1923 the Interzone system was introduced with the European and American zones and Inter-zone finals preceding the Challenge Round. A third zone, Eastern, was not introduced until 1952 and in 1966 came the European A and B zones. The competition was again interrupted by war from 1940–5. In 1971 it was agreed that the Challenge Round would be abolished as from the following year. By then the Cup had been won 23 times by the US, 22 by Australasia/Australia, nine by Great Britain/British Isles and six by France. In fact the six French victories came between 1927 and 1932 during the glorious years of the 'Four Musketeers', Borotra, Brugnon, Lacoste and Cochet. Among them they played 164 rubbers for France and won 120. The 1928 entry was then a record 33 but the overall record entry was achieved in 1972 with 55 countries. The record for the longest rubber was in 1973 when Stan Smith and Erik Van Dillen (US) beat Jaime Fillol and Pat Cornejo (Chile) 7-9, 37-39, 8-6, 6-1, 6-3 in the American zone final – a total of 122 games. The previous record was achieved in 1969, when Wilhelm Bungert and Christian Kuhnke (Germany) beat Mark Cox and Peter Curtis 10-8, 17-19, 13-11, 3-6, 6-2 (95 games) in Birmingham, England. Before that, in 1958, Alex Olmedo and Ham Richardson (US) beat Mal Anderson and Neale Fraser (Australia) 10-12, 3-6, 16-14, 6-3, 7-5 (82 games).

The Davis Cup has always produced its share of tennis dramas and tragedies, upsets and upheavals, and, more recently, political manoeuvrings. In the 1960s and 1970s some competing nations protested against the South African policy of apartheid, leading to that country's suspension in 1970 and rejection in 1971. Anti-apartheid crowd protests have led to matches being interrupted. In 1967 the mighty US was defeated in the American zone final by lowly Ecuador and Australia beat Spain over three rubbers, losing only 27 games – the most one-sided tie since 1904, when Britain lost only 17 games in beating Belgium. In 1928 Finland, entering for the first time, had to play a tie at two venues when rain flooded the courts at Zagreb and the last two singles against Yugoslavia were played in Belgrade four days later. In 1933 Britain had a winning margin against the US in the Inter-zone final at the Roland Garros Stadium when Fred Perry (GB) faced Ellsworth Vines. Leading two sets to one and 3-2 in the fourth set, Vines hurt his ankle and in the fifth, with Perry at 1-6, 6-0, 4-6, 7-5, 7-6 and 40-15 match point, the American fainted and could not continue. The Davis Cup legends are legion.

Up to 1973 control and organisation of the cup was each year in the hands of the country holding the trophy. However, at the annual meeting of Davis Cup nations of 1973 it was agreed that the championship should henceforth by supervised by a management committee appointed by the annual meeting. The competition is generally open only to full members of the ILTF and nations pay subscriptions when they enter and when they win a round. The host nation in each tie pays a percentage of receipts to a special travelling expenses fund and from this grants are made to countries incurring heavy expenses. A country in which gate receipts are low can, in this way, pay visiting team expenses with help from the fund.

DAVIS, Dwight Filley, USA
Born July 1879, St Louis, Missouri, died November 1945. The donor of the Davis Cup in 1900, Dwight Davis was the son of a wealthy St Louis family who was educated at an exclusive preparatory school and then went on to Harvard. In 1899 he teamed with Holcombe Ward, a fellow varsity student, to win the first of three consecutive US doubles championships and prove himself a fine left-handed tennis player. In that year he conceived the idea of the Davis Cup for international competition and when the first match was played against Great Britain he won both his singles and the doubles partnered by Ward. Another Harvard colleague was Malcolm Whitman, the US singles champion, was also in the first US Davis Cup team. In the second match in 1902, Davis played with Ward again in the doubles but lost to the famous Doherty brothers. In 1923 he became president of the USLTA and from 1925–9 was US Secretary of War, afterwards becoming Governor General of the Philippines until 1932, when he retired from the post. During World War II he was Director General of the US Army Specialist Corps.

The cup which he presented is a massive silver bowl lined with gold and was originally valued at $700; it holds 37 bottles of champagne and it has been cracked three times, dented and modified on several occasions. In 1920, because the bowl itself was already fully inscribed with winners' names, Dwight Davis added a $400 tray similarly decorated.

US All-Comers singles r/u 1898 (M D Whitman won, 3-6, 6-2, 6-2, 6-1), r/u Challenge Round 1899 (J P Paret won, 7-5, 8-10, 6-3, 2-6, 6-3); men's doubles won 1899 (beat L Ware/ G Sheldon, 6-4, 6-4, 6-3), won 1900 (beat F Alexander/R Little, 6-4, 9-7, 12-10), won 1901 (beat Ware/B Wright, 6-3, 9-7, 6-1), r/u 1902 (R Doherty/L Doherty won, 11-9, 12-10, 6-4), all with H Ward.

Wimbledon men's doubles r/u 1901 with Ward (Roper Barrett/G Simond won, 7-5, 6-4, 6-4).

DECUGIS, Max, France
Born September 1882, Paris. Decugis and his protégé André Gobert, were the first players to bring a serious challenge across the channel from France to Wimbledon and in 1911 they won the men's doubles, beating the holders M J G Ritchie and New Zealander Anthony Wilding, 9-7, 5-7, 6-3, 2-6, 6-2 in the Challenge Round. That same year Decugis was the first Frenchman to get as far as the singles quarter-finals. Described as the first modern French tennis player, Decugis showed his talent by the time he was 18 and in 1903 he won his first national singles title. (The championships were restricted to French nationals from 1891 until 1924.) He went on to win the title eight times up to 1914 and was runner-up in 1920 and 1923. He also won the doubles 13 times and mixed doubles seven. Decugis always played each game with enormous energy and enjoyment, serving and smashing powerfully. He represented France in the Davis Cup in 1904–5, 1912–14 and 1919 and was a tennis Olympic gold medallist in 1912.

French men's singles (closed) won 1903–4, 1907–9, 1912–14, r/u 1920, 1923; men's doubles (closed) won 1902–14, 1920; mixed doubles (closed) won 1904–6, 1908–9, 1914, 1920.

Wimbledon men's doubles won 1911 (beat J Ritchie/A Wilding, 9-7, 5-7, 6-3, 2-6, 6-2), r/u 1912 (C Dixon/H Roper Barrett won, 3-6, 6-3, 6-4, 7-5) both with A Gobert.

DENT, Philip, Australia
Born February 1950, Sydney. At 17 Dent became the youngest player since Hoad and Rosewall to be named for the Australian Davis Cup team and in 1968 he won the Australian junior championship, the French junior championship and also reached the quarter-finals of the Australian senior event. He was then ranked No 1 in the junior lists and No 9 in the senior. He joined WCT in 1971 but in 1972 suffered a leg injury in a car accident. Back in form in 1973 he was runner-up with John Alexander in the Australian doubles and won the WCT Toronto doubles, beating fellow Australians Emerson

and Laver. He and Alexander gained their national doubles title in 1975 but lost it next year. Dent was runner-up to Jim Connors in the 1974 Australian Open and beat Borg on the way to the final. Later he took Connors to 10-8 in the final set of the Wimbledon second round. During 1976 he had further WCT singles and doubles successes (with Alexander), won the US Open mixed with Mrs King and played World Team Tennis with the champions, New York Sets. In 1977, with Alexander, he was r/u for both the Australian and Wimbledon doubles.

Australian men's singles r/u 1974 (J Connors won, 7-6, 6-4, 4-6, 6-3); doubles r/u 1970 (R Lutz/S Smith won), r/u 1973 (J Newcombe/M Anderson won), r/u 1977–8 (A Stone/R Ruffels won, 7-6, 7-6), all with J Alexander. Brisbane singles r/u 1976; Perth singles r/u 1976.

US Open mixed doubles won 1976 with Mrs L W King (beat F McMillan/Miss B Stöve, 3-6, 6-2, 7-5). WCT doubles finals r/u 1974 with Alexander (R Hewitt/McMillan won); Fort Worth WCT r/u 1976; Atlanta WCT doubles won 1976; Denver WCT doubles won 1976, both with Alexander; Woodlands ATP doubles r/u 1976 with A Stone.

Wimbledon doubles r/u 1977 with Alexander (R Case/G Masters won, 6-3, 6-4, 3-6, 8-9, 6-4).

Devonshire Park, Eastbourne, GB

One of the six major tennis centres in Britain, Devonshire Park has been the venue for the Inter-County championships, the Registered Professional Coaches' championships (from 1912), the British junior grass court championships (from 1970), the Junior National Invitation championship for under-12s (from 1972), under-14s (from 1970) and under-16s (from 1970). Tennis was first played at the Park in 1870, the South of England grass court championships began there in 1881 and many Davis Cup ties have been staged there. It has 21 grass courts and six hard courts.

Dewar Cup

Sponsored by John Dewar and Sons Ltd, the whisky distillers, the Dewar Cup began in 1968 with the idea of taking top-class international indoor tennis to the provinces which seldom had the opportunity of seeing the sport's stars. In the first year tournaments were held in Aberavon (Wales), Perth (Scotland), Stalybridge (Cheshire) and Torquay (Devon). The finals were divided between the Queen's Club, London, where the British covered court championships had been seeing mixed fortunes for some years, and the Crystal Palace, London. They incorporated the covered court championships. First winners were R Hewitt (South Africa) and Mrs M Court (Australia). In 1969 the Queen's Club matches were dropped and in 1970 Perth gave place to the larger new Meadowbank stadium, Edinburgh. The finals were staged at the Royal Albert Hall, London. Two other 1970 innovations were the use of yellow balls, more easily seen under artificial lighting, and synthetic grass surfaces. In 1971 the qualifying tournaments were in Edinburgh, Billingham (Teesside), Aberavon and Torquay. The next major change came in 1972, when the grand finals also became the final tournament of the Commercial Union GP series for men. Previously the eight-point qualifiers had gone through to the finals; now the men's singles included 32 players and the matches were split between Nottingham University Sports Hall and the Albert Hall, the quarter-finalists competing at the latter venue. Torquay was dropped as a venue in 1973.

DIBBS, Eddie, USA

Born February 1951, Miami Beach, Florida. A steadily improving player with a two-fisted backhand, Dibbs first came to international attention in 1973 when he won the German singles championship, defeating Fassbender and Meiler on the way to the title and also having wins over Connors, Smith, Tiriac, Newcombe and Tanner during the season. He retained the German title in 1974, lost it in 1975 and regained it in 1976, by which time his overall performance had taken him to fourth place on the WCT and

Grand Prix circuits and into the world's top ten rankings for 1977.

German Open men's singles won 1973 (beat K Meiler, 6-1, 3-6, 7-6, 6-3), won 1974 (beat H Plotz, 6-2, 6-2, 6-3), won 1976 (beat M Orantes, 6-4, 4-6, 6-1, 2-6, 6-1).

Paris Indoor Open won 1976 (beat J Fillol). Monterrey WCT won 1976 (beat H Solomon); Mexico City WCT r/u 1976 (R Ramirez won); Washington WCT doubles won 1976 with Solomon; Barcelona WCT singles won 1976 (beat E Drysdale); Cincinnati singles r/u 1976 (Tanner won). Oviedo GP won 1977.

DIBLEY, Colin, Australia

Born September 1944, Marrickville, Sydney. A former Customs Immigration Officer, Dibley has one of the strongest serves in tennis. Though his main successes have been as a doubles player, he has also played consistently in singles.

New South Wales hard court championship won 1970–1; South Australian championship r/u 1972. New Zealand BP championship won 1970–1. Reached WCT doubles finals Montreal 1973 with T Addison; American Airlines doubles won 1976 with A Mayer.

DIXON, Charles Percy, GB

Born February 1873, Grantham, Lincolnshire, died April 1939. A solicitor and in 1912 a tennis Olympic gold medallist, Dixon and H Roper Barrett won the Wimbledon men's doubles back from Decugis and Gobert of France in that year, when Dixon was 39 and his partner 38. They retained it against the challenge of the Germans Kleinschroth and Rahe in 1913 but were deposed by Brookes (Australia) and Wilding (New Zealand) next year. With Cecil Parke he also won the Australian doubles and helped Britain win the Davis Cup from Australia in 1912. A rackets 'blue' for Cambridge University, he was in the British Davis Cup team in 1909, 1911–13.

Wimbledon men's singles All-Comers r/u 1901 (A W Gore won, 6-4, 6-0, 6-3), All-Comers r/u 1911 (H Roper Barrett won, 5-7, 4-6, 6-4, 6-3, 6-1); men's doubles won 1912 (beat M Decugis/A Gobert, 3-6, 6-3, 6-4, 7-5), won 1913 (beat H Kleinschroth/F Rahe, 6-2, 6-4, 4-6, 6-2), r/u 1914 (N Brookes/A Wilding won, 6-1, 6-1, 5-7, 8-6), all with Roper Barrett.

Australian men's doubles won 1912 with J C Parke (beat A Beamish/F Lowe).

DOD, Charlotte (Lottie), GB

Born September 1871, Bebington, Cheshire, died June 1960. The youngest-ever Wimbledon champion at age 15 years 10 months in 1887 and five times holder of the women's title, Lottie was an outstanding all-round athlete. She took part in archery, was British Ladies Golf Champion in 1904, played hockey for England in 1889–90 and enjoyed ice skating. The affection in which she was held and the delight of her performance created interest in the women's game which it had not previously received. Lottie, a tall tomboy, learned her tennis with her sister and two brothers and then modelled her game on the style of the Renshaw brothers, introducing the smash, speed and attacking net play to the women's game. Even before her remarkable Wimbledon debut, she had made her mark by beating the reigning ladies champion, Maud Watson, at Bath in 1886. It was Miss Watson's first defeat in 55 matches and Lottie was aged 14. Lottie never lost at Wimbledon and dropped only one set there. At the age of 21 she gave up tennis to devote her talents to golf.

Wimbledon women's singles won 1887 (beat Miss B Bingley, 6-2, 6-0), won 1888 (beat Mrs G Hillyard, 6-3, 6-3), won 1891 (wo), won 1892 (beat Mrs Hillyard, 6-1, 6-1), won 1893 (beat Mrs Hillyard, 6-8, 6-1, 6-4).

Irish women's singles won 1887 (beat Miss M Langrishe).

DOEG, John Hope, USA

Born December 1908, Sonora Co, Mexico. A left-hander and a protégé of Bill Tilden, Doeg had a brilliant service. Though he won the US singles title in 1930 and replaced Tilden as No 1 in the American rankings, he never fulfilled his early promise.

US men's singles won 1930 (beat F Shields, 10-8, 1-6, 6-4, 16-14); men's doubles won 1929 (beat B Bell/L White, 10-8, 16-14, 6-1), won 1930 (beat J Van Ryn/W Allison, 8-6, 6-3, 4-6, 13-15, 6-4), both with G M Lott. US Davis Cup team 1930.

Wimbledon men's doubles r/u 1930 (Van Ryn/Allison won, 6-3, 6-3, 6-2).

DOHERTY, Hugh Lawrence (Laurie), GB

Born October 1876, Wimbledon, London, died August 1919. Younger of the Doherty brothers (see R F Doherty) and generally acknowledged to be the finest exponent of tennis before World War I, Laurie set a high standard in skill and sportsmanship. He won the Wimbledon singles title five times and, with his brother, the doubles eight times. He was the first non-American to take the US singles title (1903) and he won every one of the 12 Davis Cup rubbers he played. Between 1897 and 1906 no Wimbledon singles final was played without one of the Doherty brothers being involved and between them they did much to revive popular interest in tennis at Wimbledon at a time when it was flagging. Laurie, the shorter and more athletic of the two was nicknamed 'Little Do'.

Wimbledon men's singles r/u 1898 (R Doherty won 6-3, 6-3, 2-6, 5-7, 6-1), won 1902 (beat A Gore, 6-4, 6-3, 3-6, 6-0), won 1903 (beat D F Riseley, 7-5, 6-3, 6-0), won 1904 (beat Riseley, 6-1, 7-5, 8-6), won 1905 (beat N Brookes, 8-6, 6-2, 6-4), won 1906 (beat Riseley, 6-4, 4-6, 6-2, 6-2); men's doubles 1897 All-Comers won (beat C Cazalet/S H Smith, 6-2, 7-5, 2-6, 6-2), won Challenge Round 1898 (beat C Hobart/H Nisbet, 6-4, 6-4, 6-2), won 1899 (beat Hobart/

Right: Reggie Doherty (pictured here) and his brother Laurie dominated tennis for a decade (1900–1909).

Nisbet, 7-5, 6-0, 6-2), won 1900 (beat Nisbet/Roper Barrett, 9-7, 7-5, 4-6, 3-6, 6-3), won 1901 (beat D Davis/H Ward, 4-6, 6-2, 6-3, 9-7), r/u 1902 (Riseley/Smith won, 4-6, 8-6, 6-3, 4-6, 11-4), won 1903 (beat Riseley/Smith, 6-4, 6-4, 6-4), won 1904 (beat Riseley/Smith, 6-3, 6-4, 6-3), won 1905 (beat Riseley/Smith, 6-2, 6-4, 6-8, 6-3), r/u 1906 (Riseley/Smith won, 6-8, 6-4, 5-7, 6-3, 6-3), all with R Doherty.

US men's singles won 1903 (beat W A Larned, 6-0, 6-3, 10-8); men's doubles won 1902 (beat Ward/Davis, 11-9, 12-10, 6-4), won 1903 (beat K Collins/L Waidner, 7-5, 6-3, 6-3), both with R Doherty.

Irish championships singles won 1902; doubles won 1898–1902, all with R Doherty; mixed doubles won 1901–2.

Davis Cup team 1902–6. Won two Olympic gold medals (1900).

DOHERTY, Reginald Frank (Reggie), GB

Born October 1874, Wimbledon, London, died December 1910. Though his playing career was dogged by poor health, some contemporary commentators believed he was a better player than his brother Laurie. Tall and thin he was nicknamed 'Big Do'. He won the Wimbledon singles title four times and the doubles eight times with his brother, and also gained the Irish Open singles title on three occasions and won the South African singles in 1909. The decade of dominance by the Doherty brothers and their services to the game are commemorated at the All England Club, Wimbledon by 'The Doherty Gates'.

Wimbledon men's singles won 1897 (beat H Mahony, 6-4, 6-4, 6-3), won 1898 (beat L Doherty, 6-3, 6-3, 2-6, 5-7, 6-1), won 1899 (beat A Gore, 1-6, 4-6, 6-2, 6-3, 6-3), won 1900 (beat S H Smith 6-8, 6-3, 6-1, 6-2), r/u 1901 (Gore won, 4-6, 7-5, 6-4, 6-4); men's doubles r/u 1896, won 1897–1901, r/u 1902, won 1903–5, r/u 1906 (*see* H L Doherty above for scores).

US men's singles r/u 1902 (W Larned won, 4-6, 6-2, 6-4, 8-6); men's doubles won 1902–3 (*see* H L Doherty).

South African men's singles won 1909.

Irish Championships singles won 1899–1901; doubles won 1898–1902; mixed doubles won 1899–1900.

Davis Cup team 1902–6. Won three Olympic gold medals (1900, two, and 1908).

DOUGLASS, Dorothea *see* Chambers, Dorothea Lambert

DOWDESWELL, Colin, Rhodesia

Born May 1955, London, England, emigrated to Salisbury, Rhodesia and studied at University of Witwatersrand. Runner-up to Billy Martin of America in 1973 Wimbledon junior invitation and Pepsi junior at the US Open. Dowdeswell created a stir in 1975 when he reached the finals of the Wimbledon men's doubles when paired with Allan Stone, with whom he had never before played. They beat two seeded pairs, Okker/Riessen and Hewitt/McMillan before losing to Gerulaitis/Mayer.

Rothmans' Surrey hard court championships men's singles 1973 divided with N Holmes (6-4, 0-2); Rothmans' Connaught singles r/u 1973.

Carroll's Irish Open singles r/u 1974; doubles won 1974 with J Yuill; mixed doubles won 1974 with Mrs J Chanfreau.

Rhodesia Open singles won 1974.

Wimbledon men's doubles r/u 1975 with A Stone (V Gerulaitis/A Mayer won, 7-5, 8-6, 6-4).

Cologne doubles r/u with M Estep (R Hewitt/F McMillan won, 6-1, 3-6, 7-6).

Swedish Open doubles r/u 1977 with Hewitt (J Fassbender/K Meiler won, 6-4, 7-6).

DROBNÝ, Jaroslav, Czechoslovakia

Born October 1921, Prague. A refugee from Czechoslovakia in 1945, Drobný became a naturalised Egyptian in 1950 and is now a British subject. One of the great post-war players on clay, Drobný possessed a deadly left-hand service and smash, yet could use a delicate touch when necessary. He was always popular with the crowds and Wimbledon was swept by a wave of emotion when in 1954 at the age of 33 he beat the 19-year-old Ken Rosewall and finally won the men's singles – the first left-hander to do so since Norman Brookes of Australia in 1914. It was his eleventh attempt. In 1953, in the third round at Wimbledon he met 'Budge' Patty and played for 4 hours 20 minutes (from 5.00 PM to 9.20PM) before winning the 93-game match 8-6, 16-18, 3-6, 8-6, 12-10 – the longest Wimbledon

Left: Jaroslav Drobný possessed a deadly left-hand smash and service but was also capable of the gentle touch. In 1954 he won the men's singles at Wimbledon, the first left-hander to do so since 1914.

singles to that date. In 1938, at the age of 16, he had taken Don Budge to five sets in a match in Prague, where he was a ball boy. In 43 Davis Cup rubbers he won 37 and in his career he won 12 major international championships, often after a series of failures or when having to drag an apparently lost match back into his favour.

Wimbledon men's singles r/u 1949 (F Schroeder won, 3-6, 6-0, 6-3, 4-6, 6-4), r/u 1952 (F Sedgman won, 4-6, 6-2, 6-3, 6-2), won 1954 (beat K Rosewall, 13-11, 4-6, 6-2, 9-7); men's doubles r/u 1951 with E Sturgess (K McGregor/Sedgman won, 3-6, 6-2, 6-3, 3-6, 6-3).

Australian men's doubles r/u 1950 with Sturgess (A Quist/J Bromwich won, 6-3, 5-7, 4-6, 6-3, 8-6).

French singles r/u 1946 (M Bernard won, 3-6, 2-6, 6-1, 6-4, 6-3), r/u 1948 (F Parker won, 6-4, 7-5, 5-7, 8-6), r/u 1950 (J Patty won, 6-1, 6-2, 3-6, 5-7, 7-5), won 1951 (beat Sturgess 6-3, 6-3, 6-3), won 1952 (beat Sedgman, 6-2, 6-0, 3-6, 6-4); men's doubles won 1948 with L Bergelin (beat

H Hopman/Sturgess, 8-6, 6-1, 12-10), r/u 1950 with Sturgess (W Talbert/M Trabert won, 6-2, 1-6, 10-8, 6-2); mixed doubles won 1948 with Mrs P Todd (beat Sedgman/Miss D Hart, 6-3, 3-6, 6-3).

Italian singles won 1950, 1951, 1953; doubles won 1951 with R Savitt, won 1952 with Sedgman, won 1954 with E Morea, won 1956 with L Hoad.

DRYSDALE, Clifford, South Africa

Born May 1941, Nelspruit, Transvaal. A right-hander with a two-fisted backhand and occasional two-handed forehand, Drysdale is also an accomplished golfer. Though he has not won a major international singles title in Australia, Britain, France or the US, he has been successful in WCT doubles events. During the 1967 Wimbledon meeting he married Jean Forbes. He was first president of the ATP in 1973, when he also became resident professional at the WCT Lakeway Center.

South African men's singles won 1965.
German singles won 1965, r/u 1968.
US men's singles r/u 1965 (M Santana won, 6-2, 7-9, 7-5, 6-1); men's doubles won 1972 with R Taylor (beat O Davidson/J Newcombe, 6-4, 7-6, 6-3).
Barcelona WCT r/u 1976 (E Dibbs won, 6-1, 6-1).
Johannesburg WCT r/u 1976 (O Parun won, 7-6, 6-3).
Gunze Tokyo Open singles r/u 1976 (M Orantes won).

Dublin, Ireland

Home of the Irish Open championships, the second oldest championships in the world, which are administered by the Fitzwilliam Club, founded in Dublin in 1877. The men's events were held for 24 years in Dublin's Fitzwilliam Square but the women played on the club's courts for greater privacy. Until 1973 the championships were on grass but since the club moved to new premises, they have been on hard courts. The new club has seven hard courts, four grass, an indoor court and squash courts. Dublin is also the home of the Irish LTA, established in 1908 and affiliated to the British LTA. In 1923 the Irish association became an independent national organisation and two years later affiliated to the ILTF.

DUPONT, Laura, USA

Born May 1949, Kentucky. While a university student, she won the US National Intercollegiates in 1970 aged 21 and in 1971 was runner-up in the US National Amateur grass championships and the National Bank Open. She has since maintained a consistent performance, winning the New Zealand hard court singles and doubles in 1975, when she was also runner-up in the Canadian Open and in 1976 the

South American championship singles and r/u in the South African Open. She beat Nancy Richey to win the US clay court singles in 1977.
US clay courts doubles r/u 1976 with Miss W Turnbull (Miss L Boshoff/Miss I Kloss won, 6-2, 6-3; singles won 1977 (beat Miss N Richey, 6-4, 6-3).
Canadian Open r/u 1975 (Miss M Louis won, 6-1, 4-6, 6-4).
German championships doubles r/u 1976 with Miss W Turnbull.
New Zealand hard court singles won 1975; doubles won 1975; New Zealand Open doubles r/u 1975 with Miss C Martinez (Miss E Goolagong/Miss Turnbull won, 6-3, 4-6, 6-4).
South American Open singles won 1976 (beat Miss B Araujo).
South African Open r/u 1976 (Miss B Cuypers won, 6-7, 6-4, 6-1).

duPONT, Margaret Evelyn (*née Osborne*), USA

Born March 1918, Joseph, Oregon. An outstanding exponent of the serve-and-volley technique, Margaret Osborne duPont is probably best remembered for her long run of successes in doubles with Louise Brough as well as some classic singles matches against her doubles partner. With W F Talbert she held the US mixed doubles title for four successive years and she was also US singles champion for three consecutive years. She still ranks as one of the best servers the women's game has ever produced and was among those who established the American supremacy in women's tennis from 1946.
US women's singles r/u 1944 (Miss P Betz won, 6-3, 8-6), r/u 1947 (Miss Brough won, 8-6, 4-6, 6-1), won 1948 (beat Miss Brough, 4-6, 6-4, 15-13), won 1949 (beat Miss D Hart, 6-4, 6-1), won 1950 (beat Miss Hart, 6-3, 6-3); women's doubles won 1941 with Mrs E Cooke, won 1942–3, won 1944 (beat Miss P Betz/Miss Hart, 4-6, 6-4, 6-3), won 1945 (beat Miss Betz/Miss Hart, 6-4, 6-4), won 1946 (beat Mrs D A Prentiss/Mrs P Todd, 6-2, 6-0), won 1947 (beat Miss Hart/Mrs Todd, 5-7, 6-3, 7-5), won 1948 (beat Miss Hart/Mrs Todd, 6-4, 8-10, 6-1), won 1949 (beat Miss Hart/Miss S Fry, 6-4, 8-6), won 1950 (beat Miss Hart/Miss Fry, 6-2, 6-2), r/u 1953 (Miss Fry/Miss Hart won, 6-3, 7-9, 9-7), r/u 1954 (Miss Fry/Miss Hart won, 6-4, 6-4), won 1955 (beat Miss Hart/Miss Fry, 6-3, 1-6, 6-3), won

Left (centre): Margaret duPont (née Osborne) still ranks as one of the best servers the women's game has ever produced.
Left: Françoise Durr is the best woman player France has produced in 40 years.

1956 (beat Miss Fry/Mrs B Pratt, 6-3, 6-0), won 1957 (beat Miss A Gibson/Miss D R Hard, 6-2, 7-5), all with Miss Brough; mixed doubles won 1943, won 1944 (beat W McNeill/Miss D Bundy, 6-2, 6-3), won 1945 (beat R Falkenburg/Miss Hart, 6-4, 6-4), won 1946 (beat R Kimbell/Miss Brough, 6-3, 6-4), all with W F Talbert, r/u 1948 T Brown/Miss Brough won, 6-4, 6-4), r/u 1949 (E Sturgess/Miss Brough won, 4-6, 6 3, 7-5), both with Talbert, won 1950 with K McGregor (beat F Sedgman/Miss Hart, 6-4, 3 6, 6-3), r/u 1954 (E Seixas/Miss Hart won, 4-6, 6-1, 6-1), won 1956 (beat L Hoad/Miss Hard, 9-7, 6-1), both with K Rosewall, won 1958 (beat A Olmedo/Miss M Bueno, 6-4, 3-6, 9-7), won 1959 (beat R Mark/Miss J Hopps, 7-5, 13-15, 6-2), won 1960 (beat A Palafox/Miss Bueno, 6-3, 6-2), all with N Fraser.

French women's singles won 1946 (beat Miss Betz, 1-6, 8-6, 7-5), won 1949 (beat Mrs N Adamson, 7-8, 6-2); women's doubles won 1946 (beat Miss Betz/Miss Hart, 6-4, 0-6, 6-1), won 1947 (beat Miss Hart/Mrs Todd, 7-5, 6-2), won 1949 (beat Mrs B Hilton/Miss J Gannon, 7-5, 6-1), r/u 1950 (Miss Hart/Miss Fry won, 1-6, 7-5, 6-2), all with Miss Brough.

Wimbledon women's singles won 1947 (beat Miss Hart, 6-2, 6-4), r/u 1949 (Miss Brough won, 10-8, 1-6, 10-8), r/u 1950 (Miss Brough won, 6-1, 3-6, 6-1); women's doubles won 1946 (beat Miss Betz/Miss Hart, 6-3, 2-6, 6-3), r/u 1947 (Miss Hart/Mrs Todd won, 3-6, 6-4, 7-5), won 1948 (beat Miss Hart/Mrs Todd, 6-3, 3-6, 6-3), won 1949 (beat Miss G Moran/Mrs Todd, 8-6, 7-5), won 1950 (beat Miss Fry/Miss Hart, 6-4, 5-7, 6-1), r/u 1951 (Miss Fry/Miss Hart won, 6-3, 13-11), won 1954 (beat Miss Fry/Miss Hart, 4-6, 9-7, 6-3), all with Miss Brough, r/u 1958 with Miss M Varner (Miss Bueno/Miss Gibson won, 6-3, 7-5); mixed doubles r/u 1954 with K Rosewall (Seixas/Miss Hart won, 5-7, 6-4, 6-3), won

1962 with N Fraser (beat R Ralston/Miss A Haydon, 2-6, 6-3, 13-11).

Wightman Cup 1946–50, 1954–5, 1957, 1962 (unbeaten in 18 rubbers); captain 1953–5, 1957–8, 1961–3, 1965.

DURR, Françoise (Mrs B J Browning), France Born December 1942, Algiers. Despite an unorthodox style, she is the most outstanding French woman player in 40 years. Before turning professional in 1968 she became, in 1967, the first French woman to win her country's singles title in over 20 years. A deceptively frail-looking red-head, she appears almost ungainly in play. Her chief successes have been in doubles events and she was French doubles champion for five years running. In 1968 she was signed by George McCall for the National Tennis League professional group and in 1971 joined Gladys Heldman's team of women professionals on the Virginia Slims circuit, earning $50,000 in her first year. She is a consistent and popular competitor on the world professional circuit. In 1977 her successes included winning the Colgate Inaugural doubles with Virginia Wade.

French women's singles won 1967 (beat Miss L Turner, 4-6, 6-3, 6-4); women's doubles r/u 1965 with Miss J Lieffrig (Miss Turner/Miss M Smith won, 6-3, 6-1), won 1967 with Miss G Sherriff (beat Miss A Van Zyl/Miss P Walkden, 6-2, 6-2), won 1968 (beat Mrs L W King/Miss R Casals, 7-5, 4-6, 6-4), won 1969 (beat Mrs B M Court/Miss N Richey, 6-0, 4-6, 7-5), both with Mrs A Jones, won 1970 (beat Miss Casals/Mrs King, 6-3, 1-6, 6-3), won 1971 (beat Miss H Gourlay/Miss K Harris, 6-4, 6-1), both with Mrs G Chanfreau, r/u 1973 with Miss B Stöve (Mrs Court/Miss V Wade won, 6-2, 6-3); mixed doubles won 1968 (beat O Davidson/Mrs King, 6-1, 6-4), r/u 1969 (M Riessen/Mrs Court won, 7-5, 6-4), r/u 1970 (R Hewitt/Mrs King won, 3-6,

84

6-3, 6-2), won 1971 (beat T Lejus/Miss W Shaw, 6-2, 6-4), r/u 1972 (K Warwick/Miss E Goolagong won, 6-3, 6-4), won 1973 (beat P Dominguez/Miss Stöve, 6-1, 6-4), all with J C Barclay.

US women's doubles won 1969 with Miss Hard (beat Miss Court/Miss Wade, 0-6, 6-3, 6-4), r/u 1971 with Mrs Chanfreau (Miss Casals/Mrs R D Dalton won, 6-3, 6-3), won 1972 with Miss Stöve (beat Mrs Court/Miss Wade, 6-3, 1-6, 6-3); mixed doubles r/u 1969 with R Ralston (M Riessen/Mrs Court won, 7-5, 6-3).

Wimbledon women's doubles r/u 1968 with Mrs A Jones (Miss Casals/Mrs King won, 3-6, 6-4, 7-5), r/u 1970 with Miss Wade (Miss Casals/Mrs King won, 6-2, 6-3), r/u 1972 with Mrs Dalton (Mrs King/Miss Stöve won, 6-2, 4-6, 6-3), r/u 1973 (Miss Casals/Mrs King won, 6-1, 4-6, 7-5), r/u 1975 (Miss A Kiyomura/Miss K Sawamatsu won, 7-5, 1-6, 7-5), both with Miss Stöve; mixed doubles won 1976 with A D Roche (beat R Stockton/Miss Casals, 6-3, 9-8).

Italian championship doubles won 1969 with Mrs A Jones (beat Miss Casals/Mrs King, 6-3, 3-6, 6-2).

German championships singles won 1967.

Colgate Inaugural singles r/u 1976 (Miss Evert won), Colgate Inaugural doubles won 1977 with Miss Wade (beat Mrs H Gourlay Cawley/Miss J Russell, 6-1, 4-6, 6-4).

Virginia Slims Houston doubles won 1976 (beat Miss Evert/Miss Navratilova), V S San Francisco doubles r/u 1976, V S Philadelphia doubles r/u 1976, V S Boston doubles r/u 1976, all with Miss Casals.

US Indoor Atlanta doubles won with Miss Casals 1976 (beat Miss Wade/Miss Stöve). Federation Cup 1963, 1966, 1971–3.

Eastern Grass Court Championships, USA
The official championships of the Eastern LTA of America, the Eastern grass court championships were first staged in 1927 at the Westchester Biltmore Country Club (now the Westchester Country Club), Rye, New York. In 1946 they transferred to the Orange Lawn Tennis Club, South Orange, New Jersey. Many players who won the championship titles were either nationally or internationally famous at the time or later became so.

EBBINGHAUS, Katja (*née* **Burgemeister**), Germany
Born January 1948, Karlsruhe. West German mixed doubles r/u 1974 with H Pohmann; Head Cup, Kitzbuhel won 1972, Dusseldorf r/u 1972, won 1974; Mannerheim r/u 1975; Kitzbuhel r/u 1975, Klagenfurt won 1975.

French women's doubles r/u 1974 with Mrs G Chanfreau (Miss C Evert/Miss O Morozova won).

USLTA, New York r/u 1973 (Miss C Evert won).

South American doubles won 1974 with H Masthoff.

Austrian doubles won 1974 with Masthoff, r/u 1976.

EDMONDSON, Mark, Australia
Born June 1954, Gosford, NSW. Coached from the age of ten by the famous Australian spotter of future tennis stars, Charlie Hollis, Edmondson shot to prominence in 1976 after a successful junior record. That year, unseeded, he won the Australian Open, beating Phil Dent, Dick Crealy, Ken Rosewall and John Newcombe. Later he also beat Raul Ramirez in the US clay courts before losing to 'Buster' Mottram.

Australian hard courts junior r/u 1972; New South Wales junior hard courts won 1972; NSW junior grass r/u 1972; won Rothmans' Sutton doubles 1975; Australian Open won 1976 (beat J Newcombe, 6-7, 6-3, 7-6, 6-1), won Brisbane 1976.

Ellis Park, Johannesburg, South Africa
The stadium at Ellis Park was built in 1923 on the site of a disused brickyard and consisted of two centre courts enclosed by a covered stand at the north end and three open stands on the remaining sides. Today the stadium itself is covered and has seating for 6000 around the main Centre Court. The complex of 20 additional courts includes seating for over 4000. In 1964 a Tennis Patrons' Club was built at a cost of over $200,000 with a luxury box overlooking the Centre Court and a glass-fronted viewing area overlooking outside courts. All courts are cement surfaced, due to the problems of maintaining any other surface in temperatures of around 110° and torrential rains.

EMERSON, Roy Stanley, Australia
Born November 1936, Blackheat, Queensland. One of the band of Australian players who dominated tennis in the 1950s and 1960s, Emerson transferred his notable schoolboy prowess as an athlete – at 14 he ran the 100 yards in 10.6 seconds – to tennis, using his speed, agility and powerful forehand to gain no fewer than 32 'Big Four' titles. He won the Wimbledon singles title in 1964 and 1965 and, seeded No 1 in 1966, looked set to equal Fred Perry's record of three successive Wimbledon men's singles titles. However, in the quarter-finals, playing against his fellow countryman Owen Davidson, he crashed at speed into the umpire's chair and injured a shoulder. Though he continued the match he was badly hampered and lost 1-6, 6-3, 6-4, 6-4. The tall, lean Australian nevertheless won his country's singles title six times, including five in succession, took every major singles title in the world except the Italian and won 36 of 40 Davis Cup rubbers. Apart from his speed, Emerson always presented a business-like calm and efficiency in play and never appeared upset

Left : Roy Emerson won no fewer than 32 'Big Four' titles.

by decisions which went against him. He turned professional in 1968. With Rod Laver he spends considerable time running tennis clinics for promising youngsters.

Australian men's singles won 1961 (beat R Laver, 1-6, 6-3, 7-5, 6-4), r/u 1962 (Laver won 8-6, 0-6, 6-4, 6-4), won 1963 (beat K Fletcher, 6-3, 6-3, 6-1), won 1964 (beat F Stolle, 6-3, 6-4, 6-2), won 1965 (beat Stolle, 7-9, 2-6, 6-4, 7-5, 6-1), won 1966 (beat A Ashe, 6-4, 6-8, 6-2, 6-3), won 1967 (beat Ashe, 6-4, 6-1, 6-4); men's doubles r/u 1958 with R Mark (A Cooper/N Fraser won, 7-5, 6-8, 3-6, 6-3, 7-5), r/u 1960 with Fraser (Laver/Mark won, 1-6, 6-2, 6-4, 6-4), r/u 1961 with M Mulligan (Laver/Mark won, 6-3, 7-5, 3-6, 9-11, 6-2), won 1962 with Fraser (beat R Hewitt/Stolle, 4-6, 4-6, 6-1, 6-4, 11-9), r/u 1964 with Fletcher (Hewitt/Stolle won, 6-4, 7-5, 3-6, 4-6, 14-12), r/u 1965 with Stolle (Newcombe/A Roche won, 3-6, 4-6, 13-11, 6-3, 6-4), won 1966 with Stolle (beat Newcombe/Roche, 7-9, 6-3, 6-8, 14-12, 12-10), won 1969 with Laver

(beat Rosewall/Stolle, 6-4, 6-4, best of three sets); mixed doubles r/u 1956 with Mrs M Hawton (Fraser/Miss B Penrose won, 6-2, 6-4). Davis Cup team 1959–67.

French men's singles r/u 1962 (Laver won, 3-6, 2-6, 6-3, 9-7, 6-2), won 1963 (beat P Darmon, 3-6, 6-1, 6-4, 6-4), won 1967 (beat Roche, 6-1, 6-4, 2-6, 6-2); men's doubles r/u 1959 (O Sirola/N Pietrangeli won, 6-3, 6-2, 14-12), won 1960 (beat J Arilla/A Gimeno, 6-2, 8-10, 7-5, 6-4), both with Fraser, won 1961 with Laver (beat R Howe/Mark, 3-6, 6-1, 6-1, 6-4), won 1962 with Fraser (beat W Bungert/C Kuhnke, 6-3, 6-4, 7-5), won 1963 with M Santana (beat G Forbes/A Segal, 6-2, 6-4, 6-4), won 1964 with Fletcher (beat Newcombe/Roche, 7-5, 6-3, 3-6, 7-5), won 1965 with Stolle (beat Fletcher/ Hewitt, 6-8, 6-3, 8-6, 6-2), r/u 1967 with Fletcher (Newcombe/Roche won, 6-3, 9-7, 12-10), r/u 1968 (Rosewall/Stolle won, 6-3, 6-4, 6-3), r/u 1969 (Newcombe/Roche won, 4-6, 6-1, 3-6, 6-4, 6-4), both with Laver; mixed doubles r/u

1960 with Miss A Haydon (Howe/Miss M Bueno won, 1-6, 6-1, 6-2).

US men's singles won 1961 (beat Laver, 7-5, 6-3, 6-2), r/u 1962 (Laver won, 6-2, 6-4, 5-7, 6-4), won 1964 (beat Stolle, 6-4, 6-1, 6-4); men's doubles won 1959 (beat A Olmedo/E Buchholz, 3-6, 6-3, 5-7, 6-4, 7-5), won 1960 (beat Laver/Mark, 9-7, 6-2, 6-4), both with Fraser, won 1965 (beat F Froehling/C Pasarell, 6-4, 10-12, 7-5, 6-3), won 1966 (beat R Ralston/C Graebner, 6-4, 6-4, 6-4), both with Stolle, r/u 1970 with Laver (P Barthès/N Pilić won, 6-3, 7-6, 4-6, 7-6).

Wimbledon singles won 1964 (beat Stolle, 6-4, 12-10, 4-6, 6-3), won 1965 (beat Stolle, 6-2, 6-4, 6-4); men's doubles won 1959 (beat Laver/Mark, 8-6, 6-3, 14-16, 9-7), won 1961 (beat Hewitt/Stolle, 6-4, 6-8, 6-4, 6-8, 8-6), both with Fraser, r/u 1964 (Hewitt/Stolle won, 7-5, 11-9, 6-4), r/u 1967 (Hewitt/F McMillan won, 6-2, 6-3, 6-4), both with Fletcher, won 1971 with Laver (beat Ashe/Ralston, 4-6, 9-7, 6-8, 6-4, 6-4).

Italian championship doubles won 1959, 1961, 1966; mixed doubles won 1961. Became professional 1968; joined WCT 1971–2.

ESTEP, Mike, USA

Born July 1949, Dallas, Texas. A political science graduate, Estep gained himself the nickname 'Mighty Mouse' as a promising young left-hander who took America to victory in the Sunshine Cup for under-21s in 1966 and again in 1968. In between he was runner-up in the Wimbledon junior invitation to Manuel Orantes and was US junior champion on grass. In 1975 he reached the last 16 at Wimbledon with a 63-game win over fellow Texan Sherwood Stewart. He has shown himself to be an exceptionally strong doubles player with an excellent forehand.

Wimbledon junior r/u 1967. US junior grass champion 1967; won Orange Bowl 1968; Washington WCT doubles won 1975, Houston WCT doubles r/u 1975, both with J Simpson; Cologne Cup doubles r/u 1976 with C Dowdeswell. Played World Team Tennis for Boston Lobsters.

EVERT, Christine Marie, USA

Born December 1954, Fort Lauderdale, Florida. In 1971 'Chrissie' Evert became the youngest player ever to represent the United States. Aged 16 years and 8 months she played a crucial part in America's Wightman Cup win and had 46 consecutive singles wins in that year before being defeated by Billie Jean King in the US women's semi-finals. It was an auspicious start to what has become an extraordinarily brilliant tennis career bringing Chris Evert fame and a fortune which would have been impossible for women players less than a decade ago. In 1974 she became the fourth youngest winner of the Wimbledon title at 19 years 196 days and she won it again in 1976 and retained the US title which she gained from Mrs King in 1975. The 1976 final against Evonne Cawley gave her her

101st successive clay court win.

Coached by her father, Jim Evert, himself a tennis professional, she had already beaten Billie Jean and Margaret Court when only 15 – before her Wightman Cup selection – and had been playing since she was six years old. After beating Virginia Wade – ten years her senior – in that cup match she coolly told a press conference that 'After all, I've had plenty of experience. I've had ten years'!

Her coolness, sometimes described as icy, has been one of her chief assets in her climb to become the world's number one player; this and her total dedication, her searing two-handed backhand and immaculate precision, which have placed her among the all-time 'greats' at an early age. In 1974, when both Chris and Jimmy Connors were blazing a youngsters' trail through the ranks of hardened professionals, they were engaged for a time but later in the year went their separate ways on the tennis circuit – Miss Evert to complete a run of 56 consecutive wins which was again ended by Mrs King. Her successes continued in 1976 with wins in 12 out of 17 tournaments and another exceptional winning run without a break of 41 matches.

Though she lost her Wimbledon title to Virginia Wade in 1977 and at one stage of the season confessed to the need for a break from tennis, she remained formidable as a player and an earner and again won the US Open singles. She picked up $78,620 by beating Mrs King in the Colgate final and avenged herself on Miss Wade, defeating her 7-5, 7-6 in the Wightman Cup. In the Virginia Slims championships of 1977 she beat Sue Barker, dropping one set. She has become increasingly active in promoting the interests of women professionals – having turned professional at 18 – and gaining them parity in prize money with men. In 1977 she earned $343,368 from tournaments. She is a former president of the Women's Tennis Association. Chris Evert is perhaps today's most formidable woman contestant.

US women's singles won 1975 (beat Mrs King, 5-7, 6-4, 6-2), won 1976 (beat Mrs Cawley, 6-3, 6-0), won 1977 (beat Miss W Turnbull, 7-6, 6-2); US mixed doubles r/u 1974. US clay courts championship won 1972–5.

French women's singles r/u 1973 (Mrs B M Court won, 6-7, 7-6, 6-4), won 1974 (beat Mrs O Morozova, 6-1, 6-2), won 1975 (beat Miss Navratilova, 2-6, 6-2, 6-1); doubles won 1974 with Mrs Morozova, won 1975 with Miss Navratilova.

Wimbledon women's singles r/u 1973 (Mrs King won 6-0, 7-5), won 1974 (beat Mrs Morozova, 6-0, 6-4), won 1976 (beat Mrs Cawley, 6-3, 4-6, 8-6); doubles won 1976 with Miss Navratilova (beat Mrs King/Miss B Stöve, 6-1, 3-6, 7-5).

Italian championships singles r/u 1973, won 1974–5.

Virginia Slims Houston r/u 1976 (Miss Navratilova won, 6-3, 6-4), doubles r/u with Miss

Navratilova (Miss Durr/Miss Casals won, 6-0, 7-5); V S Washington won 1976 (beat Miss Wade, 6-2, 6-1); V S Detroit won 1976 (beat Miss R Casals, 6-4, 6-2); doubles r/u (Miss A Kiyomura/Mrs M Guerrant won, 6-3, 6-4); V S Saratoga won 1976 (beat Mrs Cawley, 6-3, 6-0); V S San Francisco won 1976 (Mrs Cawley, 7-5, 7-6); V S Philadelphia r/u 1976 (Mrs Cawley won, 6-3, 7-6); V S championships r/u 1976

(Mrs Cawley won, 6-3, 5-7, 6-3), won 1977 (beat Miss Barker, 2-6, 6-1, 6-1).

Dewar Cup r/u 1976 (Miss Wade won, 6-2, 6-2).

Wightman Cup team 1971 – including unbeaten run of 10 singles to 1976 and won 1976 doubles with Miss Casals.

Colgate Inaugural singles won 1977 (beat Mrs King, 6-2, 6-2).

Above: Chrissie Evert is one of the all-time greats and is still on the road to further fame and glory.

EVERT, Jeanne, USA
Born October 1957, Fort Lauderdale, Florida. Younger sister of Chris, she beat her sister's record as the youngest player ever to represent America when she was selected for the Wightman Cup team of 1973 aged 15 years 10 months and 10 days. In 1973 on her US Open debut she beat Rosemary Casals. Her style of play and her appearance are similar to those of her sister and she can also maintain long rallies with accuracy. However, she lacks the same 'killer instinct' necessary to follow in Christine's footsteps.

US amateur clay court r/u 1973, Southern championships won 1973, 1975; Gunze Open, Japan, doubles r/u 1975 with Mrs O Morozova.

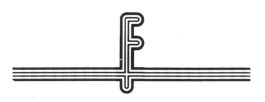

FABYAN, Mrs M *see* Palfrey, Sarah Hammond

FAIRLIE, Brian, New Zealand
Born June 1948, Christchurch. Consistently in the top ten national rankings, Fairlie showed early promise when he was selected as New Zealand's No 2 Davis Cup player to travel to Britain in 1966 aged 18 and that year was runner-up to V Korotkov of Russia in the Wimbledon junior invitation and was junior champion of New South Wales and Victoria. Ten years later he won the Wimbledon Men's Singles Plate and was runner-up to Onny Parun in the New Zealand Open. Son of a former national billiards champion and himself an excellent golfer, Fairlie's career in the decade between has been patchy. His best years have

been 1973, when, unseeded, he won the Rothmans' Albert Hall, was r/u to Kodes in the Cologne championships and performed consistently well on the WCT circuit, and 1976 when he was also r/u in Mexico City WCT doubles, Brisbane doubles, Japan Open doubles and won the Sydney doubles, all with El Shafei.

New Zealand Open singles r/u 1975 (O Parun won, 4-6, 6-4, 6-4, 6-7, 6-4); doubles r/u 1975 with Parun (R Carmichael/R Ruffels won, 7-6, retired); NZ Open singles r/u 1976 (Parun won, 6-2, 6-3, 4-6, 6-3); NZ hard courts singles won 1975; Wellington won 1971. Australia junior championships won 1967; Brisbane doubles r/u 1976 with I El Shafei; Sydney doubles won 1976 with El Shafei.

London hard courts singles won 1969; North of England championships r/u 1969; Rothmans' International Albert Hall, won 1973 (beat M Cox, 2-6, 6-2, 6-2, 7-6).

Cologne professional championships r/u 1973 (J Kodeš won, 6-1, 6-3, 6-1). Mexico City WCT doubles r/u 1976 with El Shafei (B Gottfried/R Ramirez won, 6-4, 7-6); Japan Open, Tokyo doubles r/u 1976 with El Shafei (Carmichael/Rosewall won, 6-4, 6-4).

FALKENBURG, Robert, USA/Brazil
Born January 1926, New York. During the late 1940s and early 1950s Bob Falkenburg was credited with having the fastest serve in American tennis. He is, however, probably best remembered both for his surprise win over Australian John Bromwich in the 1948 Wimbledon finals and for his unpopular habit of deliberately slowing a game down in order to take a rest. The tall, lean American appeared to be all arms and legs as he bounded about the court – earning him the nickname 'Daddy Longlegs' – and his performance of crouching down ostensibly to tie his laces but in effect to 'take a breather', led to another nickname: the 'Praying Mantis'. His win over Bromwich in 1948 after being three match points down came about through a combination of flashes of bril'iant play and persistent 'rest periods' during which he threw away points, and 'breathers' which clearly unsettled his opponent and displeased spectators. Later in his career, however, Falkenburg was warmly greeted in Britain when he represented Brazil (by virtue of residence in Rio de Janeiro) in the Davis Cup and his sportsmanship was then unquestionable.

He had a very powerful serve and had all the confidence to take risky shots on important points.

US men's doubles won 1944 with W McNeill (beat W Talbert/F Segura, 7-5, 6-4, 3-6, 6-1); mixed doubles, r/u 1945 with Miss D Hart (Talbert/Miss M Osborne won, 6-4, 6-4).

Wimbledon men's singles won 1948 (beat Bromwich, 7-5, 0-6, 6-2, 3-6, 7-5); men's doubles won 1947 with J Kramer (beat A Mottram/O Sidwell, 8-6, 6-3, 6-3).

Brazil Davis Cup team 1954–5.

Left (centre): In the early 1950s and late 1940s Bob Falkenburg was credited with having the fastest serve in American tennis.
Left: Jurgen Fassbender has proved himself a competent doubles player on the professional circuit.

FASSBENDER, Jurgen, Germany

Born May 1948. The son of a professional tennis coach, Fassbender was twice West German junior champion and has been doubles champion twice and mixed doubles three times. He was seeded No 8 in the 1973 Wimbledon draw after the withdrawal of 79 professionals in the dispute between the ATP and the ILTF. He reached the men's quarter-finals but lost to Sandy Mayer. He has proved himself a powerful doubles player with consistent form on the professional circuit and in 1973 was top doubles money earner with Karl Meiler on the USLTA circuit. With Meiler he won the 1977 Swedish Open doubles.

West German men's doubles won 1973 (beat I Tiriac/M Orantes 7-6, 7-6, 7-6), won 1974, both with H Pohmann; mixed doubles won 1971 (beat J Barclay/Miss C Truman, 2-6, 6-0, 6-4); men's doubles won 1972, won 1974, all with H Orth; German indoor closed singles won 1972.

US clay courts doubles r/u 1974 with Pohmann; US Indoor Open championship doubles won 1973 with J Gisbert (beat C Graebner/I Năstase, 2-6, 6-4, 6-3). Commercial Union Masters doubles second 1975 with Pohmann.

South Africa mixed doubles won 1973 with Miss E Goolagong (beat B Mitton/Miss I Kloss, 6-3, 6-2).

Canadian Open doubles r/u 1974 with Pohmann.

Swiss Open doubles won 1976 with Pohmann (beat P Bertolucci/A Panatta, 7-5, 6-3, 6-3). Swedish Open doubles won 1977 with Meiler (beat Dowdeswell/Hewitt, 6-4, 7-6).

Davis Cup 1968; King's Cup 1967.

Federation Cup

Inaugurated in 1963, the Federation Cup filled the long-felt need for an international team contest for women. The ILTF, celebrating its 50th anniversary, donated the trophy, which is a large silver flower bowl. The competition is held in various international tennis centres with some nations seeded. Each round includes two singles matches and one doubles. All full member nations of the ILTF are eligible. Regulations allow for the matches to be played on any surface. The first competition in 1963 was won by the USA with Australia as runner-up and these two teams have tended to dominate the event since, though South Africa (1972) and Czechoslovakia (1975) have also won.

FIBAK, Wojtek, Poland

Born August 1952. An excellent doubles player, Fibak, who was a law student and multi-linguist, has done much to boost Polish tennis on the international scene and has also achieved some fine singles results. He made his Davis Cup debut in both singles and doubles in 1974 and beat Arthur Ashe in Barcelona. In 1976 he had spectacular wins over the world's leading players thanks to intelligent play and in his first Commercial Union Masters final he put up a determined resistance to Manuel Orantes before losing 5-7, 6-2, 0-6, 7-6, 6-1, to take second place. He has had recent wins over Borg, Vilas, Năstase, Ramirez, Gottfried, Smith, Lutz, Mottram, Dibbs, Ashe, Orantes, and Franulović. He was again ranked No 1 in Poland in 1977 and with Jan Kodeš was runner-up in the French Open doubles, and the US Professional with Tom Okker.

Helsinki singles r/u 1975 (I Năstase won); ATP Madrid doubles won 1975 with J Kodeš; German Open doubles r/u 1975 (M Orantes/J Gisbert won, 6-3, 7-6); Spanish championships doubles r/u 1975 with K Meiler (B Borg/G Vilas won, 3-6, 6-4, 6-3).

US clay courts singles r/u 1976 (Connors won, 6-2, 6-4); US clay courts doubles r/u 1975 with H Pohmann (Gisbert/Orantes won, 7-5, 6-0). US Professional doubles r/u 1977 with Okker (F McMillan/R Hewitt won, 6-1, 1-6, 6-3).

French Open doubles r/u 1977 with Kodeš (B Gottfried/R Ramirez won, 7-6, 4-6, 6-3, 6-4). French Indoor doubles won 1975 with Meiler. Dewar Cup doubles won 1975 with Meiler (J Connors/Năstase, 6-1, 7-5). Stockholm WCT singles won 1976 (beat Năstase, 6-4, 7-6); WCT doubles final won 1976 with Meiler (beat R Lutz/S Smith, 6-3, 2-6, 3-6, 6-3, 6-4). Canadian Open singles r/u 1976 (Vilas won, 6-4, 7-6, 6-2).

Il Trofeo Gillette, Madrid men's doubles won with Ramirez in 1976 (beat R Hewitt/F McMillan, 4-6, 7-5, 6-3); Fischer Grand Prix, Vienna, singles won 1976 (beat Ramirez, 6-7, 6-3, 6-4, 2-6, 6-1); Commercial Union Masters' singles r/u 1976 (Orantes won, 5-7, 6-2, 0-6, 7-6, 6-1); Monte Carlo doubles won 1976 with Meiler (beat Borg/Vilas, 7-6, 6-1); Coca-Cola British hard court singles won 1976 (beat Orantes, 6-2, 7-9, 6-2, 6-2), doubles won with F McNair (beat Gisbert/Orantes, 4-6, 7-5, 7-5).

FILLOL, Jaime, Chile

Born June 1946. Now living in Santiago, Fillol, who is a trained physical education teacher, has shown himself to be capable of putting up a good performance on all types of surface, making full use of the whole court. In 1974 he became the first secretary of the Association of Tennis Professionals and worked hard on the Association's behalf on the 'political' side of the game. In the second round of the 1976 US Open he was close to beating Borg when 6-4, 2-6 and 5-2 third set but the Swede recovered to take the decisive set 7-6. He was been particularly successful in doubles with his fellow countryman Patricio Cornejo, with whom he won the 1977 US clay court doubles. He was r/u to Vilas in the 1977 Argentine Open.

US Open doubles r/u 1974 with P Cornejo; Washington Indoors won 1971; Dewar Cup, Billingham won 1971; Toronto WCT doubles won 1976 with F McMillan; Dayton singles won 1976. US clay court doubles won 1977 with Cornejo (beat R Crealy/C Letcher, 6-7, 6-4, 6-3).

French Open doubles r/u 1972 with Cornejo; mixed doubles r/u 1975 with Miss P Teeguarden; Paris Indoor singles r/u 1976; Belgian doubles r/u 1972 with Cornejo.

South African professional singles r/u 1973.

British hard courts championship doubles r/u 1971 with Cornejo.

Argentine Open r/u 1977. Davis Cup 1970–

FLEITZ, Mrs Beverly (née Baker), USA

Born March 1930, Providence, Rhode Island. One of the most attractive players of her day, Mrs Fleitz was ambidextrous, free-hitting and a fast mover. She brought both grace and pace to her game but never achieved a major international win. In 1955 she came close, beating Doris Hart in the Wimbledon semi-finals to meet the 32-year-old Louise Brough in the final, when, though she led 5-4 in both sets, she lost 7-5 and 8-6. In the following year she reached the quarter-finals but, feeling unwell, consulted the championship chairman, Colin Gregory, who was a family doctor. He diagnosed pregnancy and Mrs Fleitz withdrew.

French women's doubles won 1955 with Miss D Hard (beat Miss S Bloomer/Miss P Ward, 7-5, 6-8, 13-11).

Wimbledon women's singles r/u 1955 (Miss A Brough won, 7-5, 8-6); women's doubles r/u 1959 with Miss C Truman (Miss J Arth/Miss Hard won, 2-6, 6-2, 6-3). Wightman Cup 1949, 1956, 1959.

Right: Wojtek Fibak is Poland's No 1 ranked player. Right (centre): Beverly Fleitz (née Baker) was an attractive ambidextrous, graceful player of the mid-1950s.

FLETCHER, Kenneth Norman, Australia/Hong Kong

Born June 1940, Queensland. One of the great Australian players of the 1960s, Fletcher tended to be overshadowed by Laver, Emerson and Fraser, mainly because he was essentially a doubles player and was rarely at his best in major singles events. In 1963 he achieved the mixed doubles 'Grand Slam' (Australian, French, US and Wimbledon titles) with Margaret Smith. He was once men's doubles champion at Wimbledon and three times runner-up, four times mixed doubles champion and twice runner-up. He was never selected for the Australian Davis Cup team. In 1965 he emigrated to Hong Kong and in 1969 retired from the international tennis circuit.

Australian men's singles r/u 1963 (R Emerson won, 6-3, 6-3, 6-1); men's doubles r/u 1963 with J Newcombe (R Hewitt/F Stolle won, 6-2, 3-6, 6-3, 3-6, 6-3), r/u 1964 with Emerson (Hewitt/Stolle won, 6-4, 7-5, 3-6, 4-6, 14-12); mixed doubles won 1963 (beat Stolle/Miss L Turner, 7-5, 5-7, 6-4), won 1964 (beat M Sangster/Miss J Lehane, 6-3, 6-2), both with Miss Smith.

French men's doubles won 1964 with Emerson (beat Newcombe/A Roche, 7-5, 6-3, 3-6, 7-5), r/u 1965 with Hewitt (Emerson/Stolle won, 6-8, 5-3, 8-6, 6-2), r/u 1967 with Emerson (Newcombe/Roche won, 6-3, 9-7, 12-10); mixed doubles won 1963 (beat Stolle/Miss Turner, 6-1, 6-2), won 1964 (beat Stolle/Miss Turner, 6-3, 6-4), won 1965 (beat Newcombe/Miss M Bueno, 6-4, 6-4), all with Miss Smith.

US mixed doubles won 1963 with Miss Smith (beat E Rubinoff/Miss J Tegart, 3-6, 8-6, 6-2).

Wimbledon men's doubles r/u 1964 with Emerson (Hewitt/Stolle won, 7-5, 11-9, 6-4), r/u 1965 with Hewitt (Newcombe/Roche won, 7-5, 6-3, 6-4), won 1966 with Newcombe (beat W Bowrey/O Davidson, 6-3, 6-4, 3-6, 6-3), r/u 1967 with Emerson (Hewitt/F McMillan won, 6-2, 6-3, 6-4); mixed doubles won 1963 (beat Hewitt/Miss Hard, 11-9, 6-4), r/u 1964 (Stolle/Miss Turner won, 6-4, 6-4), won 1965 (beat Roche/Miss Tegart, 12-10, 6-3), won 1966 (beat R Ralston/Mrs L W King, 4-6, 6-3, 6-3), all with Miss Smith, r/u 1967 with Miss Bueno (Davidson/Mrs King won, 7-5, 6-2), won 1968 with Mrs B M Court (beat A Metreveli/Miss O Morozova, 6-1, 14-12). British hard courts champion 1966.

Flushing Meadows, USA

A new tennis complex to replace the crowded and outdated facilities at Forest Hills as America's leading tennis centre, Flushing Meadows was due for completion at a cost of $10-million in August 1978. In addition to 25 outdoor courts with acrylic surfaces which are slower than grass but faster than clay, there are indoor courts and a massive new Centre Court with seats for 20,000 and 600 glass-fronted, air-conditioned boxes. A lesser, tiered stadium adjoining the centre court will have room for 6000 spectators. The tree-lined and landscaped site covers 16 acres (6.48 hectares) near Manhattan and is to have every facility for players, officials, press, radio, television and public. The 1978 US Open is due to be held there.

Forest Hills, USA

Formed in 1892, the West Side Tennis Club had three homes before it moved in 1915 to Forest Hills, a part of Queens, some eight miles from Manhattan. In that year the national men's singles championships were transferred from the Newport Casino to Forest Hills and were held there annually until 1977 apart from a break of three years (1921–3). The US women's singles have been staged there since 1921, the men's doubles and women's doubles since 1968 and the mixed doubles since 1969.

In 1923 the West Side Club opened the new Forest Hills stadium, a horseshoe-shaped tennis arena which was the second largest in the world (next to Wimbledon) with 23 clay and 22 grass courts and seating for about 14,000. The first international tournament staged there was the 1923 Wightman Cup in which the US women (Miss H Wills, Mrs M Mallory, Mrs G Wightman and Miss E Goss) decisively beat Great Britain (Miss K McKane, Mrs R Clayton, Mrs A Beamish and Mrs B Covell) 7-0.

The 1927 mens' final between W T Tilden and J R Lacoste was watched by over 13,000 people and 14,000 people attended on successive days in 1937 to see Baron von Cramm defeat Bobby Riggs in the semi-finals. Though tournaments did not stop during World War II, events were restricted but the Armistice saw an upsurge in interest and in 1946 the gates of Forest Hills were closed and thousands turned away; 1947 saw the same packed crowds. In 1965 the attendance record for the US amateur championships was 90,000 and in 1970, 122,990 watched

Left (centre): Australian-born Ken Fletcher was an inspired doubles player who rarely excelled in singles competition. He retired in 1969.

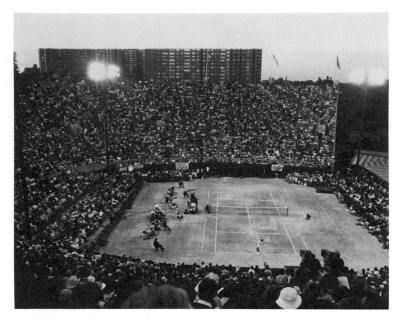

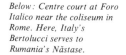

Above: Centre court at the West Side Tennis Club, Forest Hills. This Club is second only to Wimbledon in size. Here we see Borg serving to Connors.

Below: Centre court at Foro Italico near the coliseum in Rome. Here, Italy's Bertolucci serves to Rumania's Năstase.

the Open championships. That record only lasted until 1972, when 130,000 attended, with day records of 14,683 and 14,696 on the last two days.

In 1942 all five major national grass court championship events for men and women were held at Forest Hills for the first time. However, from 1946 until 1967 the men's and women's doubles were staged at Longwood Cricket Club, Chestnut Hill, Massachusetts, while the men's and women's singles and mixed doubles remained at Forest Hills. With the coming of the Open championships in 1968 all five events were again staged at Forest Hills. The 'clay courts' are in fact covered with a fairly slow surface of granite chippings and the grass courts have presented problems for some years because of the subsoil which, after heavy rain, distorts and gives an uneven playing surface. The last Open was held at Forest Hills in 1977 and its new home at Flushing Meadows was due to be completed by the summer of 1978.

See **Flushing Meadows.**

Foro Italico, Rome, Italy

Built close to the ancient Coliseum in Rome in 1925, the Foro Italico stadium complex encloses six courts in paired sections. The stadium and complex present a majestic sight with pine trees, potted plants, neat hedges and giant statues. The stands at the Number One and Two courts have seating for about 5000 and the other four courts have room for a further 5000 in all. Spectators sit on cement tiers except in the exclusive club house, where a parapet with large picture windows overlooks the main arena. The courts are clay with a topping of red brick dust, which gives a slow surface.

Four Musketeers, France

The four players who made France pre-eminent in international tennis during the 1920s and into the 1930s were Jean Borotra, Jacques Brugnon, Henri Cochet and René Lacoste. One or other of them carried off the French singles title from 1924 to 1932 and the Wimbledon singles from 1924 to 1929. They played 164 Davis Cup rubbers among them, winning 120 and retaining the Cup from 1927–32. *See* separate entries for individual records.

France

Two clubs claim to have been the first to play lawn tennis in France and both were founded by Englishmen. The Dinnard Tennis Club, Brittany, was started by holidaying Englishmen in 1878 and went on to produce future champions. The Le Havre Athletic Club was founded by graduates from the Universities of Oxford and Cambridge in 1872, its members playing rugby and football. It was apparently not until 1884 that the first three grass courts were marked out. Later they were turned into hard courts and four more were added. In 1882 the Racing Club of France was founded in Paris, followed in 1883 by the *Stade Français* also in the capital. Two years later the famous sporting society of the *Île de Puteaux* was formed and became the scene of the first French championships in 1891. Early in its history the *Île de Puteaux*, where tennis is still played, became the meeting place

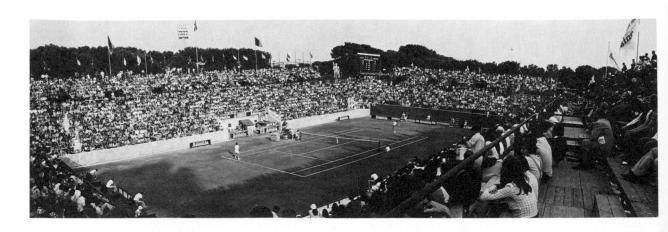

Left (centre): The 'Four
Musketeers'. Left to right –
J Borotra, R Lacoste
J Brugnon, H Cochet.

for tennis players and did much to establish the sport in France. Women were admitted to the championships there in 1897. Meanwhile many other clubs were founded across the country, including the Tennis Club of Paris (1895), which remains one of the largest clubs in the city and is next to the great covered-courts arena, the Pierre de Coubertin Stadium, which opened in 1938, when King Gustav V of Sweden attended the Challenge Round match between France and Sweden in the King's Cup, which he had presented. The stadium was wrecked by air raids during World War II but has been rebuilt and is the centre for major events in tennis and other sports.

The early 1900s saw the emergence of one of the greatest of French tennis players, Max Decugis, and three other players who helped spread the popularity of tennis, Maurice Germot, André Gobert and William Laurentz. Decugis won the men's singles closed championships eight times in all between 1903, when he was 21, and 1914 and has been called the first Frenchman to play modern tennis, using the volley, with a powerful serve and smash. With the small, precise 'Fifi' Germot, he formed an indestructible doubles partnership and won the championship on ten occasions between 1904 and 1920. Germot, who was thin and supple, also won the doubles title with Gobert and with Marcel DuPont and interrupted the Decugis singles reign in 1905–6. In complete contrast, Gobert was 6 ft 4 in (1.92 m) tall and extremely athletic but could be too easily distracted from concentration. He won the singles title in 1911 and again when competition was resumed in 1920 after World War I. Despite his weakness of concentration he became a golf player and was French champion. The fourth of these early 'Musketeers', Laurentz, played a fast accurate game which brought him international fame for 15 years and made him 'world champion' at Saint Cloud in 1920.

Another French tennis star of this era whose name has become legend was Suzanne Lenglen who in 1914, at the age of 15, burst upon the scene to win the World clay court championship singles and doubles. Two weeks earlier she had been runner-up to Marguerite Broquedis, the reigning champion, in the French championships. Miss Lenglen went on to dominate international women's tennis from 1919–26. In that period she won the French closed championships singles four times, the national championships twice, the Wimbledon women's title six times and gained no fewer than 19 French and British titles in doubles and mixed doubles.

The extraordinary reign of the four players who became known as France's 'Four Musketeers', Jean Borotra, Jacques Brugnon, Henri Cochet and René Lacoste, came about after Borotra and Cochet had played each other for the first time in 1921 in the final of the Criterium at the Racing Club of France (Cochet won). Next year they were in the Davis Cup team

Below: An engraving of a
French 'real' tennis court,
1767.

and in 1923 were joined by the other two. Their playing careers are detailed elsewhere in this work: suffice to say that the 'Musketeers' gave France a new pride in tennis and an international dominance which it has not enjoyed since. Though France had entered the Davis Cup since 1904, it was not until 1919 that it gained its first victory to reach the final round, when it lost to Britain. At last, in 1927, after successes in zone and inter-zone events in the intervening years, France won the Challenge Round for the first time.

For the defence of the Davis Cup, France required a suitable new tennis stadium and working together the *Stade Français* and the Racing Club of France built the *Stade Roland Garros* on a site given by the city of Paris to the French Lawn Tennis Federation. Originally the stadium had seating for 8000 but enlargement has made room for some 13,000 and there are nine clay and two hard courts. The opening event in May 1928 was a women's tournament between France and Britain, then, in July the Davis Cup was successfully defended, the French team beating the US 4-1.

The Cup did not leave France until 1933, when it went to Britain. It was the end of the golden years; not until 1946 and after would French players shine again on the international scene. Then Yvon Petra won the Wimbledon singles and French doubles and Marcel Bernard won the French singles and doubles (having previously won the latter in 1936 and the mixed in 1935–6). In 1948 Mrs Nelly Landry, who had been born in England but was French by marriage, won the women's singles, having reached the quarter-finals in 1936 and 1946 and been runner-up in 1938. With French titles being taken increasingly by overseas players, some honour was restored in 1967, when Françoise Durr won the French singles and doubles and the German singles. She has since taken 11 other doubles and mixed doubles international titles and has proved herself the outstanding French woman player of four decades.

The French national championship, held annually at different centres, was founded by the *Fédération Française de Lawn-Tennis* in 1951 as a closed championship for French players. Usually 16 men and 8 women qualify for the final, though certain players can qualify without either ranking in the national first series or, through the second series, reaching the quarter-finals of the *Critérium* of France or semi-finals of the women's *Critérium*. Other major tennis events include the club team championships, the team championships of Paris, the Marcel Porée Cup, the clay courts *Critérium* of France for men and women ranked in the second series, the *Espérance de France* for those ranked in the third series, the *Omnium* for non-classified players and the French international covered court championships.

The FFLT which governs French tennis was founded in 1920 with Henry Wallet, who had been president of the previous controlling commission, as its first president. He was also to be one of four French presidents of the ILTF, in the founding of which France played an important role. The first exploratory meeting to consider founding an international tennis organisation was held in Paris in 1912 and the inaugural meeting, also in Paris, in 1913.

In addition to adult tournaments held under the FFLT there are schemes for the coaching of junior and young players and several hundred tennis schools exist. In 1970 the Federation, with the backing of the Ministry for Youth and Sports started an experiment by electing a dozen boys from among the best young players and taking them to Nice, where they attend the Lycée for normal education and also have daily training in tennis and physical exercise.

The ranking of players is an intricate annual affair involving some 3000 men and 1000 women players who send in their playing records to the FFLT at the end of each season. They are then divided into three categories: first series players, who usually number 20 men and 12 women; second series, in which men are handicapped owe 15 to receive 15; and third series grading from 15/2 to 30. The rankings involve successively the regional commissioners of the FFLT leagues, inter-regional and national commissioners and appeals can be made to the Federal Bureau, which will accept or modify rankings.

FRANULOVIĆ, Zeljko, Yugoslavia

Born June 1947, Split. After proving himself a tough opponent on clay courts early in his career, Franulović became successful on all surfaces and achieved some good international tournament results. His career was threatened by a persistent shoulder injury in 1971 and he has struggled to retain earlier form. He joined WCT in 1973 and in 1975 was suspended for a time by the Yugoslav federation for playing in South Africa. His best performance since injury was in 1976 when he had 11 straight King's Cup victories and two wins on clay over the Polish Wojtek Fibak.

French men's singles r/u 1970 (J Kodeš won, 6-2, 6-4, 6-0).

Belgian r/u 1969 (T Okker won, 6-4, 1-6, 6-2, 6-2).

US clay courts championships won 1969 (beat A Ashe), won 1971 (beat C Richey, 6-3, 6-4, 0-6, 6-3).

South American championships won 1969, 1970–1; São Paulo r/u 1973.

British hard courts championships r/u 1971 (G Battrick won, 6-3, 6-2, 5-7, 6-0).

Hilversum singles r/u 1975; doubles r/u with J Lloyd.

FRASER, Neale Andrew, Australia

Born October 1933, St Kilda, Melbourne. The son of an Australian judge, Fraser was a left-hander of enormous determination, with a clean fast service and excellent volley. With his

contemporaries, Rod Laver, Roy Emerson, Ashley Cooper, Lew Hoad and Ken Rosewall, he helped to keep Australia in the forefront of world tennis in the late 1950s and early 1960s. He was particularly effective as a doubles player but also won the US singles twice (1959–60) and Wimbledon once (1960). His 1959 fourth-round Wimbledon win against Orlando Sirola was over 71 games. In the Australian singles final of 1960 he saved six match points against Laver before losing 5-7, 3-6, 6-3, 8-6, 8-6, but later that year beat him at Wimbledon and Forest Hills. Perhaps the finest three days of his entire career were in 1959 when he led the Australian bid to recapture the Davis Cup from America at Forest Hills. He won both his singles and the doubles with Emerson for Australia to take the Cup 3-2.

In 21 Davis Cup rubbers between 1958 and 1963 he won 18 and in 1973 he was non-playing captain of the team which again recaptured the trophy from the US, winning 5-0 in Cleveland.

Australian men's singles r/u 1957 (A Cooper won, 6-3, 9-11, 6-4, 6-2), r/u 1959 (A Olmedo won, 6-1, 6-2, 3-6, 6-3), r/u 1960 (R Laver won, 5-7, 3-6, 6-3, 8-6, 8-6); men's doubles r/u 1954 with C Wilderspin (R Hartwig/M Rose won, 6-3, 6-4, 6-2), won 1957 with L Hoad (beat Cooper/M Anderson, 6-3, 8-6, 6-1), won 1958 with Cooper (beat R Emerson/R Mark, 7-5, 6-8, 3-6, 6-3, 7-5), r/u 1960 (Laver/Mark won, 1-6, 6-2, 6-4, 6-4), won 1962 (beat R Hewitt/F Stolle, 4-6, 4-6, 6-1, 6-4, 11-9), both with Emerson; mixed doubles won 1956 with Miss B Penrose (beat Emerson/Mrs M Hawton, 6-2, 6-4).

Davis Cup 1955–63.

French men's doubles won 1958 with Cooper (beat R Howe/A Segal, 3-6, 8-6, 6-3, 7-5), r/u 1959 (O Sirola/N Pietrangeli won, 6-3, 6-2, 14-12), won 1960 (beat J Arilla/A Gimeno, 6-2, 8-10, 7-5, 6-4), won 1962 (beat W Bungert/C Kuhnke, 6-3, 6-4, 7-5), all with Emerson.

US men's singles won 1959 (beat Olmedo, 6-3, 5-7, 6-2, 6-4), won 1960 (beat Laver, 6-4, 6-4, 10-8); men's doubles won 1957 with Cooper (beat G Mulloy/J Patty, 4-6, 6-3, 9-7, 6-3), won 1959 (beat Olmedo/E Buchholz, 3-6, 6-3, 5-7, 6-4, 7-5), won 1960 (beat Laver/Mark, 9-7, 6-2, 6-4), both with Emerson; mixed doubles won 1958 (beat Olmedo/Miss M Bueno, 6-4, 3-6, 9-7), won 1959 (beat Mark/Miss J Hoggs, 7-5, 13-15, 6-2), won 1960 (beat A Palafox/Miss Bueno, 6-3, 6-2), all with Mrs duPont.

Wimbledon men's singles r/u 1958 (Cooper won 3-6, 6-3, 6-4, 13-11), won 1960 (beat Laver, 6-4, 3-6, 9-7, 7-5); men's doubles r/u 1955 with Rosewall (R Hartwig/L Hoad won, 7-5, 6-4, 6-3), r/u 1957 with Hoad (Mulloy/Patty won, 8-10, 6-4, 6-4, 6-4), r/u 1958 with Cooper (S Davidson/U Schmidt won, 6-4, 6-4, 8-6), won 1959 (beat Laver/Mark, 8-6, 6-3, 14-16, 9-7), won 1961 (beat Hewitt/Stolle, 6-4, 6-8, 6-4, 6-8, 8-6), both with Emerson, r/u 1973 with Cooper (J Connors/I Năstase won, 3-6, 6-3, 6-4, 8-9, 6-1); mixed doubles r/u 1957 with Miss A Gibson (M Rose/Miss D Hard won, 6-4, 7-5), r/u 1959 with Miss Bueno (Laver/Miss Hard won, 6-4, 6-3), won 1962 with Mrs duPont (beat R Ralston/Miss A Haydon, 2-6, 6-3, 13-11).

FROMHOLTZ, Dianne Lee, Australia
Born August 1956, Sydney. A left-hander with a powerful backhand and plentiful athletic prowess, Miss Fromholtz came to international prominence in 1973 on her first trip to Europe during which she won ten tournaments. She travelled the circuit in a mobile home accompanied by her mother, sister and a friend. She was ranked in the world's top ten for the first time in 1976, when she was one of only four players to beat Chris Evert – in the first round of the Virginia Slims Boston – and also won the Futures of Tallahassee, beating Virginia Ruzici of Rumania. She was runner-up to Kerry Reid for the 1977 Australian singles and won the doubles.

Australian hard court singles won 1973, singles r/u 1977 (Mrs K Reid won, 7-5, 6-2); doubles won 1977 with Miss Gourlay (beat Mrs Reid/Miss Nagelsen, 5-7, 6-1, 7-5); New Zealand hard courts won 1973.

South African Open r/u 1974 (Miss K Melville won), doubles r/u with Mrs B M Court.

US clay court r/u 1975 (Miss Evert won, 6-3, 6-4); Futures of Tallahassee won 1976 (beat Miss Ruzici); Phoenix WTA r/u 1976 (Miss Evert won).

Rothmans' Connaught singles won 1973 (beat Miss I Kloss, 6-1, 3-6, 6-4); Chichester singles won 1973 (beat Miss B Cuypers, 6-1, 6-0); Surrey hard courts won 1973 (beat Miss K Sawamatsu, 7-5, 6-3); Green Shield Welsh championships r/u 1973 (Miss J Heldman won, 1-6, 6-1, 11-9); Green Shield Beckenham won 1973 (beat Miss J Newberry, 7-5, 0-6, 6-1); West of Scotland hard courts won 1974; Irish Open doubles won 1974 with Miss R Giscafre.

FRY, Joan (Mrs T A Lakeman), GB
Born May 1906, Horsham, Sussex. At the age of 19 in 1925 Miss Fry made her first appearance at Wimbledon and won through to the women's final, despite having been overlooked by her county selection committee. She faced the legendary Suzanne Lenglen and became her sixth singles finals victim at Wimbledon.

Wimbledon women's singles r/u 1925 (Miss S Lenglen won, 6-2, 6-0); mixed doubles r/u 1929 with I Collins (F Hunter/Miss H Wills won, 6-1, 6-4).

US women's doubles r/u 1927 with Miss B Nuthall (Mrs L Godfree/Miss E Harvey won, 6-1, 4-6, 6-4).

Wightman Cup 1925–7, 1930.

FRY, Shirley June (Mrs K E Irvin), USA
Born June 1927, Akron, Ohio. Although often overshadowed by the brilliance of contemporary players such as Louise Brough, Margaret duPont, Doris Hart, and the young Maureen Connolly, she was an outstanding all-round player and gained particular success in women's doubles. In 1953 she won the Wimbledon doubles with Miss Hart, beating Miss Connolly and Miss Sampson, 6-0, 6-0 and losing only four games in the whole event. Her first important win was as US junior champion in 1944, her last, the Australian singles title in 1957. Between 1949 and 1956 she helped America continue its 21-year dominance of the Wightman Cup, playing in 1949, 1951–3 and 1955–6.

US women's singles r/u 1951 (Miss Connolly won, 6-3, 1-6, 6-4), won 1956 (beat Miss A Gibson, 6-3, 6-4); women's doubles r/u 1949 (Miss Brough/Mrs duPont won, 6-4, 8-6), r/u 1950 (Miss Brough/Mrs duPont won, 6-2, 6-2), won 1951 (beat Mrs P Todd/ Mrs N Chaffee, 6-4, 6-2), won 1952 (beat Miss Brough/Miss Connolly, 10-8, 6-4), won 1953 (beat Mrs duPont/Miss Brough, 6-3, 7-9, 9-7), won 1954 (beat Mrs duPont/Miss Brough, 6-4, 6-4), r/u 1955 (Miss Brough/Mrs duPont won, 6-3, 1-6, 6-3), all with Miss Hart, r/u 1956 with Mrs B Pratt (Miss Brough/Mrs duPont won, 6-3, 6-0); mixed doubles r/u 1951 with M Rose (F Sedgman/Miss Hart won, 6-3, 6-2), r/u 1955 with G Mulloy (E Seixas/Miss Hart won, 7-5, 5-7, 6-2).

French women's singles r/u 1948 (Mrs N Landry won, 6-2, 0-6, 6-0), won 1951 (beat Miss Hart, 6-3, 3-6, 6-3), r/u 1952 (Miss Hart won, 6-4, 6-4); women's doubles r/u 1948 with Mrs M Prentiss (Miss Hart/Mrs Todd won, 6-4, 6-2), won 1950 (beat Mrs duPont/Miss Brough, 1-6, 7-5, 6-2), won 1951 (beat Mrs B Bartlett/Miss B

Scofield, 10-8, 6-3), won 1952 (beat Mrs H Redick-Smith/Mrs J Wipplinger, 7-5, 6-1), won 1953 (beat Miss Connolly/Miss Sampson, 6-4, 6-3), all with Miss Hart; mixed doubles r/u 1952 with E Sturgess (Sedgman/Miss Hart won, 6-8, 6-3, 6-3).

Wimbledon women's singles r/u 1951 (Miss Hart won, 6-1, 6-0), won 1956 (beat Miss A Buxton, 6-3, 6-1); women's doubles r/u 1950 (Miss Brough/Mrs duPont won, 6-4, 5-7, 6-1), won 1951 (beat Miss Brough/Mrs duPont, 6-3, 13-11), won 1952 (beat Miss Brough/Miss Connolly, 8-6, 6-3), won 1953 (beat Miss Connolly/Miss Sampson, 6-0, 6-0), r/u 1954 (Miss Brough/Mrs duPont won, 4-6, 9-7, 6-3), all with Miss Hart; mixed doubles r/u 1953 with E Morea (Seixas/Miss Hart won, 9-7, 7-5), won 1956 with Seixas (beat Mulloy/Miss Gibson, 2-6, 6-2, 7-5).

Australian singles won 1957 (beat Miss Gibson, 6-3, 6-4); women's doubles won 1957 with Miss Gibson (beat Mrs K Hawton/Miss F Muller, 6-2, 6-1).

Italian doubles won 1951 with Miss Hart; mixed doubles won 1951 with F Ampon.

Left: Gerulaitis is one of the most promising American players on today's circuit.

Galea Cup

Presented in 1950 by Mme Edmond de Galea, the Galea Cup is intended to provide an international men's team competition for young players between the junior and Davis Cup standards. Entry is for players under 21 and the event includes two cross singles and one double; rubbers are the best of three sets until the final stages, when they are best of five. The first competition was held at Deauville and won by Italy, who had competed against France, Belgium and Spain. The following year the cup went to France and since 1952 the finals have been at Vichy and the competition has been organised on a zonal basis.

GARLAND, Charles Stedman, USA

Born October 1898, Pittsburgh, Pennsylvania, died January 1971. Secretary of the US Lawn Tennis Association, 1921–2, he won the Wimbledon men's doubles of 1920 with R Williams, defeating A Kingscote and J Parke (GB) 4-6, 6-4, 7-5, 6-2 in the All-Comers and gaining a walk-over from P O'Hara Wood and R V Thomas (Australia) in the Challenge Round.

GEEN, Mrs A C *see* Boothby, Penelope

GERULAITIS, Vitas, USA

Born July 1954, Brooklyn, New York. After first gaining attention in 1972 by winning all the major US junior titles except the under-18, Gerulaitis was also runner-up to Borg in the Orange Bowl and runner-up in the US amateur grass courts championship. He had a sensational start to 1975 when he beat Okker, Ramirez, Gerken and Alexander to reach the final of the US professional indoor championship before losing to Riessen in a tough match. A walk-over from Connors gave him the IPA New York title and with Sandy Mayer he took the Wimbledon doubles title against all expectations and they created a record by going through without playing a seeded pair. He led the World Team Tennis Pittsburgh Triangles to the WTT championship. In the 1976 Wimbledon he defeated the defending champion, Arthur Ashe in the fourth round and he came within one match of reaching the WCT finals at Dallas after a good all-round season. He won the Italian 1977 Open after dropping a set to Zugarelli and dropped two to John Lloyd in winning the Australian Open.

US amateur grass court singles r/u 1973; US amateur clay court doubles won 1973 with Teacher; Salt Lake City doubles won 1974 with Connors; Roanoke doubles won with Mayer; US professional indoor r/u 1975 (M Riessen won, 7-6, 5-7, 6-2, 6-7, 6-3). US Open mixed doubles r/u 1977 with Mrs King (F McMillan/Miss B Stöve won, 6-2, 3-6, 6-3).

Wimbledon men's doubles won 1975 with Mayer (beat C Dowdeswell/A Stone, 7-5, 8-6, 6-4).

Oslo Open doubles r/u 1974 with J Borowiak.

WCT Indianapolis r/u 1976; WCT Charlotte r/u 1976; WCT Toronto r/u 1976; finished 9 in WCT.

Italian Open won 1977 (beat A Zugarelli, 6-2, 7-6, 3-6, 7-6).

Right: Althea Gibson

GIBSON, Althea (Mrs W A Darbon), USA
Born August 1927, Silver, South Carolina. Oldest of four children of a poor sharecropper, Althea Gibson, the first black to become a world-class player, was brought up in the ghettos of New York and, as a tough tomboy, learned to box, play basketball and paddle tennis on the sidewalks of Harlem. Bought secondhand lawn tennis rackets by a local social worker, Althea was spotted by school-teacher Juan Serrell, who had her admitted to the Cosmopolitan Tennis Club. Aged 15 in 1942, she entered her first tournament, the New York State Open, and won the girls' singles. Later that year she lost at the black players' American Tennis Association girls' tournament at Lincoln University, Pennsylvania, but returned to win in 1944–5. She made her debut in the ATA national women's singles at 18 and was runner-up. Althea became a protégée of Dr

H A Eaton and Dr R W Johnson, of Virginia, who gave her training sessions and she went on to capture the ATA title for ten consecutive years. Now recognised as a leading player she was invited to enter the National Indoors championships in 1949 and 1950 but no invitation came from the national championship organisers at Forest Hills until they responded to public pressure in 1951. Then she became the first black player to appear on the Forest Hills Center Court, losing in the second round to champion Louise Brough after picking up one set in a match which spread into two days because of a thunder storm.

Althea took up a job teaching physical education at Lincoln University, Jefferson, in 1953 but without any major tournament wins, had to be dissuaded from giving up tennis by part-time professional Sydney Llewellyn. He changed her grip, taught her the tactics of play and renewed her determination. In 1955 she went on a tennis tour of India, Pakistan, Burma and Ceylon, then Sweden, Germany and Egypt, sponsored by the State Department. With this added experience and now a tough, determined player with a service as powerful as a man's, forceful ground strokes and decisive volleys, the sturdy Althea entered the French championships in 1956 and became the first black player to win the women's singles, against Angela Mortimer, 6-3, 11-9. Next year she gained her first Wimbledon title when she was aged almost 30, beating 16-year-old Christine Truman on the way to the final in which she beat Darlene Hard in straight sets. Returning to a heroine's reception in New York, she won the national championship by defeating Louise Brough 6-3, 6-2. In 1958 she again beat Angela Mortimer, this time in the Wimbledon final, and Darlene Hard in the US National and then turned professional, recognised as the greatest woman player in the world.

US women's singles r/u 1956 (Miss S Fry won, 6-3, 6-4), won 1957 (beat Miss L Brough, 6-3, 6-2), won 1958 (beat Miss D Hard, 3-6, 6-1, 6-2); women's doubles r/u 1957 with Miss Hard (Miss Brough/Mrs W duPont won, 6-2, 7-5), r/u 1958 with Miss M Bueno (Miss J Arth/Miss Hard won, 6-2, 6-3); mixed doubles won 1957 with K Nielson (R Howe/Miss Hard won, 6-3, 9-7). US Wightman Cup team 1957–8.

French women's singles won 1956 (beat Miss A Mortimer, 6-0, 12-10); doubles won 1956 with Miss A Buxton (beat Mrs D Knode/Miss Hard, 6-8, 8-6, 6-1).

Wimbledon singles won 1957 (beat Miss Hard, 6-3, 6-2), won 1958 (beat Miss Mortimer, 8-6, 6-2); women's doubles won 1956 with Miss Buxton (beat Miss F Muller/Miss D Seeney, 6-1, 8-6), won 1957 with Miss Hard (beat Mrs K Hawton/Mrs T Long, 6-1, 6-2), won 1958 with Miss Bueno (beat Mrs duPont/Miss M Varner, 6-3, 7-5); mixed doubles r/u 1957 with N Fraser (M Rose/Miss Hard won, 6-4, 7-5), r/u 1958 with Nielson (R Howe/Miss L Coghlan won,

6-3, 13-11).

Australian singles r/u 1957 (Miss S Fry won, 6-3, 6-4); doubles won 1957 with Miss Fry (beat Mrs Hawton/Miss Muller, 6-2, 6-1).

GIMENO, Andrés, Spain
Born August 1937, Barcelona. After a brief amateur career Gimeno, who was ranked No 1 in Spain for several years, turned professional in 1960 but gave up contract professional tennis in 1971. His tournament progress was frequently halted by the Australian professionals Rod Laver, Roy Emerson and Ken Rosewall, with each of whom he had some tough battles. He was in the Spanish Davis Cup team of 1958–60.

British Queen's Club Indoor singles won 1960; Wembley professional championships singles r/u 1967 (Laver won); British hard court doubles r/u 1968 with R Gonzalez (Emerson/Laver won, 8-6, 4-6, 6-3, 6-2).

US men's doubles r/u 1968 with A Ashe (R Lutz/S Smith won, 11-9, 6-1, 7-5).

Australian men's singles r/u 1969 (Laver won, 6-3, 6-4, 7-5).

French men's singles won 1972 (beat P Proisy, 4-6, 6-3, 6-1, 6-1); men's doubles r/u 1960 with J Arilla (Emerson/Fraser won, 6-2, 8-10, 7-5, 6-4).

Italian Open men's doubles r/u 1971 with R Taylor (J Newcombe/A Roche won, 6-4, 6-4).

West German Open singles won 1971 (beat P Szoke, 6-3, 6-2, 6-2); men's doubles won 1971 with J Alexander (beat R Crealy/A Stone, 6-4, 7-5, 7-9, 6-4).

GISBERT, Juan, Spain
Born May 1942, Barcelona. Son of a hotel owner and the possessor of a law degree, Gisbert has proved himself an outstanding clay court player and a doggedly determined competitor who refuses to go down without fighting. He has had some excellent doubles results, particularly in recent seasons partnered by Manuel Orantes.

Australian men's singles r/u 1968 (W Bowrey won, 7-5, 2-6, 9-7, 6-4).

Italian doubles r/u with I Năstase (T Okker/M Riessen won).

British hard court championship doubles won 1973–4 with Năstase, won 1975 with M Orantes.

Swedish Open doubles r/u 1976 with W Fibak (F McNair/S Stewart won).

US clay court doubles won with Orantes 1975 (beat Fibak/H Pohmann, 7-5, 6-0).

Canadian doubles r/u with Orantes 1976 (R Hewitt/R Ramirez won, 6-2, 6-1).

West German Open doubles won 1975 with Orantes (beat J Kodeš/Fibak, 6-3, 7-6).

Barcelona ATP singles r/u 1975 (Orantes won, 7-6, 7-6); doubles won 1975 with Orantes (beat N Spear/K Kronk, 6-7, 6-2, 6-4).

Munich doubles won 1976 with Orantes (beat Fassbender/Pohmann).

Tehran doubles won 1976 with Orantes (beat Fibak/Ramirez).

Qualified for Commercial Union GP doubles finals, 1976, finishing 8 in CUGP doubles.

GODFREE, Mrs L A (née Kitty McKane), GB
Born May 1897, Bayswater, London. Twice Wimbledon women's champion, Mrs Godfree was one of the outstanding British women players of the 1920s. She and her husband, Leslie, were the only married couple ever to win the Wimbledon mixed doubles (1926) and Kitty was the only player to beat Helen Wills Moody in singles at Wimbledon. This she did in 1924, her first title year, when she defeated the US champion 4-6, 6-4, 6-4. However, Helen avenged the defeat when she beat her 3-6, 6-0, 6-2 in the US final the following year. Their personal battle was also carried on in the Wightman Cup: in the first competition in 1923 Kitty lost all her matches, including one to Helen, and the US won 7-0. In the two succeeding years, when Britain won the cup, Kitty beat Helen four times in singles and doubles.

In 1922 Kitty had forced the invincible French champion Suzanne Lenglen to a 7-5 set at Wimbledon and in the 1923 championships the most games Suzanne lost were four to Kitty in the final. Two years later the French tennis queen whitewashed her (6-0, 6-0) in the semi-finals.

Throughout her career Kitty Godfree, as she became in 1926, showed remarkable athleticism and the determined ability to drag herself back from the brink of defeat. She was All-England Badminton champion in singles, 1920–2 and 1924 and in doubles in 1921 and 1924 and mixed doubles in 1924–5. In 1920 she gained an Olympic tennis gold medal and in 1923–7, 1930, 1934 she was a member of the Wightman Cup team.

Wimbledon women's singles r/u 1923 (Miss Lenglen won, 6-2, 6-2), won 1924 (beat Miss Wills, 4-6, 6-4, 6-4), won 1926 (beat Miss L de Alvarez, 6-2, 4-6, 6-3); doubles r/u 1922 with Mrs A Stocks (Miss Lenglen/Miss E Ryan won, 6-0, 6-4), r/u 1924 with Mrs B Covell (Mrs G Wightman/Miss Wills won, 6-4, 6-4), r/u 1926 with Miss E Colyer (Miss M Browne/Miss Ryan won, 6-1, 6-1); mixed doubles won 1924 with J Gilbert (beat L Godfree/Mrs S Barron, 6-3, 3-6, 6-3), won 1926 (beat H Kinsey/Miss Browne, 6-3, 6-4), r/u 1927 (F Hunter/Miss Ryan won, 8-6, 6-0), both with L A Godfree.

US women's singles r/u 1925 (Miss Wills won, 3-6, 6-0, 6-2); doubles won 1923 with Mrs Covell (beat Mrs Wightman/Miss E Goss, 2-6, 6-2, 6-1), won 1927 with Miss E Harvey (beat Miss J Fry/Miss B Nuthall, 6-1, 4-6, 6-4); mixed doubles r/u 1923 (W Tilden/Mrs M Mallory won, 6-3, 2-6, 10-8), won 1925 (beat V Richards/Miss Harvey, 6-2, 6-4), both with J Hawkes.

French women's singles r/u 1925 (Miss Lenglen won, 6-1, 6-2); doubles r/u 1925 (Miss Lenglen/Miss D Vlasto won, 6-1, 9-11, 6-2), r/u 1926 (Miss Lenglen/Miss Vlasto won, 6-1, 6-1), both with Miss Colyer.

GODFREE, Leslie Allison, GB

Born April 1885, Brighton, Sussex, died November 1971. The man who hit the first ball on the new Centre Court at Church Road, Wimbledon after the 1922 move from Worple Road, Godfree was captain of the British Davis Cup team in 1925 and a team member from 1923-7.

Wimbledon men's doubles won 1923 with R Lycett (beat E Flaquer/Count de Gomar, 11-9, 4-6, 6-4, 3-6, 7-5; mixed doubles r/u 1924 with Mrs D Shepherd-Barron (J Gilbert/Miss K McKane won, 6-3, 3-6, 6-3), won 1926 with Mrs Kitty Godfree (beat H Kinsey/Miss M Browne, 6-3, 6-4), r/u 1927 with Mrs Godfree (F Hunter/Miss E Ryan won, 8-6, 6-0).

GONZALEZ, Ricardo Alonzo (Pancho), USA

Born May 1928, Los Angeles, California. One of the sport's greatest players of all time and certainly world No 1 during the 1950s, Pancho Gonzalez was the angry man of tennis throughout his brilliant career, starting from his suspension from tournaments for playing truant as a teenager and lasting to his court battle with promoter Jack Kramer in the mid-1960s. Temperamental as a youngster, he could still explode into anger as an experienced professional, arguing with officials and spectators. Yet he was one of the great crowd-pullers and his tennis demanded admiration. At 6 ft 3 in (1.90 m), black haired, bronzed and handsome, women adored him. His service was timed at 110 mph (177 kmh), he had cat-like movements, speed, tremendous reflexes, grim determination and the keenest tactical brain in the game.

Pancho's first break in tennis came after he had finally convinced his Mexican parents to let him concentrate on the game which he had been skipping school to play. His mother bought him a cheap racket when he was 12 and he soon began to enter junior tournaments. At the age of 19, in 1947, he won his first im-

portant tournament, the Southern California championships, beating Herbert Flam 8-10, 8-6, 6-4. That year he beat Drobný, Parker and Falkenburg in the Pacific Southwest championship but lost to Schroeder. Next year he won, beating Eric Sturgess and in 1949 he beat Schroeder in a 67-game national final to assure his place as America's No 1. In that year he signed professional forms with Bobby Riggs to tour with Kramer; they won their round-robin duel 123 games to 27. He was not re-signed in 1950 and went into a forced retirement, buying a tennis goods shop, until Kramer bought up the Riggs circus and took Pancho on to the professional tour circuit again in 1954. Their stormy relationship continued until 1958 when Gonzalez sued Kramer for an increase in his money from 20 to 25 per cent of the gross. He lost; Kramer sold his promoting interest to Tony Trabert and the feud continued until Pancho again retired until 1964. He returned to the circuit, still a great player, and with the advent of Open tennis in 1968 was able to enter many of the events which had been closed to him as a professional at his peak. In 1969, aged 41, he won one of the greatest matches of all time when he beat Charles Pasarell in a Wimbledon first round match of 112 games (22-24, 1-6, 16-14, 6-3, 11-9), lasting a record 5 hours 12 minutes. He joined WCT from the National Tennis League in 1970 but did not sign contract professional forms in 1971.

US men's singles won 1948 (beat Sturgess, 6-2, 6-3, 14-12), won 1949 (beat Schroeder, 16-18, 2-6, 6-1, 6-2, 6-4). US Indoor championship singles won 1949. US National clay court singles won 1948-9. Pacific Southwest won 1949, won 1969, won 1971; doubles won 1949 with Parker. Howard Hughes Open singles won 1969.

French men's doubles won 1949 with F Parker (beat E Fannin/Sturgess, 6-3, 8-6, 5-7, 6-3).

Wimbledon men's doubles won 1949 with Parker (beat G Mulloy/Schroeder, 6-4, 6-4, 6-2).

World professional championships, Wembley, won 1952; World professional tournament won 1966.

London professional championships won 1950-2, r/u 1953, won 1956. US Davis Cup team 1949.

GOOLAGONG, Miss Evonne see Cawley, Mrs Evonne

GORE, Arthur William Charles (Wentworth), GB

Born January 1868, Lyndhurst, Hampshire, died December 1928. In a playing career which spanned 39 years, Gore competed in 182 matches at Wimbledon and won 121, including the singles championship three times. A hard-working businessman who played tennis to relax, he was fit, fast and had a fierce forehand drive. In 1901 he briefly interrupted the reign of the legendary Doherty brothers by winning the title from Reggie Doherty. He remains the oldest Wimbledon men's singles champion, having won in 1909 aged 41 years 7 months, and the oldest finalist at 44 in 1912. He was in the first British Davis Cup team of 1900 which lost to America and competed again in 1907 and 1912. He last played at Wimbledon in 1927, the year before his death.

Wimbledon men's singles r/u 1899 Challenge Round (R Doherty won, 1-6, 4-6, 6-2, 6-3, 6-3), r/u 1900 All-Comers (S Smith won, 6-4, 4-6, 6-2, 6-1), won 1901 Challenge Round (beat R Doherty, 4-6, 7-5, 6-4, 6-4), r/u 1902 (L Doherty won, 6-4, 6-3, 3-6, 6-0), r/u 1906 All-Comers (F Riseley won, 6-3, 6-3, 6-4), r/u 1907 All-Comers (N Brookes won, 6-4, 6-2, 6-2), won 1908 (wo), won 1909 (beat M Ritchie, 6-8, 1-6, 6-2, 6-2, 6-2), r/u 1910 (A Wilding won, 6-4, 7-5, 4-6, 6-2), r/u 1912 (Wilding won, 6-4, 6-4, 4-6, 6-4); men's doubles r/u 1889 All-Comers with G Mewburn (wo), r/u 1899 All-Comers with H Roper Barrett (C Hobart/H Nisbet won, 6-4, 6-1, 8-6), r/u 1904 All-Comers with G Caridia (Riseley/Smith won, 6-3, 6-4, 6-3), r/u 1908 All-Comers (Ritchie/Wilding won, 6-1, 6-2, 1-6, 1-6, 9-7), won 1909 Challenge Round (wo), r/u 1910 (Ritchie/Wilding won, 6-1, 6-1, 6-2), all with Roper Barrett. Won two Olympic tennis gold medals, 1908.

GORE, Spencer William, GB
Born March 1850, Wimbledon, Surrey, died April 1906. The first Wimbledon champion in 1877, defeating W C Marshall 6-1, 6-2, 6-4, and runner-up in the 1878 Challenge Round to P F Hadow, who won 7-5, 6-1, 9-7. A surveyor by profession and son of the Hon C A Gore and Lady Augusta L P Ponsonby, Dowager Countess of Kerry, Gore did not return to Wimbledon and later wrote scathingly about lawn tennis in comparison with 'real' tennis and rackets, both of which he played.

GORMAN, Thomas Warner, USA
Born January 1946, Seattle, Washington. A stylish and attractive player, Gorman's career has been limited by a weakness in his back. He has reached the semi-finals of four major international singles championships – French (twice), US and Wimbledon – but despite a promising start to 1976, which made him look ready for title successes, his back injury again hampered him.

French men's doubles r/u 1971 with S Smith (A Ashe/M Riessen won, 6-8, 4-6, 6-3, 6-4, 11-9).

Dewar Cup, Albert Hall r/u 1970; Dewar Cup final r/u 1972.

Hong Kong singles won 1975 (beat S Mayer).

Indian International won (beat V Amritraj).

Vancouver singles won 1973.

Copenhagen doubles won 1973 with E Van Dillen.

Osaka Open doubles won 1973 with J Borowiak.

Stockholm singles won 1973.

Ranier International, Seattle r/u 1972.

Pacific N West doubles won 1973 with T Okker.

Cincinnati won 1975.

Baltimore won 1976 (beat Năstase).

Sacramento ATP won 1976, doubles won with S Stewart.

GOSS, Eleanor, USA
Three times winner of the US women's doubles (1918–20) and twice runner-up (1923–4), once runner-up for the singles, Miss Goss earned her place in the tennis history books for the longest Wightman Cup doubles match. Playing with Mrs Hazel Wightman (donor of the cup) against Miss Covell and Miss McKane of Britain, in the first match in 1923, the American pair won 10-8, 5-7, 6-4, a total of 40 games. Miss Goss remained in the cup team until 1928, during which time America took the cup on three occasions (1923, 1926–7).

GOTTFRIED, Brian Edward, USA
Born January 1952, Baltimore, Maryland. After an outstanding career as a junior during which he won three national titles in 1969 and 14 national junior titles in all, Gottfried has established himself as a fine player on all surfaces, excelling at doubles. His younger brother, Larry, was US under-16 No 1 in 1975 and under-18 No 1 in 1976. Brian has beaten many of the world's top players in recent seasons, including Ashe, Borg, Connors, Dibbs, Emerson, Laver, Năstase, Ramirez and Vilas. He has had a particularly effective doubles partnership with Ramirez, with whom he won the 1977 French and Italian doubles and was r/u in the US Open doubles.

French Open singles r/u 1977 (G Vilas won,

6-0, 6-3, 6-0); men's doubles won 1975 (beat J Alexander/P Dent, 6-4, 2-6, 6-2, 6-4), r/u 1976 (F McNair/S Stewart won, 7-6, 6-3, 6-1), won 1977 (beat W Fibak/J Kodeš, 7-6, 4-6, 6-3, 6-4), all with Ramirez.

South African Open singles r/u 1975 (H Solomon won, 6-2, 6-4, 5-7, 6-1), r/u 1976 (Solomon won, 6-2, 6-7, 6-3, 6-4); doubles won 1976 with Stewart (beat S Smith/J Gisbert, 1-6, 6-1, 6-2, 7-6).

Italian men's doubles won 1974–7 with Ramirez.

Wimbledon doubles won 1976 (beat R Case/ G Masters, 3-6, 6-3, 8-6, 2-6, 7-5) with Ramirez.

Benson and Hedges doubles won 1977 with McMillan (beat B Gottfried/R Ramirez 6-3, 7-6).

US Open doubles r/u 1977 with Ramirez (R Hewitt/F McMillan won, 6-4, 6-0); US clay court doubles won 1976 with M Orantes (beat W Fibak/H Pohmann, 7-5, 6-0).

(beat M Cox/C Drysdale, 7-6, 6-7, 6-2, 7-6), WCT Monterrey doubles won 1976, WCT Richmond r/u 1976, WCT Caracas won 1976; Barcelona doubles won 1976; Vienna doubles won 1976; Commercial Union G P doubles r/u 1976; Washington doubles r/u 1976, all with Ramirez. San Francisco singles r/u 1976, doubles r/u with R Hewitt; Pacific Southwest singles won 1976.

GOURLAY, Helen (Mrs H G Cawley), Australia
Born December 1946, Launceston, Tasmania. Though short on stamina as a junior, Miss Gourlay has since come to the fore as a consistently good player at international level. In 1971 she was runner-up to Evonne Goolagong Cawley in the French women's final and r/u in the Italian Open doubles with Lesley Bowrey and in 1972 and 1976 she won the Australian doubles.

She had an excellent 1977 season, winning the Australian doubles with Dianne Fromholtz at the start of the season and reaching the final of the same event on its re-arranged date at the end of the year, when the final was rained off and the title shared by her and Evonne Cawley with Kerry Reid and Mona Guerrant. She was also runner-up for the 1977–8 singles title, losing to Mrs Cawley, won the New South Wales doubles with her and was r/u for the French and Colgate Inaugural doubles titles with different partners.

Right: Helen Gourlay (Mrs Cawley)

Australian women's singles r/u 1977 (Mrs E Cawley won, 6-3, 6-0); doubles won 1972 with Miss K Harris (beat Miss P Coleman/Miss K Krantzcke, 6-0, 6-4), won 1976 with Mrs Cawley (beat Mrs W W Bowrey/Miss R Tomanova, 8-1, one set only), won 1977 with Miss Fromholtz (beat Mrs K Reid/Miss B Nagelsen, 5-7, 6-1, 7-5), shared 1977–8 with Mrs Cawley (Mrs Guerrant/Mrs Reid, rained off); NSW doubles won 1977 with Mrs Cawley (beat Mrs Reid/Mrs Guerrant, 6-0, 6-0).

French singles r/u 1971 (Miss Goolagong won, 6-3, 7-5); doubles r/u 1977 with Miss R Fox (Miss R Marsikova/Miss P Teeguarden won, 5-7, 6-4, 6-1).

Italy doubles r/u 1971 with Miss L Bowrey (Miss V Wade/Mrs H Masthoff won, 5-7, 6-2, 6-2).

Wimbledon doubles r/u 1974 with Miss Krantzcke (Miss Goolagong/Miss M Michel won, 2-6, 6-4, 6-3); British hard court singles won 1972.

South African doubles won 1972 with Miss Goolagong.

Colgate Inaugural doubles r/u 1977 with Miss J Russell (Miss Wade/Miss F Durr won, 6-1, 4-6, 6-4).

GRAEBNER, Clark Edward, USA
Born November 1943, Cleveland, Ohio. Until he turned to using the new Wilson steel racket in 1967, Graebner had been a middle-ranking player in America. Already a powerful server who used the serve-volley technique and enjoyed a forcing game, he increased the speed of his service to a recorded 112 mph with the new racket and went through to the US national singles final for the first time, losing to Newcombe. Among nine US titles, he gained the US clay court in 1968, hard court 1969 and Indoor Open in 1971 and won the clay court doubles a record six times between 1963 and 1970. He became an independent professional in 1969 and in 1973 signed with WTT. He was a member of the US Davis Cup team, 1965–8.

US singles r/u 1967 (Newcombe won, 6-4, 6-4, 8-6); doubles r/u 1966 with M Riessen (R Emerson/F Stolle won, 6-4, 6-4, 6-4), US Indoors r/u 1968, 1971; doubles r/u 1973 with I Năstase.

French doubles won 1966 with Ralston (beat I Năstase/I Tiriac, 6-3, 6-3, 6-0); mixed doubles r/u 1966 with Mrs A Jones (F McMillan/Miss A Van Zyl won, 1-6, 6-3, 6-2).

Grand Slam
The winning of the four major international championships in one season – Australian, French, US and Wimbledon – is known as the 'Grand Slam'. It is applied to winning all four singles, or doubles or mixed doubles. The 'Slam' has been achieved twice in singles by Rod Laver of Australia (1962 and 1969), and once by Don Budge (1938), Maureen Connolly (1953) and Margaret Court (1970). The doubles

Grand Slam has been achieved only by Frank Sedgman and Ken McGregor of Australia in 1951.

GREGORY, Dr John Colin, GB

Born July 1903, Beverley, Yorkshire, died 1959. As non-playing captain of the British Davis Cup team in 1952 he took to the court against Yugoslavia when injury depleted the team and, aged 48, helped to win the doubles event. He was chairman of the All England Club from 1955 until his sudden death in 1959. Gregory was a good all-round player.

Wimbledon men's doubles r/u 1929 with I G Collins (W Allison/J Van Ryn won, 6-4, 5-7, 6-3, 10-12, 6-4).

Australian men's singles won 1929 (beat R Schlesinger, 6-2, 6-2, 5-7, 7-5).

Davis Cup team 1926–30, captain 1952.

GUERRANT, Ramona Anne (née Schallau), USA

Born November 1948, Iowa City. Coached by Don Klotz and Denis van der Meer, Mrs Guerrant has developed as a fine doubles player and has achieved some excellent results on the Virginia Slims circuit. With Kerry Reid she was runner-up in the NSW doubles in Australia in 1977. She was warned for using a radio on court to communicate with her husband, Terry, during a singles match in the event.

V S Dallas doubles r/u 1975 with Miss J Anthony (Miss F Durr/Miss B Stöve won), won 1976 with Miss A Kiyomura (beat Miss G Stevens/Miss M Redondo); V S Washington doubles r/u 1976 with Miss W Overton (Miss O Morozova/Miss Wade won); V S Akron doubles won 1976 with Miss B Cuypers (beat Miss G Coles/Miss F Mihai); V S Detroit doubles won 1976 (beat Miss C Evert/Miss Stöve); V S Sarasota doubles won 1976 (beat Miss M Navratilova/Miss Stöve); V S Boston doubles won 1976 (beat Miss Durr/Miss R Casals), all with Miss Kiyomura. Pacific Coast Indoor r/u

Left: Clark Graebner was a middle-ranking player until he discovered the steel racket.

1976 (Miss T Holladay won).

Australian hard court championship singles r/u 1971. NSW Open doubles r/u 1977 with Miss K Reid (Mrs E Cawley/Mrs H Gourlay Cawley won, 6-0, 6-0).

GULYÁS, Istvan, Hungary

Born October 1941, Budapest. An exceptional hard court player who began playing tennis at age 13, Gulyás won the Hungarian championship singles 15 times and doubles 18 times. He was runner-up in the French and closed German championships in 1966 and received the International Coubertin and Hungarian Fair Play Awards in 1967. Between 1958 and 1972 he played 59 Davis Cup rubbers for Hungary. He was ranked No 1 in Hungary for 13 years, dropping to No 2 behind Szabolcs Baranyi in 1970 but returning to top the following year.

French men's singles r/u 1966 (A Roche won, 6-1, 6-4, 7-5). German singles r/u 1966 (F Stolle won).

GUNTER, Mrs K S see Richey, Nancy

HACKETT, Harold Humphrey, USA

Born July 1878, died November 1937. Hackett and Fred Alexander were among the first 'multi-winners' of the US men's doubles, gaining the title four times consecutively from 1907–10. Previously R D Sears had won six years running but with a change of partner and H Ward had twice won three years in succession, from 1899–1901 with D F Davis and from 1904–6 with B C Wright.

US men's doubles r/u 1905 (Ward/Wright won, 6-3, 6-1, 6-2), r/u 1906 (Ward/Wright won, 6-3, 3-6, 6-3, 6-3), won 1907 (beat W Larned/W Clothier, 6-3, 6-1, 6-4), won 1908 (beat R Little/Wright, 6-1, 7-5, 6-2), won 1909 (beat G James/M McLoughlin, 6-4, 6-1, 6-0), won 1910 (beat T Bundy/T Hendrick, 6-1, 8-6, 6-3), r/u 1911 (Little/G Touchard won, 7-5, 13-15, 6-2, 6-4), all with Alexander. Davis Cup team 1908–9, 1913.

HADOW, Patrick Francis, GB

Born January 1855, Regent's Park, Middlesex, died June 1946. Hadow entered the Wimbledon championships in their second year (1878) and beat Spencer Gore, the first champion 7-5, 6-1, 9-7, playing while on leave from Ceylon (now Sri Lanka), where he was a tea planter. He never again played the game. He was captain of cricket at Harrow school and played county cricket for Middlesex. In 1926 he attended the Wimbledon 50th anniversary celebrations, re-ceived a former champion's Jubilee medal and watched his first tournament anywhere since he had won the title.

HAMBEUCHER, Lesley H (née Hunt)
Australia

Born May 1950, Perth. From a successful junior, Lesley Hunt developed into an athletic, all-court player of intelligence. She captured world headlines in 1974 when she played a superb second-round match against the eventual champion Chris Evert at Wimbledon, taking her to 8-6, 5-7, 11-9. She married her agent, Jim Hambeucher in 1976.

Australian junior champion 1968–9.

French junior champion 1968.

Canadian singles r/u 1976 (Miss M Jausovec won, 6-2, 6-0).

Italian singles r/u 1976 (Miss Jausovec won, 6-1, 6-3); doubles won 1972 with Miss O Morozova.

Wimbledon junior invitation r/u 1968.

HAMILTON, Willoughby James (Willoby), Ireland

Born December 1864, Monasterevin, Co Kildare, died 1943, Dublin. So frail-looking that he was known as 'The Ghost', Hamilton's performance belied his appearance and upset the run of the Renshaw brothers, William and Ernest, when he won the men's title at Wimbledon in 1890, beating Willie in the Challenge Round over five sets. An Irish soccer international and Irish singles champion in 1889, he was famous for a running forehand which became known as the 'Irish drive'.

Wimbledon men's singles won 1890 (beat W Renshaw, 6-8, 6-2, 3-6, 6-1, 6-1).

Irish championship singles won 1889; doubles won 1886–8; mixed won 1889.

HAMMERSLEY, Mrs S H see James, Winifred

Hampton Court Palace, GB

A keen player of 'real' tennis, Henry VIII had a court built at Hampton Court Palace, near Richmond, Surrey, when he dispossessed Cardinal Wolsey of the palace, following his disgrace in 1529.

Though largely restored during the reign of William and Mary, whose monogram is on the wall beside the net, some of the original brickwork remains. The tennis court is still used. Henry also had a court included in St James's Palace, built for Anne Boleyn.

HANSELL, Ellen (Mrs E Allerdice), USA

Winner of the first US championship women's singles in 1887, when she beat Miss L Knight 6-1, 6-0, Miss Hansell did not defend her title in the Challenge Round the following year and Miss B B Townsend won by default. The women's championship events were staged by the Chestnut Hill LTC on the grass courts of the Philadelphia Cricket Club.

Bob Hewitt (left) and Frew McMillan (right) – South Africa (both)

Brian Gottfried – United States of America

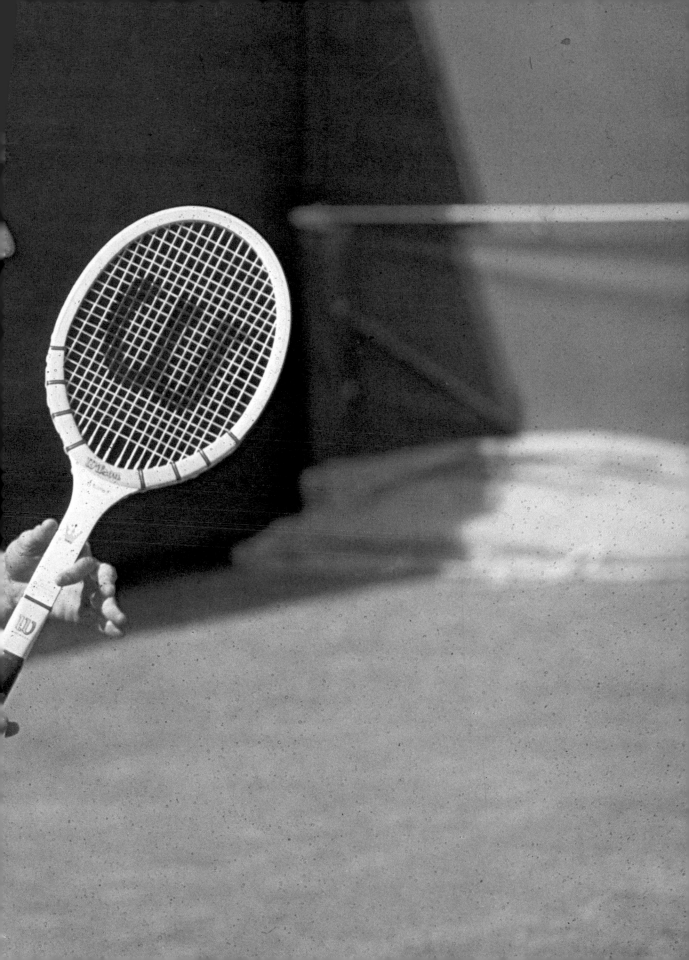

PREVIOUS
4
5

Ann Jones – Great Britain

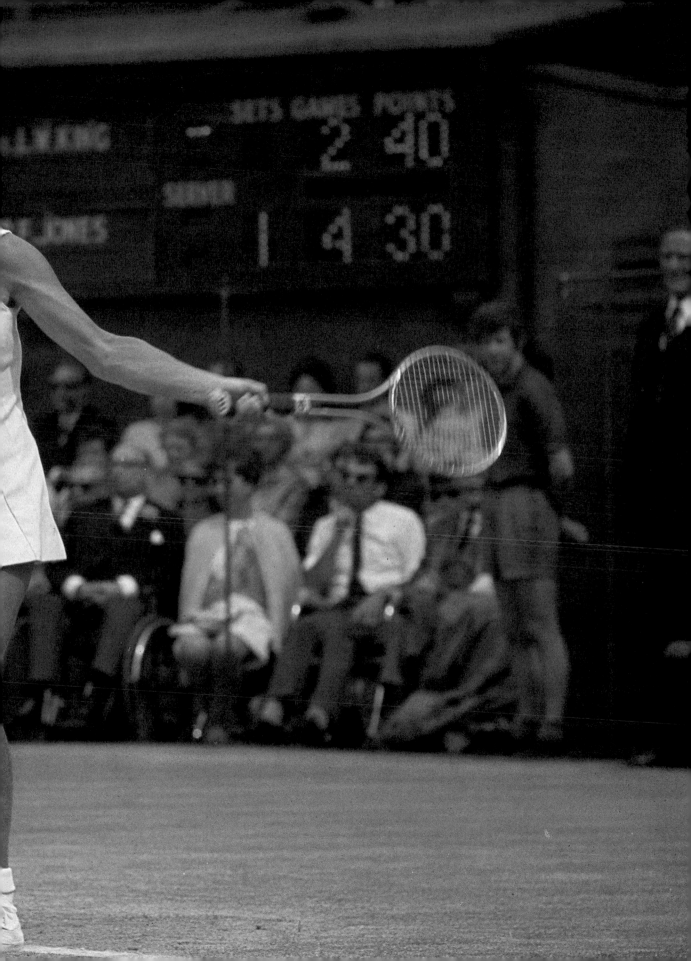

Jan Kodeš – Czechoslovakia

Billie Jean King – United States of America

Billie Jean King – United States of America

Left: Darlene Hard, an aggressive extrovert on court, won 22 international titles.

HANTZE, Karen *see* **Susman, Mrs J R**

HARD, Darlene R, USA

Born January 1936, Los Angeles. A sturdy, bounding player, Miss Hard was a vivacious extrovert on court, playing a powerful mannish game with aggressive volleys, striding about slapping her thighs and talking sternly to herself. She was an outstanding doubles player of the 1950s and 1960s and in 1960 won the doubles titles of the US, France and Wimbledon, losing only one set in the three events – to Karen Hantze and Janet Hopps in the Wimbledon semi-final. She also had some international success in singles and in 1960 took the French and US titles. She retained the US title in 1961.

In all Miss Hard, a former waitress, won 22 international titles. She took part in a notable series of matches partnered by Miss Bueno in which the pair won five titles and were runners-up twice.

US women's singles r/u 1958 (Miss A Gibson won, 3-6, 6-1, 6-2), won 1960 (beat Miss M Bueno, 6-4, 10-12, 6-4), won 1961 (beat Miss A Haydon, 6-3, 6-4), r/u 1962 (Miss M Smith won, 9-7, 6-4); doubles r/u 1957 with Miss Gibson (Miss L Brough/Mrs W duPont won, 6-2, 7-5), won 1958 (beat Miss Gibson/Miss Bueno, 2-6, 6-3, 6-4), won 1959 (beat Miss Bueno/Miss S Moore, 6-2, 6-3), both with Miss J Arth, won 1960 with Miss Bueno (beat Miss Haydon/Miss D Catt, 6-1, 6-1), won 1961 with Miss L Turner (beat Miss E Buding/Miss Y Ramirez, 6-4, 5-7, 6-0), won 1962 (beat Miss B J Moffitt/Mrs J Susman, 4-6, 6-3, 6-2), r/u 1963 (Miss R Ebbern/Miss Smith won, 4-6, 10-8, 6-3), both with Miss Bueno; mixed doubles r/u 1956 with L Hoad (K Rosewall/Mrs duPont won, 9-7, 6-1), r/u 1957 with R Howe (K Nielsen/Miss Gibson won, 6-3, 9-7), r/u 1961 with R Ralston (R Mark/Miss Smith won, wo). Wightman Cup team 1957, 1959–60, 1962–3. Federation Cup 1963.

Australian doubles r/u 1962 with Mrs M Reitano (Miss Ebbern/Miss Smith won, 6-4, 6-4); mixed doubles r/u 1962 with R Taylor (F Stolle/Miss Turner, 6-3, 9-7).

French singles won 1960 (beat Miss Ramirez, 6-3, 6-4); doubles won 1955 with Mrs J Fleitz (beat Miss S Bloomer/Miss P Ward, 7-5, 6-8, 13-11), r/u 1956 with Mrs D Knode (Miss Gibson/Miss A Buxton won, 6-8, 8-6, 6-1), won 1957 with Miss Bloomer (beat Miss Ramirez/Miss S Reyes, 7-5, 4-6, 7-5), won 1960 (beat Miss R Hales/Miss Haydon, 6-2, 7-5), r/u 1961 (Miss S Reynolds/Miss R Schuurman won, scratched), both with Miss Bueno; mixed doubles won 1955 with G Forbes (beat L Ayala/Miss J Staley, 5-7, 6-1, 6-2), r/u 1956 with R Howe (Ayala/Mrs T Long won, 4-6, 6-4, 6-1), won 1961 with R Laver (beat J Javorsky/Miss V Pužejová, 6-0, 2-6, 6-3).

Wimbledon singles r/u 1957 (Miss Gibson won, 6-3, 6-2), r/u 1959 (Miss Bueno won, 6-4, 6-3); doubles won 1957 with Miss Gibson (beat Mrs K Hawton/Mrs Long, 6-1, 6-2), won 1958 with Miss Arth (beat Mrs Fleitz/Miss Truman, 2-6, 6-2, 6-3), won 1960 (beat Miss Reynolds/Miss Schuurman, 6-4, 6-0), won 1963 (beat Miss Ebbern/Miss Smith, 8-6, 9-7), both with Miss Bueno; mixed doubles won 1957 with M Rose (beat N Fraser/Miss Gibson, 6-4, 7-5), won 1959 (beat Fraser/Miss Bueno, 6-4, 6-3), won 1960 (beat Miss Howe/Miss Bueno, 13-11, 3-6, 8-6), both with Laver, r/u 1963 with R Hewitt (K Fletcher/Miss Smith won, 11-9, 6-4).

Italian women's doubles won 1962 with Miss Bueno.

HARPER, Mrs S *see* **Lance, Sylvia**

HART, Doris Jane, USA
Born June 1925, St Louis, Missouri. At the age of six Doris Hart took up tennis as a remedial exercise after being struck by polio, which it was then thought might leave her crippled for life. Thirty years later she was ranked as one of the world's greatest players and had won 35 major titles in 'Big Four' events. To see her performing gracefully and almost majestically on court it was virtually impossible to realise that her mobility was restricted. She was one of the greatest women servers of all time and possessed a delicacy of touch in her dropshots which has rarely been matched. She was three times a triple champion, winning the singles, doubles and mixed doubles at Wimbledon in 1951 (when she lost only one set, in the mixed doubles), in France in 1952 and at Forest Hills in 1954. In 1948 she was part of the all-American semi-final at Wimbledon with Louise Brough, Margaret duPont and Pat Todd – probably the four greatest women players in the world at that time. She won the mixed doubles titles at Wimbledon and Forest Hills in five successive years (1951–5) during an exceptional run of international successes first with Frank Sedgman and then with Vic Seixas. It was said of her

that she was one of the few women who could approach the class of Maureen Connolly and she proved this by being the victor twice in 'Little Mo's' only four first-class match defeats. Miss Hart became a professional in 1955. Wightman Cup team 1946–55.

US singles r/u 1946 (Miss P Betz won, 11-9, 6-3), r/u 1949 (Mrs duPont won, 6-4, 6-1), r/u 1950 (Mrs duPont won, 6-3, 6-3), r/u 1952 (Miss Connolly won, 6-3, 7-5), r/u 1953 (Miss Connolly won, 6-2, 6-4), won 1954 (beat Miss Brough, 6-8, 6-1, 8-6), won 1955 (beat Miss P Ward, 6-4, 6-2); doubles r/u 1942 (Miss Brough/Miss Osborne won), r/u 1943 (Miss Brough/Miss Osborne won), r/u 1944 (Miss Brough/Miss Osborne won, 4-6, 6-4, 6-3), r/u 1945 (Miss Brough/Miss Osborne won, 6-4, 6-4), all with Miss Betz, r/u 1947 (Miss Brough/Miss Osborne won, 5-7, 6-3, 7-5), r/u 1948 (Miss Brough/Mrs duPont won, 6-4, 8-10, 6-1), both with Mrs P Todd, r/u 1949 (Miss Brough/Mrs duPont won, 6-4, 8-6), r/u 1950 (Miss Brough/Mrs duPont won, 6-2, 6-2), won 1951 (beat Mrs Todd/Miss N Chaffee, 6-4, 6-2), won 1952 (beat Miss Brough/Miss Connolly, 10-8, 6-4), won 1953 (beat Mrs duPont/Miss Brough, 6-3, 7-9, 9-7), won 1954 (beat Mrs duPont/Miss Brough, 6-4, 6-4), r/u 1955 (Miss Brough/Mrs duPont won, 6-3, 1-6, 6-3), all with Miss S Fry; mixed doubles r/u 1945 with R Falkenburg (W Talbert/Miss Osborne won, 6-4, 6-4), r/u 1950 (K McGregor/Mrs duPont won, 6-4, 3-6, 6-3), won 1951 (beat M Rose/Miss Fry, 6-3, 6-2), won 1952 (beat L Hoad/Mrs T Long, 6-3, 7-5), all with Sedgman, won 1953 (beat R Hartwig/Miss J Sampson, 6-2, 4-6, 6-4), won 1954 (beat Rosewall/Mrs duPont, 4-6, 6-1, 6-1), won 1955 (beat G Mulloy/Miss Fry, 7-5, 5-7, 6-2), all with Seixas.

Australian women's singles won 1949 (beat Mrs N Bolton, 6-3, 6-4), r/u 1950 (Miss Brough won, 6-4, 3-6, 6-4); doubles won 1950 with Miss Brough (beat Mrs Bolton/Mrs Long, 6-2, 2-6, 6-3); mixed doubles won 1949 (beat J Bromwich/

Miss J Fitch, 6-1, 5-7, 12-10), won 1950 (beat E Sturgess/Miss Fitch, 8-6, 6-4), both with Sedgman.

French singles r/u 1947 (Mrs Todd won, 6-3, 3-6, 6-4), won 1950 (beat Mrs Todd, 6-4, 4-6, 6-2), r/u 1951 (Miss Fry won, 6-3, 3-6, 6-3), won 1952 (beat Miss Fry, 6-4, 6-4), r/u 1953 (Miss Connolly won, 6-2, 6-4); doubles r/u 1946 with Miss Betz (Miss Brough/Miss Osborne won, 6-4, 0-6, 6-1), r/u 1947 (Miss Brough/Miss Osborne won, 7-5, 6-2), won 1948 (beat Miss Fry/Mrs M Prentiss, 6-4, 6-2), both with Mrs Todd, won 1950 (beat Mrs duPont/Miss Brough, 1-6, 7-5, 6-2), won 1951 (beat Mrs Bartlett/Miss B Scofield, 10-8, 6-3), won 1952 (beat Mrs H Redick-Smith/Mrs J Wipplinger, 7-5, 6-1), won 1953 (beat Miss Connolly/Miss Sampson, 6-4, 6-3), all with Miss Fry; mixed doubles r/u 1948 (J Drobný/Mrs Todd won, 6-3, 3-6, 6-3), won 1951 (beat Rose/Mrs Long, 7-5, 6-2), won 1952 (beat Sturgess/Miss Fry, 6-8, 6-3, 6-3), both with Sedgman, won 1953 with Seixas (beat Rose/Miss Connolly, 4-6, 6-4, 6-0).

Wimbledon singles r/u 1947 (Miss Osborne won, 6-2, 6-4), r/u 1948 (Miss Brough won, 6-3, 8-6), won 1951 (beat Miss Fry, 6-1, 6-0), r/u 1953 (Miss Connolly won, 8-6, 7-5); doubles r/u 1946 with Miss Betz (Miss Brough/Miss Osborne won, 6-3, 2-6, 6-3), won 1947 (beat Miss Brough/Miss Osborne, 3-6, 6-4, 7-5), r/u 1948 (Miss Brough/Mrs duPont won, 6-3, 3-6, 6-3), both with Mrs Todd, r/u 1950 (Miss Brough/Mrs duPont won, 6-4, 5-7, 6-1), won 1951 (beat Miss Brough/Mrs duPont, 6-3, 13-11), won 1952 (beat Miss Brough/Miss Connolly, 8-6, 6-3), won 1953 (beat Miss Connolly/Miss Sampson, 6-0, 6-0), r/u 1954 (Miss Brough/Mrs duPont won, 4-6, 9-7, 6-3), all with Miss Fry; mixed doubles r/u 1948 (Bromwich/Miss Brough won, 6-2, 3-6, 6-3), won 1951 (beat Rose/Mrs Bolton, 7-5, 6-2), won 1952 (beat E Morea/Mrs Long, 4-6, 6-3, 6-4), all with Sedgman, won 1953 (beat Morea/Miss Fry, 9-7, 7-5), won 1954 (beat Rosewall/Mrs duPont, 5-7, 6-4, 6-3), won 1955 (beat Morea/Miss Brough, 8-6, 2-6, 6-3), all with Seixas.

HARTIGAN, Joan Marcia, Australia

Born June 1912, Sydney. The first Australian woman player to achieve notice overseas, Miss Hartigan reached the semi-finals at Wimbledon in 1934–5.

Australian women's singles won 1933 (beat Mrs C Buttsworth, 6-4, 6-3), won 1934 (beat Mrs M Molesworth, 6-1, 6-4), won 1936 (beat Miss N Wynne, 6-4, 6-4); doubles r/u 1933 with Mrs J Van Ryn (Mrs Molesworth/Mrs V Westacott won, 6-3, 6-3); mixed doubles won 1934 with E Moon (beat R Dunlop/Mrs Westacott, 6-3, 6-4).

HARTLEY, Rev John Thorneycroft, GB

Born January 1849, Tong, Shropshire, died August 1935. Like many of the early Wimbledon champions, Hartley was a product of Harrow

Above: Australian Rex Hartwig's international career was primarily based on his ability to play doubles well.

school. In 1879 he did not expect to reach the semi-finals at Wimbledon. On the Saturday, after winning his quarter-final, he returned to his parish in the north of Yorkshire, to conduct Sunday services. On the Monday he travelled back to Wimbledon, arriving just in time for his semi-final, which he won. Then he went on to become the champion when P F Hadow failed to defend his title. He won again in 1880 (beat H Lawford, 6-3, 6-2, 2-6, 6-3) and was r/u to Willie Renshaw in 1881 (Renshaw won, 6-0, 6-1, 6-1). Hartley won the Oxford University Rackets championship in 1869 and Tennis championship in 1870.

HARTWIG, Rex Noel, Australia

Born September 1929, Culcairn, NSW. After winning the Australian junior doubles championship in 1947, Hartwig went on to have an international career which was notable for his doubles successes. He won the American doubles in 1953 and the Australian and Wimbledon doubles in 1954, all with Mervyn Rose. That year he was singles r/u in Australia to Rose and in America to Vic Seixas. In 1955 he turned professional.

Australian singles r/u 1954 (Rose won, 6-2, 0-6, 6-4, 6-2); doubles won 1954 with Rose (beat N Fraser/C Wilderspin, 6-3, 6-4, 6-2); mixed doubles won 1953 with Miss J Sampson (beat H Richardson/Miss M Connolly, 6-4, 6-3), won 1954 with Mrs T Long (beat J Bromwich/Miss B Penrose, 4-6, 6-1, 6-2).

French mixed doubles r/u 1954 with Mrs J Patorni (L Hoad/Miss Connolly won, 6-4, 6-3).

Wimbledon doubles r/u 1953 (Hoad/K Rosewall won, 6-4, 7-5, 4-6, 7-5) (beat Seixas/M Trabert, 6-4, 6-4, 3-6, 6-4), both with Rose, won 1955 with Hoad (beat Fraser/Rosewall, 7-5, 6-4, 6-3).

US singles r/u 1954 (Seixas won, 3-6, 6-2, 6-4, 6-4); doubles won 1953 with Rose (beat G

Mulloy/W Talbert, 6-4, 4-6, 6-2, 6-4); mixed doubles r/u 1953 with Miss Sampson (Seixas/Miss D Hart won, 6-2, 4-6, 6-4). Davis Cup, 1953–5.

HAWKES, John Bailey, Australia
Born June 1889. One of the leading Australian players of the 1920s, both in his own country and abroad, Hawkes was on the losing end of the longest Australian men's singles final when he took Gerald Patterson to 71 games in 1927. During the fourth set Hawkes had match points.

Australian singles won 1926 (beat J Willard, 6-1, 6-3, 6-1), r/u 1927 (Patterson won, 3-6, 6-4, 3-6, 18-16, 6-3); men's doubles won 1922 (beat J Anderson/N Peach, 8-10, 6-0, 6-0, 7-5), won 1926 (beat Anderson/P O'Hara Wood, 6-1, 6-4, 6-2), won 1927 (beat O'Hara Wood/I McInnes, 8-6, 6-2, 6-1), all with Patterson, r/u 1930 (J Crawford/H Hopman won, 8-6, 6-1, 2-6, 6-3). Davis Cup 1921, 1923, 1925.

US doubles r/u 1925 (R Williams/V Richards won, 6-2, 8-10, 6-4, 11-9), r/u 1928 (G Lott/F Hennessey won, 6-2, 6-1, 6-2), both with Patterson; mixed doubles r/u 1923 (W Tilden/Miss M Mallory won, 6-3, 2-6, 10-8), won 1925 (beat Richards/Miss E Harvey, 6-2, 6-4), both with Miss K McKane, won 1928 with Miss H Wills (beat E Moon/Miss E Cross, 6-1, 6-3).

Wimbledon doubles r/u 1928 with Patterson (J Brugnon/H Cochet won, 13-11, 6-4, 6-4).

HAWTON, Mary K, Australia
Four times women's doubles champion of Australia, Mrs Hawton was never able to achieve the same success in her overseas tournaments, though she reached the Wimbledon doubles finals in 1957 and the French in 1958 and was r/u to foreign challenges three times in her own country.

Australian doubles r/u 1951 with Miss J Fitch (Mrs N Bolton/Mrs T Long won, 6-2, 6-1), r/u 1952 with Mrs R Baker (Mrs Bolton/Mrs Long won, 6-1, 6-1), r/u 1953 (Miss M Connolly/Miss J Sampson won, 6-4, 6-2), won 1954 (beat Mrs H Redick-Smith/Mrs J Wipplinger, 6-3, 8-6), won 1955 (beat Mrs H Hopman/Mrs A Thiele, 7-5, 6-1), all with Miss B Penrose, won 1936 with Mrs Long (beat Miss Penrose/Miss M Carter, 6-2, 5-7, 9-7), r/u 1957 with Miss F Muller (Miss S Fry/Miss A Gibson won, 6-2, 6-1), won 1958 with Mrs Long (beat Miss A Mortimer/Miss L Coghlan, 7-5, 6-8, 6-2), r/u 1961 with Miss J Lehane (Mrs M Reitano/Miss M Smith won, 6-4, 3-6, 7-5).

French doubles r/u 1958 with Mrs Long (Miss Y Ramirez/Miss R Reyes won, 6-4, 7-5).

Wimbledon doubles r/u 1957 with Mrs Long (Miss Gibson/Miss D Hard won, 6-1, 6-2).

HAYDON, Adrianne Shirley (Ann) *see* Jones, Mrs Ann

HAYGARTH, Mrs P *see* Schuurman, Miss Renee

HEAD, Dorothy *see* Knode, Mrs Dorothy

HEATH, Rodney Wilfred, Australia
Born 1887, Melbourne. Winner of the first Australian championship in 1905, Heath won again in 1910. He took the doubles title in 1906 and 1911 and in 1919 was runner-up with Englishman Randolph Lycett in the Wimbledon All-Comers' doubles.

Australian singles won 1905 (beat A H Curtis), won 1910 (beat H M Rice); doubles won 1906 with A Wilding (beat H Parker/C Cox), r/u 1910 with J O'Dea (Rice/A Campbell won), won 1911 with Lycett (beat N Brookes/J Addison). Davis Cup 1911–12.

Wimbledon doubles r/u All-comers 1919 with Lycett (P O'Hara Wood/R Thomas won, 6-4, 6-2, 4-6, 6-2).

HEINE, Esther (Bobbie) *see* Miller, Mrs Esther H

HELDMAN, Julie, USA
Born December 1945, Berkeley, California. The daughter of Julius Heldman, a former US junior champion and regular competitor on the veterans' circuit, and Gladys, publisher and editor of the US magazine *World Tennis*, Julie turned to TV commentating and writing when her promising career was ended by injuries in 1976. She had showed herself a shrewd tactician on court and in her last season (1975) finished sixth on the Virginia Slims circuit. She played in the US Federation Cup team in 1966, 1969–70, 1974–5 and the Wightman Cup in 1969–71 and 1974, with five wins out of nine rubbers.

US 18 champion 1963; US clay court doubles won 1974, r/u 1975, both with Mrs G Chanfreau.

Italian singles won 1969, r/u 1970.

Canadian singles won 1965, r/u 1974; doubles won 1974 with Mrs Chanfreau.

British hard court doubles won 1974 with Miss V Wade.

Swedish singles won 1968.

Chile singles won 1968.

Russian singles won 1969.

Belgian singles won 1970.

South American singles won 1973.

HELWIG, Helen (Mrs H R Pouch), USA

A pioneer of the American women's game, Helen Helwig won the US women's singles title in 1894 and the doubles in 1894–5 with Miss J Atkinson, who took the singles title from her in 1895.

HENKEL, Henner Ernst Otto, Germany

Born October 1915, Posen, died in German offensive outside Stalingrad, 1943. With Baron von Cramm, Henkel made a formidable partnership in the Davis Cup team between 1935 and 1939, helping Germany to the inter-zone finals four times. Had he survived the war his career might well have matched that of von Cramm. He was German junior champion in 1932–3, won the German singles in 1937 and 1939 and the doubles in 1935 with H Denker and 1939 with R Menzel.

Australian men's doubles r/u 1938 with von Cramm (A Quist/J Bromwich won 7-5, 6-4, 6-0).

French singles won 1937 (beat H W Austin, 6-1, 6-4, 6-3); doubles won 1937 with von Cramm (beat N Farquharson/V Kirby, 6-4, 7-3, 3-6, 6-1).

US doubles won 1937 with von Cramm (beat J Budge/C Mako, 6-4, 7-5, 6-4).

Wimbledon doubles r/u 1938 with G von Metaxa (Budge/Mako won, 6-4, 3-6, 6-3, 8-6); mixed doubles r/u 1938 with Mrs S P Fabyan (Budge/Miss A Marble won, 6-1, 6-4).

HEWITT, Robert Anthony John, Australia/South Africa

Born January 1940, Sydney, NSW. Though born in Australia, Hewitt settled in Johannesburg in 1964, married a former model, Delaille Nicholas, and now runs a sports shop while continuing his tennis career. He was one of the players who helped give Australia international tennis dominance but he has achieved his greatest successes, both in South Africa and abroad, since emigrating and is a particularly aggressive doubles player. He had an outstanding run of 39 doubles wins with Frew McMillan in 1967, including South Africa, Wimbledon, British hard courts, Italy and Germany and in that year was undefeated in Davis Cup singles or doubles for South Africa. He has taken four Wimbledon doubles titles with his sturdy, forceful attacking game. In 1977 he won the US Open doubles and US Professional doubles with McMillan and the Wimbledon mixed doubles with Greer Stevens.

Australian doubles r/u 1962 (R Emerson/N Fraser won, 4-6, 4-6, 6-1, 6-4, 11-9), won 1963 (beat K Fletcher/J Newcombe, 6-2, 3-6, 6-3, 3-6, 6-3), won 1964 (beat Emerson/Fletcher, 6-4, 7-5, 3-6, 4-6, 14-12), all with F Stolle; mixed doubles won 1961 with Miss J Lehane (beat J Pearce/Mrs M Reitano, 9-7, 6-2).

French doubles r/u 1965 with Fletcher (Emerson/Stolle won, 6-8, 6-3, 8-6, 6-2), won 1972 with McMillan (beat P Cornejo/J Fillol, 6-3, 8-6, 3-6, 6-1); mixed doubles won 1970 with Mrs L W King (beat J C Barclay/Miss F Durr, 3-6, 6-3, 6-2).

Wimbledon doubles r/u 1961 (Emerson/Fraser won, 6-4, 6-8, 6-4, 6-8, 8-6), won 1962 (beat B Jovanovic/N Pilić, 6-2, 5-7, 6-2, 6-4), won 1964 (beat Emerson/Fletcher, 7-5, 11-9, 6-4), all with Stolle, r/u 1965 with Fletcher (Newcombe/A Roche won, 7-5, 6-3, 6-4), won

Right: Bob Hewitt is a particularly aggressive doubles player.
Centre right: Blanche Hillyard (née Bingley) was one of the pioneers of women's tennis. She played in the first women's single event at Wimbledon in 1884.

1967 (beat Emerson/Fletcher, 6-2, 6-3, 6-4), won 1972 (beat S Smith/E van Dillen, 6-2, 6-2, 9-7), all with McMillan; mixed doubles r/u 1963 with Miss D Hard (Fletcher/Miss M Smith won, 11-9, 6-4), won 1977 with Miss G Stevens (beat McMillan/Miss B Stöve, 3-6, 7-5, 6-4).

South African doubles won 1967, r/u 1969, won 1970, 1972, 1974, all with McMillan. South African Davis Cup 1967–74.

German doubles won 1967, 1970 with McMillan, r/u 1972 with I Tiriac.

Rothmans' British hard court doubles won 1969, 1972 with McMillan; mixed doubles won 1970 with Mrs King.

Italian singles r/u 1968 (Okker won); doubles won 1967 with McMillan.

US Open doubles won 1977 (beat Ramirez/Gottfried, 6-4, 6-0); US Professional doubles won 1977 (beat Fibak/Okker, 6-1, 1-6, 6-3) both with McMillan.

WCT doubles champion 1974, r/u 1975, both with McMillan; WCT Columbus doubles won 1976 (beat A Ashe/Okker); US Professional Indoor doubles won 1976, both with McMillan; San Francisco doubles r/u 1976 with B Gottfried. Swedish Open doubles won 1977 with Dowdeswell (Fassbender/Meiler r/u 6-4, 7-6).

HIGUERAS, José, Spain

Born March 1953. He led the Spanish under-21 team which won the Galea Cup for the first time in 1973 and in the same year he beat Borg in the second round of the Melia Trophy and played in the Davis Cup and King's Cup.

Swiss Open doubles won 1974 with T Okker; Swedish Open singles r/u 1975 (M Orantes won); São Paulo singles r/u 1976 (G Vilas won). Davis Cup team 1973

HILLYARD, Mrs Blanche (née Bingley), GB

Born November 1863, Greenford, Middlesex, died August 1946. One of the pioneers of women's tennis, she played in the first women's singles championship event at Wimbledon in 1884, reaching the semi-final. She entered 24 times in all up to 1913, winning six singles titles and reaching the semi-finals at the age of 48 on her last appearance. Her husband, Commander George Hillyard, was secretary of the All England Club from 1907 to 1924.

Wimbledon singles r/u All-Comers 1885 (Miss M Watson won, 6-1, 7-5), won Challenge Round 1885 (beat Miss Watson, 6-3, 6-3), r/u 1887 (Miss C Dod won, 6-2, 6-0), r/u 1888 (Miss Dod won, 6-3, 6-3), won 1889 (wo), r/u All-Comers 1891 (Miss Dod won, 6-2, 6-1), r/u Challenge Round 1892 (Miss Dod won, 6-1, 6-1), r/u 1893 (Miss Dod won, 6-8, 6-1, 6-4), won 1894 (wo), won 1897 (beat Miss C Cooper, 5-7, 7-5, 6-2), won 1899 (beat Miss Cooper, 6-2, 6-3), won 1900 (beat Miss Cooper, 4-6, 6-4, 6-4), r/u 1901 (Mrs A Sterry won, 6-2, 6-2); doubles non-championship events, won 1899 with Miss B Steedman, r/u 1900 with Miss L Martin, won 1901 with Mrs Sterry, won 1906 with Miss M Sutton.

German championship singles won 1897, 1900.

Irish championship singles won 1888, 1894, 1897; mixed doubles won 1894, 1897.

Welsh championship singles won 1888.

HOAD, Lewis Alan (Lew), Australia

Born November 1934, Glebe, NSW. One of the all-time greats, Hoad began playing tennis at the age of nine, was a seasoned tournament player by 15 and went on his first world tour aged 17. Teamed with his long-time rival from schooldays, Ken Rosewall, they became the great driving force of Australian tennis suprem-

acy and in 1953, both aged 19, were responsible for retaining the Davis Cup. In his singles meeting with Tony Trabert, Hoad played one of the greatest Davis Cup matches ever seen. The first set lasted 90 minutes before he won it 13-11. Then he took the next 6-3 but Trabert came back strongly to take the next two 6-2, 6-3. Playing in heavy rain, they went to 5-5 in the fifth and with Hoad 0-30 down it looked as if he was broken. But, as it was throughout his career, he played his best under the greatest pressure and amazingly, after taking a crashing fall, Hoad rallied to win that game and went on to set and match at 7-5. Chunky in build, the blond Hoad was innately lazy but reached his

peak on the occasions when it was most needed, using his 110 mph service and strong forearm devastatingly.

In 1956 Hoad, having won the Australian, French and Wimbledon titles, was robbed of the Grand Slam by Rosewall, who beat him at Forest Hills before signing professional forms with Jack Kramer. Next year, with awesome ferocity, Hoad crushed Ashley Cooper, beating him 6-2, 6-1, 6-2 in just 57 minutes. He then signed with Kramer for a record $125,000 but recurring back trouble – he had sustained a back injury in the 1956 French finals – spoiled his professional career and defeated his hopes of a comeback in Open tennis in 1968.

Australian men's singles r/u 1955 (Rosewall won, 9-7, 6-4, 6-4), won 1956 (beat Rosewall, 6-4, 3-6, 6-4, 7-5); doubles won 1953 (beat D Candy/M Rose, 9-11, 6-4, 10-8, 6-4), r/u 1955 (E Seixas/A Trabert won, 6-4, 6-2, 2-6, 3-6, 6-1), won 1956 (beat Rose/Candy, 10-8, 13-11, 6-4), all with Rosewall, won 1957 with N Fraser (Cooper/M Anderson, 6-3, 8-6, 6-1); mixed doubles r/u 1955 with Miss J Staley (G Worthington/Mrs T Long won, 6-2, 6-1). Davis Cup team 1953–6.

French singles won 1956 (beat S Davidson, 6-4, 8-6, 6-3); doubles won 1953 (beat M Rose/C Wilderspin, 6-2, 6-1, 6-1), r/u 1954 (Seixas/Trabert won, 6-4, 6-2, 6-1), both with Rosewall r/u 1956 with Cooper (Candy/R Perry won, 7-5, 6-3, 6-3); mixed doubles won 1954 with Miss M Connolly (beat R Hartwig/J Patorni, 6-4, 6-3).

US singles r/u 1956 (Rosewall won, 4-6, 6-2, 6-3, 6-3); doubles r/u 1954 (Seixas/Trabert won, 3-6, 6-4, 8-6, 6-3), won 1956 (beat H Richardson/Seixas, 6-2, 6-2, 3-6, 6-4), both with Rosewall; mixed doubles r/u 1952 with Mrs Long (F Sedgman/Miss D Hart won, 6-3, 7-5), r/u 1956 with Miss D Hard (Rosewall/Mrs W duPont won, 9-7, 6-1).

Wimbledon singles won 1956 (beat Rosewall, 6-2, 4-6, 7-5, 6-4), won 1957 (beat Cooper, 6-2, 6-1, 6-2); doubles won 1953 with Rosewall (beat Hartwig/Rose, 6-4, 7-5, 4-6, 7-5), won 1955 with Hartwig (beat Fraser/Rosewall, 7-5, 6-4, 6-3), won 1956 with Rosewall (beat N Pietrangeli/O Sirola, 7-5, 6-2, 6-1), r/u 1957 with Fraser (G Mulloy/J Patty won, 8-10, 6-4, 6-4, 6-4).

Italian singles won 1956; doubles won 1956 with J Drobný, won 1957 with Fraser.

HOLCROFT, Phoebe Catherine *see* **Watson, Phoebe**

HOLLADAY, Terry, USA
Born November 1955, Charlotte, North Carolina. A left-hander who started playing at the age of 10, coached by Lester Stoefen and Bill Bond Senior and Junior, Miss Holladay made her Wightman Cup debut in 1976, when she came in to replace the injured Billie Jean King. The tall and lean American won her singles against Glynis Coles 3-6, 6-1, 6-4. She has had good seasons on the Virginia Slims circuit and won the Pacific Coast Indoor singles 1976, beating Mrs Guerrant.

HOPMAN, Harry, Australia
Born August 1906, Sydney, NSW. An excellent tennis player of the 1930s and member of the Australian Davis Cup team from 1928 to 1932. Hopman will be best remembered for his exceptional qualities as a trainer/coach and non-playing captain of the team from 1950 to 1969, during which time Australia won 15 times and lost only four. The sandy-haired Hopman, who settled in America and became president of Port Washington Tennis Academy, Long Island,

was a tough disciplinarian whose strict training methods included road running, calisthenics, athletics and fines on players who broke curfew or training. Nicknamed 'The Fox' and 'Miracle Man', he succeeded in bringing already great players to a peak of fitness and performance. They included Hoad, Rosewall, Laver, McGregor, Anderson, Emerson, Fraser, Newcombe and Roche. He won the Australian mixed doubles four times, all with his wife Nell. He was three times Australian squash champion (1933–4, 1936).

Australian men's singles r/u 1930 (E Moon won, 6-3, 6-1, 6-3), r/u 1931 (J Crawford won, 6-4, 6-2, 2-6, 6-1), r/u 1932 (Crawford won, 4-6, 6-3, 3-6, 6-3, 6-1); doubles won 1929 (beat R Cummings/Moon, 6-1, 6-8, 4-6, 6-1, 6-3), won 1930 (beat J Hawkes/Fitchett, 8-6, 6-1, 2-6, 6-3), r/u 1931 (C Donohoe/R Dunlop won, 8-6, 6-2, 5-7, 7-9, 6-4), all with Crawford, r/u 1932 with G Patterson (Crawford/Moon won, 12-10, 6-3, 4-6, 6-4); mixed doubles won 1930 with Miss N Hall (beat Crawford/Miss M Cox, 11-9, 3-6, 6-3), won 1936 (beat A Kay/Miss M Blick, 6-2, 6-0), won 1937 (beat D Turnbull/Miss D Stevenson, 3-6, 6-3, 6-2), won 1939 (beat J Bromwich/Miss M Wilson, 6-8, 6-2, 6-3), all with Mrs N Hopman.

French doubles r/u 1930 with J Willard (H Cochet/J Brugnon won, 6-3, 9-7, 6-3), r/u 1948 with F Sedgman (L Bergelin/J Drobný won, 8-6, 6-1, 12-10).

US mixed doubles won 1939 with Miss A Marble.

Wimbledon mixed doubles r/u 1932 with Miss J Sigart (E Maier/Miss E Ryan won, 7-5, 6-2), r/u 1935 with Mrs Hopman (F Perry/Miss D Round won, 7-5, 4-6, 6-2).

HOPMAN, Nell, Australia
Born March 1909, Sydney NSW, died January 1968. Australian women's singles r/u 1939 (Mrs V Westacott won, 6-1, 6-2), r/u 1947 (Mrs N

Bolton won, 6-3, 6-2); doubles r/u 1935 with Miss L Bickerton (Miss E Dearman/Miss N Lyle won, 6-3, 6-4), r/u 1937 with Mrs Westacott (Miss T Coyne/Miss N Wynne won, 6-2, 6-2), r/u 1955 with Mrs A Thiele (Mrs M Hawton/Miss B Penrose won, 7-5, 6-1).

French women's doubles won 1954 with Miss M Connolly (beat Mrs M Galtier/Miss S Schmitt, 7-5, 4-6, 6-0). *See* **H Hopman** for mixed doubles results.

HOTCHKISS, Hazel V *see* Wightman, Mrs G W

HOWE, Robert Neville, Australia

Born August 1925, Sydney, NSW. An unusual player in that his greatest successes came from mixed doubles. In 1958 he and Lorraine Coghlan were the first Australian pair to win the Wimbledon mixed doubles. He also won the Australian mixed doubles once and the French twice.

Australian men's doubles r/u 1959 with D Candy (R Laver/R Mark won, 9-7, 6-4, 6-2); mixed doubles won 1958 with Mrs M Hawton (beat P Newman/Miss A Mortimer, 9-11, 6-1, 6-2).

French doubles r/u 1958 with A Segal (A Cooper/N Fraser won, 3-6, 8-6, 6-3, 7-5), r/u 1961 with Mark (R Emerson/R Laver won, 3-6, 6-1, 6-1, 6-4); mixed doubles r/u 1956 with Miss D Hard (L Ayala/Mrs T Long won, 4-6, 6-4, 6-1), r/u 1958 with Miss Coghlan (N Pietrangeli/Miss S Bloomer won, 9-7, 6-8, 6-2), won 1960 with Miss M Bueno (beat Emerson/Miss A Haydon, 1-6, 6-1, 6-2), won 1962 with Miss R Schuurman (beat F Stolle/Miss L Turner, 6-1, 6-2).

US mixed doubles r/u 1957 with Miss Hard (K Nielson/Miss A Gibson won, 6-3, 9-7).

Wimbledon mixed doubles won 1958 with Miss Coghlan (beat Nielson/Miss Gibson, 6-3, 13-11), r/u 1960 with Miss Bueno (Laver/Miss Hard won, 13-11, 3-6, 8-6), r/u 1961 with Miss E Buding (Stolle/Miss Turner won, 11-9, 6-2).

Hoylake, Cheshire, GB

From 1970 to 1973 the major Hoylake tournament was the Rothmans' Open, previously known as 'the North of England' and 'the Hoylake and West Kirby'. It was unique in Britain in two ways: held after Wimbledon in July, it was the only major tournament played in a public park – at West Kirby, near Liverpool – and the only tournament played solely in the evenings. Hoylake was in the LTA official lists from 1949, at which time John White, secretary of the Cheshire County LTA and of what had previously been a local tennis event at Hoylake, persuaded the local municipal authority to provide financial backing. Players of county standard were then attracted and by 1959 support from the *Liverpool Daily Post* was ensuring participation by internationals. The Commercial Union women's Grand Prix was also played there but when both Rothmans' and the CU withdrew their sponsorships Hoylake Park fell out of the list of major tournaments. However, there were plans to revive it as a venue in the Colgate International series for women in 1978.

HREBEČ, Jiři, Czechoslovakia

Born September 1950, lives in Prague. Tall and talented, Hrebeč made a good international impression in 1973 when he took a set off Britain's Roger Taylor at Wimbledon, and beat John Newcombe of Australia in four sets in the Davis Cup inter-zone final before losing to Rod Laver. In 1976 he twice came close to beating Jim Connors, leading 3-1 in the final set of the US Professional Indoor championships third round before losing 6-2, 2-6, 3-6, and had match point in the Cologne quarter-finals.

Czechoslovakia International men's doubles r/u 1971 with P Hutka (J Kodeš/J Kukal won, 6-2, 1-6, 6-3); National championship singles won 1971 (beat Hutka, 7-5, 6-4, 6-3); Prague singles won 1973 (beat Kodeš, 4-6, 6-1, 3-6, 6-0, 7-5).

Southern Australia singles won 1973; Swiss Indoor won 1975 (beat I Năstase); WCT Memphis singles r/u 1975 (H Solomon won); ATP Basle r/u 1976 (Kodeš won). Davis Cup 1973–

HUGHES, George Patrick, GB

Born December 1902, Sutton Coldfield, Warwickshire. Pat Hughes was one of the three British players to reach the Wimbledon quarter-finals in 1931 (Perry and Austin were the others) – the best since 1923 and not equalled since. He found fame as a doubles player partnered by Perry and later by Raymond Tuckey, member of a leading British tennis family. He and Perry gained the French doubles in 1933, and the Australian in 1934.

Wimbledon doubles r/u 1932 with Perry (J Borotra/J Brugnon won, 6-0, 4-6, 3-6, 7-5, 7-5), won 1936 (beat C Hare/F Wilde, 6-4, 3-6, 7-9, 6-1, 6-4), r/u 1937 (J Budge/G Mako won, 6-0, 6-4, 6-8, 6-1), both with Tuckey.

Australian doubles won 1934 (beat A Quist/D Turnbull, 6-8, 6-3, 6-4, 3-6, 6-3), r/u 1935 (J Crawford/V McGrath won, 6-4, 8-6, 6-2), both with Perry.

French doubles won 1933 with Perry (beat Quist/McGrath, 6-2, 6-4, 2-6, 7-5), r/u 1936 with Tuckey (Borotra/M Bernard won, 6-2, 3-6, 9-7, 6-1). Davis Cup team 1929, 1931–6.

HUNT, Lesley *see* Hambeucher, Lesley H

HUNTER, Francis Townsend, USA

Born June 1894, New York. Among the world's leading tennis players of the 1920s, it was Hunter's misfortune to be overshadowed by contemporaries such as 'Little Bill' Johnston, 'Big Bill' Tilden and the 'Four Musketeers' of France, Borotra, Brugnon, Cochet and Lacoste, by all of whom he was frequently relegated to runner-up. He was never able to achieve a US singles title, though he was r/u to Cochet (1928) and

Tilden (1929), or a Wimbledon title, where Johnston beat him in the 1923 final. However, with Tilden he took the US and Wimbledon doubles in 1927. After turning professional in 1930 he joined Tilden and the Czech Karel Koželuh on a tour series in 1931 and in 1937 became a promoter himself with S Howard Voshill. Their first act was to sign Britain's Fred Perry as a professional.

US singles r/u 1928 (Cochet won, 4-6, 6-4, 3-6, 7-5, 6-3), r/u 1929 (Tilden won, 3-6, 6-3, 4-6, 6-2, 6-4); men's doubles won 1927 with Tilden (beat R Williams/Johnston, 10-8, 6-3, 6-3). Davis Cup 1927–9. Olympic gold medal 1924.

French mixed doubles r/u 1928 (Cochet/Miss E Bennett won, 3-6, 6-3, 6-3), r/u 1929 (Cochet/Miss Bennett won, 6-3, 6-2), both with Miss Wills.

Wimbledon singles r/u 1923 (Johnston won, 6-0, 6-3, 6-1); doubles won with V Richards (beat W Washburn/Williams, 6-3, 3-6, 8-10, 8-6, 6-3), won 1927 with Tilden (beat Brugnon/Cochet, 1-6, 4-6, 8-6, 6-3, 6-4); mixed doubles won 1927 with Miss E Ryan (beat L Godfree/Mrs K Godfree, 6-3, 6-4), won 1929 with Miss Wills (beat I Collins/Miss J Fry, 6-1, 6-4).

Inter-County Championships, GB

Inter-county championships on grass and hard courts are staged each year by the British LTA and cover England, Scotland and Wales. The grass court championships began in 1895 for men only and were won by Gloucestershire. In 1899 the first women's county championship was won by Surrey. Since 1925 the championships have been held at various centres during one week in July and became known as Inter-County week. The grass court events are played by six counties in each of seven groups of men and seven of women and the bottom two of each group are relegated while the top two of five groups are promoted. The men's inter-county title has been won by Middlesex 33 times, Gloucestershire nine times, Surrey 14, Warwickshire five, Lancashire four, Yorkshire and Essex twice and Staffordshire once. The women's title has gone to Surrey 33 times, Middlesex 20, Warwickshire four, Devonshire three, and Kent, Cheshire, Durham and Sussex once each. In 1973 the Prudential Assurance Company began sponsoring the championships, which became known as the Prudential County Cup.

The first hard court championships for men and women were held in 1921, Surrey winning both titles. Played as an elimination event it is organised on the basis of geographical groupings and played in five stages during the year. The semi-finals and finals have been held at the West Hampshire Club in Bournemouth since 1965. Middlesex has won the men's title 18 times, Surrey 16, Warwickshire six, Essex five, Lancashire twice and Yorkshire once; the women's title has gone to Surrey 26 times, Middlesex 17, Warwickshire twice, and to Kent, Yorkshire and Devonshire once each.

International Lawn Tennis Clubs

Established in 1924 by A Wallis Myers, the International LTC of Great Britain has the aim of promoting through social union and match play, good fellowship and friendly rivalry among players of all nationalities.

International Lawn Tennis Federation

The International Lawn Tennis Federation was founded in Paris at a meeting of the *Union des Sociétés Françaises de Sports Athlétiques* on 1 March 1913. Until that date there had been no international organisation responsible for the developing sport, though it was generally accepted that the British LTA was the parent body and could make the rules. It was, in fact, Hungary which suggested the formation of an international body, sending Mr Arthur Yolland (a British resident who had played for Hungary) to London to put forward the suggestion in 1909. A similar suggestion came in 1910 from Ireland and impetus was given to the idea when representatives of the British Isles and France met during the Davis Cup tie at Folkestone in 1912. The result of their discussions was a meeting in Paris in October attended by representatives from Australasia, Austria, the British Isles, Belgium, France, Spain and Switzerland. There it was agreed to press forward with the formation of an international body. In Paris the following March the inaugural meeting of the ILTF was attended by official representatives of the lawn tennis associations of 12 countries: Australasia, Austria, Belgium, the British Isles, Denmark, France, Germany, Holland, Russia, South Africa, Sweden and Switzerland. The United States was represented informally, without a vote, and did not affiliate for ten years.

In the 1920s the ILTF was given the right to lay down the rules of the game, which were to be 'forever in the English language', and abolished the 'world championships' title which had become attached to the Wimbledon championships. Instead the ILTF official championships were created; these were, in fact, the national championships of member countries. There are two types of membership: full and associate, the former have voting rights which depend on size and importance as a tennis nation, while the latter are regarded as not yet having qualified for full membership. Each LTA sends two or three delegates to the annual meeting and every other year a president and committee of management of 11 are elected. The committee is elected from each country which has won the Davis Cup three times (Australia, Britain, France and the USA) with the other seven members including at least one from Asia and from South America and at least two from Europe. The ILTF has headquarters in Paris and London but effectively it is the latter city which has become the centre of ILTF administration.

For more than half a century one of the greatest causes of difference between members was that of amateurism and the place of the professional in the game. Amateurs were allowed to receive 'expenses' but not to earn money from the game and officially ILTF championships were strictly for amateurs. It was, however, well known that many players received financial rewards beyond the approved expenses limit. Even so, the ILTF continued to ignore suggestions for 'open' tournaments to be recognised. After lengthy debate and considerable delay the ILTF's hand was forced by the British LTA in 1967 when it passed a resolution that all reference to amateurs and professionals be deleted from the rules of the LTA. In March of the following year an emergency meeting of the ILTF decided that each country could determine the status of its players and approved the principle of open tournaments, though the distinction between amateurs, who would not play for money, and professionals, who would, remained. That year Wimbledon, which had been 'closed' to many top flight players who had turned professional, was open for the first time.

The way had been opened for many more players to sign contracts which would earn them big money in tournaments all over the world – and for sponsors to offer large sums in support of major events in the ILTF's Grand Prix tournament series. However, in 1971 the leading professional promoters, World Championship Tennis (WCT) came into conflict with the ILTF when it insisted on receiving substantial payments in addition to the prize money available to players, that it should receive a percentage of television fees and should even select the make of ball to be used and charge the manufacturer a fee. The ILTF rejected the demands and closed its official tournaments to WCT players. Eventually WCT realised that it was limiting the earnings of its players – and itself – and reached a compromise with the ILTF. In 1972 after contract professionals had withdrawn from Wimbledon, it was agreed by the ILTF that contract professionals could play in ILTF circuit tournaments and that WCT could arrange its own series of open-to-all tournaments for a limited period each year on that circuit.

International Lawn Tennis Federation Grand Prix
The introduction of the ILTF Grand Prix tournament series in 1968 was an attempt to dissuade top rank professionals from becoming contract players by offering the inducement of substantial cash prizes provided by sponsors. Tournaments selected as part of the Grand Prix series had to pay the ILTF ten percent of the advertised prize money into a pool and also pay the Federation a small fee. The money formed a

pool from which leading players were paid on a points system based on a table compiled from their overall tournament results at the end of each year. First Grand Prix sponsors, in 1970–1, were Pepsi-Cola Inc, followed by the Commercial Union Assurance Company from 1972–6, and Colgate-Palmolive in 1977. The first Grand Prix in 1970 was for men and included 20 tournaments. The American Cliff Richey won ($25,000) with Arthur Ashe second. In 1971 a women's Grand Prix of 18 events was introduced and was won by Mrs Billie Jean King ($10,000); the men's events covered 31 tournaments and another American, Stan Smith ($25,000) was the winner. Commercial Union increased the prize money in 1972 when Ilie Năstase of Rumania won $55,000 in the 33-event men's series and Mrs King $22,500 in the 31-event women's Grand Prix. Năstase won the men's GP again in 1973 ($55,000) and Christine Evert the women's GP ($23,750). The 1974 winner was Guillermo Vilas of Argentina, who won again in 1975, when his singles and doubles bonus pool money was $103,750 and GP tournament prize money totalled $133,642. In 1976 the Mexican Raul Ramirez headed the GP table with a total bonus of $190,000 in a series which included 46 tournaments.

Tournaments have to fulfil certain conditions before they can be part of the GP series; these include the amount of prize money offered, the number of players in the draw and the prestige of the tournament. Depending on these the tournaments are classified. Players receive more points for winning a major title such as Forest Hills or Wimbledon than for lesser tournaments offering, for example, prize money of $50,000 to $75,000. Players taking part in Davis Cup ties can also earn points depending upon their results and thus are not handicapped in the Grand Prix by representing their countries. The Grand Prix series is rounded off by the Grand Prix Masters' event which is open to top-of-the-table men in singles and doubles.

International Lawn Tennis Federation official championships
The ILTF recognises the championships of Australia, Britain, France, Italy and the USA, which are organised by those countries' LTAs, and the championships of Asia, South America and Scandinavia. Official championships must be open to amateurs and non-contract professionals so long as the players' national LTAs are affiliated to the ILTF and they are themselves in good standing with their LTAs and the Federation. Touring professionals can compete in official championships which are open to all categories of players so long as they are in good standing with the host country's LTA and with the ILTF.

The LTAs of other countries can also apply to have their championships officially recognised on a temporary basis which can lead to permanent recognition.

Ireland

Lawn tennis is known to have been played in Ireland before 1877, when the famous Fitzwilliam Club, Dublin was founded, though no exact date of the game's introduction can be given. The Irish LTA was founded in 1908 in Dublin and, having been given the status of an English county, was affiliated to the LTA of Great Britain. The Irish championships were staged annually at the Fitzwilliam from 1879 (except in 1922 and during the two World Wars) and in that year Ireland became the first country to hold a women's singles championship. The honour of being the world's first women's tennis champion fell to Miss May Langrishe, who also won in 1883 and 1886.

In 1923, after Southern Ireland became the Irish Free State, the association elected to become an independent national body and in 1925 it affiliated to the ILTF, covering both the Irish Republic (Eire, Southern Ireland) and Northern Ireland . Since that date Ireland as a whole has entered the Davis Cup on over 50 occasions. The Irish LTA works through four provincial councils and a general council, overseeing tennis leagues and provincial club competitions. Inter-provincial championships for adults, juniors and intermediate players are held annually.

Irish Open Championships

The second oldest of all major championships, the Irish Open was first held in 1879 and is now staged in Dublin a week after Wimbledon, which pre-dated it by two years. The Irish Open was the first championship to hold a women's singles event and a mixed doubles in their first year. The championships have always been administered by the Fitzwilliam Club but while the men's events were held for 24 years in Fitzwilliam Square, the women's were staged less publicly on the club's courts.

The first Irish men's champion was 'St Leger' Goold (Vere Thomas St Leger Goold, younger son of an Irish baronet), who won from an entry of 15. He later achieved notoriety when he and his French wife Violet were found guilty of murdering a Danish widow. Mrs Goold, who was sentenced to death, in fact died in Montpellier Prison in 1914 and 'St Leger' Goold died on Devil's Island in 1909 aged 55.

Among early champions were Willie and Ernest Renshaw and Herbert Lawford, all of whom were Wimbledon title holders. Ernest Renshaw won the Irish title four times and the other two, three times each. The first Irish-born winner since Goold was Willoughby Hamilton in 1889. Other early men's champions included the Doherty brothers, Reggie and Laurie, Wilfred Baddeley, Joshua Pim; women's champions after May Langrishe (the first, in 1879) included Maud Watson the first Wimbledon women's champion, the young Lottie Dod and Blanche Hillyard. Between 1904 and 1913 James Cecil Parke won the men's championship

eight times and Miss L (Molly) Martin gained the women's title nine times between 1889 and 1903.

From World War I and until the coming of Open tennis in 1968 the championships did not attract as many top class international players. From 1968, however, the championships – now sponsored by P J Carroll and Co Ltd, brewers – have seen such famous winners as Tom Okker, Bob Hewitt, Tony Roche, Cliff Drysdale, Mark Cox, Margaret Court (who also won in 1966), Virginia Wade, Billie Jean King and Evonne Goolagong.

When the Fitzwilliam Club moved to new premises in 1973 the surface for the championship was changed from grass to hard courts.

IRVIN, Mrs K E *see* Fry, Shirley June

Israel

The LTA of Israel has been a full member of the ILTF since 1950 and has competed in the Davis Cup regularly since 1957. Israel took part in the Federation Cup in 1972. The LTA stages two international tournaments, a team competition for some 70 affiliated clubs and junior championships.

Italy

An English lawn tennis club was founded in Bordighera, Italy, in 1878 and was followed by clubs in Rome and Turin in 1890. In fact tennis had been played in a field in Turin as early as 1880. Other clubs soon followed in Genoa and Milan in 1893, Viareggio (1896), Premeno and Arezzo (1899). The Italian LTA was founded in 1894 but lasted only four years mainly because most of its members preferred to play rather than administer the game. In 1898 the English player Wilfred Baddeley was the author of the first tennis manual published in Italy but it was not until 1910 that the Tennis Club of Florence took the initiative to found the national association. A year later the association transferred to Genoa and in 1913 a new constitution was approved and Beppe Croce, who had drawn it up, was appointed chairman. That year the association affiliated to the ILTF. By 1929, when Croce retired from office, he could report that there were 94 affiliated clubs with some 7000 members; that there had been 50 major tournaments in 1928 and Italy had competed in six Davis Cup ties and four international friendly matches, with Belgium, Czechoslovakia, Spain and Switzerland. Expansion of the sport has continued and gathered momentum over the years and by the early 1970s there were 1358 affiliated clubs with 80,000 members and 3081 courts. In 1971 no fewer than 744 tournaments were held.

The first Italian international championships were held in Milan in 1930, the men's singles being won by the American Bill Tilden and the women's by Miss L de Alvarez. In 1935 the championships were held in Rome but were then suspended from 1936 to 1949, held again in Rome in 1950 and suspended in 1951. Since 1952, however, they have been staged regularly. Since the National Olympic Committee, which oversees the Italian Tennis Federation, gave permission for advertising on the Centre Court in 1971 it has been possible to interest sponsors in supporting the game and the Italian Open is now sponsored by an insurance company.

Since first taking part in the Davis Cup in 1922 Italy has had a good record in the event, which it won for the first time in 1976, beating Chile 4-1. In 1928 and 1930, with Uberto de Morpurgo and Giorgio de Stefani – the first Italians in the World's top ten rankings – and Placido Gaslini, Italy won the European zone but lost the inter-zone finals each time to the US. In 1952 Italy first won an inter-zone final, beating India 3-2 but again losing to the US (5-0). Since then Italy has reached the inter-zone finals six times and in 1960 and 1961 Nicola Pietrangeli and Orlando Sirola reached the Challenge (final) Round, losing to the Australian trio Emerson, Fraser and Laver 4-1 and 5-0 respectively. Since the abolition of the Challenge Round in 1972 Italy has reached the quarter finals four times.

Among Italy's other leading players have been Giovanni Palmieri, the former ball boy who was national champion from 1932–6 and won the Italian International in 1934, Gianni Cucelli, who was ranked No 1 in Italy from 1946–9 and was national champion in 1946, 1948; Pietrangeli, who has played a record 164 Davis Cup rubbers, won record numbers of Cup singles and doubles, won the Championship singles in 1957 and 1961 as well as some 20 other international titles; Adriano Panatta, who won the national singles a record six times, (1970–5) and the Italian Open in 1976 and was in the world's top ten in 1977; Corrado Barazzutti, Antoni Zugarelli, Paulo Bertolucci.

The Italian Tennis Federation, which was founded in 1946 as the new national body, has its own tennis school and runs children's courses at its Centri Federali Estivi. In 1971 the country did particularly well in international competition for young players: the Roland Garros junior tournament and the Orange Bowl world junior championships were won by Barazzutti, and the Bonfiglio Trophy for under-21s by Panatta. Italy also won the King's Cup in that year and again in 1974. Other international trophy successes include the under-20s Galea Cup won in 1950, 1952, 1954–5 and the Dubler Cup in 1958, 1960–5.

JACOBS, Helen Hull, USA

Born August 1908, Globe, Arizona. One of the world's best women players between the World Wars, Miss Jacobs took part in some classic matches with her great rival Helen Wills Moody. She was twice robbed of the satisfaction of beating her in a final: in 1933, Mrs Moody retired through injury when losing 6-8, 6-3, 0-3; two years later, at Wimbledon, when the two were meeting for the ninth time, Helen Jacobs lost an apparently easy match point in the third set and Mrs Moody recovered to take the title 7-5. Neither Miss Jacobs nor Mrs Moody had lost a set in reaching the final. The following year Miss Jacobs gained her only Wimbledon title when Mrs Moody did not defend. She had beaten Miss Jacobs in eight of their nine matches. They met again in the Wimbledon 1938 final when Miss Jacobs lost once more, this time playing with a bandaged ankle after injuring an Achilles tendon in practice the day before. That year Mrs Moody gained her record eighth title. Miss Jacobs won the US title in four successive years until 1936, when Alice Marble, who had recovered from tuberculosis, returned to Forest Hills to take it from her. In 1934 Miss Jacobs took the US 'Triple Crown', winning the singles, doubles and mixed doubles. Between 1923 and 1938 Miss Jacobs played 30 rubbers in 12 Wightman Cup matches – a record at that time. In 1931 with Helen Wills Moody, she helped recapture the Cup for the US, where it remained until 1958.

US singles r/u 1928 (Miss Wills won, 6-2, 6-1), won 1932 (beat Miss C Babcock, 6-2, 6-2), won 1933 (beat Mrs Moody, 8-6, 3-6, 3-0, retired),

Left: American Helen Jacobs was one of the best women players between the wars.

won 1934 (beat Miss S Palfrey, 6-1, 6-4), won 1935 (beat Mrs Palfrey Fabyan, 6-1, 6-4), r/u 1936 (Miss Marble won, 4-6, 6-3, 6-2), r/u 1939 (Miss Marble won, 6-0, 8-10, 6-4), r/u 1940 (Miss Marble won, 6-2, 6-3); doubles r/u 1931 with Miss D Round (Miss B Nuthall/Mrs E Whittingstall won, 6-2, 6-4), won 1932 (beat Mrs Painter/Miss Marble, 8-6, 6-1), won 1934 (beat Miss Babcock/Mrs D Andrus, 4-6, 6-3, 6-4), won 1935 (beat Miss Babcock/Mrs Andrus, 6-4, 6-2), r/u 1936 (Mrs J Van Ryn/Miss Babcock won, 9-7, 2-6, 6-4) all with Mrs Palfrey Fabyan; mixed doubles r/u 1932 with E Vines (F Perry/Miss Palfrey won, 6-3, 7-5), won 1934 with G Lott (beat L R Stoefen/Miss E Ryan, 4-6, 13-11, 6-2).

French singles r/u 1930 (Mrs Moody won, 6-2, 6-1), r/u 1934 (Miss M Scriven won, 7-5, 4-6, 6-1); doubles r/u 1934 with Miss Palfrey (Mrs R Mathieu/Miss Ryan won, 3-6, 6-4, 6-2).

Wimbledon singles r/u 1929 (Miss Wills won, 6-1, 6-2), r/u 1932 (Mrs Moody won, 6-3, 6-1), r/u 1934 (Miss Round won, 6-2, 5-7, 6-3), r/u 1935 (Mrs Moody won, 6-3, 3-6, 7-5), won 1936 (beat Miss S Sperling, 6-2, 4-6, 7-5), r/u 1938 (Mrs Moody won, 6-4, 6-0); doubles r/u 1932 with Miss Ryan (Miss D Metaxa/Miss J Sigart won, 6-4, 6-3), r/u 1936 with Mrs Fabyan (Miss F James/Miss K Stammers won, 6-2, 6-1), r/u 1939 with Miss A Yorke (Miss Marble/Mrs Fabyan won, 6-1, 6-0).

Right: Christine Janes (née Truman) was always popular with British fans, and was the darling of the Wimbledon centre court.

JAMES, Winifred Alice (Freda), (Mrs S H Hammersley), GB

Born January 1911, Nottingham. Partnered by Kay Stammers, Miss James twice took the Wimbledon women's doubles (1935–6) and with Betty Nuthall gained the 1933 title when Mrs Helen Wills Moody and 'Bunny' Ryan were forced to retire after Mrs Moody had hurt her back in the women's singles final against Helen Jacobs.

Wimbledon doubles r/u 1933 with Miss A Yorke (Mrs R Mathieu/Miss Ryan won, 6-2, 9-11, 6-4), won 1935 (beat Mrs Mathieu/Mrs S Sperling, 6-1, 6-4), won 1936 (beat Mrs S Fabyan/Miss H Jacobs, 6-2, 6-1). Wightman Cup 1933–9.

US doubles won 1933 with Miss Nuthall (Mrs Moody/Miss Ryan retired).

JANES, Christine (née Truman), GB

Born January 1941, Loughton, Essex. A great favourite with British crowds, part of Christine Truman Janes' attraction was the exuberance and uninhibited manner of her play, her powerful forehand and her sporting behaviour. At the age of 17 she achieved a spectacular win against Althea Gibson in the 1958 Wightman Cup, beating the US and Wimbledon champion 2-6, 6-3, 6-4 and helping Britain to her first Cup win since 1930. The following year she became the youngest winner of the French women's singles title at 18 years 5 months, and in 1961, with the crowd very much favouring her, she had

a winning lead over Angela Mortimer in the first all-British women's final since 1914. Christine had already had a magnificent win against Margaret Smith, the reigning French and Australian champion, after surviving two match points. In the final it appeared that Christine was in such devastating form that a straight sets win was likely but in the second set with a winning lead, she fell heavily and hurt her left thigh. Though she continued to play well she appeared slower and lost the next set and despite fighting back in the third, lost that 7-5. After her marriage in 1967 she was partnered in Wightman Cup doubles by her sister, Nell Truman, in 1968–9 and 1971.

Wimbledon singles r/u 1961 (Miss Mortimer won, 4-6, 6-4, 7-5); doubles r/u 1959 with Mrs J Fleitz (Miss J Arth/Miss D Hard won, 2-6, 6-2, 6-3). Wightman Cup 1957–63, 1967–9, 1971.

Australian doubles won 1960 with Miss M Bueno (beat Miss Smith/Miss L Robinson, 6-2, 5-7, 6-2).

French singles won 1959 (beat Mrs Z Körmöczy, 6-4, 7-5).

US singles r/u 1959 (Miss Bueno won, 6-1, 6-4).

Japan

Tennis was introduced to Japan in 1880 by an American, George Adams Leland, who had been appointed by the Japanese government as an instructor at the Training Institute for Physical Education Teachers at Tokyo Higher Normal School (now Tokyo University of Education). Because the equipment which Leland had brought with him was expensive to replace by importing it, the Japanese started to use rubber balls without the conventional flannel covering. When these were found to be suitable an order for their manufacture was placed with a Japanese company. Thus began the unique soft-ball Japanese version of tennis which was spread rapidly through the country by graduate teachers from the Physical Education Institute. Schools and universities began their own soft-ball tennis clubs and the first inter-university match took place in 1898 between Tokyo Higher Norman School and the Higher Commercial School (now Hitotsubashi University); Higher Normal won.

There are a number of differences between soft-ball and lawn tennis: the court dimensions are the same but with net poles standing 5 ft 3 in (1.6 m). The standard racket has a frame of $12\frac{3}{5}$ in (32 cm), $8\frac{3}{4}$ in (22 cm) at the widest point and a handle of $14\frac{3}{5}$ in (37 cm), giving an overall length of $27\frac{1}{5}$ in (69 cm). The ball is thinly rubber covered, $2\frac{3}{5}$ in (66 mm) in diameter, weighs $1\frac{1}{10}$ oz (30.5 g) with a bounce of $25\frac{3}{5}$–$31\frac{1}{2}$ in (65–80 cm) dropped from 4 ft 11 in (150 cm).

Scoring is 1, 2, 3 and game, 3-3 being deuce. Most usually the game is played as doubles and here the greatest difference from lawn tennis is apparent: each pair includes a 'rearguard' who serves and plays only in the back of the court, and an 'advance guard' who plays at the net. Matches are of one set and the first pair to win five games takes the match.

Though Leland introduced lawn tennis officially to Japan, it had previously been played privately among some American, British and Canadian Christian missionaries and a few Japanese. Probably the first Open tennis tournament in Japan was played in 1902 or 1903 at Karaizawa, a summer resort north of Tokyo, the development of which had been encouraged by the missionaries from 1886. In 1887 Mr Hugh Frazer, the British Minister in Tokyo, allowed the two courts at the British Legation to be used by an international group of enthusiasts and sponsored a number of Japanese. Prince Hirobumi, the Prime Minister, and members of the government, became interested and in 1890 a grant of grounds in Tokyo was made by the Ministry of Education for the provision of tennis courts. From this stemmed the foundation of the Tokyo Lawn Tennis Club at the start of the century. The Japan LTA was founded in 1925 and affiliated to the ILTF that year.

Japan first took part in the Davis Cup in 1921 and having, at their first attempt, reached the Challenge Round – an achievement which astonished the tennis world – were defeated 5-0 by the holders, USA, but by no means disgraced. Competing in the American zone up to 1929, Japan twice reached the inter-zone finals (1926–7). In 1930, in the European zone, they reached the zone final but lost 3-2 to Italy. Then in 1955 Japan entered the new Eastern zone, established three years previously, and beat the Philippines in the zone final before losing 4-0 in the inter-zone to Australia, the eventual Challenge Round winners.

Zenzo Shimidzu, the first Japanese entrant at Wimbledon in 1920, reached the All-Comers final to face Bill Tilden. Shimidzu was 4-1 up in the first set, 4-2 in the second and 5-2 in the third but Tilden went on to win 6-4, 6-4, 13-11. In the following year Shimidzu reached the semi-finals. The next Japanese showing at Wimbledon came in 1933 when Jiro Satoh beat Britain's H W 'Bunny' Austin 7-5, 6-3, 2-6, 2-6, 6-2 in the quarter-finals but went down 6-3, 6-4, 2-6, 6-4 to Jack Crawford (Australia) in the semi-finals. That year, too, Satoh and R Nunoi reached the finals of the men's doubles but lost to the Frenchmen Borotra and Brugnon. No Japanese male entrants in singles or doubles have done as well since, but in 1934 Ryuki Miki won the mixed doubles with Dorothy Round (UK). Miss Kazuko Sawamutsu won the 1969 junior invitation and reached the quarter-finals of the mixed doubles and in 1970 went to the quarter-finals of the women's doubles with her sister Junko. In 1975, she and Ann Kiyomura (US), who is of Japanese–American extraction, won the women's doubles, beating Françoise Durr and Betty Stöve 7-5, 1-6, 7-5.

JAUFFRET, François, France

Born February 1942, Bordeaux. At his best on hard courts, Jauffret is one of four talented tennis-playing brothers. Formerly director of tennis at the International Club de Lys, he represents Slazengers in France. He has been national champion of France on six occasions (1964, 1969, 1971–4). In 1974 he reached the semi-finals of the French Open by beating Jan Kodeš, who then insisted on Jauffret taking a dope test, which proved negative. In 1976 he had one of the best matches of his career when he took Borg to two sets all, before losing 8-10 in the final set of the French Open quarter-finals. He beat Emerson and then Franulović to win the 1970 South American singles and in 1975, partnered by Kodeš, won the Dusseldorf doubles. Davis Cup 1973– .

JAUSOVEC, Mima, Yugoslavia

Born July 1956. After winning the French junior title in 1973, aged 17, and reaching the quarter-finals of the West German championships, Miss Jausovec made excellent progress to become one of the world's top ten women players in 1976 and ranked No 1 in her own country. In 1974 she won the Wimbledon junior invitation without losing a set, was r/u in the US Open junior singles and won the Argentine Open. She has shown consistently good if unspectacular results on the Virginia Slims circuit but her best result was in winning the

1977 French Open singles.

French Open singles won 1977 (beat Miss F Mihai, 6-2, 6-7, 6-1). Kitzbuhel singles r/u 1974. Italian Open singles won 1976 (beat Miss L Hunt). Canadian Open singles won 1976 (beat Miss Hunt). Ranked world No 7 in 1977.

JEDRZEJOWSKA, Jadwiga (Jed), Poland

Born October 1912, Krakow. The overseas successes of Miss Jedrzejowska in the 1930s and late 1940s were the greatest achievement for Polish tennis. She was champion of Poland, Hungary, Austria, Wales and Ireland and reached the finals of Wimbledon and Forest Hills in 1937. Among the world-class players she defeated were Helen Jacobs, Kay Stammers, Simone Mathieu and Alice Marble, whom she beat four times in the 1937 season.

French women's singles r/u 1939 (Mrs R Mathieu won, 6-3, 8-6); women's doubles r/u 1936 with Miss S Noel (Mrs Mathieu/Miss A Yorke won, 2-6, 6-4, 6-4), won 1939 with Mrs Mathieu; mixed r/u 1947 with C Caralulis (E Sturgess/Mrs S Summers won, 6-0, 6-0).

US women's singles r/u 1937 (Miss A Lizana won, 6-4, 6-2); doubles r/u 1938 with Mrs Mathieu (Mrs S Fabyan/Miss A Marble won, 6-8, 6-4, 6-3).

Wimbledon singles r/u 1937 (Miss D Round won, 6-2, 2-6, 7-5).

JESSUP, Marion (*née* Zinderstein), USA

Four times women's doubles champion of America, Mrs Jessup won three of the titles in successive years (1918–20) with the same partner, Eleanor Goss and the fourth, in 1922, with Helen Wills.

US women's singles r/u 1919 (Mrs G Wightman won, 6-1, 6-2), r/u 1920 (Mrs M Mallory won, 6-3, 6-1); doubles won 1918 (beat Miss M Bjurstedt/Mrs J Rogge, 7-5, 8-6), won 1919–20, all with Miss Goss, won 1922 with Miss Wills (beat Mrs Mallory/Miss Sigourney, 6-4, 7-9, 6-3), r/u 1924 with Miss Goss (Mrs Wightman/Miss Wills won, 6-4, 6-3); mixed doubles won 1919 with V Richards (beat W Tilden/Miss F Ballin).

Wightman Cup 1924, 1926.

JOHNSON, Wallace Ford, USA

Born July 1899, Merion, Pennsylvania. The foremost artist of the chop or underspin during the early 1900s, Johnson was, nevertheless, unable to beat W T 'Big Bill' Tilden when he decided to play Johnson at his own game. He was destined to be runner-up to Tilden when they met in the US finals. Johnson won the US mixed doubles four times between 1907 and 1920.

US men's singles r/u 1912 (M McLoughlin won, 3-6, 2-6, 6-2, 6-4, 6-2), r/u 1921 (Tilden won, 6-1, 6-3, 6-1); mixed doubles won 1907 with Miss M Sayers, won 1909, won 1911 (beat H M Tilden/Miss E Wildey, 6-4, 6-4), both with Miss H V Hotchkiss, won 1920 with Mrs G Wightman. Davis Cup 1913.

JOHNSTON, William M (Little Bill), USA

Born November 1894, San Francisco, died May 1946. Thin and frail-looking, Johnston, who stood 5 ft 8½ in (1.7 m), was nicknamed 'Little Bill' and is best remembered for his rivalry with the tall 'Big Bill' Tilden, and for the lion-heartedness of his play against opponents who were physically far stronger. With Tilden he shared America's Davis Cup triumph from 1920 to 1927, regaining the trophy from Australia in 1920 and personally winning all but three of 21 rubbers in the eight years. 'Little Bill's' interest in tennis began when he used to watch players at the Golden Gate Park in San Francisco. He took up the game at the age of 12 and later recalled that he adopted the Western grip, in which the racket face is turned down to meet the rising ball, from playing so often on cement surfaces which made the ball rise sharply. When America entered World War I, he was already on his way up having won the national final in 1915, been beaten in a thrilling spectacular over five sets by Dick Williams in 1916 and won the doubles in 1915–16. He joined the Navy and came out at his peak in 1919. With 'Big Bill' Tilden now showing his potential, 'Little Bill' beat him in the clay court championships and in the national final of 1919, exploiting Tilden's weak backhand and making full use of his own service spin and fine forehand. Next year, however, Johnston found that Tilden had spent the winter working on his backhand and had so improved his game that he won the national title 6-1, 1-6, 7-5, 5-7, 6-3. It was the first of Tilden's seven US titles and of five defeats Johnston was to suffer at his hands in the finals. In 1922 Tilden had to recover from two sets down to win but in 1923 and 1924 he won in three sets.

Johnston's only Wimbledon title came in 1923 when the American challenge included Frank Hunter and 20-year-old Vince Richards but lacked Tilden. 'Little Bill' played seven matches and lost only one set on the way to the title. In the Wimbledon final of that year he dropped just four games to Hunter.

US men's singles won 1915 (beat M McLoughlin, 1-6, 6-0, 7-5, 10-8), r/u 1916 (R Williams won, 4-6, 6-4, 0-6, 6-2, 6-4), won 1919 (beat Tilden, 6-4, 6-4, 6-3), r/u 1920 (Tilden won, 6-1, 1-6, 7-5, 5-7, 6-3), r/u 1922 (Tilden won, 4-6, 3-6, 6-2, 6-3, 6-4), r/u 1923 (Tilden won, 6-4, 6-1, 6-4), r/u 1924 (Tilden won, 6-1, 9-7, 6-2), r/u 1925 (Tilden won, 4-6, 11-9, 6-3, 4-6, 6-3); doubles won 1915 (beat McLoughlin/T Bundy, 6-2, 3-6, 4-6, 6-3, 6-3), won 1916 (beat McLoughlin/W Dawson, 6-4, 6-3, 5-7, 6-3), won 1920 (beat W Davis/R Roberts, 6-2, 6-2, 6-3), all with C J Griffin, r/u 1927 with Williams (Tilden/Hunter won, 10-8, 6-3, 6-3); mixed doubles won 1921 with Miss M Browne.

Wimbledon singles won 1923 (beat Hunter, 6-0, 6-3, 6-1).

World hard court championships singles won 1923.

Kerry Melville – Australia

Rod Laver – Australia

Frew McMillan – South Africa

Buster Mottram – Great Britain

Ilie Năstase – Rumania

John Newcombe – Australia

JONES, Marion, USA

The first American woman to play at Wimbledon in 1900, Miss Jones reached the quarter-finals. She had already gained the United States women's title the previous year and did so again in 1902.

US women's singles r/u 1898 (Miss J Atkinson won, 6-3, 5-7, 6-4, 2-6, 7-5), won 1899 (Miss Atkinson, default), All-Comers r/u 1901 (Miss E Moore won, 4-6, 1-6, 9-7, 9-7, 6-3), won 1902 Challenge Round (beat Miss Moore, 6-1, 1-0 retired), r/u 1903 (Miss Moore won, 7-5, 8-6); doubles won 1902 with Miss J Atkinson; mixed doubles won 1901 with R D Little.

JONES, Mrs Adrienne (Ann), (née Haydon), GB

Born October 1938, Birmingham, England. Five times runner-up for a world table tennis championship and twice English table tennis doubles champion (1956, 1958), left-hander Ann Haydon was British junior tennis champion in 1954–5 and in 1956 won the Wimbledon junior invitation. She decided to concentrate on tennis after being disappointed at being only runner-up in three world table tennis championships in 1957. She achieved her fame as much by sheer tenacity and dogged determination as by her flashes of brilliance and exuberant power shots. In 1958, with Christine Truman and Shirley Bloomer, she shocked the American Wightman Cup opposition by helping to pull off a surprise 4-3 victory, which was repeated in 1960. She established a British record by winning 16 of her 32 Wightman Cup rubbers in 12 ties.

Between 1958 and 1968 she reached the semi-finals at Wimbledon seven times and in 1967 was runner-up to Billie Jean King. Married in 1962 to P F 'Pip' Jones, then president of Warwickshire LTA, Ann had won the French singles in 1961 and 1966, the Italian in 1966 and was runner-up for the US title in 1961 and 1967. But she had to wait until 1969 to gain her Wimbledon triumph. After losing a 22-game first set to Margaret Court in the semi-finals, she won the next two comfortably. In the final against Billie Jean King she again lost the first set but then dropped her usual defensive style to disconcert the triple champion and win the next two 6-3, 6-2, helped considerably by the vociferous support of the crowd. She went on to take the mixed doubles title with Fred Stolle. After signing professional forms with the National Tennis League in 1968, she had successes on the Virginia Slims circuit but played reduced

Above: Left-handed Ann Jones (née Haydon) was a table tennis champion as well as a tennis champion.

circuits in 1971 and 1972, virtually retiring in 1973, though she played doubles in the winning Wightman Cup team of 1975.

Wimbledon singles r/u 1967 (Mrs King won, 6-3, 6-4), won 1969 (beat Mrs King, 3-6, 6-3, 6-2); doubles r/u 1968 with Miss F Durr (Miss R Casals/Mrs King won, 3-6, 6-4, 7-5); mixed doubles r/u 1962 with R Ralston (N Fraser/Mrs W duPont won, 2-6, 6-3, 13-11), won 1969 with Stolle (beat A Roche/Miss J Tegart, 6-3, 6-2). Wightman Cup team 1957–70, 1975; captain 1971–2.

Federation Cup team 1963–7, 1971.

French singles won 1961 (beat Miss Y Ramirez, 6-2, 6-1), r/u 1963 (Miss L Turner won, 2-6, 6-3, 7-5), won 1966 (beat Miss N Richey, 6-3, 6-1), r/u 1968 (Miss Richey won, 5-7, 6-4, 6-1), r/u 1969 (Mrs Court won, 6-1, 4-6, 6-3); doubles r/u 1960 with Mrs R Hales (Miss M Bueno/Miss D Hard won, 6-2, 7-5), won 1963 with Miss R Schuurman (Miss Bueno/Miss Hard scratched), won 1968 (beat Mrs King/Miss Casals, 7-5, 4-6, 6-4), won 1969 (beat Mrs Court/Miss Richey, 6-0, 4-6, 7-5), both with Miss Durr; mixed doubles r/u 1960 with R Emerson (R Howe/Miss Bueno won, 1-6, 6-1, 6-2), r/u 1966 with C Graebner (F McMillan/Miss A Van Zyl won, 1-6, 6-3, 6-2), r/u 1967 with I Tiriac (O Davidson/Mrs King won, 6-3, 6-1).

US singles r/u 1961 (Miss Hard won, 6-3, 6-4), r/u 1967 (Mrs King won, 11-9, 6-4); women's doubles r/u with Miss D Catt (Miss Bueno/Miss Hard won, 6-1, 6-1).

Italian singles r/u 1960, won 1966; doubles won 1969.

South American Open won 1968.

World Professional Championships, Caesar's Palace, won 1971.

KANDERAL, Peter, Switzerland
Born January 1948, Zurich. National champion of Switzerland in 1972–3 and r/u in 1974, he was ranked No 1 in 1973–4 and again in 1976. Swiss GP won 1972–3, 1975, r/u 1976; Swiss National Indoor singles won 1974. Davis Cup 1973– , King's Cup 1973– .

KEMINER, Miss K *see* **Shaw, Kristien**

Kent Grass Court Championships, GB
Founded in 1886 at Beckenham, the first Kent championships were played on grass courts marked out on the outfield of the town's cricket club. For many years they have attracted the world's leading players and in 1905 the great Australian Norman Brookes made his British debut there and won the men's singles to become the first overseas winner of the event, beating A W Gore and going on to win the Wimbledon All-Comers'.

Lt Col Algernon Kingscote won a record six men's titles (1914, 1919–22, 1924); Dorothea Lambert Chambers won seven women's titles, four as Miss Douglass (1901–2, 1904, 1906) and three as Mrs Chambers (1910–11, 1913) and the Californian Miss Elizabeth Ryan also claimed seven (1919–21, 1923–5, 1928) though the 1920 title was shared with Mrs R McNair when the final was rained off. In 1926 two foreign ladies met for the first time in a British final outside Wimbledon, Mrs M Mallory, from Norway but playing for the US, losing to Señorita Lili de Alvarez of Spain, 4-6, 2-6 in the women's final.

Two 17-year-olds, Anna Dmitrieva and Andrei Potanin, played in the 1958 junior and senior events and three weeks later were the first Russians to compete at Wimbledon, playing in the girls' and boys' junior invitation events. Twelve years later Alex Metreveli and Olga Morozova became the first Russians to win the men's and women's singles respectively at the same British tournament. Metreveli won again in 1973 and Morozova in 1976.

Margaret Court and John Newcombe have achieved notable successes for Australia, Mrs Court taking the women's title five times (1961, 1963–5, 1968), though in 1964 she shared with Miss M Bueno, and Newcombe winning the men's title in three successive years (1964–6). The championships have been variously sponsored in recent years by Rothmans', West and Nally, Green Shield and Robertson's.

KING, Billie Jean (*née* **Moffitt**), USA
Born November 1943, Long Beach, California. One of the most remarkable women players of all time, not only in terms of her devastating form but also of her influence on the political side of the women's game, Billie Jean has been loved and hated by the crowds and players alike. The hate stems from her brute-force aggression, her often sharp tongue and her sheer ruthless dedication; the love grows from admiration for the complete 'professional' who can overcome disappointment, injury and defeat to come out on top, playing superb, sometimes breathtaking tennis.

Daughter of a Californian fireman, who played baseball, basketball and was a track runner, and a mother who was a good swimmer, Billie Jean preferred baseball and football as a youngster, until she was bought an $8 tennis racket. Then she went to parks professional Clyde Walker who, though impressed by her tendency to rush to the net, insisted she first learned the ground strokes. She became dedicated to improving her game and took up early morning training and practise. At age 14 in 1958 she won the Southern California 14-and-under

girls' championships and Long Beach residents raised money to send her to the national girls championships at Middletown, Ohio, where she reached the quarter-finals. Playing on grass in 1959 she met Maria Bueno for the first time and was beaten by her. It was to be the first of many encounters. Next year she was runner-up to Karen Hantze in the national 18 and made her first visit, aged 17, to Wimbledon where, with 18-year-old Karen, she won the doubles. Later she admitted that she preferred playing at Wimbledon to playing at Forest Hills and she has gained more titles at the British home of tennis than anywhere else.

Billie Jean reached her first Wimbledon singles final in 1963 but was beaten by Margaret Smith. The following year she met her future husband, law student Larry King, himself a tennis enthusiast, who encouraged her to go to Australia that winter for the experience and rigorous conditioning it offered. She returned with a new determination and confidence which made her attack every ball as if it was an adversary and which sent her bounding about the

court. She could clearly be heard lecturing herself on court to do better and be seen grimacing fiercely. Even though she lost again in 1965 to Margaret Smith, this time at Forest Hills, she had the look of greatness and in 1966 she gained her first Wimbledon singles final, beating Miss Bueno. Next year came her second Wimbledon crown and her first US singles title. Each was gained by beating Ann Haydon Jones. She made a clean sweep at Forest Hills, also taking the doubles and mixed doubles title and the Wimbledon singles win was also accompanied by the 'Triple Crown' when she won the doubles with Rosemary Casals and the mixed doubles with Owen Davidson. Billie Jean's third Wimbledon win in 1968, was the first time for 15 years that the title had been won in three consecutive years (Maureen Connolly, 1952–4). That year she signed professional forms with the National Tennis League and began a new, lucrative career on the developing 'pro' circuit.

The years since have seen her become increasingly vociferous in advocating better terms for women professionals and parity with men in

Above: Billie Jean King has made her influence felt both on the courts and in the tennis political arena where she has fought for the equality of women in the field of tennis.

prize money; at the same time she has continued to gather in titles in record numbers, has survived a serious knee operation and returned to the top. She has won over 50 championships and in 1971 became the first woman to win more than $100,000 in a year. In 1977, to put the seal on her come-back after the operation, Billie Jean won her two Wightman Cup singles, beating Britain's Sue Barker 6-1, 6-4 and, in what has been described as an all-time classic, defeating Wimbledon champion Virginia Wade 6-4, 3-6, 8-6 over two-and-a-half hours in a 7-0 American whitewash. She then beat Miss Wade again twice; in the singles final of the new Bremar Cup at Crystal Palace, London, and in the doubles, where she was partnered by Miss Tomanova.

US women's singles r/u 1965 (Mrs M Court won, 8-6, 7-5), won 1967 (beat Mrs A Jones, 11-9, 6-4), r/u 1968 (Miss V Wade won, 6-4, 6-2), won 1971 (beat Miss R Casals, 6-4, 7-6), won 1972 (beat Miss K Melville, 6-3, 7-5), won 1974 (beat Miss E Goolagong, 3-6, 6-3, 7-5); doubles r/u 1962 (Miss Bueno/Miss D Hard won, 4-6, 6-3, 6-2), won 1964 (beat Miss M Smith/Miss L Turner, 3-6, 6-2, 6-4), r/u 1965 (Mrs C Graebner/Miss N Richey won, 6-4, 6-4), all with Mrs J Susman, r/u 1966 (Miss Bueno/Miss Richey won, 6-3, 6-4), won 1967 (beat Miss M Eisel/Mrs D Fales, 4-6, 6-3, 6-4), r/u 1968 (Miss Bueno/Mrs Court won, 4-6, 9-7, 8-6), r/u 1973 (Mrs Court/Miss Wade won, 3-6, 6-3, 7-5), won 1974 (beat Miss F Durr/Miss B Stöve, 7-6, 6-7, 6-4), r/u 1975 (Mrs Court/Miss Wade won, 7-5, 2-6, 7-6), all with Miss Casals; mixed doubles won 1967 (beat S Smith/Miss Casals), won 1971 (beat R Maud/Miss B Stöve, 6-3, 7-5), won 1973 (beat M Riessen/Mrs Court, 6-4, 3-6, 7-5), all with O Davidson, r/u 1975 with F Stolle (R Stockton/Miss Casals won, 6-3, 6-7, 6-3), won 1976 with P Dent (beat F McMillan/Miss Stöve, 3-6, 6-2, 7-5), r/u 1977 with V Gerulaitis (McMillan/Miss Stöve won, 6-2, 3-6, 6-3).

Australian singles won 1968 (beat Mrs Court, 6-1, 6-2), r/u 1969 (Mrs Court won, 6-4, 6-1); doubles r/u 1965 with Miss Ebbern (Miss Smith/Miss Turner won, 1-6, 6-2, 6-3), r/u 1969 with Miss Casals (Mrs Court/Miss J Tegart won, 6-4, 6-4); mixed doubles won 1968 with R Crealy (beat A Stone/Mrs Court, wo).

French singles won 1972 (beat Miss E Goolagong, 6-3, 6-3); doubles won 1972 with Miss Stöve (beat Miss W Shaw/Miss F E Truman, 6-1, 6-2); mixed doubles won 1967 with Davidson (beat I Tiriac/Mrs Jones, 6-3, 6-1), r/u 1968 (J C Barclay/Miss Durr won, 6-1, 6-4), won 1970 with R Hewitt (beat Barclay/Miss Durr, 3-6, 6-3, 6-2).

Wimbledon singles r/u 1963 (Miss Smith won, 6-3, 6-4), won 1966 (beat Miss Bueno, 6-3, 3-6, 6-1), won 1967 (beat Mrs Jones, 6-3, 6-4), won 1968 (beat Miss Tegart, 9-7, 7-5), r/u 1969 (Mrs Jones won, 3-6, 6-3, 6-2), r/u 1970 (Mrs Court won, 14-12, 11-9), won 1972 (beat Miss Goolagong, 6-3, 6-3), won 1973 (beat Miss Evert, 6-0, 7-5), won 1975 (beat Mrs E Cawley, 6-0, 6-1); doubles won 1961 with Miss K Hantze (beat Miss J Lehane/Miss Smith, 6-3, 6-4), won 1962 (beat Mrs L Price/Miss R Schuurman, 5-7, 6-3, 7-5), r/u 1964 (Miss Smith/Miss Turner won, 7-5, 6-2), both with Mrs Susman, won 1965 with Miss Bueno (beat Miss Durr/Miss J Lieffrig, 6-2, 7-5), won 1967 (beat Miss Bueno/Miss Richey, 9-11, 6-4, 6-2), won 1968 (beat Miss Durr/Mrs Jones, 3-6, 6-4, 7-5), won 1970 (beat Miss Durr/Miss Wade, 6-2, 6-3), won 1971 (beat Mrs Court/Miss Goolagong, 6-3, 6-2), all with Miss Casals, won 1972 with Miss Stöve (beat Mrs D Dalton/Miss Durr, 6-2, 4-6, 6-3), won 1973 with Miss Casals (beat Miss Durr/Miss Stöve, 6-1, 4-6, 7-5), r/u 1976 with Miss Stöve (Miss Evert/Miss N Navratilova won, 6-1, 3-6, 7-5); mixed doubles r/u 1966 with Ralston (K Fletcher/Miss Smith won, 4-6, 6-3, 6-3), won 1967 with Davidson (beat Fletcher/Miss Bueno, 7-5, 6-2), won 1971 (beat Riessen/Mrs Court, 3-6, 6-2, 15-13), won 1973 (beat R Ramirez/Miss S Newberry, 6-3, 6-2), won 1974 (beat M Farrell/Miss L Charles, 6-3, 9-7).

Bremar Cup won 1977 (beat Miss Wade, 6-3, 6-1); doubles won with Miss Tomanova (Miss Wade/Miss Stöve, 6-2, 6-3).

Italian singles won 1970; doubles won 1970 with Miss Casals.

German singles won 1971; doubles won 1971 with Miss Casals.

South African singles won 1966-7, 1969; doubles won 1967, 1970, both with Miss Casals; mixed doubles won 1967 with Davidson.

US Indoor won 1966-8, 1971. US hard courts won 1966. US clay courts won 1971.

Argentine singles won 1967.

Irish Open singles won 1963, 1969.

Austrian singles won 1971.

Led New York sets to WTT championships 1976.

Colgate Inaugural singles r/u 1977 (beat Miss Evert, 6-2, 6-2); doubles r/u 1976 with Miss Stöve.

Commercial Union GP won 1971-2.

Gunze Tokyo won 1977 (beat Miss Navratilova, 7-5, 5-7, 6-1).

US Wightman Cup team 1961-7, 1970, 1977, including longest set in competition, 17-19, against Christine Truman, Cleveland, 1963.

Federation Cup 1963-7, 1976-7.

Defeated Bobby Riggs (Wimbledon men's champion, 1939), 6-4, 6-3, 6-3, in Houston, 1973, in most publicised match ever.

KING, Mrs M R see Mudford, Phyllis Evelyn

KINGSCOTE, Algernon R F, GB

Born December 1888, India, died December 1964. After being Wimbledon All-Comers r/u in 1919 (G Patterson won, 6-2, 6-1, 6-3), Kingscote surprisingly took 'Big Bill' Tilden to five sets before losing in the fourth round of the 1920

Left: American Ann Kiyomura is one of the USA's best women's doubles players.

championship. In 1919 he was Australian men's singles champion (beat E Pockley, 6-4, 6-0, 6-3) and in 1920 with J C Parkes was Wimbledon All-Comers' doubles r/u (C Garland/R Williams won, 4-6, 6-4, 7-5, 6-2). Davis Cup team 1919–1920, 1922, 1924.

King's Cup

Donated in 1936 by HM King Gustav V of Sweden for international competition by men's teams, the King's Cup was intended to be the indoor equivalent of the Davis Cup, though it has never attracted as much international support. The tournament was originally played on the Davis Cup basis, with the holder meeting the winner of the All-Comers' rounds in a Challenge Round. The competition, under the control of the European Tennis Association, was altered after World War II so that all countries competed from the beginning, except the host country for the finals, which was automatically drawn to play at home. From January 1976 the format was changed to a league basis. From the first competition in 1936 and until the 1976 change, Sweden won seven times, Denmark six, Great Britain four, France three, Italy twice and Czechoslovakia, Germany, Hungary, Spain and Yugoslavia once each. The original trophy was won by Germany in 1938 and could not be found after the war; a new trophy was donated when the competition re-started in 1952.

KINSEY, Howard, USA

Born December 1899, St Louis, Missouri, died 1966. Winner of the US doubles in 1924, partnered by his brother Robert, Kinsey was the only non-Frenchman in the 1926 semi-finals at Wimbledon. He was faced by three of the 'Four Musketeers' of France – Cochet, Brugnon and Borotra. In the semi-finals he unexpectedly beat Brugnon, 6-4, 4-6, 6-3, 3-6, 9-7, but lost to Borotra in the final in three sets. Later in the year he signed professional forms with Charles C Pyle, who also signed Vincent Richards and Suzanne Lenglen, among others, for a successful professional tour of America. In 1927, with Richards, he helped found and lead the US Professional Lawn Tennis Association.

US doubles won 1924 with Robert Kinsey (beat G Patterson/P O'Hara Wood, 7-5, 5-7, 7-9, 6-3, 6-4); mixed doubles r/u 1922 with Miss H Wills (W Tilden/Mrs M Mallory won, 6-4, 6-3).

Wimbledon singles r/u 1926 (J Borotra won, 8-6, 6-1, 6-3); doubles r/u 1926 with Richards (J Brugnon/H Cochet won, 7-5, 4-6, 6-3, 6-2); mixed doubles r/u 1926 with Miss M Browne (L Godfree/Mrs Godfree won 6-3, 6-4).

French doubles won 1926 with Richards (beat Cochet/Brugnon, 6-4, 6-1, 4-6, 6-4).

KIYOMURA, Ann, USA

Born August 1955, San Mateo, California. Of Japanese-American extraction, Miss Kyomura won 14 US national junior championships and in 1975, aged 19, when unseeded, won the Wimbledon doubles with Kazuko Sawamutsu (Japan), beating Françoise Durr and Betty Stöve. She has continued to show good form, particularly in Virginia Slims circuit doubles events.

US national under-18 champion 1972; Virginia Slims Detroit doubles won 1976; V S Dallas doubles won 1976; V S Boston doubles won 1976; Bridgestone doubles won 1976, all with Miss R Guerrant; V S Philadelphia won 1976; V S Sarasota r/u 1976.

Wimbledon junior invitation won 1973 (beat Miss M Navratilova); women's doubles won 1975 with Miss Sawamutsu (beat Miss Durr/Miss Stöve, 7-5, 1-6, 7-5).

KLOSS, Ilana, South Africa

Born March 1956, Johannesburg. A left-hander, Miss Kloss first showed international promise when she won the US Open junior singles in 1974, also winning the South African Open doubles that year and being runner-up in 1976 with Linda Boshoff. Her doubles record with Miss Boshoff has been excellent and includes the US Open 1976 (beat Miss O Morozova/Miss V Wade, 6-1, 6-4), Austin Futures 1976, Pensacola Futures 1976, US Family Circle 1976, US clay court 1976 (beat Miss L Dupont/Miss W Turnbull, 6-2, 6-3), and 1977 (beat Miss M Carillo/Miss W Overton, 5-7, 7-5, 6-3), and the Italian 1976.

KNIGHT, William Arthur (Billy), GB

Born November 1935, Northampton. A leading British player of the 1950s and early 1960s, Billy Knight was a redoubtable left-hander who was at his best on hard courts rather than grass. In 1960 he was ranked among the top ten hard court players in the world. He was the only British player ever to win the Australian junior championship singles (1954) and was triple British junior champion in both 1952 and 1953. He won the Canadian championships in 1958, when he also took the first of his three British hard court singles and mixed doubles titles. A

rugged competitor who was a stalwart of the British Davis Cup team from 1955 to 1964, winning 27 of 43 rubbers, his best progress at Wimbledon was in 1959. As top-seeded pair he and Yola Ramirez reached the quarter-finals of the mixed doubles.

British hard court championship singles won 1958, 1963–4; doubles won 1960; mixed won 1958–60. British covered court championship singles won 1960; mixed won 1955, 1960.

French mixed won 1959 with Miss Ramirez (beat R Laver/Miss R Schuurman, 6-4, 6-4).

Canadian singles won 1958.

German singles won 1959; mixed won 1959.

KNODE, Mrs Dorothy (*née* Head), USA

Born July 1925, Richmond, California. Though she never gained a major title in any of the 'Big Four' tennis countries, Mrs Knode had a long and successful career in both singles and doubles and was first in the US 'top ten' women's list in 1943. She won the singles and doubles of Germany in 1950, 1952, the singles of Austria (1950), India, US clay courts (1951), Switzerland (1952), Egypt, Holland, Yugoslavia, Germany (1953), US clay court singles and doubles (1955), doubles (1956). She was also r/u in the French singles in 1955 and 1957 and of the doubles in 1956 with Miss D Hard, and r/u of the Italian singles in 1957. Wightman Cup team 1955–8, 1960. She retired in 1960 after winning the US clay court singles again.

KOCH, Thomas, Brazil

Born May 1945, Porto Alegre. Rated the best 18-year-old in the world in 1963, when he reached the quarter-finals of the US championships, Koch came within a game of taking Brazil into the 1966 Davis Cup Challenge Round. Leading R Krishnan of India by two sets to one and 5-2 in the fourth set, he lost the match.

US indoor championship doubles won 1968 with T Okker (beat R Lutz/S Smith, 6-3, 10-12, 8-6); singles r/u 1970.

French Open mixed doubles won 1975 with Miss F Bonicelli (beat J Fillol/Miss P Teeguarden, 6-4, 7-6).

Wimbledon Plate won 1969.

Nuremberg ATP singles r/u 1976, Khartoum ATP r/u 1976.

KODEŠ, Jan, Czechoslovakia

Born March 1946, Prague. Originally a player used to hard courts, Kodeš once declared that play on grass courts was 'a joke'. Even so, he reached the final of the 1971 US Open – on grass – as an unseeded player, having already won the 1970 and 1971 French titles. He lost the US final to Stan Smith and was again runner-up in 1973, when he took John Newcombe to five sets. In 1973 he was originally seeded 15 at Wimbledon but when 79 members of the ATP (which he had not then joined) withdrew in dispute with the ILTF, he was re-seeded No 2. In a struggling, rain-interrupted semi-final he beat Britain's Roger Taylor, 8-9, 9-7, 5-7, 6-4, 7-5 and in the final beat the Russian Alex Metreveli after another tie breaker in the second set.

French singles won 1970 (beat Z Franulović, 6-2, 6-4, 6-0), won 1971 (beat I Năstase, 8-6, 6-2, 2-6, 7-5); doubles r/u 1977 with W Fibak (B Gottfried/R Ramirez won, 7-6, 4-6, 6-3, 6-4).

US singles r/u 1971 (Smith won, 3-6, 6-3,

6-2, 7-6), r/u 1973 (Newcombe won, 6-1, 1-6, 4-6, 6-2, 6-3).

Wimbledon singles won 1973 (beat Metreveli, 6-1, 9-8, 6-3).

Italian singles r/u 1970 (Năstase won), r/u 1971 (R Laver won), r/u 1972 (M Orantes won).

German doubles won 1972 with Năstase; singles r/u 1975.

Basle ATP Open won 1976.

Kitzbuhel ATP r/u 1976; doubles won 1976 with J Hrebeč.

Madrid CUGP won 1975.

Czech Davis Cup team 1966– .

Kooyong, Australia

One of the sites for the Australian national championships and major international tournaments, the Kooyong stadium is on the outskirts of Melbourne. The horse shoe-shaped stadium which encloses three courts, is part of a 17-acre (6.8 hectare) tennis complex of some 40 courts surrounded by gardens and walkways. Designed by the architectural firm of Bates, Smart and McCutcheon in 1932, the stadium is dug out of a former Aboriginal hunting ground. Spectators enter at ground level and look down on the Centre Court. During the height of Australian tennis enthusiasm in the mid-1950s, the stadium's capacity was increased to take nearly 13,000 spectators. The grass surfaced courts are fast and virtually flawless and are kept green by the Meeri Creek river for most of the season, which ends in April. Other Australian tennis stadiums are White City, Sydney; the Memorial, Adelaide; the Milton Courts, Brisbane; and King's Park, Perth.

KÖRMÖCZY, Zsuzsi, Hungary

Born August 1924, Budapest. A popular player at Wimbledon, Mrs Körmöczy first visited England as a 14-year-old schoolgirl and beat many of the country's best players in a series of tournaments. Persistent to the last, it was 22 years before she won her only major title – the 1958 French singles, beating Shirley Bloomer in the final. After losing the title to Christine Truman in 1959 she suffered an ankle injury which eventually curtailed her career in 1960, though she won the Italian title in that year.

French singles won 1958 (beat Miss Bloomer, 6-4, 1-6, 6-2), r/u 1959 (Miss Truman won, 6-4, 7-5). Italian singles won 1960 (beat Miss A Haydon, 6-4, 4-6, 6-1).

KRAHWINKEL, Hilda see Sperling, Mrs H

KRAMER, John Albert (Jack), USA

Born August 1921, Las Vegas, Nevada. No single person has had a greater influence on the development of the modern game of tennis than Jack Kramer, as a player, a professional, a promoter and a writer and broadcaster. He has been one of the outstanding players of the immediate post-war years and the best exponent of the 'big serve, big volley' game which is so popular today. A man with an essentially warm personality, he became a ferocious killer on court and, later, a cool, calculating businessman in promotion deals. In play he had a strong service, an excellent volley and a devastatingly accurate forehand.

As a youngster, Jack, who was to become known as 'The King' and 'Big Jake', wanted to be a top baseball player and spent his spare time playing baseball, basketball and football. After a series of football batterings he was persuaded to take up tennis, of which he at first disapproved. Finding he had a natural aptitude, he was enrolled in the Los Angeles Tennis Club at 13 and came under the lasting influence of Perry Jones, the club's director and patron of several great players. In 1936, at 15, he won the national junior title and in 1939 was selected for the Davis Cup team against Australia. With Ted Schroeder he won the national doubles in the next two years and also gained the mixed doubles with Sarah Palfrey Cooke in 1941.

His career was well on its way when it was interrupted by the first of a series of illnesses and misfortunes. On the eve of the 1942 nationals he had to withdraw with appendicitis and then, after another good year, was struck down with ptomaine poisoning just before the 1943 nationals. Next came service in the US Coast Guards during World War II, from which he emerged short of tennis training. He might well have won the 1946 Wimbledon men's final against Drobný but for a blistered hand – which

Below: Evonne Cawley (née Goolagong) defeats Chris Evert in the 1973–74 Australian Open at Kooyong stadium on the outskirts of Melbourne.

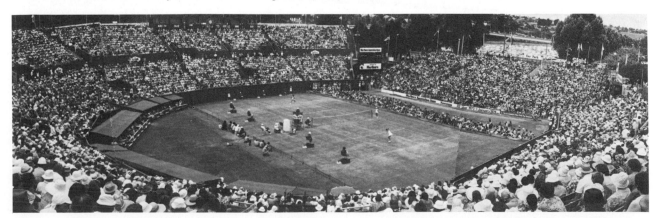

Right: American Jack Kramer was a player, a professional, a promoter, a writer and a broadcaster – one of tennis' all-rounders.

he refused to use as an excuse. That December he won the US title and with Schroeder helped recapture the Davis Cup from Australia. In 1947 he beat Tom Brown in the Wimbledon final in just 45 minutes and went on to gain his second US title. At the end of the year he turned professional and beat the great Bobby Riggs 69–20 in a cross-country tour.

In 1952 he took up promotion and persuaded such players as Sedgman, Ken McGregor, Tony Trabert, Pancho Gonzales, Ken Rosewall, Lew Hoad, Ashley Cooper and Mal Anderson to sign lucrative contracts. He gave up promoting in 1960 and turned increasingly to writing and broadcasting on tennis.

US men's singles r/u 1943 (J Hunt won, 6-3, 6-8, 10-8, 6-0), won 1946 (beat T Brown, 9-7, 6-3, 6-0), won 1947 (beat F Parker, 4-6, 2-6, 6-1, 6-0, 6-3); doubles won 1940 (beat G Mulloy/H Prussoff), won 1941 (beat W Sabin/Mulloy), both with Schroeder; won 1943 with Parker (beat W Talbert/D Freeman), won 1947 with Schroeder (beat Talbert/O Sidwell, 6-4, 7-5, 6-3); mixed doubles won 1941 with Mrs S Cooke. US Davis Cup team 1939, 1946–7.

Wimbledon singles won 1947 (beat T Brown, 6-1, 6-3, 6-2); doubles won 1946 with T Brown (beat G Brown/D Pails, 6-4, 6-4, 6-2), won 1947 with R Falkenburg (beat A Mottram/Sidwell, 8-6, 6-3, 6-3).

KRANTZCKE, Karen, Australia

Born February 1947, Sydney, died April 1977. The promising career of this lanky 6 ft 1 in (1.85 m) Australian was interrupted by a wrist operation which kept her out of the game from mid-1975 until late in 1976. It ended with her sudden death at the tragically early age of 30. Since winning the Australian junior title in 1966 Miss Krantzcke had been prominent on the international circuit, gaining a particularly good doubles record. With Kerry Melville she won the Australian doubles in 1968 and was r/u in 1970 and 1972, won the West German doubles in 1970 and was r/u in the 1970 South African doubles. In 1974 with Helen Gourlay she was r/u at Wimbledon, losing to Evonne Goolagong and Peggy Michel.

Australian doubles won 1968 (beat Miss L Turner/Miss J Tegart, 6-4, 3-6, 6-2), r/u 1970 (Mrs J Dalton/Mrs M Court won, 6-3, 6-1), r/u 1972 (Miss K Harris/Miss Gourlay won, 6-0, 6-4) all with Miss Melville. Australian hard court singles r/u 1969 (Miss Melville won, 6-3, 8-10, 6-1).

Wimbledon doubles r/u 1974 with Miss Gourlay (Miss Goolagong/Miss Michel won, 2-6, 6-4, 6-3). Women's Plate won 1972.

South Africa doubles r/u 1970.

West German doubles won 1970, both with Miss Melville.

Dutch singles r/u 1969.

New Zealand singles r/u 1969.

West Berlin singles won 1969.

KRISHNAN, Ramanathan, India

Born April 1937, Madras. Consistently India's top player for over 15 years, Krishnan was a superb touch player with a masterly half-volley. In his thirteenth year of Davis Cup play in 1966 he took India into the Challenge Round but they lost to Australia. Though he won no 'Big Four' titles, he was the first Indian to reach the Wimbledon semi-finals in 1960 and he did so again in 1961.

KROSHINA, Marina, USSR

Born 1953, Alma Ata. A promising new Russian player on the international scene, Marina Kroshina was runner-up in the Wimbledon junior invitation event in 1970 and 1974 and won it in 1971. In 1972 she was in the Soviet team which won the Annie Soisbault Cup, beating Britain, and that year won the European amateur championships and was r/u in the Moscow International. She won the US Women's indoor doubles with Olga Morozova and they were the first Russian players to take a national title in the US.

KUHNKE, Christian, Germany

Born April 1939. Son of a banker, Kuhnke, a left-hander, is a lawyer who dropped out of tennis from 1966 to 1969 to complete his studies after making his mark in the West German Davis Cup team. On his return he played the longest ever Davis Cup doubles match with Bungert – 95 games – to beat Cox and Curtis of Britain at Birmingham. In 1970 his losing Davis Cup singles match against Ashe went to a record 86 games in Cleveland.

KUYKENDALL, Kathy, USA

Born November 1956, Houston. At the age of 16 she became the world's youngest tennis professional and on the Virginia Slims circuit in 1973 had wins over Françoise Durr, Karen Krantzcke, Lesley Hunt and Kerry Harris and also showed well against Rosie Casals. In 1974 she played World Team Tennis with Philadelphia Freedoms and Baltimore Banners and in 1975 was with the Hawaii Leis. She reached the finals of the Virginia Slims but was beaten by Martina Navratilova.

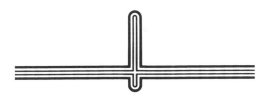

LACOSTE, Jean René, France

Born July 1905, Paris. The youngest of the famous 'Four Musketeers' of France, Lacoste first played tennis at the age of 15 when staying in England. His father, a wealthy businessman, gave him five years in which to make the tennis grade or join him in the automobile business. He was not as brilliant a player as his fellow Musketeers – Borotra, Brugnon and Cochet – and had an awkward-looking way of holding his racket in the middle of the handle. Not physically robust, he was frequently troubled by poor health, yet his persistence and his habit of noting down the styles (and weaknesses) of contemporary players turned him into a great ground-stroke player and astute tactician. He kept every one of the notebooks containing his jottings and refused to part with them. From 1924 to 1929 one or other of the four Frenchmen won the singles title at Wimbledon, Lacoste taking it in 1925, from Borotra, and 1928, from Cochet. He won the doubles that year with Borotra and was singles and doubles champion of France for the first time. He took the French singles again in 1927 and 1929 and the doubles also in 1929.

Lacoste first played in the Davis Cup in 1923, when the Musketeers made their cup debut together. Up to his last Davis Cup appearance in 1928 he played in 51 rubbers and won the crucial rubbers in the 1927 Challenge Round against America, beating 'Big Bill' Tilden and 'Little Bill' Johnston and bringing the cup to France for the first time. In 1926 and 1927 he took the US singles title, beating Borotra in the first final and Tilden, the favourite, in the second. In fact, Tilden always regarded Lacoste as his most formidable opponent and was beaten by him on at least six occasions.

Lacoste retired from tennis in 1929 because of ill health. His book, *Lacoste on Tennis*, which is largely compiled from his notebooks, is regarded as one of the best works on tennis.

French men's singles r/u 1924 (closed championship, Borotra won), won 1925 (beat Borotra, 7-5, 6-1, 6-4), r/u 1926 (Cochet won, 6-2, 6-4, 6-3), won 1927 (beat Tilden, 6-4, 4-6, 5-7, 6-3, 11-9), r/u 1928 (Cochet won, 5-7, 6-3, 6-1, 6-3), won 1929 (beat Borotra, 6-3, 2-6, 6-0, 2-6, 8-6); doubles r/u 1923, won 1924 (both closed championships), won 1925 (beat Cochet/Brugnon, 7-5, 4-6, 6-3, 2-6, 6-3), r/u 1927 (Cochet/Brugnon won, 2-6, 6-2, 6-0, 1-6, 6-4), won 1929 (beat Cochet/Brugnon, 6-3, 3-6, 6-3, 3-6, 8-6), all with Borotra. Davis Cup 1923–8.

US singles won 1926 (beat Borotra, 6-4, 6-0, 6-4), won 1927 (beat Tilden, 11-9, 6-3, 11-9); mixed doubles r/u 1926 (Borotra/Miss E Ryan won, 6-4, 7-5), r/u 1927 (Cochet/Miss E Bennett won, 2-6, 6-0, 6-2), both with Mrs G W Wightman.

Wimbledon singles r/u 1924 (Borotra won, 6-1, 3-6, 6-1, 3-6, 6-4), won 1925 (beat Borotra, 6-3, 6-3, 4-6, 8-6), won 1928 (beat Cochet, 6-1, 4-6, 6-4, 6-2); doubles won 1925 with Borotra (beat R Casey/J Hennessey, 6-4, 11-9, 4-6, 1-6, 6-3).

LAMBERT CHAMBERS, Mrs D *see* **Chambers, Dorothea Katherine Lambert**

LAKERNAN, Mrs T A *see* **Fry, Joan**

LANCE, Sylvia (Mrs S Harper), Australia
Born October 1895. One of the early pioneers of women's tennis, Miss Lance won the Australian doubles and mixed doubles in 1923 and the singles and doubles in 1924. She was runner-up for the singles in 1927 and 1930 and for the doubles in 1927, 1929–30.

LANDRY, Mrs Nelly (*née* Adamson), Belgium/France
Born December 1916, Tilbury, England. The daughter of Belgian parents, but French by marriage, Mrs Landry became the best woman player in France in the late 1940s, winning the French title in 1948 by beating Britain's Shirley Fry. She also won the French covered court singles and doubles in 1948. A left-hander, she never achieved great success in the remaining 'Big Four' tennis countries but won the singles, doubles and mixed doubles of Egypt and of the Scandinavian covered court championships also in 1948. She became a professional in 1956.

French women's singles r/u 1938 (Mrs R Mathieu won, 6-0, 6-3), won 1948 (beat Miss Fry, 6-2, 0-6, 6-0), r/u 1949 (Mrs W duPont won, 7-5, 6-2); doubles r/u 1938 with Mrs A Halff (Mrs Mathieu/Miss A Yorke won, 6-3, 6-3).

LANGRISHE, Mary Isabella (May), Ireland
The world's first women's singles champion, May Langrishe won the Irish ladies' singles title in 1879, when the Irish championships of Dublin's Fitzwilliam Club included the first women's singles and mixed doubles events ever held. Miss Langrishe won again in 1883 and 1886.

LARCOMBE, Mrs Ethel (*née* Thomson), GB
Born June 1879, Islington, London, died August 1965. Runner-up in the non-championship women's All-Comers' final of 1903, when Miss Dorothea Douglass (later Mrs Lambert Chambers) won, Mrs Larcombe had to wait nine years before she won her Wimbledon title with a walk-over from Mrs Chambers in 1912. She was again runner-up in 1914, when she won the mixed doubles with J C Parke and was r/u in the doubles with Mrs G Hannam. She won the non-championship doubles in 1904–5 and non-championship mixed in 1903–4 and 1912. A good all-round athlete, she was five times All-England badminton singles champion, four times doubles champion and twice mixed champion. Her other tennis titles included the Irish singles and mixed doubles (1912), the Scottish singles and doubles (1910–12) and mixed 1910 and 1912. Mrs Larcombe became a professional in 1922. Her husband, Major Dudley Larcombe, was secretary of the All England Club from 1925 to 1939.

Wimbledon singles won 1912 (wo), r/u 1914 (Mrs Lambert Chambers won, 7-5, 6-4); All-Comers non-championship singles r/u 1903 (Miss Douglass won, 4-6, 6-4, 6-2); doubles r/u 1914 (Miss A M Morton/Miss E Ryan won, 6-1, 6-3); mixed doubles r/u 1913 (H Crisp/Mrs C O Tuckey won, 3-6, 5-3 retired), won 1914 (beat A F Wilding/Miss M Broquedis, 4-6, 6-4, 6-2), both with Parke; non-championship mixed doubles won 1903 (beat C Hobart/Miss J Bromfield, 6-2, 6-3), won 1904 (beat W Eaves/Mrs R Winch, 7-5, 12-10), both with S H Smith, won 1912 with Parke (beat A Prebble/Miss D Boothby, 6-4, 6-2).

LARNED, William A, USA
Born December 1872, died December 1926. One of the great early champions of America, Bill Larned was a colourful character who rode with Teddy Roosevelt's 'Rough Riders' in the Spanish–American War. A graduate of Cornell University, he was tough, stocky and broad-shouldered and loved nothing more than a fast, attacking game in which his shooting backhand could be used with devastating accuracy close to the lines. He took his first US championship at the age of 28 in 1901, successfully defended it the following year against Britain's Reggie 'Big Do' Doherty but lost it next year to his brother Laurie, 'Little Do'. He did not regain it until 1907 but then won five times in a row, the last occasion in 1911. He was then aged 38 and remains the oldest US men's title winner.

US singles r/u 1892 All-Comers' (F H Hovey won, 6-0, 6-2, 7-5), r/u 1894 All-Comers' (M Goodbody won, 4-6, 6-1, 3-6, 7-5, 6-2), r/u All-

Comers' 1895 (Hovey won, 6-1, 9-7, 6-4), r/u 1900 Challenge Round (won M D Whitman, 6-4, 1-6, 6-2, 6-2), won 1901 (wo), won 1902 (beat R Doherty, 4-6, 6-2, 6-4, 8-6), r/u 1903 (L Doherty won, 6-0, 6-3, 10-8), won 1907 (wo), won 1908 (beat B C Wright, 6-1, 6-2, 8-6), won 1909 (beat W J Clothier, 6-1, 6-2, 5-7, 1-6, 6-1), won 1910 (beat T C Bundy, 6-1, 5-7, 6-0, 6-8, 6-4), won 1911 (beat M McLoughlin, 6-4, 6-4, 6-2); doubles r/u 1907 with Clothier (H Hackett/ F B Alexander won, 6-3, 6-1, 6-4). Davis Cup 1902-3, 1905, 1908-9, 1911.

LARSEN, Arthur D (Art), USA

Born April 1925. A left-hander who developed into a fine touch-player, Larsen won the US singles title in 1950, beating Herbie Flam. In 1954 he was r/u to Tony Trabert in the French singles and in his two Davis Cup years, 1951-2, he won all four of his rubbers. His career was ended when he sustained severe head injuries in a motorcycling accident in 1957.

US singles won 1950 (beat H Flam, 6-3, 4-6, 5-7, 6-4, 6-3).

French singles r/u 1954 (A Trabert won, 6-4, 7-5, 6-1).

LAVER, Rodney George, Australia

Born August 1938, Rockhampton, Queensland. An unlikely-looking champion for any sport, small-framed, comparatively short and slightly bandy-legged, the red-haired Rod Laver was certainly the greatest player of his time and will probably rank among the greatest ever. His father, cattle rancher Roy, was a tennis enthusiast and had hopes for his two older sons, Trevor and Bob, as top tournament winners. However, Charlie Hollis, a coach in Rockhampton, had faith in the puny youngster with the sunken chest and began training him and building him up. Even so, when Rod first met Australia's Davis Cup captain Harry Hopman, he was dubbed with the sarcastic nickname 'Rocket'. It was, however, a name he was to live up to with pride when, after many disappointments and years of intensive training and exercising, he became the fast, relentless left-handed attacker who could out-smart or out-manoeuvre most rivals.

Laver began playing at the age of ten on a rough clay court at home and did not tread a grass court until he was 13, after winning the under-14 state championship at Brisbane. Introduced to Hopman when he was 16, Laver impressed him with some scorching sample services. In 1956 Hopman accompanied Rod Laver and Bob Mark on a world tour which took in Wimbledon, Europe and Canada, where Laver won the junior title before going on to gain the US junior.

In 1957 he was picked by Hopman for the Davis Cup squad but did not play and in 1958 he was in the team which lost the Cup to America. Then, in 1959, he began to attract serious attention, playing in Challenge Round matches of both the singles and doubles at Forest Hills

after playing a phenomenal 800 games in five days. Not surprisingly he lost both but his performance had been enough to impress, particularly in a marathon semi-final in which he beat Barry MacKay 11-13, 11-9, 10-8, 7-9, 6-3 – 87 games. He had been runner-up earlier in the year at Wimbledon and was relegated to the same position in 1960 by fellow-Australian Neale Fraser, though in both years he won the mixed doubles with Darlene Hard. He was r/u in the US nationals in 1960, again to Fraser, but had beaten him in the Australian championships earlier in the year.

Laver was now on his way to greatness, armed with a spinning service, slicing drives from forehand and backhand, a powerful wrist and a delivery so accurate and high-kicking that it could devastate his opponents. He was a relentless attacker who moved in close to the net to return service balls as they rose. His first Wimbledon singles title came in 1961 when he beat Chuck McKinley but, playing with an injured wrist, he lost the Australian title. Then, in 1962 came the first of his two Grand Slams, duplicating the record of Don Budge. He took the Wimbledon title by beating Martin Mulligan, and the Australian, French and American, beating Roy Emerson in each. In addition he won the Italian and German titles to set a new record. Early in 1963 he turned professional, signing a contract with the International Professional Tennis Association for $100,000 over three years. Though his early career on the circuit was not particularly successful, he regained his champion's form in 1966 and began winning the major professional events and in 1969 came the fulfilment of his ambition – the second Grand Slam – which firmly established him as the world's No 1. In 1970 he was awarded the MBE and joined WCT. In 1971 his career winnings topped $1-million and his successes have continued, though in 1975 he underwent two knee operations and lost a $100,000 challenge match against Jim Connors in Las Vegas.

Australia singles won 1960 (beat N Fraser, 5-7, 3-6, 6-3, 8-6, 8-6), r/u 1961 (R Emerson won, 1-6, 6-3, 7-5, 6-4), won 1962 (beat Emerson, 8-6, 0-6, 6-4, 6-4), won 1969 (beat A Gimeno, 6-3, 6-4, 7-5); doubles won 1959 (beat D Candy/ R Howe, 9-7, 6-4, 6-2), won 1960 (beat Emerson/ Fraser, 1-6, 6-2, 6-4, 6-4), won 1961 (beat Emerson/M Mulligan, 6-3, 7-5, 3-6, 9-11, 6-2), all with R Mark, won 1969 with Emerson (beat K Rosewall/F Stolle, 6-4, 6-4); mixed doubles r/u 1959 with Miss R Schuurman (Mark/Miss S Reynolds won, 4-6, 13-11, 6-2). Australian indoors won 1973; doubles won 1976 with R D Ralston, 1973. Australian Davis Cup team 1959-62.

French singles won 1962 (beat Emerson, 3-6, 2-6, 6-3, 9-7, 6-2), r/u 1968 (Rosewall won, 6-3, 6-1, 2-6, 6-2), won 1969 (beat Rosewall, 6-4, 6-3, 6-4); doubles won 1961 (beat Howe/Mark, 3-6, 6-1, 6-1, 6-4), r/u 1968 (Rosewall/Stolle won, 6-3, 6-4, 6-3), r/u 1969 (J Newcombe/A Roche

won, 4-6, 6-1, 3-6, 6-4, 6-4) all with Emerson; mixed doubles r/u 1959 with Miss Schuurman. (W Knight/Miss Y Ramirez won, 6-4, 6-4), won 1961 with Miss D Hard (beat J Javorsky/Miss V Pužejová, 6-0, 2-6, 6-3).

US singles r/u 1960 (Fraser won, 6-4, 6-4, 10-8), r/u 1961 (Emerson won, 7-5, 6-3, 6-2), won 1962 (beat Emerson, 6-2, 6-4, 5-7, 6-4), won 1969 (beat Roche, 7-9, 6-1, 6-3, 6-2); doubles r/u 1960 with Mark (Emerson/Fraser won, 9-7, 6-2, 6-4), r/u 1970 with Emerson (P Barthès/N Pilić won, 6-3, 7-6, 4-6, 7-6), r/u 1973 with Rosewall (O Davidson/Newcombe won, 7-5, 2-6, 7-5, 7-5). US professional indoors won 1974.

Wimbledon singles r/u 1959 (A Olmedo won, 6-4, 6-3, 6-4), r/u 1960 (Fraser won, 6-4, 3-6, 9-7, 7-5), won 1961 (beat C McKinley, 6-3, 6-1, 6-4), won 1962 (beat Mulligan, 6-2, 6-2, 6-1), won 1968 (beat Roche, 6-3, 6-4, 6-2), won 1969 (beat Newcombe, 6-4, 5-7, 6-4, 6-4); doubles r/u 1959 with Mark (Emerson/Fraser won, 8-6, 6-3, 14-16, 9-7), won 1971 with Emerson (beat A Ashe/Ralston, 4-6, 9-7, 6-8, 6-4, 6-4); mixed doubles won 1959 (beat Fraser/Miss M Bueno, 6-4, 6-3), won 1960 (beat Howe/Miss Bueno, 13-11, 3-6, 8-6), both with Miss Hard.

Italian singles won 1962, 1971; doubles won 1962 with J Fraser.

London professional championships, Wembley, won 1964–7; Wimbledon professional

singles won 1967; Wembley professional championships won 1968. WCT record winning 4 straight tournaments, 23 matches, 1975. World invitation singles r/u 1975; mixed doubles won with Miss H Gourlay; doubles won 1976 with Ashe.

LAWFORD, Herbert F, GB

Born May 1851, London, died April 1925. Remembered for the famous 'Lawford stroke' which many tried to copy – a strong, sweeping forehand drive with top spin – Herbert Lawford was four times runner-up for the Wimbledon singles title before he gained it in 1887, aged 36, when he had a walk-over from the reigning champion, Willie Renshaw. The other Renshaw, Ernest, took the title from him the following year. In one match in the 1880 championship Lawford and E Lubbock had a rally of 81 strokes.

Wimbledon singles r/u 1880 (J Hartley won, 6-3, 6-2, 2-6, 6-3), r/u 1884 (W Renshaw won, 6-0, 6-4, 9-7), r/u 1885 (W Renshaw won, 7-5, 6-2, 4-6, 7-5), r/u 1886 (W Renshaw won, 6-0, 5-7, 6-3, 6-4), won 1887 (wo), r/u 1888 (E Renshaw won, 6-3, 7-5, 6-0); doubles won 1879 with L R Erskine (beat F Durant/G Tabor). (The doubles were held at Oxford until 1884.)

Lawn Tennis Associations

The world's first governing body for lawn tennis was the Marylebone Cricket Club of London, which, when tennis came in vogue in the late 1800s, already controlled rackets and real tennis. The MCC issued the first official rules for lawn tennis in 1875. Control then passed to the All England Croquet and Lawn Tennis Club, which drew up rules for the first Wimbledon championships of 1877. In 1881 the United States formed the first national association, the United States National Lawn Tennis Association, now the USLTA. It was not until 1888 that Britain, the 'home' of lawn tennis, formed a Lawn Tennis Association which took over the administration of the game. Since then LTAs have spread with the game throughout the world, the majority being affiliated to the world controlling body, the ILTF, as associate or full members.

Leamington Lawn Tennis Club, GB

The Leamington LTC in Warwickshire, England, is believed to have been the first club ever to be formed exclusively for tennis. It was founded in 1872 – five years before the first championships at Wimbledon – with Major Harry Gem, who had marked out a lawn tennis court with Mr J B Perera at the latter's home in Birmingham in 1858, as its president. The Leamington club no longer exists but its place in the history of the game was marked by the unveiling of a plaque on the site of Major Gem's home to celebrate the centenary of its founding in 1972.

LEHANE, Jan (Mrs C O'Neill), Australia

Born July 1941. A strong and determined baseline player with a double-fisted left-hand shot, Miss Lehane was four times runner-up to Margaret Smith Court for the Australian women's singles and once for the Wimbledon doubles. Her only international titles were the Australian mixed doubles of 1960–1. In the 1959–60 season she scored three victories over Christine Truman.

Australian singles r/u 1960 (Miss M Smith won, 7-5, 6-2), r/u 1961 (Miss Smith won, 6-1, 6-4), r/u 1962 (Miss Smith won, 6-0, 6-2), r/u

Above left: Herbert Lawford was best remembered for the 'Lawford stroke', a strong sweeping forehand drive with top spin. He is seen here in 1887.
Above: Leamington Lawn Tennis Club celebrated its centenary in 1972 by having a game played in the 'olde' fashioned way.

Above: Suzanne Lenglen of France was virtually unbeatable from 1919 to 1926.

1963 (Miss Smith won, 6-2, 6-2); doubles r/u 1961 with Mrs M Hawton (Mrs M Reitano/Miss Smith won, 6-4, 3-6, 7-5), r/u 1963 with Miss L Turner (Miss R Ebbern/Miss Smith won, 6-1, 6-3); mixed doubles won 1960 with T Fancutt (beat R Mark/Mrs Reitano, 6-2, 7-5), won 1961 with R Hewitt (beat J Pearce/Mrs Reitano, 9-7, 6-2), r/u 1964 with M Sangster (K N Fletcher/Miss Smith won, 6-3, 6-2).

Wimbledon doubles r/u 1961 with Miss Smith (Miss K Hantze/Miss B J Moffitt won, 6-3, 6-4).

LENGLEN, Suzanne, France

Born May 1899, Paris, died 1938. One of the legendary figures of tennis, Miss Lenglen was virtually invincible and from 1919 to 1926, when she turned professional, she only failed to win one single match when she was forced by illness to retire from the 1921 US championships. She won the French singles title three times, the Wimbledon six, the French doubles six times and the Wimbledon five, the French mixed doubles seven times and the Wimbledon three times.

Never robust and inclined to asthma attacks, Suzanne practised for hours as a girl, coaxed and lectured by her doting parents, who accompanied her everywhere and drove her continually to greater efforts. At the age of 15 she won the world hard court championships in Paris and a long series of successes in French tournaments established her as the great French player of the time. Armed with this reputation she travelled to Wimbledon for the first time in 1919 and, after first shocking the crowd by appearing in a low-cut, one-piece dress which reached to her mid-calves, shocked them further by beating the great Mrs Lambert Chambers. In fact Mrs Chambers had been 1-4 down in the decisive third set, pulled back to 6-5 and 40-15 with two match points and then saw Suzanne return two lucky shots and go on to win the set and match. She won her first French singles in 1920 and retained Wimbledon. In 1921, having won Wimbledon for a third time, she beat the American champion, Mrs Molla Mallory in the French hard court championships and pressure grew for her to go to America.

Against her father's advice but backed by her mother, Suzanne accepted the idea of a challenge match against Mrs Mallory in aid of war-torn French villages. Once in America she was also persuaded to enter the championships. On the way over, however, she had suffered a bad attack of asthma and when she appeared in the second round (her first round opponent having defaulted) she was far from fit. Suzanne found her opponent was none other than Mrs Mallory, who, backed by an obviously pro-Mallory crowd, won the first set 6-2. In the second, the French girl lost her first service point and double faulted in the second. In tears, she left the court saying she was too ill to continue and then scratched from the charity match a few days later. The American press accused her of being a 'quitter' and she returned to France disenchanted and depressed.

Even so, in France and in England she was the darling of the tennis public, drawing packed crowds wherever she appeared. Supple, cat-like and graceful, she was phenomenally accurate in her placing of the ball and determinedly methodical in her attack on every opponent. She was also temperamental and highly strung and could engage in bitter rows with officials.

In 1922 Suzanne again faced Mrs Mallory, this time in the Wimbledon final, and with their rivalry boosted by press stories of personal animosity (which was denied) Suzanne beat the American comfortably, 6-2, 6-0 and confirmed her superiority later with a 6-0, 6-0 win against Mrs Mallory in Nice. Her fifth Wimbledon title came in 1923 but in 1924 an attack of jaundice kept her out of the French championship and made her Wimbledon appearance seem doubtful. In fact, she played one round but then withdrew. The following year came her fifth French and sixth Wimbledon titles, while across the Atlantic Helen Wills was being hailed as the new great. Miss Wills challenged Suzanne to a match which was eventually held before a capacity crowd of some 3000 at the Carlton Club, Cannes. With the loud support of her home crowd, the French prima donna won 6-3, 8-6 and in 1926 won her next French title, Miss Wills having to withdraw from the championship with appendicitis.

At Wimbledon 1926 was Jubilee Year, with royalty and past and present champions in attendance. Suzanne beat the American Mary Browne in her first round match and then left without being escorted by an official, as had become customary with her, to the referee's office to check the time of the next day's match. Referee Frank Burrows then put her down to play a singles on the Centre Court, followed by a doubles. But the next day, with Queen Mary sitting in the Royal box, Miss Lenglen did not appear. On hearing that she had been drawn for the two matches, she had sent a message to Burrows asking to play only the doubles. Burrows, however, did not receive the message and when Miss Lenglen arrived to play her doubles match officials were in uproar and she could, according to the rules, have been disqualified from the singles. Upset and angry, the champion retreated to her dressing room and refused to play either match. The fuss was front page news and by the time Miss Lenglen and her partner

Didi Vlasto appeared for the doubles match next day, the crowd was hostile and there were mutterings of the Queen having been insulted. The French pair lost 3-6, 9-7, 6-2 to 'Bunny' Ryan and Mary Browne. The delayed singles against Evelyn Dewhurst was postponed until Friday because of the rain. When it was played, Suzanne won 6-2, 6-2 and on the Saturday took the court with Jean Borotra for her mixed doubles against H Aitken and Miss B Brown. Again the crowd, which usually cheered her, was anti-Lenglen and after the match, which the French pair won 6-3, 6-0, Suzanne scratched from the singles and mixed doubles and left Wimbledon for good. She had played 32 singles matches and won them all, played 66 sets and won 64, of which 29 were won 6-0.

Later in 1926 she signed professional forms with Charles C Pyle for a successful tour which brought her $75,000. Then she set up a tennis school in Paris but in 1938 at the age of 39 died of pernicious anemia.

French women's singles won 1920–3 (closed championships), won 1925 (beat Miss K McKane, 6-1, 6-2), won 1926 (beat Miss Browne, 6-1, 6-0); doubles won 1920–3 (closed), won 1925 (beat Miss McKane/Miss E Colyer, 6-1, 9-11, 6-2), won 1926 (beat Mrs L Godfree/ Miss Colyer, 6-1, 6-1), both with Miss Vlasto; mixed doubles won 1914, 1920–3 (closed), won 1925 (beat Cochet/Miss Vlasto, 6-2, 6-2), won 1926 (beat Borotra/Mrs Le Besnerais, 6-4, 6-3), both with Brugnon.

Wimbledon singles won 1919 (beat Mrs Lambert Chambers, 10-8, 4-6, 9-7), won 1920 (beat Mrs Chambers, 6-3, 6-0), won 1921 (beat Miss Ryan, 6-2, 6-0), won 1922 (beat Mrs Mallory, 6-2, 6-0), won 1923 (beat Miss McKane, 6-2, 6-2), won 1925 (beat Miss J Fry, 6-2, 6-0); doubles won 1919 (beat Mrs Chambers/Mrs D Larcombe, 4-6, 7-5, 6-3), won 1920 (beat Mrs Chambers/Mrs Larcombe, 6-4, 6-0), won 1921 (beat Mrs A Beamish/Mrs G Peacock, 6-1, 6-2), won 1922 (beat Miss McKane/Mrs A Stocks, 6-0, 6-4), won 1923 (beat Miss J Austin/ Miss Colyer, 6-3, 6-1), won 1925 (beat Mrs A Bridge/Mrs C McIlquham, 6-2, 6-2), all with Miss E Ryan; mixed doubles won 1920 with G Patterson (beat R Lycett/Miss Ryan, 7-5, 6-3), won 1922 with P O'Hara Wood(beat Lycett/ Miss Ryan, 6-4, 6-3), won 1925 with Borotra (beat H de Morpurgo/Miss Ryan, 6-3, 6-3).

World hard court championship singles won 1914, 1921–3; doubles won 1914, 1921–2; mixed doubles won 1921–3. Olympic gold medals (two) 1920.

LEWIS, Ernest Wool, GB
Born April 1867, Hammersmith, London, died April 1930. A noted volleyer, Lewis seemed to enjoy taking games to their full five sets and dragging them back to his favour. Though he gained the Wimbledon doubles title in 1892 with Harvey Barlow, he never achieved the singles title but was four times All-Comers

Right: David Lloyd and his brothers John Lloyd (far right) and Tony Lloyd (not pictured here) make a fairly strong team of tennis-playing Britons.

runner-up and won the Irish Open singles 1890–1, doubles 1889, 1892 and mixed doubles 1888.

Wimbledon singles r/u 1886 All-Comers (H Lawford won, 6-2, 6-3, 2-6, 4-6, 6-4), r/u 1888 All-Comers (E Renshaw won, 7-9, 6-1, 8-6, 6-4), r/u 1892 All-Comers (J Pim won, 2-6, 5-7, 9-7, 6-3, 6-2), r/u 1894 All-Comers (W Baddeley won, 6-0, 6-1, 6-0); doubles 1889 r/u Challenge Round (E Renshaw/W Renshaw won, 6-4, 6-4, 3-6, 0-6, 6-1), r/u 1890 All-Comers (Pim/F Stoker won, 6-0, 7-5, 6-4), both with G W Hill-yard, won 1892 Challenge Round (beat H Baddeley/W Baddeley, 4-6, 6-2, 8-6, 6-4), r/u 1893 (Pim/Stoker won, 4-6, 6-3, 6-1, 2-6, 6-0), both with H S Barlow, r/u 1895 with W V Eaves (H Baddeley/W Baddeley won, 8-6, 5-7, 6-4, 6-3).

LITTLE, Mrs D L *see* **Round, Dorothy**

LIZANA, Anita (Mrs R T Ellis), Chile
Born 1915, Santiago. The first world-class player to come from Latin America, Miss Lizana was a great favourite with Wimbledon crowds in the 1930s. She was famous for her superb drop shots. In 1937 she gained the US women's title from 'Jed' Jedrzejowska (6-4, 6-2), interrupting the reign of Alice Marble, who was ill that year.

LLOYD, David, GB
Born January 1948, Leigh-on-Sea, Essex. British junior champion in 1965 and runner-up in 1964 and 1966, Lloyd joined the British rankings at No 8 in 1969, when he was in the King's Cup team for the first time and beat Năstase on the Dewar Cup circuit. In 1972 he and his brother John were named for the British Davis Cup team – the first brothers to be named since the

Dohertys in 1906 – but did not play. In the 1973 Davis Cup he was paired with Roger Taylor in the doubles against Germany. He is married to Veronica, sister of Taylor's wife. Lloyd took up a coaching appointment in Toronto in 1975 but returned to Britain to pair with his brother in the 1976 Davis Cup against France and had a dramatic win over Adriano Panatta and Paulo Bertolucci in the match against Italy in the European zone finals. In a 74-game match the brothers won 6-8, 3-6, 6-3, 18-16, 6-2. Davis Cup team 1972– , King's Cup 1969– .

LLOYD, John, GB
Born August 1954, Leigh-on-Sea, Essex. The middle of the three tennis-playing Lloyd brothers (the third is Tony), John had his most successful season in 1977 in a career which has previously shown flashes of brilliance. He reached the final of the Benson and Hedges tournament, having beaten Mark Cox and Brian Gottfried on the way, but lost to Björn Borg in straight sets in the final. Lloyd who has had wins over Borg, Tanner, John Alexander and Smith, was taught to play at the age of eleven by his father. He has an aggressive attack, particularly with his back-hand cross-court return of service and at his best his forehand passing shot is hard to match. In previous years he has admitted to being so depressed by his patchy results that he con-sidered giving up tennis. A poor sleeper, he frequently stays out until after midnight before a match. He is currently Davis Cup and King's Cup No 2. He had a good start to 1978 with a brilliant run to the final of the Australian Open, in which he took two sets off Gerulaitis before losing 6-3, 7-6, 5-7, 3-6, 6-2.

British National Green Shield won 1970; British junior covered court r/u 1970–1, won 1972; BP Shield won 1970; British junior championship r/u 1972; New Zealand hard court won 1974; WCT Albert Hall r/u 1974; Dewar Cup doubles won 1976 with brother. Benson and Hedges r/u 1977 (Borg won, 6-4, 6-4, 6-2). Australian Open r/u 1977 (Gerulaitis won, 6-3, 7-6, 5-7, 3-6, 6-2). Davis Cup 1972– , King's Cup 1972– .

London Grass Court Championships, GB

First held in 1890 as a men's singles event only, the championships were staged at the Queen's Club, London, in the week before Wimbledon and have produced surprise results, chiefly because leading players are often not prepared to play at full stretch so close to Wimbledon. The Queen's Club event was sponsored by Rothmans' from 1970 until 1974, when they withdrew from major tennis sponsorship. Winners of the men's events included Dr Joshua Pim, Harold Mahony, Tony Wilding, Don Budge, Ted Schroeder, Frank Sedgman, Rod Laver, Roy Emerson and John Newcombe – all of whom went on to complete the 'double' by winning that year's Wimbledon singles – and M J G Ritchie, who, with Wilding and Emerson, won the singles four times.

In the women's events Charlotte Sterry won the singles a record five times and completed the 'double', as did Ethel Larcombe, Pauline Betz, Louise Brough, Ann Jones and Margaret Court. In 1973, the last year of the London championships, the singles winners were Ilie Năstase and Olga Morozova; the men's doubles was won by Tom Okker and Martin Riessen, and the women's by Billie Jean King and Rosie Casals.

London Professional Indoor Championships, GB

Held between 1951 and 1967 at the Empire Pool, Wembley, the London professional indoor championships enabled the world's leading professionals to compete in London in a tournament from which they could not be barred by the ILTF. Played on a fast wood surface the tournament did not at first attract much public support but in its final years was drawing near-capacity crowds of more than 8000 to see players such as Pancho Gonzales, Lew Hoad, Rod Laver, Ken Rosewall, Frank Sedgman, Pancho Segura and Tony Trabert. There was no tournament in 1954–5 but when it was revived in 1956 the event made history with a superb match between Gonzalez and Sedgman which lasted two hours 55 minutes, ending in a win for Pancho, 4-6, 11-9, 11-9, 9-7, after midnight. In part the crowd-pulling ability of the competition and the very high standard of play helped bring about the introduction of Open tennis in 1968 – which put an end to the London professional championships as such. However, in their place the Jack Kramer tournament of champions was held at Wembley in 1968, the W D & H O Wills championships in 1969 and the Embassy Trophy in 1970–1 which held purses of £20,000.

LONG, Mrs Thelma (*née* Coyne), Australia

Born May 1918, Sydney, NSW. One of Australia's finest and most consistent women players, Mrs Long's career stretched from 1935, when she won the Australian girl's singles championship, to 1959. She was a particularly fine doubles player and astute tactician. In 1952 she took a set off Maureen Connolly in the Wimbledon quarter-finals – one of only two singles sets 'Little Mo' ever lost at Wimbledon. Mrs Long was doubles champion of Australia eleven times and twice gained the singles title.

Australian singles r/u 1951 (Mrs N Bolton won, 6-1, 7-5), won 1952 (beat Miss H Angwin, 6-2, 6-3), won 1954 (beat Miss J Staley, 6-3, 6-4), r/u 1955 (Miss B Penrose won, 6-4, 6-3), r/u 1956 (Miss M Carter won, 3-6, 6-2, 9-7); doubles won 1936 (beat Miss M Blick/Miss K Woodward, 6-2, 6-4), won 1937 (beat Mrs H Hopman/Mrs V Westacott, 6-2, 6-2), won 1938 (beat Miss D M Bundy/Miss D Workman, 9-7, 6-4), won 1939 (beat Mrs Westacott/Miss M Hardcastle, 7-5, 6-4), won 1940, all with Miss N Wynne, won 1947 (beat Miss J Fitch/Miss M Bevis, 6-3, 6-3), won 1948 (beat Miss Bevis/Miss N Jones, 6-3, 6-3), won 1949 (beat Miss D Toomey/Miss M Toomey, 6-0, 6-1), r/u 1950 (Miss D Hart/Miss L Brough won, 6-2, 2-6, 6-3), won 1951 (beat Mrs M Hawton/Miss Fitch, 6-2, 6-1), won 1952 (beat Mrs R Baker/Mrs Hawton, 6-1, 6-1), all with Mrs Bolton, won 1956 (beat Miss Penrose/Miss Carter, 6-2, 5-7, 9-7), won 1958 (beat Miss A Mortimer/Miss L Coghlan, 7-5, 6-8, 6-2), both with Mrs Hawton; mixed doubles r/u 1948 with O Sidwell (C F Long/Mrs Bolton won, 7-5, 4-6, 8-6), won 1951 (beat J May/Miss C Proctor, 6-4, 3-6, 6-2), won 1952 (beat T Warhurst/Mrs A R Thiele, 9-7, 7-5), both with G Worthington, won 1954 with R N Hartwig (beat J Bromwich/Miss Penrose, 4-6, 6-1, 6-2), won 1955 with Worthington (beat L Hoad/Miss Staley, 6-2, 6-1).

French doubles r/u 1958 with Mrs Hawton (Miss Y Ramirez/Miss R M Reyes won, 6-4, 7-5); mixed doubles r/u 1951 with M Rose (F Sedgman/Miss Hart won, 7-5, 6-2), won 1956 with L Ayala (beat R Howe/Miss D Hard, 4-6, 6-4 ,6-1).

US mixed doubles r/u 1938 with Bromwich (D Budge/Mrs Fabyan won, 6-2, 8-10, 6-0), r/u 1952 with Hoad (Sedgman/Miss Hart won, 6-3, 7-5).

Wimbledon doubles r/u 1957 with Mrs Hawton (Miss A Gibson/Miss Hard won, 6-1, 6-2); mixed doubles r/u 1952 with A Morea (Sedgman/Miss Hart won, 4-6, 6-3, 6-4).

LOTT, George Martin, USA

Born October 1906, Springfield, Illinois. A bustling cheerful player, Lott gained fame from two doubles matches at Wimbledon in which, with different partners, he defeated three of the famous French 'Four Musketeers'. In 1931, with J Van Ryn, he beat Jacques Brugnon and Henri Cochet in a dramatic 64-game final and three years later, with L R Stoefen, beat Brugnon and Borotra in straight sets. Lott won US doubles five times. He became a professional in 1934.

US singles r/u 1931 (E Vines won, 7-9, 6-3, 9-7, 7-5); doubles won 1928 with J F Hennessey (beat G Patterson/J Hawkes, 6-2, 6-1, 6-2), won 1929 (beat B Bell/L White, 10-8, 16-14, 6-1), won 1930 (beat J Van Ryn/W Allison, 8-6, 6-3, 4-6, 13-15, 6-4), both with J H Doeg, won 1933 (beat F Shields/F Parker, 11-13, 9-7, 9-7, 6-3), won 1934 (beat Allison/Van Ryn, 6-4, 9-7, 3-6, 6-4), both with Stoefen; mixed doubles won 1929 (beat H W Austin/Mrs B Covell, 6-3, 6-3), won 1931 (beat Allison/Mrs L A Harper, 6-3, 6-3), both with Miss B Nuthall, r/u 1933 with Miss S Palfrey (Vines/Miss E Ryan won, 11-9, 6-1), won 1934 with Miss H Jacobs (beat Stoefen/Miss Ryan, 4-6, 13-11, 6-2). Davis Cup team 1928–31, 1933–4.

French doubles won 1931 with Van Ryn (beat J G Kirby/M Farquharson, 6-4, 6-3, 6-4).

Wimbledon doubles r/u 1930 with Doeg (Allison/Van Ryn won, 6-3, 6-3, 6-2), won 1931 with Van Ryn (beat Brugnon/Cochet, 6-2, 10-8, 9-11, 3-6, 6-3), won 1934 with Stoefen (beat Brugnon/Borotra, 6-2, 6-3, 6-4); mixed doubles won 1931 with Mrs L A Harper (beat L Collins/Miss J Ridley, 6-3, 1-6, 6-1).

LOVERA, Gail (*née* Sherriff, formerly Mrs Chanfreau), France

Born April 1945, Bondi, Australia. Eldest daughter of a well-known Australian veteran player and niece of Fred Sherriff (who once ordered Alvarez off court in the French championships), Gail and her sister Carol played each other in the second round at Wimbledon in 1966 – probably the first matching of sisters since that of Gillian and Maud Watson in 1884. She has been French national singles champion five times and four times French Open doubles champion, three times with Françoise Durr. In 1970, when she won the French nationals for the second time her then husband, Jean Baptiste Chanfreau, won the men's singles.

French national championship singles won 1969–74; French Open doubles won 1967 (beat Miss A Van Zyl/Miss P Walkden, 6-2, 6-2), won 1970 (beat Miss R Casals/Mrs L W King, 6-2, 1-6, 6-3), won 1971 (beat Miss H Gourlay/Miss K Harris, 6-4, 6-1), all with Miss Durr, r/u 1974 with Mrs K Ebbinghaus, won 1976 with Miss F Bonicelli (beat Miss K Harter/Mrs H Masthoff, 6-4, 1-6, 6-3).

US clay courts singles won 1969, r/u 1970, 1974; US Open doubles r/u 1971 with Miss Durr (Miss Casals/Mrs R Dalton won, 6-3, 6-3).

Wimbledon Plate r/u 1967 (Miss P Hogan won, 6-2, 9-7); British hard court mixed doubles won 1972 with F McMillan.

Italian doubles r/u 1972 with Miss Vido.

West German doubles won 1967 with Miss Durr.

Swiss Open singles r/u 1976.

LUTZ, Robert Charles, USA

Born August 1947, Lancaster, Pennsylvania. With Stan Smith, Lutz formed the only men's doubles partnership to win US titles on four different surfaces and also the only American pair to win three Davis Cup Challenge Round doubles. Lutz has also achieved an excellent singles record since becoming US national 18 champion in 1965. In eight Davis Cup wins out of eight played, seven were in doubles. He joined WCT in 1970.

US national singles r/u 1969; US amateur r/u 1968, US professional championship singles won 1972; US professional indoors r/u 1973; US Open doubles won 1968 (beat A Ashe/A Gimeno, 11-9, 6-1, 7-5); US national doubles won 1968; US indoors won 1966, 1969; US clay court doubles won 1968; US hard court doubles won 1966, all with Smith; US hard court doubles won 1969 with E Van Dillen.

Australian Open men's doubles won 1970 (beat J Alexander/P Dent, 8-6, 6-3, 6-4), Australian amateur doubles won 1970.

WCT doubles finals r/u 1976 (W Fibak/K Meiler won, 6-3, 2-6, 3-6, 6-3, 6-4), WCT Indianapolis 1976 doubles won; WCT Rome 1976 doubles r/u, both with Smith; WCT Rotterdam singles r/u 1976, Pacific SW doubles won 1976 with Smith.

LYCETT, Randolph, GB

Born August 1886, Birmingham, died 1935. Lycett learned to play tennis in Australia but in 1911 declined to play for the Australian Davis Cup team. In the Wimbledon quarter-finals of 1921 he created a stir by bringing on to court a bottle of champagne which he used for refreshment. Towards the end of the match against the Japanese Zenzo Shimidzu, Lycett was seen to be reeling and staggering and eventually lost, though managing to stay upright for five sets. In 1922 he took part in all three Wimbledon finals and was runner-up to Gerald Patterson in the singles, winner of the doubles with James Anderson and r/u with Elizabeth Ryan in the mixed doubles. He won the doubles in three successive years with different partners: in 1921 with Max Woosnam and 1923 with Leslie Godfree.

Wimbledon singles r/u 1922 (Patterson won, 6-3, 6-4, 6-2); doubles r/u 1919 with R Heath (P O'Hara Wood/R Thomas won, 6-4, 6-2, 4-6, 6-2), won 1921 with Woosnam (beat A Lowe/F Lowe, 6-3, 6-0, 7-5), won 1922 with Anderson (beat O'Hara Wood/Patterson, 3-6, 7-9, 6-4, 6-3, 11-9), won 1923 with Godfree (beat E Flaquer/Count de Gomar, 6-3, 6-4, 3-6, 6-3); mixed doubles won 1919 (beat A Prebble/Mrs Lambert Chambers, 6-0, 6-0), r/u 1920 (Patterson/Miss S Lenglen won, 7-5, 6-3), won 1921 (beat Woosnam/Miss P Howkins, 6-3, 6-1), r/u 1922 (O'Hara Wood/Miss Lenglen won, 6-4, 6-3), won 1923 (beat L Deane/Mrs D Sheppard-Barron, 6-4, 7-5), all with Miss Ryan. British Davis Cup team 1921, 1923.

Australian men's doubles won 1905 with T Tatchell (beat E Barnett/B Spence), won 1911 with R W Heath (beat N Brookes/J Addison).

McATEER, Myrtle, USA
Winner of the 1900 US women's singles and twice winner of the doubles.

US singles won 1900 (beat Miss M Jones, default), r/u 1901 (Miss E Moore won, 6-4, 3-6, 7-5, 2-6, 6-2); doubles won 1899 with Miss J Craven, r/u 1900 with Miss M Weimer (Miss E Parker/Miss H Champlin won, 9-7, 6-2, 6-2), won 1901 with Miss J P Atkinson.

McGRATH, Vivian B, Australia
Born February 1916, NSW. The first of the noted double-fisted players, McGrath spearheaded Australia's new Davis Cup team of 1933 with Jack Crawford which unsuccessfully attempted for five years to gain the Cup which Australasia had last held in 1919. In 1932, aged 17, he had defeated the great American, Wilmer Allison, in Sydney. He won the Australian singles title in 1937, defeating John Bromwich in a hard-fought five set match.

Australian singles won 1937 (beat J Bromwich, 6-3, 1-6, 6-0, 2-6, 6-1); doubles won 1935 (beat F Perry/G Hughes, 6-4, 8-6, 6-2), r/u 1936 (A Quist/D Turnbull won, 6-8, 6-2, 6-1, 3-6, 6-2), both with Crawford. Australian Davis Cup 1933-7.

French doubles r/u 1933 with Quist (Hughes/Perry won, 6-2, 6-4, 2-6, 7-5), r/u 1934 with Crawford (J Borotra/J Brugnon won, 11-9, 6-3, 2-6, 4-6, 9-7), r/u 1935 with Turnbull (Crawford/Quist won, 6-1, 6-4, 6-2).

McGREGOR, Kenneth Bruce, Australia
Born June 1929, Adelaide. A big-game player of the 1950s and Wimbledon runner-up to Dick Savitt in 1951, McGregor gained the doubles 'Grand Slam' in 1951 with Frank Sedgman. In 1950 at Wimbledon the pair beat Gardnar Mulloy and Bill Talbert in a 64-game third round match and then took part in a record-breaking quarter-final against 'Budge' Patty and Tony Trabert. In a rain-interrupted match they were beaten by the Americans 6-4, 31-29, 7-9, 6-2. The total of 94 games for the match and the 60-game second set both set records. McGregor beat Sedgman to become Australian singles champion in 1952. In 1950 he and Sedgman helped Australia win the Davis Cup 4-1 from the US and were in the winning teams of 1951-2. McGregor, who was also known as a good Australian-rules footballer, became a tennis professional in 1953.

Australian singles r/u 1950 (Sedgman won, 6-3, 6-4, 4-6, 6-1), r/u 1951 (Savitt won, 6-3, 2-6, 6-3, 6-1), won 1952 (beat Sedgman, 7-5, 12-10, 2-6, 6-2); doubles won 1951 (beat J Bromwich/A Quist, 11-9, 2-6, 6-3, 4-6, 6-3), won 1952 (beat M Rose/D Candy, 6-4, 7-5, 6-3), both with Sedgman. Australian Davis Cup team 1950-2.

French doubles won 1951 (beat Mulloy/Savitt, 6-2, 2-6, 9-7, 7-5), won 1952 (beat Mulloy/Savitt, 6-3, 6-4, 6-4), both with Sedgman.

US doubles won 1951 (beat Candy/Rose, 10-6, 6-4, 4-6, 7-5), r/u 1952 (Rose/E Seixas won, 3-6, 10-8, 10-8, 6-8, 8-6), both with Sedgman; mixed doubles won 1950 with Mrs W duPont (beat Sedgman/Miss D Hart, 6-4, 3-6, 6-3).

Wimbledon singles r/u 1951 (Savitt won, 6-4, 6-4, 6-4); doubles won 1951 (beat J Drobný/E Sturgess, 3-6, 6-2, 6-3, 3-6, 6-3), won 1952 (beat Seixas/Sturgess, 6-3, 7-5, 6-4).

Left: Australia's Ken McGregor not only was an excellent tennis player but also a good Australian-rules footballer.

McKINLEY, Charles Robert (Chuck), USA

Born January 1941, St Louis, Missouri. A short, bouncing, leaping player with incredible speed of movement, McKinley credited a season spent in Australia for toughening him and giving him the experience and confidence to win the 1963 Wimbledon title. He led the Davis Cup team of 1963 which brought back the trophy from Australia and he also headed the winning 1964 squad. He gave up tennis for a stock exchange career in Wall Street in 1966, having three times won the US doubles.

US doubles won 1961 (beat R Osuna/A Palafox, 6-3, 6-4, 3-6, 13-11), r/u 1962 (Osuna/Palafox won, 6-4, 10-12, 1-6, 9-7, 6-3), won 1963 (beat Osuna/Palafox, 9-7, 4-6, 5-7, 6-3, 11-9), won 1964 (beat M Sangster/G Stilwell, 6-3, 6-2, 6-4), all with R D Ralston. US Davis Cup team 1960–5.

Wimbledon singles r/u 1961 (R Laver won, 6-3, 6-1, 6-4), won 1963 (beat F Stolle, 9-7, 6-1, 6-4).

McLOUGHLIN, Maurice Evans, USA

Born January 1890, Carson City, Nevada, died 1957. Known as the 'Californian Comet', McLoughlin was the first player of international standard to use the 'cannonball service', the speed of which devastated many of his opponents. A redhead, he was constantly on the move, attacking every ball, moving fast and playing everything at full power. In 1914, playing in the Davis Cup against Australian Norman Brookes in ·the newly-opened Forest Hills stadium, McLoughlin won a 50-game match 17-15, 6-3, 6-3. When he had travelled to Wimbledon the year before, his reputation had preceded him and his first round match against Roper Barrett drew such crowds that the gates had to be closed. The match went to the American 8-6 in the final set and the 'Comet' then blasted his way to the Challenge Round. There, with the Centre Court packed, hundreds turned away and ticket touts asking £10.00 for a seat, he met Tony Wilding, the reigning champion. The New Zealander's wiles proved more powerful than McLoughlin's attack and he retained the title chiefly by advancing to meet the cannonball service and by playing on the American's weak backhand. McLoughlin won the US title twice; first in 1912 after the Challenge Round had been abolished and again in 1913. He also took the doubles title three times with T C Bundy.

US singles r/u 1909 All-Comers (beat W Clothier, 7-5, 6-4, 9-11, 6-3), r/u 1911 Challenge Round (W Larned won, 6-4, 6-4, 6-2), won 1912 (beat W F Johnson, 3-6, 2-6, 6-2, 6-4, 6-2), won 1913 (beat R Williams, 6-4, 5-7, 6-3, 6-1), r/u 1914 (Williams won, 6-3, 8-6, 10-8), r/u 1915 (W M Johnston won, 1-6, 6-0, 7-5, 10-8); doubles r/u 1909 with G J James (H Hackett/F B Alexander won, 6-4, 6-1, 6-0), won 1912 (beat R Little/G Touchard, 3-6, 6-2, 6-1, 7-5), won 1913 (beat J Strachan/C Griffin, 6-4, 7-5, 6-1), won 1914 (beat G Church/D Mathey, 6-4, 6-2, 6-4), r/u 1915 (Johnston/Griffin won, 6-2, 3-6, 4-6, 6-3, 6-3), all with T C Bundy, r/u 1916 with W Dawson (Johnston/Griffin won, 6-4, 6-3, 5-7, 6-3). US Davis Cup team 1909, 1911, 1913–14.

Wimbledon men's singles r/u 1913 (Wilding won, 8-6, 6-3, 10-8).

McMILLAN, Frew Donald, South Africa

Born May 1942, Springs, Transvaal. A fine player who uses a two-fisted grip on both left and right sides, McMillan has an exceptional doubles record since the mid 1960s. Always recognisable by his white cap, McMillan has won over 20 international doubles titles on all surfaces and at the 1967 Wimbledon, partnered, as so often, by Bob Hewitt, he never lost his service or a set on the way to the doubles championship. In the same year McMillan and Hewitt did not lose a Davis Cup match and their defeat in the fourth round of the French championship was the first in 40 matches. McMillan has been doubles champion of his own country four times. He became a contract professional with WCT in 1970–1 and in 1976 was player-coach for the WTT Golden Gaters. He had an excellent doubles season in 1977, winning the US Open and professional doubles with Bob Hewitt, the Open mixed with Betty Stöve, with whom he was r/u at Wimbledon; he was winner of the 1977 Benson and Hedges doubles with Sandy Mayer.

South African singles r/u 1970; doubles won 1967, r/u 1968–9, won 1970, 1972, 1974, all with Hewitt; mixed doubles r/u 1970 with Miss P Walkden, r/u 1972 with Mrs Q C Pretorius.

French doubles won 1972 (beat P Cornejo/ J Fillol, 6-3, 8-6, 3-6, 6-1); mixed doubles won 1966 with Miss A Van Zyl (beat C Graebner/ Mrs A Jones, 1-6, 6-3, 6-2).

US mixed r/u 1970 with Mrs R D Dalton (M Reissen/Mrs M Court won, 6-4, 6-4), r/u 1976 with Miss Stöve (P Dent/Mrs B J King won, 3-6, 6-2, 7-5), won 1977 with Miss Stöve (beat V Gerulaitis/Mrs King, 6-2, 3-6, 6-3); US clay court doubles won 1973 with B Carmichael (beat M Orantes/I Tiriac, 6-3, 6-4); US indoors singles r/u 1974; doubles won 1974 with J Connors. WCT doubles championships won 1974, r/u 1975, both with Hewitt. US professional indoors doubles r/u 1976 with Hewitt. US professional doubles won 1977 with Hewitt (beat W Fibak/T Okker, 6-1, 1-6, 6-3).

Wimbledon doubles won 1967 (beat R Emerson/K Fletcher, 6-2, 6-3, 6-4), won 1972 (beat S Smith/E van Dillen, 6-2, 6-2, 9-7); mixed doubles r/u 1977 with Miss Stöve (Hewitt/Miss G Stevens won, 3-6, 7-5, 6-4). British hard court championship doubles won 1967, 1969, 1972, all with Hewitt, mixed doubles won 1971 with Mrs Dalton, won 1972 with Mrs Chanfreau. Benson and Hedges Wembley doubles won 1977 with S Mayer (beat B Gottfried/R Ramirez, 6-3, 7-6).

West German doubles won 1967, 1970 both with Hewitt; mixed doubles won 1970 with Mrs Dalton. Italian doubles won 1967 with Hewitt, r/u 1972 with L Hoad. Baltimore indoor doubles won 1976, Madrid doubles r/u 1976, Barcelona doubles r/u 1976, Vienna doubles won 1976, Cologne doubles won 1976, Stockholm doubles won 1976, all with Hewitt; Nuremburg ATP doubles won 1976 with K Meiler, Basle doubles won 1976 with T Okker, WCT Toronto doubles won 1976 with Fillol, Cologne singles r/u 1976.

McNAIR, Frederick, USA
Born July 1950, Washington. Mother Iranian. He and his father had the unusual distinction of being US father-and-son champions six times –

Above: Madison Square Garden, New York

three on grass (1971–3) and three clay (1965, 1969–70). He has developed as a good doubles player and in 1975 reached the Commercial Union Master's doubles, where he won two out of three matches to finish third. His best doubles year so far was 1976 with Sherwood Stewart when they won the US indoor, Bournemouth, French Open, South Orange, Paris indoor and the CU Masters doubles. He was r/u in the 1977 Italian Open doubles with Stewart, losing to Brian Gottfried and Raul Ramirez.

McNEILL, W Donald, USA
Born April 1916, Chickasha, Oklahoma. The first American to win the French men's singles, McNeill in fact defeated another American, Bobby Riggs, to gain the 1939 title. With C Harris, he also won the French doubles that year and again defeated Riggs in 1940 for the US singles title.

US singles won 1940 (beat Riggs, 8-6, 6-8, 6-3, 7-5); doubles won 1944 with R Falkenburg (beat W Talbert/F Segura, 7-5, 6-4, 3-6, 6-1), r/u 1946 with F Guernsey (G Mulloy/Talbert won, 3-6, 6-4, 2-6, 6-3, 20-18).

French singles won 1939 (beat Riggs, 7-5, 6-0, 6-3); doubles won with C Harris.

Madison Square Garden, New York, USA
Probably the most famous indoor sports arena in the world, the present Garden over Pennsylvania Station, 7th Avenue, is the fourth to bear the name. It is a 13-storey complex which includes a main arena seating over 20,000, an auditorium for 5000, plus art gallery, theatre-cinema, exhibition area and bowling centre. Work on the building began in 1963 and it was opened in February 1968. The original Garden in the disused New York and Harlem Railroad depot was destroyed in 1890 and a new one built in the same year. Sixteen years later its architect, Stanford White, was murdered in the roof garden. In 1925 this second building was demolished and a new one opposite the Poly-

clinic Hospital was opened in December of that year to accommodate nearly 19,000 but it became obsolete in the early 1960s.

The Garden has traditionally been the main centre for professional tennis promotions since the days of such promoters as Charles C (Cash-and-Carry) Pyle in the mid-1920s. In 1925 he signed the legendary Suzanne Lenglen of France for $50,000 to play Mary K Browne, three times US champion before World War I. The gate for their tournament was $40,000. In 1934 the professional debut of Ellsworth Vines to play Bill Tilden attracted a record crowd of 16,000; then in 1937 Fred Perry, also making his pro' debut, attracted 17,630 people who paid $58,119 to see him beat Vines. During the war, after a poor response to a 1941 matching of Riggs and Budge, Perry and Frank Koracs, it was decided to close down tennis promotions at the Garden except for war charity events. Then in 1947 a crowd of 15,114 battled through a blizzard to see Jack Kramer meet and be beaten by Bobby Riggs, both of whom were themselves to become promoters using the Garden as a starting place for many of their professional tours by the world's top players. Madison Square Garden again became the venue for the leading professional matches and tournaments, which grew in popularity while arguments continued about whether world tennis should become 'open' to professionals.

MAHONY, Harold Segerson, Ireland

Born February 1867, Edinburgh, Scotland, died 1905, Co Kerry, Ireland. Despite his birthplace, Mahony was an Irish player and a colourful character who was popular with the Wimbledon crowds. The genial Irishman was said to have the worst forehand in the game but attacked with volley, smash and backhand. A regular Wimbledon entrant, he eventually won the men's singles in 1896 from Wilfred Baddeley. He won the Irish singles in 1898 and mixed doubles in 1895–6. Mahony was killed when he was thrown from his bicycle at the foot of Caragh Hill in County Kerry, Ireland.

Wimbledon singles r/u 1893 All-Comers (J Pin won, 9-7, 6-3, 6-0), won 1896 Challenge Round (beat Baddeley, 6-2, 6-8, 5-7, 8-6, 6-3), r/u 1897 (R Doherty won, 6-4, 6-4, 6-3), r/u 1898 All-Comers (H Doherty won, 6-1, 6-2, 4-6, 2-6, 14-12); doubles r/u 1892 All-Comers with Pim (H Barlow/E Lewis won, 8-10, 6-3, 5-7, 11-9, 6-1), r/u 1903 All-Comers with M Ritchie (H Doherty/R Doherty won, 8-6, 6-2, 6-2).

US men's doubles r/u 1897 with H A Nisbet (L Ware/G Sheldon won, 11-13, 6-2, 9-7, 1-6, 6-1).

MAIER, Enriqué Gerado, Spain

Born December 1910, Barcelona. In 1932 Maier partnered Helen Wills Moody in the Wimbledon mixed doubles, helping her to the seventeenth of her 19 Wimbledon titles. Three years later he and Mrs Sarah Palfrey Fabyan took the US

mixed doubles title. He was a member of the Spanish Davis Cup team from 1929 to 1934.

Wimbledon mixed doubles won 1932 with Mrs Moody (beat H Hopman/Miss J Sigart, 7-5, 6-2).

US mixed doubles won 1935 with Mrs Fabyan (beat R Menzel/Miss K Stammers, 6-3, 3-6, 6-4).

MAKO, Constantine Gene, USA

Born January 1916, Budapest, Hungary. Gene Mako was brought up in California where he learned to play tennis. In 1933 he was beaten by Don Budge in the junior championships at Culver, Indiana. Then the two became firm friends and later that year entered the national clay court championship doubles together. It was the first pairing in a partnership which was to become world famous. At first Mako tended to be regarded as the senior partner but as Budge grew in fame he took over the leadership. In 1938 Mako helped Budge towards his Wimbledon Triple Crown, partnering him in the doubles, which they had first won the year before. (It was in 1938 that Budge also achieved the 'Grand Slam'.) Mako also partnered another all-time great, Alice Marble, in mixed doubles. He and Budge were the first doubles pair to stand in on each others' returns, a tactic which each used when partnering Miss Marble. Mako became a professional in 1946.

US singles r/u 1938 (Budge won, 6-3, 6-8, 6-2, 6-1); doubles r/u 1935 (W Allison/J Van Ryn won, 6-4, 6-2, 3-6, 2-6, 6-1), won 1936 (beat Allison/Van Ryn, 6-4, 6-2, 6-4), r/u 1937 (G von Cramm/H Henkel won, 6-4, 7-5, 6-4), won 1938 (beat A Quist/J Bromwich, 6-3, 6-2, 6-1), all with Budge; mixed doubles won 1936 with Miss Marble (beat Budge/Mrs S Fabyan, 6-3, 6-2). Davis Cup team 1935–8.

French doubles r/u 1938 with Budge (B Destremau/Y Petra won, 3-6, 6-3, 9-7, 6-1).

Wimbledon doubles won 1937 (beat G Hughes/C Tuckey, 6-0, 6-4, 6-8, 6-1), won 1938 (beat Henkel/G von Metaxa, 6-4, 3-6, 6-3, 8-6).

MALLORY, Molla (née Bjurstedt), USA

Born 1892, Norway, died 1959. Though Norwegian by birth Molla Bjurstedt became American by marriage and was the greatest woman player that country had seen before the emergence of Helen Wills Moody. Seven times winner of the US singles (she also won the 1917 National Patriotic Tournament), she was the only player to beat Suzanne Lenglen in singles after World War I – a victory achieved in the first round of the 1921 US championships, which Mrs Mallory went on to win. Though she had a remarkably weak service, a largely defensive backhand and rarely practised, she ruled the court by her fighting endurance and a mighty forehand drive.

Champion of her native Norway for ten years, Molla went to America in 1914 and became US champion in 1915 (Mary Browne defaulted in the Challenge Round), having already won the US indoor championships. She won the national title for four consecutive years (including the National Patriotic) until Mrs Wightman broke the run in 1919. Then, as Mrs Mallory, she won again in 1920–2 and after Helen Wills had reigned for three years, came back to win yet again in 1926. Her 1921 victory against Miss Lenglen came after the French woman had defeated her in the French championships the same year, and in June Suzanne Lenglen beat her again at Wimbledon. Determined to level the score at least, Mrs Mallory challenged Miss Lenglen to a match at Nice. While Molla and her husband Frank enjoyed the bright lights and night life, Suzanne practised hard and overwhelmed the American 6-0, 6-0.

Mrs Mallory won four mixed doubles titles with Bill Tilden – two on grass and two indoors – and two US women's doubles titles with Eleonora Sears in 1916–17. She played in the first Wightman Cup match of 1923 and her last competitive match was the Wightman Cup of 1928, when, with a knee injury, she was beaten. She retired in 1929 and died in 1959 in Stockholm aged 67.

US singles won 1915 (Miss Browne defaulted), won 1916 (beat Mrs E Raymond, 6-0, 6-1), won National Patriotic 1917 (beat Miss M Vanderhoef, 4-6, 6-0, 6-2), won 1918 (beat Miss F Goss, 6-4, 6-3), won 1920 (beat Miss M Zinderstein, 6-3, 6-1), won 1921 (beat Miss Browne, 4-6, 6-4, 6-2), won 1922 (beat Miss Wills, 6-3, 6-1), r/u 1923 (Miss Wills won, 6-2, 6-1), r/u 1924 (Miss Wills won, 6-1, 6-2), won 1926 (beat Miss E Ryan, 4-6, 6-4, 9-7); doubles won 1916 (beat Miss E Wilder/Mrs E Raymond, 4-6, 6-2, 10-8), won 1917 National Patriotic (beat Mrs R LeRoy/Miss P Walsh, 6-2, 6-4), both with Miss Sears; r/u 1918 with Mrs J Rogge (Miss Zinderstein/Miss Goss won, 7-5, 8-6), r/u 1922 with Miss Sigourney (Mrs J B Jessup/Miss Wills won, 6-4, 7-9, 6-3); mixed doubles r/u 1915 (H Johnson/Mrs Wightman won, 6-0, 6-1), won 1917 (beat Tilden/Miss F Ballin, 10-12, 6-1, 6-3), both with I C Wright, r/u 1918 with F B Alexander

Left: Alice Marble (seen here at Wimbledon in 1937) was one of the pioneers of women's power tennis.

(Wright/Mrs Wightman won, 6-2, 6-4), won 1922 (beat H Kinsey/Miss Wills, 6-4, 6-3), won 1923 (beat J Hawkes/Miss K McKane, 6-3, 2-6, 10-8), r/u 1924 (V Richards/Miss Wills won, 6-8, 7-5, 6-0), all with Tilden. Wightman Cup team 1923–5, 1927–8.

Wimbledon singles r/u 1922 (Miss Lenglen won, 6-2, 6-0).

MARBLE, Miss Alice, USA

Born September 1913, Plumas County, California. Four times American singles, doubles and mixed doubles champion, Alice Marble was one of the pioneers of women's power tennis before World War II, playing a serve-volley technique previously seen only among men. The blonde Californian farmer's daughter ranks among the ten greatest women players of all time not only for the standard of her play but also for the courage which she brought to it in defeating serious illness and then coming back to her peak.

She started playing tennis at the age of 13 when her older brother, Don, gave her a racket. Ten years later she won the first of her national titles. In between, her tennis career had been threatened as the result of a day of marathon tennis at the Maidstone Club, Long Island. Here, in 1933, she was drawn to play the semi-finals and finals of both doubles and singles in a tournament on one day. Having won her semi-final in the morning, she played her two finals with a temperature of 104, and lost both. As she left court she fainted after getting through 108 games in the day. Pleurisy was diagnosed. However, the next year she collapsed on court in Paris and was found to have tuberculosis. Complete rest was part of the long intensive treatment and she did not return to competitive tennis until 1936.

Alice seemed a better, fitter, faster player than ever. She was 5 ft 7 in (1.7 m) of unrestrained athleticism, free in motion, relaxed, cool and armed with a cannonball service and killer volley.

She won that year's national singles title from Helen Jacobs, who had held it for four years, and also took the mixed doubles with Gene Mako. Though she won the Wimbledon mixed doubles with Don Budge and US doubles with Mrs Sarah Palfrey Fabyan in 1937, her form that year was generally below its best. However, she came back in 1938 to win the Wimbledon doubles and mixed doubles and the national 'Triple Crown'. She took just 20 minutes to beat Nancye Wynne in the US singles final, 6-0, 6-3. In 1939 she took the Wimbledon 'Triple Crown', defeating Kay Stammers with the loss of only two games for the singles title. Back in America she gained her third 'Triple Crown' and in 1940, before turning professional, took her fourth singles and mixed doubles.

US singles won 1936 (beat Miss Jacobs, 4-6, 6-3, 6-2), won 1938 (beat Miss Wynne, 6-0, 6-3), won 1939 (beat Miss Jacobs, 6-0, 8-10, 6-4), won 1940 (beat Miss Jacobs, 6-2, 6-3); doubles r/u 1932 with Mrs Painter (Miss Jacobs/Miss Palfrey won, 8-6, 6-1), won 1937 (beat Miss C Babcock/Mrs J Van Ryn, 7-5, 6-4), won 1938 (beat Mrs R Mathieu/Miss J Jedrzejowska, 6-8, 6-4, 6-3), won 1939 (beat Miss Stammers/Mrs S Hammersley, 6-4, 8-6), won 1940, all with Mrs S P Fabyan; mixed doubles won 1936 with Mako (beat Budge/Mrs Fabyan, 6-3, 6-2), won 1938 with Budge (beat J Bromwich/Miss T Coyne, 6-1, 6-2), won 1939 with H Hopman, won 1940 with R Riggs. US Wightman Cup team 1933, 1937–9.

Wimbledon singles won 1939 (beat Miss Stammers, 6-2, 6-0); doubles won 1938 (beat Mrs Mathieu/Miss A Yorke, 6-2, 6-3), won 1939 (beat Miss Jacobs/Miss Yorke, 6-1, 6-0), both with Mrs Fabyan; mixed doubles won 1937 (beat Y Petra/Mrs Mathieu, 6-2, 6-4), won 1938 (beat H Henkel/Mrs Fabyan, 6-1, 6-4), both with Budge, won 1938 with Riggs (beat F Wilde/Miss N Brown, 9-7, 6-1).

MARK, Robert, Australia

Born November 1937, Albury, NSW. A tall, dark, rugged Australian of considerable talent, Mark's career suffered from his sometimes ungovernable temper. In 1956 he went with the young Rod Laver on a world tour accompanied by Harry Hopman. When the Australian LTA imposed restrictions in 1961 on players leaving the country to compete overseas, Mark was among several who not only objected but left the country. He went to South Africa, where he won the men's singles the following year – his only international singles title, though he had won doubles and mixed doubles in America (1961) and Australia (1959–61).

Australian doubles r/u 1958 with R Emerson (A Cooper/N Fraser won, 7-5, 6-8, 3-6, 6-3, 7-5), won 1959 (beat D Candy/R Howe, 9-7, 6-4, 6-2), won 1960 (beat Emerson/Fraser, 1-6, 6-2, 6-4, 6-4), won 1961 (beat Emerson/M Mullison, 6-3, 7-5, 3-6, 9-11, 6-2), all with Laver; mixed doubles won 1959 with Miss S Reynolds

(beat Laver/Miss R Schuurman, 4-6, 13-11, 6-2), r/u 1960 with Mrs M Reitano (T Fancutt/Miss J Lehane won, 6-2, 7-5).

French doubles r/u 1961 with Howe (Emerson/Laver won, 3-6, 6-1, 6-1, 6-4).

US doubles r/u 1960 with Laver (Emerson/Fraser won, 9-7, 6-2, 6-4); mixed doubles r/u 1959 with Miss J Hopps (Fraser/Mrs W duPont won, 7-5, 13-15, 6-2), won 1961 with Miss M Smith (beat R Ralston/Miss D Hard, wo).

Wimbledon doubles r/u 1959 with Laver (Emerson/Fraser won, 8-6, 6-3, 14-16, 9-7).

MARTIN, Billy, USA

Born December 1956, Evanston, Illinois. When Martin showed promise as a youngster his family moved to Palos Verdes, California for the sake of his tennis. Coached by John Newcombe and 'Pancho' Segura, he has developed into a good circuit professional after a difficult start in 1975. He first attracted international attention when he represented America in the 1973 BP under-21 matches at Torquay, England. Right-handed, he has a two-handed backhand. His junior successes included the US national 14 championships in 1969–70, national 16 singles and doubles in 1971, national 18 singles and doubles in 1973, when he led the US to win the Sunshine Cup and also won the Orange Bowl. In 1973 and 1974 he won the US Open junior championship and Wimbledon junior invitation event.

MASKELL, Dan, GB

Born April 1908, England. Sixteen times British professional champion (1928–36, 1938–9, 1946–53), Dan Maskell became the first permanent coach to the All England Club in 1929, having started his tennis career as a Wimbledon ball boy. After World War II he returned to the post he had left in 1939 and continued as coach

Left: Germany's Helga Masthoff (née Niessen) is a tall (6' 1") graceful player who is particulatly effective on clay courts.
Left (centre): Dan Maskell commentating at Wimbledon, 1977.

until 1955, also becoming LTA training manager in 1953, a post he held for over 20 years. He is now an LTA consultant and well known as a tennis commentator with the British Broadcasting Corporation on radio and TV.

MASTERS, Geoff, Australia

Born May 1950, Brisbane. Coached by the South African Trevor Francutt, Masters has achieved a good Davis Cup record and shown particularly well in doubles events. He won the Australian Open doubles in 1974 and in 1976 he reached the doubles finals of Australia, Wimbledon and Italy. He and Ross Case won the Wimbledon event in 1977.

Australian Open doubles r/u 1972 (K Rosewall/O Davidson won, 3-6, 7-6, 6-2), won 1974 (beat R Giltinan/S Ball, 6-7, 6-3, 6-4), r/u 1976 (J Newcombe/A Roche won, 7-6, 6-4), r/u 1977 (Newcombe/Roche won, 6-7, 6-3, 6-1), all with R Case; Australian hard courts singles r/u 1971; doubles won 1972 with Case.

Italian Open doubles r/u 1973 with Case, r/u 1976 with Newcombe.

Wimbledon doubles r/u 1976 (B Gottfried/R Ramirez won, 3-6, 6-3, 8-6, 2-6, 7-5), won 1977 (beat J Alexander/P Dent, 6-3, 6-4, 3-6, 8-9, 6-4), both with Dent.

Manila singles r/u 1973; Washington doubles won 1973, with Case; WCT São Paulo doubles won 1975-6, St Louis doubles r/u 1975, Melbourne doubles won 1975, Sydney doubles r/u 1975, WCT Monterrey doubles r/u 1976, Manila doubles won 1976, all with Case.

Masters Tournament see Grand Prix

MASTHOFF, Helga (née Niessen), Germany

Born November 1941, Essen. At 6 ft 1 in (1.84 m) Mrs Masthoff is an elegant player who has achieved consistently good results in recent seasons and has performed particularly well on clay courts. In 1970 she became the first German woman to reach a postwar singles final of one of the Big Four – the French Open. She won the West German singles for the third successive year in 1974, was doubles champion with Heide Orth from 1971-3 and German national singles champion in 1965-6 and 1968. In 1976 she shared the Benson and Hedges Auckland title with Sue Barker when the match had to be suspended because of darkness and bad weather. She plays with studied persistence rather than brilliance.

West German singles r/u 1969-70, won 1972-4; doubles won 1971-3 with Mrs Orth. German national champion 1965-6, r/u 1967, won 1968, 1972-3.

French singles r/u 1970 (Mrs M Court won, 6-2, 6-4); doubles r/u 1976 with Miss K Harter (Miss F Bonicelli/Mrs G Lovera won, 6-4, 1-6, 6-3).

South American singles won 1969, 1971.

Dutch singles r/u 1973.

Italian doubles won 1971 with Miss V Wade, r/u 1974 with Mrs Orth.

British hard court singles r/u 1972.

Japanese Open r/u 1973.

Canadian Open r/u 1973.

MATHIEU, Mrs Simone (née Passemard), France

Born January 1908, Neuilly-Sur-Seine. The leading French woman player of the 1930s, Mme Mathieu, as she liked to be called, was a determined fighter who could sustain long rallies and never gave up a point easily. She had a fierce forehand and tended to play from the baseline. Her greatest successes came in doubles: she won the French doubles six times and Wimbledon three. She dominated French tennis for more than a decade and in 1934 partnered

'Bunny' Ryan in her nineteenth and last Wimbledon victory.

French singles r/u 1929 (Miss H Wills won, 6-3, 6-4), r/u 1932 (Mrs H Moody won, 6-2, 6-1), r/u 1933 (Miss M Scriven won, 6-2, 4-6, 6-4), r/u 1935 (Mrs H Sperling won. 6-2, 6-1), r/u 1936 (Mrs Sperling won, 6-3, 6-4), r/u 1937 (Mrs Sperling won, 6-2, 6-4), won 1938 (beat Mrs N Landry, 6-0, 6-3), won 1939 (beat Miss J Jedrzejowska, 6-2, 6-3); doubles r/u 1930 with Miss S Barbier (Mrs Moody/Miss E Ryan won, 6-3, 6-1), won 1933 (beat Mrs S Henrotin/Miss C Rosambert, 6-1, 6-3), won 1934 (beat Miss H Jacobs/Miss S Palfrey, 3-6, 6-4, 6-2), both with Miss Ryan, won 1936 (beat Miss S Noel/Miss Jedrzejowska, 2-6, 6-4, 6-4), won 1937 (beat Mrs D Andrus/Mrs Henrotin, 3-6, 6-2, 6-2), won 1938 (beat Mrs A Halff/Mrs Landry, 6-3, 6-3), all with Miss A M Yorke, won 1939 with Miss Jedrzejowska; mixed doubles won 1937 with Y Petra (beat R Journu/Miss M Horn, 7-5, 7-5), won 1938 with D Mitic (beat C Boussus/Miss N Wynne, 2-6, 6-3, 6-4).

US doubles r/u 1938 with Miss Jedrzejowska (Mrs S P Fabyan/Miss A Marble won, 6-8, 6-4, 6-3).

Wimbledon doubles won 1933 (beat Miss F James/Miss Yorke, 6-2, 9-11, 6-4), won 1934 (beat Mrs Andrus/Mrs Henrotin, 6-3, 6-3), both with Miss Ryan, r/u 1935 with Mrs Sperling (Miss James/Miss K Stammers won, 6-1, 6-4), won 1937 (beat Mrs M R King/Mrs J Pittman, 6-3, 6-3), r/u 1938 (Miss Marble/Mrs Fabyan won, 6-2, 6-3), both with Miss Yorke; mixed doubles r/u 1937 with Petra (D Budge/Miss Marble won, 6-4, 6-1).

MAUD, Robert, South Africa

Born August 1946, Johannesburg. Now a company director, Maud was selected for the South African Davis Cup team at the age of 19 – the youngest ever to be selected. He won the Wimbledon Plate in 1970 and with Lew Hoad was r/u in the 1972 South African doubles. In 1967 and 1969 he was British hard court mixed doubles champion with Virginia Wade and with her was also r/u in the 1969 South African mixed doubles.

MAYER, Alexander (Sandy), USA

Born April 1952, Flushing, New York. Coached by his father, Alex Sr, who played doubles for Hungary and Yugoslavia, Sandy Mayer had a remarkable debut at Wimbledon in 1973 when, unseeded, he beat the favourite, Ilie Năstase, in four sets and reached the semi-finals before losing to Alex Metreveli. In 1975 he and Vitas Gerulaitis won the doubles in an upset of seeded pairs which brought them up against a last-minute partnership of Colin Dowdeswell and Allan Stone. With Frew McMillan he won the Benson and Hedges 1977 doubles.

US amateur grass court singles r/u 1972.

IPA Fairfield singles r/u 1975; doubles r/u with I Tiriac; IPA Roanoke doubles won 1975 with Gerulaitis.

WCT Fort Worth doubles won 1976; WCT Houston doubles r/u 1976, both with Gerulaitis; finished No 1 in WCT singles and played for champions, New York Sets.

Wimbledon doubles won 1975 with Gerulaitis (beat Dowdeswell/Stone, 7-5, 8-6, 6-4).

Benson and Hedges Wembley doubles won 1977 with F McMillan (beat B Gottfried/R Ramirez, 6-3, 7-6).

MEILER, Karl, Germany

Born April 1949, Munich. A talented but unpredictable player, Meiler made a good impression when he beat Ken Rosewall in the Australian Open of 1973, beat Roger Taylor in the Davis Cup and took Björn Borg to five sets before losing at Wimbledon. He also reached the semi-final of that year's Wimbledon doubles with Jurgen Fassbender, with whom he had won the King's Cup doubles against Britain in 1967, and was r/u in the West German Championship singles. In 1976 he won the WCT doubles finals in Kansas City with Fibak, with whom he also won the WCT doubles at Monte Carlo, was r/u at Barcelona and Atlanta and won the Nice and Dusseldorf doubles. He was runner-up in the 1975 Swiss Open singles and the South African Open doubles with Charles Pasarell and he won the Philippines Grand Prix 1977 singles with a walk-over from Manuel Orantes. In 1977 he and Fassbender won the Swedish Open doubles in a well-fought match.

MELVILLE, Kerry (Mrs K Reid), Australia

Born August 1947, Sydney, NSW. After showing a consistently good record over a number of years Miss Melville (now Mrs Reid) had her best season to date in 1977, when she won the Australian singles and was runner-up with

Right: Australia's Kerry Melville (Mrs Reid) is one of Australia's consistently successful players on the international circuit.

Betsy Nagelsen in the doubles. She reached the singles and doubles finals of the Colgate International and the doubles final of the NSW Open and the 1977–8 Australian Open with Mona Guerrant. In 1972 she beat Chris Evert and was r/u to Billie Jean King in the US Open. As a teenager she beat Mrs King in the 1966 US nationals. In 1968 she and Margaret Court pulled off a 3-0 Federation Cup victory over the Netherlands and in 1974 she had a surprise, though deserved, victory over her compatriot, Evonne Goolagong in the Wimbledon quarter-finals. She married US ranked player Grover 'Raz' Reid in 1975.

Australian Open singles r/u 1970 (Mrs Court won, 6-1, 6-3), won 1977 (beat Miss D Fromholtz, 7-5, 6-2); doubles won 1968 (beat Miss L Turner/Miss J Tegart, 6-4, 3-6, 6-2), r/u 1970 (Mrs J Dalton/Mrs Court won, 6-3, 6-1), both with Miss K Krantzcke, r/u 1973 (Mrs Court/Miss V Wade won, 6-4, 6-4), r/u 1974 (Miss Goolagong/Miss M Michel won, 7-5, 6-3), both with Miss K Harris, r/u 1977 with Miss Nagelsen (Miss Fromholtz/Miss Gourlay won, 5-7, 6-1, 7-5), shared 1977–8 with Mrs Guerrant (Mrs E Cawley/Mrs H Gourlay Cawley, rained off). NSW doubles r/u 1977 with Mrs Guerrant (Mrs Cawley/Mrs Gourlay Cawley won, 6-0, 6-0). Australian hard courts won 1969; Australian junior champion doubles won 1965, r/u 1966.

Dutch singles won 1969, r/u 1970.

South African doubles r/u 1970 with Miss Krantzcke.

Italian singles r/u 1969.

US singles r/u 1972 (Mrs King won, 6 3, 7-5).

Colgate International r/u 1977 (Mrs Cawley won, 6-1, 6-3); doubles shared 1977 with Miss G Stevens (Mrs Cawley/Miss B Stöve, 6-2, 1-3, abandoned).

MENZIES, Mrs M *see* **Stammers, Katherine**

METREVELI, Alexander, USSR
Born November 1944, Tbilisi, Georgia. The first Russian player to reach the Wimbledon singles finals (1973) and the first to reach the mixed doubles final (with Olga Morozova in 1968), Alex Metreveli is a Master of Soviet Sport and a trained journalist and broadcaster. In 1972 he and Miss Morozova became the first Russians to win their singles events at a British tournament – the Kent grass court championships at Beckenham – and in 1973 he scored another 'first' by becoming the first Russian to join WCT. His prize money goes to the Lawn Tennis Federation of the USSR, which meets all his expenses. Metreveli now coaches promising young soviet players.

Russian national junior champion 1961; Davis Cup debut 1963.

Wimbledon singles r/u 1973 (J Kodeš won, 6-1, 9-8, 6-3); mixed doubles r/u 1968 (K Fletcher/Mrs M Court won, 6-1, 14-12), r/u 1970 (I Năstase/Miss R Casals won, 6-3, 4-6, 9-7), both with Miss Morozova.

MICHEL, Margaret (Peggy), USA
Born February 1949, Pacific Palisades, California. Formerly a student in teaching mentally retarded children, Peggy Michel was out of the international tennis circuit for three years following an attack of hepatitis after an impressive 1969 Wimbledon in which she was doubles runner-up with Patti Hogan. In 1974 she won the Australian doubles, unseeded, and Wimbledon doubles with Evonne Goolagong, and in 1975 she and Miss Goolagong retained the Australian title, defeating Margaret Court and Martina Navratilova in the final. A shoulder injury in 1976 severely curtailed her playing.

MICHELL, Peggy (*née*** Saunders),** GB
Born January 1905, Chiswick, Middlesex, died June 1941. Playing with Mrs Phoebe Watson, Mrs Michell won the Wimbledon doubles in 1928 and 1929 and the pair also gained the US doubles in 1929. In the same two years Mrs Michell won both her Wightman Cup doubles.

Wimbledon doubles won 1928 (beat Miss E Bennett/Miss E Harvey, 6-2, 6-3), won 1929 (beat Mrs B Covell/Mrs D Shepherd-Barron, 6-4, 8-6), both with Mrs Watson. Wightman Cup team 1928-9, 1932.

French doubles r/u 1927 with Mrs Watson (Mrs I Peacock/Miss E Herne won, 6-2, 6-1).

US doubles won 1929 with Mrs Watson (beat Mrs Covell/Mrs Shepherd-Barron, 2-6, 6-3, 6-4).

Midland Counties Championship, GB
First held in 1899 at Edgbaston, Birmingham, the Midland Counties lawn tennis championship was for many years one of the leading tournaments in the British tennis calendar but declined in popularity and the standard of players it was able to attract during the mid-1960s.

Left: Alex Metreveli was the first tennis player from the USSR to reach the Wimbledon singles final and the mixed final.

Sydney Smith of Stroud, Gloucestershire, who won the Wimbledon doubles in 1902 and 1906, was winner of the Midland singles title a record six consecutive times (1900–5) – an achievement made the more remarkable by the fact that he had one leg encased in a metal support. Because of that he developed one of the most powerful forehand drives ever seen, the 'Smith Punch', which he used so accurately that he rarely needed to move from the baseline. The first winner of the Wimbledon men's singles title to win the Midland was Bill Tilden in 1920; the next was Jaroslav Drobný in 1954. Among women players the names of Wimbledon champions such as Charlotte Cooper, Dora Boothby, Doris Hart, Ethel Larcombe, Angela Mortimer and Dorothy Round are on the Edgbaston champions list. In 1963 The Birmingham Post and Mail newspaper company took over sponsorship of the championships for three years and Roy Emerson won the men's title that year, beating Rafael Osuna. In 1965 Margaret Court beat Virginia Wade in the women's finals. The championships have since become more a local event. In 1975 Mrs P F Jones (Miss Ann Haydon), the Birmingham-born tennis star, won the women's title.

MIKI, Tatsuyoshi (Ryuki), Japan

Born February 1904, Takamotsu, died January 1967. One of Japan's pioneer overseas players, though not the first, Miki won the Wimbledon mixed doubles with Dorothy Round in 1934 and was captain of the Japanese Davis Cup team in that year.

Wimbledon mixed doubles won 1934 with Miss Round (beat H W Austin/Mrs D Shepherd-Barron, 3-6, 6-4, 6-0).

MILLER, Esther (née Heine), South Africa

Born December 1910, Estcourt, Natal. One of the finest players produced by South Africa, Bobbie Heine was a tall, attractive player who made an impressive overseas debut in 1927, aged 17, when she won the French doubles with Mrs Irene Peacock and also with her was runner-up in the Wimbledon doubles. The next year she won the first of her five South African national singles titles and at 19 won the British hard court singles. She won her last major event in 1937.

South African singles won 1928, 1931–2, 1936–7.

French doubles won 1927 with Mrs Peacock (beat Mrs P Watson/Miss P Saunders, 6-2, 6-1), r/u 1929 with Mrs Neave (Miss L de Alvarez/Miss K Bouman won, 7-5, 6-3).

Wimbledon doubles r/u 1927 with Mrs Peacock (Miss H Wills/Miss E Ryan won, 6-3, 6-2).

MOFFIT, Billie Jean see King, Mrs Billie Jean

MOLINA, Ivan, Colombia

Born June 1946. A left-hander, Molina is a protégé of Willie Alvarez, from whom he learned the international game in the 1960s. He has since been a consistent performer on the circuit without achieving brilliant results. He can always be relied upon to give a good performance and on top form is capable of beating world leaders such as Laver, Ashe, John Lloyd, Dibley, Crealy and Orantes.

French mixed doubles won 1974 with Miss M Navratilova, won 1977 with Miss F Mihai (beat J McEnroe/Miss M Carillo, 7-6, 6-3), won Head Cup Kitzbuhl doubles 1974 with J Velasco; ATP Nice r/u 1975; doubles r/u with Velasco; Aryamehr Cup r/u 1975.

MOODY, Helen (née Wills, afterwards Mrs A Roark), USA

Born October 1905, Berkeley, California. One of the greatest of all women players and second only to Suzanne Lenglen in her invincibility, Helen Wills Moody won Wimbledon a record eight times out of nine challenges and the US singles seven times. From 1927 up to 1932 she did not lose a single set in any match. The daughter of a doctor, whose heavy adult racket she used to borrow to take to school, Helen did not play tennis regularly until she was 13. Then her father noticed her potential and enrolled her in the Berkeley Tennis Club, where she came under the eye of the club's part-time coach, William 'Pop' Fuller. Visiting San Francisco she saw 'Little Bill' Johnston playing and was enthralled by the power the small man put into his shots. Modelling herself on him, she developed her own forceful style with a devastating forehand. Though she was not a fast mover, her groundstrokes were so accurate and powerful that this did not matter. On court she appeared totally mechanised, cool and unemotional and this earned her the nickname 'Miss Poker Face'; yet off court she could be a giggling, effervescent and charming personality. No one quite knew which was the real Helen. Apart from her coolness, her trademark on court was the white and green eye shade she always wore.

At 15, having won a string of junior and senior tournaments on the American Eastern circuit, Helen became US 18 champion in 1921. Retaining the title next year, she also reached the national women's final but lost 6-3, 6-1 to Mrs Molla Mallory. In 1923 she was picked for the first Wightman Cup team and won the first match played on the new Forest Hills Center Court. That year, too, she beat Molla Mallory, 6-2, 6-1 for her first US women's title. Next came her introduction to overseas tennis when she travelled to Britain in 1924 for the Wightman Cup and Wimbledon, losing in both. However, she went on to Paris to win Olympic gold medals for singles and doubles and returned to America to retain the women's title.

In 1926 Suzanne Lenglen, rated as the world's greatest woman player, bowed to pressure for her to play Helen. They met in front of a 3000 crowd at the Carlton Club, Cannes, and though

the American lost 6-3, 8-6, and never again played Miss Lenglen, she later described it as her own greatest match. Appendicitis interrupted her run of US titles in 1926 but next year she won the first of her Wimbledon singles championships, the last of which came in 1938, when she was aged 32. Then she met her long time rival Helen Jacobs, who had also been coached by 'Pop' Fuller. Back in the 1933 US final the two Helens had met and 'Little Helen' Jacobs had taken the first set 8-6. 'Queen Helen' Wills Moody, as she now was, took the second 6-3 but in the third 'Little Helen' twice broke the older Helen's service to lead 3-0. Without warning 'Queen Helen' walked off court and said she could not continue. She later blamed a back injury sustained earlier in the year in her garden

and though she was criticised by the press for being 'a quitter', she did, in fact, have to have an operation and treatment which kept her out of the 1934 season.

She returned to Wimbledon to win a classic match and her seventh title in 1935, beating Miss Jacobs 6-3, 3-6, 7-5. In 1937 she turned down a professional contract and divorced her first husband. A year after her record eighth Wimbledon title she married Aidan Roark and thereafter played only social tennis, devoting her time to writing novels, tennis books, a syndicated newspaper column, painting, creating fashion designs and interior decor.

US singles r/u 1922 (Mrs Mallory won, 6-3, 6-1), won 1923 (beat Mrs Mallory, 6-2, 6-1), won 1924 (beat Mrs Mallory, 6-1, 6-2), won

Above: Helen Wills Moody won Wimbledon eight out of nine times and won the US Open seven times in her remarkable career. From 1927 to 1932 she did not lose a single set in any match.

1925 (beat Miss K McKane, 3-6, 6-0, 6-2), won 1927 (beat Miss B Nuthall, 6-1, 6-4), won 1928 (beat Miss Jacobs, 6-2, 6-1), won 1929 (beat Mrs P Watson, 6-4, 6-2), won 1931 (beat Mrs E F Whittingstall, 6-4, 6-1), r/u 1933 (Miss Jacobs won, 8-6, 3-6, 3-0 retired); doubles won 1922 with Mrs J B Jessup (beat Mrs Mallory/Miss Sigourney, 6-4, 7-9, 6-3), won 1924 with Mrs G Wightman (beat Miss E Goss/Mrs Jessup, 6-4, 6-3), won 1925 with Miss M K Browne (beat Mrs M Bundy/Miss E Ryan, 6-4, 6-3), won 1928 with Mrs Wightman (beat Miss E Cross/Mrs L Harper, 6-2, 6-2), r/u 1933 with Miss Ryan (Miss Nuthall/Miss F James won, retired); mixed doubles r/u 1922 with H Kinsey (W Tilden/Mrs Mallory won, 6-4, 6-3), won 1924 with V Richards (beat Tilden/Mrs Mallory, 6-8, 7-5, 6-0), won 1928 with J B Hawkes (beat E Moon/Miss E Cross, 6-1, 6-3).

French singles won 1928 (beat Miss E Bennett, 6-1, 6-2), won 1929 (beat Mrs R Mathieu, 6-3, 6-4), won 1930 (beat Miss Jacobs, 6-2, 6-1), won 1932 (beat Mrs Mathieu, 7-5, 6-1); doubles won 1930 (beat Mrs Mathieu/Miss S Barbier, 6-3, 6-1), won 1932 (beat Mrs Whittingstall/Miss Nuthall, 6-1, 6-3), both with Miss Ryan; mixed doubles r/u 1928 (H Cochet/Miss E Bennett won, 3-6, 6-3, 6-3), r/u 1929 (Cochet/Miss Bennett won, 6-3, 6-2), both with F Hunter, r/u 1932 with S Wood (F Perry/Miss Nuthall won, 6-4, 6-2). Wightman Cup team 1923–5, 1927–32, 1938.

Wimbledon singles r/u 1924 (Miss McKane won, 4-6, 6-4, 6-4), won 1927 (beat Miss L de Alvarez, 6-2, 6-4), won 1928 (beat Miss de Alvarez, 6-2, 6-3), won 1929 (beat Miss Jacobs, 6-1, 6-2), won 1930 (beat Miss E Ryan, 6-2, 6-2), won 1932 (beat Miss Jacobs, 6-3, 6-1), won 1933 (beat Miss D Round, 6-4, 6-8, 6-3), won 1935 (beat Miss Jacobs, 6-3, 3-6, 7-5), won 1938 (beat Miss Jacobs, 6-4, 6-0); doubles won 1924 with Mrs Wightman (beat Mrs B Covell/Miss McKane, 6-4, 6-4), won 1927 (beat Miss E Heine/Mrs I Peacock, 6-3, 6-2), won 1930 (beat Miss Cross/Miss S Palfrey, 6-2, 9-7), both with Miss Ryan; mixed doubles won 1929 with E Hunter (beat I Collins/Miss I Fry, 6-1, 6-4).

MOORE, Elisabeth Holmes, USA
Born 1877, died 1959. One of the American pioneer women tennis players, Miss Moore was involved in an early marathon match when she beat Marion Jones in a 58-game US All-Comers final 1901, 4-6, 1-6, 9-7, 9-7, 6-3 on the way to take the singles title for the second of four times. She was also winner of the doubles and the mixed doubles twice.

US singles r/u 1891 All-Comers (Miss M Cahill won, 6-5, 6-3, 6-4, 4-6, 6-2), r/u 1892 Challenge Round (Miss Cahill won), won 1896 (beat Miss J Atkinson, 6-4, 4-6, 6-3, 6-2), r/u 1897 (Miss Atkinson won, 6-3, 6-3, 4-6, 3-6, 6-3), won 1901 (beat Miss M McAteer, 6-4, 3-6, 7-5, 2-6, 6-2), r/u 1902 (Miss Jones won, 6-1, 1-0, retired), won 1903 (beat Miss Jones, 7-5, 8-6),

r/u 1904 (beat Miss M Sutton, 6-1, 6-2), won 1905 (beat Miss Sutton by default); doubles won 1896 with Miss Atkinson, won 1903 with Miss C B Neely; mixed doubles won 1902, 1904, both with W C Grant.

MOORE, Ray, South Africa
Born August 1946, Johannesburg. In 1968 Moore set the fashion, now commonplace, for men players to have long hair. It was a style he showed in many places on the international tennis circuit as he joined WCT that year. Though he is by no means a power player, he has shown that he is able to beat the best players of his day. He was South African junior champion in 1965 and two years later made his Davis Cup debut.

South African Open doubles won 1969 with R Gonzalez, r/u 1971–2 with G Goven. Joined WCT 1968 for two years. Berlin Open singles won 1969. Scandinavian Open singles r/u 1972. Rejoined WCT 1973. Canadian Open doubles won 1975 with C Drysdale. American Airlines doubles r/u 1976 with E Van Dillen. Dusseldorf doubles r/u 1976 with R Carmichael.

MORAN, Gertrude (Gorgeous Gussy), USA
Born September 1923, Santa Monica, California. Miss Moran made Wimbledon fashion history in 1949 when, aged 25, she defied convention by appearing for her matches wearing lace panties under a short ballerina skirt – a costume created by the designer Teddy Tinling, who was also an assistant in the referee's office at Wimbledon for many years. Her outfit attracted the attention of the world's press and Miss Moran, a trim, attractive girl, became known as 'Gorgeous Gussy'. With Mrs Pat Todd she reached that year's doubles final, losing to Miss Brough and Mrs duPont. She became a professional in 1951, signing for Bobby Riggs.

US national girls' doubles won 1941 with Miss Brough; US national hard courts won 1949: Egyptian championships singles won 1950, doubles won with Mrs Todd, mixed doubles won with J Washer.

Wimbledon doubles r/u 1949 with Mrs Todd (Miss Brough/Mrs duPont won, 8-6, 7-5).

MOREA, Enricqué, Argentina
Born April 1924, Buenos Aires. A particularly successful doubles player, Morea was ranked No 1 in his own country for some 20 years. His first Argentinian titles were the doubles and mixed doubles of 1943. He took the singles title in 1944, 1945 and 1954–7 and the doubles 1954–5, 1957, 1960. He played in the Davis Cup in 1948, 1952 and 1955. In 1953 he won the South American singles for the third time, was Wimbledon mixed doubles r/u for the second time and won the British hard courts singles for the only time.

Wimbledon mixed doubles r/u 1952 with Mrs T Long (F Sedgman/Miss D Hart won, 4-6,

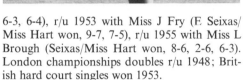

6-3, 6-4), r/u 1953 with Miss J Fry (E Seixas/Miss Hart won, 9-7, 7-5), r/u 1955 with Miss L Brough (Seixas/Miss Hart won, 8-6, 2-6, 6-3). London championships doubles r/u 1948; British hard court singles won 1953.

French doubles r/u 1946 with F Segura (M Bernard/Y Petra won, 7-5, 6-3, 0-6, 1-6, 10-8); mixed doubles won 1950 with Miss B Scofield (beat W Talbert/Mrs P C Todd, retired).

MOROZOVA, Olga (Mrs O Rubenova), USSR
Born February 1949, Moscow. Alex Metreveli and Miss Morozova were the first Soviet players to reach a Wimbledon final when they were runners-up in the mixed doubles of 1968. In 1972 she became the first Soviet player to reach the singles final of a major championship, when she was r/u to Miss L Tuero in the Italian singles and in 1973 she and Marina Kroschina were the first Russians to win an American title – the US indoor doubles. She upset the Wimbledon seedings in 1974 when she defeated Billie Jean King in the women's quarter-finals, playing a better net game – which she favours – than the American. In the next round she beat Virginia Wade after losing the first set, but in the final she lost in two straight sets to give Christine Evert her first Wimbledon title.

French singles r/u 1974 (Miss Evert won, 6-1, 6-2); doubles won 1974 with C Evert (beat Mrs C Chanfreau/Miss K Ebbinghaus, 6-4, 2-6, 6-1), r/u 1975 with Miss J Anthony (Miss Evert/Miss Navratilova won, 6-3, 6-2).

Italian singles r/u 1972 (beat Miss Tuero); doubles won 1973 with Miss Wade, won 1974 with Miss Evert.

Australian doubles r/u 1975 with Mrs M Court (Miss E Goolagong/Miss P Michel won, 7-6, 7-6).

US Open doubles r/u 1976 with Miss Wade (Miss L Boshoff/Miss I Kloss won, 6-1, 6-4). US indoors won 1973 with Miss Kroschina (beat Miss Goolagong/Miss J Young, 6-2, 6-4). Virginia Slims Chicago won 1976, VS Washington doubles won 1976, both with Miss Wade.

Wimbledon singles r/u 1974 (Miss Evert won, 6-0, 6-4); mixed doubles r/u 1968 (K Fletcher/Mrs Court won, 6-1, 14-12), r/u 1970 (I Năstase/Miss R Casals won, 6-3, 4-6, 9-7), both with Metreveli.

MORTIMER, Angela (Mrs J Barrett), GB
Born April 1932, Plymouth, Devon. The first British winner in 1961 of the women's singles at Wimbledon for 24 years (Dorothy Round in 1937), Miss Mortimer was, with Christine Truman, in the first all-British Wimbledon women's final since 1914 (Mrs D R Larcombe and Mrs Lambert Chambers). In 1955, with Anne Shilcock, she took part in the first all-British final at Wimbledon since 1937 when they won the women's doubles against Shirley Bloomer and Pat Ward. That year she also became the first British woman for 18 years to win a major singles title anywhere when she took the French women's singles after a final against Dorothy Knode lasting two hours four minutes. Miss Mortimer, who played her 1961 final when temporarily deaf – which she later said was an advantage against distractions – was well-liked and admired by players and spectators for her resolution and patience. Her stroke play was not particularly strong but her persistence frequently wore down the opposition. A fall by Christine Truman in the second set of the final certainly affected her and Miss Mortimer was a good enough tactician to play on Christine's injured thigh to advantage, taking the title by 4-6, 6-4, 7-5.

Wimbledon singles r/u 1958 (Miss A Gibson won, 8-6, 6-2), won 1961 (beat Miss Truman, 4-6, 6-4, 7-5); doubles won 1955 with Miss Shilcock (beat Miss Bloomer/Miss Ward, 7-5, 6-1).

Australian singles won 1958 (beat Miss L Coghlan, 6-3, 6-4); doubles r/u 1958 with Miss Coghlan (Mrs T D Long/Mrs K M Hawton won, 7-5, 6-8, 6-2); mixed doubles r/u 1958 with P Newman (R Howe/Mrs Hawton won, 9-11, 6-1, 6-2). British Wightman Cup team 1953, 1955–6, 1959–61.

French singles won 1955 (beat Mrs Knode,

2-6, 7-5, 10-8), r/u 1956 (Miss A Gibson won, 6-0, 12-10).

MORTON, Agnes Mary (Agatha), GB

Born March 1872, Halstead, Essex, died 1952. Winner of the Wimbledon doubles in 1914 with the American Elizabeth Ryan, Miss Morton had twice won the event before it became an official championship – in 1902 and 1909 – and had been mixed doubles non-championship winner in 1909 and runner-up in the non-championship All-Comers doubles in 1905–7. She was singles runner-up in the All-Comers in 1902, 1904 and 1908–9. In 1925 she became Lady Hugh Stewart.

MOTTRAM, Christopher (Buster), GB

Born April 1955, Kingston, Surrey. Son of Tony Mottram, the British Davis Cup player and former national coach, 'Buster' Mottram is a 6 ft 3 in (1.90 m) giant of a player who became the youngest winner of the British under-21 title in 1971, aged 16, and in the following year was the youngest player ever named for the British Davis Cup team. In 1975, when ranked No 3 in Britain, he had an excellent WCT tour, beating Borg and Okker at Johannes-burg and during the season having wins over Panatta, Hewitt, Tanner, Kodeš, Amritraj and Ashe. He had to withdraw from Wimbledon with an arm injury and defaulted in the South African Open with an ear infection after beating Fillol. His 1976 year, though consistent, did not live up to the promise of the previous season and in 1977 it was disclosed that his career was being hampered by susceptibility to some allergies. He was runner-up to Vilas in the South African men's singles of 1977.

British junior championship r/u 1969, won 1971; British junior covered court singles r/u 1970, won 1971–2. Wimbledon junior invitation r/u 1972 (Borg won). British junior under-21 champion 1971–2. Won Rothmans' Cumberland singles, 1973. French junior champion 1972. South African singles r/u 1977 (Vilas won, 7-6, 6-3, 6-4).

MOTTRAM, Linda, GB

Born May 1957, Wimbledon. Sister of 'Buster', Linda was also coached by her father. An attractive blonde, she is affected even more than her brother by her proneness to allergies and during 1977 underwent a series of tests to determine the extent of her susceptibility which is affecting her career. In 1970 she was British junior under-14 champion and in 1971 runner-up in the under-16 championships. In 1973 she beat Sue Barker to become British junior covered court champion and was runner-up to Miss Barker in the British junior championship. Aged 15, she also completed a unique family double by winning the Cumberland women's singles – Buster having won the men's – beating Virginia Wade on the way. In 1976 she won the singles at Perth, Bournemouth and Aberavon and had good results in America on the Virginia Slims circuit. In recent years she appears to suffer from an inability to concentrate on the match at hand.

Rothmans' Cumberland singles won 1973, 1975; Sutton singles won 1975, r/u 1976. Pernod Paddington singles won 1975; doubles r/u 1976 with Miss B Thompson. New Zealand Open r/u 1975 (Miss Goolagong won). French Open junior r/u 1975 (Miss R Marsikova won). Member of winning Annie Soisbault team 1975 and Connolly Cup team 1975–6.

MUDFORD, Phyllis Evelyn (Mrs M R King), GB

Born August 1905, Wallington, Surrey. Miss Mudford won the Wimbledon doubles in 1931 with Mrs Dorothy Shepherd-Barron and in 1937 was runner-up with Mrs J B Pittman. She was a member of the winning British Wightman Cup team of 1930 and again in the team in 1931–2 and 1935, when the United States won. In 1938 she was non-playing captain.

Wimbledon doubles won 1931 with Mrs Shepherd-Barron (beat Miss D Metaxa/Miss J Sigart, 3-6, 6-3, 6-4), r/u 1937 with Mrs Pittman (Mrs R Mathieu/Miss A Yorke won, 6-3, 6-3).

Below: Linda Mottram has won many junior titles in spite of bad allergy problem.

Tom Okker – Netherlands

Charlie Pasarell – United States of America

Nancy Richey – United States of America

Manuel Santana – Spain

Ken Rosewall – Australia

Tony Roche – Australia

MULLIGAN, Martin F, Australia/Italy
Born October 1940, Sydney, NSW. One of several players who objected to the Australian LTA's ban in 1961 on top players leaving the country to play in overseas competitions without permission, Mulligan moved to Rome in 1964 and became a member of the Italian Davis Cup team in 1968, winning nine out of 11 rubbers. In 1962 Mulligan reached the Wimbledon final unseeded but was beaten by Rod Laver 6-2, 6-2, 6-1. (The last four were all Australians and there were no Americans in the last eight for the first time since 1922.) He had a spectacular junior career, including winning an under-19 match at age 16 without losing a point and being junior champion in 1958. He played in 22 finals at 27 tournaments in 1967 and won 17 of them.

Australian doubles r/u 1961 with R Emerson (R Laver/R Mark won, 6-3, 7-5, 3-6, 9-11, 6-2). Australian hard court singles won 1960-4, doubles won 1960-4.

Italian singles won 1963, 1965, 1967. German singles won 1963, doubles won 1962 with R Hewitt. South African mixed won 1972 with Miss Wade. Swedish singles won 1967-8. Austrian singles won 1967-8. Spanish singles won 1967-8. Japanese Open singles won 1971.

MULLOY, Gardnar Putnam, USA
Born November 1913, Washington DC. Apart from being a leading American player for nearly 20 years, Gardnar Mulloy was an outspoken advocate for taking the 'starchiness' out of tennis, insisting that the word 'love' in scoring was detrimental to the popularity and that the rules that players should wear all-white and spectators should remain silent were archaic. He was an excellent athlete of ideal build and at the age of 43 years seven months became the oldest player to win a Wimbledon championship when he won the doubles with Patty in 1957.

He was in the top ten US rankings 14 times between 1939 and 1954 and ranked No 1 in 1952. In the 1960s he and his former doubles partner, William Talbert, were involved in a company settling inflatable plastic domes to make indoor courts weather-proof.

US singles r/u (F Sedgman won, 6-1, 6-2, 6-3); doubles won 1942 (beat F Schroeder/S Wood), won 1945 (beat R Falkenburg/J Tuero, 12-10, 8-10, 12-10, 6-2), won 1946 (beat W McNeill/F Guernsey, 3-6, 6-4, 2-6, 6-3, 20-18), won 1948 (beat F Parker/Schroeder, 1-6, 9-7, 6-3, 3-6, 9-7), r/u 1950 (J Bromwich/F Sedgman won, 7-5, 8-6, 3-6, 6-1), r/u 1953 (M Rose/R Hartwig won, 6-4, 4-6, 6-2, 6-4), all with W F Talbert, r/u 1957 with J Patty (A Cooper/N Fraser won, 4-6, 6-3, 9-7, 6-3); mixed doubles r/u 1955 with Miss S Fry (E Seixas/Miss D Hart won, 7-5, 5-7, 6-2). US Davis Cup team 1946, 1948-50, 1952-3, 1957.

French doubles r/u 1951 (K McGregor/Sedgman won, 6-2, 2-6, 9-7, 7-5), r/u 1952 (McGregor/Sedgman won, 6-3, 6-4, 6-4), both with R Savitt.

Wimbledon doubles r/u 1948 with T Brown (Bromwich/Sedgman won, 5-7, 7-5, 7-5, 9-7), r/u 1949 with Schroeder (R Gonzalez/Parker won, 6-4, 6-4, 6-2), won 1957 with Patty (beat Fraser/L Hoad, 8-10, 6-4, 6-4, 6-4); mixed doubles r/u 1956 with Miss A Gibson (Seixas/Miss Fry won, 2-6, 6-2, 7-5).

MURRAY, R Lindley, USA
Born November 1893, San Francisco, California, died 1970. After winning the US National Patriotic tournament of 1917, held to raise money for World War I charities, left-hander Murray beat the young 'Big Bill' Tilden in the 1918 US final, 6-3, 6-1, 7-5.

Musketeers, Four *see* **Four Musketeers**

NĂSTASE, Ilie, Rumania

Born July 1946, Bucharest. Undoubtedly one of the world's greatest players, Năstase has proved himself a man of mercurial talents and temperament since he arrived on the international tennis scene in 1969. He has shown himself to be a supremely masterful player with hardly a weakness of stroke – if not of orthodox style – to mark against him. Yet he can throw a game quite deliberately when annoyed and has been involved in more disputes with tournament officials and with spectators than probably any other player in the game's history, many of them resulting in disqualifications, fines or suspensions. He made his first impression in 1969 when he and fellow Rumanian Ion Tiriac took their country to the Davis Cup Challenge Round against America. The following year saw him winning the Italian singles and doubles, the French doubles, the US indoors and becoming the first Rumanian to have his name on the Wimbledon championships roll when he won the mixed doubles with Rosemary Casals.

Năstase reached his first Wimbledon singles final in 1972, by which time his dark good looks were attracting the sort of teenage adulation usually reserved for 'pop' stars. (In 1973 he and the young Borg had to be supplied with police escorts to protect them from screaming hordes of fans.) In the 1972 final he faced Australian Stan Smith, in his coolness a complete contrast to Năstase. The Rumanian was obviously nervous and he spent the first four sets constantly plucking the strings of his rackets and changing them until, in the fifth, he finally settled on one with a tension which was to his liking. By then it was too late and Smith won 4-6, 6-3, 6-3, 4-6, 7-5, in a match described as the best final since the Crawford–Vines final of 1933. However, Năstase took his revenge at Forest Hills, where he defeated Smith on the way to winning the US Open, after dropping two sets to Arthur Ashe in the final. In 1973 he was at his electrifying best in beating Nikki Pilić in the French finals without dropping a set – a record for the event. Here he displayed his true genius, playing with daring, dash, confidence and artistry, using searing smashes and drives, passing shots, thunderous volleys and whip-lash services.

This was the year in which members of the ATP were in dispute with the ILTF over its suspension of Pilić for refusing to play in the Yugoslavian Davis Cup team. Wimbledon suffered when 79 ATP members withdrew from the championships. Among those who still played was Năstase, who moved from No 2 to No 1 in the re-seeding and claimed the Rumanian ATP had instructed him to play. Though he won the doubles with Jim Connors, he was out of the singles in the fourth round, losing to Sandy Mayer. Earlier in the year his temperament had lost him the British hard court title when he persisted in arguing and exchanging insults with people in the stands, while his opponent, Adriano Panatta got on with winning. It was a display of bad behaviour which was to make the nickname 'Nasty' increasingly well-known to newspaper readers and to convince tennis experts that but for his extraordinary outbursts Năstase would be winning even more titles. Even so, he topped the ATP prize-money table in 1973, winning $228,750.

It was not until 1976 that he reached the Wimbledon finals again and then it was only to fall victim to the mettlesome brilliance of Borg, playing at his inspired best. Until the final Năstase had played superbly and with a dedicated determination which put him through without losing a set. He led 3-0 in the first set and had three break points in the fourth game but Borg was playing faultlessly and twice had runs of three winning games in quick succession to take the set 6-4. The match was played at immense pace and the next set went quickly to Borg 6-2. In the final set, after Borg had earlier broken service, Năstase made a last desperate bid and broke back to 7-7. Then Borg broke through again and took the last game to love.

In 1977 Năstase, who is married and has one daughter, was ranked No 3 in the world but was unranked in his own country, for whom he did not play in the 1976 Davis Cup because it clashed with the WCT-Avis Cup, in which he defeated both Borg, in the semi-final, and Ashe in the final. He had few major tournament wins and took none of the 'Big Four' titles in 1977.

French singles r/u 1971 (J Kodeš won, 8-6, 6-2, 2-6, 7-5), won 1973 (beat Pilić, 6-3, 6-3, 6-0); doubles r/u 1966 (C Graebner/R Ralston won, 6-3, 6-3, 6-0), won 1970 (beat Ashe/C Pasarell, 6-2, 6-4, 6-3), both with Tiriac, r/u 1973 with J Connors (J Newcombe/T Okker won, 6-1, 3-6, 6-3, 5-7, 6-4).

US Open won 1972 (beat Ashe, 3-6, 6-3, 6-7, 6-4, 6-3); doubles won 1975 with Connors (beat Okker/M Riessen, 6-4, 7-6); mixed doubles r/u 1972 with Miss Casals (Riessen/Mrs M Court won, 6-3, 7-5). US indoor won 1970–1, r/u 1972. US indoor, Salisbury, won 1976. US clay courts doubles won 1974 with Connors. Commercial Union Masters won 1971–3, r/u 1974, won 1975. Smash 77 won 1977 (beat Newcombe, 7-6, 6-7, 6-2).

Italian singles won 1970, 1973, r/u 1974; doubles won 1970, 1972, both with Tiriac, r/u 1974 with J Gisbert.

Canadian Open won 1972, r/u 1975.

Wimbledon singles r/u 1972 (Smith won, 4-6, 6-3, 6-3, 4-6, 7-5), r/u 1976 (Borg won, 6-4, 6-2, 9-7); doubles won 1973 with Connors (beat A Cooper/N Fraser, 3-6, 6-3, 6-4, 8-9, 6-1); mixed doubles won 1970 (beat A Metreveli/Miss O Morozova, 9-11, 6-3, 6-4), won 1972 (beat K

Warwick/Miss E Goolagong, 6-4, 6-4), both with Miss Casals.

WCT Avis Cup won 1976, WCT Caracas r/u 1976, WCT Stockholm won 1976, Hong Kong r/u 1976; WCT doubles r/u 1976 with Amritraj.

Gunze Tokyo r/u 1977 (K Rosewall won, 4-6, 7-6, 6-4).

Above: Rumania's Ilie Năstase is a masterful but moody player and tends to become involved in arguments with officials and crowds.

NAVRATILOVA, Martina, Czechoslovakia

Born October 1956, Bernice, Prague. A talented, aggressive left-hander, Miss Navratilova defected to America in 1975 after her best tennis season. She refused to return to Czechoslovakia after the US Open at Forest Hills, in which she reached the semi-finals of both the singles and doubles. Coached by her father, she had been women's champion of Czechoslovakia for three years until 1974. During the 1967 season she had been runner-up in the Italian singles and won the doubles with Christine Evert, runner-up in the Australian and French singles and won the French doubles, also with Miss Evert, with whom she formed an increasingly strong partnership to win the Wimbledon doubles in 1976. In 1977 she and Betty Stöve took the US Open doubles and she was r/u in the Smash 77 and Gunze tournaments.

Czechoslovakia national women's singles won 1972–4.

US Open doubles won 1977 with Miss Stöve (beat Miss R Richards/Miss B Stuart, 6-2, 3-6, 6-3).

World Invitation doubles r/u 1976 with Miss V Wade; Colgate Inaugural doubles won 1976 with Miss Evert.

Australian singles r/u 1975 (Miss E Goolagong won, 6-3, 6-2); doubles r/u 1975 with Miss M Court (Miss Goolagong/Miss M Michel won, 7-6, 7-6). Colgate Sydney singles won 1976 (beat Miss Stöve).

French singles r/u 1975 (Miss Evert won, 2-6, 6-2, 6-1); doubles won 1975 with Miss Evert (beat Miss J Anthony/Miss O Morozova, 6-3, 6-2).

Italian singles r/u 1974–5; doubles r/u 1973 with Miss R Tomanova, won 1975 with Miss Evert.

Wimbledon doubles won 1976 with Miss Evert (beat Mrs L W King/Miss Stöve, 6-1, 3-6, 7-5), r/u 1977 with Miss Stöve (Mrs Cawley/Miss J Russell won, 6-3, 6-3) ; won 1978.

West German singles r/u 1974; doubles r/u 1974 with Miss Tomanova.

Virginia Slims finals r/u 1975 (Miss Evert won); VS Houston singles won 1976; VS Chicago doubles won 1970 with Mrs E Cawley; VS Dallas singles won 1976. Smash 77 r/u 1977 (Mrs Cawley won, 6-1, 6-4). Gunze Tokyo r/u 1977 (Mrs King won, 7-5, 5-7, 6-1).

Nestlé Schools Tournament, GB

Founded in 1963 by the Nestlé Company in Britain, the Nestlé schools tournament has its finals at Queen's Club, London, and over 30,000 boy and girl entrants from all parts of Britain compete. The winners of the English, Irish, Scottish and Welsh finals compete together in the 'International' final. The tournament is organised by the Lawn Tennis Foundation of Great Britain.

NEWBERRY, Janet, USA

Born August 1953, Los Angeles. Step-daughter of Edward Turville, US Davis Cup captain 1970–1, Miss Newberry's impressive career beginnings were temporarily halted in 1976 by a knee injury sustained during her first Virginia Slims event of the year. However, she made a good comeback after an operation and seemed set for future success. Before her injury she had won eight national junior titles and in 1975 qualified for the Virginia Slims finals. That year she held match point against Virginia Wade in the Wimbledon third round. Her best success on return to the circuit was to win the 1976 US Open doubles with Mrs P M Doerner. In 1977 she won the Italian Open, beating Renata Tomanova in straight sets.

NEWCOMBE, John David, Australia

Born May 1944, Sydney, NSW. One of the seemingly endless stream of talented tennis players to come out of Australia, John Newcombe established himself as the world's top amateur player in 1967, when he won the singles and doubles at Wimbledon and Forest Hills and the doubles of France and Australia. A superbly fit and strong player who enjoys a relentless, forcing game, he was pitched in at the deep end of international tennis when, at 19, he was in the 1963 team bidding to regain the Davis Cup from America. He lost both his singles and Australia were crushed 3-2. He gave notice of his re-emerging confidence when he won the Wimbledon doubles of 1965 with Owen Davidson and the Australian doubles with Tony Roche, who was to be his long-time partner. His second Wimbledon doubles came in 1966 but it was his successes of 1967 which gave him the title 'Player of the Year' and confirmed him as a power player whose no-nonsense game would bring him a place in tennis history books.

After winning the Wimbledon singles again

in 1970 and 1971 he was denied the chance of three successive wins when he, like all contract professionals with WCT, was banned from Wimbledon in 1972. However, 1973 saw him back in the honours lists of world tennis with his second US Open singles and third doubles, his first Australian singles and third doubles, his third French doubles and second Italian. In addition he was Australia's Davis Cup hero in their 5-0 victory over the holders, America. At the US Open he had been seeded No 10 but by the end of the season he achieved his ambition and was seeded World No 1.

Since 1974 the titles have not come so fast, though he gained his sixth Wimbledon doubles that year (the fifth with Roche), and his 1976 career was blighted by arm and shoulder injuries, although he reached the final of the Australian Open. He was elected president of the ATP in succession to Arthur Ashe, during Wimbledon. He started 1977 well when he won the Australian doubles with Roche for the fifth time and for his sixth time, beating Case and Masters, 6-7, 6-3, 6-1.

Australian singles won 1973 (beat O Parun, 6-3, 6-7, 7-5, 6-1), won 1975 (beat J Connors, 7-5, 3-6, 6-4, 7-5), r/u 1976 (M Edmondson won, 6-7, 6-3, 7-6, 6-1); doubles won 1965 (beat R Emerson/F Stolle, 3-6, 4-6, 13-11, 6-3, 6-4), r/u 1966 (Emerson/Stolle won, 7-9, 6-3, 6-8, 14-12, 12-10), won 1967 (beat O Davidson/W Bowrey, 3-6, 6-3, 7-5, 6-8, 8-6), won 1971 (beat M Riessen/T Okker, 6-2, 7-6), all with Roche; won 1973 with M J Anderson (beat J Alexander/P Dent, 6-3, 6-4, 7-6), won 1976 (beat S Smith/C Pasarell, 4-6, 7-6, 6-2), won 1977 (beat R Case/G Masters, 6-7, 6-3, 6-1), both with Roche.

French doubles r/u 1964 (Emerson/K Fletcher won, 7-5, 6-3, 3-6, 7-5), won 1967 (beat Emerson/Fletcher, 6-3, 9-7, 12-10), won 1969 (beat Emerson/R Laver, 4-6, 6-1, 3-6, 6-4, 6-4), all with Roche; won 1973 with Okker (beat Connors/I Năstase, 6-1, 3-6, 6-3, 5-7, 6-4).

US singles r/u 1961 (Stolle won, 4-6, 12-10, 6-3, 6-4), won 1967 (beat C Graebner, 6-4, 6-4, 8-6), won 1973 (beat J Kodeš, 6-4, 1-6, 4-6, 6-2, 6-3); doubles won 1967 with Roche (beat Davidson/Bowrey, 6-8, 9-7, 6-3, 6-3), won 1971 with R Taylor (beat Smith/E Van Dillen, 6-7, 6-3, 7-6, 4-6, 5-3 tie break), r/u 1972 (C Drysdale/Taylor won, 6-4, 7-6, 6-3), won 1973 (beat Laver/K Rosewall, 7-5, 2-6, 7-5, 7-5), both with Davidson; mixed doubles won 1964 with Miss M Smith (beat E Rubinoff/Miss J Tegart, 3-6, 8-6, 6-2). Smash 77 r/u 1977 (I Năstase won 7-6, 6-7, 6-2).

Wimbledon singles won 1967 (beat W Bungert, 6-3, 6-1, 6-1), r/u 1969 (Laver won, 6-4, 5-7, 6-4, 6-4), won 1970 (beat Rosewall, 5-7, 6-3, 6-2, 3-6, 6-1), won 1971 (beat Smith, 6-3, 5-7, 2-6, 6-4, 6-4); doubles won 1965 with Roche (beat Fletcher/R Hewitt, 7-5, 6-3, 6-4), won 1966 with Fletcher (beat Bowrey/Davidson, 6-3, 6-4, 3-6, 6-3), won 1968 (beat Rosewall/Stolle, 3-6, 8-6, 5-7, 14-12, 6-3), won 1969 (beat Okker/Riessen, 7-5, 11-9, 6-3), won 1970 (beat Rosewall/Stolle, 10-8, 6-3, 6-1), won 1974 (beat R Lutz/Smith, 8-6, 6-4, 6-4), all with Roche. British hard court singles won 1969.

Italian singles won 1969; doubles won 1971 with Roche, won 1973 with Okker; mixed doubles won 1964 with Miss Smith. Canadian singles won 1971. West German singles won 1968.

Newport, Monmouthshire, GB

The home of the Welsh championships since 1897, Newport Athletic Club was founded in 1875 to provide facilities for Rugby football and

Above: The Newport Casino in Rhode Island has been the venue for tennis championships (amateur and professional) since 1881.

cricket. Previously the Welsh championships had been held in Cardiff and Penarth after their inception in 1886. The Newport Club had its first indoor tennis court in 1890 – one of the earliest in Britain – and also has facilities for athletics, badminton, bowls, hockey, netball and table tennis. Although they are the *Welsh* championships, this major tennis event in Wales only ever had two native-born winners – Peter Freeman in 1920 and D H Williams in 1927. The championships had numerous famous international players on their honours rolls, including Maud Watson, the first women's title holder, Elizabeth Ryan, Angela Mortimer, Ann Haydon, Maria Bueno, Judy Tegart, Margaret Court, Evonne Goolagong and Virginia Wade. Among the recent winners of the men's title, until the end of the championships in 1975 through increasing costs, were Jaroslav Drobný, Mike Sangster, Bob Hewitt, Roy Emerson, John Newcombe, Ken Rosewall and Roger Taylor.

Newport, Rhode Island, USA

The Newport Casino in Rhode Island was the venue for the US national championships from their inception in 1881 until 1915, when they were transferred to Forest Hills. To fill the gap left, the Newport men's invitation singles and doubles tournament was founded in that year and attracted most of the leading US players. The winner was Richard Norris Williams II, the current national champion, who beat the 1913–14 champion Maurice Loughlin. A Japanese entrant, Ichiya Kumagai, was the first foreign winner, in 1916, while the famous Australian pair, Norman Brookes and Gerald Patterson were the first overseas doubles winners, in 1919. Only six players have won the singles more than once: William Talbert, Ted Schroeder, Frank Sedgman, Hamilton Richardson, Don McNeill and Neale Fraser. Australians have figured prominently on the winners' list – Emerson, Laver, Newcombe, Rosewall and Stolle. Neale Fraser won the doubles three times with different partners. The last Newport

invitation amateur tournament was held in 1967 and it then became a professional event. In 1972 the casino became a venue for the women's Virginia Slims professional circuit.

New Zealand

The first tennis club in New Zealand was the Parnell LTC in Auckland, founded in 1872 for croquet, which was later followed by tennis. Some 800 clubs have since been formed. Court surfaces include many fine grass courts, asphalt/ bitumen and locally-designed porous quick-drying concrete courts. The New Zealand LTA was formed in 1886 and from 1904 to 1922 it was affiliated to the LTA of Australasia. During this period Australasia won the Davis Cup in 1907–9 and 1911, 1914 and 1919. In 1923 New Zealand affiliated separately to the ILTF and has taken part in its own right in the Davis Cup since 1924. The major tennis event each year is the national senior championships held at Auckland, Christchurch or Wellington. Another important tennis event is the Auckland Open which, like the national, attracts leading players from overseas as well as from New Zealand. During the season there are district representative matches held under the auspices of the 21 district associations. These include events for the men's Wilding Shield, named after the leading player of the early 1900s, Tony Wilding, the women's Nunneley Casket, the boys' Slazenger Shield and girls' Howe Shield.

The main season, when most local tournaments are held, runs from October to April for grass and longer for hard-courts. Coaching plays an important role in development of the game and the New Zealand Lawn Tennis Professional Coaches Association provides some 25 part-time or full-time coaches. As a result of improved standards of play New Zealand became an annual entrant in the Australian Linton and Wilson Cups for juniors and in 1973 hosted the events for the first time. National and international business concerns have played an important part in sponsoring tennis since the advent of the Open game.

NIESSEN, Helga *see* Masthoff, Helga

Northern Lawn Tennis Championships, GB

The Northern Club, now based in Didsbury, Manchester, is one of the oldest tennis clubs in Britain and was founded in the late 1870s. In 1881, when records of the club begin, it was based at Old Trafford, Manchester, but prior to that date there was a Northern LTA under which a tournament was first played on the Broughton Cricket Club's ground in 1880, attracting 30 competitors. The second tournament, in 1881, was held at a cricket club in Kersal and in 1882 it was held in Liverpool. The Northern Club took control of the event in 1884 and it alternated between Liverpool and Manchester until the late 1920s. By 1909 membership of the club at Old Trafford had fallen away considerably as the district became increasingly industrialised and in that year it moved headquarters to Didsbury. Here the playing area, which gradually became one of the finest in the country, was developed over the years with good grass courts, three hard courts and three all-weather, a covered court, six squash courts and a croquet lawn.

The tournament continued to attract leading players and became known as 'the Wimbledon of the North'. However, since 1970 the event has declined in importance.

NORTON, Brian, I C, South Africa

Born October 1899, Cape Province, died 1957. Winner of the US men's doubles in 1923, partnered by 'Big Bill' Tilden, Norton took part in a controversial Wimbledon Challenge Round singles match against his doubles partner in 1921. Three weeks before the match Tilden had undergone a minor operation in Paris and was not fully match fit when he met Norton, a friend of his. Norton won the first two sets without much difficulty, 4-6, 2-6 and Tilden was seen to be looking tired and strained. At this time a section of the Wimbledon Centre Court crowd began shouting disparaging remarks at Tilden, who was a homosexual. However, it was Norton, not the champion, who reacted and virtually threw away the third and fourth sets, which went 6-1, 6-0 to Tilden. Now level, the match became a real contest in the last set which Norton led 4-2. Tilden fought back to 4-4 but Norton led again, 5-4 with Tilden to serve. In the tenth game Norton led 30-40 and Tilden played a shot he thought was out but which the linesman gave as in. Norton's return was out but he went on to gain a second match point. This time though, Tilden's service was a winner and he won the next two games, to take the match and title 4-6, 2-6, 6-1, 6-0, 7-5. He did not return to Wimbledon for five years.

US doubles won 1925 with Tilden (beat R N Williams/W M Washburn, 3-6, 6-3, 6-3, 5-7, 6-2).

NUTHALL, Betty (Mrs F C Shoemaker), GB

Born May 1911, Surbiton, Surrey. The first overseas player to win the US women's singles title (1930), the attractive Miss Nuthall also won the US doubles with Miss Sarah Palfrey the same year. In 1927, when she reached the Wimbledon quarter-finals for the first time, she was already a British idol, yet though she could be an extremely good player elsewhere she was never at her best at Wimbledon. In 1927, the year of the first fully seeded draw, she was unseeded. She beat Molla Mallory convincingly in the second round but was put out by Joan Fry in the quarter-final.

US singles r/u 1927 (Miss H Wills won, 6-1, 6-4), won 1930 (beat Mrs L A Harper, 6-4, 6-1); doubles r/u 1927 with Miss Fry (Mrs L A Godfree/Miss E Harvey won, 6-1, 4-6, 6-4), won 1930 with Miss Palfrey (beat Miss E Cross/Mrs Harper, 3-6, 6-3, 7-5), won 1931 with Mrs E F Whitingstall (beat Miss D Round/Miss H Jacobs, 6-2, 6-4), won 1933 with Miss F James (Mrs F S Moody/Miss E Ryan retired); mixed doubles won 1929 (beat H W Austin/Mrs B Covell, 6-3, 6-3), won 1931 (beat W Allison/Mrs Harper, 6-3, 6-3), both with G Lott.

French singles r/u 1931 (Miss C Aussem won, 8-6, 6-1); doubles won 1931 (beat Miss Ryan/Miss Aussem, 9-7, 6-2), r/u 1932 (Mrs Moody/Miss Ryan won, 6-1, 6-3), both with Mrs Whitingstall; mixed doubles won 1931 with P D B Spence (beat Austin/Mrs D Shepherd-Barron, 6-3, 5-7, 6-3), won 1932 (beat S B Wood/Mrs Moody, 6-4, 6-2), r/u 1933 (J Crawford/Miss M Scriven won, 6-2, 6-3), both with F Perry.

British Wightman Cup team 1927–9, 1931–4, 1939.

OKKER, Tom, Netherlands

Born February 1944, Amsterdam. The best male player ever to join the international circuit from the Netherlands, Okker has maintained a consistently high standard and achieved an outstanding doubles record with the American Martin Riessen, with whom he won the US Open doubles in 1976. In 1977 he was runner-up in the US professional doubles with Wojtek Fibak, losing to Frew McMillan and Bob Hewitt of Australia. In the first US Open in 1968 he took Ashe to 14-12 in the first set of the singles final and to the full five sets before Ashe won the title.

Dutch singles won 1970, 1973. Stockholm doubles won 1976 with Riessen. Belgian singles won 1970. Canadian singles won 1973.

Australian doubles r/u 1971 with Riessen (J Newcombe/A Roche won, 6-2, 7-6).

French doubles won 1973 with Newcombe (beat J Conners/I Năstase, 6-1, 3-6, 6-3, 5-7, 6-4). French covered court won 1967; Paris indoor doubles won 1976 with Riessen.

US singles r/u 1968 (A Ashe won, 14-12, 5-7, 6-3, 3-6, 6-3); doubles won 1976 with Riessen (beat P Kronk/C Letcher, 6-4, 6-4). US indoor doubles won 1968 with T Koch (beat R Lutz/S Smith, 6-3, 10-12, 8-6); US professional doubles r/u 1977 with Fibak (McMillan/Hewitt won, 6-1, 1-6, 6-3).

WCT doubles r/u 1973 with Riessen; WCT Columbus doubles r/u 1976; WCT Richmond doubles r/u 1976; WCT Rotterdam doubles r/u 1976, all with Ashe. Commercial Union GP r/u 1973.

Wimbledon Plate won 1965; Wimbledon doubles r/u 1969 with Riessen (Newcombe/Roche won, 7-5, 11-9, 6-3). Dewar Cup won 1969. British hard court singles r/u 1966, won 1970; doubles won 1970 with Roche.

Italian singles won 1968; doubles divided 1969 with Riessen (Newcombe/Roche), won 1973 with Newcombe.

South African singles won 1967, 1969; doubles won 1967 with Riessen, won 1973 with Ashe, r/u 1974 with Riessen; mixed doubles won 1969 with Mrs J du Plooy.

West German singles r/u 1969, won 1970; doubles won 1969 with Riessen.

OLMEDO, Alejandro (Alex), USA

Born March 1936, Arequipa, Peru. The first Peruvian to become a world-ranked player, Olmedo was of mixed Aztec and Spanish descent and gained a tennis scholarship to the University of Southern California, where he impressed Perry Jones, the director of Los Angeles Tennis Club and President of the Pacific South West Tennis Association. Olmedo was selected for the 1958 US Davis Cup team when Jones was named its captain.

Though not armed with particularly powerful strokes, Olmedo moved with grace and speed and had a beautiful touch and feel. He had remarkable anticipation and a superb volley. He justified his Davis Cup selection by winning both his singles and his doubles in America's 3-2 win to regain the cup from Australia. With Ham Richardson he won the 1958 US doubles and soon afterwards Olmedo became the first American – having taken out citizenship papers – to win the Australian singles since Dick Savitt had done so in 1951. That same year he defeated Rod Laver to take the Wimbledon title without losing a set to the Australian. After reaching the 1959 US finals of both the singles and doubles Olmedo turned professional, touring with Pancho Gonzalez, Ken Rosewall and Pancho Segura.

US singles r/u 1959 (N Fraser won, 6-3, 5-7, 6-2, 6-4); doubles won 1958 with Richardson (beat S Giammalva/B MacKay, 6-4, 3-6, 6-3, 6-4), r/u 1959 with E Buchholz (R Emerson/N Fraser won, 3-6, 6-3, 5-7, 6-4, 7-5); mixed doubles r/u 1958 with Miss M Bueno (Fraser/Mrs W duPont won, 6-4, 3-6, 9-7). US Davis Cup team 1958–9.

Australian singles won 1959 (beat Fraser, 6-1, 6-2, 3-6, 6-3).

Wimbledon singles won 1959 (beat Laver, 6-4, 6-3, 6-4).

Olympic Tennis

Lawn tennis was accepted as an official Olympic sport at Athens (1896), Paris (1900), St Louis (1904), London (1908), Stockholm (1912), Antwerp (1920) and Paris (1924). However, by the last occasion there was considerable dispute between the international Olympic Committee and the ILTF over the definition of an 'amateur' and it was obvious to many that 'shamateurism' was increasing among tennis players. Tennis therefore ceased to be accepted as an official Olympic sport. It was included in the 1968 Games in Mexico only as a demonstration sport. In fact, even when it was acceptable, Olympic tennis did not always attract either the interest or the standard of player hoped for and did not feature as a major sporting attraction of the games. Among the leading players who took part were Suzanne Lenglen, Kitty McKane, Helen Wills, Hazel Wightman, Tony Wilding, André Gobert, the Doherty brothers, Max Decugis and Charles Dixon.

Orange Bowl, USA

The annual Orange Bowl championships are held at Miami Beach, Florida, each December and are for boys and girls aged under 18 and under 16. The championships were first held in

1947 and were won by Lew McMasters and Joan Johnson. Manuel Orantes was the first unseeded player to win in 17 years in 1966.

O'NEILL, Mrs C *see* **Lehane, Jan**

ORANTES, Manuel, Spain
Born February 1949, Granada. One of the greatest players to come from Spain, left-hander Orantes made an early international mark when he won the 1966 Orange Bowl, unseeded, and followed up by winning the Wimbledon junior invitation title in 1967, when he was picked to play in the Davis Cup Challenge Round. Coached by Andres Gimeno, he has achieved notable singles successes to rank among the world's top ten players. In 1976 he overcame arm and back troubles to win five of his last eight tournaments in superb form. He was ranked No 6 in the world in 1977 and beat Connors to win the US clay court singles. Orantes has gained rapidly in popularity as crowds have increasingly appreciated not only his undoubted talent but also his sportsmanship. With his excellent judgement and anticipation together with topspin lobs, withering volleys, and cracking passing shots, he is recognised as one of the greatest hard court players.
  Spanish Open singles won 1971, 1976. Madrid singles won 1976; Barcelona singles won 1976.
  French Open singles r/u 1974 (B Borg won, 2-6, 6-7, 6-0, 6-1, 6-1).
  US Open singles won 1975 (beat J Connors, 6-4, 6-3, 6-3). US clay court singles won 1975 (beat A Ashe, 6-2, 6-2), won 1977 (beat Connors, 6-1, 6-3). Commercial Union Masters won 1976 (beat W Fibak, 5-7, 6-2, 0-6, 7-6, 6-1); CU Grand Prix 2nd 1976.
  Italian singles won 1972, r/u 1973, 1975. Belgian singles won 1971. Canadian singles r/u

1973, won 1975. Sweden singles won 1972, r/u 1973–4; Stockholm r/u 1976. South African r/u 1973, won 1975. South America r/u 1970, 1974. West Germany won 1972, 1975. Tehran won 1976. Gunze Open r/u 1976. Dewar Cup r/u 1976.

ORTH, Heide (*née* **Schildknecht),** Germany
Born August 1942. A former junior slalom skiing champion and then a tennis doubles specialist, Mrs Orth holds over 30 national and international titles in West Germany. She won the West German indoor championships four times (1969, 1971–3) and has been doubles champion of West Germany twice (1972–3) and runner-up once (1971) all with Helga Masthoff, and mixed doubles champion three times (1971–2, 1974), with Jurgen Fassbender. A knee injury in 1975 forced her retirement from the world circuit.

OSBORNE, Margaret *see* **duPont, Margaret Evelyn**

OSUNA, Rafael Herrera, Mexico
Born September 1938, Mexico City, died June 1969. Rated the finest-ever Mexican player, Osuna was killed in an air crash near Monterrey, Mexico. He was fleet-footed and had a beautifully delicate touch. Apart from reigning supreme for more than a decade in Mexico he made his mark on international tennis by winning the US singles title in 1963, beating Frank Froehling, the US doubles in 1962 and the Wimbledon doubles in 1960 and 1963.
  US singles won 1963 (beat Froehling, 7-5, 6-4, 6-2); doubles r/u 1961 (C R McKinley/ R D Ralston won, 6-3, 6-4, 2-6, 13-11), won 1962 (beat McKinley/Ralston, 6-4, 10-12, 1-6, 9-7, 6-3), r/u 1963 (McKinley/Ralston won, 9-7,

4-6, 5-7, 6-3, 11-9), all with A Palafox.

Wimbledon doubles won 1960 with Ralston (beat M Davies/R Wilson, 7-5, 6-3, 10-8), won 1963 with Palafox (beat J C Barclay/P Darmon, 4-6, 6-2, 6-2, 6-2).

Mexican Davis Cup team 1958–68.

OVERTON, Wendy, USA

Born March 1947, Glen Cove, Long Island. Coached by Ed Faulkner and Doris Hart, Miss Overton turned professional in 1971, having made her mark as a junior by winning the US under-18 in 1964 and US 18 doubles in 1969. In 1972 she was runner-up in the West German doubles with Valerie Ziegenfuss and with the same partner won her Wightman Cup doubles against Virginia Wade and Mrs J Williams. She had a disappointing season in 1976 and though she was on the circuit and played WTT for Cleveland Nets she devoted some time to TV commentating. However, she showed signs of a comeback in 1977, reaching the finals of the US clay court doubles with Miss Carillo but losing 5-7, 7-5, 6-3, to 'Linky' Boshoff and Ilana Kloss.

Pacific Coast Championships, USA

Like many other lawn tennis tournaments, the Pacific Coast championships were originally a men-only event. Founded in 1889 with men's singles and doubles titles, they were held at Del Monte, northern California, until 1908. Women's events began in 1890. From 1909 there were two Pacific Coast sectional championships in men's doubles, one for southern California and the other for northern. Since 1962 the Pacific Coast international championships men's doubles have also carried the northern sectional title.

The tournament was staged at the California Tennis Club in San Francisco in its early years and from 1951 to 1971 it was held at the Berkley Tennis Club. From 1962 it became the Pacific Coast international and in 1969 became an open event. In 1971 it was made part of the ILTF and WCT Grand Prix circuits and in 1972, after the women's events had been dropped when the WTA professional circuit began, the championships moved to Albany, California. Then in 1973 under new sponsorship the name was changed completely and the Fireman's Fund international championships came into being, first held at Alamo, California and now at San Francisco.

Holders of the Pacific Coast titles have included many who went on to become national grass court champions: Maurice McLoughlin, Bill Johnston (ten times Pacific Coast winner), Ellsworth Vines, Fred Perry, Don Budge, Bobby Riggs, Jack Kramer, Ted Schroeder, Art Larsen, Tony Trabert, Ashley Cooper, Rafael Osuna, Manuel Santana, Fred Stolle, Stan Smith, Arthur Ashe and Rod Laver. Among women winners who were national grass court champions were Louise Brough, Margaret duPont, Pauline Betz, Shirley Fry, Maureen Connolly, Althea Gibson, Darlene Hard, Maria Bueno and Margaret Court.

Pacific Southwest Championships, USA

Started in 1927 by the Tennis Patrons Association of southern California, the Pacific Southwest tennis championships were intended to attract leading national and international players to southern California. From the outset they succeeded and the first winner was Bill Tilden, who won the singles, the doubles with Francis Hunter and mixed doubles with Molla Mallory.

Originally the championships were held on the cement courts of the Los Angeles Tennis Club but in 1975 they moved to the University of California's 8000-seat Pauley Pavilion in Los Angeles when Arthur Ashe, who had won in 1963, was the winner again. In 1976 he was runner-up to Brian Gottfried. For 38 years until his death in 1938 Perry T Jones, president of the Southern California Tennis Association and patron of many tennis players, had directed the championships. Frank Parker (1941–2, 1944–5) and Roy Emerson of Australia (1959, 1962, 1964 and 1967) won the singles four times; Fred Perry (1932–4), Don Budge (1935–7), Jack Kramer (1943, 1946–7), Vic Seixas (1952, 1954, 1957) and Pancho Gonzalez (1949, 1969, 1971), all won three times.

The doubles were won four times by Kramer, twice with Schroeder (1941, 1947), once with Charles Olewine (1942), and once with Parker (1943). Parker also won the title with five other partners. Australian Lew Hoad took the doubles four times, three of them with Ken Rosewall and one with Rex Hartwig. Another Australian, Roy Emerson, took the title five times, twice each with Laver and Fred Stolle and once with Bob Hewitt.

Among winners of the women's events, there have been overseas singles winners in Kea Bouman of Holland (1927), Betty Nuthall (1929), Dorothy Round (1933), Ann Haydon (1960), all of Britain, and Maria Bueno (1964, 1966). Other winners have included Beverly Baker Fleitz (1947, 1955, 1958–9), Betty Nuthall, Alice Marble, Sarah Palfrey Cooke, Pauline Betz (1942, 1944, 1946), Louise Brough, Maureen Connolly, Shirley Fry, Althea Gibson, Maria Bueno, Darlene Hard, Rosemary Casals and Billie Jean King.

In 1971 the two finalists, Miss Casals and Miss King, walked off the court when referee Jack Kramer refused to replace a lineswoman and a double default was declared.

The doubles title was won six times by Margaret Osborne duPont and Louise Brough and the latter won a seventh time with Midge Gladman Van Ryn.

Padder Tennis

A hybrid form of tennis played on a court half the size of that for lawn tennis, 39 ft by 18 ft (11.9 m by 5.5 m), without tramlines and with the net at 2 ft 6 in (0.76 m) at the posts and 2 ft 3 in (0.69 m) at the centre, Padder tennis makes an excellent introduction to lawn tennis. It is played with a conventional lawn tennis ball and wooden bats 15 in (38.1 cm) long and 8 in (20.3 cm) wide.

Another hybrid form of tennis similar to padder tennis is known as platform tennis because it was originally played in New York on a platform built to overcome the problems of snow. The platform was surrounded by chicken wire netting 8 ft (2.44 m) high. Again wooden 'paddles' are used but the tennis ball is replaced by one of sponge rubber. The game was invented in 1928 by Fassbender Blanchard and James Cogswell.

Today the size of the court is 44 ft by 20 ft (13.4 m by 6.1 m) and the surrounding netting is 12 ft (3.66 m) high. The game spread to New England and was governed by the Paddle Tennis Association which became the American Platform Tennis Association in 1950. Basically, the same rules apply as in tennis but only one service is allowed and the ball can be hit after it has bounced off the wire surround before it has bounced a second time. *See also* **Czechoslovakia.**

PAILS, Dennis Robert (Dinny), Australia

Born November 1921, Nottingham, England. Seeded No 1 for the first post war Wimbledon championships in 1946, Pails could be said to have lost his chance of the men's title to the London underground tube trains. He made good progress through the early rounds but then, on his way to play his quarter-final match on the Centre Court in front of Queen Mary, he lost his way. He arrived at the ground twenty minutes late and in a state of nervous tension which undoubtedly did not help his game against Yvon Petra of France, who beat him 7-5, 7-5, 6-8, 6-4 and went on to take the title. Pails was runner-up in the doubles and in 1947, before turning professional, won the Australian singles.

Australian singles r/u 1946 (J Bromwich won, 5-7, 6-3, 7-5, 3-6, 6-2), won 1947 (beat Bromwich, 4-6, 6-4, 3-6, 7-5, 8-6).

Wimbledon doubles r/u 1946 with G Brown (T Brown/J Kramer won, 6-4, 6-4, 6-2).

PALAFOX, Antonio, Mexico

Born April 1936, Guadalajara. Younger brother of Gustavo Palafox, who played for Mexico in the Davis Cup for many years, Antonio achieved his major successes as a doubles player. He won the US doubles in 1962 and Wimbledon doubles in 1963, partnered by Rafael Osuna. In 1959 he took Neale Fraser and Rod Laver to five sets in the American zone Mexico Davis Cup match against Australia. He became a professional in 1966.

US men's doubles r/u 1961 (C R McKinley/ R Ralston won, 6-3, 6-4, 2-6, 13-11), won 1962 (beat McKinley/Ralston, 6-4, 10-12, 1-6, 9-7, 6-3), r/u 1963 (McKinley/Ralston won, 9-7, 4-6, 5-7, 6-3, 11-9), all with Osuna.

Wimbledon doubles won 1963 with Osuna (beat J C Barclay/P Darmon, 4-6, 6-2, 6-2, 6-2).

Mexican Davis Cup team 1959–65.

PALFREY, Sarah Hammond (Mrs M Fabyan, Mrs E T Cooke, Mrs J Danzig), USA

Born September 1912, Sharon, Massachusetts. A fine volleyer and outstanding doubles player, Sarah Palfrey won the US women's doubles title nine times between 1930 and 1941 including four times with Alice Marble and three with Helen Jacobs. She also won the US mixed doubles title four times, the singles twice late in her amateur career (1941 and 1945), and the Wimbledon doubles twice, partnered by Alice Marble. On the second occasion she helped Miss Marble win the 'Triple Crown' of Wimbledon when they beat Miss Jacobs and Miss A Yorke in straight sets, dropping only one game. Her career spanned nearly 20 years; in 1929 she was ranked No 4 in America and in 1945 was No 1. She became a professional in 1946. She played in ten Wightman Cup matches, winning 14 out of 21 rubbers.

US singles r/u 1934 (Miss Jacobs won, 6-1, 6-4), r/u 1935 (Miss Jacobs won, 6-1, 6-4), won 1941 (beat Miss P Betz, 6-1, 6-4), won 1945 (beat Miss Betz, 3-6, 8-6, 6-4); doubles won 1930 with Miss B Nuthall (beat Miss E Cross/ Mrs L Harper, 3-6, 6-3, 7-5), won 1932 (beat Mrs Painter/Miss Marble, 8-6, 6-1), won 1934 (beat Miss C Babcock/Mrs D Andrus, 4-6, 6-3, 6-4), won 1935 (beat Miss Babcock/Mrs Andrus, 6-4, 6-2), r/u 1936 (Mrs J Van Ryn/Miss Babcock won, 9-7, 2-6, 6-4), all with Miss Jacobs; won 1937 (beat Miss Babcock/Mrs Van Ryn, 7-5, 6-4), won 1938 (beat Mrs R Mathieu/Miss J Jedrzejowska, 6-8, 6-4, 6-3), won 1939 (beat Miss K Stammers/Mrs S Hammersley, 6-4, 8-6), won 1940, all with Miss Marble; won 1941 with Miss Osborne; mixed doubles won 1932 with F Perry (beat H Vines/Miss Jacobs, 6-3, 7-5), r/u 1933 with G Lott (Vines/Miss Ryan won, 11-9, 6-1), won 1935 with E Maier (beat R Menzel/Miss Stammers), r/u 1936 (C G Mako/ Miss Marble won, 6-3, 6-2), won 1937 (beat Y Petra/ Mrs S Henrotin, 6-2, 8-10, 6-0), both with D Budge; won 1941 with J Kramer. US Wightman Cup team 1930–9.

French doubles r/u 1934 with Miss Jacobs (Mrs Mathieu/Miss Ryan won, 3-6, 6-4, 6-2); mixed doubles won 1939 with E T Cooke.

Wimbledon doubles r/u 1930 with Miss Cross (Mrs H Moody/Miss Ryan won, 6-2, 9-7), r/u 1936 with Miss Jacobs (Miss F James/ Miss Stammers won, 6-2, 6-1), won 1938 (beat Mrs Mathieu/Miss Yorke, 6-2, 6-3), won 1939 (beat Miss Jacobs/Miss Yorke, 6-1, 6-0), both with Miss Marble; mixed doubles r/u 1936 with Budge (Perry/Miss D Round won, 7-9,

*Centre left: Adriano Panatta
was Italy's No 1 in 1977 and
remained in the world's top
ten.*
*Centre right: Frank Parker
was among America's top ten
players for 17 years, 1932–49.*

7-5, 6-4), r/u 1938 with H Henkel (Budge/Miss
Marble won, 6-1, 6-4).

Pan-American Games

Tennis was included in the Pan-American
games as the Pan-American tennis championships, on five occasions: in Buenos Aires (1951),
Mexico City (1955), Chicago (1959), São Paulo
(1963), and Winnipeg (1967). Thereafter it was
excluded from the games. During those five
games Mexico gained 26 medals (ten gold,
ten silver and six bronze). Of these Palafox won
five gold and two bronze and Miss Yola Ramirez
won four gold, two silver and one bronze. The
United States, which did not compete in 1951,
was second in the medals table with 17 (five gold,
three silver, nine bronze), followed by Argentina, 13 (four gold, seven silver, two bronze),
Brazil, 11 (five gold, two silver, four bronze),
Chile, three (one gold, one silver, one bronze),
Ecuador, three (one gold, two bronze), and
Canada, two (one silver, one bronze).

PANATTA, Adriano, Italy

Born July 1950, Rome. After winning the
Italian national singles titles a record six times
up to 1975, Panatta had a poor season in 1976,
losing his championship to Corrado Barazzutti,
and winning only the Italian and French Opens.
His only other success was in the Italian Davis
Cup 4-1 victory over Chile, in which he won
both his singles and his doubles with Bertolucci.
Even so, he retained his No 1 ranking in Italy
and started 1977 still in the world top ten. He
shot to prominence in 1970 when, aged 20, he
beat Willy Bungert in the West Berlin Open and
won the Italian national for the first time, beating
Pietrangeli. He made a good impression on his
first Wimbledon appearance in 1972 and the
following year beat Năstase in the final of the
British hard courts. He had another poor year
in 1974 but returned to form in 1975 with wins
over Borg, Vilas, Ashe, Orantes, Parun and
Connors.

Italian Open singles won 1976 (beat K
Warwick); Italian national singles won 1970–5.

French Open singles won 1976 (beat H
Solomon, 6-1, 6-4, 4-6, 7-6).

West German r/u 1972.

Swiss Open r/u 1972, 1976; doubles r/u 1976
with Bertolucci.

WCT Stockholm doubles r/u 1976 with T
Okker.

British hard courts won 1973 (beat Năstase,
6-8, 7-5, 6-3, 8-6); doubles r/u 1973 with I
Tiriac.

PARKE, James Cecil, Ireland

Born July 1881, Clones, Co Monaghan, died
1946. A noted all-round athlete, Parke won the
Australian singles and doubles in 1912, the
Wimbledon mixed doubles in 1914. His Davis
Cup career spanned World War I and he was
selected in 1908–9, 1912–14 and 1920. He won
the Irish championships eight times, including

six successive wins – both records. He played
Rugby football for Ireland 20 times between
1903–7, was captain three times and was a
scratch golfer.

Irish singles won 1904–5, 1908–13.

Wimbledon doubles r/u All-Comers 1911 with
S Hardy (M Decugis/A Gobert won, 6-2, 6-1,
6-2), r/u All-Comers 1912 (C Dixon/H Roper
Barrett won, 6-8, 6-4, 3-6, 6-3, 6-4), r/u All-
Comers 1913 (H Kleinschroth/F Rahe won, 6-3,
6-2, 6-4), both with A Beamish, r/u All-Comers
1920 with A Kingscote (C Garland/R Williams
won, 4-6, 6-4, 7-5, 6-2); mixed doubles r/u 1913
(H Crisp/Mrs C O Tuckey won, 3-6, 5-3, retired), won 1914 (beat A Wilding/Miss M
Broquedis, 4-6, 6-4, 6-2).

Australian singles won 1912 (beat A Beamish,
3-6, 6-2, 1-6, 6-1, 7-5); doubles won 1912 with
Dixon (beat Beamish/F G Lowe).

PARKER, E F, Australia

Winner of the Australian singles in 1913 and
the doubles in 1909 and 1913, Parker was a good
Australian player of the pre-World War I era
whose career was overshadowed by that of the
great Norman Brookes.

PARKER, Frank Andrew, USA

Born January 1916, Milwaukee. Parker, son of
Polish parents, was originally named Franciszek
Andzej Paikowski. A protégé of Mercer Beasley,
he was at his best on slow hard courts and, lacking the powerful shots of some of his contemporaries, achieved success through hard work
and dedication coupled with a formidable ball
control and deadly accurate service. Slender
and bespectacled, he showed little emotion
during play. He was among America's top ten
players for 17 consecutive years to 1949, when
he turned professional. His greatest success

was in winning the US singles title in 1944 and 1945, each time beating off the challenge of William Talbert. He also won the French singles in 1948 and the singles and doubles in 1949.

US singles r/u 1942 (F Schroeder won, 8-6, 7-5, 3-6, 4-6, 6-2), won 1944 (beat Talbert, 6-4, 3-6, 6-3, 6-3), won 1945 (beat Talbert, 14-12, 6-1, 6-2), r/u 1947 (J Kramer won, 4-6, 2-6, 6-1, 6-0, 6-3); doubles r/u 1933 with F X Shields (G Lott/L Stoefen won, 11-13, 9-7, 9-7, 6-3), won 1943 with Kramer (beat Talbert/D Freeman), r/u 1948 with Schroeder (G Mulloy/Talbert won, 1-6, 9-7, 6-3, 3-6, 9-7). US Davis Cup team 1937, 1939, 1946, 1948.

French singles won 1948 (beat J Drobný, 6-4, 7-5, 5-7, 8-6), won 1949 (beat J Patty, 6-3, 1-6, 6-1, 6-4); doubles won 1949 with R Gonzalez (beat E Fannin/E Sturgess, 6-2, 1-6, 10-8, 6-2).

Wimbledon doubles won 1949 with Gonzalez (beat Mulloy/Schroeder, 6-4, 6-4, 6-2).

PARUN, Onny, New Zealand

Born April 1944, Wellington, NZ, of Yugoslav and Australian parents. Parun has achieved a good record in major grass court tournaments but had a disappointing season after not recovering fully from an ankle injury during 1976, when playing Ilie Năstase at Forest Hills. Parun reached his first 'Big Four' final, the Australian singles, in 1973, losing to John Newcombe. In 1970, when he gained his first New Zealand national singles title, he was runner-up in the US indoor doubles with Brian Fairlie. He has taken the national singles title three times since then and won the Open singles in 1973 and again in 1976.

New Zealand Open singles won 1973, r/u 1974, won 1976. New Zealand national singles won 1970–2, 1974. Australian Open singles r/u 1973 (Newcombe won, 6-3, 6-7, 7-5, 6-1).

French doubles won 1974 with R Crealy (beat R Lutz/S Smith, 6-3, 6-2, 3-6, 5-7, 6-1).

US hard courts r/u 1973; US indoor doubles r/u 1970 with Fairlie.

WCT Johannesburg won 1976, WCT Washington r/u 1976.

PASARELL, Charles Manuel, USA

Born February 1944, San Juan, Puerto Rico. The son of two former Puerto Rican champions, Pasarell has twice made Wimbledon history. In 1967 he beat the reigning champion, Manuel Santana within two hours of the Wimbledon championships opening. Then in 1969, aged 25, he took part in a cliff-hanger of a match against the 41-year-old Mexican, Pancho Gonzalez which proved to be the longest in any event in the history of Wimbledon – 112 games in five hours twelve minutes. The first round match began at 6.30 PM and it was almost 9.00 PM before the first set was completed, Pasarell winning it 24-22. As the light faded, Gonzalez asked for a postponement but referee Michael Gibson decreed the match should continue. Angered, Gonzalez lost the second set 1-6 before a halt was called. Resuming next afternoon Gonzalez played possibly the best tennis of his entire career and won the third set 16-14. By then 83 games had been played and the Mexican was not finished: he took the next set 6-3 before Pasarell fought back magnificently. Seven times he was at match point and twice Gonzalez was 0-40 down. Yet he saved the set and match after 20 games, winning by 11-9 to thunderous applause.

Pasarell has won five US men's titles and five US junior titles and continues to be a formidable doubles and singles player.

US Open doubles r/u 1969 with R Ralston (K Rosewall/F Stolle won, 2-6, 7-5, 13-11, 6-3); US 18 doubles won 1961 with C Graebner; US national doubles r/u 1965 with F Froehling; US intercollegiate singles won 1966; US indoor singles won 1966–7, doubles won 1967 with A Ashe; Pacific Southwest doubles r/u 1976 with Ashe.

Below: Puerto Rican Charlie Pasarell is best remembered in Britain for the mammoth game he lost to Pancho Gonzalez after 112 games and five hours and 12 minutes at Wimbledon in 1969.

French doubles r/u 1970 with Ashe (I Năstase/ I Tiriac won, 6-2, 6-4, 6-3).

PASSEMARD, Simone *see* **Mathieu, Mrs Simone**

PATTERSON, Gerald Leighton, Australia
Born December 1895, Melbourne, Victoria, died 1967. The first man to win the Wimbledon singles title when the Challenge Round was abolished in 1922. Patterson had previously won the title in 1919 when he beat fellow-Australian Norman Brookes, losing only one set through the All-Comers rounds. He had a dynamite service and strong net attack, which put him among the first of the power players. In 1920 he won the mixed doubles with Suzanne Lenglen, enabling her to win the 'Triple Crown'. Patterson won the Australian doubles five times, partnered on three occasions by J Hawkes. He was a member of the Australasian Davis Cup team in 1919–20 and 1922, the Australian team in 1924–5 and 1928 and was non-playing captain in 1946.

Australian singles r/u 1914 (A O'Hara Wood won, 6-4, 6-3, 5-7, 6-1), r/u 1922 (J Anderson won, 6-0, 3-6, 3-6, 6-3, 6-2), r/u 1925 (Anderson won, 11-9, 2-6, 6-2, 6-3), won 1927 (beat J Hawkes, 3-6, 6-4, 3-6, 18-16, 6-3); doubles won 1914 with A Campbell (beat R Heath/A O'Hara Wood, 7-5, 3-6, 6-3, 6-3), won 1922 with Hawkes (beat Anderson/N Peach, 8-10, 6-0, 6-0, 7-5), r/u 1924 (Brookes/Anderson won, 6-2, 6-4, 6-3), won 1925 (beat Anderson/F Kalms, 6-4, 8-6, 7-5), both with P O'Hara Wood; won 1926 (beat Anderson/P O'Hara Wood, 6-1, 6-4, 6-2), won 1927 (beat P O'Hara Wood/I McInnes, 8-6, 6-2, 6-1), both with Hawkes.

US doubles won 1919 with Brookes (beat W Tildin/V Richards, 8-6, 6-3, 4-6, 6-2).

Wimbledon singles won 1919 (beat Brookes, 6-3, 7-5, 6-2), r/u 1920 (Tilden won, 2-6, 6-3, 6-2, 6-4), won 1922 (beat R Lycett, 6-3, 6-4, 6-2); doubles r/u 1922 with P O'Hara Wood (Anderson/Lycett won, 3-6, 7-9, 6-4, 6-3, 11-9), r/u 1928 with Hawkes (J Brugnon/H Cochet won, 13-11, 6-4, 6-4); mixed doubles won 1920 with Miss Lenglen (beat Lycett/Miss E Ryan, 7-5, 6-3).

PATTY, John Edward (Budge), USA
Born February 1924, Fort Smith, Arkansas. Though American by birth, Patty's game was largely shaped by European influence when he took up residence in Europe after service in World War II. A player with impeccable timing, classic style and famous for his forehand volley and passing shots, he won the Wimbledon and French singles in 1950, beating his great friend and rival, Jaroslav Drobný in the latter. He was the first man to win this 'double' since Don Budge in 1938. It was with Drobný that he played his most famous match, the third round of the Wimbledon singles in 1953. The two battled through an enthralling four hours 23 minutes and 93 games before Drobný won 8-6,

16-18, 3-6, 8-6, 12-10 as the scoreboard lights shone brightly through the darkness gathering about the Centre Court.

In 1957 Patty, aged 33, partnered by Gardnar Mulloy, 43, reached the Wimbledon doubles final unseeded and pulled off a spectacular and unexpected win over Lew Hoad and Neale Fraser to end seven years' Australian domination of the event.

US doubles r/u 1957 with Mulloy (A Cooper/ Fraser won, 4-6, 6-3, 9-7, 6-3). US Davis Cup team 1951.

French singles r/u 1949 (F Parker won, 6-3, 1-6, 6-1, 6-4), won 1950 (beat Drobný, 6-1, 6-2, 3-6, 5-7, 7-5); mixed doubles won 1946 with Miss P Betz (beat T Brown/Miss D Bundy, 7-5, 9-7).

Wimbledon singles won 1950 (beat F Sedgman, 6-1, 8-10, 6-2, 6-3); doubles won 1957 with Mulloy (beat Fraser/Hoad, 8-10, 6-4, 6-4, 6-4).

PENROSE, Beryl (Mrs B Collier), Australia
Born December 1930, Sydney, NSW. Miss Penrose won the Australian doubles in 1954 and 1955 with Mrs M Hawton, the singles in 1955, beating Mrs T D Long, the previous year's champion, and the mixed doubles in 1956 with Neale Fraser.

Australian singles won 1955 (beat Mrs Long, 6-4, 6-3); doubles r/u 1953 (Miss M Connolly/ Miss J Sampson won, 6-4, 6-2), won 1954 (beat Mrs H Redick-Smith/Mrs J Wipplinger, 6-3, 8-6), won 1955 (beat Mrs H Hopman/Mrs A Thiele, 7-5, 6-1), all with Mrs Hawton; mixed doubles r/u 1954 with J Bromwich (R Hartwig/ Mrs Long won, 4-6, 6-1, 6-2), won 1956 (beat R Emerson/Mrs Hawton, 6-2, 6-4).

Pepsi-Cola, USA
The American soft drinks manufacturers, Pepsi-Cola, a division of Pepsico Inc, were the original sponsors of the ILTF Grand Prix for two years (1970–1), committing about $250,000 each year.

Far left: American-born 'Budge' Patty took up residence in Europe after World War II.
Left: Fred Perry is seen here at Wimbledon 27 July 1935.

In 1970 Cliff Richey of America won the first prize of $25,000 and in 1971 another American, Stan Smith, won the same sum. In that year Billie Jean King won the $10,000 prize in the first Pepsi-Cola women's Grand Prix.

Pepsi-Cola also sponsored the Masters' Tournament for the first time in 1970, when Smith won, and again in 1971, when Ilie Năstase was the winner. Thereafter the company gave up its Grand Prix and Masters' sponsorship, which was taken up by the Commercial Union Assurance Company.

PERRY, Frederick John, GB

Born May 1909, Stockport, Cheshire, later became a US citizen. Son of a Labour Member of Parliament, Fred Perry, the man who restored British tennis prestige in the 1930s, did not become interested in the game until he was aged 19. His great love was table tennis at which he was world singles champion in 1929. Within a year of taking up tennis Perry had won the mixed doubles junior title for Middlesex county in 1928. He brought to the game the strong whip-lash wrist which was to stand him in good stead in future years on tennis courts throughout the world and help him become the first man to be singles champion of Australia, France, America and Wimbledon. By the time he turned professional in 1937 Perry had won every major title in the amateur game, had ended France's six-year Davis Cup reign in 1933 with Bunny Austin and helped retain the Cup for three more years, had won Wimbledon three times running and the US singles three times in all.

Tall, dark-haired and good-looking, Perry was supremely self-confident and never seemed to tire on court. He had a long, easy stride which made him a speedy mover, a devastating forehand, bolt-like serve and lethal smash. He liked to move quickly into the net behind his forcing shots. Apart from the speedy delivery of his serves, he liked to serve quickly, without pausing and this sometimes upset opponents,

Centre left: Yvon Petra was born in Indo-China and from there he travelled to France where he began his tennis career.
Centre right: Italian-born Nicola Pietrangeli played 164 Davis Cup rubbers between 1954 and 1972.

who called for a let.

His great years began in 1933 with the Davis Cup victory against France followed by his first US singles title when he beat Australian Jack Crawford. He defeated Crawford again for his first Wimbledon victory in 1934 and retained the US crown in a tough battle with Wilmer Allison, who squared the match after being two sets down but lost the fifth 8-6. In 1935 Perry took the French title from Baron von Cramm and later the two met again in the final at Wimbledon. Once more Perry won, but in 1936, when he faced that German across the Centre Court at Wimbledon again, the story was different: the Baron had beaten Perry in the French final. Perry had lost one set on his way to the Wimbledon final, von Cramm two. In the second game von Cramm, noted for his sportsmanship, injured a thigh muscle but successfully disguised the fact for some time. The first game went to deuce ten times and a long battle seemed inevitable. Instead, it was over in less than 45 minutes. Perry winning, 6-1, 6-1, 6-0 – and equalling Wilfred Renshaw's defeat of John Hartley in 1881 as the briefest final.

Perry signed as a professional at the end of 1936, by which time he had played 52 Davis Cup rubbers and won 45 of them – a percentage record unequalled by anyone playing over 50 rubbers. He made his professional debut at Madison Square Garden, New York, in 1937 against Ellsworth Vines who, in the subsequent tour, won 32 of the 61 matches. However, Perry's contract gave him $91,335 while Vines picked up only $34,195. Next year they co-promoted a less successful tour, Vines won 48 matches, Perry 35 and they divided $34,000. Later Perry became a teaching professional, continuing to play into his fifties and also establishing a reputation as a writer and broadcaster.

Wimbledon singles won 1934 (beat Crawford, 6-3, 6-0, 7-5), won 1935 (beat von Cramm, 6-2, 6-4, 6-4), won 1936 (beat von Cramm, 6-1, 6-1, 6-0); doubles r/u 1932 with G Hughes (J Borotra/J Brugnon won, 6-0, 4-6, 3-6, 7-5, 7-5); mixed doubles won 1935 (beat H Hopman/Mrs Hopman, 7-5, 4-6, 6-2), won 1936 (beat D Budge/Mrs S P Fabyan, 7-9, 7-5, 6-4) both with Miss D Round. British Davis Cup team 1931–6.

Australian singles won 1934 (beat Crawford, 6-3, 7-5, 6-1), r/u 1935 (Crawford won, 2-6, 6-4, 6-4, 6-4); doubles won 1934 (beat A Quist/D Turnbull, 6-8, 6-3, 6-4, 3-6, 6-3), r/u 1935 (Crawford/V McGrath won, 6-4, 8-6, 6-2), both with Hughes.

French singles won 1935 (beat von Cramm, 6-3, 3-6, 6-1, 6-3), r/u 1936 (von Cramm won, 6-0, 2-6, 6-2, 2-6, 6-0); doubles won 1933 with Hughes (beat Quist/McGrath, 6-2, 6-4, 2-6, 7-5); mixed doubles won 1932 (beat S Wood/Mrs H Moody, 6-4, 6-2), r/u 1933 (Crawford/Miss M Scriven won, 6-2, 6-3), both with Miss B Marshall.

US singles won 1933 (beat Crawford, 6-3, 11-13, 4-6, 6-0, 6-1), won 1934 (beat Allison, 6-4, 6-3, 3-6, 1-6, 8-6), won 1936 (beat Budge, 2-6, 6-2, 8-6, 1-6, 10-8); mixed doubles won 1932 with Miss S Palfrey (beat H Vines/Miss H Jacobs, 6-3, 7-5).

PETRA, Yvon François Marie, France
Born March 1916, Cholon, Indo-China. Petra learned to play in bare feet in Indo-China, now Vietnam. He travelled with his parents to France and became a barman and part-time tennis player. During World War II he was seriously wounded in the leg and taken prisoner. Instead of the amputation which seemed likely, a German doctor treated and saved the leg. Before the war he had won the French doubles.

A giant player who appeared, deceptively, to shamble, Petra was a whirlwind performer with a big serve but little polish to his game. Nevertheless in the first postwar Wimbledon of 1946, he disposed of players who were undoubtedly his betters in terms of strokes and experience. He simply blasted his way to the final, where he quickly went two sets up against Geoff Brown. Using his height and thundering forehand against the shorter Brown, Petra found that his opponent was also a power player with great accuracy. Brown took the third set but dropped behind in the fourth until Petra was serving for the match at 40-15. Then Brown unleashed two lightning two-fisted returns which flashed past the Frenchman and levelled the match. Recovering from those returns, which had left him and the crowd stunned, Petra took the final set 6-4 to win the title.

Earlier that year he had won his second French doubles title. (He had, in fact won the men's singles in 1943–5 and doubles in 1942–4 when France had unofficial closed championships.) He became a professional in 1948.

French doubles won 1938 with B Destreman (beat D Budge/G Mako, 3-6, 6-3, 9-7, 6-1), won 1946 with M Bernard (beat E Morea/F Segura, 7-5, 6-3, 0-6, 1-6, 10-8); mixed doubles won 1937 with Mrs R Mathieu (beat R Journu/Miss M Horn, 7-5, 7-5). French Davis Cup team 1937–9, 1946–7.

US mixed doubles r/u 1937 with Mrs S Henrotin (Budge/Mrs S P Fabyan won, 6-2, 8-10, 6-0).

Wimbledon singles won 1946 (beat Brown, 6-2, 6-4, 7-9, 5-7, 6-4); mixed doubles r/u 1937 with Mrs Mathieu (Budge/Miss A Marble won, 6-4, 6-1).

PIERCEY, Miss S *see* **Summers, Sheila**

PIETRANGELI, Nicola, Italy
Born September 1933, Tunis. The son of a French father and Russian mother, Pietrangeli had an unusual start to what became a brilliant tennis career. He was introduced to the game by his father and the two used to play together often. When the father was a prisoner of war he was allowed to organise a tennis tournament and Nicola, who was visiting the camp, was persuaded to enter. His first tournament victory came then: he beat his father. He went on to win over 20 major titles, be awarded the Italian Gold Medal for Athletic Valour and achieve a remarkable Davis Cup record. Between 1954 and 1972 he played 164 Davis Cup rubbers (more than anyone in the history of the Cup), won the most rubbers (120), played the most singles (110) and won most (78), played the most doubles (54) and won most (42) and played in more ties (66) than anyone else. He was twice French singles champion (1959–60) and once doubles champion (1959), won the Italian Open singles twice (1957, 1961), the German singles once (1960) and reached the Wimbledon doubles

final once (1956). Though he had a superb touch and fine timing, he tended to be inconsistent in performance. He was at his best on clay courts.

Italian singles won 1957 (beat G Merlo), won 1961 (beat R Laver); doubles r/u 1957. Divided 1960 (R Emerson/N Fraser), both with O Sirola.

French singles won 1959 (beat I C Vermaak, 3-6, 6-3, 6-4, 6-1), won 1960 (beat L Ayala, 3-6, 6-3, 6-4, 4-6, 6-3), r/u 1961 (M Santana won, 4-6, 6-1, 3-6, 6-0, 6-2), r/u 1964 (Santana won, 6-3, 6-1, 4-6, 7-5); doubles r/u 1955 (E Seixas/A Trabert won, 6-1, 4-6, 6-2, 6-4), won 1959 (beat Emerson/Fraser, 6-3, 6-2, 14-12); mixed doubles won 1958 with Miss S Bloomer (beat R Howe/Miss L Coghlan, 9-7, 6-8, 6-2).

Wimbledon doubles r/u 1956 with Sirola (L Hoad/K Rosewall won, 7-5, 6-2, 6-1).

PILIĆ, Nicolo (Nikki), Yugoslavia
Born August 1939, Split. A talented left-hander, Pilić has won the Yugoslavian national singles title five times since 1962. During the 1971

Above: Yugoslavian Nikki Pilić became a WCT contract professional in 1968.

Wimbledon meeting he married actress Mia Adamovič. In 1973 he captured world headlines when he was suspended by his own LTA for refusing to play in the Davis Cup. When the ILTF upheld the suspension but reduced it from nine months to one month, the ATP instructed its members to withdraw from Wimbledon and 79 players obeyed the instruction. He became a WCT contract professional in 1968.

In 1966 he and Gene Scott took part in a 98-game Wimbledon first round doubles match against Cliff Richey and Torben Ulrich, winning 19-21, 12-10, 6-4, 4-6, 9-7. The record still stands.

Yugoslavia singles won 1962–4, 1966–7.

French singles r/u 1973 (I Năstase won, 6-3, 6-3, 6-0).

US Open doubles won 1970 with P Barthès (beat R Emerson/R Laver, 6-3, 7-6, 4-6, 7-6).

Wimbledon doubles r/u 1962 with B Jovanovic (R Hewitt/F Stolle won, 6-2, 5-7, 6-2, 6-4).

Stockholm Indoor Open won 1969.

Wills Indoor Open won 1970.

Rothmans' Albert Hall r/u 1971.

PIM, Dr Joshua, Ireland

Born May 1869, Bray, Co Wicklow, died 1942. A colourful Irish doctor, Pim was part of the 'invasion' of Wimbledon by Ireland in 1890, when the two singles championships and the doubles (Pim and F O Stoker) went to Irish players. The following year, playing with an injured hand, he reached the All-Comers final but was beaten by Wilfred Baddeley, who was aged 19 years five months 23 days – the youngest male winner of a major singles grass championship. In 1892 Baddeley won again in the Challenge Round but in 1893 and 1894 Pim beat Baddeley for the title. He also won the doubles again in 1893 and the Irish singles 1893–5. In 1902, for some obscure reason of Irish humour, he was nominated for the British Isles Davis Cup team as 'Mr X'; he lost both his singles.

Wimbledon singles r/u 1891 All-Comers (W Baddeley won, 6-4, 1-6, 7-5, 6-0), r/u 1892 Challenge Round (Baddeley won, 4-6, 6-3, 6-3, 6-2), won 1893 (beat Baddeley, 3-6, 6-1, 6-3, 6-2), won 1894 (beat Baddeley, 10-8, 6-2, 8-6); doubles won 1890 (wo), r/u 1891 (H Baddeley won, 6-1, 6-3, 1-6, 6-2), both with Stoker, r/u 1892 All-Comers with H Mahony (H S Barlow/E W Lewis won, 8-10, 6-3, 5-7, 11-9, 6-1), won 1893 Challenge Round with Stoker (beat Barlow/Lewis, 4-6, 6-3, 6-1, 2-6, 6-0).

PINNER, Uli, Germany

Born February 1954, Zittan, West Germany. A young player of promise, Piller started his international career well and reached the final of the French junior championships in 1972, losing to Britain's 'Buster' Mottram. The following year he went as far as the semi-finals of the German indoor singles and won the national

singles title. He won the Australian hard court singles in 1974. Though he has had wins over V Amritraj, Franulovic, Cornejo, Crealy, Fibak and Pilić, he has not recently achieved top international successes.

PLAYER, John & Sons, GB

One of Britain's leading tobacco companies, John Player & Sons entered the field of tennis sponsorship in 1970 through the Nottingham tournament, introducing a round robin prize-money event. The tournament forms part of the Grand Prix 'AA' group.

PLOTZ, Hans-Joachim, Germany

Born February 1944, Berlin. Considered one of Europe's best clay court players, Plotz has achieved his best results on his home territory. He was national champion in 1968 and runner-up in 1967 and 1970, won the doubles five years running, 1967–71, and again in 1974, when he also won the national mixed doubles.

POHMANN, Hans Jurgen, Germany

Born May 1947, Cologne. A talented player with a double-handed backhand, Pohmann has consistency on his side and regularly turns in good performances on the world circuit. In 1976 he was the centre of a characteristic but unusually unpleasant loss of temper by Rumanian Ilie Năstase during the US Open. Năstase felt that Pohmann was allowed too long to recover from cramps and that, rightly, he should not have been treated on court by a doctor. 'Nasty' was at his nastiest, rowing with the officials, screaming abuse at the crowd (which itself had nothing to be proud of in its taunting) and finally spitting at Pohmann. He went on to win 7-6, 4-6, 7-6, was fined $1000 and suspended for three weeks.

West German national singles won 1970; doubles won 1973–4, both with J Fassbender; mixed doubles r/u 1972 with Mrs H Masthoff, r/u 1974 with Mrs K Ebbinghaus; Munich doubles r/u 1976, Berlin doubles r/u 1976; Kitzbuhel doubles r/u 1976; Swiss Open doubles won 1976, all with Fassbender.

US Professional doubles r/u 1974 with M Riessen; US clay courts doubles r/u 1974; Canadian Open doubles r/u 1974, both with Fassbender.

POUCH, Mrs H R see Helwig, Helen

PRICE, Sandra (née Reynolds), South Africa

Born March 1939, Bloemfontein. An attractive player, Miss Reynolds had her most successful year in 1960 when, though deprived by Bernice Vukovich of her previous year's South African title, she beat Darlene Hard and Ann Haydon to reach the final of the Wimbledon singles. Though defeated by Maria Bueno, she later beat Christine Truman and Miss Bueno to win the German championship.

Australian women's doubles won 1959 with

Miss R Schuurman (beat Mrs M Reitano/Miss L Coghlan, 7-5, 6-4); mixed doubles won 1959 with R Mark (beat R Laver/Miss Schuurman, 4-6, 13-11, 6-2).

French doubles won 1959 (beat Miss Y Ramirez/Miss L M Reyes, 2-6, 6-0, 6-1), won 1961 (Miss Bueno/Miss Hard scratched), won 1962 (beat Miss M Smith/Miss J Bricka, 6-4, 6-4), all with Miss Schuurman.

Wimbledon singles r/u 1960 (Miss Bueno won, 8-6, 6-0); doubles r/u 1960 (Miss Bueno/Miss Hard won, 6-4, 6-0), r/u 1962 (Miss B J Moffitt/Mrs J R Susman won, 5-7, 6-3, 7-5), both with Miss Schuurman.

Professional World Tournament *see* **London Professional Indoor Championships**

PROISY, Patrick, France
Born September 1949, Evreux. After making a rapid advance on the international circuit in 1972–3, Proisy's career was hampered by back and elbow injuries in 1974 and he has had difficulty in returning to his best form. He was French junior champion in 1967, when he was also a member of the winning Galea Cup team. In 1968 he was again in the cup team which lost to Spain in the final. He won the World Student Games singles finals in 1970 and in 1971 was runner-up for the first time in the French nationals, a position he reached again in 1972–3.

French Open r/u 1972 (A Gimeno won, 6-4, 6-3, 6-1, 6-1); Benson and Hedges Open New Zealand r/u 1973; Coca Cola Bournemouth r/u 1975; Florence ATP r/u 1976.

Prudential Cup
The Prudential County Cup is awarded by the Prudential Assurance Company to the winning county in the British inter-county grass court championships. The company first started sponsoring the Inter-County Week in 1973 by putting up £7500.

PUŽEJOVÁ, Miss V *see* **Suková, Vera**

Queen's Club, London, GB
At one time the famous Queen's Club in London was a centre for almost every type of ball game, as well as athletics and cycling. It is situated on some 13 acres (about 5 hectares) of land, the 'Queen's field', at Baron's Court, which was bought in 1887 for the foundation of an athletic club when the old Prince's Club in Hans Place, Knightsbridge, closed. In addition to lawn tennis courts, there were two real tennis courts, two rackets courts and two covered lawn tennis courts, Eton fives courts and an asphalt skating rink. Outside there were also Rugby and football pitches and an athletics track.

Lack of space for spectators forced the athletics and football activities to end in the 1920s and more space was taken for tennis, which now has 15 grass courts, 13 hard courts and five covered courts. The London grass court championships were held there until 1973 and the British covered courts championships until 1968. During World War II the club was hit by bombs on several occasions and two covered courts built on the site of the skating rink were destroyed, as were two squash courts. One of the two real tennis courts and the Eton fives courts were damaged.

The club has been owned by the LTA since 1954 and has been a training ground for the LTA special courses. The Davis Cup and King's Cup have been staged there in the past and in 1963 it was the venue for the first Federation Cup.

QUIST, Adrian Karl, Australia
Born August 1913, Medindia, Southern Australia. One of Australia's finest players and the outstanding exponent of the doubles game, Quist won ten successive doubles titles in the Australian championships. Of this string of victories, eight were scored with John Bromwich, with whom he developed an exceptional playing understanding which proved virtually unbeatable. There were 15 years between his first and last Wimbledon doubles victories: 1935 with Jack Crawford and 1950 with Bromwich. Quist also won the French doubles in 1935 with Crawford and the 1939 US doubles with Bromwich. A sturdy figure, he produced powerful shots and had excellent placement. In addition to his doubles brilliance, he was a considerable singles player, taking the Australian title three times. In 1936, during his long membership of the Australian Davis Cup team, he beat Wilmer Allison in the singles of the American zone final and then, partnered by Crawford, beat Don Budge and Gene Mako in the doubles after being two sets down, 4-6, 2-6, 6-4, 7-5, 6-4.

Australian singles won 1936 (beat Crawford, 6-2, 6-3, 4-6, 3-6, 9-7), r/u 1939 (Bromwich won, 6-4, 6-1, 6-3), won 1940 (beat Crawford), won 1948 (beat Bromwich, 6-4, 3-6, 6-3, 2-6, 6-3); doubles r/u 1934 (F Perry/G Hughes won, 6-8, 6-3, 6-4, 3-6, 6-3), won 1936 (beat Crawford/V B McGrath, 6-8, 6-2, 6-1, 3-6, 6-2), won 1937 (beat Bromwich/J Harper, 6-2, 9-7, 1-6, 6-8, 6-4), all with D Turnbull, won 1938 (beat G von Cramm/H Henkel, 7-5, 6-4, 6-0), won 1940, won 1946, won 1947 (beat F Sedgman/G Worthington, 6-1, 6-3, 6-1), won 1948 (beat Sedgman/C F Long, 1-6, 6-8, 9-7, 6-3, 8-6), won 1949 (beat G Brown/O Sidwell, 1-6, 7-5, 6-2, 6-3), won 1950 (beat E Sturgess/J Drobný, 6-3, 5-7, 4-6, 6-3, 8-6), r/u 1951 (Sedgman/K McGregor won, 11-9, 2-6, 6-3, 4-6, 6-3), all with Bromwich. Australian Davis Cup team 1933–9, 1946, 1948.

French doubles r/u 1933 with McGrath (Hughes/Perry won, 6-2, 6-4, 2-6, 7-5), won 1935 with Crawford (beat McGrath/Turnbull, 6-1, 6-4, 6-2); mixed doubles r/u 1934 with Miss E Ryan (Borotra/Miss C Rosambert won, 6-2, 6-4).

US doubles won 1939 with Bromwich (beat Crawford/H Hopman, 8-6, 6-1, 6-4).

Wimbledon doubles won 1935 with Crawford (beat W Allison/J van Ryn, 6-3, 5-7, 6-2, 5-7, 7-5), won 1950 with Bromwich (beat Brown/Sidwell, 7-5, 3-6, 6-3, 3-6, 6-2).

RALSTON, Richard Dennis, USA

Born July 1942, Bakersfield, California. At the age of 17 years 11 months in 1960 Ralston became Wimbledon male champion when he and Rafael Osuna won the men's doubles unseeded. In was a year which accurately summed up the amateur career of this tempestuous player. Against expectations he reached the semi-final of the US championship singles yet he unexpectedly lost in the third round of the US clay court championships and failed to retain the national junior title he had won the year before. An extremely powerful player with a thundering service and great accuracy, his great weakness was his temper, which too often boiled over at the wrong moments. Even so, he won the US doubles three times and the French doubles once, in 1966 shortly before turning professional.

US doubles won 1961 (beat Osuna/A Palafox, 6-3, 6-4, 2-6, 13-11), r/u 1932 (Osuna/Palafox won, 6-4, 10-12, 1-6, 9-7, 6-3), won 1963 (beat Osuna/Palafox, 9-7, 4-6, 5-7, 6-3, 11-9), won 1964 (beat M Sangster/G Stilwell, 6-3, 6-2, 6-4), all with C R McKinley, r/u 1966 with C Graebner (R Emerson/F Stolle won, 6-4, 6-4, 6-4), r/u 1969 with C Pasarell (K Rosewall/Stolle won, 2-6,

7-5, 13-11, 6-3); mixed doubles r/u 1961 with Miss D Hard (R Marble/Miss M Smith won, wo), r/u 1969 with Miss F Durr (M Riessen/Mrs M Court won, 7-5, 6-3). US Davis Cup team 1960–6; non-playing captain 1972–4.

French doubles won 1966 with Graebner (I Năstase/I Tiriac, 6-3, 6-3, 6-0).

Wimbledon singles r/u 1966 (M Santana won, 6-4, 11-9, 6-4); doubles won 1960 with Osuna (beat M Davies/R Wilson, 7-5, 6-3, 10-8), r/u 1971 with Ashe (Emerson/Laver won, 4-6, 9-7, 6-8, 6-4, 6-4); mixed doubles r/u 1962 with Miss A Haydon (N Fraser/Mrs W duPont won, 2-6, 6-3, 13-11), r/u 1966 with Mrs B J King (K Fletcher/Miss Smith won, 4-6, 6-3, 6-3).

RAMIREZ, Raul Carlos, Mexico

Born June 1953, Ensenada. A former US junior champion, Ramirez was coached by the late Rafael Osuna and by George Tooley and has established himself as one of the world's leading players in only a few seasons. He first made an impression when, in 1973, the year he turned professional, he had wins against Ashe, Borg, Connors, Lutz, Gorman, Năstase and Newcombe. He and Brian Gottfried have formed an American–Mexican doubles partnership of considerable success, combining subtlety with pace. They have gained more than a dozen major doubles titles and a host of lesser successes. In 1977 they won the French Open for the second time and the Italian Open doubles for the third time since 1974, and were runners-up to Hewitt and McMillan in the US Open. With Gottfried he was runner-up in the Benson and Hedges 1977 doubles and he lost in straight sets to Dibbs in the 1977 Oviedo GP singles final.

US Open doubles r/u 1977 (R Hewitt/F McMillan won, 6-4, 6-0); US clay courts doubles won 1976 (beat F McNair/S Stewart, 6-2, 6-2); WCT championship doubles won 1975; WCT Richmond won 1976, WCT Monterey won 1976; Barcelona doubles won 1976; Commercial Union Masters doubles r/u 1976 (McNair/

Left: Raul Ramirez was a top junior who turned professional when he was only 20. He has had great success in both singles and doubles matches.

Stewart won, 6-3, 5-7, 5-7, 6-4, 6-4), all with Gottfried; WCT Caracas won 1976, WCT Mexico City won 1976; doubles won with Gottfried; WCT Jackson won 1976; Washington singles r/u 1976, doubles won with Gottfried.

French doubles won 1975 (beat J Alexander/ P Dent, 6-4, 2-6, 6-2, 6-4), r/u 1976 (McNair/ Stewart won, 7-6, 6-3, 6-1), won 1977 (beat W Fibak/J Kodeš, 7-6, 4-6, 6-3, 6-4).

Wimbledon doubles won 1976 with Gottfried (beat R Case/G Masters, 3-6, 6-3, 8-6, 2-6, 7-5); mixed doubles r/u 1973 with Miss J Newberry (O Davidson/Mrs B J King won, 6-3, 6-2).

Italian singles won 1975; doubles won 1974, 1976, 1977, all with Gottfried.

Swiss Open singles won 1976 (beat A Panatta).

Canadian Open doubles won 1976 with R Hewitt.

Vienna singles won 1976; doubles r/u with Gottfried.

Dewar Cup won 1976 (beat M Orantes).

Benson and Hedges doubles r/u 1977 with Gottfried (S Mayer/McMillan won, 6-3, 7-6).

Mexican Davis Cup team 1973– .

RAMIREZ, Yola, Mexico

Born March 1935, Mexico City. The best-known woman player from Mexico, Miss Ramirez was ranked No 1 in Mexico and No 10 in the world in 1959, when she beat Christine Truman at Wimbledon, won the French mixed doubles and was runner-up for the French doubles, which she had won the previous year.

French singles r/u 1960 (Miss D Hard won,

6-3, 6-4), r/u 1961 (Miss A Haydon won, 6-2, 6-1); doubles r/u 1957 (Miss Hard/Miss S Bloomer won, 7-5, 4-6, 7-5), won 1958 (beat Mrs M Hawton/Mrs T Long, 6-4, 7-5), r/u 1959 (Miss S Reynolds/Miss R Schuurman won, 2-6, 6-0, 6-1), all with Miss R Reyes; mixed doubles won 1959 with W Knight (beat R Laver/Miss Schuurman, 6-4, 6-4).

US doubles r/u 1961 with Miss E Buding (Miss Hard/Miss L Turner won, 6-4, 5-7, 6-0).

German singles won 1957.

REDONDO, Marita, USA
Born February 1956, National City, California. One of nine children of a Californian mother and Filipino father, Miss Redondo learned her tennis on cement surfaces and made her big-time debut in 1973 at age 17 when she played in the US Wightman Cup team and also defeated Evonne Goolagong and took a set off Chris Evert at Akron, Ohio. Since then she has stamped her personality and game – both of which sparkle – on the circuits and maintained steady performances until late 1976 when form slipped.

US amateur grass courts won 1971; US national 18 r/u 1971; Pacific Southwest won 1971; won Maureen Connolly Award for promise; Pacific Coast indoors r/u 1973; Midland Fixtures won 1976.

REID, Kerry see Kerry Melville

REITANO, Mary (née Carter), Australia
Born November 1934, Sydney, NSW. Twice winner of the Australian women's singles title and once of the doubles, Mrs Reitano twice won the junior championships and went on to improve her game by touring in Europe.

Australian singles won 1956 (beat Mrs T Long, 3-6, 6-2, 9-7), won 1959 (beat Miss R Schuurman, 6-2, 6-3); doubles r/u 1956 with Miss B Penrose (Mrs M Hawton/Mrs Long won, 6-2, 5-7, 9-7), r/u 1959 with Miss L Coghlan (Miss E Reynolds/Miss Schuurman won, 7-5, 6-4), won 1961 with Miss M Smith (beat Mrs Hawton/Miss J Lehane, 6-4, 3-6, 7-5), r/u 1962 with Miss D Hard (Miss R Ebbern/Miss Smith won, 6-4, 6-4); mixed doubles r/u 1960 with R Mark (T Fancutt/Miss Lehane won, 6-2, 7-5), r/u 1961 with J Pearce (R Hewitt/Miss Lehane won, 9-7, 6-2).

RENSHAW, James Ernest and William Charles, GB
Identical twins born January 1861, Leamington, Warwickshire. Ernest died 1899; William, 1904. Between them the Renshaw twins (William was the eldest by 15 minutes) won no fewer than 28 tennis titles, including 13 at Wimbledon. They are generally regarded as the creators of modern tennis in that, though they did not invent the smash or overhead service, they exploited and perfected them as attacking weapons. In effect, they turned what had been a social 'vicarage lawn' game into a thriving sport which saw the beginnings of today's mass spectator support. Both had warm personalities and were loved by the crowds. William, the more dominant of the two, was bolder, had greater power and a cooler judgement than Ernest, who had quicker footwork and a delightful touch. William delighted in leaping to take a ball at the top of its bounce, from which came the description 'The Renshaw Smash'.

In 1881, the year he won his first title, William beat Herbert Lawford in the All-Comers semi-final. It was the first of many clashes over a decade and which drew the crowds into Wimbledon. In that year's Challenge Round, William beat the Rev John Hartley 6-0, 6-1, 6-1 in just 37 minutes – the shortest men's singles final on record. In 1883 Ernest beat Lawford in a first round match in which the score blew with the strong wind gusting down the court. Favoured in turn by that wind Lawford took the first set 5-6, Renshaw the next 6-1, Lawford the third 3-6 and Renshaw the fourth 6-2. Then, when 5-0 down in the final set, Renshaw found his spin and a gust of wind in his favour; Lawford lost the point and Ernest went on to win 6-5 and go through to challenge his brother, losing 6-1, 2-6, 4-6, 6-2, 6-2. That year the twins accepted a challenge from the American brothers C M and J S Clark and beat them in two matches at the All-England Club – 6-4, 8-6, 3-6, 6-1, and 6-3, 6-2, 6-3. The Clarks took back to America news of this new, faster style of tennis.

The men's doubles event was brought to Wimbledon in 1884, having previously been held at Oxford (and won by the twins in 1880–1). The Renshaws promptly put their mark on that trophy and William again beat Lawford in the Challenge Round to take his fourth title. Next year Lawford beat Ernest in the All-Comers but once more lost to William in the Challenge Round, though the latter, having dropped the third set, had to fight back from 0-4, 15-40 in the fourth to take it 7-5. Though spectators loved the duels between the Renshaws and Lawford, other competitors were not so happy about losing the limelight and entrants dropped from 60 in 1880 to just 16 in 1887.

In 1886 Ernest lost in the semi-final to Lawford, who beat E W Lewis in the All-Comers before again losing to William. However, his turn was to come. In 1887, at his tenth challenge, Lawford won the All-Comers against Ernest (who at one stage was leading two sets to one) and took the Challenge Round when he had a walk-over because tennis elbow prevented William from defending. The following year the Lawn Tennis Association came into being and on 26 January William Renshaw was made president. At Wimbledon he had to play through in his bid to regain the title but lost to the colourful Irishman, Willoughby Hamilton, who then lost to Ernest in the semi-final. It was to be Ernest's year: he went on to beat Lewis in the All-Comers and Lawford in the Challenge

Round. Then, in 1889, William played through again and met Ernest in the Challenge Round, winning 6-4, 6-1, 3-6, 6-0 and gaining his seventh title, a record never equalled in men's events.

In the doubles event William and Ernest won at Oxford in 1880–1 and at Wimbledon in 1884–5, in 1886, when a Challenge Round was introduced, and in 1888–9. After that victory they retired.

Ernest: Wimbledon singles r/u 1882 (W Renshaw won, 6-1, 2-6, 4-6, 6-2, 6-2), r/u 1883 (W Renshaw won, 2-6, 6-3, 6-3, 4-6, 6-3), r/u 1885 All-Comers (Lawford won, 5-7, 6-1, 0-6, 6-2, 6-4), r/u 1887 All-Comers (Lawford won, 1-6, 6-3, 3-6, 6-4, 6-4), won 1888 Challenge Round (beat Lawford, 6-3, 7-5, 6-0), r/u 1889 (W Renshaw won, 6-4, 6-1, 3-6, 6-0); doubles won 1880 (beat C Cole/O Woodhouse), won 1881 (beat W Down/H Vaughan), won 1884 (beat E Lewis/E Williams, 6-3, 6-1, 1-6, 6-4), won 1885 (beat C Farrer/J Stanley, 6-3, 6-3, 10-8), won 1886 (beat Farrer/Stanley, 6-3, 6-3, 4-6, 7-5), won 1888 (beat P Bowes-Lyon/H W Wilberforce, 2-6, 1-6, 6-3, 6-4, 6-3), won 1889 (beat G Hillyard/Lewis, 6-4, 6-4, 3-6, 0-6, 6-1), all with William. Irish singles won 1883, 1887–8, 1892; Irish doubles, *see* William.

William: Wimbledon singles won 1881 (beat J Hartley, 6-0, 6-1, 6-1), won 1882 (beat E Renshaw, 6-1, 2-6, 4-6, 6-2, 6-2), won 1883 (beat E Renshaw, 2-6, 6-3, 6-3, 4-6, 6-3), won 1884 (beat Lawford, 6-0, 6-4, 9-7), won 1885 (beat Lawford, 7-5, 6-2, 4-6, 7-5), won 1886 (beat Lawford, 6-0, 5-7, 6-3, 6-4), won 1889 (beat E Renshaw, 6-4, 6-1, 3-6, 6-0); Wimbledon doubles, *see* Ernest. Irish singles won 1880–1, 1882; doubles won 1881, 1883–5, all with Ernest.

REYNOLDS, Sandra *see* Price, Mrs L E G

RICE, Helena Bertha Grace (Lena), Ireland
Born June 1866, Co Tipperary, Ireland, died 1907. Miss Rice, who was All-Comers runner-up at Wimbledon in 1889, became champion in the following year after playing only two matches because there were just four entries that year and she had a walk-over in the Challenge Round!

Wimbledon singles r/u 1889 All-Comers (Mrs G W Hillyard won, 4-6, 8-6, 6-4), won 1890 (wo).

RICHARDS, Vincent, USA
Born March 1903, New York, died 1959. Vin Richards became the new 'Boy Wonder' of American tennis when, with Bill Tilden, ten years his senior, he won the US doubles in 1918 at the age of 15. Together they won the doubles again in 1921–2 and Richard took the title again in 1925–6 with R Norris-Williams. Armed with one of the greatest volleys of the time, Richards, with Williams, twice helped repel the Davis Cup challenges of the French in 1925–6. He also had

successes against some of the famous 'Four Musketeers' of France at Wimbledon, where he beat Brugnon in the 1923 fourth round before losing to fellow-American 'Little Bill' Johnston. It was at the 1923 Wimbledon meeting that Richards provided evidence of the 'super-star' quality with which top players were beginning to be invested: he arrived at the ground with an entourage which included a typist, a secretary and a doctor. In 1924 Richards lost to Borotra in the quarter-finals but, with Frank Hunter, beat Lacoste and Borotra to take the doubles title. Then, with Howard Kinsey, he beat Cochet and Brugnon for the 1926 French doubles.

Richards became a professional in 1926, signing with C C Pyle for the 'circus' which was to tour with Suzanne Lenglen and Mary Browne. In 1927, with Howard Kinsey, he set up the US Professional Tennis Association and the following year went into the promotion business.

US doubles won 1918 (beat F B Alexander/B C Wright, 6-3, 6-4, 3-6, 2-6, 6-2), r/u 1919 (N Brookes/G Patterson won, 8-6, 6-3, 4-6, 4-6, 6-2), won 1921 (beat R Williams/W Washburn, 13-11, 12-10, 6-1), won 1922 (beat Patterson/P O'Hara Wood, 4-6, 6-1, 6-3, 6-3), all with Tilden, won 1925 (beat Patterson/J Hawkes, 6-2, 8-10, 6-4, 11-9), won 1926 (beat Tilden/A Chaplin, 6-4, 6-8, 11-9, 6-3), both with Williams; mixed doubles won 1919 with Miss M Zinderstein (beat Tilden/Miss F Ballin), won 1924 with Miss H Wills (beat Tilden/Mrs M Mallory, 6-8, 7-5, 6-0), r/u 1925 with Miss E Harvey (Hawkes/Miss K McKane won, 6-2, 6-4). US Davis Cup team 1922–6.

French doubles won 1926 with Kinsey (beat H Cochet/J Brugnon, 6-4, 6-1, 4-6, 6-4).

Wimbledon doubles won 1924 with Hunter (beat Washburn/Williams, 6-3, 3-6, 8-10, 8-6, 6-3), r/u with Kinsey (Brugnon/Cochet won, 7-5, 4-6, 6-3, 6-2).

RICHARDSON, Hamilton, USA
Born August 1933, Baton Rouge, Louisiana. Though Richardson proved himself a fine, powerful player and had some good international results he never achieved the major title wins among the 'Big Four' tennis nations which always seemed just around the corner. He began playing at the age of 12 and competed in his first tournament in 1946. The following year he won the US boys doubles and in 1948 the singles. By 1955 he was achieving results in senior events and was runner-up in the US indoor singles and in 1956 reached the semi-finals of the Wimbledon singles and doubles, and won the doubles at Queen's Club. His overall performance during the year gained him the William Johnston Trophy for his 'outstanding contribution to tennis'. In 1958 he won the US doubles title with Olmedo. He was a member of the US Davis Cup team in 1952, 1956, 1958 and 1965.

US doubles r/u 1956 with E Seixas (L Hoad/

K Rosewall won, 6-2, 6-2, 3-6, 6-4), won 1958 with Olmedo (beat S Giammalva/B MacKay, 6-4, 3-6, 6-3, 6-4).

RICHEY, George Clifford (Cliff), USA

Born December 1946, San Angelo, Texas. Son of a tennis professional, Cliff Richey had his most successful season in 1970, when he played a leading role in America's 5-0 Davis Cup win against West Germany, won the Grand Prix and reached the semi-finals of the French and US Opens. He took part in a record 98-game doubles with Torben Ulrich at the 1966 Wimbledon and in 1968 he had a dramatic and unexpected victory over Tony Roche in the second round, beating the Australian 3-6, 3-6, 19-17, 14-12, 6-3 before losing to Ray Ruffels. Then, in 1971, he took part in one of his finest matches, again at Wimbledon, when he faced Ken Rosewall in the quarter-final. Using all his power, his whipping forehand and his speed of movement, Richey took a two set lead and was 4-2 up in the third set, with the Australian 0-30 down. Amazingly Rosewall, now in the twentieth year of his career, turned the tables with a display of his full repertoire of strokes. He won the third and then, after trailing 6-7, took the fourth to level. By now the Centre Court was packed and the noise could be heard of the hundreds of fans clamouring outside. In the fifth set Rosewall was leading 5-4 when he lost four match points. He trailed 15-40 at 5 games all but took the eleventh game and went to his fifth match point against Richey, a man who was playing with courage and determination before a largely pro-Rosewall crowd. At last, in a fraction under four hours, Rosewall sent over a speeding backhand winner to go through to the semi-finals.

US junior champion 1963; US clay courts won 1966, 1970, r/u 1971; US indoors won 1968, r/u 1970-1. South Africa won 1972;

South America won 1966–7; Canada won 1969; Baltimore doubles r/u 1976 with Năstase.

RICHEY, Nancy (Mrs K S Gunter), USA

Born August 1942, San Angelo, Texas. Sister of Cliff, she played as Nancy Gunter for a time after her marriage in 1970 to Kenneth Gunter but has now reverted to her maiden name. One of the finest clay court players America has produced, she won the US clay courts singles a record six times in a row (1963–8) and was runner-up in 1977. She has won numerous singles and doubles titles throughout the world. Coached by her father, she became a grim, determined and generally cool baseliner who seldom goes in to the net. She has excellent ball placement both on her forehand and backhand. In 1965 she reluctantly shared the American No 1 ranking with Billie Jean King, her great rival. It was not until 1968 that the two actually met on court to settle their rivalry over that equal 'billing'. Then, in an invitation tournament at Madison Square Garden Miss Richey, still an amateur, faced Mrs King, who was playing her last match before becoming a professional. Mrs King took the first set 6-4 and led 5-3 and match point in the second when she missed a comparatively simple overhead shot. Immediately Miss Richey stepped in and took a staggering ten straight games to win the match 4-6, 7-5, 6-0. In 1968 Miss Richey also won the first French Open championship, beating Britain's Ann Jones.

US singles r/u 1966 (Miss M Bueno won, 6-3, 6-1), r/u 1969 (Mrs M Court won, 6-2, 6-2); doubles won 1963 with Mrs C Graebner (beat Miss B J Moffitt/Mrs J Susman, 6-4, 6-4), won 1966 with Miss Bueno (beat Mrs B J King/ Miss R Casals, 6-3, 6-4). US clay court singles won 1963–8, r/u 1977; doubles won 1964–5 with Mrs Graebner, won 1968 with Miss V

Left (centre): Marty Riessen is an all-round player who has enjoyed most of his successes in doubles play.
Left: Bobby Riggs is the only player to win all three Wimbledon events at his first and only challenge in 1939 but he is remembered nowadays for his 'grudge' matches against Margaret Court and Billie Jean King.

Ziegenfuss. US indoor singles won 1965; doubles won 1970 with Miss J Bartkowicz. US hard court singles won 1961; doubles won 1965 with Mrs Graebner, won 1966 with Miss Bueno. US Wightman Cup team 1962–8; Federation Cup 1964, 1968–9 (played 17 rubbers, won 15).

Australian singles r/u 1966 (Miss M Smith won, default), won 1967 (beat Miss L Turner, 6-1, 6-4); doubles won 1966 with Mrs Graebner (beat Miss Smith/Miss Turner, 6-4, 7-5).

French singles r/u 1966 (Mrs A Jones won, 6-3, 6-1), won 1968 (beat Mrs Jones, 5-7, 6-4, 6-1); doubles r/u 1969 with Mrs Court (Miss F Durr/Mrs Jones won, 6-0, 4-6, 7-5).

Wimbledon doubles won 1966 (beat Miss Smith/Miss J Tegart, 6-3, 4-6, 6-4), r/u 1967 (Miss Casals/Mrs King won, 9-11, 6-4, 6-2), both with Miss Bueno.

Italian singles r/u 1965. South African singles r/u 1969; doubles r/u 1969 with Miss V Wade. South American singles won 1964–5; doubles won 1966 with Miss N Baylon.

RIESSEN, Martin Claire (Marty), USA

Born December 1941, Hinsdale, Illinois. Son of a tennis coach at Northwestern University, Riessen is a fine all-round sportsman who has achieved his main successes in doubles and after being a semi-finalist six times, eventually won the US Open doubles in 1976 with Tom Okker. He became a contract professional in 1968, by which time he had won more than a dozen national and international titles. He has shared many mixed doubles titles with Margaret Court including the US Open mixed in 1969, 1970 and 1972, the French in 1969 and the Wimbledon in 1975.

US doubles won 1976 with Okker (beat P Kronk/C Letcher, 6-4, 6-4); mixed doubles won 1969 (beat R Ralston/Miss F Durr, 7-5, 6-3), won 1970 (beat F McMillan/Mrs R Dalton, 6-4,

6-4), won 1972 (beat I Năstase/Miss R Casals, 6-3, 7-5), r/u 1973 (O Davidson/Mrs King won, 6-4, 3-6, 7-5), all with Mrs Court. US clay court mixed doubles won 1969, 1970, 1972, r/u 1973, all with Mrs Court.

WCT Johannesburg doubles won 1976, WCT Memphis doubles r/u 1976, both with R Tanner.

Australian doubles r/u 1971 with Okker (J Newcombe/A Roche won, 6-2, 7-6).

French doubles won 1971 with A Ashe (beat T Gorman/S Smith, 6-8, 4-6, 6-3, 6-4, 11-9); mixed doubles won 1969 with Mrs Court (beat J C Barclay/Miss Durr, 7-5, 6-4). Paris indoor doubles won 1976 with Okker.

Wimbledon doubles r/u 1969 with Okker (Newcombe/Roche won, 7-5, 11-9, 6-3); mixed doubles r/u 1971 (Davidson/Mrs King won, 3-6, 6-2, 15-13), won 1975 (beat A Stone/Miss B Stöve, 6-4, 7-5), both with Mrs Court.

Italian doubles won 1968, divided 1969, both with Okker; mixed doubles won 1968 with Mrs Court.

West German doubles won 1968 with Okker; mixed doubles won 1969 with Miss J Tegart.

Canadian doubles won 1970 with W Bowrey, won 1971 with Okker.

Stockholm doubles r/u 1976.

World doubles r/u 1973, both with Okker.

South African singles won 1968; mixed doubles won 1968 with Miss P Walkden, won 1970, 1974, both with Mrs Court.

RIGGS, Robert Lorimer, USA

Born February 1918, Los Angeles, California. Riggs is unique in being the only player to win all three Wimbledon events at his first and only challenge in 1939. He has since made a mark as 'the champion who would not lie down' through much publicised challenge matches played when he was 55 against Margaret Court and Billie Jean King in 1973. He beat Mrs Court 6-2, 6-1 at Ramona, California, and lost to Mrs King 6-4, 6-3, 6-3 at the Houston Astrodome in front of 30,500 paying spectators and a television audience estimated at 50 million. Riggs, who became a professional in 1941, after winning the US singles title for the second time, might well have had a more successful career had not World War II come when he was at his peak. He was a confident match player with an excellent repertoire of shots, quick brain and excellent tactics which made up for his comparatively small stature. He had a steel-like wrist and played high-and-long or low-and-short equally accurately. Riggs started playing at the age of 12 and was spotted by Esther and Jerry Bartosh, whose protégé he became. By the age of 15 he was already winning senior tournaments and at 16 he defeated the US No 2 ranker, Frank Shields. After becoming a professional and joining the touring 'circus' he took up promoting in 1947. He is now an active veteran player in America.

US singles won 1939 (beat S W Van Horn, 6-4, 6-2, 6-4), r/u 1940 (W D McNeill won, 8-6, 6-8, 6-3, 7-5), won 1941 (beat F Kovacs, 5-7, 6-1, 6-3, 6-3); mixed doubles won 1940 with Miss A Marble. US Davis Cup team 1938–9.

French singles r/u 1939 (McNeill won, 7-5, 6-0, 6-3).

Wimbledon singles won 1939 (beat E Cooke, 2-6, 8-6, 3-6, 6-3, 6-2); doubles won 1939 with Cooke (beat C Hare/F Wilde, 6-3, 3-6, 6-3, 9-7); mixed doubles won 1939 with Miss Marble (beat Wilde/Miss N Brown, 9-7, 6-1).

RISELEY, Frank Lorymer, GB
Born July 1877, Clifton, Bristol, died 1959. Riseley, who was three times runner-up for the Wimbledon singles title, never achieved it but instead took the doubles crown twice (1902, 1906) with Sydney Smith. On each occasion they succeeded in breaking the stranglehold on the championships by the famous Doherty brothers, Laurie and Reggie, combining Smith's devastatingly accurate forehand with Riseley's power and speed at the net. Eighteen years separated Riseley's two Davis Cup appearances – 1904 and 1922.

Wimbledon singles r/u 1903 (L Doherty won, 7-5, 6-3, 6-0), r/u 1904 (L Doherty won, 6-1, 7-5, 8-6), r/u 1906 (L Doherty won, 6-4, 4-6, 6-2, 6-3); doubles r/u 1900 All-Comers (H A Nisbet/H Roper Barrett won, 6-2, 2-6, 6-8, 8-6, 6-2), won 1902 (beat L Doherty/R Doherty, 4-6, 8-6, 6-3, 4-6, 11-9), r/u 1903 (L Doherty/R Doherty won, 6-3, 6-4, 6-4), r/u 1904 (L Doherty/R Doherty won, 6-3, 6-4, 6-3), r/u 1905 (L Doherty/R Doherty won, 6-2, 6-4, 6-8, 6-3), won 1906 (beat L Doherty/R Doherty, 6-8, 6-4, 5-7, 6-3, 6-3).

Irish singles won 1906; doubles 1906; mixed doubles 1906.

RITCHIE, Major Josiah George, GB
Born October 1870, Westminster, London, died

1955. A regular competitor at Wimbledon at the turn of the century, Ritchie came closest to the coveted singles title in 1909, when he was runner-up to Arthur Gore. Twenty years later he was still entering. However, Ritchie twice won the doubles title with New Zealander Tony Wilding. On the first occasion in 1908, the scorebook entry was one of the most unusual seen at Wimbledon since Wilding had won the title the previous year with Australian Norman Brookes, who was not defending in the 1908 Challenge Round. Thus the entry read 'A F Wilding and M J G Ritchie (challengers) wo A F Wilding and N E Brookes (holders)'! It is the only occasion on which a champion walked-over himself to remain champion!

Wimbledon singles r/u 1902 All-Comers (L Doherty won, 8-6, 6-3, 7-5), r/u 1903 All-Comers F Riseley won, 1-6, 6-3, 8-6, 13-11), r/u 1904 All-Comers (Riseley won, 6-0, 6-1, 6-2), r/u 1909 Challenge Round (A Gore won, 6-8, 1-6, 6-2, 6-2, 6-2); doubles r/u All-Comers 1903 (L Doherty/R Doherty won, 8-6, 6-2, 6-2), won 1908 (wo), won 1910 (beat Gore/H Roper Barrett, 6-1, 6-1, 6-2), r/u 1911 (M Decugis/A Gobert won, 9-7, 5-7, 6-3, 2-6, 6-2), all with Wilding. Davis Cup 1908.

River Oaks, USA
The first River Oaks invitation tournament held at the River Oaks Country Club, Houston, Texas in April 1931 was won by Ellsworth Vines, shortly before he won his first US singles title. In those days there was a crowd capacity of 1200, including 900 in a covered grandstand, but before the next tournament this was doubled. For the next 40 years the invitation event was held annually – except between 1942–5 – and attracted many of the country's leading players and then famous internationals.

The only player to win the men's event four times was Brian 'Bitsy' Grant (1934–7), each time defeating Wilmar Allison. Gardnar Mulloy took the title three times (1946, 1952–3) and several players won twice. Apart from Vines and Allison, other US champions who won the River Oaks were Frank Parker and Rod Laver. Eleven Wimbledon champions also won: Vines, Riggs, Kramer, Falkenburg, Schroeder, Savitt, Trabert, Laver, Emerson, Santana and Newcombe. In 1973 River Oaks became part of the WCT circuit.

Women's events were held from 1932 (Miss A M Reichert won) until 1960, apart from the war years, and again in 1968–9, when Miss Bueno and Mrs Court were the winners. The first national women's champion to win at River Oaks was Sarah Palfrey Fabyan in 1940.

ROARK, Mrs A (*née* **Helen Wills**) *see* **Mrs F S Moody**

ROBB, Muriel Evelyn, GB
Born May 1878, Newcastle-upon-Tyne, died 1907. Winner of the 1902 non-championship

Wimbledon women's final, Miss Robb established a record which still stands for the longest women's final. Playing Mrs Charlotte Sterry, the reigning title-holder, she was leading 4-6, 13-11 when rain stopped play for the day. When the match was resumed the following day it was replayed and this time Miss Robb won 7-5, 6-1. The total number of games played was 53.

Wimbledon singles won 1902 (beat Mrs Sterry, 7-5, 6-1). Irish singles won 1901; Scottish singles won 1901; Welsh singles won 1899.

ROCHE, Anthony Dalton, Australia
Born May 1945, Wagga Wagga, NSW. One of the remarkable breed of Australian players of the 1960s left-hander Roche earns a place in tennis history books as much for his courageous fight back to the top after serious injury as for his brilliance as a doubles player. Junior champion of Australia in 1964 he was in among the international titles only a year later and continued to pull them in, particularly as doubles partner of fellow-Australian John Newcombe, until 1970 when tennis elbow threatened his career. He struggled against the injury until 1974, when a faith healer in the Philippines restored full use of the arm. Immediately he began to reappear in the world's winners' lists and confirmed his re-emergence among the world's top players when he won the Australian doubles with Newcombe for the fifth time in 1977, defeating Wimbledon champions Roger Case and Geoff Masters. Together Roche and Newcombe present a doubles partnership of sweeping power and agility which for more than a decade has ruled courts throughout the world. In 1969 they became the first pair to win three Wimbledon doubles titles since the abolition of the Challenge Round in 1922. He and Newcombe became contract professionals in 1968.

Australian doubles won 1965 (beat A Emerson/F Stolle, 3-6, 4-6, 13-11, 6-3, 6-4), r/u 1966 (Emerson/Stolle won, 7-9, 6-3, 6-8, 14-12, 12-10), won 1967 (beat O Davidson/W Bowrey, 3-6, 6-3, 7-5, 6-8, 8-6), won 1971 (beat M Riessen/T Okker, 6-2, 7-6), won 1976 (beat Case/Masters, 7-6, 6-4), won 1977 (beat Case/Masters, 6-7, 6-3, 6-1), all with Newcombe; mixed doubles won 1966 (beat Bowrey/Miss R Ebbern, 6-1, 6-3), r/u 1967 (Davidson/Miss L Turner won, 9-7, 6-4), both with Miss J Tegart.

French singles r/u 1965 (Stolle won, 3-6, 6-0, 6-2, 6-3), won 1966 (beat I Gulyas, 6-1, 6-4, 7-5), r/u 1967 (Emerson won, 6-1, 6-4, 2-6, 6-2); doubles won 1965 (beat K Fletcher/R Hewitt, 6-8, 6-3, 8-6, 6-2), won 1967 (beat Emerson/Fletcher, 6-3, 9-7, 12-10), won 1969 (beat Emerson/R Laver, 4-6, 6-1, 3-6, 6-4, 6-4), all with Newcombe.

US singles r/u 1969 (Laver won, 7-9, 6-1, 6-3, 6-2), r/u 1970 (K Rosewall won, 2-6, 6-4, 7-6, 6-3); doubles won 1967 with Newcombe (beat Davidson/Bowrey, 6-8, 9-7, 6-3, 6-3).

Wimbledon singles r/u 1968 (Laver won, 6-3, 6-4, 6-2); doubles won 1965 (beat Fletcher/Hewitt, 7-5, 6-3, 6-4), won 1968 (beat Rosewall/Stolle, 3-6, 8-6, 5-7, 14-12, 6-3), won 1969 (beat Okker/Riessen, 7-5, 11-9, 6-3), won 1970 (beat Rosewall/Stolle, 10-8, 6-3, 6-1), won 1974 (beat R Lutz/S Smith, 8-6, 6-4, 6-4) all with J Newcombe; mixed doubles r/u 1965 (Fletcher/Miss M Smith won, 12-10, 6-3), r/u 1969 (Stolle/Mrs A Jones won, 6-3, 6-2), both with Miss Tegart, won 1976 with Miss F Durr (beat R Stockton/Miss R Casals, 6-3, 2-6, 7-5).

Italian singles won 1966, r/u 1967, 1969; doubles r/u 1964, divided 1969, won 1971, all with Newcombe.

ROOSEVELT, Ellen and Grace, USA
Winner of the third US women's championship in 1890, Miss Ellen Roosevelt defeated her sister, Grace, in the All-Comers final before beating the title holder, Bertha Townsend, in the Challenge Round. She and Grace then won the first doubles title, held the same year. With C Hobart, Ellen won the mixed doubles in 1893.

ROSE, Mervyn Gordon, Australia
Born January 1930, Coffs Harbour, NSW. A gifted, individualistic left-hander, Rose scored doubles and singles successes in many parts of the world and in 1958, his last year as an amateur, won the singles titles of France), Germany and Italy. He gained the Australian singles and doubles titles in 1954, when he also won the Wimbledon doubles. He was a fine touch player and an excellent tactician. In 1964 as a player-coach, he spent three months working on Billie Jean King's game, improving her service and racket action.

Australian singles r/u 1953 (K Rosewall won, 6-0, 6-3, 6-4), won 1954 (beat R Hartwig, 6-2, 0-6, 6-4, 6-2); doubles r/u 1952 (F Sedgman/K McGregor won, 6-4, 7-5, 6-3), r/u 1953 (L Hoad/Rosewall won, 9-11, 6-4, 10-8, 6-4), both with D Candy, won 1954 with Hartwig (beat N Fraser/C Wilderspin, 6-3, 6-4, 6-2), r/u 1956

Left (centre): The partnership of Tony Roche (pictured here) and John Newcombe (picture page 181) has ruled world doubles matches for more than a decade.

with Candy (Hoad/Rosewall won, 10-8, 13-11, 6-4). Australian Davis Cup team 1950–7.

French singles won 1958 (beat L Ayala, 6-3, 6-4, 6-4); doubles r/u 1953 with Wilderspin (Hoad/Rosewall won, 6-2, 6-1, 6-1), r/u 1957 with Candy (M Anderson/A Cooper won, 6-3, 6-0, 6-3); mixed doubles r/u 1951 with Mrs T Long (Sedgman/Miss D Hart won, 7-5, 6-2), r/u 1953 with Miss M Connolly (E Seixas/Miss Hart won, 4-6, 6-4, 6-0).

US doubles r/u 1951 with Candy (McGregor/ Sedgman won, 10-8, 6-4, 4-6, 7-5), won 1952 with Seixas (beat McGregor/Sedgman, 3-6, 10-8, 10-8, 6-8, 8-6), won 1953 with Hartwig (beat G Mulloy/W Talbert, 6-4, 4-6, 6-2, 6-4); mixed doubles r/u 1951 with Miss S Fry (Sedgman/Miss Hart won, 6-3, 6-2).

Wimbledon doubles r/u 1953 (Hoad/Rosewall won, 6-4, 7-5, 4-6, 7-5), won 1954 (beat Seixas/ A Trabert, 6-4, 6-4, 3-6, 6-4), both with Hartwig; mixed doubles r/u 1951 with Mrs N Bolton (Sedgman/Miss Hart won, 7-5, 6-2), won 1957 with Miss Hard (beat Fraser/Miss A Gibson, 6-4, 7-5).

ROSEWALL, Kenneth Robert, Australia

Born November 1934, Sydney, NSW. Though Rosewall never won the Wimbledon singles title, it was the only one of the 'Big Four' singles crowns to elude him. His supremely classical style, impeccable backhand and fine groundstroke play set him among the all time 'greats'. He was a leader of postwar tennis as an amateur, a professional and a popular competitor in Open tennis from 1968. Although he lacked the power of his contemporary, Lew Hoad, the dark-haired, deceptively frail-looking Rosewall was a masterful handler of the racket with a delightful touch and crispness in executing his shots.

With Hoad, Rosewall went on a world tour in 1952, aged 17, after the potential of both youngsters had been spotted by the Australian LTA. The two had first met as 12-year-olds in a school tournament which Rosewall won. In 1946 they played an exhibition match at the famous Kooyong courts, Melbourne, and Rosewall again won. When Hoad lost a third time he gave up tennis for two years, but the two remained firm friends and excellent doubles partners. In 1953 both played in the Davis Cup Challenge Round, when Australia retained the Cup 3-2 against America and Rosewall won the decisive singles against Seixas. America took the Cup in 1954 but Hoad and Rosewall spearheaded the successful challenge of 1955 and the defence in 1956, after which Rosewall signed a contract with Jack Kramer.

By then he had won the American singles and doubles twice, the US singles, doubles and mixed doubles once, the French singles and doubles once and the Wimbledon doubles twice. He was by no means at the end of his winning days and went on to collect seven more 'Big Four' singles and doubles titles. He was world professional champion from 1960 until 1965 and in 1971, after joining WCT, won the US professional championships. In 1974 he reached his fourth Wimbledon singles final, 20 years after his first. He was decisively beaten by Jim Connors, who again won when they met in the US final that year. In 1977, at 42, he was again runner-up to Connors, this time in the Australian Open, which he has now won four times.

Australian singles won 1953 (beat M Rose, 6-0, 6-3, 6-4), won 1955 (beat Hoad, 9-7, 6-4, 6-4), r/u 1956 (Hoad won, 6-4, 3-6, 6-4, 7-5), won 1971 (beat A Ashe, 6-1, 7-5, 6-3), won 1972 (beat M Anderson, 7-6, 6-3, 7-5), r/u 1977 (Connors won, 7-5, 6-4, 6-2); doubles won 1953 (beat D Candy/Rose, 9-11, 6-4, 10-8, 6-4), r/u 1955 (E Seixas/A Trabert won, 6-4, 6-2, 2-6, 3-6, 6-1), won 1956 (beat Rose/Candy, 10-8, 13-11, 6-4), all with Hoad, r/u 1969 with F Stolle (R Emerson/R Laver won, 6-4, 6-4), won 1972 with O Davidson (beat G Masters/R Case, 3-6, 7-6, 6-2).

French singles won 1953 (beat Seixas, 6-3, 6-4, 1-6, 6-2), won 1968 (beat Laver, 6-3, 6-1, 2-6, 6-2), r/u 1969 (Laver won, 6-4, 6-3, 6-4); doubles won 1953 (beat Rose/C Wilderspin, 6-2, 6-1, 6-1), r/u 1951 (Seixas/Trabert won, 6-4, 6-2, 6-1), both with Hoad, won 1968 with Stolle (beat Laver/Emerson, 6-3, 6-4, 6-3).

US singles r/u 1953 (Trabert won, 9-7, 6-3, 6-3), won 1956 (beat Hoad, 4-6, 6-2, 6-3, 6-3), won 1970 (beat A Roche, 2-6, 6-4, 7-6, 6-3), r/u 1974 (Connors won, 6-1, 6-0, 6-1); doubles r/u 1954 (Seixas/Trabert won, 3-6, 6-4, 8-6, 6-3), won 1956 (beat H Richardson/Seixas, 6-2, 6-2, 3-6, 6-4), both with Hoad, won 1969 with Stolle (beat C Pasarell/R Ralston, 2-6, 7-5, 13-11, 6-3), r/u 1973 with Laver (Davidson/J Newcombe won, 7-5, 2-6, 7-5, 7-5); mixed doubles r/u 1954 (Seixas/Miss D Hart won, 4-6, 6-1, 6-1), won

1956 (beat Hoad/Miss D Hard, 9-7, 6-1), both with Mrs W duPont.

Wimbledon singles r/u 1954 (J Drobný won, 13-11, 4-6, 6-2, 9-7), r/u 1956 (Hoad won, 6-2, 4-6, 7-5, 6-4), r/u 1970 (Newcombe won, 5-7, 6-3, 6-2, 3-6, 6-1), r/u 1974 (Connors won, 6-1, 6-1, 6-4); doubles won 1953 with Hoad (beat R Hartwig/Rose, 6-4, 7-5, 4-6, 7-5), r/u 1955 with Fraser (Hartwig/Hoad won, 7-5, 6-4, 6-3), won 1956 with Hoad (beat N Pietrangeli/O Sirola, 7-5, 6-2, 6-1), r/u 1968 (Newcombe/Roche won, 10-8, 6-3, 6-1), both with Stolle; mixed doubles r/u 1954 with Mrs duPont (Seixas/Miss Hart won, 5-7, 6-4, 6-3).

Italian doubles won 1953 with Hoad. British hard court singles won 1968. WCT finals won 1971–2. South African singles won 1971; doubles won 1971 with Stolle. London professional championship singles won 1957, 1960–3, r/u 1964, 1966–8. World professional tournament, Wimbledon, r/u 1967; World professional BBC-2 invitation r/u 1968; Wembley tournament of champions won 1968. US professional championships won 1972. WCT Jackson won 1976; WCT Houston r/u 1976, doubles won with Laver. Hong Kong singles won 1976. Gunze Tokyo r/u 1977 (I Năstase won, 4-6, 7-6, 6-4).

ROUND, Dorothy Edith (Mrs D L Little), GB Born July 1909, Dudley, Worcestershire. With Fred Perry gaining world successes in men's

Right: Dorothy Round (Mrs Little) dominated the British women's tennis scene from 1933 to 1937.

running she went out in the Wimbledon quarter-finals in 1936, losing to Hilda Sperling, the eventual runner-up, but winning the mixed doubles again with Perry. In 1937 she became the second British woman since the end of World War I to take the title twice (Kitty McKane Godfree was the other, in 1924 and 1926). To do so she beat the Polish player Miss 'Jed' Jedrzejowska after dropping the second set and having to pull back to 7-5 in the decisive third.

Wimbledon singles r/u 1933 (Mrs F S Moody won, 6-4, 6-8, 6-3), won 1934 (beat Miss H Jacobs, 6-2, 5-7, 6-3); mixed doubles won 1934 with R Miki (beat H W Austin/Mrs D C Shepherd-Barron, 3-6, 6-4, 6-0), won 1935 (beat H Hopman/Mrs Hopman, 7-5, 4-6, 6-2), won 1936 (beat D Budge/Mrs S A Fabyan, 7-9, 7-5, 6-4), both with Perry. British Wightman Cup team 1931-6.

Australian singles won 1935 (beat Miss N M Lyle, 1-6, 6-1, 6-3).

US doubles r/u 1931 with Miss Jacobs (Miss B Nuthall/Miss S Palfrey won, 3-6, 6-3, 7-5).

Royal Albert Hall, London, GB *see* **Albert Hall**

RUBENOVA, Mrs O *see* **Morozova, Olga**

RUFFELS, Ray, Australia

Though rated the top Australian junior in 1964, where he had won every possible state junior title, Ruffels never gained the national junior title but was representing his country in the Sunshine Cup when that year's championships were held. He was selected for the Australian team to defend the Davis Cup in 1968 at a time when the country's leading players had turned professional. Despite a valiant effort at the Memorial Drive courts, Adelaide, Ruffels lost to Arthur Ashe 6-8, 7-5, 6-3, 6-3. (An indication of the decline in spectator interest in tennis was that fewer than 6000 watched the Challenge Round – compared with 26,000 at White City, Sydney in 1954.) Australia lost the Cup 4-1, Ruffels also losing his second singles against Graebner 3-6, 8-6, 2-6, 6-3, 6-1. Though he has won no major 'Big Four' singles titles, the hard-serving left-hander has been a steady if unspectacular competitor on the world circuit since joining WCT in 1970 and won the Australian doubles of 1977–8 with Allan Stone. In 1973 a heel injury kept him out of the season until he received treatment from the same Philippines faith healer who successfully attended to Tony Roche's elbow injury.

Australian doubles won 1977–8 with Stone (beat J Alexander/P Dent, 7-6, 7-6). New Zealand Open doubles won 1975 with R Carmichael. South African mixed doubles r/u 1971 with Miss P Walkden; r/u NSW Open 1976; Arkansas doubles won 1976 with S Ball; US professional doubles won 1976 with A Stone; Bermuda doubles r/u 1976 with R Crealy; Manila singles r/u 1976. Australian Davis Cup team 1968–70.

events, Dorothy Round was the other half of a pair who re-established the prestige of British tennis in the mid-1930s. In 1934 she and Perry delighted British tennis fans when they provided the country with two champions as each won their Wimbledon singles event for the first time. Miss Round, who beat America's Helen Jacobs, was a formidable opponent armed with accurate ground strokes which often had the power of a male player. In 1934 she also won the mixed doubles with the popular Japanese player Ryuki Miki. Though she lost her singles crown the following year she retained the mixed doubles playing with Perry. In 1935 she also became the first overseas challenger to gain the Australian women's singles title. For the second year

RUZICI, Virginia, Rumania
Born January 1955, Bucharest. A natural athlete and good volleyer Miss Ruzici made her international mark as a member of the Federation Cup team in 1973 when she won the decisive doubles match against Britain and was the only winner in Rumania's loss to South Africa. Ranked No 1 in Rumania she won the national women's title in 1973 4 and had an excellent season in 1976, when she reached the quarter-final of the French and US Opens and the Futures championship and was runner-up in the Italian Open doubles with Mariana Simionescu, fiancée of Björn Borg, and in the Australian Open. She was runner-up to Betty Stöve for third place in the 1977 Bremar Cup tournament, London.

RYAN, Elizabeth Montague (Bunny), USA
Born February 1892, Anaheim, Los Angeles. Miss Ryan had a playing record which is unlikely ever to be equalled in today's style of tennis: in a playing career of more than 20 years she competed in at least 365 tournaments and won at least 662 events, including 193 singles, 255 doubles and 214 mixed doubles. Her last tournament success before becoming a professional in 1934 was in winning the Pacific Southwest championship doubles in Los Angeles with Caroline Babcock. She won 19 Wimbledon doubles events – 12 women's, including six with Suzanne Lenglen, and seven mixed – but never gained the singles title there. Her first tournament in Britain, where she mainly lived, was in 1912 at Surbiton, Surrey. She won her first singles match there and went on to a handicap tournament at Stratford-upon-Avon, where she won the singles, the doubles with her sister, and the mixed doubles. That year she played 19 tournaments in Britain – and did so again in

1934, her last competition year. In 1914 she won the last women's title of Imperial Russia and in 1924, at her peak, played in 35 tournaments, winning 75 titles from 88 finals. She was a strong volleyer and used a cunningly chopped forehand approach.

US doubles won 1926 with Miss E Goss (beat Miss M Browne/Mrs A Chapin, 3-6, 6-4, 12-10); mixed doubles won 1926 with J Borotra (beat R Lacoste/Mrs G Wightman, 6-4, 7-5), won 1933 with H E Vines (beat G Lott/Miss S Palfrey, 11-9, 6-1). US Wightman Cup team 1926.

French doubles won 1930 (beat Mrs R Mathieu/Miss S Barbier, 6-3, 6-1), won 1932 (beat Mrs E Whittingstall/Miss B Nuthall, 6-1, 6-3), both with Mrs F S Moody; won 1933 (beat Mrs S Henrotin/Miss C Rosambert, 6-1, 6-3); won 1934 (beat Miss H Jacobs/Miss Palfrey, 3-6, 6-4, 6-2), both with Mrs Mathieu.

Wimbledon doubles won 1914 with Mrs A Morton (beat Mrs D Larcombe/Mrs G Hannam, 6-1, 6-1), won 1919 (beat Mrs R Lambert Chambers/Mrs Larcombe, 4-6, 7-5, 6-3), won 1920 (beat Mrs Lambert Chambers/Mrs Larcombe, 6-4, 6-0), won 1921 (beat Mrs A Beamish/Mrs G Peacock, 6-1, 6-2), won 1922 (beat Miss K McKane/Mrs A Stocks, 6-0, 6-4), won 1923 (beat Miss J Austin/Miss E Colyer, 6-3, 6-1), won 1925 (beat Mrs A Bridge/Mrs C McIlquham, 6-2, 6-2), all with Miss Lenglen, won 1926 with Miss Browne (beat Mrs L Godfree/Miss Colyer, 6-1, 6-1), won 1927 with Miss H Wills (beat Miss E Heine/Mrs Peacock, 6-3, 6-2), won 1930 with Mrs Moody (beat Miss E Cross/Miss Palfrey, 6-2, 9-7), won 1933 (beat Miss F James/Miss A Yorke, 6-2, 9-11, 6-4), won 1934 (beat Mrs D Andrus/Mrs Henrotin, 6-3, 6-3), both with Mrs Mathieu; mixed doubles won 1919 (beat A Prebble/Mrs Lambert Chambers, 6-0, 6-0), won 1921 (beat M Woosnam/Miss P Howkins, 6-3, 6-1), won 1923 (beat L Deare/Mrs D Shepherd-Barron, 6-4, 7-5), all with R Lycett, won 1927 with F Hunter (beat L Godfree/Mrs Godfree, 8-6, 6-0), won 1928 with P D B Spence (beat J Crawford/Miss D Akhurst, 7-5, 6-4), won 1930 with Crawford (beat D Prenn/Miss H Krahwinkel, 6-1, 6-3), won 1932 with E Maier (beat H Hopman/Miss J Segart, 7-5, 6-2).

World hard court championship doubles won 1914, 1922; mixed doubles won 1913–14.

Italian singles won 1933; doubles won 1934; mixed doubles won 1934.

SAKAI, Toshiro, Japan
Born November 1947, Tokyo. Captain and No 1 of the Japanese Davis Cup team, Sakai has won the national indoor championships of Japan six times (1968, 1970, 1972–4, 1976, and the doubles

Left (centre): Elizabeth Ryan won more titles at Wimbledon than any other player. In her 20 years of competition she won at least 662 events.

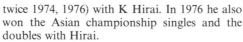

twice 1974, 1976) with K Hirai. In 1976 he also won the Asian championship singles and the doubles with Hirai.

SANGSTER, Michael, GB

Born September 1940, Torquay, Devon. Considered the most promising young British player of 1959–60, when he beat Drobný, Nielsen and Pietrangeli, Sangster was briefly the most successful British player of the early 1960s. In July 1963 his formidable service was timed at 154 mph (247 kmh). The overwhelming power of his shots made him a devastating opponent. In 1960 he became a member of the British Davis Cup team and in 1963 was its main strength in reaching the inter-zone finals, where Britain lost 5-0 to America. From 1960 to 1968 he won 43 of the 65 Davis Cup rubbers he played. He was Western Australia champion in 1961; mixed doubles r/u of Australia in 1964 and won the British covered court championship of 1964. That year he was also US doubles runner-up with Graham Stilwell.

SANTANA, Manuel, Spain

Born May 1939, Madrid. So genial and sportsmanlike was this brilliant player that he might have been nicknamed the 'Smiling Spaniard'. His cheerfulness and his knack of producing superb tennis under pressure made him extremely popular. Without doubt the finest Spanish player of all time, Santana was rated the world's best amateur on clay, employing a heavy topspin on forehand and backhand. Despite his preference for hard surfaces, he still flourished on grass and took the US singles title against Cliff Drysdale on the fast Forest Hills surface in 1965, having already won the French title twice. In 1966 he won his only Wimbledon title when he defeated Dennis Ralston in the singles final. The son of a groundsman at Madrid Tennis Club, where he began as a ball boy, Santana set the seal on his career with this victory. However, he retained his championship, the first won by a European at Wimbledon since Fred Perry, for less than two hours in 1967, losing in the first round to Charles Pasarell 10-8, 6-3, 2-6, 8-6. He led the Spanish Davis Cup team to the Challenge Round twice against Australia (1965 and 1967) and won 91 of his 119 Davis Cup rubbers between 1958 and 1973.

Spanish national champion 1958, 1960–4, 1968–9. Spanish Open won 1971.

US singles won 1965 (Drysdale beat, 6-2, 7-9, 7-5, 6-1).

French singles won 1961 (beat N Pietrangeli, 4-6, 6-1, 3-6, 6-0, 6-2), won 1964 (beat Pietrangeli, 6-3, 6-1, 4-6, 7-5); doubles won 1963 with R Emerson (beat G Forbes/A Segal, 6-2, 6-4, 6-4).

Wimbledon singles won 1966 (beat Ralston, 6-4, 11-9, 6-4).

Italian singles r/u 1965.

South African championships won 1967.

SAUNDERS, Peggy *see* Michell, Peggy

Betty Stöve – Netherlands

Stan Smith – United States of America

Roscoe Tanner – United States of America

Guillermo Vilas – Argentina

Kim Warwick – Australia

Left: Ted Schroeder was a great scrambler and was known off-court for his Popeye corncob pipe. Centre: Richard Savitt was the second overseas winner of the Australian men's singles in 1951. (The first was Don Budge in 1938.)

SAVITT, Richard, USA

Born March 1927, Bayonne, New Jersey. In 1951 this tall, hard-hitting American became the first overseas winner of the Australian men's singles since Don Budge in 1938. Armed with an overspin on his backhand, weighty shots and solid groundstrokes of great accuracy, he went on to become one of the few to win a Wimbledon title at the first attempt when he beat McGregor, who had been his victim in Australia, in straight sets. The following year he won the Canadian singles. Despite his obvious talent Savitt was only selected to play comparatively easy Davis Cup ties against Japan and Canada.

Australian singles won 1951 (beat K McGregor, 6-3, 2-6, 6-3, 6-1).

French doubles r/u 1951 (McGregor/F Sedgman won, 6-2, 2-6, 9-7, 7-5), r/u 1952 (McGregor/Sedgman won, 6-3, 6-4, 6-4), both with G Mulloy.

Wimbledon singles won 1951 (beat McGregor, 6-4, 6-4, 6-4).

US Davis Cup team 1951.

SAWAMATSU, Kazuko (Mrs M Yoshida), Japan

Born January 1951, Nishinomiya. National champion of Japan at the age of 16, Miss Sawamatsu won the Wimbledon junior invitation in 1969, was Swiss champion in 1972 and reached the high spot of her career in 1975 when she won the Wimbledon doubles with Ann Kiyomura, who is of American–Japanese extraction. She had good results on the world circuit, sometimes playing with her sister Junko and showing her best on clay.

Wimbledon doubles won 1975 with Miss Kiyomura (beat Miss F Durr/Miss B Stöve, 7-5, 1-6, 7-5).

Scandinavian Championships

The Scandinavian championships were first held in 1936 as a tournament staged to mark the 30th anniversary of the Swedish LTA in Stockholm and were immediately recognised by the ILTF as one of their official championships.

The event was thereafter played as the only official championships indoors and attracted many of the world's leading players. Denmark, Finland, Norway and Sweden shared in responsibility for staging the championships once each every four years in Copenhagen, Helsinki, Oslo and Stockholm. Events included singles and doubles for men and women, the mixed doubles having been dropped in 1970. Qualifying rounds were introduced in 1967 to give younger players the opportunity of playing several matches in a few days and also to concentrate the tournament-proper into a shorter period. With the coming of Open tennis in 1968 it was found increasingly difficult to meet the rising costs and without sponsorship it proved impossible to maintain the standard of the tournament as the official ILTF world covered court event.

Scarborough Lawn Tennis Club

The centre of lawn tennis in Yorkshire from the early 1920s until 1968, Scarborough was for many years the home of the Yorkshire county championships and the North of England championships. Increasing maintenance costs created financial problems and major events could no longer be held on the club's 19 excellent grass courts.

SCHALLAU, Miss R A *see* Guerrant, Mrs Mona

SCHILDKNECHT, Miss H *see* Orth, Heide

SCHROEDER, Frederick Rudolph (Ted), USA

Born July 1921, Newark, New Jersey. Built more like a boxer than a tennis player, Ted Schroeder had muscular arms, broad shoulders and bandy legs. Off court he seemed always to be sucking at a corn-cob pipe; on court he was determined, hard hitting, agile and cool, playing his best under pressure. Another protégé of southern Californian Perry Jones, he won the national junior singles in 1939, and in 1940 and 1941 won the national doubles with Jack

Kramer. In 1942 he beat Frank Parker for the singles title after dropping the third and fourth sets. He and Kramer paired again to take the doubles a third time in 1947 before the latter became a professional. In 1946 they had led the successful US attack to regain the Davis Cup from Australia at Kooyong, Melbourne.

Schroeder resisted offers to sign lucrative contracts and began a personal battle with the colourful Pancho Gonzalez to establish who was the best American amateur. Eventually they met in a tense Forest Hills final in 1949. Gonzalez lost the first two sets, was upset by a doubtful 'out' call and angered when Schroeder broke off to change into spike shoes on the slippery court (Gonzalez could also have done so but he had none). Gonzalez fought back to level and – after again dropping behind – took the fifth 6-4.

Schroeder, however, had the satisfaction of winning the Wimbledon title at his first and only attempt. As was his habit, he ran several of his matches close, was match point down against Frank Sedgman in the quarter-final and for the third time at the meeting went to five sets in the final against Jaroslav Drobný before winning. In taking the title he beat Henri Cochet's cliffhanging performance of 1927 on the way to the championships: Cochet lost seven sets and 114 games; 'Lucky' Schroeder lost eight sets and 119 games.

US singles won 1942 (beat Parker, 8-6, 7-5, 3-6, 4-6, 6-2), r/u 1949 (Gonzalez won, 16-18, 2-6, 6-1, 6-2, 6-4); doubles won 1940 (beat G Mulloy/H Prussoff), won 1941 (beat W Sabin/Mulloy), won 1947 (beat W Talbert/O Sidwell, 6-4, 7-5, 6-3), all with Kramer; mixed doubles won 1942 with Miss L Brough. US Davis Cup team 1946–51.

Wimbledon singles won 1949 (beat Drobný, 3-6, 6-0, 6-3, 4-6, 6-4); doubles r/u 1949 with Mulloy (Gonzalez/Parker won, 6-4, 6-4, 6-2).

SCHUURMAN, Renée (Mrs P Haygarth), South Africa.

Born October 1939, Durban, Natal. The daughter of a South African baseball player, Miss Schuurman was junior champion of Natal at the age of 13 and two years later, in 1955, won both the junior and senior titles. With Sandra Reynolds (Mrs L E G Price), she toured the world's tennis circuits for three years and by 1959 had made her mark as a leading singles player and in doubles with Miss Reynolds. In 1957 they had reached the semi-final of the Wimbledon doubles, and did so again in 1959. Also in 1959 their successes included the Australian, French and US clay court titles. In 1960 they were runners-up in the Wimbledon doubles. This redoubtable pair won the French doubles three times and Miss Schuurman took the title a fourth time with Ann Jones of Britain in 1963.

French doubles won 1959 (beat Miss Y Ramirez/Miss R Reyes, 2-6, 6-0, 6-1), won 1961 (Miss M Bueno/Miss D Hard scratched), won 1962 (beat Miss M Smith/Miss J Bricks, 6-4, 6-4), all with Miss S Reynolds, won 1963 with Mrs A Jones (beat Miss Smith/Miss R Ebbern, 7-5, 6-4).

Australian singles r/u 1959 (Mrs M Reitano won, 6-2, 6-3); doubles won 1959 with Miss Reynolds (beat Mrs Reitano/Miss L Coghlan, 7-5, 6-4); mixed doubles r/u 1959 with R Laver (R Mark/Miss Reynolds won, 4-6, 13-11, 6-2).

Wimbledon doubles r/u 1960 with Miss Reynolds (Miss Bueno/Miss Hard won, 6-4, 6-0), r/u 1962 with Mrs Price (Miss B J Moffitt/Mrs J Susman won, 5-7, 6-3, 7-5).

Scotland

Lawn tennis was first played in Scotland on the Grange Cricket Ground, Edinburgh, in 1875 and in 1878 – a year after the first Wimbledon championships – the first Scottish championships were held with singles and doubles events for men played on two covered courts. Women's singles were introduced in 1886 and the mixed doubles were introduced in 1904 and doubles not until 1909.

The men's singles trophy was donated by the St Andrews Club, the women's singles and doubles cups by the Dyvours Club and the other doubles trophy by Edinburgh University Club. These clubs originally controlled the championships but in 1894, after some players had become dissatisfied with the arrangement, the Scottish LTA was formed and the first championships held under its auspices were in 1895 at Moffat, Dumfriesshire, where they remained until moved in 1908 to Bridge of Allan, Stirlingshire. The LTA now has nine affiliated district associations: North, North East, Midland Counties, Central, East, Border Counties, West, Southwest and Ayrshire. Training courses are held at schools, colleges and clubs under the Scottish LTA's national coaching scheme. Four teams enter the inter-county championships, representing North, South, East and West Scotland.

Since 1947 the Scottish championships have been held at Craiglockhart, Edinburgh. The first Scottish champion was J Patten Mac-Dougall, who was Registrar General of Scotland. Among early champions were the Doherty brothers, Arthur Gore and Tony Wilding, and Muriel Robb. Later champions during the mid-1920s and thirties included Ian Collins, Dr John Gregory, Don MacPhail, Jack Crawford, Joan Ridley, Charlotte Sterry, Winnie Mason and Anita Lizana of Chile. In 1966 Winnie Shaw (Mrs Wooldridge), daughter of Winnie Mason, won the women's singles. Joyce Barclay won the championship in 1960 aged 15 and went on to win it nine times. More recent winners among the men have included Adrian Quist, Eric Sturgess, Billy Knight, Bob Wilson, John Clifton, Ray Ruffels and David Lloyd.

SCRIVEN, Margaret Croft (Mrs F H Vivian), GB

Born August 1912, Leeds. British junior champion at the age of 17, Miss Scriven, a left-hander, was a 'natural' player who never had a tennis lesson. With a punishing forehand and awkward style, she won her events by patient determination. She twice won the French singles title, beating Renée Mathieu and Helen Jacobs.

French singles won 1933 (beat Mrs Mathieu, 6-2, 4-6, 6-4), won 1934 (beat Miss Jacobs, 7-5, 4-6, 6-1).

Sears Cup, USA

A team competition for women, the Sears Cup began in 1927 when New England beat the Eastern states, 5-2. The cup was named after Eleonora Randolph Sears, who won the US doubles four times (1911, 1917–19) and mixed doubles once (1916).

SEARS, Richard Dudley, USA

Born October 1861, Boston, Massachusetts, died 1943. The winner of the first US championships at the age of 19, Sears went on to hold the title for seven years. He also won the doubles for six years in succession. Both records still stand.

US singles won 1881 (beat W Glyn, 6-0, 6-3, 6-2), won 1882 (beat C Clark, 6-1, 6-4, 6-0), won 1883 (beat J Dwight, 6-2, 6-0, 9-7), won 1884 (beat H Taylor, 6-0, 1-6, 6-0, 6-2), won 1885 (beat G Brinley, 6-3, 4-6, 6-0, 6-3), won 1886 (beat R Beeckman, 4-6, 6-1, 6-3, 6-4), won 1887 (beat H Slocum, 6-1, 6-3, 6-2); doubles won 1882 (beat W Nightingale/G Smith), won 1883 (beat A Van Rensselaer/A Newbould), won 1884 (beat Van Rensselaer/W Berry), all with J Dwight, won 1885 with J Clark (beat Slocum/W Knapp, 6-3, 6-0, 6-2), won 1886 (beat Taylor/Brinley), won 1887 (beat Taylor/Slocum), both with Dwight.

SEDGMAN, Frank Allan, Australia

Born October 1927, Mount Albert, Victoria.

Left: Frank Sedgman never lost a doubles match in the Davis Cup.

Winner of the doubles 'Grand Slam' in 1951 (Australia, France, US and Wimbledon), Sedgman was also the first Australian to win the US singles title (1951), the first to win the Wimbledon singles after World War II in 1952 and in that year also gained the Wimbledon 'Triple Crown' by winning the doubles and mixed doubles. He possessed uncanny anticipation, ease of movement and a brilliant forehand. Before he became a professional in 1953, tennis fans of Australia attempted to dissuade him by raising a fund to keep him as an amateur. As a result he gained a petrol station to keep him out of professional ranks for a year. Sedgman was teamed by Australian Davis Cup coach Harry Hopman with the then lesser known Ken McGregor for the 1950 Challenge Round and though the Americans were favoured to retain the cup for a fifth year Sedgman, McGregor and John Bromwich pulled off a spectacular 4-1 win. The doubles pair remained together in the winning teams of 1951–2. When he turned professional he signed with Jack Kramer for a guaranteed $75,000 or 30 percent of the gate but despite his excellent record as an amateur, American crowds were not over enthusiastic about the Australian. In his amateur career Sedgman took 22 'Big Four' titles in singles, doubles and mixed doubles, took the Italian singles and doubles in 1952 and never lost a Davis Cup double. In 1956 he was matched against the fiery Pancho Gonzalez and the clash was regarded as one of the finest ever seen at Wimbledon. Gonzalez won 4-6, 11-9, 11-9, 9-7.

Australian singles won 1949 (beat J Bromwich, 6-3, 6-3, 6-2), won 1950 (beat McGregor, 6-3, 6-4, 4-6, 6-1), r/u 1952 (McGregor won, 7-5, 12-10, 2-6, 6-2); doubles r/u 1947 with G Worthington (A Quist/J Bromwich won 6-1, 6-3, 6-1), r/u 1948 with C Long (beat Quist/Bromwich, 1-6, 6-8, 9-7, 6-3, 8-6), won 1951 (beat Bromwich/

Above: American Vic Seixas whose chief assets on the court were his tenacity, stamina and his exploitation of the topspin lob.

Quist, 11-9, 2-6, 6-3, 4-6, 6-3), won 1952 (beat M Rose/D Candy, 6-4, 7-5, 6-3), both with McGregor; mixed doubles won 1949 (beat Bromwich/Miss J Fitch, 6-1, 5-7, 12-10), won 1950 (beat E Sturgess/Miss Fitch, 8-6, 6-4), both with Miss D Hart. Australian Davis Cup team 1949–52.

French singles r/u 1952 (J Drobný won, 6-2, 6-0, 3-6, 6-4); doubles r/u 1948 with H Hopman (L Bergelin/Drobný won, 8-6, 6-1, 12-10), won 1951 (beat G Mulloy/R Savitt, 6-2, 2-6, 9-7, 7-5), won 1952 (beat Mulloy/Savitt, 6-3, 6-4, 6-4), both with McGregor; mixed doubles r/u 1948 (Drobný/Mrs P Todd won, 6-3, 3-6, 6-3), won 1951 (beat Rose/Mrs T D Long, 7-5, 6-2), won 1952 (beat Sturgess/Miss S Fry, 6-8, 6-3, 6-3), both with Miss Hart.

US singles won 1951 (beat E Seixas, 6-4, 6-1, 6-1), won 1952 (beat Mulloy, 6-1, 6-2, 6-3); doubles won 1950 with Bromwich (beat Mulloy/W Talbert, 7-5, 8-6, 3-6, 6-1), won 1951 (beat Candy/Rose, 10-8, 6-4, 4-6, 7-5), r/u 1952 (Rose/Seixas won, 3-6, 10-8, 10-8, 6-8, 8-6), both with McGregor; mixed doubles r/u 1950 (McGregor/Mrs L Dupont won, 6-4, 3-6, 6-3), won 1951 (beat Rose/Miss Fry, 6-3, 6-2), won 1952 (beat L Hoad/Mrs Long, 6-3, 7-5), all with Miss Hart.

Wimbledon singles r/u 1950 (J Patty won, 6-1, 8-10, 6-2, 6-3), won 1952 (beat Drobný, 4-6, 6-2, 6-3, 6-2); doubles won 1948 with Bromwich (beat T Brown/Mulloy, 5-7, 7-5, 7-5, 9-7), won 1951 (beat Drobný/Sturgess, 3-6, 6-2, 6-3, 3-6, 6-3), won 1952 (beat Seixas/Sturgess, 6-3, 7-5, 6-4), both with McGregor; mixed doubles r/u 1948 (Bromwich/Miss L Brough won, 6-2, 3-6, 6-3), won 1951 (beat Rose/Mrs N Bolton, 7-5, 6-2), won 1952 (beat E Morea/Mrs Long, 4-6, 6-3, 6-4), all with Miss Hart.

SEGURA, Francisco (Pancho), Ecuador

Born June 1921, Guayquil. Though he never won a major tennis title, Segura was a popular and often spectacular player both as an amateur and a professional. He brought immense enthusiasm and determined fighting qualities to his game and had a remarkably accurate double-handed forehand and penetrating low volley. After turning professional in 1947 he increased his reputation as an enthusiastic performer on all types of surface.

US doubles r/u 1944 with W Talbert (W McNeill/R Falkenburg won, 7-5, 6-4, 3-6, 6-1); mixed doubles r/u 1947 with Miss G Moran (J Bromwich/Miss L Brough won, 6-3, 6-1). US clay court singles r/u 1944; doubles won 1944–5 with Talbert. US indoor singles won 1946. Pacific Southwest doubles won 1945 with F Parker, won 1946 with P Pelliza. London championships won 1946.

French doubles r/u 1946 with E Morea (M Bernard/Y Petra won, 7-5, 6-3, 0-6, 1-6, 10-8).

SEIXAS, Elias Victor, USA

Born August 1923, Philadelphia, Pennsylvania. A dark-haired six-footer who did not reach full tennis maturity until his late twenties. Vic Seixas then set about making up for lost time and rapidly collected about him 15 'Big Four' titles in only four years. By no means a stylist, he had a looping forehand, sliced backhand and exploited top spin lobs and drop shots. His greatest weapon was his tenacity; he appeared able to carry on playing for ever. With Tony Trabert he succeeded in 1954 in bringing back from Australia the Davis Cup which they had failed to retrieve in 1953. From 1951–7 he played 55 Davis Cup rubbers – more than any other American – winning 38 in 19 ties. He won the Wimbledon mixed doubles four times in successive years, three with Doris Hart. In 1953 he took the Wimbledon singles title and in 1954 the US singles.

US singles r/u 1951 (F Sedgman won, 6-4, 6-1, 6-1), r/u 1953 (M Trabert won, 6-3, 6-2, 6-3), won 1954 (beat R Hartwig, 3-6, 6-2, 6-4, 6-4); doubles won 1952 with M Rose (beat K McGregor/F Sedgman, 3-6, 10-8, 10-8, 6-8, 8-6), won 1954 with Trabert (beat L Hoad/K Rosewall, 3-6, 6-4, 8-6, 6-3), r/u 1956 with H Richardson (Hoad/Rosewall won, 6-2, 6-2, 3-6, 6-4); mixed doubles won 1953 (beat Hartwig/Miss J Sampson, 6-2, 4-6, 6-4), won 1954 (beat Rosewall/Mrs W duPont, 4-6, 6-1, 6-1), won 1955 (beat G Mulloy/Miss S Fry, 7-5, 5-7, 6-2), all with Miss Hart.

Australian doubles won 1955 with Trabert (beat Hoad/Rosewall, 6-4, 6-2, 2-6, 3-6, 6-1).

French singles r/u 1953 (Rosewall won, 6-3, 6-4, 1-6, 6-2); doubles won 1954 (beat Hoad/Rosewall, 6-4, 6-2, 6-1), won 1955 (beat N Pietrangeli/O Sirola, 6-1, 4-6, 6-2, 6-4), both with Trabert; mixed doubles won 1953 with Miss Hart (beat Rose/Miss M Connolly, 4-6, 6-4, 6-0).

Wimbledon singles won 1953 (beat K Nielsen, 9-7, 6-3, 6-4); doubles r/u 1952 with E Sturgess (McGregor/Sedgman won, 6-3, 7-5, 6-4), r/u 1954 with Trabert (Hartwig/Rose won, 6-4, 6-4,

3-6, 6-4); mixed doubles won 1953 (beat Morea/Miss Fry, 9-7, 7-5), won 1954 (beat Rosewall/Mrs duPont, 5-7, 6-4, 6-3), won 1955 (beat Morea/Miss L Brough, 8-6, 2-6, 6-3), all with Miss Hart; won 1956 with Miss Fry (beat Mulloy/Miss A Gibson, 2-6, 6-2, 7-5).

SHAW, Kristien (Miss K Keminer), USA

Born July 1952, San Diego. A left-hander, Mrs Shaw started her junior career spectacularly, winning ten national junior titles. In 1967 she won the National 16 singles, in 1970 the National 18 doubles, and from 1968–70 the clay court doubles. Other successes have included being runner-up in the South Australian singles, the Buenos Aires singles and the West German doubles of 1973 with Miss L Rossouw.

SHAW, Winnie (Mrs K Wooldridge), GB

Born January 1947, Clarkston, Glasgow. Her mother, Winifred Mason, won the Scottish title in 1930 and 1933 and Miss Shaw first won the title in 1966 and again in 1970. She was British junior champion in 1964, Under-21 champion in 1965 and made her debut in the Federation Cup and Wightman Cup competitions in 1966. She was a promising player in her youth.

French Open mixed doubles r/u 1971 with T Lejus (J C Barclay/ Miss F Durr won, 6-2, 6-4). German doubles r/u 1968 with Miss J Tegart. British hard court singles r/u 1968; Rothmans' London championship singles r/u 1969. Scottish indoors won 1971; Scottish championships won 1966, 1970, r/u 1971.

SHEPHERD-BARRON, Mrs Dorothy (née Shepherd), GB

Born November 1897, Beighton, Norfolk, died 1953. A frequent competitor at Wimbledon and in America in the 1920s Mrs Shepherd-Barron won the women's doubles at Wimbledon in 1931 – the only title she ever won, though she was twice runner-up for the mixed doubles, and once each for the Wimbledon and US women's doubles. She was a member of the 1924, 1926, 1929 and 1931 Wightman Cup team and non-playing captain in 1951.

Wimbledon women's doubles r/u 1929 with Mrs B Covell (Mrs M Watson/Mrs L R C Michell won, 6-4, 8-6), won 1931 with Miss P Mudford (beat Miss D Metaxa/Miss J Sigart, 3-6, 6-3, 6-4); mixed doubles r/u 1923 with L Deane (R Lycett/Miss E Ryan won, 6-4, 7-5), r/u 1924 with L Godfree (J Gilbert/Miss K McKane won, 6-3, 3-6, 6-3).

US doubles r/u 1929 with Mrs Covell (Mrs P Watson/Mrs Michell won, 2-6, 6-3, 6-4).

French mixed doubles r/u 1931 with H W Austin (P D B Spence/Miss B Nuthall won, 6-3, 5-7, 6-3).

SHERRIFF, Gail *see* Lovera, Gail

SHOEMAKER, Mrs F C *see* Nuthall, Betty

SIMIONESCU, Mariana, Rumania

Born November 1956, Bucharest. Miss Simionescu, the brightest young tennis star to emerge recently from Rumania, made her Federation Cup debut in 1973 at the age of 17, and was in the team which reached the semi-final. In the following year she used as her chief weapon a strong forehand to win the French junior championship, beating Britain's Sue Barker in the final, and was also runner-up to Mima Jausovec of Yugoslavia in the Wimbledon invitation. She was runner-up for the Rumanian national title and played for the first time on the Virginia Slims circuit. In 1976 she paired with Virginia Ruzici to reach the final of the Italian Open doubles. She became engaged to Björn Borg in late 1976.

SIROLA, Orlando, Italy

Born April 1928, Fiume. A 6 ft 6 in (1.98 m) unpredictable player, Sirola was one of the leaders of Italy's tennis revival after World War II and shared with Nicolo Pietrangeli the credit for Italy's successes in the European zone of the Davis Cup in 1955–6, 1958–9. He formed a notable doubles partnership with Pietrangeli and they were finalists in the French championships in 1955 and at Wimbledon in 1956 before winning the French title in 1959. A strong, powerful player, he would strike unexpected bad periods during which his play was languid. In his ten years (1953–63) in the Italian Davis Cup team he won 57 of 89 rubbers in 45 ties.

French doubles r/u 1955 (V Seixas/A Trabert won, 6-1, 4-6, 6-2, 6-4), won 1959 (beat R Emerson/N Fraser, 6-3, 6-2, 14-12), both with Pietrangeli.

Wimbledon doubles r/u 1956 with Pietrangeli (L Hoad/K Rosewall won, 7-5, 6-2, 6-1). Wimbledon Plate r/u 1960.

Swiss covered court singles won 1954.

SLOCUM, Henry Warner, USA

Born May 1862. Successor to the young Richard Sears as American singles champion, Slocum had to wait seven years to become the second holder of the title in 1888, after Sears had retired undefeated. Slocum retained the title in 1889 but lost to Oliver Campbell in the 1890 Challenge Round. He won the doubles with Howard Taylor in 1889.

US singles r/u 1887 (Sears won, 6-1, 6-3, 6-2), won 1888 (wo), won 1889 (beat Q Shaw, 6-3, 6-1, 4-6, 6-2), r/u 1890 (Campbell won, 6-2, 4-6, 6-3, 6-1); doubles r/u 1885 with W Knapp (Sears/J Clark won, 6-3, 6-0, 6-2), r/u 1887 (Sears/J Dwight won), won 1889 (beat V Hall/O Campbell), both with Taylor.

SMITH, Miss M *see* Court, Margaret

SMITH, Stanley Roger, USA

Born December 1946, Pasadena, California. Although the tall (6 ft 4 in, 1.9 m), powerful Smith did not start winning major championships

Above: American Stan Smith's methodical play lead him to win more than 25 American titles and even more international ones.

until he was 24 (he gained his US singles title in 1971), he has since more than made up for his late arrival on the list of tennis 'greats' and has won some 25 US titles – he and Bob Lutz are the only men's pair to win titles on four surfaces. In 1972 he beat Ilie Năstase in the Wimbledon singles final and later faced Năstase and Ion Tiriac in the Challenge Round of the Davis Cup in Bucharest. With only the assistance of Eric Van Dillen and faced by a hostile crowd and extraordinarily bad behaviour on the part of the two Rumanians, Smith fought sportingly for America to retain the Cup.

He is a painstaking, methodical performer with few frills to his game. Erect as a soldier and always appearing to be without emotion, his power play is grindingly wearing on the opposition and he has apparently total fitness as well as unconquerable determination to add to his armoury.

US singles won 1971 (beat J Kodeš, 3-6, 6-3, 6-2, 7-6); doubles won 1968 with Lutz (beat A Ashe/A Gimeno, 11-9, 6-1, 7-5), r/u 1971 with Van Dillen (J Newcombe/R Taylor won, 6-7, 6-3, 7-6, 4-6, 5-3 tie-break), won 1974 with Lutz (beat P Cornejo/J Fillol, 6-3, 6-3); US national singles won 1969; US Indoor Open singles won 1970, doubles won 1970 with Ashe; US indoor singles won 1969, 1972, doubles won 1966, 1969, both with Lutz, won 1970 with Ashe; US hard court singles won 1966–8, doubles won 1966 with Lutz; US clay court doubles won 1968 with Lutz; US professional indoor singles won 1973, doubles won 1974 with Lutz. WCT Memphis singles r/u 1976; WCT doubles finals, Kansas City, r/u 1976 with Lutz; WCT Barcelona doubles won, 1976; WCT Rome doubles won 1976, Pacific Southwest doubles won 1976, all with Lutz. Grand Prix r/u 1972; Grand Prix Masters won 1970. World Doubles won 1973 with Lutz. Dewar Cup won 1968.

Australian doubles won 1970 with Lutz (beat J Alexander/P Dent, 8-6, 6-3, 6-4).

French doubles r/u 1971 with T Gorman (Ashe/M Riessen won, 6-8, 4-6, 6-3, 6-4, 11-9), r/u 1974 with Lutz (R Crealy/O Parun won, 6-3, 6-2, 3-6, 5-7, 6-1).

Wimbledon singles r/u 1971 (J Newcombe won, 6-3, 5-7, 2-6, 6-4, 6-4), won 1972 (beat Năstase, 4-6, 6-3, 6-3, 4-6, 7-5); doubles r/u 1972 with Van Dillen (R Hewitt/F McMillan won, 6-2, 6-2, 9-7), r/u 1974 with Lutz (Newcombe/A Roche won, 8-6, 6-4, 6-4). British covered court doubles won 1968 with Lutz; mixed doubles won 1968 with Mrs M Court.

SMITH, Sydney Howard, GB

Born February 1872, Stroud, Gloucestershire, died 1947. Twice doubles champion at Wimbledon Sydney Smith and his partner Frank Riseley carried on a four-year running battle with the Doherty brothers, Laurie and Reggie, who took the title from them in 1903 and held it until Smith and Riseley regained the title in an exciting five-set match in 1906. Smith was a colourful character who played with one leg in an iron support but was nevertheless a formidable opponent. His flat powerful forehand was known as the 'Smith Punch' and was so accurate that he could afford to spend most of his time on the baseline while his opponents ran. He won the Midland Counties championship at Edgbaston, Birmingham, a record six times (1900–5).

Wimbledon singles r/u 1899 All-Comers (A W Gore won, 3-6, 6-2, 6-1, 6-4), r/u 1890 Challenge Round (R Doherty won, 6-8, 6-3, 6-1, 6-2), r/u 1905 All-Comers (N E Brookes won, 1-6, 6-4, 6-1, 1-6, 7-5); doubles r/u 1897 All-Comers with C Cazalet (L Doherty/R Doherty won, 6-2, 7-5, 2-6, 6-2), r/u 1898 All-Comers with G Hillyard (C Hobart/H Nisbet won, 2-6, 6-2, 6-2, 6-3), r/u 1900 (Nisbet/Roper-Barrett won, 6-2, 2-6, 6-8, 8-6, 6-2), won Challenge Round 1902 (beat L Doherty/R Doherty, 4-6, 8-6, 6-3, 4-6, 11-9), r/u 1903 (L Doherty/R Doherty won, 6-4, 6-4, 6-4), r/u 1904 (L Doherty/R Doherty won, 6-3, 6-4, 6-3), r/u 1905 (L Doherty/R Doherty won, 6-2, 6-4, 6-8, 6-3), won 1906 (beat L Doherty/R Doherty, 6-8, 6-4, 5-7, 6-3, 6-3). British Davis Cup team 1905–6.

Soft-Ball Tennis

Developed in Japan in the 1890s, soft-ball tennis uses a rubber ball, has scoring similar to that in lawn tennis and is usually played as doubles with one partner as a rearguard always playing in the back court and serving, and an advance guard, who plays at the net. *See also* **Japan.**

SOLOMON, Harold, USA

Born September 1952, Washington. Originally regarded as solely a clay court player, Solomon, who stands only 5 ft 6 in (1.70 m), has established a reputation on other surfaces, thanks largely to winning the South African Open in 1975 and 1976 in addition to being runner-up in the 1976

French Open.

US 18 clay courts won 1970; US interschool won 1970; US amateur clay court won 1971; Orange Bowl won 1969, 1971; WCT Washington won 1976, WCT Houston won 1976, WCT Monterey r/u 1976; US professional championships r/u 1976.

South African Open won 1975–6. French Open r/u 1976 (A Panatta won, 6-1, 6-4, 4-6, 7-6).

South Africa

Lawn tennis was introduced in the 1870s to South Africa by a Mr L Nevill, an Englishman, who, with a few fellow-countrymen, launched the game in Natal. The earliest recorded events took place in 1881 and one of the first tournaments was in Durban. In 1882 the Berea LTC, Durban and the Port Elizabeth Club were formed, the latter becoming the main centre of tennis in South Africa in the early years of the game. In 1891 the club took on the functions of the national governing body for tennis and founded annual championships, whose first winners were L A Richardson (1891–2) and Miss H Grant (1891–4). Control passed to the South African Lawn Tennis Union in 1903, the year it was founded, and the Port Elizabeth Club was honoured as the venue of the first official national championships in that year. In 1913 South Africa affiliated to the ILTF as a founder member and in 1931 the championships, which had been held in several venues, were settled in Ellis Park, Johannesburg. Originally the associations of seven provinces came under the control of the SALTU: Eastern Province, Border, Tranvaal, Western Province, Natal, Griqualand West, and Orange Free State. Later Transvaal and Western Province were divided into new areas: Northern, Eastern, Western and Boland.

The non-white tennis body, the South African National Lawn Tennis Union, which has 14 provincial associations, affiliated to SALTU in 1968 with full voting powers on a national level. South Africa has concentrated on improving tennis standards in recent years and there are provincial coaching schemes at all centres and tennis has been part of the curriculum of Afrikaans schools since 1967. The country has competed regularly in international competitions, the first being the 1908 Olympic Games in London. In the 1912 games in Stockholm Charlie Winslow (later national champion) won the singles and, with H A Kitson, the doubles, and in 1920 Louis Raymond won the singles at Antwerp. Both Kitson and Raymond were national champions, the latter from 1921–4 and 1930–1. The country first entered the Davis Cup in 1913 and was an irregular entrant until 1927, when it entered every other year until 1959. Thereafter it became an annual competitor but because of its government's policy of apartheid was barred in 1970–2. The European B-zone final of 1967 was the first Davis Cup match held in South Africa, when the home team beat Brazil 5-0 and went on to the inter-zone final, losing 2-3 to Spain in Johannesburg.

South Africa has competed in the Federation Cup each year since the competition began in 1963 and won the cup for the first time in 1972 in Johannesburg. The country also competed against Australia for the Anza Trophy at irregular intervals between 1952 and 1968. Of the six matches played, South Africa won four, drew one and lost one. Leading junior male players have taken part in the Orange Bowl and Sunshine Cup events since 1959. Over the years the tennis authorities have made it a policy to invite teams of leading international tennis players to the country, the first being that led by G W Hillyard of Britain in 1908–9. In 1928 the first Australian women's team visited and later other teams came from France, Australia, Czechoslovakia, Germany, the United States and Yugoslavia and from the International Lawn Tennis Club of Great Britain.

Major home events include the national championships, which became the South African Open in 1969, and the tournaments of the Sugar Circuit, started in 1962 and embracing the provincial championships at Bloemfontein, Port Elizabeth, East London, Cape Town and Durban.

Among leading South African players who have achieved international reputations are Brian Norton (South African champion 1920), who caused a sensation by 'throwing' his Wimbledon finals match against his friend Bill Tilden in 1921; Eric Sturgess (1939–40, 1946, 1948–54, 1957), twice winner of the Wimbledon mixed doubles; Norman Farquharson (1934–6, 1938), who beat champion Fred Perry in the 1937 Wimbledon first round; P D B Spence, who won the 1928 Wimbledon mixed doubles; Bob Hewitt, formerly of Australia, and Frew McMillan, who became a formidable international doubles partnership winning several titles; and Cliff Drysdale, winner of the US doubles in 1972 partnered by Roger Taylor (GB).

Among women players the most notable internationals have included Sandra Reynolds Price (1959, 1961) and Renée Schuurman Haygarth, who won the French doubles three times (Miss Schuurman gaining a fourth title with Ann Jones of Britain); Bobby Heine Miller (1928, 1931–2, 1936–7), who won the French doubles with Mrs Irene Peacock and reached the Wimbledon finals, won the British hard courts title in 1929 aged 19 and gained many other titles; Annette Van Zyl, later Mrs du Plooy (1963), who was the youngest national singles champion at 17 years seven months; Mrs Pat Pretorias and Brenda Kirk, who took South Africa to their 1972 Federation Cup victory.

South American Championships

Organised by the South American Tennis confederation, the championships include the Mitre

Cup for men (founded in 1921 and won by Argentina) the Osorio Cup for women (1957, Chile), the Bolivia Cup for Boys of 18 (1953, Brazil), the Columbia Cup for Girls 18 (1965, Argentina), the Harten Cup for Boys 15 (1963, Brazil), and the Chile Cup for Girls 15 (1965, Chile). All ten South American LTAs belong to the confederation, which was founded in 1948.

SPEAR, Nikola, Yugoslavia

Born February 1944. A language student who speaks seven languages, Spear was Yugoslav national champion in 1969 and 1972–3 and won the Yugoslavian international tournament in 1971. He makes use of intelligent tactical play to beat players who are often ranked higher than he and has scored victories over Franulović, Kodeš, Lutz, Năstase and Richey.

SPENCE, Patrick Dennis Benham, South Africa

Born February 1898, Queenstown, Cape Colony. Educated at Edinburgh University, Scotland, and a qualified doctor, Spence was a good rugby player and qualified by residence in Britain to play in many 'closed' tournaments. In 1928 he won the Wimbledon mixed doubles partnered by the American Bunny Ryan and with Betty Buthall he took the French mixed doubles title in 1931.

Wimbledon mixed doubles won with Miss E Ryan (beat J Crawford/Miss D Akhurst, 7-5, 6-4).

French mixed doubles won 1931 with Miss Nuthall (beat H W Austin/Mrs D Shepherd-Barron, 6-3, 5-7, 6-3).

South African Davis Cup team 1924–31.

SPERLING, Mrs Hilda (née Krawinkel), Germany/Denmark

Born March 1908, Essen, Germany, Danish by marriage. An interminable baseline battler who gained her successes by stolid indomitability, Mrs Sperling competed originally as a German entrant at Wimbledon, but it was not until she had married and thereby become Danish that she gained her first title, the mixed doubles of 1933 with Baron von Cramm. The tall, long-legged girl took part in the first all-German women's final at Wimbledon in 1931, when Cilly Aussem won 6-2, 7-5. Both players took part with badly blistered feet which slowed still further the usually somewhat tedious pace of Miss Krawinkel's game. In 1935 she won the first of her three successive French singles titles, beating Mrs Simone Mathieu in straight sets, as she did in the next two years. She was German singles champion five times.

German singles won 1933–5, 1937, 1939; doubles 1932, 1937; mixed doubles 1932–4.

French singles won 1935 (beat Mrs Mathieu, 6-2, 6-1), won 1936 (beat Mrs Mathieu, 6-3, 6-4), won 1937 (beat Mrs Mathieu, 6-2, 6-4); doubles r/u 1935 with Miss Adamoff (Miss M Scriven/Miss K Stammers won, 6-4, 6-0).

Wimbledon singles r/u (Miss Aussem won, 6-2, 7-5), r/u 1936 (Miss H Jacobs won, 6-2, 4-6, 7-5); doubles r/u 1935 with Mrs Mathieu (Miss F James/Miss Stammers won, 6-1, 6-4); mixed doubles r/u 1930 with D Prenn (J Crawford/Miss E Ryan won, 6-1, 6-3), won 1933 with von Cramm (beat N Farquharson/Miss M Heeley, 7-5, 8-6).

Sphairistiké

The form of lawn tennis invented and patented by Major Walter Clopton Wingfield, member of the Honourable Corps of Gentlemen-at-Arms to Queen Victoria, in 1874 was named 'Sphairistiké', after the Greek game known as *Sphairisis*. The first record of Major Wingfield playing the game was at Lansdowne House, London, in 1869, with a net two feet high (0.6 m). The Greek name was contracted to 'Sticky' and later gave place to 'Lawn Tennis'. Sets of equipment for the game were sold by Major Wingfield all over Britain at five guineas (£5.25) and included four rackets, balls and the net. By 1875, when the major issued the fifth edition of his booklet on the game a list of people playing it included 11 princes and princesses, seven dukes, 14 marquises, three marchionesses, 54 earls, six countesses, 105, viscounts, 41 barons, 44 ladies, 44 honourables, five right honourables and 55 baronets and knights.

The court was wider at the baselines than at the net, giving it an hourglass shape. It was 60 ft (18.3 m) long – 18 ft (5.5 m) shorter than the modern court – 21 ft (6.4 m) wide at the net and 30 ft (9.14 m) wide at the baselines compared with today's standard 27 ft (8.23 m). The height of the net was 4 ft 8 in (1.42 m) at the posts.

There are rival claimants to the invention of lawn tennis, including Major Harry Gem and J B Perera, of Birmingham, England, whose rules for tennis were published in 1870, and J H Hale, who invented 'Germains tennis', named after his village in Buckinghamshire. Sets for this were sold by John Wisden & Co, also at five guineas (£5.25) in 1874.

Stade Roland Garros, France

When France won the Davis Cup for the first time, in 1927, there was no tennis stadium suitable for the country's defence of the Cup the following year until the *Stade Français* and the Racing Club of France built the Stade Roland Garros on a site at Porte d'Auteil given by the City of Paris to the French Lawn Tennis Federation. Originally the stadium, which was opened in May 1928 with a tournament between women's teams from France and Britain, had space for 8000 spectators. Subsequent enlargements made room for some 14,000 in the concrete stadium around the centre court with a dozen courts outside. The slow red courts have often proved a frustration to visiting players and the French championships were won exclusively by Frenchmen for 41 years from their inception in 1891 until the Australian Jack Crawford beat Henri Cochet in 1933. The Stade was the scene

of many of the triumphs of the legendary
French 'Four Musketeers', Henri Cochet, Jean
Borotra, Jacques Brugnon and René Lacoste.

**STAMMERS, Katherine (Kay) Esther (Mrs M
Menzies, later Mrs T Bullitt), GB**
Born April 1914, St Albans, Hertfordshire.
Winner of the Wimbledon women's doubles in
1935 at the age of 19 with Freda James, Kay
Stammers was an attractive and popular player
who did much to help restore confidence in
British tennis in the 1930s. The doubles victory of
that year was the third British triumph at
Wimbledon, since Fred Perry and Dorothy
Round had taken the mixed doubles and Perry
the men's singles. Miss Stammers and Miss James
won again in 1936. A left-hander, Miss Stammers
was a fluent, stylish stroke player. In 1939 she
beat Helen Jacobs and Sarah Palfrey Fabyan to
reach the singles final, there losing to Alice
Marble. The years of World War II would have
seen her at her peak; nevertheless she was back
in 1946 and 1947, reaching the singles quarter-
finals and doubles semi-finals. She represented
Britain in the Wightman Cup team from 1935–9
and was non-playing captain, 1946–8.

Wimbledon singles r/u 1939 (Miss Marble
won, 6-2, 6-0); doubles won 1935 (beat Mrs R
Mathieu/Mrs H Sperling, 6-1, 6-4), won 1936
(beat Mrs S P Fabyan/Miss H Jacobs, 6-2, 6-1),
both with Miss James.

French doubles won 1935 with Miss M Scriven
(beat Miss Adamoff/Mrs Sperling, 6-4, 6-0).

US doubles r/u 1939 with Mrs S Hammersley
(Mrs Fabyan/Miss Marble won, 6-4, 8-6);
mixed doubles r/u 1935 with R Menzel (E
Maier/Mrs Fabyan won, 6-3, 3-6, 6-4).

STERRY, Mrs Charlotte (née Cooper), GB
Born September 1870, Ealing, London, died
1966. Five times singles champion of Wimbledon, Mrs Sterry was one of the four early
stalwarts and 'multi-winners' of women's events
in the first 31 singles championships. From
their inception in 1884 until 1914 there were only
ten champions and among them Mrs Lambert
Chambers, Mrs Hillyard, Miss Dod and Mrs
Sterry won 23 of the titles. An engaging and
lively personality, known as 'Chattie', she was
unusually strong and active for a girl, according
to a contemporary writer. Her greatest strength
was her volleying and she liked to come in to the
net as often as possible. In 1902 Mrs Sterry
took part in a unique final against Muriel Robb.
The champion had won the first set 6-4 but lost
the second 11-13 when rain interrupted play for
the rest of the day. Next day the umpire decreed
that the whole match should be replayed and
Miss Robb emerged the winner, 7-5, 6-1 having
played a record match of 43 games.

Wimbledon singles won 1895 (wo), won 1896
(beat Mrs W Pickering, 6-2, 6-3), r/u 1897 (Mrs
G Hillyard won, 5-7, 7-5, 6-2), won 1898 (wo),
r/u 1899 (Mrs Hillyard won, 6-2, 6-3), r/u 1900
(Mrs Hillyard won, 4-6, 6-4, 6-4), won 1901

(beat Mrs Hillyard, 6-2, 6-2), r/u 1902 (Miss
Robb won, 7-5, 6-1), r/u 1904 (Miss D K Douglass won, 6-0, 6-3), r/u 1906 All-Comers (Miss
Douglass won, 6-2, 6-2), won 1908 (wo), r/u
1912 All-Comers (Mrs D Larcombe won, 6-3,
6-1); doubles won 1901 non-championship with
Mrs Hillyard (beat Miss Adams/Mrs W Pickering, 6-3, 6-0), won 1902 non-championship with
Miss A Morton (beat Miss H Lane/Miss C
Wilson, wo), r/u 1913 with Mrs Lambert
Chambers (Mrs R McNair/Miss D Boothby
won, 4-6, 2-4 retired); mixed doubles won 1901
non-championship (beat W Eaves/Mrs N Dur-
lacher, 6-2, 6-3), won 1902 non-championship
(beat C Cazalet/Miss Robb, 6-4, 6-3), both with
L Doherty.

Irish singles won 1895, 1898; mixed doubles
won 1895–6, 1899–1900, Scottish singles won
1899. Olympic gold medals (two) 1900.

STEWART, Sherwood, USA
Born June 1946, Goose Creek, Texas. In recent
years Stewart has achieved singles wins over a
number of leading players but it has been in
doubles that he has made most progress,
particularly in partnership with Fred McNair,
with whom he was runner-up to Gottfried and
Ramirez in the 1977 Italian Open doubles. In
1976 he and McNair won the French, German,
Swedish, Commercial Union Masters, and US
indoor doubles. He and Gottfried won the South
African doubles.

US indoor doubles won 1976 (beat S Krule-
vitz/T Waitke, 6-3, 6-3); CU Masters doubles
won 1976 (beat B Gottfried/R Ramirez, 6-3, 5-7,
5-7, 6-4, 6-4); Swedish doubles 1976 (beat J
Gisbert/W Fibak, 6-3, 6-4); German doubles
1976 (beat B Bertram/J Yuill, 6-2, 6-3); French
doubles 1976 (beat Gottfried/Ramirez, 7-6, 6-3,
6-1), all with McNair; South African doubles
with Gottfried (beat S Smith/Gisbert, 1-6, 6-1,
6-2, 7-6); Italian doubles r/u 1977 with McNair
(Gottfried/Ramirez won, 6-7, 7-6, 7-5).

*Above: Kay Stammers (Mrs
Menzies/Mrs Bullitt) is seen
here at the Hertfordshire
Championships at Harpenden
in June 1937.*

Right: New York-born Dick Stockton holds a record of 20 US national junior titles.

STOCKTON, Dick, USA

Born February 1951, New York. Holder of a record number of US national junior titles (20), Stockton beat Jim Connors in the final of the 1977 US professional championship in a hard-fought match over five sets. The position was reversed in the WCT 1977 finals in Dallas. In 1976 he and Rosie Casals were World mixed doubles champions and in 1975 he was runner-up in the US professional indoor doubles with Erik van Dillen.

STOEFEN, Lester Rollo, USA

Born March 1911, Des Moines, Iowa, died 1970. World amateur doubles champion in 1934 with George Lott, Stoefen, who had a powerful and accurate service, was twice doubles champion of America and once at Wimbledon with the same partner. He and Lott became professionals in 1934, signing for Bill Tilden's 1935 tour.

US doubles won 1933 (beat F Shields/F Parker, 11-13, 9-7, 9-7, 6-3), won 1934 (beat W Allison/J Van Ryn, 6-4, 9-7, 3-6, 6-4), both with Lott; mixed doubles r/u 1934 with Miss E Ryan (Lott/Miss H Jacobs won, 4-6, 13-11, 6-2). US Davis Cup team 1934.

Wimbledon doubles won 1934 with Lott (beat J Borotra/J Brugnon, 6-2, 6-3, 6-4).

STOKER, Frank Owen, Ireland

Born May 1867, Dublin, died 1939. Frank Stoker was part of the 'Irish invasion' of Wimbledon in the 1890s, when titles were falling to men such as Willoughby Hamilton, Joshua Pim, Harold Mahony and himself. With Dr Pim, Stoker twice took the men's doubles by a walk-over in 1890, lost it to the Baddeley brothers, Wilfred and Herbert in 1891, did not play as a pair in 1892 and then regained it in 1893 from Harry Barlow and Ernest Lewis.

Wimbledon doubles won 1890 (wo), r/u 1891 (H Baddeley/W Baddeley won, 6-1, 6-3, 1-6, 6-2), won 1893 (beat Barlow/Lewis, 4-6, 6-3, 6-1, 2-6, 6-0).

STOLLE, Frederick Sydney, Australia

Born October 1938, Hornsby, NSW. Once a bank clerk in Sydney, Fred Stolle first attracted notice in tennis as a doubles specialist but eventually came to be recognised as a successful singles player. He was a powerful server and volleyer and had a dogged determination and consistency in his return of service. With the German, Baron Gottfried von Cramm, he shares the doubtful distinction of being a three-times loser in the Wimbledon singles finals in successive years. In 1963 he lost to Chuck McKinley and in 1964-5 he was beaten by fellow Australian Roy Emerson. However, he won the French singles in 1965 and the US and German singles in 1966. In 1965 he also won the French and US doubles with Emerson, who successfully partnered him for the Australian, Italian and US doubles of 1966. He was a notable Davis Cup player and between 1964-6 he won 13 out of 16 rubbers. He became a contract professional in 1967 and the following year was runner-up with Ken Rosewall in the Wimbledon doubles.

Australian singles r/u 1964 (Emerson won, 6-3, 6-4, 6-2), r/u 1965 (Emerson won, 7-9, 2-6, 6-4, 7-5, 6-1); doubles r/u 1962 (Emerson/N Fraser won, 4-6, 4-6, 6-1, 6-4, 11-9), won 1963 (beat K Fletcher/J Newcombe, 6-2, 3-6, 6-3, 3-6, 6-3), won 1964 (beat Emerson/Fletcher, 6-4, 7-5, 3-6, 4-6, 14-12), all with R Hewitt, r/u 1965 (Newcombe/A Roche won, 3-6, 4-6, 13-11, 6-3, 6-4), won 1966 (beat Newcombe/Roche, 7-9, 6-3, 6-8, 14-12, 12-10), both with Emerson; r/u 1969 with Rosewall (Emerson/R Laver won, 6-4, 6-4); mixed doubles r/u 1962 (beat R Taylor/Miss D Hard, 6-3, 9-7), r/u 1963 (Fletcher/Miss M Smith won, 7-5, 5-7, 6-4), both with Miss L Turner. Australian Davis Cup team 1964-6.

French singles won 1965 (beat Roche, 3-6, 6-0, 6-2, 6-3); doubles won 1965 with Emerson (beat Fletcher/Hewitt, 6-8, 6-3, 8-6, 6-2), won 1968 with Rosewall (beat Laver/Emerson, 6-3, 6-4, 6-3); mixed doubles r/u 1962 (R Howe/Miss R Schuurman won, 3-6, 6-4, 6-4), r/u 1963 (Fletcher/Miss Smith won, 6-1, 6-2), r/u 1964 (Fletcher/Miss Smith won, 6-3, 6-4), all with Miss Turner.

US singles r/u 1964 (Emerson won, 6-4, 6-1, 6-4), won 1966 (beat Newcombe, 4-6, 12-10, 6-3, 6-4); doubles won 1965 (beat F Froehling/C Pasarell, 6-4, 10-12, 7-5, 6-3), won 1966 (beat R Ralston/C Graebner, 6-4, 6-4, 6-4), both with Emerson, won 1969 with Rosewall (beat Pasarell/Ralston, 2-6, 7-5, 13-11, 6-3); mixed doubles won 1962 (beat Froehling/Miss Turner, 7-5, 6-2), won 1965 (beat Froehling/Miss J Tegart, 6-2, 6-2), both with Miss Smith.

Wimbledon singles r/u 1963 (McKinley won, 9-7, 6-1, 6-4), r/u 1964 (Emerson won, 6-4, 12-10, 4-6, 6-3), r/u 1965 (Emerson won, 6-2, 6-4, 6-4); doubles r/u 1961 (Emerson/Fraser won, 6-4, 6-8, 6-4, 6-8, 8-6), won 1962 (beat B Jovanovic/N Pilić, 6-2, 5-7, 6-2, 6-4), won 1964 (beat Emerson/Fletcher, 7-5, 11-9, 6-4), all with

Hewitt, r/u 1968 (Newcombe/Roche won, 3-6, 8-6, 5-7, 14-12, 6-3), r/u 1970 (Newcombe/ Roche won, 10-8, 6-3, 6-1), both with Rosewall; mixed doubles won 1961 (beat Howe/E Buding, 11-9, 6-2), won 1964 (beat Fletcher/Miss Smith, 6-4, 6-4), both with Miss Turner, won 1969 with Mrs A Jones (beat Roche/Miss Tegart, 6-3, 6-2).

Italian doubles won 1963–4, with Hewitt, 1906 with Emerson; mixed doubles won 1962 with Miss Turner.

STONE, Allan, Australia

Born October 1935, Launceston, Tasmania. Stone has achieved an excellent doubles record on the international circuit, initially with Dick Crealy, with whom he won the Australian

doubles in 1968, the US nationals in 1969 and reached the West German finals in 1971. In 1975 he paired for the first time with Colin Dowdeswell and they sensationally reached the final of the Wimbledon doubles, beating established stars such as Hewitt and McMillan, Okker and Riessen before losing to Gerulaitis and Mayer. Stone has since continued to build on his doubles reputation with a variety of partners on all surfaces and won the Australian doubles of 1977–8 with Ray Ruffels. In singles he came close to causing another Wimbledon upset in 1969 when, in the first round, he beat Stan Smith 22-20 in the first set and took him to 87 games in five sets before losing 20-22, 6-4, 9-7, 4-6, 6-3. He joined WCT in 1970 and is

Above: Fred Stolle of South Africa was most successful in doubles competitions.

player coach with WTT Indiana Loves.

Australian doubles won 1968 with Crealy (beat T Addison/R Keldie, 10-8, 6-4, 6-3), r/u 1975 with R Carmichael (J Alexander/P Dent won, 6-3, 7-6), won 1977–8 with Ruffels (beat J Alexander/P Dent, 7-6, 7-6); mixed doubles r/u 1968 with Mrs M Court (Crealy/Mrs B J King won, wo). New Zealand singles r/u 1971.

US national doubles won 1969 with Crealy (W Bowrey/C Pasarell, 9-11, 6-3, 7-5); US professional doubles won 1976 with R Ruffels (M Cahill/J Whitlinger, 3-6, 6-3, 7-6). WCT São Paulo doubles r/u 1976, WCT Houston doubles r/u 1976, both with Pasarell; ATP Woodlands doubles r/u 1976 with Dent.

Wimbledon doubles r/u 1975 with Dowdeswell (Gerulaitis/Mayer won, 7-5, 8-6, 6-4); mixed doubles r/u 1975 with Miss B Stöve (M Riessen/Mrs M Court won, 6-4, 7-5).

West German doubles r/u 1971 with Crealy; Italian doubles r/u 1968 with N Kalogeropoulos.

STÖVE, Betty Flippina, Netherlands

Born June 1945, Rotterdam. Runner-up in the 1977 Wimbledon singles, Miss Stöve is the outstanding woman player from the Netherlands to reach the top of the international circuit by consistently good performance over recent years. A formidable figure of a woman, she has a powerful volley and strong backhand. Despite her size, she can move remarkably fast on court. With Billie Jean King she formed an extremely successful doubles partnership which took the French and Wimbledon titles in 1972. In the same year she and Françoise Durr took the US doubles. Her success has been achieved as much by her dogged determination as by brilliance and she has proved an amiable and popular competitor with a particularly strong following at Wimbledon. Her consistency has kept her high on the Virginia Slims prize-money table. Her 1977 successes included winning the US Open doubles with Martina Navratilova and mixed doubles with Frew McMillan, with whom she was also Wimbledon runner-up. She was also runner-up in the Wimbledon doubles with Miss Navratilova and took third place in the new Bremar Cup. With Mrs Cawley she shared the Colgate Inaugural doubles with Mrs K Reid and Miss Stevens.

French doubles won 1972 with Mrs King (beat Miss W Shaw/Miss N Truman, 6-1, 6-2), r/u 1973 with Miss Durr (Mrs M Court/Miss V Wade won, 6-2, 6-3); mixed doubles r/u 1973 with P Dominguez (J C Barclay/Miss Durr won, 6-1, 6-4).

US doubles won 1972 (beat Mrs Court/Miss Wade, 6-3, 1-6, 6-3), r/u 1974 (Miss R Casals/ Mrs King won, 7-6, 6-7, 6-4), both with Miss Durr, won 1977 with Miss Navratilova (beat Miss R Richards/Miss B Stuart, 6-2, 3-6, 6-3); mixed doubles r/u 1971 with R Maud (O Davidson/Mrs King won, 6-3, 7-5), r/u 1976 (P Dent/Mrs King won, 3-6, 6-2, 7-5), won 1977 (beat V Gerulaitis/Mrs King, 6-2, 3-6, 6-3),

both with McMillan. Philadelphia doubles won 1976; San Francisco doubles won 1976; Bridgestone doubles won 1976; Colgate Inaugural doubles r/u 1976, all with Mrs King; Colgate Inaugural doubles 1977 with Mrs Cawley divided (Mrs K Reid/Miss G Stevens, 6-2, 1-3 abandoned). US indoor r/u 1976; doubles r/u 1976 with Miss V Wade.

Wimbledon Plate r/u 1971; singles r/u 1977 (Miss Wade won, 4-6, 6-3, 6-1); doubles won 1972 with Mrs King (beat Mrs D Dalton/Miss Durr, 6-2, 4-6, 6-3), r/u 1973 (Miss Casals/Mrs King won, 6-1, 4-6, 7-5), r/u 1975 (Miss A Kiyomura/Miss K Sawamatsu won, 7-5, 1-6, 7-5), both with Miss Durr, r/u 1976 with Mrs King (Miss C Evert/Miss Navratilova won, 6-1, 3-6, 7-5), r/u 1977 with Miss Navratilova (Mrs Cawley/Miss J Russell won, 6-3, 6-3); mixed doubles r/u 1975 with A Stone (M Riessen/Mrs Court won, 6-4, 7-5), r/u 1977 with McMillan (R Hewitt/Miss Stevens won, 3-6, 7-5, 6-4). Rothmans' British hard court doubles r/u 1972 with Mrs King.

Bremar Cup 1977 3rd place; doubles r/u 1977 with Miss Wade (Mrs King/Miss Tomanova won, 6-2, 6-3).

Dutch singles won 1970, 1972–3.

Federation Cup 1963– .

STURGESS, Eric William, South Africa

Born May 1920, Johannesburg. One of South Africa's finest players, Sturgess was comparatively slight in build and did not rely on power so much as superb accuracy and control of his groundstrokes. His play was graceful and full of determination. He was eleven times singles champion of South Africa – first at the age of 18 in 1939 – eight times doubles champion and six times mixed doubles, at which he also gained international success. In 1949 he won the French,

Left: Karen Susman (née Hantze) was a determined and athletic player.
Left (centre): Eric Sturgess won the South African singles title a record 11 times.

Wimbledon and US mixed doubles titles, though his own country's eluded him that year.

Australian doubles r/u 1950 with J Drobný (A Quist/J Bromwich won, 1-6, 7-5, 6-2, 6-3); mixed doubles r/u 1950 with Miss J Fitch (F Sedgman/Miss D Hart won, 8-6, 6-4).

French singles r/u 1947 (J Asboth won, 8-6, 7-5, 6-4), r/u 1951 (J Drobný won, 6-3, 6-3, 6-3); doubles won 1947 (beat T Brown/O Sidwell, 6-4, 4-6, 6-4, 6-3), r/u 1949 (R Gonzalez/F Parker won, 6-3, 8-6, 5-7, 6-3), both with E Fannin; r/u 1950 with Drobný (W Talbert/A Trabert won, 6-2, 1-6, 10-8, 6-2); mixed doubles won 1947 (beat C Caralulis/Miss J Jedrzejowska, 6-0, 6-0), won 1949 (beat G Oakley/Miss J Quertier, 6-1, 6-1), both with Mrs S A Summers, r/u 1952 with Miss Fry (Sedgman/Miss Hart won, 6-8, 6-3, 6-3).

US singles r/u 1948 (Gonzalez won, 6-2, 6-3, 14-12); mixed doubles won 1949 with Miss L Brough (beat Talbert/Mrs W duPont, 4-6, 6-3, 7-5).

Wimbledon doubles r/u 1951 with Drobný (K McGregor/Sedgman won, 3-6, 6-2, 6-3, 3-6, 6-3), r/u 1952 with V Seixas (McGregor/Sedgman won, 6-3, 7-5, 6-4); mixed doubles won 1949 with Mrs Summers (beat Bromwich/Miss Brough, 9-7, 9-11, 7-5), won 1950 with Miss Brough (beat G Brown/Mrs P Todd, 11-9, 6-1, 1-4).

South African singles won 1939-40, 1946, 1948-54, 1957; doubles won 1946-8, 1951-3, 1955, 1957; mixed doubles 1940, 1946-9, 1951, 1953. Davis Cup team 1947-51.

SUKOVÁ, Vera (née Pužejová), Czechoslovakia Born 1931, Uherské Hradiště. One of the greatest players ever produced by Czechoslovakia, Mrs Suková originally concentrated on basketball and did not start playing tennis until her late teens. Even so, she was national champion for the first time after three years and held the title from 1954-60. She won the French mixed doubles with Jiři Javorsky in 1957 and in 1962 reached the final of the Wimbledon singles, losing to Karen Susman 6-4, 6-4. She was also

singles champion of Hungary and Austria. After her international career she became a coach employed by the state.

SUMMERS, Sheila (née Piercey), South Africa Born March 1919, Johannesburg. Winner of the Wimbledon mixed doubles in 1949 with her compatriot, Eric Sturgess, Mrs Summers also gained the French mixed doubles with him in that year. In all she was mixed doubles champion of South Africa six times with Sturgess, singles champion three times and doubles twice.

French mixed doubles won 1947 (beat C Caralulis/Miss J Jedrzejowska, 6-0, 6-0), won 1949 (beat G Oakley/Miss J Quertier, 6-1, 6-1), both with Sturgess.

Wimbledon mixed doubles won 1949 with Sturgess (beat J Bromwich/Miss L Brough, 9-7, 9-11, 7-5).

South African singles won 1948-9, 1951; doubles won 1940, 1953; mixed doubles won 1940, 1946-8, 1951, 1953.

Sunshine Cup

Run on Davis Cup lines, the Sunshine Cup is for international competition by teams of boys aged under 18. It is held annually in Miami Beach, Florida, and was first staged in 1959, when the Brazilian team won.

SUSMAN, Karen (née Hantze), USA
Born December 1942, San Diego, California. Coached by the famous Eleanor 'Teach' Tennant, who also coached Alice Marble and Maureen Connolly, Mrs Susman was an aggressively athletic player. She competed at Wimbledon for the first time in 1960 and reached the quarter-finals that year and in 1961, when she also won the doubles. Then, in 1962, she reached the final and defeated the Czech Vera Suková. That year she won the doubles again with Billie Jean Moffitt and was runner-up in the US doubles with her, winning two years later.

US doubles r/u 1962 (Miss M Bueno/Miss D Hard won, 4-6, 6-3, 6-2), won 1964 (beat Miss M Smith/Miss L Turner, 3-6, 6-2, 6-4), r/u 1965

(Mrs C Graebner/Miss N Richey won, 6-4, 6-4), all with Miss B J Moffitt. US Wightman Cup team 1960–2, 1965.

Wimbledon singles won 1962 (beat Mrs Suková, 6-4, 6-4); doubles won 1961 (beat Miss J Lehane/Miss Smith, 6-3, 6-4), won 1962 (beat Mrs L Price/Miss R Schuurman, 5-7, 6-3, 7-5), r/u 1964 (Miss Smith/Miss Turner won, 7-5, 6-2), all with Miss Moffitt.

SUTTON, May *see* **Bundy, Mrs T C**

TALBERT, William F, USA

Born September 1918, Cincinnati, Ohio. One of America's leading doubles players after World War II, Talbert was also a member of the US Davis Cup team from 1946–54 and captain from 1953–7. He won the doubles and mixed doubles four times and also took the French doubles title in 1950. After giving up tournament tennis he became a successful tennis writer.

US men's singles r/u 1944 (F Parker won, 6-4, 3-6, 6-3, 6-3), r/u 1945 (Parker won, 14-12, 6-1, 6-2); doubles won 1942 with G Mulloy (beat F Schroeder/S B Wood), r/u 1943 with D Freeman (J Kramer/Parker won), r/u 1944 with F Segura (W McNeill/R Faulkenburg won, 7-5, 6-4, 3-6, 6-1), won 1945 (beat Falkenburg/J Tuero, 12-10, 8-10, 12-10, 6-2), won 1946 (beat McNeill/F Guernsey, 3-6, 6-4, 2-6, 6-3, 20-18), both with Mulloy, r/u 1947 with O Sidwell (Kramer/Schroeder won, 6-4, 7-5, 6-3), won 1948 (beat Parker/Schroeder, 1-6, 9-7, 6-3, 3-6, 9-7), r/u 1950 (J Bromwich/F Sedgman won, 7-5, 8-6, 3-6, 6-1), r/u 1953 (M Rose/R Hartwig won, 6-4, 4-6, 6-2, 6-4), all with Mulloy; mixed doubles won 1943, won 1944 (beat McNeill/Miss D Bundy, 6-2, 6-3), won 1945 (beat Falkenburg/Miss D Hart, 6-4, 6-4), won 1946 (beat R Kimbell/Miss L Brough, 6-3, 6-4), all with Miss M Osborne, r/u 1948 (T Brown/Miss Brough won, 6-4, 6-4), r/u 1949 (E Sturgess/Miss Brough won, 4-6, 6-3, 7-5), with Mrs W duPont.

French doubles won 1950 with A Trabert (beat J Drobný/Sturgess, 6-2, 1-6, 10-8, 6-2); mixed doubles r/u 1950 with Mrs P Todd (retired, E Morea/Miss B Schofield won).

TANNER, Roscoe, USA

Born October 1951, Chattanooga. A tough left-hander with a scorchingly fast service which has been timed at 140 mph, Tanner is one of the few players who can match the power of Jim Connors and has beaten him on a number of occasions. On form, he has a winning forehand, sure volley, and blistering smashes. He won the 1977 New South Wales Open and was runner-up in the WCT Challenge Cup, but his overall performance did not match that of his previous

seasons. In 1976 he beat Connors in the Wimbledon quarter-finals in straight sets, playing at his powerful best and reversing a defeat in the semi-final in 1975.

US amateur championship singles won 1970; US amateur indoor singles won 1971, doubles won 1971 with A Mayer; US amateur clay court doubles won 1971 with Mayer; US 18 won 1969. WCT Challenge Cup r/u 1977 (Connors won, 6-2, 5-6, 3-6, 6-3, 6-5), WCT Memphis doubles r/u 1976 with M Riessen. Cincinnati singles won 1976. Columbus singles won 1976; San Francisco singles won 1976, doubles won with R Stockton; Maui doubles r/u 1976 with Stockton.

Benson and Hedges, Wembley, r/u 1976 (Connors won, 3-6, 7-6, 6-4); New South Wales Open won 1977 (beat B Teacher, 6-3, 3-6, 6-3, 6-7, 6-3). Japan Open won 1976 (beat C Barazzutti, 6-3, 6-2).

TAYLOR, Roger, GB

Born October 1941, Sheffield. One of the great hopes of British tennis in the 1960s and 1970s, the sturdy left-hander Roger Taylor has never quite achieved his full potential or fulfilled the hopes of the vast following he has had in Britain. In 1967 he became the second British male player to reach a Wimbledon semi-final since before the war, when he beat Ray Ruffels (Mike Sangster was the other in 1961) and in 1970 he became the only Briton since 1938 to do so twice, beating the reigning champion, Rod Laver, and then Graebner, before losing to Rosewall. In 1973 he defied the ATP ban on member players appearing at Wimbledon because of the association's dispute with the ILTF. Taylor, who had been seeded 16, was re-seeded No 3 and again reached the semi-finals before losing to the eventual champion, Jan Kodeš, 7-9, 9-7, 5-7, 6-4, 7-5. That year he became the first Briton to reach the WCT finals, losing to Rosewall. In 1971 he had also achieved another distinction when he won the US doubles with John Newcombe and became the first British man to get his name on the US championship roll since the war; with Cliff Drysdale he won again in 1972. Between 1964 and 1967 he won 13 of his 14 King's Cup singles and in 1967 joined WCT.

Wimbledon Plate won 1966; Welsh Open r/u 1971, won 1973.

US doubles won 1971 with Newcombe (beat S Smith/E van Dillen, 6-7, 6-3, 7-6, 4-6, 5-3 tie break), won 1972 with Drysdale (beat Laver/K Rosewall, 7-5, 2-6, 7-5, 7-5).

Australian mixed doubles r/u 1962 with Miss D Hard (F Stolle/Miss L Turner won, 6-3, 9-7).

New Zealand singles r/u 1966, won 1970.

WCT finals q/f 1973 (Rosewall won Group B, 4-6, 6-2, 6-7, 6-1, 6-4).

Dutch singles r/u 1969, 1970. Canadian singles r/u 1970. Swiss singles r/u 1970. Italian doubles r/u 1971 with A Gimeno. South African doubles r/u 1970 with Drysdale.

TEGART, Judy *see* **Dalton, Mrs D E**

THOMPSON, Ethel W *see* **Larcombe, Mrs Dudley**

TILDEN, William Tatem, USA
Born February 1893, Germantown, Philadelphia, died 1953. Acknowledged as one of the greatest players of all time, 'Big Bill' Tilden gathered about him an extraordinary number of records and during his ten years as the world's top player was the centre either of adulation usually reserved for film stars, or of dispute regarding his private life or his playing career. A frustrated actor and later a successful author, the lanky, stoop-shouldered six-footer delighted in the attention and remained a showman. The second son of a well-to-do Germantown wool-merchant, 'Big Bill' was introduced to tennis by his older brother, Herbert, but though he won a tournament for boys aged 13 and under when he was only eight, he showed no particular interest in the game and did not mature as a player until his mid-twenties. Once having done

so, however, he was virtually unbeatable and went on to win seven US singles titles (six in succession), five doubles and four mixed doubles, three Wimbledon singles titles (the last at the age of 37), 13 of 14 Davis Cup singles between 1920–6, and numerous other titles in his own country and abroad.

In 1913, at the age of 20, he was spotted by the US women's champion Mary K Browne, who suggested they should play in the national mixed doubles: they won two years in succession. He played in his first national singles championship in 1916, losing in an early round. Next year he was ranked No 2 behind William (Little Bill) Johnston, who was to become his chief rival, and in 1918 reached the singles final, losing to Lindley Murray. By 1920 he was ranked No 1 and remained there for ten years. Over the years the clashes between Tilden and Johnston became routine and great crowd-pullers. Though at first honours were fairly even, Johnston was coming to the end of his great career as Tilden was on the way up and gradually the tall man gained supremacy. Together they formed a partnership which won the Davis Cup back from Australia in 1920. It was to remain in America for seven years, until the coming of the 'Four Musketeers' of France. In 1920, too, Tilden won his first Wimbledon title, beating the Australian Gerald Patterson in the final and becoming the first American to take the title. Then he returned to America to beat Johnston and take the first of his seven US singles titles.

It was now that Tilden's supreme mastery of the game really showed itself. He possessed a fluid grace and long strides which took him across the court effortlessly; a cannonball service, powerful forehand and backhand drives and a full repertoire of shots into which he put a considerable amount of spin. If a stroke was not perfect, Tilden went away to change or practise until it was; he spent the winter of 1919 remodelling his backhand after losing to 'Little Bill'; in 1922 after he had the tip of a finger on his right hand amputated, he successfully re-styled his grip. He was a temperamental player, given to petulance and though he did not rant and rave like some, he had been known to walk off court in disgust. His withering stare, hand on hip, at a linesman who had earned his disfavour became famous, as did his habit of deliberately 'throwing' a point if he thought a call had been made wrongly to his advantage.

Throughout his career he suffered a series of accidents and illnesses. In the 1920 Wimbledon All-Comers Final he severely agitated an old cartilage injury while playing the Japanese Zenzo Shimizu but managed to win; in 1922 he sustained a finger injury when he ran into wire netting; in 1925 he suffered ptomaine poisoning during the Davis Cup Challenge Round but was able to beat René Lacoste and Henri Cochet in his two singles matches after being two sets down to each, and in 1926 his knee gave way during the US nationals and Cochet ended his

six-year run. He took his seventh US title at the age of 36 in 1929 – the oldest winner. His third Wimbledon title the next year made him the oldest winner there since World War I and from 1920 to 1930 he played in a record 28 Davis Cup Challenge Round rubbers, winning 21.

Tilden became a professional in 1931 and began a series of successful one-night-stand tours starting from Madison Square Garden. He quickly established himself as the dominating professional. When he finally retired from the professional circuit he continued to play exhibition matches and enter first-class tournaments. He was planning to enter a tournament in Cleveland when he collapsed and died from a heart attack in June 1953, aged 60.

US singles r/u 1918 (W M Johnston won, 6-3, 6-1, 7-5), r/u 1919 (Johnston won, 6-4, 6-4, 6-3), won 1920 (beat Johnston, 6-1, 1-6, 7-5, 5-7, 6-3), won 1921 (beat W F Johnson, 6-1, 6-3, 6-1), won 1922 (beat W M Johnston, 4-6, 3-6, 6-2, 6-3, 6-4), won 1923 (beat Johnston, 6-4, 6-1, 6-4), won 1924 (beat Johnston, 6-1, 9-7, 6-2), won 1925 (beat Johnston, 4-6, 11-9, 6-3, 4-6, 6-3), r/u 1927 (R Lacoste won, 11-9, 6-3, 4-6, 6-3), r/u 1927 (Lacoste won, 11-9, 6-3, 11-9), won 1929 (beat F Hunter, 3-6, 6-3, 4-6, 6-2, 6-4); doubles won 1918 (beat F Alexander/B Wright, 6-3, 6-4, 3-6, 2-6, 6-2), r/u 1919 (N Brookes/G Patterson won, 8-6, 6-3, 4-6, 4-6, 6-2), both with V Richards, won 1920 with C Griffin (beat W Davis/R Roberts, 6-2, 6-2, 6-3), won 1921 beat R Williams/W Washburn, 13-11, 12-10, 6-1), won 1922 (beat Patterson/P O'Hara Wood, 4-6, 6-1, 6-3, 6-4), both with Richards, won 1923 with B I C Norton (beat Williams/Washburn, 3-6, 6-2, 6-3, 5-7, 6-2), r/u 1926 with A Chapin (Williams/Richards won, 6-4, 6-8, 11-9, 6-3), won 1927 with Hunter (beat Williams/Johnston, 10-8, 6-3, 6-3); mixed doubles won 1913 (beat C Rogers/Miss D Green, 7-5, 7-5), won 1914 (beat J Rowlands/Miss A Myers, 6-1, 6-4), both with Miss M K Browne; r/u 1916 (W Davis/Miss E Sears won, 6-4, 7-5), r/u 1917 (I Wright/Miss M Bjursted won, 10-12, 6-1, 6-3), r/u 1919 (Richards/Miss M Zinderstein won), all with Miss F Ballin, won 1922 (beat H Kinsey/Miss H Wills, 6-4, 6-3), won 1923 (beat J Hawkes/Miss K McKane, 6-3, 2-6, 10-8), r/u 1924 (Richards/Miss Wills won, 6-8, 7-5, 6-0), all with Mrs M Mallory.

Wimbledon singles won 1920 (beat Patterson, 2-6, 6-3, 6-2, 6-4), won 1921 (beat Norton, 4-6, 2-6, 6-1, 6-0, 7-5), won 1930 (beat W Allison, 6-3, 9-7, 6-4); doubles won 1927 with Hunter (beat J Brugnon/H Cochet, 1-6, 4-6, 8-6, 6-3, 6-4).

French singles r/u 1927 (Lacoste won, 6-4, 4-6, 5-7, 6-3, 11-9), r/u 1930 (Cochet won, 3-6, 8-6, 6-3, 6-1); mixed doubles r/u 1927 with Miss L de Alvarez (J Borotra/Mrs M Bordes won, 6-4, 2-6, 6-2), won 1930 with Miss C Aussem (beat Cochet/Mrs F Whittingstall, 6-4, 6-4).

Italian singles won 1930; doubles won 1930.

TIRIAC, Ion, Rumania

Born May 1939, Rumania. One of the two greatest Rumanian players – and mentor of the other (Ilie Năstase), Tiriac was champion of his own country for eight years in succession, 1959–1966, and has proved himself a tenacious player on the world circuit. He and Năstase formed a formidable partnership which took Rumania into the Davis Cup Challenge Rounds in 1969, 1971–2. The pair were runners-up in the French doubles in 1966 and won in 1970 and also won the Italian doubles in 1970 and 1972. A qualified PE teacher and hockey international for Rumania, Tiriac is a renowned gamesman; like his compatriot Năstase, he is not above employing disconcerting histrionics on court. He has recently spent time coaching Guillermo Vilas and announced his intention of concentrating in future on coaching and promoting.

French doubles r/u 1966 (C Graebner/R Ralston won, 6-3, 6-3, 6-0), won 1970 (beat A Ashe/C Pasarell, 6-2, 6-4, 6-3), both with Năstase. US indoor singles won 1972. Italian doubles won 1970, 1972, both with Năstase. British hard court doubles r/u 1972 with Năstase, r/u 1973 with A Panatta. West German doubles r/u 1972 with R Hewitt, r/u 1973 with M Orantes.

TODD, Mary Patricia (*née* Canning), USA

Born July 1922, San Francisco, California. A statuesque player who possessed a fluent command of strokes and used the full court gracefully, Pat Todd might have achieved greater success had she not been at the height of her career at the same time as Louise Brough, Margaret Osborne duPont and Doris Hart, by whom she was outshone. Her greatest success came in 1947 when she beat Miss Hart, her frequent doubles partner, to take the French singles title and then, with her, defeated the reigning Wimbledon doubles champions, Miss Brough and Miss Osborne for her only Wimbledon title. The following year she and Miss Hart also took the French doubles.

US women's doubles r/u 1946 with Mrs D A Prentiss (Miss Brough/Miss Osborne won, 6-2,

6-0), r/u 1947 (Miss Brough/Miss Osborne won, 5-7, 6-3, 7-5), r/u 1948 (Miss Brough/Miss Osborne won, 6-4, 8-10, 6-1), all with Miss Hart, r/u 1951 with Miss N Chaffee (Miss S Fry/Miss Hart won, 6-4, 6-2). US Wightman Cup team 1947–51.

French singles won 1947 (beat Miss Hart, 6-3, 3-6, 6-4), r/u 1950 (Miss Hart won, 6-4, 4-6, 6-2); doubles r/u 1947 (Miss Brough/Miss Osborne won, 7-5, 6-2), won 1948 (beat Miss Fry/Mrs Prentiss, 6-4, 6-2), both with Miss Hart; mixed doubles won 1948 with J Drobný (beat F Sedgman/Miss Hart, 6-3, 3-6, 6-3), r/u 1950 with W Talbert (retired, E Morea/Miss B Scofield won).

Wimbledon doubles won 1947 (beat Miss Brough/Miss Osborne, 3-6, 6-4, 7-5), r/u 1948 (Miss Brough/Mrs duPont won, 6-3, 3-6, 6-3), both with Miss Hart, r/u 1949 with Miss G Moran (Miss Brough/Mrs duPont won, 8-6, 7-5); mixed doubles r/u 1950 with G Brown (E Sturgess/Miss Brough won, 11-9, 6-1, 6-4).

TOMANOVA, Renata, Czechoslovakia

Born December 1954. Coached by her country's greatest woman player, Vera Suková, Miss Tomanova is an attractive forceful player who until recently was overshadowed by her former fellow-countrywoman, Martina Navratilova. She began to achieve her potential in 1976 and 1977 with a run of good results in major singles and doubles events. She was runner-up to Janet Newberry in the Italian Open of 1977 and with Mrs King won the doubles in the new Bremar Cup London event.

Australian singles r/u 1976 (Mrs E Cawley won, 6-2, 6-2); doubles r/u 1976 with Mrs W Bowrey (Mrs Cawley/Miss H Gourlay won, 8-1 one set only).

French singles r/u 1976 (Miss S Barker won, 6-2, 0-6, 6-2).

Italian singles r/u 1977 (Miss J Newberry won); doubles r/u 1973 with Miss Navratilova (Mrs M Court/Miss V Wade won).

German singles r/u 1976 (Miss Barker won).

Bremar Cup, London, doubles won 1977 with Mrs L W King (beat Miss Wade/Miss B Stöve, 6-2, 6-3).

Torquay, Devon, GB

The famous seaside holiday resort became well known as a tennis centre after the Palace Hotel tournament was first staged there in 1936, when the hotel opened two covered courts. The first tournament, held with the support of the Dunlop company, attracted only 16 men, from whom Harry Lee emerged the winner, and 14 women, of whom the Chilean Anita Lizana was champion. After World War II handicap events were introduced and tournaments rapidly increased in popularity. From 1968 to 1972 the event was part of the Dewar Cup circuit. Sponsorship is now by the sports equipment manufacturers, Slazengers.

Many of the top international players have played at Torquay which has also become the venue for the Southwest junior tournament and is an important training ground which has produced such players as Angela Mortimer, Sue Barker, Joan Curry, Mike Sangster and Paddy Roberts, son of the resident coach Arthur Roberts.

TRABERT, Marion Anthony, USA

Born August 1930, Cincinnati, Ohio. A strapping basketball player from the University of Cincinnati, Tony Trabert became a powerful and commanding tennis champion in the mid-1950s as a result of dependable rather than spectacular play. He was one of the few players of the time to add overspin to an already strong backhand, possessed a scorching service and played every shot to be a winner. A protégé of Bill Talbert, he had a classic match at Wimbledon in 1950 when he paired with Budge Patty to play his mentor and Ken McGregor in the doubles quarter-finals. The match, which was interrupted by rain, lasted four hours and resulted in a win for Patty and Trabert, 6-4,

31-29, 7-9, 6-2. The 60-game second set and 94-game match were both records.

In 1952 and 1953 he and Vic Seixas were sent to Australia with hopes of regaining the Davis Cup for America; on the first occasion they were beaten by Frank Sedgman and McGregor and on the second came up against Lew Hoad and Ken Rosewall, both aged 19. Again they lost despite a superb battle by Trabert to defeat Hoad, who eventually emerged the winner by 13-11, 6-3, 2-6, 3-6, 7-5 in a breathtaking match. The following year the Americans avenged their defeat and brought back the Cup, though it stayed with them for only a year. The two Davis Cup colleagues were adversaries in the US singles final of 1953, when Trabert defeated Seixas for the crown. In 1955 Trabert won the French title for the second successive year, gained the Wimbledon title against the Dane Kurt Nielsen and again won the US title, defeating Ken Rosewall, who had robbed him of the 'Grand Slam' by beating him in the Australian championship. It was his best year and the last before he signed professional forms with Jack Kramer and in winning Wimbledon and Forest Hills he did not drop a single set in any round.

US singles won 1953 (beat Seixas, 6-3, 6-2, 6-3), won 1955 (beat Rosewall, 9-7, 6-3, 6-3);

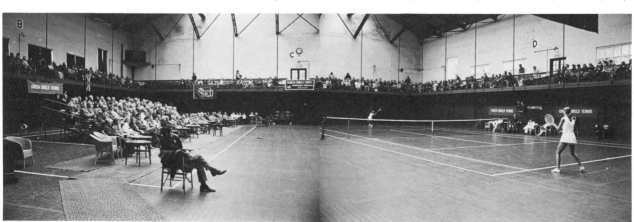

doubles won 1954 with Seixas (beat Hoad/ Rosewall, 3-6, 6-4, 8-6, 6-3). US Davis Cup team 1951–5; captain 1976.

Australian doubles won 1955 with Seixas (beat Hoad/Rosewall, 6-4, 6-2, 2-6, 3-6, 6-1).

French singles won 1954 (beat A Larsen, 6-4, 7-5, 6-1), won 1955 (beat S Davidson, 2-6, 6-1, 6-4, 6-2); doubles won 1950 with Talbert (beat J Drobný/E Sturgess, 6-2, 1-6, 10-8, 6-2), won 1954 (beat Hoad/Rosewall, 6-4, 6-2, 6-1), won 1955 (beat N Pietrangeli/O Sirola, 6-1, 4-6, 6-2, 6-4), both with Seixas.

Wimbledon singles won 1955 (beat Nielsen, 6-3, 7-5, 6-1), doubles r/u 1954 with Seixas (R Hartwig/M Rose won, 6-4, 6-4, 3-6, 6-4).

TRUMAN, Christine *see* **Janes, Mrs C**

TUCKEY, Charles Raymond Davys, GB
Born June 1910, Godalming, Surrey. A regular British Army officer and member of a well-known English tennis family, Tuckey found his greatest success as a doubles partner with Pat Hughes, with whom he won the Wimbledon doubles in 1936. In 1934 he took a set off Fred Perry in the first round of the singles and in 1931 and 1932 partnered his mother, Mrs C O Tuckey, in the mixed doubles. He gained his Cambridge University 'blue' in 1931.

Wimbledon doubles won 1936 with Hughes (beat C Hare/F Wilde, 6-4, 3-6, 7-9, 6-1, 6-4), r/u 1937 (J Budge/G Mako won, 6-0, 6-4, 6-8, 6-1). British Davis Cup team 1935–7.

TUCKEY, Agnes Katherine Raymond (*née* **Daniell),** GB
Born July 1877, Marylebone, London, died 1972. Mrs Tuckey and Hope Crisp won the Wimbledon mixed doubles in 1913, the first year in which the event was given full championship status. Their win came after one of the defending title holders, J C Parke, struck the other, Mrs D R Larcombe, in the eye with the ball. Mrs Larcombe was unable to continue or to defend her singles title. In 1931 and 1932 Mrs Tuckey partnered her son Raymond in the mixed doubles. In 1951 her daughter, Kay Tuckey, a Wightman Cup player for three years, succeeded in denting American dominance of the Wimbledon women's singles event when she and Jean Walker-Smith succeeded in reaching the last eight.

Wimbledon mixed doubles won 1913 with Crisp (beat J C Parke/Mrs D R Larcombe, 3-6, 5-3 retired).

TURNBULL, Wendy, Australia
Born November 1952, Brisbane. Coached by her father, Don Turnbull, and by Daphne Seeney Fancutt, Miss Turnbull first visited Europe in 1972 and had modest tournament successes. Since then her form has improved considerably both in singles and doubles. She was runner-up to Chris Evert in the 1977 US Open singles but gained some revenge in the

Federation Cup doubles when she and Kerry Reid beat Miss Evert and Rosie Casals, 6-3, 6-3, though Australia lost 2-1 to America. She was runner-up to Evonne Cawley in the Toyota Classic.

New Zealand Open doubles r/u 1974 with Miss M Michel, won 1975 with Miss E Goolagong; NZ hard court singles r/u 1975; doubles r/u 1974 with Miss A Kiyomura; NZ championship doubles won 1975 with Miss Goolagong.

German Open doubles r/u 1976 with Miss L Dupont.

Australian Open singles won 1976.

Swiss Open doubles won 1976 with Miss B Nagelsen.

US Open singles r/u 1977 (Miss Evert won, 7-6, 6-2); US clay court doubles r/u 1976 with Miss Dupont. Toyota Classic r/u 1977 (Mrs Cawley won, 6-4, 6-1).

TURNER, Lesley *see* **Bowrey, Mrs W W**

Above: Charles Tuckey as he appeared at Wimbledon in 1937.

ULRICH, Torben, Denmark
Born October 1928, Copenhagen. For many years a colourful character on tennis courts round the world, Torben Ulrich, a left-hander of considerable skill, had a wild piratical look, with a wild beard and his flowing hair held by a bandana. Brother of another good tennis player, Jorgen Ulrich, Torben has been the most con-

sistent of Wimbledon entrants since the war and had competed there 22 times from 1948 to 1977. The brothers are sons of Denmark's most famous tennis international, Einar Ulrich and between them they played a world record number of Davis Cup matches – over 200. In 1966 Torben was defaulted when defending his national title because he left the court to watch the World Cup soccer final on television. He has proved a successful competitor among the over-45s on the Grand Masters circuit and won the Grand Masters final in 1976.

Union of Soviet Socialist Republics

Imperial Russia was a founder member of the ILTF in 1913 and tennis has been played there for about 100 years. The last Russian championships were held in Leningrad (then St Petersburg) in 1914. The game survived the Revolution and in 1922 the Lawn Tennis Federation of the USSR was founded, becoming affiliated to the ILTF in 1956. An intensive coaching and training programme backed by the state is a feature of the game in the USSR with special sports schools for boys and girls aged eight or nine and intensive training for oustanding young players.

The USSR championships have been held since 1924, when the first champions were A Stoliarov (men's singles) and T Sukhodolskaya (women's singles). The Moscow international tournament, which attracts players from many countries, has been held since 1957. The USSR has competed in the Davis Cup regularly since 1962 and a women's team first competed in the Federation Cup in 1968.

Players who have achieved international success include Alex Metreveli, Tomas Lejus, Sergei Likhachev, Teimuraz Kakulia, Andreyev Potanin, Olga Morozova, Marina Kroschina, Natasha Chmyreva and Anna Dmitrieva.

United States Championships

The first tennis championships in the United States were held at the Newport Casino on Rhode Island from 31 August to 3 September 1881, when 26 players entered the men's singles, played on grass courts. The event was won by Richard Sears and the doubles went to C M Clark and F W Taylor. The championships, officially organised by the USNLTA, remained at the Casino for 34 years, until 1914. In 1884 the Challenge Round system as used at Wimbledon was introduced but was dropped in 1912. The championships moved to Forest Hills, New York, in 1915 and remained there until 1920, though in 1917 only a patriotic tournament was staged because of World War I. From 1921 to 1923 the championships were held at Germantown Cricket Club, Philadelphia, but returned to the West Side Club's new stadium at Forest Hills in 1924, remaining there until 1977.

The women's singles championships began in 1887, staged by the Chestnut Hill LTC on the grass courts of the Philadelphia Cricket Club until 1891, when the cricket club took over the running of the event until 1920. From 1921 the women's singles has been held at the West Side Club. The women's doubles and the mixed doubles were played with the women's singles championships but in 1921 the mixed doubles transferred to the national doubles programme, followed by the women's doubles in 1935. All five major championship events were held at the same venue – Forest Hills – for the first time in 1942 but from 1946 until 1967 the men's and women's doubles were held at Longwood Cricket Club, Chestnut Hill, while the two singles and the mixed doubles remained at Forest Hills.

The men's doubles event was held with the singles from 1881 but between 1890 and 1906 separate doubles tournaments were held in the East and West, the sectional winners then playing off for the right to meet the reigning champions in the Challenge Round. The doubles event was held as an elimination tournament in 1918 but reverted to the sectional qualifying system the next year. However, in 1920 the Challenge Round was abolished.

After Richard Sears, who won the singles seven years in succession, the next multi-winners were Bill Tilden (seven times, including six in a row) and William A Larned (seven times, including five in succession). The first foreign winners of the doubles were Reggie and Laurie Doherty of Great Britain, who won in 1902–3. In 1951 Frank Sedgman and Ken McGregor of Australia completed the only doubles 'Grand Slam' when they won the US event, having already won at Wimbledon and in Australia and France.

The first women's singles champion was Ellen Hansell. The title was taken eight times by Molla Bjurstedt Mallory and seven by Helen Wills Moody. Margaret Smith Court won the singles and the doubles six times each. Ellen Roosevelt and her sister Grace were the first women's doubles winners in 1890 and the most successful pairing was Louise Brough and Margaret Osborne duPont, who won 12 titles. Margaret duPont also won with Sarah Palfrey Fabyan Cooke, who herself won eight doubles titles.

United States Clay Court Championships

The USNLTA's clay court championships were first held in 1910 at the Omaha Field Club, Nebraska, where the winner was Melville Long. Fred Anderson and Walter Hayes (singles champion of 1911) won the first doubles. When the women's singles event was introduced in 1912 May Sutton took the title. Other winners have included several national grass court champions, such as Bill Tilden, who was six times clay court champion, Frank Parker (five) and Bobby Riggs (three). In 1971 the championships became open and were won by Zeljko Franulović of Yugoslavia, the first overseas champion.

The clay court event has been held at several venues over the years, including River Forest Tennis Club, Illinois; the Woodstock Country Club, Indianapolis; Pittsburgh Athletic Association; Cincinnati Tennis Club; Lakewood Tennis Club, Ohio; Triple A Club, St Louis; Detroit Tennis Club; Rockhill Tennis Club, Kansas City; University Club, Memphis; Chicago Town and Tennis Club; Salt Lake Tennis Club, Utah; Atlanta LTA and Milwaukee Town Club.

In a number of years the women's championship was not held (1913, 1924–39, 1942) and though usually held with the men's events, occasionally it was staged separately. Nancy Richey won the title six times in succession, Dorothy Head Knode four times. The women's doubles, which began in 1914, were also not always held (1915–16, 1921, 1924–39, 1942, 1948–9). Doris Hart won four times, twice with Pauline Betz, and Darlene Hard won four times with different partners.

United States Indoor Championships

There were 30 entrants in the first USNLTA indoor championships, held at the Winter Lawn Tennis Club, Newton Center, Massachusetts in 1898 and won by Leonard Ware. The event was not held in 1899 but in 1900 the Seventh Regiment Tennis Club in New York took over the championship, which was staged there until 1963, apart from 1941, when it was held at Oklahoma City, and 1924–5 when it was not staged. In 1964 the men's championship moved to Salisbury, Maryland. Wylie Grant won the men's singles five times (1903–4, 1906, 1908, 1912), Gustave Touchard four times (1910, 1913–15), Jean Borotra four times (1925, 1927, 1929, 1931) and Gregory Mangin four times (1932–3, 1935–6). The doubles championship began in 1900 when Calhoun Cragin and J Paret won. Wylie Grant won six times, three with Robert LeRoy. Harold Hackett and Frederick Alexander won the title together three times and Alexander also won twice with Theodore Pell and once with William Rosenbaum. Bill Talbert won five times, three with Don McNeill. Jean Borotra won four times with different partners.

The women's indoor singles began in 1907 at the Seventh Regiment Tennis Club, when Elizabeth Moore was the winner. The doubles followed in 1908 and Miss Moore won with Helen Helwig Pouch. During the war years, 1942–5, when the men's championship was not held, the women's events were held at Longwood covered courts, Chestnut Hill, and remained there until 1966. In 1967 the championship transferred to Winchester Tennis Club, Massachusetts, until 1972, when a women's amateur indoor championship was held at East Providence, Rhode Island.

Among singles champions have been Marie Wagner, who won six times, Molla Bjurstedt (five), Pauline Betz (four) and Billie Jean King (four). Mrs Hazel Hotchkiss Wightman, donor of the Wightman Cup, won the doubles ten times, including five with Sarah Palfrey and four with Marion Zinderstein. Katherine Hubbell won five times, twice with Lois Felix and the rest with different partners, and Mary Eisel won five times, three with Carol Hanks Aucamp. Marjorie Gladman Buck won four times, twice with Nancy Chaffee.

United States Lawn Tennis Association

The first really national lawn tennis association to be founded was the United States National Lawn Tennis Association, which was formed in 1881 and dropped the 'National' from its title in 1920. It adopted the All England Club's rules for its own championships and on its formation represented 34 tennis clubs. The first official championship was held in 1881 at the new Newport Casino, Rhode Island. Dr James Dwight of Boston, who was the President of the association for 21 years, was the first American to play at Wimbledon in 1884. By 1895 there were 106 member clubs of the USNLTA and they represented all parts of the country, though the major tournaments were in Chicago, Minneapolis and San Francisco or on the Atlantic seaboard. Though membership of the association dropped in 1900 because of the growth of interest in golf and the intervention of the Spanish-American war, the start of the Davis Cup in 1900 was a greater stimulus to the game and membership rose to 115 in 1908, by which time all but three states held their own championships. The finances of the association improved considerably and it was able to introduce championships for boys and girls by 1918, thereby beginning the junior development programme which was to lead to American supremacy in the game in later years. In 1923, the year that Forest Hills Stadium opened, the USLTA joined the ILTF. By this time the association had changed its rules so that its authority was no longer exercised directly on clubs but through sectional associations. As a result LTAs were formed in the West, California, the Pacific Northwest, Missouri, New York, the East, New England and the South over the course of the next few years. Today there are 17 sectional associations representing nearly 3000 clubs.

In 1935 the USLTA introduced a new programme of training and development for young players in the form of the junior Davis Cup programme, which was followed in 1938 by the junior Wightman Cup programme. Though tennis activity did not halt during World War II, events were restricted and many were held to raise funds for the war effort or war charities. After the war interest in tennis rose and in 1946 the gates of Forest Hills had to be closed for the first time since 1937. Development of the junior game was further boosted with official tennis centres and an increased number of tournaments for juniors. In 1958 Los Angeles was chosen by the USLTA as the centre for junior training and a programme to bring tennis to parks and high schools was sponsored by the National Tennis Educational Foundation, founded in 1951, and the Southern Californian Tennis Association. The foundation's 'clinics' attracted 100,000 students and were followed by others in many cities.

Though the question of Open tennis had been raised periodically since the 1930s it was not until the British LTA openly defied the ILTF in 1968 and held an Open Wimbledon that the USLTA supported Britain in adopting a resolution allowing member nations to decide for themselves whether or not to hold Open tournaments.

United States Professional Tennis Association

The United States Professional Lawn Tennis Association was formed in 1927 (it dropped 'Lawn' from the title in 1970) at the instigation of Vincent Richards, who took over professional tennis promotions started by C C Pyle. The association brought in European players as well as Americans as the professional ranks attracted increasing numbers of the world's top amateurs. It elected officers, framed a constitution and fixed an 'acceptable standard' for its members, who paid an initiation fee of $10.

VAN DILLEN, Erik, USA

Born February 1951, San Mateo, California. An outstanding doubles player, van Dillen made his reputation with an exceptional performance in the US Davis Cup Challenge Round win against Rumania in 1972. With Stan Smith as his partner, he helped defeat Ilie Năstase and Ion Tiriac in straight sets to secure a 3-2 win. In 1973, however, he and Smith lost their Challenge Round doubles against Newcombe and Laver after a previously exemplary record. He is the only player to win American junior titles in singles and doubles in four age divisions. In 1969 he won the US hard courts doubles and US amateur doubles, when he was National 18 champion. He became an independent professional in 1970 and in 1971 was runner-up in the Open doubles with Smith. In 1973 he and Smith played a record doubles rubber of 123 games in the Davis Cup against Fillol and Cornejo (Chile), winning 7-9, 37-39, 8-6, 6-1, 6-3.

US Open doubles r/u 1971 with Smith (J Newcombe/R Taylor won, 6-7, 6-3, 7-6, 4-6, 5-3, tie break). US hard court doubles won 1969 with R Lutz (beat M Lara/J Loyo-Mayo, 6-3, 5-7, 8-6). US amateur doubles won 1969 with T Leonard (beat J McKinley/R Stockton, 6-4, 7-5, 6-3). US professional indoor doubles r/u 1975 with Stockton (B Gottfried/R Ramirez won, 6-3, 3-6, 7-6), won Memphis doubles 1975, won Volvo doubles 1975, both with Stockton. Birmingham doubles won 1976 with

J Connors; Cincinnati doubles won 1976 with Smith. US Davis Cup team 1971– .

VAN RYN, John William, USA

Born June 1906, Newport News, Virginia. Three times winner of the Wimbledon doubles van Ryn formed a powerful partnership with Wilmer Allison, with whom he twice took the US doubles and twice the Wimbledon. His other winning partner was George Lott, his partner for the third Wimbledon victory and their only French doubles title.

US men's doubles r/u 1930 (Lott/J Doeg won, 8-6, 6-3, 4-6, 13-15, 6-4), won 1931 (beat G Mangin/B Bell, 6-4, 8-6, 6-3), r/u 1932 (H E Vines/K Gledhill won, 6-4, 6-3, 6-2), r/u 1934 (Lott/L Stoefen won, 6-4, 9-7, 3-6, 6-4), won 1935 (beat J Budge/G Mako, 6-4, 6-2, 3-6, 2-6, 6-1), r/u 1936 (Budge/Mako won, 6-4, 6-2, 6-4), all with Allison. US Davis Cup team 1926–36.

French doubles won 1931 with Lott (beat V Kirby/N Farquharson, 6-4, 6-3, 6-4).

Wimbledon doubles won 1929 (beat I Collins/J Gregory, 6-4, 5-7, 6-3, 10-12, 6-4), won 1930 (beat Doeg/Lott, 6-3, 6-3, 6-2), both with Allison, won 1931 with Lott (beat J Brugnon/H Cochet, 6-2, 10-8, 9-11, 3-6, 6-3), r/u 1935 with Allison (J Crawford/A Quist won, 6-3, 5-7, 6-2, 5-7, 7-5).

VASS

The Van Alen Streamlined Scoring system (VASS) was invented by a Rhode Island millionaire tennis enthusiast, James Van Alen, to shorten matches and help make the programming of events easier in the new television age of tennis. Instead of the traditional scoring of love, 15, 30, 40, deuce, game the system relies on single points and players change service every five points, as in table tennis. Each run of five points is called a 'hand'. A full set is 31 points but if time is short the set can be cut to 21 points. If the score reaches 30-30 a nine point tie-break is operated. No advantage point or game is played in VASS; the first player to win four points wins the game and the first to win six games takes the set. At five games all the tie-break decides the eleventh game and, thus, set.

Veteran International Tennis Association

Officially recognised by the ILTF, the Veteran International Association was founded in 1956 as the international governing body for veteran players. The official team competition is the Dubler Cup, which began in 1958, when Italy defeated Germany 3-1. In the same year VITA started its international championship of Europe, which was won by Francesco Garnero, of Italy.

VILAS, Guillermo, Argentina

Born August 1952, Mar del Plata. A brilliant left-hander who has firmly established himself

in the top half-dozen players in the world Guillermo Vilas first attracted international attention when he reached the last 16 of the French Open singles at his first attempt in 1972. Thereafter he maintained his consistent improvement and had his best year so far in 1977 when his wins included beating Jim Connors in the final of the US Open, beating Brian Gott- fried for the French title and beating 'Buster' Mottram in the South African final. In this last event Mottram was leading 3-0 in the first set tie-break at 6-6 when Vilas stormed back to take seven points in a row. By the beginning of 1978 he was challenging Borg and Connors for world No 1 spot. No player in recent years has made such a remarkably rapid advance. In

Above: Guillermo Vilas of Argentina has firmly established himself near the top. By 1978 he was challenging Borg and Connors for the world No 1 spot.

1974 he won the Commercial Union Grand Prix and, beating Năstase in the Melbourne final, won the Masters. In 1975 he again won the Grand Prix and was runner-up in the French Open and US professional (both to Borg) and ended second on the prize-money list with $247,675. In 1977 he won $175,000 in GP events alone.

US Open won 1977 (beat Connors, 2-6, 6-3, 7-6, 6-0); US professional r/u 1975 (Borg won, 6-3, 6-4, 6-2).

Canadian Open won 1974, 1976.

South American Open won 1973–4; doubles won 1974 with M Orantes.

Western professional runner-up 1972.

Argentine Open won 1977 (beat J Fillol, 6-2, 7-5, 3-6, 6-3).

South African Open won 1977 (beat Mottram, 7-6, 6-3, 6-4).

Dutch Open won 1974. Italian Open r/u 1976.

French Open r/u 1975 (Borg won, 6-2, 6-3, 6-4), won 1977 (beat Gottfried, 6-0, 6-3, 6-0).

VINES, Henry Ellsworth, USA

Born September 1911, Los Angeles. A star who flashed all too briefly across the tennis sky in the early 1930s. Ellsworth Vines had the potential to become the world's greatest player had he stayed around longer. Instead, having caused a sensation both as an amateur and professional, he gave up tennis in favour of golf at which he also became a successful professional. The tall, tousle-headed Vines learned his tennis on the Los Angeles park courts and at the age of 17 in 1929 won the national junior doubles with Keith Gledhill. In 1931 he emerged as a sensational tennis 'find' beating Fred Perry from two sets down in the US semi-finals and then going on to put down George Lott 7-9, 6-3, 9-7, 7-5 in the final. Next year he beat 'Bunny' Austin in the Wimbledon final, losing only six games, and took his second US singles when he thrashed the great Frenchman Henri Cochet in straight sets.

Vines had a cannon-ball service and supreme accuracy in his shots, skimming the net or smashing to within a fraction of the line. It was said that none ever hit a ball harder or with less margin for error. He withstood tempting offers to become a professional during 1932 to play another amateur season but lost to Crawford at Wimbledon and to Bryan 'Bitsy' Grant in the US fourth round. Then he signed a professional contract and drew a crowd of 14,637 to his first match at Madison Square Garden before going on tour playing Bill Tilden. He won 47 matches to Tilden's 26. He became the No 1 professional and confirmed this in 1938 by beating Perry 49 matches to 35. However, the following year he lost over all to Don Budge and chose to swap the courts for the golf courses.

US singles won 1931 (beat Lott, 7-9, 6-3, 9-7, 7-5), won 1932 (beat Cochet, 6-4, 6-4, 6-4); doubles won 1932 with Gledhill (beat W Allison/ J Van Ryn, 6-4, 6-3, 6-2); mixed doubles won 1933 with Miss E Ryan (beat Lott/Miss S Palfrey, 11-9, 6-1). United States Davis Cup team 1932–3.

Australian doubles won 1933 with Gledhill (beat J Crawford/E Moon, 6-4, 10-8, 6-2); mixed doubles r/u 1933 with Mrs J Van Ryn (Crawford/Mrs T Crawford won, 3-6, 7-5, 13-11).

Wimbledon singles won 1932 (beat H W Austin 6-4, 6-2, 6-0), r/u 1933 (Crawford won, 4-6, 11-9, 6-2, 2-6, 6-4).

Virginia Slims Circuit

Set up in 1970 and carrying the brand name of the American tobacco company, Philip Morris, the Virginia Slims circuit began when Gladys Heldman, publisher of *World Tennis*, was asked to organise a tournament for eight women in Houston, Texas. The event was in direct competition with the established Pacific Southwest championships in Los Angeles, where promoter Jack Kramer was offering $50,000 in men's prize money and only $7500 for women. Billie Jean King and Rosie Casals approached Mrs Heldman and asked her to organise a women's boycott of the championships. Instead, Mrs Heldman proposed the tournament for the top eight women players, with $7500 prize money, much of which came from Philip Morris. Because the women were strictly still amateurs and could only take the prize money 'unofficially', they all signed professional contracts with Mrs Heldman for $1.00 (one dollar) for one week. They were suspended by the USLTA.

The women replied by setting up a series of contract professional tournaments for the 1971–72 winter and spring season and signed up a further ten players. Thus was born the World Tennis Women's Professional Tour and the Virginia Slims Circuit which rapidly fired the enthusiasm of the tennis-going public, though not of the USLTA, which introduced sanctions against the women. The Women's Pro Tour founded its own players' organisation, the Women's International Tennis Federation, to look after their interests and negotiate prize money and fees. Eventually in 1973 agreement was reached between the USLTA and the ILTF on the one hand and the WITF on the other which allowed the women to compete in international events and in Virginia Slims tournaments, which were to be limited in number. Since then the Virginia Slims Circuit has in fact grown in size and in the amount of prize money offered and the Virginia Slims championship ranks in importance with the women's titles of Wimbledon and America. Prize money for the 1977–8 Virginia Slims 'season' covering some 12 weeks was a $1,250,000 guaranteed from Philip Morris – amounting to over $100,000 a week.

VIVIAN, Mrs F H *see* Scriven, Margaret

VON CRAMM, Baron Gottfried *see* Cramm, Baron Gottfried von

WADE, Sarah Virginia, GB

Born July 1945, Bournemouth. The high point of Virginia Wade's career was reached in 1977 when, in the Queen's Jubilee Year, she won the singles title at the Centenary Wimbledon to give Britain its first Wimbledon 'queen' since Ann Jones in 1969. To take the title she beat the gallant Betty Stöve 4-6, 6-3, 6-1 in a final which, by no means great, was played in an atmosphere of fervent patriotism. It was a victory which came 16 years after her first attempt, since when she had six times reached the quarter-finals and twice the semi-finals and it was probably her greatest triumph since becoming the winner of the first US Open in 1968. In the years between she had been Britain's great tennis hope, had won numerous titles, become a leading professional – and had also shown an extraordinary unpredictability. Potentially her game is as good as any in the world, particularly with her powerful penetrating service and when given the chance to attack, which she likes to do all the time. In the past, however, she has proved unequal to the big occasion or the unexpected from opponents. Once thrown from her superbly rhythmic attack, she can tense up and play a set or more of mediocre tennis. Crowds who for years had asked 'Is this going to be Virginia's year?' had come to recognise the signs of a grim, determined Miss Wade showing all the symptoms of pre-match nerves as she strode on to court. Recently, however, she has learned to relax more and her game has flowed more easily as a result.

After winning Wimbledon Miss Wade, though still playing brilliantly in many of her matches, came up against the revitalised Billie Jean King, who was in devastating form on her return to the circuit. Virginia finished third in the 1977 Colgate Inaugural, behind Chris Evert and Billie Jean, won the doubles with Françoise Durr but was beaten by Mrs King in the final of the new Bremar Cup in London and lost again to her in a 2½-hour Wightman Cup singles after the US had already clinched the trophy. Virginia, who became a Member of the British Empire (MBE) in 1973, has frequently shown inspired captaincy of the Wightman Cup team and had hoped to bring the Cup back to Britain as an additional Jubilee Year success. At the end of the year she gained the coveted Sports Personality of the Year award of the BBC.

Wimbledon singles won 1977 (beat Miss Stöve, 4-6, 6-3, 6-1); doubles r/u 1970 with Miss Durr (Mrs King/Miss R Casals won, 6-2, 6-3); Wimbledon Plate won 1968 (beat Miss K M Harter, 6-2, 12-10). Rothmans' British hard court singles won 1967-8, r/u 1970, won 1973-4; doubles won 1967, 1974 with Miss J Heldman;

mixed doubles won 1967-8 with R Howe. Bremar Cup r/u 1977 (Mrs B J King won, 6-3, 6-1); doubles r/u with Miss Stöve (Mrs King/Miss Tomanova won, 6-2, 6-3).

Australian singles won 1972 (beat Miss E Goolagong, 6-4, 6-4); doubles won 1973 with Mrs Court (beat Miss K Melville/Miss K Harris, 6-4, 6-4).

French doubles won 1973 with Mrs M Court (beat Miss Stöve/Miss Durr, 6-2, 6-3).

US Open singles won 1968 (beat Mrs King, 6-4, 6-2); doubles r/u 1972 (Miss Durr/Miss Stöve won, 6-3, 1-6, 6-3), won 1973 (beat Mrs King/Miss Casals, 3-6, 6-3, 7-5), won 1975 (beat Mrs King/Miss Casals, 7-5, 2-6, 7-6), all with Mrs Court; r/u 1976 with Miss O Morozova (Miss L Boshoff/Miss I Kloss won, 6-1, 6-4). Colgate inaugural doubles won 1977 with Miss Durr (beat H Gourlay/Miss J Russell, 6-1, 4-6, 6-4).

Argentine Open won 1972.

Italian Open singles won 1971; doubles won 1968 with Mrs Court, won 1973 with Miss Morozova.

Canadian Open r/u 1972.

South African Open singles r/u 1968; doubles r/u 1973 with Miss Evert; mixed doubles won 1972 with M Mulligan.

Dewar Cup won 1969, r/u 1972, won 1973-6.

Virginia Slims Washington singles r/u 1976, doubles won 1976; VS Chicago singles r/u 1976, doubles won 1976, both with Miss Morozova; VS Boston singles r/u 1976; VS Akron singles r/u 1976.

Wales, GB

The first record of organised tennis in Wales is in a report of the Newport Athletic Club which mentions the formation of a tennis section in 1879 and erection of a covered court in 1890. However, in 1873 Major W C Wingfield, who devised and patented a lawn tennis kit, dedicated his book of rules to 'the party assembled at Nantclwyd Hall, the seat of the Naylor-Leland family', near Ruthin, North Wales. Tennis clubs were founded in several places during the 1880s and Penarth LTC held its first championships in 1885. The Roath LTC was founded at about this time, later changing its name to the Cardiff Racquet and Lawn Tennis Club and its grounds from Roath to Cardiff Castle.

Records of the Welsh LTA were lost during World War II but it is known to have existed in 1888, when the challenge bowl awarded to the winners of the annual inter-club competition went to Cardiff Racquet and Lawn Tennis Club. This inter-club competition was run on a knock-out basis until 1903, when it was changed to a league system. In 1927 a women's team event was started on an elimination basis but then also became a Ladies League competition.

Originally held either at Penarth LTC or Roath LTC, the Welsh championships are believed to have started in 1886. From 1897 their

Above: Great Britain's Virginia Wade, winner of the 1977 Centenary Wimbledon women's singles.

home was the Newport Athletic Club. In 1908 the Dinas Powys club organised the Whitsun tournament open to members of South Wales clubs. Because of the tournament's success the club then founded the Glamorgan championships in 1911, introducing women's singles in 1914. (No championships were held during World War I or II). For financial reasons Dinas Powys had to give up the running of the event in 1965 and Cardiff LTC took over until 1972, when the championships were discontinued.

The Carmarthenshire championships were launched in 1922 by the Llanelli LTC and in 1925 the club was the venue for a ladies' international match between Wales and Australia. Llanelli became the venue for the ladies internationals between Wales and England in 1926. The Wales versus England men's international was inaugurated in 1924 at the Newport Athletic Club and the first international mixed doubles match between Wales and Ireland was held at Colwyn Bay, North Wales, in 1949, Ireland winning then and successively up to 1958.

In recent years the Welsh LTA, which has long faced financial problems, has received assistance from commercial backing by donations, grants and sponsorship from companies such as Dewars, the distillers, and Green Shield Stamps. The LTA appointed its first full-time coach and development officer in 1971 and a junior international between Wales and Ireland was held for the first time the following year at Llanelli. The first Welsh junior championships were held in 1923. Wales's best player has been Mike Davies, who was under-16 singles and doubles champion for three years, men's doubles runner-up in 1960 and had a distinguished Davis Cup career, playing 37 rubbers. He turned professional in 1961 after winning the British hard court championships of 1960. Another outstanding Welsh product and former junior champion is Gerald Battrick, of Bridgend, Glamorgan.

WARD, Holcombe, USA
Born November 1878, New York, died 1967. Six times winner of the US men's doubles and once of the singles, Holcombe Ward was a member of the first American Davis Cup team in 1900, partnering Dwight Davis, who donated the Cup, Ward and Davis together won three US national doubles titles. Ward is credited with originating the American 'twist' service, in which a high bounce is achieved by hitting across the ball with a long follow-through swing.

US singles won 1904 (beat W Larned, wo), r/u 1905 (B C Wright won, 6-1, 6-2, 11-9); doubles r/u 1898 (L Ware/G Sheldon won, 1-6, 7-5, 6-4, 4-6, 7-5), won 1899 (beat Ware/Sheldon, 6-4, 6-4, 6-3), won 1900 (beat F B Alexander/R Little, 6-4, 9-7, 12-10), won 1901 (beat I Ware/Wright, 6-3, 9-7, 6-1), r/u 1902 (R Doherty/L Doherty won, 11-9, 12-10, 6-4), all with Davis, won 1904 (beat K Collins/Little), won 1905 (beat Alexander/H Hackett, 6-3, 6-1, 6-2), won 1906 (beat Alexander/Hackett, 6-3, 3-6, 6-3, 6-3), all with Wright. US Davis Cup team 1900, 1902, 1905–6.

Wimbledon doubles r/u 1901 with Davis (R Doherty/L Doherty won, 4-6, 6-2, 6-3, 9-7).

WARWICK, Kim, Australia
Born April 1952, Sydney, NSW. After making an impressive start in international tennis while still a junior, Warwick, a protégé of Australian coach Vic Edwards, has yet to fulfil his early promise and has had some disappointing seasons. In 1972, with Evonne Goolagong, he won the French Open mixed doubles and reached the Wimbledon final, losing to Ilie Năstase and Rosie Casals. However, bad behaviour in an Italian tournament resulted in his suspension for a year by the ILTF. After an improved season in 1974 he was runner-up in the WCT Stockholm doubles with Patrice Dominguez and runner-up in the Manila doubles with Sydney Ball in 1975 but he subsequently missed some good singles and doubles title opportunities when apparently in command.

WATSON, Maud Edith Eleanor, GB
Born October 1864, Harrow, Middlesex, died June 1946. The first woman champion at Wimbledon Miss Watson and her older sister, Lilian, were among the entry of 13 women in 1884. Maud beat Miss Blanche Bingley (later Mrs G W Hillyard) who was to become a six-times champion, and then played her own sister, Lilian, in the final, winning 6-8, 6-3, 6-3. The following year she again beat Miss Bingley to retain the title but lost to her in 1886, the first year of the women's Challenge Round. In 1884–5 she also won the Irish singles and mixed doubles and in 1887 was the first Welsh women's champion.

WATSON, Phoebe Catherine (*née* Holcroft, later Mrs W L Blakstad), GB
Born October 1898, St Leonards-on-Sea, Sussex. Twice doubles champion of Wimbledon (1928–1929) with Peggy Saunders Michell, Mrs Watson also took the French doubles with Miss E Bennett in 1928. She was in the British Wightman Cup team of 1928–30.

Wimbledon women's doubles won 1928 (beat Miss Bennett/Miss E Harvey, 6-2, 6-3), won 1929 (beat Mrs B Covell/Mrs D Shepherd-Barron, 6-4, 8-6), both with Mrs Michell.

French doubles r/u 1927 with Miss Saunders (Mrs I Peacock/Miss E Heine won, 6-2, 6-1), won 1928 with Miss Bennett (beat Miss S Dévé/Mrs Lafaurie, 6-0, 6-2).

US doubles won 1929 with Mrs Michell (beat Mrs Covell/Mrs Shepherd-Barron, 2-6, 6-3, 6-4).

Welsh Championships *see* **Newport**

West of England Championships *see* **Bristol**

WHITMAN, Malcolm D, USA
Born March 1877, died December 1932. A friend of Dwight Davis, donor of the Davis Cup, Whitman was US champion for three years (1898–1900) and was a member of the first US Davis Cup team in 1900 and 1902, with Dwight Davis and Holcombe Ward, winning all four of his singles rubbers. He is credited with originating the 'reverse' service in which the ball breaks sharply to the left of the receiver when it touches the ground.

US singles won 1898 (beat R D Wrenn, wo), won 1899 (J Paret, 6-1, 6-2, 3-6, 7-5), won 1900 (beat W Larned, 6-4, 1-6, 6-2, 6-2), r/u 1902 All-Comers (R Doherty won, 6-1, 3-6, 6-3, 6-0).

WIGHTMAN, Hazel (*née* **Hotchkiss**), USA

Born December 1886, Healdsburg, California, died December 1974. Chiefly remembered today as the donor of the Wightman Cup, Mrs Wightman was one of America's great women players of the early 1900s and won innumerable titles, including the singles four times – the first in 1909 and the last in 1919, the doubles six times – first in 1909 and finally in 1928 – and the mixed doubles six times – first in 1909 to complete her 'Triple Crown' and last in 1920. She took the Triple Crown twice more, in 1910–11, and in 1924, the year she won her fifth US doubles, took her only Wimbledon title, the doubles. That year, too, she won two Olympic gold medals. She was a member of the US Wightman Cup team 1923–4, 1927, 1929 and 1931, captain in those years and also non-playing captain in 1933, 1935, 1937–9, 1946–8. She was awarded an Honorary Commander of the British Empire (CBE) in 1973 at the Jubilee Wightman Cup

match in Boston, at which time she was still coaching.

US singles won 1909 (beat Mrs M Barger-Wallach, 6-0, 6-1), won 1910 (beat Miss L Hammond, 6-4, 6-2), won 1911 (beat Miss F Sutton, 8-10, 6-1, 9-7), r/u 1912 (Miss M K Browne won, default), r/u All-Comers 1915 (Miss M Bjurstedt won, 4-6, 6-2, 6-0), won 1919 (beat Miss M Zinderstein, 6-1, 6-2); doubles won 1909–10 with Miss E E Rotch, won 1911 (beat Miss Sutton/Miss D Green, 6-4, 4-6, 6-2), won 1915 (beat Mrs M McLean/Mrs G Chapman, 10-8, 6-2), both with Miss Eleanor Sears, r/u 1923 with Miss E Goss (Miss K McKane/Mrs B Covell won, 2-6, 6-2, 6-1), won 1924 (beat Miss Goss/Mrs J Jessup, 6-4, 6-3), won 1928 (beat Miss E Cross/Mrs L Harper, 6-2, 6-2), both with Miss H Willis; mixed doubles won 1909 with W F Johnson, won 1910 with J R Carpenter, won 1911 with Johnson (beat H M Tilden/Miss E Wildey, 6-4, 6-4), won 1915 with

H C Johnson (beat I Wright/Miss Bjurstedt, 6-0, 6-1), won 1918 with Wright (beat F B Alexander/Miss Bjurstedt, 6-2, 6-4), won 1920 with W F Johnson.

Wimbledon doubles won 1924 with Miss Wills (beat Mrs Covell/Miss McKane, 6-4, 6-4).

Wightman Cup

Donated by Mrs G W Wightman, this elaborately decorated silver vase, which stands 24 in (61 cm) high, was intended to be called the 'Women's Lawn Tennis Team Championship between Great Britain and the United States', and is inscribed with those words. However the simpler 'Wightman Cup' title came naturally, as a tribute to one of America's greatest women tennis players and supreme sportswomen. Originally Mrs Wightman had hoped that the trophy, which she gave to the USLTA in 1920, would be for competition amongst several nations but other countries did not have the same enthusiasm for this 'women's Davis Cup' as did the US and Great Britain. The first match played in 1923 in the newly opened Forest Hills stadium, New York, and America won convincingly by 7-0 – as she did just 55 years later in 1977. Since its beginning Britain has won only nine times to 1977, including successively in the second year of the competition (6-1) and 1925 (4-3) and in 1974 (6-1) and 1975 (5-2). America has repeated its 7-0 'whitewash' on six other occasions plus a 6-0 win in 1954, when one match was not played. The competition was not held from 1940–5.

The matches are played annually, the venue alternating between the United States and Britain. The Cup match has consisted since the start of five singles and two doubles. The teams can consist of from four to seven players; the two doubles pairs can take part in the singles. The numbers one and two singles players cross-play but each number three player plays only her opposite and the numbers one and two doubles teams play only their counterparts. The order of singles play is determined 24-hours in advance and the doubles are played as the last match each day. The order of play can be altered by mutual consent of the captains who can be players or non-players, and of the referee.

Over the years the Wightman Cup matches have attracted increasing public attention and now have an ardent following. In America it was agreed in 1965 to spread the matches over three days in the hope of increasing the revenue and two years later the experiment proved a success with an all-time record total attendance of 16,000. Until 1957 the competition had traditionally been played on grass but in that year fast-drying composition courts, coloured green, were used. Since then the surfaces have also been of clay, cement and synthetic carpet.

The teams in the first ever Wightman Cup match which was also the first international women's team match were: United States – Mrs Wightman, Mrs Molla Bjurstedt Mallory (the then US champion), Helen Wills and Eleanor Goss; Great Britain – Kitty McKane (the 1924 Wimbledon champion), Mrs A E Beamish, Mrs R C Clayton and Mrs B C Covell. Close on 3000 spectators were at the stadium on the first day, 11 August. Since then the competition has included many of the world's leading players – admittedly mostly on the American side in recent years – and has produced some classic duels. A large number of the annual contests have been decided by the outcome of the last doubles match – as was the case in five of the first eight years. It was in this area that Britain, though not winning the trophy, tended to dominate, winning 13 of the 20 doubles matches in the first ten years.

Among the stars who have shone in the series have been Elizabeth Ryan and Mary K Browne, Kitty McKane Godfree, Mrs Dorothy Lambert Chambers, Peggy Saunders Michell, Mrs Dorothy Shepherd-Barron, the young Helen Jacobs and Betty Nuthall; Dorothy Round, Eileen Whitingstall, Freda James, Kay Stammers, Sarah Palfrey Fabyan, Dorothy Bundy, Darlene Hard, Alice Marble, Angela Mortimer, Doris Hart, Pat Ward, Louise Brough, Shirley Bloomer, Christine Truman Janes, Ann Haydon Jones, Maureen Connolly, Shirley Fry, Althea Gibson, Karen Hantze, Billie Jean Moffitt King, Margaret Osborne duPont, Mrs Pat Todd, Winifred Shaw, Virginia Wade, Rosie Casals, Nancy Richey, Chris Evert, Glynis Coles and Sue Barker – a cross-section of the best of women players in the two countries and of the history of women's tennis since the start of the competition.

WILBERFORCE, Sir Herbert William Wrangham, GB

Born February 1864, Munich, Germany, died March 1941, London, England. A barrister and great-grandson of the emancipator William Wilberforce, Herbert Wilberforce was doubles champion of Wimbledon in 1887 with Patrick Bowes-Lyon, younger brother of the 14th Earl of Strathmore. They gained the title by a Challenge Round walk-over from the Renshaw brothers, Ernest and William. A Cambridge University tennis 'blue' 1883–6 he was secretary of the All-England Club's Wimbledon championships for 1889–90, president from 1921 to 1930 and chairman from 1921–36.

WILDING, Anthony Frederick, New Zealand

Born October 1883, Christchurch, New Zealand, killed in action at Neuve Chapelle, France, May 1915 as a Captain in the Royal Marines. The greatest New Zealand tennis player of all time, Wilding won the Wimbledon singles in four successive years, the doubles four times, was three times singles champion of his own country and twice of Australia. The handsome New Zealander, who learned his tennis at Cambridge University, was a member of the Australasian (Australia and New Zealand) Davis Cup team in 1905–9 and 1914, during which years it won the cup four times and he won eight of his Challenge Round rubbers and lost four. A brilliant stylist, he formed a successful doubles partnership with the Australian, Norman

Brookes, with whom he gained two of his four Wimbledon doubles titles. It was Brookes who finally took the title from him in the 1914 Challenge Round.

Wimbledon singles won 1910 (beat A W Gore, 6-4, 7-5, 4-6, 6-2), won 1911 (beat H Roper Barrett, 6-4, 4-6, 2-6, 6-2 retired), won 1912 (beat Gore, 6-4, 6-4, 4-6, 6-4), won 1913 (beat M McLoughlin, 8-6, 6-3, 10-8), r/u 1914 (Brookes won, 6-4, 6-4, 7-5); doubles won 1907 with Brookes (wo), won 1908 (wo), won 1910 (beat Gore/Roper Barrett, 6-1, 6-1, 6-2), r/u 1911 (M Decugis/A Gobert won, 9-7, 5-7, 6-3, 2-6, 6-2), all with M Ritchie; won 1914 with Brookes (beat C Dixon/Roper Barrett, 6-1, 6-1, 5-7, 8-6); mixed doubles r/u 1914 (J Parke/Mrs

D R Larcombe won, 4-6, 6-4, 6-2).

Australian singles won 1906 (beat H Parker), won 1909 (beat E Parker); doubles won 1906 with R Heath (beat H Parker/C Cox), r/u 1908 with G Sharp (F B Alexander/A W Dunlop won), r/u 1909 with L Brooks (E Parker/J Keane won). New Zealand singles won 1906, 1908–9. Australasian Davis Cup team 1905–9, 1914.

WILLIAMS, Richard Norris, USA

Born January 1891, Geneva, Switzerland, died June 1968, Pennsylvania. Twice singles champion of America and a long-serving member of the US Davis Cup team, Williams was a fast and powerful player who was robbed of true greatness by being erratic. On form he was virtually unbeatable, playing at great pace and deep into the corners or close to the line, but on an off day he could lose to a much lesser player. He won his first tournament at the age of 12 before moving from Switzerland to the United States. His Davis Cup career spanned World War I – during which he served in the US Army and was awarded the *Chevalier de la Légion d'honneur* and *Croix de Guerre* – and he was five times a member of the winning team; of 13 rubbers he won six singles and four doubles. In 1912 he survived the sinking of the *Titanic*.

US singles r/u 1913 (M McLoughlin won, 3-6, 2-6, 6-2, 6-4, 6-2), won 1914 (beat McLoughlin, 6-3, 8-6, 10-8), won 1916 (beat W M Johnston, 4-6, 6-4, 0-6, 6-2, 6-4); doubles r/u 1921 (W Tilden/V Richards won, 13-11, 12-10, 6-1), r/u 1923 (Tilden/B Norton won, 3-6, 6-2, 6-3, 5-7, 6-2), both with W Washburn; won 1925 (beat G Patterson/J Hawkes, 6-2, 8-10, 6-4, 11-9), won 1926 (beat Tilden/A Chapin, 6-4, 6-8, 11-9, 6-3), both with Richards; r/u 1927 with Johnston (Tilden/F T Hunter won, 10-8, 6-3, 6-3); mixed doubles won 1912 with Miss M K Browne (beat W Clothier/Miss Eleonora Sears, 6-4, 2-6, 11-9). US Davis Cup team 1913–14, 1921, 1923, 1925–6.

Wimbledon doubles won 1920 with C S Garland (wo), r/u 1924 with Washburn (Hunter/Richards won, 6-3, 3-6, 8-10, 8-6, 6-3).

WILLS, Helen *see* Mrs H W Moody

Wimbledon *see* All England Club

WOOD, Patrick O'Hara, Australia

Born April 1891, Melbourne, died December 1961. A noted doubles player and Australian Davis Cup player, O'Hara Wood was four times doubles champion of his own country and once of Wimbledon. As a member of the 1922 and 1924 Davis Cup teams he played 23 singles and doubles rubbers, winning nine singles and eight doubles. His brother, Arthur, was singles and doubles champion of Australia in 1914.

Australian singles won 1920, 1923; doubles won 1919–20 with R V Thomas, won 1923 with C B St John, r/u 1929 (N Brookes/J Anderson won, 6-2, 6-4, 6-3), won 1925 (beat Anderson/F Kalms, 6-4, 8-6, 7-5), both with G Patterson; r/u 1926 with Anderson (Patterson/J Hawkes won, 6-1, 6-4, 6-2), r/u 1927 with I McInnes (Patterson/Hawkes won, 8-6, 6-2, 6-1).

Wimbledon doubles won 1919 with Anderson (wo), r/u 1922 with Patterson (Anderson/R Lycett won, 3-6, 7-9, 6-4, 6-3, 11-9).

US doubles r/u 1922 (W Tilden/V Richards won, 4-6, 6-1, 6-3, 6-1), r/u 1924 (R Kinsey/H Kinsey won, 7-5, 5-7, 7-9, 6-3, 6-4), both with Patterson.

WOOD, Sydney Durr Beardslee, USA

Born November 1911, Black Rock, Connecticut. Sydney Wood first competed at Wimbledon at the age of 15 in 1927 and became singles champion at the age of 19 years 8 months in 1931. He is the only Wimbledon singles champion to gain his title by a walk-over: his Davis Cup team mate Frank Shields hurt a knee defeating Borotra in the semi-final and had to withdraw before the final.

US singles r/u 1935 (W Allison won, 6-2, 6-2, 6-3). Wimbledon won 1931 (wo). US Davis Cup team 1931, 1934.

WOOLDRIDGE, Mrs K *see* Shaw, Winnie

WOOSNAM, Maxwell, GB

Born September 1892, Liverpool, died July 1965. A noted all-round sportsman, Max Woosnam was a Cambridge University soccer, 'blue', a 'real' tennis 'blue' and a golf 'blue' and he also played soccer for Manchester City and for England. He won the Wimbledon doubles with Randolph Lycett in 1921, beating the brothers A H and F G Lowe in the All-Comers and having a walk-over in the final. He was a member of the Davis Cup team in 1924 and 1926.

World Championship Tennis Inc (WCT)

Eight of the world's leading players signed up for WCT when it was founded in 1967 by Dave Dixon, Lamar Hunt and Al Hill Jr in America. The founding players, whose playing careers with the new organisation began in 1968 in Sydney, Australia, were: Tony Roche and John Newcombe (Australia), Pierre Barthes (France), Roger Taylor (Great Britain), Cliff Drysdale (South Africa), Dennis Ralston and 'Butch' Buchholz (United States), and Nikki Pilić (Yugoslavia). In 1968 Dixon's share was bought out by Hunt and Hill, who gave executive control to Bob Briner, who had been handling the detailed organisation. WCT was in direct competition with another professional group, the National Tennis League promoted by George MacCall. At first neither WCT nor NTL did well with their tours and WCT began reorganising, first under Briner and then under Mike Davies, the former British Davis Cup player who had been a professional under Jack Kramer's promotions. WCT and the NTL, which eventually merged with WCT, had long-running disputes with the ILTF in the early years, mainly over the promoters' insistence on the payment of 'management fees' by each tournament before the professionals appeared. In 1970 WCT announced a scheme for a $1-million world championship of tennis circuit covered by 32 players with 20 events from which the top eight players would compete in a final tournament worth $100,000 (including a $50,000 first prize).

The first world championship of tennis final was in Dallas in November 1971, when Ken Rosewall beat Rod Laver for the largest prize offered in tennis up to that time. Next year the timing of the championship was altered to fit in with television programming – TV providing important financial backing – and concluded in May. In 1971, because agreement had not been reached between WCT and the ILTF, the professionals did not compete in Open tennis but the differences were settled – or, at least, buried – in the spring of 1972, though not in time for the contract players to enter that year's contest at Wimbledon.

By now WCT was an undoubted success and had created an upsurge of interest. By 1973 the WCT circuit was split into two groups – Europe and the US – each 32-man group playing 11 matches between January and May and the top four from the groups playing off in the Dallas Final. The circuit continued to grow, as did the prize money, and in 1976 the group system was ended, 54 players competing against each other in 26 tournaments on a money-based points pool system. Prize money now totals some $2.5 million.

World Team Tennis (WTT), USA

Founded in 1973 as an American indoor league team competition, WTT was the brainchild of ice-hockey and basketball promoter Dennis Murphy. The first season, in 1974, was financially disastrous for the 16 teams involved and their promoters. The league introduced an entirely new brand of tennis: matches consisting of a women's single, a men's single, a mixed doubles; scoring on the 'no-ad' system with tie breaks at 5-5 in any set; a programme lasting $2\frac{1}{2}$ hours, to suit television's requirements; vociferous, chanting fans and a general atmosphere of high-pressure salesmanship that made tennis purists shudder. Despite the early setback and scepticism, WTT survived and is now a regular part of the American tennis scene, attracting many of the world's leading players to its teams, which have fancy names such as the Golden Gaters (San Francisco), the Phoenix Racquets, the Cleveland Nets, the Hawaii Leis, the New York Sets. The league covers ten cities and includes amongst its players Chris Evert, Billie Jean King, Evonne Cawley, Martina Navratilova, Betty Stöve, Virginia Wade, Tony Roche, Ilie Năstase, Vitas Gerulaitis, Bob Hewitt, Tom Okker, Frew McMillan, John Newcombe and Margaret Court.

WRENN, Robert D, USA

Born September 1873. A powerful left-hander who was an excellent all-round athlete, Wrenn won the US singles title four times out of five between 1893 and 1897, the first at the age of 19, making him the third youngest winner.

US singles won 1893 (wo), won 1894 (beat M Goodbody, 6-8, 6-1, 6-4, 6-4), r/u 1895 (F Hovey won, 6-3, 6-2, 6-4), won 1896 (beat Hovey, 7-5, 3-6, 6-0, 1-6, 6-1), won 1897 (beat W Eaves, 4-6, 8-6, 6-3, 2-6, 6-2); doubles won 1895 (beat J Howland/A E Foote), r/u 1896 (C Neel/S Neel won), both with M G Chace.

WRIGHT, Beals C, USA

Born December 1879, Boston, Massachusetts, died 1961. The first American to reach the All-Comers singles final at Wimbledon, in 1910, when he lost to the eventual champion, Tony Wilding, Wright was a friend of Dwight Davis, donor of the Davis Cup. A left-hander, he played in the US Davis Cup team in 1905 and 1907–8. He won the US singles in 1905 and was twice doubles champion with Holcombe Ward.

US singles r/u 1901 All-Comers (W Larned won, 6-2, 6-8, 6-4, 6-4), won 1905 Challenge Round (beat H Ward, 6-1, 6-2, 11-9), r/u 1906 (W Clothier won, 6-3, 6-0, 6-4), r/u 1908 (Larned won, 6-1, 6-2, 8-6), r/u 1910 All-Comers (T Bundy won, 6-8, 6-3, 6-3, 10-8), r/u All-Comers 1911 (M McLoughlin won, 6-4, 4-6, 7-5, 6-3); doubles r/u 1901 with I Ware (H Ward/D Davis won, 6-3, 9-7, 6-1), won 1904 (beat K Collins/R Little), won 1905 (beat F B Alexander/H Hackett, 6-3, 6-1, 6-2), won 1906 (beat Alexander/Hackett, 6-3, 3-6, 6-3, 6-3), all with Ward, r/u 1908 with Little (Hackett/Alexander won, 6-1, 7-5, 6-2), r/u 1918 with Alexander (W Tilden/V Richards won, 6-3, 6-4, 3-6, 2-6, 6-2).

Wimbledon singles r/u 1910 All-Comers (Wilding won, 4-6, 4-6, 6-3, 6-2, 6-3); doubles r/u 1907 All-Comers with K Behr (N Brookes/Wilding won, 6-4, 6-4, 6-2).

WYNNE, Nancye see Nancye Bolton

YORKE, Adeline Maud (Billie), GB

Born December 1910, Rawalpindi, Punjab, India. Winner of the Wimbledon women's doubles of 1937 with Mrs René Mathieu, Mrs Yorke also won the French doubles in three successive years with the same partner.

Wimbledon doubles won 1937 with Mrs Mathieu (beat Mrs M B King/Mrs J Pittman, 6-3 6-3).

French doubles won 1936 (beat Miss S Noel/Miss J Jedrzejowska, 2-6, 6-4, 6-4), won 1937 (beat Mrs D Andrus/Mrs S Henrotin, 3-6,

6-2, 6-2), won 1938 (beat Mrs A Haff/Mrs N Landry, 6-3, 6-3), all with Mrs Mathieu; mixed doubles won 1936 with M Bernard (beat A Legeay/Mrs Henrotin, 7-5, 6-8, 6-3).

YOSHIDA, Mrs M *see* **Sawamatsu, Kazuko**

ZIEGENFUSS, Valerie, USA
Born June 1949, San Diego, California. Three times winner of the US national Girls 18 doubles with 'Peaches' Bartkowicz, Miss Ziegenfuss beat Billie Jean King in the Pacific Southwest championships of 1966 and while still a junior beat Judy Tegart and Winnie Shaw in early rounds of the US championships. She became a professional in 1969 and has since had some good results, notably in doubles on the Virginia Slims circuit. Though major championship titles have eluded her she has been US clay court doubles champion (1968), US indoor doubles champion (1969), US hard court doubles champion (1967) and runner-up in the West German Open doubles in 1972. With Mrs Margaret duPont she won the South African Open doubles in 1976, beating Ilana Kloss and Linky Boshoff.

ZINDERSTEIN, Marion *see* **Jessup, Marion**

terms

Advantage When the score reaches 40-40 (deuce), if the next point is won by the player holding service the score is to his or her advantage. Strictly, the umpire's call is 'advantage server' but today the call is usually in the name of the server. If the point is won by the receiver, the name of the receiver is called. If the player now holding advantage wins the next point he wins the game. There is no limit to the number of deuces or advantages in a game.

If the score in games reaches 5-5 in an advantage set, one player must gain a two-game lead to win the set, except in a tie-break situation. *See also* **Tie-Break** *and* **Scoring.**

Age groups The term applied to the grouping by age of junior players in tournaments. In the United States there are many age group events ranging not only through juniors but also up to men over 70. The most junior events are for boys and girls aged under 12, the qualifying date being 1 October preceding the tournament.

In Great Britain the term is used to describe the annual tournaments held for players aged under 12, under 14 and under 16, the qualifying date being 31 December preceding the event. In France the age groupings are *poussins*, under 11, *Benjamins*, 11–12, *minimes*, 13–14, *cadets*, 15–16, and juniors, 17–18. The qualifying date is also 31 December. In Belgium the groupings are *minimes*, under 13, *cadets*, under 14, *scolaires*, under 16, and juniors, under 18.

All-Comers The All-Comers rounds in tournaments were those in which all entrants except the reigning title holders competed through every round, unless given a bye in an early round. The winners of the All-Comers rounds met the title holder in the Challenge Round. The term fell out of use with the abolition of Challenge Rounds. *See also* **Challenge Round** *and* **Bye**

Alley A colloquial term used in America for the area between the inner and outer sidelines or 'tramlines' as they are sometimes known.

Amateur One of the four categories of players recognised by the ILTF and covering those players who, after their 16th birthday, do not receive pecuniary advantage, directly or indirectly, by playing, teaching or in pursuit of the game.

American twist Another name for a 'kick service' in which the serving action tends to take the racket to the right-hand side of the body. *See also* **Service**

Australian grip Now almost extinct, the Australian grip employs the Western grip and the racket is turned over for backhand shots. The same face of the racket therefore strikes the ball in both forehand and backhand shots. *See also* **Grips**.

Backcourt The area of the court between the sidelines (including the 'tramlines' in doubles) and from the service line to the baseline.

Backhand For a right-handed player, all strokes played from the left-hand side of the body are backhand, ideally with the back of the hand towards the net and with the right foot and shoulder also towards the net.

Backhand grip There are two standard grips for the backhand: with the thumb straight up the back of the racket handle or diagonally across it. *See also* **Grips**

Backswing Swinging the racket back and behind the body builds up the power and rhythm of a stroke.

Ball When Major Harry Gem formed the first lawn tennis club in Leamington, England, he specified that the ball should be made of 'India rubber or other substance answering the purpose, punctured or not as may be agreed upon or as circumstances require'. This was because the balls used in 'real' tennis were tightly packed (with wool, hair or wool strips) and though they bounced well enough on the hard stone floors of 'real' tennis courts, they did not do so on grass.

Major Gem stipulated that the circumference of the ball should be about $7\frac{1}{2}$ in (19.05 cm) but with a latitude of $\frac{1}{2}$ in (about 1 cm) more or less. The weight was to be about $1\frac{1}{2}$ oz (42.5 g), but with an allowable variation of $\frac{1}{4}$ oz (about 7 g) either way. They were to be white or near-white to make them more easily visible. When the Marylebone Cricket Club's tennis committee published its new rules for lawn tennis in 1875 it stipulated that balls should be hollow and made of India rubber, exactly $2\frac{1}{4}$ in (5.7 cm) in diameter and weighing exactly $1\frac{1}{2}$ oz (42.52 g). They might be covered in white cloth, the rules stated.

The All England Club's rules drawn up for the first Wimbledon championships in 1877 stipulated that balls were to be $2\frac{1}{4}$ to $2\frac{5}{8}$ in (5.7 to 6.7 cm) in diameter and $1\frac{1}{4}$ to $1\frac{1}{2}$ oz (35.4 to 42.5 g) in weight. The cloth cover, which soon became standard, was cemented – instead of being hand-sewn – by Slazengers, the manufacturers, from 1924 but both types of ball were available for several years after this date. The official rules now state that the ball may be white or yellow in colour, between $2\frac{1}{2}$ and $2\frac{5}{8}$ in (6.35 and 6.7 cm) in diameter, weighing between 2 oz (56.7 g) and $2\frac{1}{16}$ oz (58.5 g). They add that it should have a bounce of more than 53 in (135 cm) and less than 58 in (147 cm) when dropped from 100 in (254 cm) onto a concrete surface.

Ball boys The boys and girls used in championships and tournaments to ensure that players are kept supplied with balls and the court is clear of them. A full complement of ball boys is six for a championship: two at each end and one on

Right: A regulation tennis court. The area shaded in is the singles court.

either side of the net. Ball girls were first used at the Wimbledon championships in 1977.

Ball in Play A ball is in play from the moment it is struck in service until a point has been scored or a let called.

Baseline The line at each end of the court parallel to the net, marking the extreme ends of the playing area into which the ball must fall.

Bound (Bounce) The upward movement of the ball after it has struck the ground. The height and direction of the bound can be affected by the nature of the surface, the amount of spin, the weather conditions and, of course, the power of the strike.

Bye The term applied when a player goes through a round without having to play in it. When entries do not number exactly 2, 4, 8, 16, 32 etc, or exactly a higher power of two, there must be byes in the first round to achieve the right number of players in the second. The number of byes equals the difference between the number of entries and the next higher power of two: if, for example, there are 27 entries there will be five byes – 32 minus 27. Byes can also be given in an artificial draw to ensure that seeded players do not have to compete in early rounds. They can be placed according to a set pattern in most draws. *See also* **Draw** *and* **Seeding**

Centre Court The term is generally associated throughout the world with Wimbledon's famous Centre Court, which, since the last Davis Cup Challenge Round there in 1936, is never used between championships. The only exception was for the professional tournament at Wimbledon in August 1967. Most major tennis venues have one main court which is called the centre court.

Centre mark A line 4 in (10.16 cm) long and 2 in (5.08 cm) wide drawn inside the court at its centre point, at right angles to the baseline. The player with service plays first from the right side of the centre mark, then, after the point has been decided, from the left. If his foot touches the ground on or beyond the mark a foot fault is called. *See also* **Foot fault**

Challenge Round The round of a tournament in which the reigning champion was challenged by the winner of that year's All-Comers round was known as the Challenge Round. The winner of that match became the new champion. A Challenge Round was introduced at Wimbledon in the 1878 men's singles and in 1886 in the men's doubles and women's singles. The rounds, which gave an advantage to the title holders because they had only to play one match, were abolished at Wimbledon in 1922. The United States introduced Challenge Rounds in the 1884 men's

singles, abolishing them in 1912, and in the women's singles in 1888 until 1919. No challenge rounds were held in the Australian and French championships. The Davis Cup Challenge Round began with the inception of the competition in 1900, when only America and Britain competed, and continued until 1972. *See also* **All-Comers**

Changing ends The players change ends after every odd-numbered game throughout a match. They are limited to one minute's break between games when changing ends.

Chop The reverse of topspin, and sometimes called 'underspin', a chop is imparted when the ball is struck from the top to the bottom so that the bottom spins towards the line of flight. Wind resistance is reduced at the top of the ball and increased at the bottom. The ball can be made to keep low or stop short, or even recoil, depending upon the surface, wind, atmospheric conditions and the amount of chop applied.

Closed tournament A closed tournament is one limited to nationals of the country staging it, as opposed to an 'Open' tournament in which all comers are welcome. It can also be used to apply to tournaments which are 'closed' to members of a particular club or association.

Continental grip Similar to the Eastern grip except that the right hand moves about $\frac{1}{2}$ in (about 1 cm) to the left until the 'V' of the thumb and index finger is centred over the left-hand bevel of the handle so that the palm is more on top of the handle.

Court dimensions In singles the court is 78 ft (23.77 m) long and 27 ft (8.23 m) wide, divided across the middle by a net suspended from a cord or metal cable of a maximum diameter of $\frac{1}{3}$ in (0.8 cm), the ends of which pass over or are attached to the tops of two posts 3 ft 6 in (1.07 m) high, the centre of which is 3 ft (0.91 m) outside the court on either side. The height of the net is 3 ft (0.91 m) at the centre, where it is held by a strap not wider than 2 in (5 cm) and kept taut. On each side of the net the service lines are drawn at a distance of 21 ft (6.4 m) from and parallel to the net. The lines bounding the ends and sides of the court are called the baselines and sidelines. The spaces on either side of the net between the service lines and the sidelines are divided into two equal parts by the centre service line which is 2 in (5 cm) wide. The areas so formed are the service courts. The baselines are bisected by an imaginary continuation of the centre service line to a line 4 in (10 cm) long and 2 in (5 cm) wide called the centre mark, drawn inside the court at right angles to and in contact with the baselines. The baselines may be 4 in (10 cm) wide and all other lines must be between 1 in (2.5 cm) and 2 in (5 cm) wide. For all official ILTF championships there must

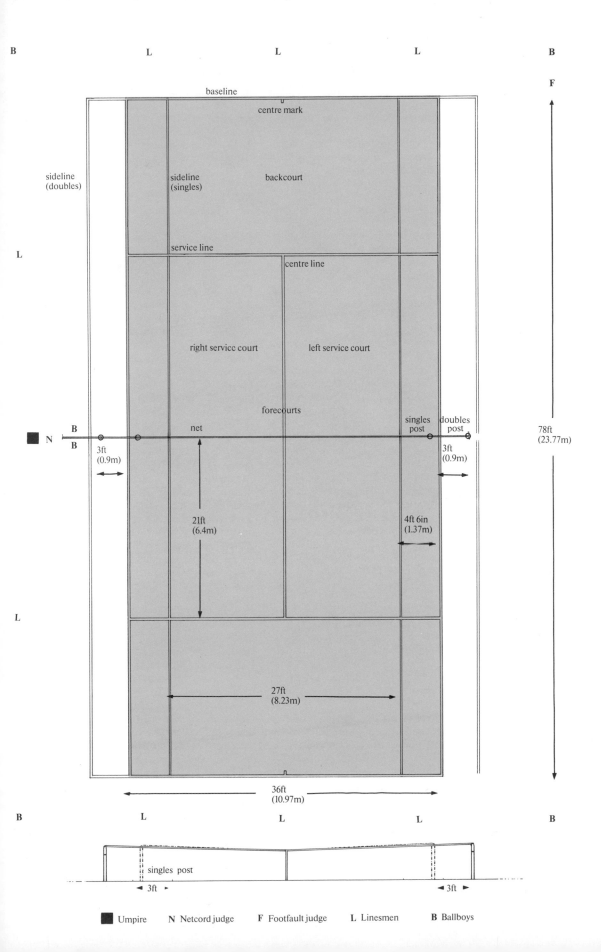

Umpire   **N** Netcord judge   **F** Footfault judge   **L** Linesmen   **B** Ballboys

be a space behind the baselines of not less than 21 ft (6.4 m) and at the sides of not less than 12 ft (3.66 m).

In doubles the court is 36 ft (10.97 m) wide and the portions of the singles sidelines between the two service lines are called the service sidelines.

In Major Walter Clopton Wingfield's 'Sphairistiké' version of tennis patented in 1874 the court was hourglass shaped. It was 60 ft (18.29 m) long, 21 ft (6.4 m) wide at the net and 30 ft (9.14 m) wide at the baseline. The server stood in a lozenge-shaped box in the middle and delivered the ball to a service court between the service line and the baseline. The net was 4 ft 8 in (1.42 m) high at the posts, which were on the sidelines.

The tennis committee of the MCC, which drew up new rules for the game in 1875, stipulated that the court should retain its hourglass shape but should be 78 ft long (23.77 m), 30 ft wide (9.14 m) at the base and 24 ft (7.31 m) at the middle. The net was 5 ft high (1.52 m) at the sides and 4 ft (1.22 m) in the centre. The service court extended 26 ft (7.92 m) from the net and delivery had to be made with one foot outside the baseline. Points were scored only by the server (15 up for a game, with 'deuce' called at 14 all). Methods of handicapping were included and the posts were made 7 ft high (2.13 m); a handicapped player had to play the ball above a cord stretched at this height.

The rules committee of the All England Club, which laid down rules for the first Wimbledon championship, stipulated that the court should be 78 ft (23.77 m) by 27 ft (8.23 m). The scoring was changed to today's system. The net at the first tournament was 5 ft high (1.52 m) at the posts and 3 ft 3 in (0.99 m) at the centre and the service line was then still 26 ft (7.92 m) from the net.

Covered courts Modern technology has made it possible to have covered courts which are out of doors. This is done by covering the courts with inflatable plastic domes. Previously, covered courts were inside permanent buildings and are still mostly found in cold or inclement countries.

Cross-court Strokes played diagonally across the court, from right to opposite right or left to opposite left, are termed cross-court shots.

Dead A ball that is out of play is 'dead'. The word is also used in reference to a match or 'rubber' which has still to be played when one side already has a winning lead.

Deuce The term used in scoring when the score is three points all in any one game, 40-40, is 'deuce'. *See also* **Advantage**

Doubles Doubles matches, between two pairs of players, are divided into three categories: men's, women's and mixed. The court for a doubles game is 4 ft 6 in (1.37 m) wider on either side than that used for singles, taking in the 'tramlines'. Service alternates between the pairs, all four players serving in turn and players receiving service must do so from the same court for the whole of a set. At the end of a set each pair may change their order of service or the court in which partners receive service.

Double fault Two successive faults in a service from the same court form a double fault and the server loses the point. *See also* **Fault**

Down the line Strokes played approximately parallel with the sidelines are described as 'down the line' as opposed to cross-court.

Draw A player's position in a tournament schedule is determined by the draw. Normally the draw is made by drawing the players' names at random, except for those of certain seeded players, whose positions in the draw are allocated in advance. *See also* **Seeding**

Drive Played on forehand or backhand, the drive is the most widely used stroke. The ball is struck hard, usually from the back of the court or behind the baseline and using either top spin or flat-faced racket.

Dropshot When the ball is hit, forehand or backhand, gently and usually with underspin, into the opposite forecourt, as close to the net as possible, the stroke is called a dropshot. It is most used to catch the opponent wrong-footed – on the retreat or far enough away to make it difficult for him to reach the ball for a return.

Eastern grip The most widely used grip for the forehand drive is the Eastern grip, so named because it was first used extensively in the Eastern United States. The palm of the hand is parallel with the racket face, flat against the back of the handle. The racket is held at its throat in the left hand so that the edge of the frame is parallel with the ground (ie: the cross-strings are perpendicular) and the handle points to the stomach. The right hand is then placed flat against the gut, parallel to the face of the racket and then drawn down the handle until it is at the end of the handle. Fingers and thumb are closed round the handle in a 'shake-hands' grip.

Fault A fault is called on service if: a) the server does not stand with both feet behind the baseline on the correct side of the centre mark and between it and the sideline; b) the ball, having been thrown into the air, strikes the ground before being hit by the racket; c) the ball is hit twice; d) the server materially changes his position before delivery; e) he touches with his foot any area other than the serving position described; f) he serves from the wrong half of

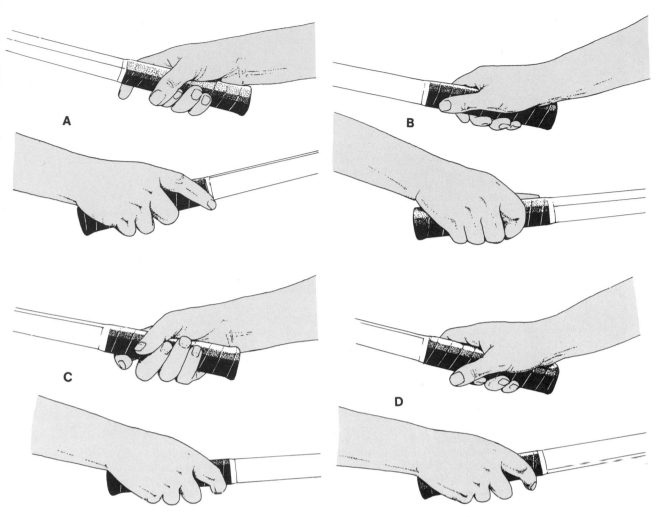

A. *Continental Forehand*
B. *Eastern Backhand*
C. *Eastern Forehand*
D. *Continental Backhand.*

the court; g) the ball does not clear the net into the opposing service court; h) the ball clears the net but falls outside the service court or on a line bounding it, and fault is also called if i) the server misses the ball as he attempts to strike it, and if j) the ball, having been delivered, strikes a permanent fixture. *See also* **Double fault, Foot fault** *and* **Let**

Follow through The path of the racket after it has connected with the ball indicates the type of shot played and is called the follow through.

Foot fault A foot fault is committed when the server materially changes his position before striking the ball by walking, running, jumping or touching with his foot any area of ground other than that behind the baseline and within the imaginary extension of the centre mark and sideline.

Footwork Correct footwork is important for proper balance and rhythm in playing strokes and for moving into position to play a shot.

Forecourt The area of the court between the sidelines (taking in the 'tramlines' in doubles) and from the net to the service line is the fore-court.

Forehand A forward stroke played by a right-handed player on his right side or by a left-handed player on his left.

Game A game begins at 'love all' (0-0). The first point scored takes the score to 15, the second to 30, the third to 40 and the fourth to 'game'. The first player to win six games wins the set. If the score in games reaches 5-5 one player must gain a two-game lead before winning the set (for example, 7-5 or 5-7). *See also* **Tie-break** *and* **Scoring**

Grand Slam The winning of the four major championships – Australia, France, US and Wimbledon – in one year is termed the Grand Slam. The first player to achieve a Grand Slam was Donald Budge in 1938. In 1951 Frank Sedgman and Ken McGregor of Australia achieved the doubles Grand Slam.

Grips Though individual players have many variations in their grip of a racket there are basically only two orthodox grips used by leading players and from which all other grips derived: the Eastern grip and the Continental grip. (See separate entries.)

Originally used on the cement courts of California, the Western grip is practically obsolete today. It was derived from the Eastern grip, this time by moving the hand about $\frac{1}{2}$ in to the right. In the Australian grip the hand is turned over for backhand shots.

For the backhand the thumb is either placed up the back of the handle or diagonally across it. For service, volley and overhead shots the Continental is the standard grip but the Eastern is also popular for volley and forehand. Players may also use two hands for all shots, except the service and smash.

An 'open' racket is one in which the face of the racket tends to be skywards from the vertical; a 'closed' racket tilts groundwards. Thus a Continental is an 'open' grip and a Western is a 'closed' grip.

Groundstroke Normally used to refer to drives, a groundstroke is one in which the ball is struck after it has bounced.

Half volley A groundstroke played immediately after the ball has bounced is a half volley and is more difficult to use accurately than an ordinary groundstroke or a volley.

Handicapping Handicapping is designed to help weaker players put up a stronger resistance to players of a higher standard and give them a better chance in tournaments. Handicaps are based on odds owed or received. If two players each handicapped to owe odds meet in a tournament the player owing the least odds is put back to scratch and the other player benefits by the difference. If two players meet who each receive odds, the one receiving the smaller odds is put to scratch and the match is played at face value between them.

No competitor may have a handicap of more than owe 50 or receive 40 and none can receive more than 30 from any opponent. But if a player is prevented by that rule from receiving his full handicap he gets the additional points up to a limit of owe 50 by way of owed odds. Two owed odds are regarded as equal to one received point.

In addition to straight owe and receive odds of, for example, 15 (in which the player concerned owes or receives 15 at the beginning of every game) there are additional tables of owed and recieved odds on which a player can receive or owe from one-sixth to five-sixths of each of 15, 30 and 40. For example, a player receiving four-sixths/15 actually receives 15 points in the first, second, fourth and sixth games of the first set and in the same games of succeeding sets. The pattern of owed and received sixths is laid down in tables and remains the same.

Junior In the United States the term 'junior' refers only to boys of 18 and under; girls of 18 and under are called Girls 18. The ILTF lays down that a player who has not reached the age of 18 on 31 December preceding the date of a competition or match is a junior. *See also* **Age groups**

Kick service *see* **Service**

Left court The left court is the area between the service line and the net and bounded by the sideline and centre line on the left of the whole court.

Let A let is ordered by the umpire as a result of a disputed or reversed linesman's decision, doubt, or the interruption of play by an untoward occurrence that might affect the players. It involves the replaying of the whole point, including two services, except where the let is over the second service, in which case only that service is replayed. *See also* **Net cord**

Line judge A full complement of court officials includes ten line judges. The baseline, centre line, sideline and service line judges decide whether the ball is in or out of court. The net cord judge decides whether the ball has touched the top of the net and the foot fault judge decides whether services have been properly delivered. *See also* **Foot fault** *and* **Umpire**

Lob When the ball is played high into the air to land as close to the baseline as possible, the stroke is called a lob. It is usually played in reply to a smash but can also be used as an attacking stroke, employing a lower trajectory.

Love A game begins at 'love all', 0-0. There has long been speculation as to how the term was derived. It was originally used in 'real' tennis and it has been suggested that 'love' is a corruption of the French *l'oeuf*, meaning the egg and representing a duck's egg, ie 'a duck' in cricket, meaning 'scored 0'. Since 'real' tennis was played long before cricket, this seems unlikely. However, it is possible that the egg-shape of the figure '0' was indeed responsible for the term.

Match A contest between two players or pairs of players is called a match and can be played over one set, or the best of three or five sets. Men's singles and doubles are normally over five sets in major international championships but otherwise are over three sets for the match.

Mixed doubles Matches played between two pairs each consisting of a man and a woman are mixed doubles. Originally these were played purely socially and did not figure in tournaments but in recent years most major tournaments have introduced mixed doubles, though they tend to be the first events to be abandoned should the tournament programme be disrupted for any reason.

Net The net is stretched across the middle of the court on a cord or metal cable attached to or passing over the net posts on either side of the court. The posts are 3 ft (0.91 m) from the sidelines and are 3 ft 6 in (1.07 m) high. The net itself drops from that height at the posts to 3 ft at the centre, where it is held by a strap not more than 2 in (5 cm) wide. A tape measuring between 2 in and $2\frac{1}{2}$ in (6.3 cm) wide covers the cord or cable.

Net cord If a service ball touches the top of the net (the net cord) and lands correctly on the other side, a let is given and the service taken again. If in ordinary play, other than a service, the ball touches the top of the net and continues over, landing correctly within the court, the stroke is a net cord.

Open The term 'open' was used from the early days of tennis to define a tournament open to all comers, as opposed to 'closed' tournaments which were for players only from the organising country (or club). Since 1968 'Open' tennis has come to mean tennis played by all four categories of players recognised by the ILTF. *See also* **Playing status**

Open grip An 'open' grip is one in which the racket face tends to incline skywards instead of being vertical. A 'closed' grip turns the racket face towards the ground from the vertical.

Order of play The order of play, setting out the daily programme for a tournament, subject to weather conditions at outdoor events, is produced by the referee. Usually it is decided before the end of play on the preceding day to give players a chance to know when they are likely to be on court. Advance knowledge of the order of play is also important to the press, radio, television, the public and, of course, the programme printers.

Order of service The order in which players serve is decided by the toss and remains constant throughout a singles match. In doubles a pair can decide to change their order of service at the end of each set.

Out of play A ball is out of play or 'dead' from the moment a point is decided and until play is started for the next point.

Overarm service *see* **Service**

Overspin Pure underspin or chop is imparted by striking the ball with a vertical downwards motion. Depending on surface conditions, atmospheric conditions and wind, the chop and the cut (imparting spin horizontally under the ball) can make the ball skid, bounce low, stop or bound sharply upwards. *See also* **Spin**

Playing status Under a ruling by the ILTF in 1968 four categories of players were officially recognised: 1) contract professionals under the jurisdiction of a promoter; 2) registered or authorised players playing for money but acknowledging the authority of their national associations; 3) coaching professionals, who receive fees for giving instruction; and 4) amateurs who, after reaching their 16th birthday, do not receive pecuniary advantage, directly or indirectly, from playing, teaching, demonstrating or in pursuit of the game.

The ILTF agreed that players who had lost their amateur status prior to the ruling could be reinstated by their national associations if they returned to fulfilling the requirements. It was left to individual countries to define the playing conditions for the last three categories themselves, or to exclude any of them if they wished. Thus, Russia and Eastern European countries generally have only amateurs, the United States has amateurs and professionals and Great Britain has only players.

Poaching In doubles, when a player intercepts a shot that would have been expected to go to his or her partner the act is known as poaching. It can be used as a surprise tactic against the opposition or, particularly in mixed doubles, to shield a weaker partner from pressure.

Point *see* **Scoring**

Press A press is a piece of equipment used to keep a racket frame straight, preventing warping by applying equal pressure to both sides. Metal frames do not require the use of a press but rackets with wood frames, particularly if tightly strung, benefit from this care.

Racket 'Real' tennis was originally played with a glove, the Italians being first to think of this form of protection for the hand. Later either the Italians or French thought of stretching a network of strings across the glove to give greater power and control of the ball. This soon evolved into a wooden-framed 'glove' to which a handle was attached and over which parchment was stretched. Later it was found that catgut was more effective than parchment.

It is thought that when Major Harry Gem first played lawn tennis with friends 'real' tennis rackets were used. These had a twist or bend in the head of the racket to facilitate return of balls close to ground level, using a 'scoop' action.

Lawn tennis rackets were introduced in 1874 when Major Walter Clopton Wingfield started to market his Sphairistiké set. His rackets had long handles and heads somewhat smaller than the 'real' tennis version. They were followed by a variety of specially designed lawn tennis rackets as the game increased in popularity. They included rackets with large heads, with widely spaced strings, diagonally strung rackets, knotted gut rackets, a racket with a curved handle, another with mercury in a hollow handle and even some with steel frames.

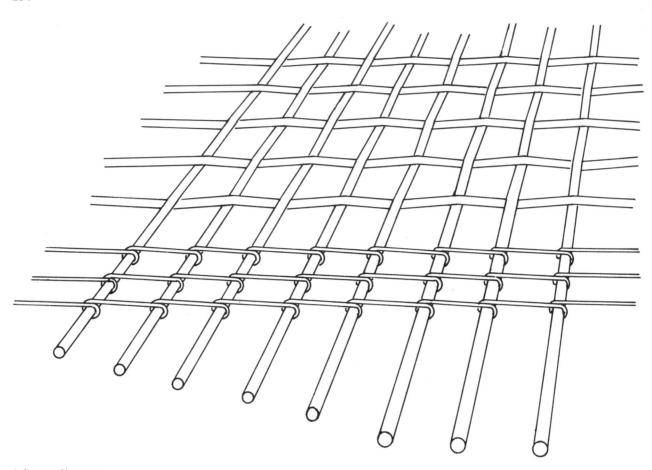

A close-up of how to string a racket.

Apart from a few weird exceptions, rackets in the past 100 years have fallen within a general specification: 25 to 27 in (63.5 to 68.6 cm) long and weighing between 12½ and 16½ oz (354.4 and 467.8 g). Though methods of construction and the materials used have altered, these size and weight specifications have remained constant. Plain wood handles gave place to leather-covered grips, rubber, foam and towelling. Head shapes varied with experimentation, from slightly bulbous tops, exaggeratedly bulbous tops, slight twists and, today, the more symmetrical shape, suitable for modern machine-stringing and uniform tension. The height of the net is often checked at its centre in 'social' games by comparing it to the length of a racket plus the width of the head, which equals approximately 3 ft (0.91 m).

Early rackets had heavier gauge gut than today and when laminated frames were introduced it was found that stringing tension could be raised and thinner gauge strings used. Nowadays synthetic strings are common but gut is still popular with many players. In 1977 a double-strung racket was produced, giving each face of the racket its own stringing and considerably increasing the speed at which the ball leaves the racket. However, after protests by several top professionals, the racket was officially banned by the ILTF until it had been tested and any necessary new legislation decided upon.

Rally The strokes played between delivery of service and completion of a point constitute a rally.

Ranking Each year national associations compile lists which grade players according to their performances in the preceding 12 months. Most countries concentrate on their top ten rankings. Today computers are often used, particularly in working out rankings, points and prize-money gained by players on the professional circuits. In America, where men's rankings began in 1885 and women's in 1913, players are now ranked in every age group. In Britain official rankings began in 1956. Various unofficial ranking lists are produced each year, notably by distinguished tennis writers.

Receiver The player who is receiving service is the receiver.

Referee A referee is appointed to control a tournament and is consulted about seedings, attends the draw and is responsible for making out the order of play. In the event of a dispute during the tournament he can be called upon to adjudicate and decides upon points of tennis law. His decision is final and can include banning or defaulting a player. If misdemeanour is committed by a player the referee can be required to report to the national association, which will decide on any penalty against the player concerned.

Return Usually the term refers to the stroke made by a player in reply to a service but it can also be applied to all counter-strokes made after service during a rally.

Right court The right court is the area between the service line and the net and bounded by the sideline and centre line on the right of the whole court.

Rough When the racket is spun in the 'toss' at the beginning of a match to decide service or side, it will come to rest presenting either the 'rough' or the 'smooth' face of strings. The thin strings at the top and bottom of the racket head are strung in such a way as to present a rough or a smooth surface against the thicker playing strings. The thin strings are known as the treblings and are used to keep the vertical, thicker strings in place.

Round Robin A tournament in which each competitor plays every other on a league basis is a Round Robin or an 'American tournament'.

Rubber The term rubber is used to describe an individual match, singles or doubles, within a team competition. The whole match between the two teams is called a tie. The Davis Cup is decided on the basis of the best of five rubbers. A 'dead' rubber is one which remains to be played after the result of a tie has already been established by a winning margin.

Scoring A game begins at 'love all' (0-0) and succeeding points are 15, 30, 40 and game. In addition to these terms there are: 'deuce', called when the score is 40-40, 'advantage server' or 'advantage . . . (name of server)', called when the server has won the next point after deuce, 'advantage receiver' or 'advantage . . . (name of receiver)', called when the receiver has won the next point after deuce. The player who gains the next point after winning the advantage point wins the game. If he loses the next point after winning the advantage the score returns to deuce and there is no limit to the number of times deuce and advantage can be played.

The player first winning six games wins a set. If the score is 5-5 one player must gain a two-game lead in an advantage set to win the set, except in the case of a tie-break situation. A match is generally either the best of three sets or, for major men's singles and doubles titles, the best of five.

Players devised their own systems of scoring when tennis began, frequently using the same as that for Rackets, with a game of 15 up and points only being scored if the server won a rally. If he lost, the receiver became the server. The All England Club was using the 'clock system' in 1876. This was based on 15 for the first quarter hour, 30 for the half hour, 45 for the three-quarter hour and game for the final point, the full hour. At some stage the 45 was changed to 40, possibly because it was easier to say and to hear. This method of scoring has remained since the first Wimbledon in 1877, with the addition of advantage sets.

In 1970 the tie-break system was used unofficially at the Philadelphia Open championships but later that year the ILTF gave permission for a nine-point tie-break system at Forest Hills and in 1971 Wimbledon was allowed to use a 12-point tie-break.

The American millionaire James Van Alen introduced the Van Alen Streamlining Scoring system (VASS) in the mid-1960s, replacing the traditional scoring with a simple points system in which service changes every five points and an official set is 31 points or, if time is short, 21 points. At 30–30 a nine-point tie-break is operated. No advantage is played. The system is also simpler to use for handicapping purposes.

Another method of scoring was used by professionals before the advent of Open tennis in 1968. In this one-set matches were played, the first player to win 10 games being the winner. If the score stood at 9-9, the first player to gain a two-game lead won. *See also* **Tie-break**

Seeding Various formulae are used to place leading players in a draw so that they do not meet each other until later rounds and this is called seeding, which, in ILTF tournaments, is restricted in numbers depending upon the entry. With not less than eight entries two players may be seeded, with not less than 16, four, with not less than 24, six, and with 32 or more, eight.

Seniors Veteran players in the United States are called seniors.

Server The player whose turn it is to serve is the server.

Service Services can be divided into three actions: flat, slice and topspin. The flat service is hit with little or no spin and has the fastest motion, tending to come off the surface extremely quickly. The ball is thrown straight up and hit with an open faced racket, the follow through being down the left side of the body. The slice imparts sidespin to the ball, making it break sharply to the right of the receiver and keep low. Here the ball is thrown up slightly to the right of the body and in front of the head and the racket is brought slightly down and across the ball to finish on the left side of the body.

The topspin service gives the opposite effect, the ball breaking to the left of the receiver and bouncing high, the follow-through still finishing to the left of the body. The ball is thrown further to the left, the body turns and bends under the ball and the racket strikes the ball a glancing blow, upwards and outwards. (Exaggeration of the action turns the service into a kick service or

'American twist'.)

Other service actions are overarm, roundarm and underarm, though these are rarely used today. The over- and roundarm actions resemble those of a bowler in cricket. In the overarm the arm comes straight up and over while with roundarm it comes round the body and slightly above the shoulder, making the ball go towards the receiver's forehand. In the underarm service the ball is thrown to about waist height in front of the body and hit upwards over the net. A server may change from over- to underarm after first advising his opponent that he is doing so.

Service line   Each half of the court has a service line 21 ft (6.4 m) from the net and parallel to it. The service court is bounded by the service line, the centre line and the inner sideline, inside which the ball must land for a service to be good.

Sideline   There are two outer and two inner sidelines, each 78 ft (23.77 m) long and bisected by the net at right angles to them. In singles the ball must land on or inside the inner sidelines and the baseline; in doubles the ball must land on or inside the outer sidelines and the baseline. The outer and inner sidelines are known as the 'tramlines' and the space between them is the 'alley'.

Singles   Singles matches are those between two players. The singles court is smaller than the doubles, being bounded by the inner sidelines and the baseline, rather than the outer sidelines.

Slice   A slice is imparted when the ball is given a mixture of underspin and sidespin, making it rotate both from top to bottom and sideways. This tends to make the ball's trajectory flatter and its bounce low.

Slow-balling   Also known as 'soft-balling', this means that the ball is hit gently, with considerable spin, so that it moves slowly and with a higher trajectory than normal. It is a useful tactic against an opponent who employs a hard-hitting pressure game since it robs him of the pace with which to counter-attack and can break the rhythm of his game.

Smash   A smash, often the most spectacular stroke and certainly the most aggressive, is similar to a service action. The ball is hit above the head, as hard as possible to counter a lob. A smash can also be made somewhat less powerfully if it is angled away from an opponent, particularly to catch him wrong-footed.

Smooth   Opposite to 'rough'. *See also* **Rough**

Spin   There is a variety of ways of imparting spin to the ball. A chop gives spin vertically downwards; a cut gives it horizontally or nearly so and a slice gives it to the side. Topspin imparts spin over the ball in the direction of flight. A combination of spins can be used to make the ball's trajectory high or low, bounce low or high, skid or 'sit-up' and even stop.

Stop netting   The netting or wire fencing at either end of the court is the stop netting and is intended to prevent the ball going too far beyond the court, thus delaying play. In first-class play the court area should be 120 by 60 ft (36.6 by 18.3 m).

Stroke   The action of hitting the ball and the resulting action combine to form a stroke. A player is deemed to have attempted a stroke if he faces up to the ball with his racket, attempts to play and misses. (*See also* **Backhand, Dropshot, Forehand, Lob, Service, Spin, Volley** etc.)

Sudden death   The term 'sudden death' was originally applied to the last game in a non-advantage set but is now applied to the nine-point tie-break.

Tennis elbow   A pain centred over the lower end of the arm's humerus (the 'funny bone') and caused by inflammation of the tendon through the exertions of tennis is known as tennis elbow. It is a term often applied today to several forms of arm injury in the same region induced by similar strains but not associated with tennis.

Tie-break   The tie-break is designed to eliminate marathon sets. James Van Alen's nine-point or 'sudden death' method is usually introduced when the score is 6-6. It involves two services from the first player, 'A', two from 'B', two more from 'A' and then three serves from 'B'. The first player winning five points wins the set 7-6. Players change ends after four points. In doubles the first three players each serve two points and the fourth serves three.

At Wimbledon a 12-point tie-break was first used in 1971. If the score reaches 8-8, one more game is played, the first player to win seven points taking the set 9-8. The player whose turn it is to serve in the last game takes one service from the right hand court; his opponent follows with two serves from the left court. Thereafter each player serves twice from alternate courts until one wins seven points. Players change ends after each series of six points but if the total is 6-6 in points they continue until one has a two-point lead. In doubles the first player has one service and thereafter each has two in turn. The tie-break is not used at Wimbledon in the final set of any match.

Topspin *see* **Spin**

Toss   The toss is made at the start of a match and is usually by spinning a racket to fall 'rough' or 'smooth', rather than by tossing a coin. The winner can choose or ask his opponent to choose whether to serve or receive, in which case the other player chooses the side, or the winner can choose or ask the opponent to choose side, in which case the other has the right to decide whether to be server or receiver. A 'toss' is also an Australian synonym for a lob.

Tramlines   The outer and inner sidelines on a court are known as the 'tramlines', though the term is tending to go out of use.

Two-handed, Two-fisted   The use of both hands to make a stroke, either backhand or forehand, makes it a two-handed or two-fisted stroke.

Umpire and officials   The most important official on court in a match is the umpire, who has control over ten line judges, a net cord judge and a foot fault judge. The umpire introduces the players, keeps the score and calls it, ensures the balls are changed at the right time and that all rules are observed. He can make a line decision if a line judge has been unsighted and can allow a let to be played. A player may appeal to the umpire against a line call but only to the referee, through the umpire, on a point of law.

Umpire's chair   The umpire has control of a match from the umpire's chair. a centrally-positioned high chair beside a net post. By tradition players keep their clothing, equipment and refreshments beside the umpire's chair and take the statutory one minute break there.

Underarm service *see* **Service**

Underspin *see* **Spin**

Veterans   The age at which a player becomes a veteran, or senior player as they are called in America, varies from country to country but most countries have clubs exclusively for them or clubs with veteran sections. In the United States men seniors (aged 45 and over) and women seniors (40 and over) come under the control of senior men's and senior women's committees of the USLTA. There are sub-committees for over 50, 55, 60, 65 and 70, each of which age group is a playing class. The first USLTA national senior championship was held in 1918 at Forest Hills and there are now over 200 tournaments for senior players with national championships on grass, clay, hard courts and indoors.

In December 1958 the Veterans' Lawn Tennis Club of Great Britain was formed and it became affiliated to the LTA in 1973. The club holds international matches as well as a series of matches against such clubs as the All England, Queen's, Hurlingham and the Navy.

Volley   If the ball is hit before it has struck the ground the stroke is known as a volley. Several different types of volley can be used: drop, lob, drive, high and low. Usually a volley is played in the forecourt area.

World circuit   The international calendar of tournaments is often called the 'world circuit'. The events are planned so that they do not clash, enabling the world's leading players to compete in as many as possible. When World Championship Tennis began and was in dispute with the ILTF some of its tournaments clashed with official ILTF events but since agreement was reached between the two bodies, dovetailing of events has been the practice. The major tournaments are still considered to be the Wimbledon, the US Open, French Open and Australian Open but events such as the WCT finals and Virginia Slims finals, and others, now rank high in terms of spectator interest and value to competitors in prize money.

AUSTRALIAN CHAMPIONSHIPS

Men's Singles

Date	Winners	Runners-up	Score
1905	R W Heath	A H Curtis	
1906	A F Wilding	H A Parker	
1907	H M Rice	H A Parker	
1908	F B Alexander	A W Dunlop	
1909	A F Wilding	E F Parker	
1910	R W Heath	H M Rice	
1911	N E Brookes	H M Rice	
1912	J C Parke	A E Beamish	3-6, 6-2, 1-6, 6-1, 7-5
1913	E F Parker	H A Parker	
1914	A O'Hara Wood	G L Patterson	6-4, 6-3, 5-7, 6-1
1915	F G Lowe	H M Rice	
1916–18	No Competition		
1919	A R F Kingscote	E O Pockley	6-4, 6-0, 6-3
1920	P O'Hara Wood		
1921	R H Gemmell		
1922	J O Anderson	G L Patterson	6-0, 3-6, 3-6, 6-3, 6-2
1923	P O'Hara Wood		
1924	J O Anderson	R E Schlesinger	6-3, 6-4, 3-6, 5-7, 6-3
1925	J O Anderson	G L Patterson	11-9, 2-6, 6-2, 6-3
1926	J B Hawkes	J Willard	6-1, 6-3, 6-1
1927	G L Patterson	J B Hawkes	3-6, 6-4, 3-6, 18-16, 6-3
1928	J Borotra	R O Cummings	6-4, 6-1, 4-6, 5-7, 6-3
1929	J C Gregory	R E Schlesinger	6-2, 6-2, 5-7, 7-5
1930	E F Moon	H C Hopman	6-3, 6-1, 6-3
1931	J H Crawford	H C Hopman	6-4, 6-2, 2-6, 6-1
1932	J H Crawford	H C Hopman	4-6, 6-3, 3-6, 6-3, 6-1
1933	J H Crawford	K Gledhill	2-6, 7-5, 6-3, 6-2
1934	F J Perry	J H Crawford	6-3, 7-5, 6-1
1935	J H Crawford	F J Perry	2-6, 6-4, 6-4, 6-4
1936	A K Quist	J H Crawford	6-2, 6-3, 4-6, 3-6, 9-7
1937	V B McGrath	J E Bromwich	6-3, 1-6, 6-0, 2-6, 6-1
1938	J D Budge	J E Bromwich	6-4, 6-2, 6-1
1939	J E Bromwich	A K Quist	6-4, 6-1, 6-3
1940	A K Quist	J H Crawford	
1941–5	No Competition		
1946	J E Bromwich	D Pails	5-7, 6-3, 7-5, 3-6, 6-2
1947	D Pails	J E Bromwich	4-6, 6-4, 3-6, 7-5, 8-6
1948	A K Quist	J E Bromwich	6-4, 3-6, 6-3, 2-6, 6-3
1949	F A Sedgman	J E Bromwich	6-3, 6-3, 6-2
1950	F A Sedgman	K McGregor	6-3, 6-4, 4-6, 6-1
1951	R Savitt	K McGregor	6-3, 2-6, 6-3, 6-1
1952	K McGregor	F A Sedgman	7-5, 12-10, 2-6, 6-2
1953	K R Rosewall	M G Rose	6-0, 6-3, 6-4
1954	M G Rose	R N Hartwig	6-2, 0-6, 6-4, 6-2
1955	K R Rosewall	L A Hoad	9-7, 6-4, 6-4
1956	L A Hoad	K R Rosewall	6-4, 3-6, 6-4, 7-5
1957	A J Cooper	N A Fraser	6-3, 9-11, 6-4, 6-2
1958	A J Cooper	M J Anderson	7-5, 6-3, 6-4
1959	A Olmedo	N A Fraser	6-1, 6-2, 3-6, 6-3
1960	R G Laver	N A Fraser	5-7, 3-6, 6-3, 8-6, 8-6
1961	R S Emerson	R G Laver	1-6, 6-3, 7-5, 6-4
1962	R G Laver	R S Emerson	8-6, 0-6, 6-4, 6-4
1963	R S Emerson	K N Fletcher	6-3, 6-3, 6-1
1964	R S Emerson	F S Stolle	6-3, 6-4, 6-2
1965	R S Emerson	F S Stolle	7-9, 2-6, 6-4, 7-5, 6-1
1966	R S Emerson	A R Ashe	6-4, 6-8, 6-2, 6-3
1967	R S Emerson	A R Ashe	6-4, 6-1, 6-4
1968	W W Bowrey	J M Gisbert	7-5, 2-6, 9-7, 6-4

Open Championship began

Date	Winners	Runners-up	Score
1969	R G Laver	A Gimeno	6-3, 6-4, 7-5
1970	A R Ashe	R D Crealy	6-4, 9-7, 6-2
1971	K R Rosewall	A R Ashe	6-1, 7-5, 6-3
1972	K R Rosewall	M J Anderson	7-6, 6-3, 7-5
1973	J D Newcombe	O Parun	6-3, 6-7, 7-5, 6-1
1974	J Connors	P Dent	7-6, 6-4, 4-6, 6-3
1975	J D Newcombe	J Connors	7-5, 3-6, 6-4, 7-5
1976	M Edmondson	J D Newcombe	6-7, 6-3, 7-6, 6-1
1977	J Connors	K Rosewall	7-5, 6-4, 6-2
1977–8	V Gerulaitis	J Lloyd	6-3, 7-6, 5-7, 3-6, 6-2

Men's Doubles

Date	Winners	Runners-up	Score
1905	T Tachell/ R Lycett	E T Barnard/ B Spence	
1906	A F Wilding/ R W Heath	H A Parker/ C C Cox	
1907	H A Parker/ W A Gregg	H M Rice/ G W Wright	
1908	F B Alexander/ A W Dunlop	A F Wilding/ G G Sharp	
1909	E F Parker/ J P Keane	A F Wilding/ L Crooks	
1910	H M Rice/ A Campbell	R W Heath/ J L O'Dea	
1911	R W Heath/ R Lycett	N E Brookes/ J J Addison	
1912	J C Parkes/ C P Dixon	A E Beamish/ F G Lowe	
1913	E F Parker/ A H Hedemann		
1914	A Campbell/ G L Patterson	R Heath/ A O'Hara Wood	7-5, 3-6, 6-3, 6-3
1915	H M Rice/ C V Todd		
1916–18	No Competition		
1919	P O'Hara Wood/ R V Thomas		
1920	P O'Hara Wood/ R V Thomas		
1921	R H Gemmell/ S H Eaton		
1922	G L Patterson/ J B Hawkes	J O Anderson/ N Peach	8-10, 6-0, 6-0, 7-5
1923	P O'Hara Wood/ C B StJohn		
1924	N E Brookes/ J O Anderson	G L Patterson/ P O'Hara Wood	6-2, 6-4, 6-3
1925	G L Patterson/ P O'Hara Wood	J O Anderson/ F Kalms	6-4, 8-6, 7-5
1926	G L Patterson/ J B Hawkes	J O Anderson/ P O'Hara Wood	6-1, 6-4, 6-2
1927	G L Patterson/ J B Hawkes	P O'Hara Wood/ I McInnes	8-6, 6-2, 6-1
1928	J Borotra/ J Brugnon	J Willard/ E F Moon	6-2, 4-6, 6-4, 6-4
1929	J H Crawford/ H C Hopman	R O Cummings/ E F Moon	6-1, 6-8, 4-6, 6-1, 6-3
1930	J H Crawford/ H C Hopman	J B Hawkes/ Fitchett	8-6, 6-1, 2-6, 6-3
1931	C Donohoe/ R Dunlop	J H Crawford/ H C Hopman	8-6, 6-2, 5-7, 7-9, 6-4
1932	J H Crawford/ E F Moon	H C Hopman/ G L Patterson	12-10, 6-3, 4-6, 6-4
1933	H E Vines/ K Gledhill	J H Crawford/ E F Moon	6-4, 10-8, 6-2
1934	F J Perry/ G P Hughes	A K Quist/ D P Turnbull	6-8, 6-3, 6-4, 3-6, 6-3
1935	J H Crawford/ V B McGrath	F J Perry/ G P Hughes	6-4, 8-6, 6-2
1936	A K Quist/ D P Turnbull	J H Crawford/ V B McGrath	6-8, 6-2, 6-1, 3-6, 6-2
1937	A K Quist/ D P Turnbull	J E Bromwich/ J E Harper	6-2, 9-7, 1-6, 6-8, 6-4
1938	A K Quist/ J E Bromwich	G von Cramm/ H Henkel	7-5, 6-4, 6-0
1939	A K Quist/ J E Bromwich	D P Turnbull/ C F Long	6-4, 7-5, 6-2
1940	A K Quist/ J E Bromwich		
1941–5	No Competition		
1946	A K Quist/ J E Bromwich		
1947	A K Quist/ J E Bromwich	F A Sedgman/ G Worthington	6-1, 6-3, 6-1
1948	A K Quist/ J E Bromwich	F A Sedgman/ C F Long	1-6, 6-8, 9-7, 6-3, 8-6
1949	A K Quist/ J E Bromwich	G E Brown/ O W Sidwell	1-6, 7-5, 6-2, 6-3
1950	A K Quist/ J E Bromwich	E W Sturgess/ J Drobný	6-3, 5-7, 4-6, 6-3, 8-6
1951	F A Sedgman/ K McGregor	J E Bromwich/ A K Quist	11-9, 2-6, 6-3, 4-6, 6-3
1952	F A Sedgman/ K McGregor	M G Rose/ D Candy	6-4, 7-5, 6-3
1953	L A Hoad/ K R Rosewall	D Candy/ M G Rose	9-11, 6-4, 10-8, 6-4
1954	R N Hartwig/ M G Rose	N A Fraser/ C Wilderspin	6-3, 6-4, 6-2
1955	E V Seixas/ M A Trabert	L A Hoad/ K R Rosewall	6-4, 6-2, 2-6, 3-6, 6-1
1956	L A Hoad/ K R Rosewall	M G Rose/ D Candy	10-8, 13-11, 6-4
1957	L A Hoad/ N A Fraser	A J Cooper/ M J Anderson	6-3, 8-6, 6-1
1958	A J Cooper/ N A Fraser	R S Emerson/ R Mark	7-5, 6-8, 3-6, 6-3, 7-5
1959	R G Laver/ R Mark	D Candy/ R N Howe	9-7, 6-4, 6-2
1960	R G Laver/ R Mark	R S Emerson/ N A Fraser	1-6, 6-2, 6-4, 6-4
1961	R G Laver/ R Mark	R S Emerson/ M F Mulligan	6-3, 7-5, 3-6, 9-11, 6-2
1962	R S Emerson/ N A Fraser	R A J Hewitt/ F S Stolle	4-6, 4-6, 6-1, 6-4, 11-9
1963	R A J Hewitt/ F S Stolle	K N Fletcher/ J D Newcombe	6-2, 3-6, 6-3, 3-6, 6-3
1964	R A J Hewitt/ F S Stolle	R S Emerson/ K N Fletcher	6-4, 7-5, 3-6, 4-6, 14-12
1965	J D Newcombe/ A D Roche	R S Emerson/ F S Stolle	3-6, 4-6, 13-11, 6-3, 6-4

Date	Winners	Runners-up	Score
1966	R S Emerson/ F S Stolle	J D Newcombe/ A D Roche	7-9, 6-3, 6-8, 14-12, 12-10
1967	J D Newcombe/ A D Roche	O K Davidson/ W W Bowrey	3-6, 6-3, 7-5, 6-8, 8-6
1968	R D Crealy/ A Stone	T Addison/ R Keldie	10-8, 6-4, 6-3

Open Championships began

Date	Winners	Runners-up	Score
1969	R S Emerson/ R G Laver	K R Rosewall/ F S Stolle	6-4, 6-4
1970	R C Lutz/ S R Smith	J Alexander/ P Dent	8-6, 6-3, 6-4
1971	J D Newcombe/ A D Roche	M C Riessen/ T S Okker	6-2, 7-6
1972	K R Rosewall/ O K Davidson	G Masters/ R Case	3-6, 7-6, 6-2
1973	J D Newcombe/ M J Anderson	J Alexander/ P Dent	6-3, 6-4, 7-6
1974	R Case/ G Masters	R Giltinan/ S Ball	6-7, 6-3, 6-4
1975	J Alexander/ P Dent	A Stone/ R Carmichael	6-3, 7-6
1976	J Newcombe/ A Roche	R Case/ G Masters	7-6, 6-4
1977	J Newcombe/ A Roche	R Case/ G Masters	6-7, 6-3, 6-1
1977–8	A Stone/ R Ruffels	J Alexander/ P Dent	7-6, 7-6

Women's Singles

Date	Winners	Runners-up	Score
1922	Mrs M Molesworth	Miss E F Boyd	6-3, 10-8
1923	Mrs M Molesworth		
1924	Miss S Lance	Miss E F Boyd	6-3, 3-6, 6-4
1925	Miss D Akhurst	Miss E F Boyd	1-6, 8-6, 6-4
1926	Miss D Akhurst	Miss E F Boyd	6-1, 6-3
1927	Miss E F Boyd	Mrs S Harper	5-7, 6-1, 6-2
1928	Miss D Akhurst	Miss E F Boyd	7-5, 6-2
1929	Miss D Akhurst	Miss L M Bickerton	6-1, 5-7, 6-2
1930	Miss D Akhurst	Mrs S Harper	10-8, 2-6, 7-5
1931	Mrs C Buttsworth	Mrs J H Crawford	1-6, 6-3, 6-4
1932	Mrs C Buttsworth	Miss K Le Messurier	9-7, 6-4
1933	Miss J Hartigan	Mrs C Buttsworth	6-4, 6-3
1934	Miss J Hartigan	Mrs M Molesworth	6-1, 6-4
1935	Miss D E Round	Miss N M Lyle	1-6, 6-1, 6-3
1936	Miss J Hartigan	Miss N Wynne	6-4, 6-4
1937	Miss N Wynne	Mrs V Westacott	6-3, 5-7, 6-4
1938	Miss D M Bundy	Miss D Stevenson	6-3, 6-2
1939	Mrs V Westacott	Mrs H C Hopman	6-1, 6-2
1940	Mrs N Bolton		
1941–5	*No Competition*		
1946	Mrs N Bolton	Miss J Fitch	6-4, 6-4
1947	Mrs N Bolton	Mrs H C Hopman	6-3, 6-2
1948	Mrs N Bolton	Miss M Toomey	6-3, 6-1
1949	Miss D J Hart	Mrs N Bolton	6-3, 6-4
1950	Miss A L Brough	Miss D J Hart	6-4, 3-6, 6-4
1951	Mrs N Bolton	Mrs T D Long	6-1, 7-5
1952	Mrs T D Long	Miss H Angwin	6-2, 6-3
1953	Miss M Connolly	Miss J Sampson	6-3, 6-2
1954	Mrs T D Long	Miss J Staley	6-3, 6-4
1955	Miss B Penrose	Mrs T D Long	6-4, 6-3
1956	Miss M Carter	Mrs T D Long	3-6, 6-2, 9-7
1957	Miss S J Fry	Miss A Gibson	6-3, 6-4
1958	Miss A Mortimer	Miss L Coghlan	6-3, 6-4
1959	Miss M Reitano	Miss R Schuurman	6-2, 6-3
1960	Miss M Smith	Miss J Lehane	7-5, 6-2
1961	Miss M Smith	Miss J Lehane	6-1, 6-4
1962	Miss M Smith	Miss J Lehane	6-0, 6-2
1963	Miss M Smith	Miss J Lehane	6-2, 6-2
1964	Miss M Smith	Miss L R Turner	6-3, 6-2
1965	Miss M Smith	Miss M E Bueno	6-4, 7-5
1966	Miss M Smith	Miss N Richey	default
1967	Miss N Richey	Miss L R Turner	6-1, 6-4
1968	Mrs L W King	Mrs B M Court	6-1, 6-2

Open Championships began

Date	Winners	Runners-up	Score
1969	Mrs B M Court	Mrs L W King	6-4, 6-1
1970	Mrs B M Court	Miss K Melville	6-1, 6-3
1971	Mrs B M Court	Miss E F Goolagong	2-6, 7-6, 7-5
1972	Miss S V Wade	Miss E F Goolagong	6-4, 6-4
1973	Mrs B M Court	Miss E F Goolagong	6-4, 7-5
1974	Miss E Goolagong	Miss C Evert	7-6, 4-6, 6-0
1975	Miss E Goolagong	Miss M Navratilova	6-3, 6-2
1976	Mrs E Cawley	Miss R Tomanova	6-2, 6-2
1977	Mrs K Reid	Miss D Fromholtz	7-5, 6-2
1977–8	Mrs E Cawley	Mrs H Gourlay Cawley	6-3, 6-0

Women's Doubles

Date	Winners	Runners-up	Score
1922	Miss E F Boyd/ Miss M Mountain	Mrs H S Utz/ Miss St George	1-6, 6-4, 7-5
1923	Miss E F Boyd/ Miss F Lance		
1924	Miss D Akhurst/ Miss S Lance/	Mrs P O'Hara Wood/ Miss K Le Messurier	7-5, 6-2
1925	Mrs S Harper/ Miss D Akhurst	Miss E F Boyd/ Miss K Le Messurier	6-4, 6-3
1926	Mrs P O'Hara Wood/ Miss E F Boyd	Miss D Akhurst/ Miss M Cox	6-3, 6-8, 8-6
1927	Mrs P O'Hara Wood/ Miss L M Bickerton	Mrs S Harper/ Miss E F Boyd	6-3, 6-3
1928	Miss D Akhurst/ Miss E F Boyd	Miss K Le Messurier/ Miss D Weston	6-3, 6-1
1929	Miss D Akhurst/ Miss L M Bickerton	Mrs P O'Hara Wood/ Mrs S Harper	6-2, 3-6, 6-2
1930	Mrs M Molesworth/ Miss E Hood	Mrs S Harper/ Miss M Cox	6-3, 0-6, 7-5
1931	Miss D A Cozens/ Miss L M Bickerton	Mrs H S Utz/ Miss N Lloyd	6-0, 6-4
1932	Mrs C Buttsworth/ Mrs J H Crawford	Miss K Le Messurier/ Miss D Weston	6-2, 6-2
1933	Mrs M Molesworth/ Mrs V Westacott	Mrs J Van Ryn/ Miss J Hartigan	6-3, 6-3
1934	Mrs M Molesworth/ Mrs V Westacott		
1935	Miss E Dearman/ Miss N M Lyle	Mrs H C Hopman/ Miss L M Bickerton	6-3, 6-4
1936	Miss T Coyne/ Miss N Wynne	Miss M Blick/ Miss K Woodward	6-2, 6-4
1937	Miss T Coyne/ Miss N Wynne	Mrs H C Hopman/ Mrs V Westacott	6-2, 6-2
1938	Miss T Coyne/ Miss N Wynne	Miss D M Bundy/ Miss D E Workman	9-7, 6-4
1939	Miss T Coyne/ Miss N Wynne	Mrs V Westacott/ Miss M Hardcastle	7-5, 6-4
1940	Miss T Coyne/ Miss N Wynne		
1941–5	*No Competition*		
1946	Miss M Bevis/ Miss J Fitch		
1947	Mrs N Bolton/ Mrs T D Long	Miss J Fitch/ Miss M Bevis	6-3, 6-3
1948	Mrs N Bolton/ Mrs T D Long	Miss M Bevis/ Miss N Jones	6-3, 6-3
1949	Mrs N Bolton/ Mrs T D Long	Miss D Toomey/ Miss M Toomey	6-0, 6-1
1950	Miss D J Hart/ Miss A L Brough	Mrs N Bolton/ Mrs T D Long	6-2, 2-6, 6-3
1951	Mrs N Bolton/ Mrs T D Long	Mrs M K Hawton/ Miss J Fitch	6-2, 6-1
1952	Mrs N Bolton/ Mrs T D Long	Mrs R Baker/ Mrs M K Hawton	6-1, 6-1
1953	Miss M Connolly/ Miss J Sampson	Mrs M K Hawton/ Miss B Penrose	6-4, 6-2
1954	Mrs M K Hawton/ Miss B Penrose	Mrs H Redick-Smith/ Mrs J Wipplinger	6-3, 8-6
1955	Mrs M K Hawton/ Miss B Penrose	Mrs H C Hopman/ Mrs A R Thiele	7-5, 6-1
1956	Mrs M K Hawton/ Mrs T D Long	Miss B Penrose/ Miss M Carter	6-2, 5-7, 9-7
1957	Miss S J Fry/ Miss A Gibson	Mrs M K Hawton/ Miss F Muller	6-2, 6-1
1958	Mrs T D Long/ Mrs M K Hawton	Miss A Mortimer/ Miss L Coghlan	7-5, 6-8, 6-2
1959	Miss S Reynolds/ Miss R Schuurman	Mrs M Reitano/ Miss L Coghlan	7-5, 6-4
1960	Miss M E Bueno/ Miss C C Truman	Miss M Smith/ Miss L Robinson	6-2, 5-7, 6-2
1961	Mrs M Reitano/ Miss M Smith	Mrs M K Hawton/ Miss J Lehane	6-4, 3-6, 7-5
1962	Miss R A Ebbern/ Miss M Smith	Miss D R Hard/ Mrs M Reitano	6-4, 6-4
1963	Miss R A Ebbern/ Miss M Smith	Miss J Lehane/ Miss L R Turner	6-1, 6-3
1964	Miss J A M Tegart/ Miss L R Turner	Miss M Smith/ Miss R A Ebbern	6-4, 6-4
1965	Miss M Smith/ Miss L R Turner	Miss B J Moffitt/ Miss R A Ebbern	1-6, 6-2, 6-3
1966	Mrs C E Graebner/ Mrs N Richey	Miss M Smith/ Miss L Turner	6-4, 7-5
1967	Miss J A M Tegart/ Miss L R Turner	Miss E Terras/ Miss L Robinson	6-0, 6-2
1968	Miss K Krantzcke/ Miss K Melville	Miss L R Turner/ Miss J A M Tegart	6-4, 3-6, 6-2

Open Championships began

Date	Winners	Runners-up	Score
1969	Mrs B M Court/ Miss J A M Tegart	Mrs L W King/ Miss R Casals	6-4, 6-4

Date	Winners	Runners-up	Score		Date	Winners	Runners-up	Score
1970	Mrs J Dalton/ Mrs B M Court	Miss K Melville/ Miss K Krantzcke	6-3, 6-1		1961	R A J Hewitt/ Miss J Lehane	J Pearce/ Mrs M Reitano	9-7, 6-2
1971	Mrs B M Court/ Miss E F Goolagong	Miss L Hunt/ Miss J Emerson	6-0, 6-0		1962	F S Stolle/ Miss L R Turner	R Taylor/ Miss D R Hard	6-3, 9-7
1972	Miss K Harris/ Miss H Gourlay	Miss P Coleman/ Miss K Krantzcke	6-0, 6-4		1963	K N Fletcher/ Miss M Smith	F S Stolle/ Miss L R Turner	7-5, 5-7, 6-4
1973	Mrs B M Court/ Miss S V Wade	Miss K Melville/ Miss K Harris	6-4, 6-4		1964	K N Fletcher/ Miss M Smith	M J Sangster/ Miss J Lehane	6-3, 6-2
1974	Miss E Goolagong/ Miss M Michel	Miss K Harris/ Miss K Melville	7-5, 6-3		1965	J D Newcombe/ Miss M Smith	O K Davidson/ Miss R A Ebbern	
1975	Miss E Goolagong/ Miss M Michel	Mrs M Court/ Miss O Morozova	7-5, 7-6		1966	A D Roche/ Miss J A M Tegart	W W Bowrey/ Miss R A Ebbern	6-1, 6-3
1976	Mrs E Cawley/ Miss H Gourlay	Mrs W W Bowrey/ Miss R Tomanova	8-1 (one set only)		1967	O K Davidson/ Miss L R Turner	A D Roche/ Miss J A M Tegart	9-7, 6-4
1977	Miss D Fromholtz/ Mrs H Gourlay	Mrs K Reid/ Miss B Nagelsen	5-7, 6-1, 7-5		1968	R D Crealy/ Mrs L W King	A Stone/ Mrs B M Court	wo
1977–8	Mrs E Cawley/ Mrs H Gourlay Cawley	Mrs M Guerrant/ Mrs K Reid	shared (rained-off)		1969–78	No Competition		

Mixed Doubles

Date	Winners	Runners-up	Score
1922	J B Hawkes/ Miss E F Boyd	H S Utz/ Mrs H S Utz	6-1, 6-1
1923	H M Rice/ Miss S Lance		
1924	J Willard/ Miss D Akhurst	G M Hone/ Miss E F Boyd	6-3, 6-4
1925	J Willard/ Miss D Akhurst	R E Schliesinger/ Mrs S Harper	6-4, 6-4
1926	J B Hawkes/ Miss E F Boyd	J Willard/ Miss D Akhurst	6-2, 6-4
1927	J B Hawkes/ Miss E F Boyd	J Willard/ Miss Y Anthony	6-1, 6-3
1928	J Borotra/ Miss D Akhurst a bye	J B Hawkes/ Miss E F Boyd retired	
1929	E F Moon/ Miss D Akhurst	J H Crawford/ Miss M Cox	6-0, 7-5
1930	H C Hopman/ Miss N Hall	J H Crawford/ Miss M Cox	11-9, 3-6, 6-3
1931	J H Crawford/ Mrs J H Crawford	A Willard/ Mrs V Westacott	
1932	J H Crawford/ Mrs J H Crawford	J Sato/ Mrs P O'Hara Wood	6-8, 8-6, 6-3
1933	J H Crawford/ Mrs J H Crawford	H E Vines/ Mrs J Van Ryn	3-6, 7-5, 13-11
1934	E F Moon/ Miss J Hartigan	R Dunlop/ Mrs V Westacott	6-3, 6-4
1935	C Boussus/ Miss L M Bickerton	V G Kirby/ Mrs Bond	1-6, 6-3, 6-3
1936	H C Hopman/ Mrs H C Hopman	A A Kay/ Miss M Blick	6-2, 6-0
1937	H C Hopman/ Mrs H C Hopman	D P Turnbull/ Miss D Stevenson	3-6, 6-3, 6-2
1938	J E Bromwich/ Miss J Wilson	C F Long/ Miss N Wynne	6-3, 6-2
1939	H C Hopman/ Mrs H C Hopman	J E Bromwich/ Miss M Wilson	6-8, 6-2, 6-3
1940	C F Long/ Miss N Wynne		
1941–5	No Competition		
1946	C F Long/ Mrs N Bolton		
1947	C F Long/ Mrs N Bolton	J E Bromwich/ Miss J Fitch	6-3, 6-3
1948	C F Long/ Mrs N Bolton	O W Sidwell/ Mrs T C Long	7-5, 4-6, 8-6
1949	F A Sedgman/ Miss D J Hart	J E Bromwich/ Miss J Fitch	6-1, 5-7, 12-10
1950	F A Sedgman/ Miss D J Hart	E W Sturgess/ Miss J Fitch	8-6, 6-4
1951	G Worthington/ Mrs T C Long	J May/ Miss C Proctor	6-4, 3-6, 6-2
1952	G Worthington/ Mrs T C Long	T Warhurst/ Mrs A R Thiele	9-7, 7-5
1953	R N Hartwig/ Miss J Sampson	H Richardson/ Miss M Connolly	6-4, 6-3
1954	R N Hartwig/ Mrs T C Long	J E Bromwich/ Miss B Penrose	4-6, 6-1, 6-2
1955	G Worthington/ Mrs T C Long	L A Hoad/ Miss J Staley	6-2, 6-1
1956	N A Fraser/ Miss B Penrose	R S Emerson/ Mrs M K Hawton	6-2, 6-4
1957	M J Anderson/ Miss F Muller	W A Knight/ Miss J Langley	7-5, 3-6, 6-1
1958	R N Howe/ Mrs M K Hawton	P Newman/ Miss A Mortimer	9-11, 6-1, 6-2
1959	R Mark/ Miss S Reynolds	R G Laver/ Miss R Schuurman	4-6, 13-11, 6-2
1960	T T Fancutt/ Miss J Lehane	R Mark/ Miss M Reitano	6-2, 7-5

DAVIS CUP

Date	Winners	Runners-up	Score
1900	United States	British Isles	3-0
1901	No Competition		
1902	United States	British Isles	3-2
1903	British Isles	United States	4-1
1904	British Isles	Belgium	5-0
1905	British Isles	United States	5-0
1906	British Isles	United States	5-0
1907	Australasia	British Isles	3-2
1908	Australasia	United States	3-2
1909	Australasia	United States	5-0
1910	No Competition		
1911	Australasia	United States	5-0
1912	British Isles	Australia	3-2
1913	United States	British Isles	3-2
1914	Australasia	United States	3-2
1915–18	No Competition		
1919	Australasia	British Isles	4-1
1920	United States	Australasia	5-0
1921	United States	Japan	5-0
1922	United States	Australasia	4-1
1923	United States	Australia	4-1
1924	United States	Australia	5-0
1925	United States	France	5-0
1926	United States	France	4-1
1927	France	United States	3-2
1928	France	United States	4-1
1929	France	United States	3-2
1930	France	United States	4-1
1931	France	Great Britain	3-2
1932	France	United States	3-2
1933	Great Britain	France	3-2
1934	Great Britain	United States	4-1
1935	Great Britain	United States	5-0
1936	Great Britain	Australia	3-2
1937	United States	Great Britain	4-1
1938	United States	Australia	3-2
1939	Australia	United States	3-2
1940–5	No Competition		
1946	United States	Australia	5-0
1947	United States	Australia	4-1
1948	United States	Australia	5-0
1949	United States	Australia	4-1
1950	Australia	United States	4-1
1951	Australia	United States	3-2
1952	Australia	United States	4-1
1953	Australia	United States	3-2
1954	United States	Australia	3-2
1955	Australia	United States	5-0
1956	Australia	United States	5-0
1957	Australia	United States	3-2
1958	United States	Australia	3-2
1959	Australia	United States	3-2
1960	Australia	Italy	4-1
1961	Australia	Italy	5-0
1962	Australia	Mexico	5-0
1963	United States	Australia	3-2
1964	Australia	United States	3-2
1965	Australia	Spain	4-1
1966	Australia	India	4-1
1967	Australia	Spain	4-1
1968	United States	Australia	4-1
1969	United States	Rumania	5-0
1970	United States	West Germany	5-0
1971	United States	Rumania	3-2
1972	United States	Rumania	3-2
1973	Australia	United States	5-0
1974	South Africa	India	wo
1975	Sweden	Czechoslovakia	3-2
1976	Italy	Chile	4-1
1977	Australia	Italy	3-1

FEDERATION CUP

Date	Winners	Runners-up	Score
1963	**United States**	Australia	2-1
1964	**Australia**	United States	2-1
1965	**Australia**	United States	2-1
1966	**United States**	West Germany	3-0
1967	**United States**	Great Britain	3-0
1968	**Australia**	Netherlands	3-0
1969	**United States**	Australia	2-1
1970	**Australia**	West Germany	3-0
1971	**Australia**	Great Britain	3-0
1972	**South Africa**	Great Britain	2-1
1973	**Australia**	South Africa	3-0
1974	**Australia**	United States	2-1
1975	**Czechoslovakia**	Australia	3-0
1976	**United States**	Australia	2-1
1977	**United States**	Australia	2-1

FRENCH CHAMPIONSHIPS

Men's Singles

Date	Winners	Runners-up	Score
1925	**R Lacoste**	J Borotra	7-5, 6-1, 6-4
1926	**H Cochet**	R Lacoste	6-2, 6-4, 6-3
1927	**R Lacoste**	W T Tilden	6-4, 4-6, 5-7, 6-3, 11-9
1928	**H Cochet**	R Lacoste	5-7, 6-3, 6-1, 6-3
1929	**R Lacoste**	J Borotra	6-3, 2-6, 6-0, 2-6, 8-6
1930	**H Cochet**	W T Tilden	3-6, 8-6, 6-3, 6-1
1931	**J Borotra**	C Boussus	2-6, 6-4, 7-5, 6-4
1932	**H Cochet**	G de Stefani	6-0, 6-4, 4-6, 6-3
1933	**J H Crawford**	H Cochet	8-6, 6-1, 6-3
1934	**G von Cramm**	J H Crawford	6-4, 7-9, 3-6, 7-5, 6-3
1935	**F J Perry**	G von Cramm	6-3, 3-6, 6-1, 6-3
1936	**G von Cramm**	F J Perry	6-0, 2-6, 6-2, 2-6, 6-0
1937	**H Henkel**	H W Austin	6-1, 6-4, 6-3
1938	**J D Budge**	R Menzel	6-3, 6-2, 6-4
1939	**W D McNeill**	R L Riggs	7-5, 6-0, 6-3
1940	*No Competition*		
1941–5	*Tournoi de France (closed)*		
1941	**B Destremau**		
1942	**B Destremau**		
1943	**Y Petra**		
1944	**Y Petra**		
1945	**Y Petra**	B Destremau	7-5, 6-4, 6-2
1946	**M Bernard**	J Drobný	3-6, 2-6, 6-1, 6-4, 6-3
1947	**J Asboth**	E W Sturgess	8-6, 7-5, 6-4
1948	**F A Parker**	J Drobný	6-4, 7-5, 5-7, 8-6
1949	**F A Parker**	J E Patty	6-3, 1-6, 6-1, 6-4
1950	**J E Patty**	J Drobný	6-1, 6-2, 3-6, 5-7, 7-5
1951	**J Drobný**	E W Sturgess	6-3, 6-3, 6-3
1952	**J Drobný**	F A Sedgman	6-2, 6-0, 3-6, 6-4
1953	**K R Rosewall**	E V Seixas	6-3, 6-4, 1-6, 6-2
1954	**M A Trabert**	A Larsen	6-4, 7-5, 6-1
1955	**M A Trabert**	S Davidson	2-6, 6-1, 6-4, 6-2
1956	**L A Hoad**	S Davidson	6-4, 8-6, 6-3
1957	**S Davidson**	H Flam	6-3, 6-4, 6-4
1958	**M G Rose**	L Ayala	6-3, 6-4, 6-4
1959	**N Pietrangeli**	I C Vermaak	3-6, 6-3, 6-4, 6-1
1960	**N Pietrangeli**	L Ayala	3-6, 6-3, 6-4, 4-6, 6-3
1961	**M Santana**	N Pietrangeli	4-6, 6-1, 3-6, 6-0, 6-2
1962	**R G Laver**	R S Emerson	3-6, 2-6, 6-3, 9-7, 6-2
1963	**R S Emerson**	P Darmon	3-6, 6-1, 6-4, 6-4
1964	**M Santana**	N Pietrangeli	6-3, 6-1, 4-6, 7-5
1965	**F S Stolle**	A D Roche	3-6, 6-0, 6-2, 6-3
1966	**A D Roche**	I Guylas	6-1, 6-4, 7-5
1967	**R S Emerson**	A D Roche	6-1, 6-4, 2-6, 6-2

Open Championships began

Date	Winners	Runners-up	Score
1968	**K R Rosewall**	R G Laver	6-3, 6-1, 2-6, 6-2
1969	**R G Laver**	K R Rosewall	6-4, 6-3, 6-4
1970	**J Kodeš**	Z Franulović	6-2, 6-4, 6-0
1971	**J Kodeš**	I Năstase	8-6, 6-2, 2-6, 7-5
1972	**A Gimeno**	P Proisy	4-6, 6-3, 6-1, 6-1
1973	**I Năstase**	N Pilić	6-3, 6-3, 6-0
1974	**B Borg**	M Orantes	6-7, 6-0, 6-1, 6-1
1975	**B Borg**	G Vilas	6-2, 6-3, 6-4
1976	**A Panatta**	H Solomon	6-1, 6-4, 4-6, 7-6
1977	**G Vilas**	B Gottfried	6-0, 6-3, 6-0

Men's Doubles

Date	Winners	Runners-up	Score
1925	**R Lacoste/** **J Borotra**	H Cochet/ J Brugnon	7-5, 4-6, 6-3, 2-6, 6-3
1926	**V Richards/** **H O Kinsey**	H Cochet/ J Brugnon	6-4, 6-1, 4-6, 6-4
1927	**H Cochet/** **J Brugnon**	J Borotra/ R Lacoste	2-6, 6-2, 6-0, 1-6, 6-4
1928	**J Borotra/** **J Brugnon**	H Cochet/ R de Buzelet	6-4, 3-6, 6-2, 3-6, 6-4
1929	**R Lacoste/** **J Borotra**	H Cochet/ J Brugnon	6-3, 3-6, 6-3, 3-6, 8-6
1930	**H Cochet/** **J Brugnon**	H C Hopman/ J Willard	6-3, 9-7, 6-3
1931	**G M Lott/** **J Van Ryn**	V G Kirby/ N J Farquharson	6-4, 6-3, 6-4
1932	**H Cochet/** **J Brugnon**	C Boussus/ M Bernard	6-4, 3-6, 7-5, 6-3
1933	**G P Hughes/** **F J Perry**	A K Quist/ V B McGrath	6-2, 6-4, 2-6, 7-5
1934	**J Borotra/** **J Brugnon**	J H Crawford/ V B McGrath	11-9, 6-3, 2-6, 4-6, 9-7
1935	**J H Crawford/.** **A K Quist**	V B McGrath/ D P Turnbull	6-1, 6-4, 6-2
1936	**J Borotra/** **M Bernard**	C R D Tuckey/ G P Hughes	6-2, 3-6, 9-7, 6-1
1937	**G von Cramm/** **H Henkel**	N G Farquharson/ V G Kirby	6-4, 7-5, 3-6, 6-1
1938	**B Destremau/** **Y Petra**	J D Budge/ C G Mako	3-6, 6-3, 9-7, 6-1
1939	**W D McNeill/** **C Harris**		
1940	*No Competition*		
1941–5	*Tournoi de France (closed)*		
1941	**B Destremau/** **C Boussus**		
1942	**B Destremau/** **Y Petra**		
1943	**M Bernard/** **Y Petra**		
1944	**M Bernard/** **Y Petra**		
1945	**H Cochet/** **P Pellizza**	Y Petra/ B Destremau	2-6, 6-4, 8-6, 3-6, 6-0
1946	**M Bernard/** **Y Petra**	E Morea/ F Segura	7-5, 6-3, 0-6, 1-6, 10-8
1947	**E Fannin/** **E W Sturgess**	T Brown/ O W Sidwell	6-4, 4-6, 6-4, 6-3
1948	**L Bergelin/** **J Drobny**	H C Hopman/ F A Sedgman	8-6, 6-1, 12-10
1949	**R A Gonzalez/** **F A Parker**	E Fannin/ E W Sturgess	6-3, 8-6, 5-7, 6-3
1950	**W F Talbert/** **M A Trabert**	J Drobny/ E W Sturgess	6-2, 1-6, 10-8, 6-2
1951	**K McGregor/** **F A Sedgman**	G Mulloy/ R Savitt	6-2, 2-6, 9-7, 7-5
1952	**K McGregor/** **F A Sedgman**	G Mulloy/ R Savitt	6-3, 6-4, 6-4
1953	**L A Hoad/** **K R Rosewall**	M G Rose/ C Wilderspin	6-2, 6-1, 6-1
1954	**E V Seixas/** **M A Trabert**	L A Hoad/ K R Rosewall	6-4, 6-2, 6-1
1955	**E V Seixas/** **M A Trabert**	N Pietrangeli/ O Sirola	6-1, 4-6, 6-2, 6-4
1956	**D W Candy/** **R M Perry**	A J Cooper/ L A Hoad	7-5, 6-3, 6-3
1957	**M J Anderson/** **A J Cooper**	D W Candy/ M G Rose	6-3, 6-0, 6-3
1958	**A J Cooper/** **N A Fraser**	R N Howe/ A Segal	3-6, 8-6, 6-3, 7-5
1959	**O Sirola/** **N Pietrangeli**	R S Emerson/ N A Fraser	6-3, 6-2, 14-12
1960	**R S Emerson/** **N A Fraser**	J Arilla/ A Gimeno	6-2, 8-10, 7-5, 6-4
1961	**R S Emerson/** **R G Laver**	R N Howe/ R Mark	3-6, 6-1, 6-1, 6-4
1962	**R S Emerson/** **N A Fraser**	W P Bungert/ C Kuhnke	6-3, 6-4, 7-5
1963	**R S Emerson/** **M Santana**	G L Forbes/ A Segal	6-2, 6-4, 6-4
1964	**R S Emerson/** **K N Fletcher**	J D Newcombe/ A D Roche	7-5, 6-3, 3-6, 7-5
1965	**R S Emerson/** **F S Stolle**	K N Fletcher/ R A J Hewitt	6-8, 6-3, 8-6, 6-2
1966	**C E Graebner/** **R D Ralston**	I Năstase/ I Tiriac	6-3, 6-3, 6-0
1967	**J D Newcombe/** **A D Roche**	R S Emerson/ K N Fletcher	6-3, 9-7, 12-10

Open Championships began

Date	Winners	Runners-up	Score
1968	**K R Rosewall/** **F S Stolle**	R G Laver/ R S Emerson	6-3, 6-4, 6-3
1969	**J D Newcombe/** **A D Roche**	R S Emerson/ R G Laver	4-6, 6-1, 3-6, 6-4, 6-4
1970	**I Năstase/** **I Tiriac**	A R Ashe/ C M Pasarell	6-2, 6-4, 6-3
1971	**A R Ashe/** **M C Riessen**	T Gorman/ S R Smith	6-8, 4-6, 6-3, 6-4, 11-9
1972	**R A J Hewitt/** **F D McMillan**	P Cornejo/ J Fillol	6-3, 8-6, 3-6, 6-1

Date	Winners	Runners-up	Score
1973	J D Newcombe/ T S Okker	J Connors/ I Năstase	6-1, 3-6, 6-3, 5-7, 6-4
1974	R Crealy/ O Parun	R Lutz/ S Smith	6-3, 6-2, 3-6, 5-7, 6-1
1975	R Ramirez/ B Gottfried	J Alexander/ P Dent	6-4, 2-6, 6-2, 6-4
1976	F McNair/ S Stewart	B Gottfried/ R Ramirez	7-6, 6-3, 6-1
1977	R Hewitt/ F McMillan	R Ramirez/ B Gottfried	6-4, 6-0

Women's Singles

Date	Winners	Runners-up	Score
1925	Miss S Lenglen	Miss K McKane	6-1, 6-2
1926	Miss S Lenglen	Miss M K Browne	6-1, 6-0
1927	Miss K Bouman	Mrs Peacock	6-2, 6-4
1928	Miss H Wills	Miss E Bennett	6-1, 6-2
1929	Miss H Wills	Mrs R Mathieu	6-3, 6-4
1930	Mrs F S Moody	Miss H H Jacobs	6-2, 6-1
1931	Miss C Aussem	Miss B Nuthall	8-6, 6-1
1932	Mrs F S Moody	Mrs R Mathieu	7-5, 6-1
1933	Miss M C Scriven	Mrs R Mathieu	6-2, 4-6, 6-4
1934	Miss M C Scriven	Miss H H Jacobs	7-5, 4-6, 6-1
1935	Mrs H Sperling	Mrs R Mathieu	6-2, 6-1
1936	Mrs H Sperling	Mrs R Mathieu	6-3, 6-4
1937	Mrs H Sperling	Mrs R Mathieu	6-2, 6-4
1938	Mrs R Mathieu	Mrs N Landry	6-0, 6-3
1939	Mrs R Mathieu	Miss J Jedrzejowska	6-3, 8-6
1940	*No Competition*		
1941–5	*Tournoi de France (closed)*		
1941	Miss A Weiwers		
1942	Miss A Weiwers		
1943	Mrs N Lafargue		
1944	Miss R Veber		
1945	Miss L D Payot	Mrs N Lafargue	6-3, 6-4
1946	Miss M E Osborne	Miss P M Betz	1-6, 8-6, 7-5
1947	Mrs P C Todd	Miss D J Hart	6-3, 3-6, 6-4
1948	Mrs N Landry	Miss S J Fry	6-2, 0-6, 6-0
1949	Mrs W duPont	Mrs N Adamson	7-5, 6-2
1950	Miss D J Hart	Mrs P C Todd	6-4, 4-6, 6-2
1951	Miss S J Fry	Miss D J Hart	6-3, 3-6, 6-3
1952	Miss D J Hart	Miss S J Fry	6-4, 6-4
1953	Miss M Connolly	Miss D J Hart	6-2, 6-4
1954	Miss M Connolly	Mrs G Bucaille	6-4, 6-1
1955	Miss A Mortimer	Mrs D P Knode	2-6, 7-5, 10-8
1956	Miss A Gibson	Miss A Mortimer	6-0, 12-10
1957	Miss S J Bloomer	Mrs D P Knode	6-1, 6-3
1958	Mrs Z Körmöczy	Miss S J Bloomer	6-4, 1-6, 6-2
1959	Miss C C Truman	Mrs Z Körmöczy	6-4, 7-5
1960	Miss D R Hard	Miss Y Ramirez	6-3, 6-4
1961	Miss A S Haydon	Miss Y Ramirez	6-2, 6-1
1962	Miss M Smith	Miss L R Turner	6-3, 3-6, 7-5
1963	Miss L R Turner	Mrs P F Jones	2-6, 6-3, 7-5
1964	Miss M Smith	Miss M E Bueno	5-7, 6-1, 6-2
1965	Miss L R Turner	Miss M Smith	6-3, 6-4
1966	Mrs P F Jones	Miss N Richey	6-3, 6-1
1967	Miss F Durr	Miss L R Turner	4-6, 6-3, 6-4

Open Championships began

Date	Winners	Runners-up	Score
1968	Miss N Richey	Mrs P F Jones	5-7, 6-4, 6-1
1969	Mrs B M Court	Mrs P F Jones	6-1, 4-6, 6-3
1970	Mrs B M Court	Miss H Niessen	6-2, 6-4
1971	Miss E F Goolagong	Miss H Gourlay	6-3, 7-5
1972	Mrs L W King	Miss E F Goolagong	6-3, 6-3
1973	Mrs B M Court	Miss C Evert	6-7, 7-6, 6-4
1974	Miss C Evert	Miss O Morozova	6-1, 6-2
1975	Miss C Evert	Miss M Navratilova	2-6, 6-2, 6-1
1976	Miss S Barker	Miss R Tomanova	6-2, 0-6, 6-2
1977	Miss M Jausovec	Miss F Mihai	6-2, 6-7, 6-1

Women's Doubles

Date	Winners	Runners-up	Score
1925	Miss S Lenglen/ Miss D Vlasto	Miss K McKane/ Miss E Colyer	6-1, 9-11, 6-2
1926	Miss S Lenglen/ Miss D Vlasto	Mrs L A Godfree/ Miss E Colyer	6-1, 6-1
1927	Mrs I E Peacock/ Miss E L Heine	Mrs P Watson/ Miss P Saunders	6-2, 6-1
1928	Mrs P Watson/ Miss E Bennett	Miss S Deve/ Mrs Lafaurie	6-0, 6-2
1929	Miss L de Alvarez/ Miss K Bouman	Miss E L Heine/ Mrs Neave	7-5, 6-3
1930	Mrs F S Moody/ Miss E Ryan	Mrs R Mathieu/ Miss S Barbier	6-3, 6-1
1931	Mrs E F Whittingstall/ Miss B Nuthall	Miss E Ryan/ Miss C Aussem	9-7, 6-2
1932	Mrs F S Moody/ Miss E Ryan	Mrs E F Whittingstall/ Miss B Nuthall	6-1, 6-3
1933	Mrs R Mathieu/ Miss E Ryan	Mrs S Henrotin/ Miss C Rosambert	6-1, 6-3

Date	Winners	Runners-up	Score
1934	Mrs R Mathieu/ Miss E Ryan	Miss H H Jacobs/ Miss S Palfrey	3-6, 6-4, 6-2
1935	Miss M C Scriven/ Miss K E Stammers	Miss Adamoff/ Mrs H Sperling	6-4, 6-0
1936	Mrs R Mathieu/ Miss A M Yorke	Miss S Noel/ Miss J Jedrzejowska	2-6, 6-4, 6-4
1937	Mrs R M Mathieu/ Miss A M Yorke	Mrs D Andrus/ Mrs S Henrotin	3-6, 6-2, 6-2
1938	Mrs R Mathieu/ Miss A M Yorke	Mrs A Halff/ Mrs N Landry	6-3, 6-3
1939	Mrs R Mathieu/ Miss J Jedrzejowska		
1940	*No Competition*		
1941–5	*Tournoi de France (closed)*		
1941	Miss A Weiwers/ Miss St Omer Roy		
1942	Miss A Weiwers/ Miss St Omer Roy		
1943	Miss A Weiwers/ Miss St Omer Roy		
1944	Mrs Grosbois/ Mrs Manescau		
1945	Mrs N Lafargue/ Mrs P Fritz	Mrs R Mathieu/ Miss Brunnarius	6-3, 6-1
1946	Miss A L Brough/ Miss M E Osborne	Miss P M Betz/ Miss D J Hart	6-4, 0-6, 6-1
1947	Miss A L Brough/ Miss M E Osborne	Miss D'J Hart/ Mrs P C Todd	7-5, 6-2
1948	Miss D J Hart/ Mrs P C Todd	Miss S J Fry/ Mrs M A Prentiss	6-4, 6-2
1949	Miss A L Brough/ Mrs W duPont	Mrs B E Hilton/ Miss J Gannon	7-5, 6-1
1950	Miss D J Hart/ Miss S J Fry	Mrs W duPont/ Miss A L Brough	1-6, 7-5, 6-2
1951	Miss D J Hart/ Miss S J Fry	Mrs B Bartlett/ Miss B Scofield	10-8, 6-3
1952	Miss D J Hart/ Miss S J Fry	Mrs H Redick-Smith/ Mrs J Wipplinger	7-5, 6-1
1953	Miss D J Hart/ Miss S J Fry	Miss M Connolly/ Miss J Sampson	6-4, 6-3
1954	Miss M Connolly/ Mrs H C Hopman	Mrs M Galtier/ Miss S Schmitt	7-5, 4-6, 6-0
1955	Mrs J F Fleitz/ Miss D R Hard	Miss S J Bloomer/ Miss P E Ward	7-5, 6-8, 13-11
1956	Miss A Gibson/ Miss A Buxton	Mrs D P Knode/ Miss D R Hard	6-8, 8-6, 6-1
1957	Miss D R Hard/ Miss S J Bloomer	Miss Y Ramirez/ Miss R M Reyes	7-5, 4-6, 7-5
1958	Miss Y Ramirez/ Miss R M Reyes	Mrs M K Hawton/ Mrs T D Long	6-4, 7-5
1959	Miss S Reynolds/ Miss R Schuurman	Miss Y Ramirez/ Miss R M Reyes	2-6, 6-0, 6-1
1960	Miss M E Bueno/ Miss D R Hard	Mrs R Hales/ Miss A S Haydon	6-2, 7-5
1961	Miss S Reynolds/ Miss R Schuurman	Miss M E Bueno/ Miss D R Hard	scratched
1962	Mrs S Price/ Miss R Schuurman	Miss M Smith/ Miss J Bricka	6-4, 6-4
1963	Mrs P F Jones/ Miss R Schuurman	Miss M Smith/ Miss R A Ebbern	7-5, 6-4
1964	Miss L R Turner/ Miss M Smith	Miss N Baylon/ Miss M Schultze	6-3, 6-0
1965	Miss L R Turner/ Miss M Smith	Miss F Durr/ Miss J Lieffrig	6-3, 6-1
1966	Miss M Smith/ Miss J A M Tegart	Miss J Blackman/ Miss Toyne	4-6, 6-1, 6-1
1967	Miss F Durr/ Miss G Sherriff	Miss A M Van Zyl/ Miss P Walkden	6-2, 6-2

Open Championships began

Date	Winners	Runners-up	Score
1968	Miss F Durr/ Mrs P F Jones	Mrs L W King/ Miss R Casals	7-5, 4-6, 6-4
1969	Miss F Durr/ Mrs P F Jones	Mrs B M Court/ Miss N Richey	6-0, 4-6, 7-5
1970	Mrs G Chanfreau/ Miss F Durr	Miss R Casals/ Mrs L W King	6-3, 1-6, 6-3
1971	Mrs G Chanfreau/ Miss F Durr	Miss H Gourlay/ Miss K Harris	6-4, 6-1
1972	Mrs L W King/ Miss B Stöve	Miss W Shaw/ Miss N Truman	6-1, 6-2
1973	Mrs B M Court/ Miss S V Wade	Miss B Stöve/ Miss F Durr	6-2, 6-3
1974	Miss C Evert/ Miss O Morozova	Mrs G Chanfreau/ Miss K Ebbinghaus	6-4, 2-6, 6-1
1975	Miss C Evert/ Miss M Navratilova	Miss J Anthony/ Miss O Morozova	6-3, 6-2
1976	Miss F Bonicelli/ Mrs G Lovera	Miss K Harter/ Mrs H Masthoff	6-4, 1-6, 6-3
1977	Miss R Marsikova/ Miss P Teeguarden	Miss R Fox/ Mrs H Gourlay Cawley	5-7, 6-4, 6-2

Mixed Doubles

Date	Winners	Runners-up	Score
1925	J Brugnon/ Miss S Lenglen	H Cochet/ Miss D Vlasto	6-2, 6-2
1926	J Brugnon/ Miss S Lenglen	J Borotra/ Mrs Le Besnerais	6-4, 6-3
1927	J Borotra/ Mrs M Bordes	W T Tilden/ Miss L de Alvarez	6-4, 2-6, 6-2
1928	H Cochet/ Miss E Bennett	F T Hunter/ Miss H Wills	3-6, 6-3, 6-3
1929	H Cochet/ Miss E Bennett	F T Hunter/ Miss H Wills	6-3, 6-2
1930	W T Tilden/ Miss C Aussem	H Cochet/ Mrs F Whittingstall	6-4, 6-4
1931	P D B Spence/ Miss B Nuthall	H W Austin/ Mrs D C Shepherd-Barron	6-3, 5-7, 6-3
1932	F J Perry/ Miss B Nuthall	S B Wood/ Mrs F S Moody	6-4, 6-2
1933	J H Crawford/ Miss M C Scriven	F J Perry/ Miss B Nuthall	6-2, 6-3
1934	J Borotra/ Miss C Rosambert	A K Quist/ Miss E Ryan	6-2, 6-4
1935	M Bernard/ Miss L D Payot	A M Legeay/ Mrs S Henrotin	4-6, 6-2, 6-4
1936	M Bernard/ Miss A M Yorke	A M Legeay/ Mrs S Henrotin	7-5, 6-8, 6-3
1937	Y Petra/ Mrs R Mathieu	R Journo/ Miss M Horn	7-5, 7-5
1938	D Mitic/ Mrs R Mathieu	C Boussus/ Miss N Wynne	2-6, 6-3, 6-4
1939	E T Cooke/ Mrs S P Fabyan		
1940	*No Competition*		
1941–5	*Tournoi de France (closed)*		
1941	R Abdesselam/ Miss A Weiwers		
1942	H Pellizza/ Mrs N Larfargue		
1943	H Pellizza/ Mrs N Larfargue		
1944	A Gentien/ Miss S Pannetier		
1945	A Jacquemet/ Mrs L D Payot		
1946	J E Patty/ Miss P M Betz	T Brown/ Miss D Bundy	7-5, 9-7
1947	E W Sturgess/ Mrs S P Summers	C Caralulis/ Miss J Jedrzejowska	6-0, 6-0
1948	J Drobny/ Mrs P C Todd	F A Sedgman/ Miss D J Hart	6-3, 3-6, 6-3
1949	E W Sturgess/ Mrs S P Summers	G D Oakley/ Miss J Quertier	6-1, 6-1
1950	E Morea/ Miss B Scofield wo	W F Talbert/ Mrs P C Todd retired	
1951	F A Sedgman/ Miss D J Hart	M G Rose/ Mrs T D Long	7-5, 6-2
1952	F A Sedgman/ Miss D J Hart	E W Sturgess/ Miss S J Fry	6-8, 6-3, 6-3
1953	E V Seixas/ Miss D J Hart	M G Rose/ Miss M Connolly	4-6, 6-4, 6-0
1954	L A Hoad/ Miss M Connolly	R N Hartwig/ Miss J Patorni	6-4, 6-3
1955	G L Forbes/ Miss D R Hard	L Ayala/ Miss J Staley	5-7, 6-1, 6-2
1956	L Ayala/ Mrs T D Long	R N Howe/ Miss D R Hard	4-6, 6-4, 6-1
1957	J Javorsky/ Miss V Puzejová	L Ayala/ Miss E Buding	6-3, 6-4
1958	N Pietrangeli/ Miss S J Bloomer	R N Howe/ Miss L Coghlan	9-7, 6-8, 6-2
1959	W A Knight/ Miss Y Ramirez	R G Laver/ Miss R Schuurman	6-4, 6-4
1960	R N Howe/ Miss M E Bueno	R S Emerson/ Miss A S Haydon	1-6, 6-1, 6-2
1961	R G Laver/ Miss D R Hard	J Javorsky/ Miss V Pužejová	6-0, 2-6, 6-3
1962	R N Howe/ Miss R Schuurman	F S Stolle/ Miss L R Turner	3-6, 6-4, 6-4
1963	K N Fletcher/ Miss M Smith	F S Stolle/ Miss L R Turner	6-1, 6-2
1964	K N Fletcher/ Miss M Smith	F S Stolle/ Miss L R Turner	6-3, 6-4
1965	K N Fletcher/ Miss M Smith	J D Newcombe/ Miss M E Bueno	6-4, 6-4
1966	F D McMillan/ Miss A M Van Zyl	C E Graebner/ Mrs P F Jones	1-6, 6-3, 6-2
1967	O K Davidson/ Mrs L W King	I Tiriac/ Mrs P F Jones	6-3, 6-1

Date	Winners	Runners-up	Score
	Open Championships began		
1968	J C Barclay/ Miss F Durr	O K Davidson/ Mrs L W King	6-1, 6-4
1969	M C Riessen/ Mrs B M Court	J C Barclay/ Miss F Durr	7-5, 6-4
1970	R A J Hewitt/ Mrs L W King	J C Barclay/ Miss F Durr	3-6, 6-3, 6-2
1971	J C Barclay/ Miss F Durr	T Lejus/ Miss W Shaw	6-2, 6-4
1972	K Warwick/ Miss E F Goolagong	J C Barclay/ Miss F Durr	6-2, 6-4
1973	J C Barclay/ Miss F Durr	P Dominguez/ Miss B Stöve	6-1, 6-4
1974	I Molina/ Miss M Navratilova	M Lara/ Mrs P Darmon	6-3, 6-3
1975	T Koch/ Miss F Bonicelli	J Fillol/ Miss P Teeguarden	6-4, 7-6
1976	K Warwick/ Miss I Kloss	C Dowdeswell/ Miss L Boshoff	5-7, 7-6, 6-2
1977	F McMillan/ Miss B Stöve	V Gerulaitis/ Mrs L W King	6-2, 3-6, 6-3

UNITED STATES CHAMPIONSHIPS

Men's Singles

Played in Newport RI

Date	Winners	Runners-up	Score
1881	R D Sears	W E Glyn	6-0, 6-3, 6-2
1882	R D Sears	C M Clark	6-1, 6-4, 6-0
1883	R D Sears	J Dwight	6-2, 6-0, 9-7

Challenge Round began

Date	Winners	Runners-up	Score
1884	R D Sears	H A Taylor	6-0, 1-6, 6-0, 6-2
1885	R D Sears	G M Brinley	6-3, 4-6, 6-0, 6-3
1886	R D Sears	R L Beeckman	4-6, 6-1, 6-3, 6-4
1887	R D Sears	H W Slocum	6-1, 6-3, 6-2
1888	H W Slocum (wo)		
1889	H W Slocum	Q A Shaw	6-3, 6-1, 4-6, 6-2
1890	O S Campbell	H W Slocum	6-2, 4-6, 6-3, 6-1
1891	O S Campbell	C Hobart	2-6, 7-5, 7-9, 6-1, 6-2
1892	O S Campbell	F H Hovey	7-5, 3-6, 6-3, 7-5
1893	R D Wrenn (wo)		
1894	R D Wrenn	M F Goodbody	6-8, 6-1, 6-4, 6-4
1895	F H Hovey	R D Wrenn	6-3, 6-2, 6-4
1896	R D Wrenn	F H Hovey	7-5, 3-6, 6-0, 1-6, 6-1
1897	R D Wrenn	W V Eaves	4-6, 8-6, 6-3, 2-6, 6-2
1898	M D Whitman (wo)		
1899	M D Whitman	J P Paret	6-1, 6-2, 3-6, 7-5
1900	M D Whitman	W A Larned	6-4, 1-6, 6-2, 6-2
1901	W A Larned (wo)		
1902	W A Larned	R F Doherty	4-6, 6-2, 6-4, 8-6
1903	H L Doherty	W A Larned	6-0, 6-3, 10-8
1904	H Ward (wo)		
1905	B C Wright	H Ward	6-1, 6-2, 11-9
1906	W J Clothier	B C Wright	6-3, 6-0, 6-4
1907	W A Larned (wo)		
1908	W A Larned	B C Wright	6-1, 6-2, 8-6
1909	W A Larned	W J Clothier	6-1, 6-2, 5-7, 1-6, 6-1
1910	W A Larned	T C Bundy	6-1, 5-7, 6-0, 6-8, 6-4
1911	W A Larned	M E McLoughlin	6-4, 6-4, 6-2

Challenge Round abolished

Date	Winners	Runners-up	Score
1912	M E McLoughlin	W F Johnson	3-6, 2-6, 6-2, 6-4, 6-2
1913	M E McLoughlin	R N Williams	6-4, 5-7, 6-3, 6-1
1914	R N Williams	M E McLoughlin	6-3, 8-6, 10-8

Transferred from Newport to Forest Hills

Date	Winners	Runners-up	Score
1915	W M Johnston	M E McLoughlin	1-6, 6-0, 7-5, 10-8
1916	R N Williams	W M Johnston	4-6, 6-4, 0-6, 6-2, 6-4

National Patriotic Tournament

Date	Winners	Runners-up	Score
1917	R L Murray	N W Niles	5-7, 8-6, 6-3, 6-3
1918	R L Murray	W T Tilden	6-3, 6-1, 7-5
1919	W M Johnston	W T Tilden	6-4, 6-4, 6-3
1920	W T Tilden	W M Johnston	6-1, 1-6, 7-5, 5-7, 6-3

Transferred to Philadelphia, Pennsylvania

Date	Winners	Runners-up	Score
1921	W T Tilden	W F Johnson	6-1, 6-3, 6-1
1922	W T Tilden	W M Johnston	4-6, 3-6, 6-2, 6-3, 6-4
1923	W T Tilden	W M Johnston	6-4, 6-1, 6-4

Transferred to Forest Hills, New York

Date	Winners	Runners-up	Score
1924	W T Tilden	W M Johnston	6-1, 9-7, 6-2
1925	W T Tilden	W M Johnston	4-6, 11-9, 6-3, 4-6, 6-3
1926	R Lacoste	J Borotra	6-4, 6-0, 6-4
1927	R Lacoste	W T Tilden	11-9, 6-3, 11-9
1928	H Cochet	F T Hunter	4-6, 6-4, 3-6, 7-5, 6-3

Date	Winners	Runners-up	Score
1929	W T Tilden	F T Hunter	3-6, 6-3, 4-6, 6-2, 6-4
1930	J H Doeg	F X Shields	10-8, 1-6, 6-4, 16-14
1931	H E Vines	G M Lott	7-9, 6-3, 9-7, 7-5
1932	H E Vines	H Cochet	6-4, 6-4, 6-4
1933	F J Perry	J H Crawford	6-3, 11-13, 4-6, 6-0, 6-1
1934	F J Perry	W L Allison	6-4, 6-3, 3-6, 1-6, 8-6
1935	W L Allison	S B Wood	6-2, 6-2, 6-3
1936	F J Perry	J D Budge	2-6, 6-2, 8-6, 1-6, 10-8
1937	J D Budge	G von Cramm	6-1, 7-9, 6-1, 3-6, 6-1
1938	J D Budge	G G Mako	6-3, 6-8, 6-2, 6-1
1939	R L Riggs	S W Van Horn	6-4, 6-2, 6-4
1940	W D McNeill	R L Riggs	8-6, 6-8, 6-3, 7-5
1941	R L Riggs	F Kovacs	5-7, 6-1, 6-3, 6-3
1942	F R Schroeder	F A Parker	8-6, 7-5, 3-6, 4-6, 6-2
1943	J R Hunt	J A Kramer	6-3, 6-8, 10-8, 6-0
1944	F A Parker	W F Talbert	6-4, 3-6, 6-3, 6-3
1945	F A Parker	W F Talbert	14-12, 6-1, 6-2
1946	J A Kramer	T Brown	9-7, 6-3, 6-0
1947	J A Kramer	F A Parker	4-6, 2-6, 6-1, 6-0, 6-3
1948	R A Gonzalez	E W Sturgess	6-2, 6-3, 14-12
1949	R A Gonzalez	F R Schroeder	16-18, 2-6, 6-1, 6-2, 6-4
1950	A Larsen	H Flam	6-3, 4-6, 5-7, 6-4, 6-3
1951	F A Sedgman	E V Seixas	6-4, 6-1, 6-1
1952	F A Sedgman	G Mulloy	6-1, 6-2, 6-3
1953	M A Trabert	E V Seixas	6-3, 6-2, 6-3
1954	E V Seixas	R N Hartwig	3-6, 6-2, 6-4, 6-4
1955	M A Trabert	K R Rosewall	9-7, 6-3, 6-3
1956	K R Rosewall	L A Hoad	4-6, 6-2, 6-3, 6-3
1957	M J Anderson	A J Cooper	10-8, 7-5, 6-4
1958	A J Cooper	M J Anderson	6-2, 3-6, 4-6, 10-8, 8-6
1959	N A Fraser	A Olmedo	6-3, 5-7, 6-2, 6-4
1960	N A Fraser	R G Laver	6-4, 6-4, 10-8
1961	R S Emerson	R G Laver	7-5, 6-3, 6-2
1962	R G Laver	R S Emerson	6-2, 6-4, 5-7, 6-4
1963	R H Osuna	F R Froehling	7-5, 6-4, 6-2
1964	R S Emerson	F S Stolle	6-4, 6-1, 6-4
1965	M Santana	E Drysdale	6-2, 7-9, 7-5, 6-1
1966	F S Stolle	J D Newcombe	4-6, 12-10, 6-3, 6-4
1967	J D Newcombe	C E Graebner	6-4, 6-4, 8-6

Open Championships began

Date	Winners	Runners-up	Score
1968	A R Ashe	T R Okker	14-12, 5-7, 6-3, 3-6, 6-3
1969	R G Laver	A D Roche	7-9, 6-1, 6-3, 6-2
1970	K R Rosewall	A D Roche	2-6, 6-4, 7-6, 6-3
1971	S R Smith	J Kodeš	3-6, 6-3, 6-2, 7-6
1972	I Năstase	A R Ashe	3-6, 6-3, 6-7, 6-4, 6-3
1973	J D Newcombe	J Kodeš	6-4, 1-6, 4-6, 6-2, 6-3
1974	J Connors	R Tanner	6-1, 6-0, 6-1
1975	M Orantes	J Connors	6-4, 6-3, 6-3
1976	J Connors	B Borg	6-4, 3-6, 7-6, 6-4
1977	G Vilas	J Connors	2-6, 6-3, 7-6, 6-0

Men's Doubles
Played in Newport, RI

Date	Winners	Runners-up	Score
1881	C M Clark/ F W Taylor	A Van Rensselaer/ A E Newbold	6-5, 6-4, 6-5
1882	R D Sears/ J Dwight	W Nightingale/ G M Smith	
1883	R D Sears/ J Dwight	A Van Rensselaer/ A E Newbold	
1884	R D Sears/ J Dwight	A Van Rensselaer/ W V R Berry	
1885	R D Sears/ J S Clark	H W Slocum/ W P Knapp	6-3, 6-0, 6-2
1886	R D Sears/ J Dwight	H A Taylor/ G M Brinley	
1887	R D Sears/ J Dwight	H A Taylor/ H W Slocum	
1888	O S Campbell/ V G Hall	C Hobart/ E P MacMullen	
1889	H W Slocum/ H A Taylor	V G Hall/ O S Campbell	
1890	V G Hall/ C Hobart	J W Carver/ J A Ryerson	
1891	O S Campbell/ R P Huntington	V G Hall/ C Hobart	
1892	O S Campbell/ R P Huntington	V G Hall/ E L Hall	
1893	C Hobart/ F H Hovey	O S Campbell/ R P Huntington	
1894	C Hobart/ F H Hovey	C B Neel/ S R Neel	
1895	M G Chace/ R D Wrenn	J Howland/ A E Foote	
1896	C B Neel/ S R Neel	R D Wrenn/ M G Chace	
1897	L E Ware/ G P Sheldon	H S Mahony/ H A Nisbet	11-13, 6-2, 9-7, 1-6, 6-1

Date	Winners	Runners-up	Score
1898	L E Ware/ G P Sheldon	H Ward/ D F Davis	1-6, 7-5, 6-4, 4-6, 7-5
1899	H Ward/ D F Davis	L E Ware/ G P Sheldon	6-4, 6-4, 6-3
1900	H Ward/ D F Davis	F B Alexander/ R D Little	6-4, 9-7, 12-10
1901	H Ward/ D F Davis	I E Ware/ B C Wright	6-3, 9-7, 6-1
1902	R F Doherty/ H L Doherty	H Ward/ D F Davis	11-9, 12-10, 6-4
1903	R F Doherty/ H L Doherty	K Collins/ L H Waidner	7-5, 6-3, 6-3
1904	H Ward/ B C Wright	K Collins/ R D Little	
1905	H Ward/ B C Wright	F B Alexander/ H H Hackett	6-3, 6-1, 6-2
1906	H Ward/ B C Wright	F B Alexander/ H H Hackett	6-3, 3-6, 6-3, 6-3
1907	H H Hackett/ F B Alexander	W A Larned/ W J Clothier	6-3, 6-1, 6-4
1908	H H Hackett/ F B Alexander	R D Little/ B C Wright	6-1, 7-5, 6-2
1909	H H Hackett/ F B Alexander	G J James/ M E McLoughlin	6-4, 6-1, 6-0
1910	H H Hackett/ F B Alexander	T C Bundy/ T W Hendrick	6-1, 8-6, 6-3
1911	R D Little/ G F Touchard	H H Hackett/ F B Alexander	7-5, 13-15, 6-2, 6-4
1912	T C Bundy/ M E McLoughlin	R D Little/ G F Touchard	3-6, 6-2, 6-1, 7-5
1913	T C Bundy/ M E McLoughlin	J R Strachan/ C J Griffin	6-4, 7-5, 6-1
1914	T C Bundy/ M E McLoughlin	G M Church/ D Mathey	6-4, 6-2, 6-4

Transferred from Newport to Forest Hills

Date	Winners	Runners-up	Score
1915	W M Johnston/ C J Griffin	M E McLoughlin/ T C Bundy	6-2, 3-6, 4-6, 6-3, 6-3
1916	W M Johnston/ C J Griffin	M E McLoughlin/ W Dawson	6-4, 6-3, 5-7, 6-3

National Patriotic Tournament

Date	Winners	Runners-up	Score
1917	F B Alexander/ H A Throckmorton	H C Johnson/ I C Wright	11-9, 6-4, 6-4
1918	W T Tilden/ V Richards	F B Alexander/ B C Wright	6-3, 6-4, 3-6, 2-6, 6-2

Transferred to Chestnut Hill, Massachusetts

Date	Winners	Runners-up	Score
1919	N E Brookes/ G L Patterson	W T Tilden/ V Richards	8-6, 6-3, 4-6, 4-6, 6-2
1920	W M Johnston/ C J Griffin	W F Davis/ R E Roberts	6-2, 6-2, 6-3
1921	W T Tilden/ V Richards	R N Williams/ W M Washburn	13-11, 12-10, 6-1
1922	W T Tilden/ V Richards	G L Patterson/ P O'Hara Wood	4-6, 6-1, 6-3, 6-4
1923	W T Tilden/ B I C Norton	R N Williams/ W M Washburn	3-6, 6-2, 6-3, 5-7, 6-2
1924	R G Kinsey/ H O Kinsey	G L Patterson/ P O'Hara Wood	7-5, 5-7, 7-9, 6-3, 6-4
1925	R N Williams/ V Richards	G L Patterson/ J B Hawkes	6-2, 8-10, 6-4, 11-9
1926	R N Williams/ V Richards	W T Tilden/ A H Chapin	6-4, 6-8, 11-9, 6-3
1927	W T Tilden/ F T Hunter	R N Williams/ W M Johnston	10-8, 6-3, 6-3
1928	G M Lott/ J F Hennessey	G L Patterson/ J B Hawkes	6-2, 6-1, 6-2
1929	G M Lott/ J H Doeg	B Bell/ I N White	10-8, 16-14, 6-1
1930	G M Lott/ J H Doeg	J Van Ryn/ W L Allison	8-6, 6-3, 4-6, 13-15, 6-4
1931	W L Allison/ J Van Ryn	G S Mangin/ B Bell	6-4, 8-6, 6-3
1932	H E Vines/ K Gledhill	W L Allison/ J Van Ryn	6-4, 6-3, 6-2
1933	G M Lott/ L R Stoefen	F X Shields/ F A Parker	11-13, 9-7, 9-7, 6-3

Transferred to Philadelphia, Pennsylvania

Date	Winners	Runners-up	Score
1934	G M Lott/ L R Stoefen	W L Allison/ J Van Ryn	6-4, 9-7, 3-6, 6-4

Transferred to Chestnut Hill, Massachusetts

Date	Winners	Runners-up	Score
1935	W L Allison/ J Van Ryn	J D Budge/ C G Mako	6-4, 6-2, 3-6, 2-6, 6-1
1936	J D Budge/ C G Mako	W L Allison/ J Van Ryn	6-4, 6-2, 6-4

Date	Winners	Runners-up	Score
1937	**G von Cramm/ H Henkel**	J D Budge/ C G Mako	6-4, 7-5, 6-4
1938	**J D Budge/ C G Mako**	A K Quist/ J E Bromwich	6-3, 6-2, 6-1
1939	**A K Quist/ J E Bromwich**	J H Crawford/ H C Hopman	8-6, 6-1, 6-4
1940	**J A Kramer/ F R Schroeder**	G Mulloy/ H J Prussoff	
1941	**J A Kramer/ F R Schroeder**	W Sabin/ G Mulloy	

Transferred to Forest Hills, NY

Date	Winners	Runners-up	Score
1942	**G Mulloy/ W F Talbert**	F R Schroeder/ S B Wood	
1943	**J A Kramer/ F A Parker**	W F Talbert/ D Freeman	
1944	**W D McNeill/ R Falkenburg**	W F Talbert/ F Segura	7-5, 6-4, 3-6, 6-1
1945	**G Mulloy/ W F Talbert**	R Falkenburg/ J Tuero	12-10, 8-10, 12-10, 6-2

Transferred to Chestnut Hill, Massachusetts

Date	Winners	Runners-up	Score
1946	**G Mulloy/ W F Talbert**	W D McNeill/ F Guernsey	3-6, 6-4, 2-6, 6-3, 20-18
1947	**J A Kramer/ F R Schroeder**	W F Talbert/ O Sidwell	6-4, 7-5, 6-3
1948	**G Mulloy/ W F Talbert**	F A Parker/ F R Schroeder	1-6, 9-7, 6-3, 3-6, 9-7
1949	**O W Sidwell/ J E Bromwich**	F A Sedgman/ G Worthington	6-4, 6-0, 6-1
1950	**J E Bromwich/ F A Sedgman**	G Mulloy/ W F Talbert	7-5, 8-6, 3-6, 6-1
1951	**K McGregor/ F A Sedgman**	D W Candy/ M G Rose	10-8, 6-4, 4-6, 7-5
1952	**M G Rose/ E V Seixas**	K McGregor/ F A Sedgman	3-6, 10-8, 10-8, 6-8, 8-6
1953	**M G Rose/ R N Hartwig**	G Mulloy/ W F Talbert	6-4, 4-6, 6-2, 6-4
1954	**E V Seixas/ M A Trabert**	L A Hoad/ K R Rosewall	3-6, 6-4, 8-6, 6-3
1955	**K Kamo/ A Miyagi**	G Moss/ W Quillan	6-2, 6-3, 3-6, 1-6, 6-4
1956	**L A Hoad/ K R Rosewall**	H Richardson/ E V Seixas	6-2, 6-2, 3-6, 6-4
1957	**A J Cooper/ N A Fraser**	G Mulloy/ J E Patty	4-6, 6-3, 9-7, 6-3
1958	**H Richardson/ A Olmedo**	S Giammalva/ B MacKay	6-4, 3-6, 6-3, 6-4
1959	**R S Emerson/ N A Fraser**	A Olmedo/ E Buchholz	3-6, 6-3, 5-7, 6-4, 7-5
1960	**R S Emerson/ N A Fraser**	R G Laver/ R Mark	9-7, 6-2, 6-4
1961	**C R McKinley/ R D Ralston**	R H Osuna/ A Palafox	6-3, 6-4, 2-6, 13-11
1962	**R H Osuna/ A Palafox**	C R McKinley/ R D Ralston	6-4, 10-12, 1-6, 9-7, 6-3
1963	**C R McKinley/ R D Ralston**	R H Osuna/ A Palafox	9-7, 4-6, 5-7, 6-3, 11-9
1964	**C R McKinley/ R D Ralston**	M J Sangster/ G Stillwell	6-3, 6-2, 6-4
1965	**R S Emerson/ F S Stolle**	F R Froehling/ C M Pasarell	6-4, 10-12, 7-5, 6-3
1966	**R S Emerson/ F S Stolle**	R D Ralston/ C E Graebner	6-4, 6-4, 6-4
1967	**J D Newcombe/ A D Roche**	O K Davidson/ W W Bowrey	6-8, 9-7, 6-3, 6-3

Open Championships began at Forest Hills, New York

Date	Winners	Runners-up	Score
1968	**R C Lutz/ S R Smith**	A R Ashe/ A Gimeno	11-9, 6-1, 7-5
1969	**K R Rosewall/ F S Stolle**	C M Pasarell/ R D Ralston	2-6, 7-5, 13-11, 6-3
1970	**P Barthès/ N Pilić**	R S Emerson/ R G Laver	6-3, 7-6, 4-6, 7-6
1971	**J D Newcombe/ R Taylor**	S R Smith/ E Van Dillen	6-7, 6-3, 7-6, 4-6, 5-3 tie break
1972	**C Drysdale/ R Taylor**	O K Davidson/ J D Newcombe	6-4, 7-6, 6-3
1973	**O K Davidson/ J D Newcombe**	R G Laver/ K R Rosewall	7-5, 2-6, 7-5, 7-5
1974	**R Lutz/ S Smith**	P Cornejo/ J Fillol	6-3, 6-3
1975	**J Connors/ I Năstase**	T Okker/ M Riessen	6-4, 7-6
1976	**M Riessen/ T Okker**	P Kronk/ C Letcher	6-4, 6-4
1977	**R Hewitt/ F McMillan**	R Ramirez/ B Gottfried	6-4, 6-0

Women's Singles

Played in Philadelphia, Pennsylvania

Date	Winners	Runners-up	Score
1887	**Miss E Hansell**	Miss L Knight	6-1, 6-0
1888	**Miss B B Townsend**	Miss E Hansell	default
1889	**Miss B B Townsend**	Miss L D Voorhees	7-5, 6-2
1890	**Miss C E Roosevelt**	Miss B B Townsend	
1891	**Miss M E Cahill**	Miss E C Roosevelt	
1892	**Miss M E Cahill**	Miss E H Moore	
1893	**Miss A M Terry**	Miss M F Cahill	default
1894	**Miss H R Helwig**	Miss A M Terry	7-5, 3-6, 6-0, 3-6, 6-3
1895	**Miss J P Atkinson**	Miss H R Helwig	6-4, 6-2, 6-1
1896	**Miss E H Moore**	Miss J P Atkinson	6-4, 4-6, 6-3, 6-2
1897	**Miss J P Atkinson**	Miss E H Moore	6-3, 6-3, 4-6, 3-6, 6-3
1898	**Miss J P Atkinson**	Miss M Jones	6-3, 5-7, 6-4, 2-6, 7-5
1899	**Miss M Jones**	Miss J P Atkinson	default
1900	**Miss M McAteer**	Miss M Jones	default
1901	**Miss E H Moore**	Miss M McAteer	6-4, 3-6, 7-5, 2-6, 6-2
1902	**Miss M Jones**	Miss E H Moore	6-1, 1-0 retired
1903	**Miss E H Moore**	Miss M Jones	7-5, 8-6
1904	**Miss M G Sutton**	Miss E H Moore	6-1, 6-2
1905	**Miss E H Moore**	Miss M G Sutton	default
1906	**Miss H Homans**	Miss E H Moore	default
1907	**Miss Evelyn Sears**	Miss H Homans	default
1908	**Mrs M Barger-Wallach**	Miss Evelyn Sears	6-2, 1-6, 6-3
1909	**Miss H V Hotchkiss**	Mrs M Barger-Wallach	6-0, 6-1
1910	**Miss H V Hotchkiss**	Miss L Hamond	6-4, 6-2
1911	**Miss H V Hotchkiss**	Miss F Sutton	8-10, 6-1, 9-7
1912	**Miss M K Browne**	Miss H V Hotchkiss	default
1913	**Miss M K Browne**	Miss D Green	6-2, 7-5
1914	**Miss M K Browne**	Miss M Wagner	6-2, 1-6, 6-1
1915	**Miss M Bjurstedt**	Miss M K Browne	default
1916	**Miss M Bjurstedt**	Mrs E Raymond	6-0, 6-1

National Patriotic Tournament

Date	Winners	Runners-up	Score
1917	**Miss M Bjurstedt**	Miss M Vanderhoef	4-6, 6-0, 6-2
1918	**Miss M Bjurstedt**	Miss E E Goss	6-4, 6-3

Challenge Round abolished

Date	Winners	Runners-up	Score
1919	**Mrs G W Wightman**	Miss M Zinderstein	6-1, 6-2
1920	**Mrs M Mallory**	Miss M Zinderstein	6-3, 6-1

Transferred to Forest Hills, New York

Date	Winners	Runners-up	Score
1921	**Mrs M Mallory**	Miss M K Browne	4-6, 6-4, 6-2
1922	**Mrs M Mallory**	Miss H Wills	6-3, 6-1
1923	**Miss H Wills**	Mrs M Mallory	6-2, 6-1
1924	**Miss H Wills**	Mrs M Mallory	6-1, 6-2
1925	**Miss H Wills**	Miss K McKane	3-6, 6-0, 6-2
1926	**Mrs M Mallory**	Miss E Ryan	4-6, 6-4, 9-7
1927	**Miss H Wills**	Miss B Nuthall	6-1, 6-4
1928	**Miss H Wills**	Miss H H Jacobs	6-2, 6-1
1929	**Miss H Wills**	Mrs P Watson	6-4, 6-2
1930	**Miss B Nuthall**	Mrs L A Harper	6-4, 6-1
1931	**Mrs F S Moody**	Mrs E F Whittingstall	6-4, 6-1
1932	**Miss H H Jacobs**	Miss C A Babcock	6-2, 6-2
1933	**Miss H H Jacobs**	Mrs F S Moody	8-6, 3-6, 3-0 retired
1934	**Miss H H Jacobs**	Miss S Palfrey	6-1, 6-4
1935	**Miss H H Jacobs**	Mrs S P Fabyan	6-1, 6-4
1936	**Miss A Marble**	Miss H H Jacobs	4-6, 6-3, 6-2
1937	**Miss A Lizana**	Miss J Jedrzejowska	6-4, 6-2
1938	**Miss A Marble**	Miss N Wynne	6-0, 6-3
1939	**Miss A Marble**	Miss H H Jacobs	6-0, 8-10, 6-4
1940	**Miss A Marble**	Miss H H Jacobs	6-2, 6-3
1941	**Mrs E T Cooke**	Miss P M Betz	6-1, 6-4
1942	**Miss P M Betz**	Miss A L Brough	4-6, 6-1, 6-4
1943	**Miss P M Betz**	Miss A L Brough	6-3, 5-7, 6-3
1944	**Miss P M Betz**	Miss M E Osborne	6-3, 8-6
1945	**Mrs E T Cooke**	Miss P M Betz	3-6, 8-6, 6-4
1946	**Miss P M Betz**	Miss D J Hart	11-9, 6-3
1947	**Miss A L Brough**	Miss M E Osborne	8-6, 4-6, 6-1
1948	**Mrs W duPont**	Miss A L Brough	4-6, 6-4, 15-13
1949	**Mrs W duPont**	Miss D J Hart	6-4, 6-1
1950	**Mrs W duPont**	Miss D J Hart	6-3, 6-3
1951	**Miss M Connolly**	Miss S J Fry	6-3, 1-6, 6-4
1952	**Miss M Connolly**	Miss D J Hart	6-3, 7-5
1953	**Miss M Connolly**	Miss D J Hart	6-2, 6-4
1954	**Miss D J Hart**	Miss A L Brough	6-8, 6-1, 8-6
1955	**Miss D J Hart**	Miss P E Ward	6-4, 6-2
1956	**Miss S J Fry**	Miss A Gibson	6-3, 6-4
1957	**Miss A Gibson**	Miss A L Brough	6-3, 6-2
1958	**Miss A Gibson**	Miss D R Hard	3-6, 6-1, 6-2
1959	**Miss M Bueno**	Miss C C Truman	6-1, 6-4
1960	**Miss D R Hard**	Miss M E Bueno	6-4, 10-12, 6-4
1961	**Miss D R Hard**	Miss A S Haydon	6-3, 6-4
1962	**Miss M Smith**	Miss D R Hard	9-7, 6-4
1963	**Miss M E Bueno**	Miss M Smith	7-5, 6-4
1964	**Miss M E Bueno**	Mrs C E Graebner	6-1, 6-0
1965	**Miss M Smith**	Miss B J Moffitt	8-6, 7-5

Date	Winners	Runners-up	Score
1966	**Miss M E Bueno**	Miss N Richey	6-3, 6-1
1967	**Mrs L W King**	Mrs P F Jones	11-9, 6-4

Open Championships began

Date	Winners	Runners-up	Score
1968	**Miss S V Wade**	Mrs L W King	6-4, 6-2
1969	**Mrs B M Court**	Miss N Richey	6-2, 6-2
1970	**Mrs B M Court**	Miss R Casals	6-2, 2-6, 6-1
1971	**Mrs L W King**	Miss R Casals	6-4, 7-6
1972	**Mrs L W King**	Miss K Melville	6-3, 7-5
1973	**Mrs B M Court**	Miss E F Goolagong	7-6, 5-7, 6-2
1974	**Mrs L W King**	Miss E Goolagong	3-6, 6-3, 7-5
1975	**Miss C Evert**	Mrs E Cawley	5-7, 6-4, 6-2
1976	**Miss C Evert**	Mrs E Cawley	6-3, 6-0
1977	**Miss C Evert**	Miss W Turnbull	7-6, 6-2

Women's Doubles

Played in Philadelphia, Pennsylvania

Date	Winners	Runners-up	Score
1890	**Miss E C Roosevelt/** **Miss G W Roosevelt**		
1891	**Miss M E Cahill/** **Mrs W F Morgan**		
1892	**Miss M E Cahill/** **Miss A M McKinley**		
1893	**Miss A M Terry/** **Miss H Butler**		
1894	**Miss H R Helwig/** **Miss J P Atkinson**		
1895	**Miss H R Helwig/** **Miss J P Atkinson**		
1896	**Miss E H Moore/** **Miss J P Atkinson**		
1897	**Miss J P Atkinson/** **Miss K Atkinson**		
1898	**Miss J P Atkinson/** **Miss K Atkinson**		
1899	**Miss J W Craven/** **Miss M McAteer**		
1900	**Miss E Parker/** **Miss H Champlin**	Miss M McAteer/ Miss M Weiwer	9-7, 6-2, 6-2
1901	**Miss J P Atkinson/** **Miss M McAteer**		
1902	**Miss J P Atkinson/** **Miss M Jones**		
1903	**Miss E H Moore/** **Miss C B Neely**		
1904	**Miss M G Sutton/** **Miss M Hall**		
1905	**Miss H Homans/** **Miss C B Neely**		
1906	**Mrs L S Coe/** **Mrs D S Platt**		
1907	**Miss M Weiwer/** **Miss C B Neely**	Miss E Wildey/ Miss N Wildey	6-1, 2-6, 6-4
1908	**Miss Evelyn Sears/** **Miss M Curtis**	Miss C B Neely/ Miss M Steever	6-3, 5-7, 9-7
1909	**Miss H V Hotchkiss/** **Miss E E Rotch**		
1910	**Miss H V Hotchkiss/** **Miss E E Rotch**		
1911	**Miss H V Hotchkiss/** **Miss Eleonora Sears**	Miss F Sutton/ Miss D Green	6-4, 4-6, 6-2
1912	**Miss D Green/** **Miss M K Browne**	Mrs M Barger-Wallach Mrs F Schmitz	6-2, 5-7, 6-0
1913	**Miss M K Browne/** **Mrs R H Williams**	Miss E Wildey/ Miss D Green	12-10, 2-6, 6-3
1914	**Miss M K Browne/** **Mrs R H Williams**	Mrs E Raymond/ Miss E Wildey	8-6, 6-2
1915	**Mrs G W Wightman/** **Miss Eleonora Sears**	Mrs M McLean/ Mrs G L Chapman	10-8, 6-2
1916	**Miss M Bjurstedt/** **Miss Eleonora Sears**	Miss E Wildey/ Mrs E Raymond	4-6, 6-2, 10-8

National Patriotic Tournament

Date	Winners	Runners-up	Score
1917	**Miss M Bjurstedt/** **Miss Eleonora Sears**	Mrs R LeRoy/ Miss P Walsh	6-2, 6-4
1918	**Miss M Zinderstein/** **Miss E Goss**	Miss M Bjurstedt/ Mrs J Rogge	7-5, 8-6
1919	**Miss M Zinderstein/** **Miss E Goss**		
1920	**Miss M Zinderstein/** **Miss E Goss**		

Transferred to Forest Hills, New York

Date	Winners	Runners-up	Score
1921	**Miss M K Browne/** **Mrs L Williams**		
1922	**Mrs J B Jessup/** **Miss H Wills**	Mrs M Mallory/ Miss Sigourney	6-4, 7-9, 6-3

Date	Winners	Runners-up	Score
1923	**Miss K McKane/** **Mrs B C Covell**	Mrs G W Wightman/ Miss E Goss	2-6, 6-2, 6-1
1924	**Mrs G W Wightman/** **Miss H Wills**	Miss E Goss/ Mrs J B Jessup	6-4, 6-3
1925	**Miss M K Browne/** **Miss H Wills**	Mrs M Bundy/ Miss E Ryan	6-4, 6-3
1926	**Miss E Ryan/** **Miss E Goss**	Miss M K Browne/ Mrs A H Chapin	3-6, 6-4, 12-10
1927	**Mrs L A Godfree/** **Miss E H Harvey**	Miss J Fry/ Miss B Nuthall	6-1, 4-6, 6-4
1928	**Mrs G W Wightman/** **Miss H Wills**	Miss E Cross/ Mrs L A Harper	6-2, 6-2
1929	**Mrs P Watson/** **Mrs L R C Michell**	Mrs B C Covell/ Mrs D C Shepherd-Barron	2-6, 6-3, 6-4
1930	**Miss B Nuthall/** **Miss S Palfrey**	Miss E Cross/ Mrs L A Harper	3-6, 6-3, 7-5
1931	**Miss B Nuthall/** **Mrs E F Whittingstall**	Miss D E Round/ Miss H H Jacobs	6-2, 6-4
1932	**Miss H H Jacobs/** **Miss S Palfrey**	Mrs Painter/ Miss A Marble	8-6, 6-1
1933	**Miss B Nuthall/** **Miss F James** a bye	Mrs F S Moody/ Miss E Ryan retired	
1934	**Miss H H Jacobs/** **Miss S Palfrey**	Miss C A Babcock/ Mrs D Andrus	4-6, 6-3, 6-4

Transferred to Chestnut Hill, Massachusetts

Date	Winners	Runners-up	Score
1935	**Miss H H Jacobs/** **Mrs S P Fabyan**	Miss C A Babcock/ Mrs D Andrus	6-4, 6-2
1936	**Mrs J Van Ryn/** **Mrs C A Babcock**	Miss H H Jacobs/ Mrs S P Fabyan	9-7, 2-6, 6-4
1937	**Mrs S P Fabyan/** **Miss A Marble**	Miss C A Babcock/ Mrs J Van Ryn	7-5, 6-4
1938	**Mrs S P Fabyan/** **Miss A Marble**	Mrs R Mathieu/ Mrs J Jedrzejowska	6-8, 6-4, 6-3
1939	**Mrs S P Fabyan/** **Miss A Marble**	Miss K E Stammers/ Mrs S H Hammersley	6-4, 8-6
1940	**Mrs S P Fabyan/** **Miss A Marble**		
1941	**Mrs E T Cooke/** **Miss M E Osborne**		

Transferred to Forest Hills, New York

Date	Winners	Runners-up	Score
1942	**Miss A L Brough/** **Miss M E Osborne**		
1943	**Miss A L Brough/** **Miss M E Osborne**		
1944	**Miss A L Brough/** **Miss M E Osborne**	Miss P M Betz/ Miss D J Hart	4-6, 6-4, 6-3
1945	**Miss A L Brough/** **Miss M E Osborne**	Miss P M Betz/ Miss D J Hart	6-4, 6-4

Transferred to Chestnut Hill, Massachusetts

Date	Winners	Runners-up	Score
1946	**Miss A L Brough/** **Miss M E Osborne**	Mrs D Arnold Prentiss/ Mrs P C Todd	6-2, 6-0
1947	**Miss A L Brough/** **Miss M E Osborne**	Miss D J Hart/ Mrs P C Todd	5-7, 6-3, 7-5
1948	**Miss A L Brough/** **Mrs W duPont**	Miss D J Hart/ Mrs P C Todd	6-4, 8-10, 6-1
1949	**Miss A L Brough/** **Mrs W duPont**	Miss D J Hart/ Miss S J Fry	6-4, 8-6
1950	**Miss A L Brough/** **Mrs W duPont**	Miss D J Hart/ Miss S J Fry	6-2, 6-2
1951	**Miss S J Fry/** **Miss D J Hart**	Mrs P C Todd/ Miss N Chaffee	6-4, 6-2
1952	**Miss S J Fry/** **Miss D J Hart**	Miss A L Brough/ Miss M Connolly	10-8, 6-4
1953	**Miss S J Fry/** **Miss D J Hart**	Mrs W duPont/ Miss A L Brough	6-3, 7-9, 9-7
1954	**Miss S J Fry/** **Miss D J Hart**	Mrs W duPont/ Miss A L Brough	6-4, 6-4
1955	**Miss A L Brough/** **Mrs W duPont**	Miss D J Hart/ Miss S J Fry	6-3, 1-6, 6-3
1956	**Miss A L Brough/** **Mrs W duPont**	Miss S J Fry/ Mrs B Pratt	6-3, 6-0
1957	**Miss A L Brough/** **Mrs W duPont**	Miss A Gibson/ Miss D R Hard	6-2, 7-5
1958	**Miss J Arth/** **Miss D R Hard**	Miss A Gibson/ Miss M E Bueno	2-6, 6-3, 6-4
1959	**Miss J Arth/** **Miss D R Hard**	Miss M E Bueno/ Miss S H Moore	6-2, 6-3
1960	**Miss M E Bueno/** **Miss D R Hard**	Miss A S Haydon/ Miss D Catt	6-1, 6-1
1961	**Miss D R Hard/** **Miss L R Turner**	Miss E Buding/ Miss Y Ramirez	6-4, 5-7, 6-0
1962	**Miss M Bueno/** **Miss D R Hard**	Miss B J Moffitt/ Mrs J R Susman	4-6, 6-3, 6-2
1963	**Miss R A Ebbern/** **Miss M Smith**	Miss D R Hard/ Miss M E Bueno	4-6, 10-8, 6-3

Date	Winners	Runners-up	Score
1964	Miss B J Moffitt/	Miss M Smith/	
	Mrs J R Susman	Miss L R Turner	3-6, 6-2, 6-4
1965	Mrs C E Graebner/	Miss B J Moffitt/	
	Miss N Richey	Mrs J R Susman	6-4, 6-4
1966	Miss M E Bueno/	Mrs L W King/	
	Miss N Richey	Miss R Casals	6-3, 6-4
1967	Miss R Casals/	Miss M A Eisel/	
	Mrs L W King	Mrs D Fales	4-6, 6-3, 6-4

Open Championships began at Forest Hills, New York

Date	Winners	Runners-up	Score
1968	Miss M E Bueno/	Miss R Casals/	
	Mrs B M Court	Mrs L W King	4-6, 9-7, 8-6
1969	Miss F Durr/	Mrs B M Court/	
	Miss D R Hard	Miss S V Wade	0-6, 6-3, 6-4
1970	Mrs B M Court/	Miss R Casals/	
	Mrs R D Dalton	Miss S V Wade	6-4, 6-3
1971	Miss R Casals/	Mrs G Chanfreau/	
	Mrs R D Dalton	Miss F Durr	6-3, 6-3
1972	Miss F Durr/	Mrs B M Court/	
	Miss S Stöve	Miss S V Wade	6-3, 1-6, 6-3
1973	Mrs B M Court/	Mrs L W King/	
	Miss S V Wade	Miss R Casals	3-6, 6-3, 7-5
1974	Mrs I W King/	Miss F Durr/	
	Miss R Casals	Miss B Stöve	7-6, 6-7, 6-4
1975	Mrs M Court/	Mrs L W King/	
	Miss V Wade	Miss R Casals	7-5, 2-6, 7-6
1976	Miss L Boshoff/	Miss O Morozova/	
	Miss I Kloss	Miss V Wade	6-1, 6-4
1977	Miss B Stöve/	Miss R Richards/	
	Miss M Navratilova	Miss B Stuart	6-2, 3-6, 6-3

Mixed Doubles

Played in Philadelphia, Pennsylvania

Date	Winners	Runners-up	Score
1892	C Hobart/		
	Miss M E Cahill		
1893	C Hobart/		
	Miss E C Roosevelt		
1894	E P Fischer/		
	Miss J P Atkinson		
1895	Miss E P Fischer/		
	Miss J P Atkinson		
1896	E P Fischer/		
	Miss J P Atkinson		
1897	D L Magruder/		
	Miss L Henson		
1898	E P Fischer/		
	Miss C B Neely		
1899	A L Hoskins/		
	Miss E J Rastall		
1900	A Codman/	G Atkinson/	
	Miss M J Hunnewell	Miss Shaw	11-9, 6-3, 6-1
1901	R D Little/		
	Miss M Jones		
1902	W C Grant/		
	Miss E H Moore		
1903	E F Allen/		
	Miss H Chapman		
1904	W Grant/		
	Miss E H Moore		
1905	C Hobart/		
	Mrs C Hobart		
1906	E B Dewhurst/		
	Miss S Coffin		
1907	W F Johnson/		
	Miss M Sayres		
1908	N W Niles/	R D Little/	
	Miss E E Rotch	Miss L Hammond	6-4, 4-6, 6-4
1909	W F Johnson/		
	Miss H V Hotchkiss		
1910	J R Carpenter/		
	Miss H V Hotchkiss		
1911	W F Johnson/	H M Tilden/	
	Miss H V Hotchkiss	Miss E Wildey	6-4, 6-4
1912	R N Williams/	W J Clothier/	
	Miss M K Browne	Miss Eleonora Sears	6-4, 2-6, 11-9
1913	W T Tilden/	C S Rogers/	
	Miss M K Browne	Miss D Green	7-5, 7-5
1914	W T Tilden/	J R Rowland/	
	Miss M K Browne	Miss M Myers	6-1, 6-4
1915	H C Johnson/	I C Wright/	
	Mrs G W Wightman	Miss M Bjurstedt	6-0, 6-1
1916	W E Davis/	W T Tilden/	
	Miss Eleonora Sears	Miss F A Ballin	6-4, 7-5

National Patriotic Tournament

Date	Winners	Runners-up	Score
1917	I C Wright/	W T Tilden/	
	Miss M Bjurstedt	Miss F A Ballin	10-12, 6-1, 6-3
1918	I C Wright/	F B Alexander/	
	Mrs G W Wightman	Miss M Bjurstedt	6-2, 6-4

Date	Winners	Runners-up	Score
1919	V Richards/	W T Tilden/	
	Miss M Zinderstein	Miss F A Ballin	
1920	W F Johnson/		
	Mrs G W Wightman		

Transferred to Chestnut Hill, Massachusetts

Date	Winners	Runners-up	Score
1921	W M Johnston/		
	Miss M K Browne		
1922	W T Tilden/	H O Kinsey/	
	Mrs M Mallory	Miss H Wills	6-4, 6-3
1923	W T Tilden/	J B Hawkes/	
	Mrs M Mallory	Miss K McKane	6-3, 2-6, 10-8
1924	V Richards/	W T Tilden/	
	Miss H Wills	Mrs M Mallory	6-8, 7-5, 6-0
1925	J B Hawkes/	V Richards/	
	Miss K McKane	Miss E H Harvey	6-2, 6-4
1926	J Borotra/	R Lacoste/	
	Miss E Ryan	Mrs G W Wightman	6-4, 7-5
1927	H Cochet/	R Lacoste/	
	Miss E Bennett	Mrs G W Wightman	2-6, 6-0, 6-2
1928	J B Hawkes/	E F Moon/	
	Miss H Wills	Miss E Cross	6-1, 6-3
1929	G M Lott/	H W Austin/	
	Miss B Nuthall	Mrs B C Covell	6-3, 6-3
1930	W L Allison/	F X Shields/	
	Miss E Cross	Miss M Morrill	6-4, 6-4
1931	G M Lott/	W L Allison/	
	Miss B Nuthall	Mrs L A Harper	6-3, 6-3
1932	F J Perry/	H E Vines/	
	Miss S Palfrey	Miss H H Jacobs	6-3, 7-5
1933	H E Vines/	G M Lott/	
	Miss E Ryan	Miss S Palfrey	11-9, 6-1

Transferred to Philadelphia, Pennsylvania

Date	Winners	Runners-up	Score
1934	G M Lott/	L R Stoefen/	
	Miss H H Jacobs	Miss E Ryan	4-6, 13-11, 6-2

Transferred to Chestnut Hill, Massacutsetts

Date	Winners	Runners-up	Score
1935	E Maier/	R Menzel/	
	Mrs S P Fabyan	Miss K E Stammers	6-3, 3-6, 6-4
1936	C G Mako/	J D Budge/	
	Miss A Marble	Mrs S P Fabyan	6-3, 6-2
1937	J D Budge/	Y Petra/	
	Mrs S P Fabyan	Mrs S Henrotin	6-2, 8-10, 6-0
1938	J D Budge/	J E Bromwich/	
	Miss A Marble	Miss T Coyne	6-1, 6-2
1939	H C Hopman/		
	Miss A Marble		
1940	R L Riggs/		
	Miss A Marble		
1941	J A Kramer/		
	Mrs E T Cooke		

Transferred to Forest Hills, New York

Date	Winners	Runners-up	Score
1942	F R Schroeder/		
	Miss A L Brough		
1943	W F Talbert/		
	Miss M E Osborne		
1944	W F Talbert/	W D McNeill/	
	Miss M E Osborne	Miss D M Bundy	6-2, 6-3
1945	W F Talbert/	R Falkenburg/	
	Miss M E Osborne	Miss D J Hart	6-4, 6-4
1946	W F Talbert/	R Kimbell/	
	Miss M E Osborne	Miss A L Brough	6-3, 6-4
1947	J E Bromwich/	F Segura/	
	Miss A L Brough	Miss G Moran	6-3, 6-1
1948	T Brown/	W F Talbert/	
	Miss A L Brough	Mrs W duPont	6-4, 6-4
1949	E W Sturgess/	W F Talbert/	
	Miss A L Brough	Mrs W duPont	4-6, 6-3, 7-5
1950	K McGregor/	F A Sedgman/	
	Mrs W duPont	Miss D J Hart	6-4, 3-6, 6-3
1951	F A Sedgman/	M G Rose/	
	Miss D J Hart	Miss S J Fry	6-3, 6-2
1952	F A Sedgman/	L A Hoad/	
	Miss D J Hart	Mrs T D Long	6-3, 7-5
1953	E V Seixas/	R N Hartwig/	
	Miss D J Hart	Miss J A Sampson	6-2, 4-6, 6-4
1954	E V Seixas/	K R Rosewall/	
	Miss D J Hart	Mrs W duPont	4-6, 6-1, 6-1
1955	E V Seixas/	G Mulloy/	
	Miss D J Hart	Miss S J Fry	7-5, 5-7, 6-2
1956	K R Rosewall/	L A Hoad/	
	Mrs W duPont	Miss D R Hard	9-7, 6-1
1957	K Neilson/	R N Howe/	
	Miss A Gibson	Miss D R Hard	6-3, 9-7
1958	N A Fraser/	A Olmedo/	
	Mrs W duPont	Miss M E Bueno	6-4, 3-6, 9-7
1959	N A Fraser/	R Mark/	
	Mrs W duPont	Miss J Hopps	7-5, 13-15, 6-2

Date	Winners	Runners-up	Score
1960	N A Fraser/	A Palafox/	
	Mrs W duPont	Miss M E Bueno	6-3, 6-2
1961	R Mark/	R D Ralston/	
	Miss M Smith	Miss D R Hard	wo
1962	F S Stolle/	F R Froehling/	
	Miss M Smith	Miss L R Turner	7-5, 6-2
1963	K N Fletcher/	E Rubinoff/	
	Miss M Smith	Miss J A M Tegart	3-6, 8-6, 6-2
1964	J D Newcombe/	E Rubinoff/	
	Miss M Smith	Miss J A M Tegart	10-8, 4-6, 6-3
1965	F S Stolle/	F R Froehling/	
	Miss M Smith	Miss J A M Tegart	6-2, 6-2
1966	O K Davidson/	E Rubinoff/	
	Mrs D Fales	Miss C Aucamp	6-3, 6-1
1967	O K Davidson/	S R Smith/	
	Mrs L W King	Miss R Casals	

Open Championships began

Date	Winners	Runners-up	Score
1968	*No Competition*		
1969	M C Riessen/	R D Ralston/	
	Mrs B M Court	Miss F Durr	7-5, 6-3
1970	M C Riessen/	F D McMillan/	
	Mrs B M Court	Mrs R D Dalton	6-4, 6-4
1971	O K Davidson/	R Maud/	
	Mrs L W King	Miss B Stöve	6-3, 7-5
1972	M C Riessen/	1 Nåstase/	
	Mrs B M Court	Miss R Casals	6-3, 7-5
1973	O K Davidson/	M C Riessen/	
	Mrs L W King	Mrs B M Court	6-4, 3-6, 7-5
1974	G Masters/	J Connors/	
	Miss P Teeguarden	Miss C Evert	6-1, 7-6
1975	R Stockton/	F Stolle/	
	Miss R Casals	Mrs L W King	6-3, 6-7, 6-3
1976	P Dent/	F McMillan/	
	Mrs L W King	Miss B Stöve	3-6, 6-2, 7-5
1977	F McMillan/	V Gerulaitis/	
	Miss B Stöve	Mrs L W King	6-2, 3-6, 6-3

WIGHTMAN CUP

1923	**United States**	Great Britain	7-0
1924	**Great Britain**	United States	6-1
1925	**Great Britain**	United States	4-3
1926	**United States**	Great Britain	4-3
1927	**United States**	Great Britain	5-2
1928	**Great Britain**	United States	4-3
1929	**United States**	Great Britain	4-3
1930	**Great Britain**	United States	4-3
1931	**United States**	Great Britain	5-2
1932	**United States**	Great Britain	4-3
1933	**United States**	Great Britain	4-3
1934	**United States**	Great Britain	5-2
1935	**United States**	Great Britain	4-3
1936	**United States**	Great Britain	4-3
1937	**United States**	Great Britain	5-1
1938	**United States**	Great Britain	5-2
1939	**United States**	Great Britain	5-2
1940-5	*No Competition*		
1946	**United States**	Great Britain	7-0
1947	**United States**	Great Britain	7-0
1948	**United States**	Great Britain	6-1
1949	**United States**	Great Britain	7-0
1950	**United States**	Great Britain	7-0
1951	**United States**	Great Britain	6-1
1952	**United States**	Great Britain	7-0
1953	**United States**	Great Britain	7-0
1954	**United States**	Great Britain	6-0
1955	**United States**	Great Britain	6-1
1956	**United States**	Great Britain	5-2
1957	**United States**	Great Britain	6-1
1958	**Great Britain**	United States	4-3
1959	**United States**	Great Britain	4-3
1960	**Great Britain**	United States	4-3
1961	**United States**	Great Britain	6-1
1962	**United States**	Great Britain	4-3
1963	**United States**	Great Britain	6-1
1964	**United States**	Great Britain	5-2
1965	**United States**	Great Britain	5-2
1966	**United States**	Great Britain	4-3
1967	**United States**	Great Britain	6-1
1968	**Great Britain**	United States	4-3
1969	**United States**	Great Britain	5-2
1970	**United States**	Great Britain	4-3
1971	**United States**	Great Britain	4-3
1972	**United States**	Great Britain	5-2
1973	**United States**	Great Britain	5-2
1974	**Great Britain**	United States	6-1
1975	**Great Britain**	United States	5-3
1976	**United States**	Great Britain	5-2
1977	**United States**	Great Britain	7-0

WIMBLEDON CHAMPIONSHIPS
CHALLENGE ROUND

Men's Singles

Date	Winners	Runners-up	Score
1877	S W Gore	W C Marshall	6-1, 6-2, 6-4
1878	P F Hadow	S W Gore	7-5, 6-1, 9-7
1879	J T Hartley	P F Hadow	
	a bye	retired	
1880	J T Hartley	H F Lawford	6-0, 6-2, 2-6, 6-3
1881	W Renshaw	J T Hartley	6-0, 6-2, 6-1
1882	W Renshaw	E Renshaw	6-1, 2-6, 4-6, 6-2, 6-2
1883	W Renshaw	E Renshaw	2-6, 6-3, 6-3, 4-6. 6-3
1884	W Renshaw	H F Lawford	6-0, 6-4, 9-7
1885	W Renshaw	H F Lawford	7-5, 6-2, 4-6, 7-5
1886	W Renshaw	H F Lawford	6-0, 5-7, 6-3, 6-4
1887	H F Lawford	W Renshaw	
	a bye	retired	
1888	E Renshaw	H F Lawford	6-3, 7-5, 6-0
1889	W Renshaw	E Renshaw	6-4, 6-1 3-6, 6-0
1890	W J Hamilton	W Renshaw	6-8, 6-2, 3-6, 6-1, 6-1
1891	W Baddeley	W J Hamilton	
	a bye	retired	
1892	W Baddeley	J Pim	4-6, 6-3, 6-3, 6-2
1893	J Pim	W Baddeley	3-6, 6-1, 6-3, 6-2
1894	J Pim	W Baddeley	10-8, 6-2, 8-6
1895	W Baddeley	J Pim	
	a bye	retired	
1896	H S Mahony	W Baddeley	6-2, 6-8, 5-7, 8-6, 6-3
1897	R F Doherty	H S Mahony	6-4, 6-4, 6-3
1898	R F Doherty	H L Doherty	6-3, 6-3, 2-6, 5-7, 6-1
1899	R F Doherty	A W Gore	1-6, 4-6, 6-2, 6-3, 6-3
1900	R F Doherty	S H Smith	6-8, 6-3, 6-1, 6-2
1901	A W Gore	R F Doherty	4-6, 7-5, 6-4, 6-4
1902	H L Doherty	A W Gore	6-4, 6-3, 3-6, 6-0
1903	H L Doherty	F L Riseley	7-5, 6-3, 6-0
1904	H L Doherty	F L Riseley	6-1, 7-5, 8-6
1905	H L Doherty	N E Brookes	8-6, 6-2, 6-4
1906	H L Doherty	F L Riseley	6-4, 4-6, 6-2, 6-3
1907	N E Brookes	H L Doherty	
	a bye	retired	
1908	A W Gore	N E Brookes	
	a bye	retired	
1909	A W Gore	M J G Ritchie	6-8, 1-6, 6-2, 6-2, 6-2
1910	A F Wilding	A W Gore	6-4, 7-5, 4-6, 6-2
1911	A F Wilding	H Roper-Barrett	6-4, 4-6, 2-6, 6-2, retired
1912	A F Wilding	A W Gore	6-4, 6-4, 4-6, 6-4
1913	A F Wilding	M E McLoughlin	8-6, 6-3, 10-8
1914	N E Brookes	A F Wilding	6-4, 6-4, 7-5
1915-18	*No Competition*		
1919	G L Patterson	N E Brookes	6-3, 7-5, 6-2
1920	W T Tilden	G L Patterson	2-6, 6-3, 6-2, 6-4
1921	W T Tilden	B I C Norton	4-6, 2-6, 6-1, 6-0, 7-5

Challenge Round abolished; subsequently holders played through

Date	Winners	Runners-up	Score
1922	G L Patterson	R Lycett	6-3, 6-4, 6-2
1923	W M Johnston	F T Hunter	6-0, 6-3, 6-1
1924	J Borotra	R Lacoste	6-1, 3-6, 6-1, 3-6, 6-4
1925	R Lacoste	J Borotra	6-3, 6-3, 4-6, 8-6
1926	J Borotra	H O Kinsey	8-6, 6-1, 6-3
1927	H Cochet	J Borotra	4-6, 4-6, 6-3, 6-4, 7-5
1928	R Lacoste	H Cochet	6-1, 4-6, 6-4, 6-2
1929	H Cochet	J Borotra	6-4, 6-3, 6-4
1930	W T Tilden	W L Allison	6-3, 9-7, 6-4
1931	S B Wood	F X Shields	
	(wo)		
1932	H E Vines	H W Austin	6-4, 6-2, 6-0
1933	J H Crawford	H E Vines	4-6, 11-9, 6-2, 2-6, 6-4
1934	F J Perry	J H Crawford	6-3, 6-0, 7-5
1935	F J Perry	G von Cramm	6-2, 6-4, 6-4
1936	F J Perry	G von Cramm	6-1, 6-1, 6-0
1937	J D Budge	G von Cramm	6-3, 6-4, 6-2
1938	J D Budge	H W Austin	6-1, 6-0, 6-3
1939	R L Riggs	E T Cooke	2-6, 8-6, 3-6, 6-3, 6-2
1940-5	*No Competition*		
1946	Y Petra	G E Brown	6-2, 6-4, 7-9, 5-7, 6-4
1947	J A Kramer	T Brown	6-1, 6-3, 6-2
1948	R Falkenburg	J E Bromwich	7-5, 0-6, 6-2, 3-6, 7-5
1949	F Schroeder	J Drobný	3-6, 6-0, 6-3, 4-6, 6-4
1950	J E Patty	F A Sedgman	6-1, 8-10, 6-2, 6-3
1951	R Savitt	K McGregor	6-4, 6-4, 6-4
1952	F A Sedgman	J Drobný	4-6, 6-2, 6-3, 6-2
1953	E V Seixas	K Nielsen	9-7, 6-3, 6-4
1954	J R Drobný	K R Rosewall	13-11, 4-6, 6-2, 9-7
1955	M A Trabert	K Nielsen	6-3, 7-5, 6-1
1956	L A Hoad	K R Rosewall	6-2, 4-6, 7-5, 6-4
1957	L A Hoad	A J Cooper	6-2, 6-1, 6-2
1958	A J Cooper	N A Fraser	3-6, 6-3, 6-4, 13-11
1959	A Olmedo	R G Laver	6-4, 6-3, 6-4
1960	N A Fraser	R G Laver	6-4, 3-6, 9-7, 7-5
1961	R G Laver	C R McKinley	6-3, 6-1, 6-4
1962	R G Laver	M F Mulligan	6-2, 6-2, 6-1

Date	Winners	Runners-up	Score
1963	**C R McKinley**	F S Stolle	9-7, 6-1, 6-4
1964	**R S Emerson**	F S Stolle	6-4, 12-10, 4-6, 6-3
1965	**R S Emerson**	F S Stolle	6-2, 6-4, 6-4
1966	**M Santana**	R D Ralston	6-4, 11-9, 6-4
1967	**J D Newcombe**	W P Bungert	6-3, 6-1, 6-1

Open championships began

Date	Winners	Runners-up	Score
1968	**R G Laver**	A D Roche	6-3, 6-4, 6-2
1969	**R G Laver**	J D Newcombe	6-4, 5-7, 6-4, 6-4
1970	**J D Newcombe**	K R Rosewall	5-7, 6-3, 6-2, 3-6, 6-1
1971	**J D Newcombe**	S R Smith	6-3, 5-7, 2-6, 6-4, 6-4
1972	**S R Smith**	I Năstase	4-6, 6-3, 6-3, 4-6, 7-5
1973	**J Kodeš**	A Metreveli	6-1, 9-8, 6-3
1974	**J Connors**	K Rosewall	6-1, 6-1, 6-4
1975	**A Ashe**	J Connors	6-1, 6-1, 5-7, 6-4
1976	**B Borg**	I Năstase	6-4, 6-2, 9-7
1977	**B Borg**	J Connors	3-6, 6-2, 6-1, 5-7, 6-4
1978	**B Borg**	J Connors	6-2, 6-2, 6-3

Men's Doubles

Founded by Oxford University

Date	Winners	Runners-up	Score
1879	**L R Erskine/**	F Durant/	
	H F Lawford	G E Tabor	
1880	**W Renshaw/**	O E Woodhouse/	
	E Renshaw	C J Cole	
1881	**W Renshaw/**	W J Down/	
	E Renshaw	H Vaughan	
1882	**J T Hartley/**	J G Horn/	
	R T Richardson	C B Russell	
1883	**C W Grinstead/**	C B Russell/	
	C E Welldon	R T Milford	

Transferred from Oxford to Wimbledon

Date	Winners	Runners-up	Score
1884	**W Renshaw/**	E W Lewis/	
	E Renshaw	E L Williams	6-3, 3-6, 6-1, 1-6, 6-4
1885	**W Renshaw/**	C E Farrar/	
	E Renshaw	A J Stanley	6-3, 6-3, 10-8

Challenge Round introduced

Date	Winners	Runners-up	Score
1886	**W Renshaw/**	C E Farrar/	
	E Renshaw	A J Stanley	6-3, 6-3, 4-6, 7-5
1887	**H W W Wilberforce/**	W Renshaw/	
	P B Lyon a bye	E Renshaw retired	
1888	**W Renshaw/**	H W W Wilberforce/	
	E Renshaw	P B Lyon	2-6, 1-6, 6-3, 6-4, 6-3
1889	**W Renshaw/**	E W Lewis/	
	E Renshaw	G W Hillyard	6-4, 6-4, 3-6, 0-6, 6-1
1890	**J Pim/**	W Renshaw/	
	F O Stoker a bye	E Renshaw retired	
1891	**W Baddeley/**	J Pim/	
	H Baddeley	F O Stoker	6-1, 6-3, 1-6, 6-2
1892	**E W Lewis/**	W Baddeley/	
	H S Barlow	H Baddeley	4-6, 6-2, 8-6, 6-4
1893	**J Pin/**	E W Lewis/	
	F O Stoker	H S Barlow	4-6, 6-3, 6-1, 2-6, 6-0
1894	**H Baddeley/**	J Pim/	
	W Baddeley a bye	F O Stoker retired	
1895	**W Baddeley/**	E W Lewis/	
	H Baddeley	W V Eaves	8-6, 5-7, 6-4, 6-3
1896	**W Baddeley/**	R F Doherty/	
	H Baddeley	H A Nisbet	1-6, 3-6, 6-4, 6-2, 6-1
1897	**R F Doherty/**	W Baddeley/	
	H L Doherty	H Baddeley	6-4, 4-6, 8-6, 6-4
1898	**R F Doherty/**	H A Nisbet/	
	H L Doherty	C Hobart	6-4, 6-4, 6-2
1899	**R F Doherty/**	H A Nisbet/	
	H L Doherty	C Hobart	7-5, 6-0, 6-2
1900	**R F Doherty/**	H Roper-Barrett/	
	H L Doherty	H A Nisbet	9-7, 7-5, 4-6, 3-6, 6-3
1901	**R F Doherty/**	D F Davis/	
	H L Doherty	H Ward	4-6, 6-2, 6-3, 9-7
1902	**S H Smith/**	R F Doherty/	
	F L Riseley	H L Doherty	4-6, 8-6, 6-3, 4-6, 11-9
1903	**R F Doherty/**	S H Smith/	
	H L Doherty	F L Riseley	6-4, 6-4, 6-4
1904	**R F Doherty/**	S H Smith/	
	H L Doherty	F L Riseley	6-1, 6-2, 6-4
1905	**R F Doherty/**	S H Smith/	
	H L Doherty	F L Riseley	6-2, 6-4, 6-8, 6-3
1906	**S H Smith/**	R F Doherty/	
	F L Riseley	H L Doherty	6-8, 6-4, 5-7, 6-3, 6-3
1907	**N E Brookes/**	S H Smith/	
	A F Wilding a bye	F L Riseley retired	
1908	**A F Wilding/**	N E Brookes/	
	M J G Ritchie a bye	A F Wilding retired	
1909	**A W Gore/**	M J G Ritchie/	
	H Roper-Barrett a bye	A F Wilding retired	

Date	Winners	Runners-up	Score
1910	**A F Wilding/**	A W Gore/	
	M J G Ritchie	H Roper-Barrett	6-1, 6-1, 6-2
1911	**A H Gobert/**	M J G Ritchie/	
	M Decugis	A F Wilding	9-7, 5-7, 6-3, 2-6, 6-2
1912	**H Roper-Barrett/**	A H Gobert/	
	C P Dixon	M Decugis	3-6, 6-3, 6-4, 7-5
1913	**H Roper-Barrett/**	F W Rahe/	
	C P Dixon	H Kleinschroth	6-2, 6-4, 4-6, 6-2
1914	**N E Brookes/**	H Roper-Barrett/	
	A F Wilding	C P Dixon	6-1, 6-1, 5-7, 8-6
1915–18	*No Competition*		
1919	**R V Thomas/**		
	P O'Hara Wood wo		
1920	**R N Williams/**	R V Thomas/	
	C S Garland a bye	P O'Hara Wood retired	
1921	**R Lycett/**	R N Williams/	
	M Woosnam a bye	C S Garland retired	

Challenge Round abolished; subsequently holders played through

Date	Winners	Runners-up	Score
1922	**J O Anderson/**	G L Patterson/	
	R Lycett	P O'Hara Wood	3-6, 7-9, 6-4, 6-3, 11-9
1923	**R Lycett/**	Count de Gomar/	
	L A Godfree	E Flaquer	6-3, 6-4, 3-6, 6-3
1924	**V Richards/**	R N Williams/	
	F T Hunter	W M Washburn	6-3, 3-6, 8-10, 8-6, 6-3
1925	**R Lacoste/**	J Hennessey/	
	J Borotra	R Casey	6-4, 11-9, 4-6, 1-6, 6-3
1926	**H Cochet/**	V Richards/	
	J Brugnon	H O Kinsey	7-5, 4-6, 6-3, 6-2
1927	**F T Hunter/**	J Brugnon/	
	W T Tilden	H Cochet	1-6, 4-6, 8-6, 6-3, 6-4
1928	**H Cochet/**	G L Patterson/	
	J Brugnon	J B Hawkes	13-11, 6-4, 6-4
1929	**W L Allison/**	J C Gregory/	
	J Van Ryn	I G Collins	6-4, 5-7, 6-3, 10-12, 6-4
1930	**W L Allison/**	J H Doeg/	
	J Van Ryn	G M Lott	6-3, 6-3, 6-2
1931	**G M Lott/**	H Cochet/	
	J Van Ryn	J Brugnon	6-2, 10-8, 9-11, 3-6, 6-3
1932	**J Borotra/**	G P Hughes/	
	J Brugnon	F J Perry	6-0, 4-6, 3-6, 7-5, 7-5
1933	**J Borotra/**	R Nunoi/	
	J Brugnon	J Sato	4-6, 6-3, 6-3, 7-5
1934	**G M Lott/**	J Borotra/	
	L R Stoefen	J Brugnon	6-2, 6-3, 6-4
1935	**J H Crawford/**	W L Allison/	
	A K Quist	J Van Ryn	6-3, 5-7, 6-2, 5-7, 7-5
1936	**G P Hughes/**	C E Hare/	
	C R D Tuckey	F H D Wilde	6-4, 3-6, 7-9, 6-1, 6-4
1937	**J D Budge/**	G P Hughes/	
	C G Mako	C R D Tuckey	6-0, 6-4, 6-8, 6-1
1938	**J D Budge/**	H Henkel/	
	C G Mako	G von Metaxa	6-4, 3-6, 6-3, 8-6
1939	**E T Cooke/**	C E Hare/	
	R L Riggs	F H D Wilde	6-3, 3-6, 6-3, 9-7
1940–5	*No Competition*		
1946	**T Brown/**	G E Brown/	
	J A Kramer	D Pails	6-4, 6-4, 6-2
1947	**R Falkenburg/**	A J Mottram/	
	J A Kramer	O W Sidwell	8-6, 6-3, 6-3
1948	**J E Bromwich/**	T Brown/	
	F A Sedgman	G Mulloy	5-7, 7-5, 7-5, 9-7
1949	**R P Gonzalez/**	G Mulloy/	
	F A Parker	F R Schroeder	6-4, 6-4, 6-2
1950	**J E Bromwich/**	G E Brown/	
	A K Quist	O W Sidwell	7-5, 3-6, 6-3, 3-6, 6-2
1951	**K McGregor/**	J Drobný/	
	F A Sedgman	E W Sturgess	3-6, 6-2, 6-3, 3-6, 6-3
1952	**K McGregor/**	E V Seixas/	
	F A Sedgman	E W Sturgess	6-3, 7-5, 6-4
1953	**L A Hoad/**	R N Hartwig/	
	K R Rosewall	M G Rose	6-4, 7-5, 4-6, 7-5
1954	**R N Hartwig/**	E V Seixas/	
	M G Rose	M A Trabert	6-4, 6-4, 3-6, 6-4
1955	**R N Hartwig/**	N A Fraser/	
	L A Hoad	K R Rosewall	7-5, 6-4, 6-3
1956	**L A Hoad/**	N Pietrangeli/	
	K R Rosewall	O Sirola	7-5, 6-2, 6-1
1957	**G Mulloy/**	N A Fraser/	
	J E Patty	L A Hoad	8-10, 6-4, 6-4, 6-4
1958	**S Davidson/**	A J Cooper/	
	U Schmidt	N A Fraser	6-4, 6-4, 8-6
1959	**R Emerson/**	R G Laver/	
	N A Fraser	R Mark	8-6, 6-3, 14-16, 9-7
1960	**R H Osuna/**	M G Davis/	
	R D Ralston	R K Wilson	7-5, 6-3, 10-8
1961	**R Emerson/**	R A J Hewitt/	
	N A Fraser	F S Stolle	6-4, 6-8, 6-4, 6-8, 8-6

Date	Winners	Runners-up	Score
1962	R A J Hewitt/ F S Stolle	B Jovanovic/ N Pilić	6-2, 5-7, 6-2, 6-4
1963	R H Osuna/ A Palafox	J C Barclay/ P Darmon	4-6, 6-2, 6-2, 6-2
1964	R A J Hewitt/ F S Stolle	R Emerson/ K N Fletcher	7-5, 11-9, 6-4
1965	J D Newcombe/ A D Roche	K N Fletcher/ R A J Hewitt	7-5, 6-3, 6-4
1966	K N Fletcher/ J D Newcombe	W W Bowrey/ O K Davidson	6-3, 6-4, 3-6, 6-3
1967	R A J Hewitt/ F D McMillan	R Emerson/ K N Fletcher	6-2, 6-3, 6-4

Open Championships began

Date	Winners	Runners-up	Score
1968	J D Newcombe/ A D Roche	K R Rosewall/ F S Stolle	3-6, 8-6, 5-7, 14-12, 6-3
1969	J D Newcombe/ A D Roche	T S Okker/ M C Riessen	7-5, 11-9, 6-3
1970	J D Newcombe/ A D Roche	K R Rosewall/ F S Stolle	10-8, 6-3, 6-1
1971	R S Emerson/ R G Laver	A R Ashe/ R D Ralston	4-6, 9-7, 6-8, 6-4, 6-4
1972	R A J Hewitt/ F D McMillan	S R Smith/ E J Van Dillen	6-2, 6-2, 9-7
1973	J S Connors/ I Năstase	J R Cooper/ N A Fraser	3-6, 6-3, 6-4, 8-9, 6-1
1974	J Newcombe/ A Roche	R Lutz/ S Smith	8-6, 6-4, 6-4
1975	V Gerulaitis/ A Mayer	C Dowdeswell/ A Stone	7-5, 8-6, 6-4
1976	B Gottfried/ R Ramirez	R Case/ G Masters	3-6, 6-3, 8-6, 2-6, 7-5
1977	R Case/ G Masters	J Alexander/ P Dent	6-3, 6-4, 3-6, 8-9, 6-4
1978	R A Hewitt/ F D McMillan	P Fleming/ J P McEnroe	6-1, 6-4, 6-2

Women's Singles

Date	Winners	Runners-up	Score
1884	Miss M Watson	Miss L Watson	6-8, 6-3, 6-3
1885	Miss M Watson	Miss Bingley	6-1, 7-5

Challenge Round introduced

Date	Winners	Runners-up	Score
1886	Miss B Bingley	Miss M Watson	6-3, 6-3
1887	Miss L Dod	Miss B Bingley	6-2, 6-0
1888	Miss L Dod	Mrs G W Hillyard	6-3, 6-3
1889	Mrs G W Hillyard a bye	Miss L Dod retired	
1890	Miss L Rice a bye	Mrs G W Hillyard retired	
1891	Miss L Dod a bye	Miss L Rice retired	
1892	Miss L Dod	Mrs G W Hillyard	6-1, 6-1
1893	Miss L Dod	Mrs G W Hillyard	6-8, 6-1, 6-4
1894	Mrs G W Hillyard a bye	Miss L Dod retired	
1895	Miss C Cooper a bye	Mrs G W Hillyard retired	
1896	Miss C Cooper	Mrs Pickering	6-2, 6-3
1897	Mrs G W Hillyard	Miss C Cooper	5-7, 7-5, 6-2
1898	Miss C Cooper a bye	Mrs G W Hillyard retired	
1899	Mrs G W Hillyard	Miss C Cooper	6-2, 6-3
1900	Mrs G W Hillyard	Miss C Cooper	4-6, 6-4, 6-4
1901	Mrs A Sterry	Mrs G W Hillyard	6-2, 6-2
1902	Miss M E Robb	Mrs A Sterry	7-5, 6-1, [match replayed after overnight score of 4-6, 13-11]
1903	Miss D K Douglass a Bye	Miss M E Robb retired	
1904	Miss D K Douglass	Mrs A Sterry	6-0, 6-3
1905	Miss M G Sutton	Miss D K Douglass	6-3, 6-4
1906	Miss D K Douglass	Miss M G Sutton	6-3, 9-7
1907	Miss M G Sutton	Mrs Lambert Chambers	6-1, 6-4
1908	Mrs A Sterry a bye	Miss M G Sutton retired	
1909	Miss D P Boothby a bye	Mrs A Sterry retired	
1910	Mrs Lambert Chambers	Miss D P Boothby	6-2, 6-2
1911	Mrs Lambert Chambers	Miss D P Boothby	6-0, 6-0
1912	Mrs D R Larcombe a bye	Mrs Lambert Chambers retired	
1913	Mrs Lambert Chambers a bye	Mrs D R Larcombe retired	
1914	Mrs Lambert Chambers	Mrs D R Larcombe	7-5, 6-4
1915–18	No Competition		
1919	Miss S Lenglen	Mrs Lambert Chambers	10-8, 4-6, 9-7
1920	Miss S Lenglen	Mrs Lambert Chambers	6-3, 6-0
1921	Miss S Lenglen	Miss E Ryan	6-2, 6-0

Challenge Round abolished

Date	Winners	Runners-up	Score
1922	Miss S Lenglen	Mrs M Mallory	6-2, 6-0
1923	Miss S Lenglen	Miss K McKane	6-2, 6-2
1924	Miss K McKane	Miss H Wills	4-6, 6-4, 6-4
1925	Miss S Lenglen	Miss J Fry	6-2, 6-0
1926	Mrs L A Godfree	Miss L de Alvarez	6-2, 4-6, 6-3
1927	Miss H Wills	Miss L de Alvarez	6-2, 6-4
1928	Miss H Wills	Miss L de Alvarez	6-2, 6-3
1929	Miss H Wills	Miss H H Jacobs	6-1, 6-2
1930	Mrs F S Moody	Miss E Ryan	6-2, 6-2
1931	Miss C Aussem	Miss H Krahwinkel	6-2, 7-5
1932	Mrs F S Moody	Miss H H Jacobs	6-3, 6-1
1933	Mrs F S Moody	Miss D E Round	6-4, 6-8, 6-3
1934	Miss D E Round	Miss H H Jacobs	6-2, 5-7, 6-3
1935	Mrs F S Moody	Miss H H Jacobs	6-3, 3-6, 7-5
1936	Miss H H Jacobs	Mrs S Sperling	6-2, 4-6, 7-5
1937	Miss D E Round	Miss J Jedrzejowska	6-2, 2-6, 7-5
1938	Mrs F S Moody	Miss H H Jacobs	6-4, 6-0
1939	Miss A Marble	Miss K E Stammers	6-2, 6-0
1940–5	No Competition		
1946	Miss P M Betz	Miss A L Brough	6-2, 6-4
1947	Miss M E Osborne	Miss D J Hart	6-2, 6-4
1948	Miss A L Brough	Miss D J Hart	6-3, 8-6
1949	Miss A L Brough	Mrs W duPont	10-8, 1-6, 10-8
1950	Miss A L Brough	Mrs W duPont	6-1, 3-6, 6-1
1951	Miss D J Hart	Miss S J Fry	6-1, 6-0
1952	Miss M Connolly	Miss A L Brough	7-5, 6-3
1953	Miss M Connolly	Miss D J Hart	8-6, 7-5
1954	Miss M Connolly	Miss A L Brough	6-2, 7-5
1955	Miss A L Brough	Mrs J G Fleitz	7-5, 8-6
1956	Miss S J Fry	Miss A Buxton	6-3, 6-1
1957	Miss A Gibson	Miss D R Hard	6-3, 6-2
1958	Miss A Gibson	Miss A Mortimer	8-6, 6-2
1959	Miss M E Bueno	Miss D R Hard	6-4, 6-3
1960	Miss M E Bueno	Miss S Reynolds	8-6, 6-0
1961	Miss A Mortimer	Miss C C Truman	4-6, 6-4, 7-5
1962	Mrs J R Susman	Mrs V Sukova	6-4, 6-4
1963	Miss M Smith	Miss B J Moffitt	6-3, 6-4
1964	Miss M E Bueno	Miss M Smith	6-4, 7-9, 6-3
1965	Miss M Smith	Miss M E Bueno	6-4, 7-5
1966	Mrs L W King	Miss M E Bueno	6-3, 3-6, 6-1
1967	Mrs L W King	Mrs P F Jones	6-3, 6-4

Open Championships began

Date	Winners	Runners-up	Score
1968	Mrs L W King	Miss J A M Tegart	9-7, 7-5
1969	Mrs P F Jones	Mrs L W King	3-6, 6-3, 6-2
1970	Mrs B M Court	Mrs L W King	14-12, 11-9
1971	Miss E F Goolagong	Mrs B M Court	6-4, 6-1
1972	Mrs L W King	Miss E F Goolagong	6-3, 6-3
1973	Mrs L W King	Miss C Evert	6-0, 7-5
1974	Miss C Evert	Miss O Morozova	6-0, 6-4
1975	Mrs L W King	Mrs E Cawley	6-0, 6-1
1976	Miss C Evert	Mrs E Cawley	6-3, 4-6, 8-6
1977	Miss V Wade	Miss B Stöve	4-6, 6-3, 6-1
1978	Miss M Navratilova	Miss C Evert	2-6, 6-4, 7-5

Women's Doubles

Full Championship event began

Date	Winners	Runners-up	Score
1913	Mrs R J McNair/ Miss D P Boothby	Mrs A Sterry/ Mrs Lambert Chambers	4-6, 2-4, retired
1914	Miss E Ryan/ Miss A M Morton	Mrs D R Larcombe/ Mrs Hannam	6-1, 6-3
1915–18	No Competition		
1919	Miss S Lenglen/ Miss E Ryan	Mrs Lambert Chambers/ Mrs D R Larcombe	4-6, 7-5, 6-3
1920	Miss S Lenglen/ Miss E Ryan	Mrs Lambert Chambers/ Mrs D R Larcombe	6-4, 6-0
1921	Miss S Lenglen/ Miss E Ryan	Mrs A E Beamish/ Mrs I E Peacock	6-1, 6-2
1922	Miss S Lenglen/ Miss E Ryan	Mrs A D Stocks/ Miss K McKane	6-0, 6-4
1923	Miss S Lenglen/ Miss E Ryan	Miss J Austin/ Miss E L Colyer	6-3, 6-1
1924	Mrs G W Wightman/ Miss H Wills	Mrs B C Covell/ Miss K McKane	6-4, 6-4
1925	Miss S Lenglen/ Miss E Ryan	Mrs A V Bridge/ Mrs C G McIlquham	6-2, 6-2
1926	Miss E Ryan/ Miss M K Browne	Miss L A Godfree/ Miss E L Colyer	6-1, 6-1
1927	Miss H Wills/ Miss E Ryan	Miss E L Heine/ Mrs I E Peacock	6-3, 6-2
1928	Mrs Holcroft-Watson/ Miss P Saunders	Miss E H Harvey/ Miss E B Bennett	6-2, 6-3
1929	Mrs Holcroft-Watson/ Mrs L R C Michell	Mrs B C Covell/ Mrs D C Shepherd-Barron	6-4, 8-6
1930	Mrs F S Moody/ Miss E Ryan	Miss S Cross/ Miss S Palfrey	6-2, 9-7
1931	Mrs D C Shepherd-Barron/	Miss D Metaxa/	

Date	Winners	Runners-up	Score
	Miss P E Mudford/	Miss J Sigart	3-6, 6-3, 6-4
1932	**Miss D Metaxa/**	Miss E Ryan/	
	Miss J Sigart	Miss H H Jacobs	6-4, 6-3
1933	**Mrs R Mathieu/**	Miss F James/	
	Miss E Ryan	Miss A M Yorke	6-2, 9-11, 6-4
1934	**Mrs R Mathieu/**	Mrs D Andrus/	
	Miss E Ryan	Mrs S Henrotin	6-3, 6-3
1935	**Miss F James/**	Mrs R Mathieu/	
	Miss K E Stammers	Mrs S Sperling	6-1, 6-4
1936	**Miss F James/**	Mrs S P Fabyan/	
	Miss K E Stammers	Miss H H Jacobs	6-2, 6-1
1937	**Mrs R Mathieu/**	Mrs M R King/	
	Miss A M Yorke	Mrs J B Pittman	6-3, 6-3
1938	**Miss S P Fabyan/**	Mrs R Mathieu/	
	Miss A Marble	Miss A M Yorke	6-2, 6-3
1939	**Mrs S P Fabyan/**	Miss H H Jacobs/	
	Miss A Marble	Miss A M Yorke	6-1, 6-0
1940–5	*No Competition*		
1946	**Miss A L Brough/**	Miss P M Betz/	
	Miss M E Osborne	Miss D J Hart	6-3, 2-6, 6-3
1947	**Miss D J Hart/**	Miss A L Brough/	
	Mrs P C Todd	Miss M E Osborne	3-6, 6-4, 7-5
1948	**Miss A L Brough/**	Miss D J Hart/	
	Mrs W duPont	Mrs P C Todd	6-3, 3-6, 6-3
1949	**Miss A L Brough/**	Miss G Moran/	
	Mrs W duPont	Mrs P C Todd	8-6, 7-5
1950	**Miss A L Brough/**	Miss S J Fry/	
	Mrs W duPont	Miss D J Hart	6-4, 5-7, 6-1
1951	**Miss S J Fry/**	Miss A L Brough/	
	Miss D J Hart	Mrs W duPont	6-3, 13-11
1952	**Miss S J Fry/**	Miss A L Brough/	
	Miss D J Hart	Miss M Connolly	8-6, 6-3
1953	**Miss S J Fry/**	Miss M Connolly/	
	Miss D J Hart	Miss J Sampson	6-0, 6-0
1954	**Miss A L Brough/**	Miss S J Fry/	
	Mrs W duPont	Miss D J Hart	4-6, 9-7, 6-3
1955	**Miss A Mortimer/**	Miss S J Bloomer/	
	Miss J A Shilcock	Miss P E Ward	7-5, 6-1
1956	**Miss A Buxton/**	Miss F Muller/	
	Miss A Gibson	Miss D G Seaney	6-1, 8-6
1957	**Miss A Gibson/**	Mrs K Hawton/	
	Miss D R Hard	Mrs T D Long	6-1, 6-2
1958	**Miss M E Bueno/**	Mrs W duPont/	
	Miss A Gibson	Miss M Varner	6-3, 7-5
1959	**Miss J Arth/**	Mrs J G Fleitz/	
	Miss D R Hard	Miss C Truman	2-6, 6-2, 6-3
1960	**Miss M E Bueno/**	Miss S Reynolds/	
	Miss D R Hard	Miss R Schuurman	6-4, 6-0
1961	**Miss K Hantze/**	Miss J Lehane/	
	Miss B J Moffitt	Miss M Smith	6-3, 6-4
1962	**Miss B J Moffitt/**	Mrs L E G Price/	
	Mrs J R Susman	Miss R Schuurman	5-7, 6-3, 7-5
1963	**Miss M E Bueno/**	Miss R A Ebbern/	
	Miss D R Hard	Miss M Smith	8-6, 9-7
1964	**Miss M Smith/**	Miss B J Moffitt/	
	Miss L R Turner	Mrs J R Susman	7-5, 6-2
1965	**Miss M E Bueno/**	Miss F Durr/	
	Miss B J Moffitt	Miss J Lieffrig	6-2, 7-5
1966	**Miss M E Bueno/**	Miss M Smith/	
	Miss N Richey	Miss J A M Tegart	6-3, 4-6, 6-4
1967	**Miss R Casals/**	Miss M E Bueno/	
	Mrs L W King	Miss N Richey	9-11, 6-4, 6-2

Open Championships began

Date	Winners	Runners-up	Score
1968	**Miss R Casals/**	Miss F Durr/	
	Mrs L W King	Mrs P F Jones	3-6, 6-4, 7-5
1969	**Mrs B M Court/**	Miss P S A Hogan/	
	Miss J A M Tegart	Miss M Michel	9-7, 6-2
1970	**Miss R Casals/**	Miss F Durr/	
	Mrs L W King	Miss S V Wade	6-2, 6-3
1971	**Miss R Casals/**	Mrs B M Court/	
	Mrs L W King	Miss E F Goolagong	6-3, 6-2
1972	**Mrs L W King/**	Mrs D E Dalton/	
	Miss B Stöve	Miss F Durr	6-2, 4-6, 6-3
1973	**Miss R Casals/**	Miss F Durr/	
	Mrs L W King	Miss B F Stöve	6-1, 4-6, 7-5
1974	**Miss E Goolagong/**	Miss H Gourlay/	
	Miss M Michel	Miss K Krantze	2-6, 6-4, 6-3
1975	**Miss A Kiyomura/**	Miss F Durr/	
	Miss K Sawamatsu	Miss B Stöve	7-5, 1-6, 7-5
1976	**Miss C Evert/**	Mrs L W King/	
	Miss M Navratilova	Miss B Stöve	6-1, 3-6, 7-5
1977	**Mrs E Cawley/**	Miss M Navratilova/	
	Miss J Russell	Miss B Stöve	6-3, 6-3
1978	**Mrs K Reid/**	Miss M Jausovec/	
	Miss W Turnbull	Miss V Ruzici	4-6, 9-8, 6-3

Mixed Doubles

Full Championship event began

Date	Winners	Runners-up	Score
1913	**H Crisp/**	J C Parke/	
	Mrs C O Tuckey	Mrs D R Larcombe	3-6, 5-3, retired
1914	**J C Parke/**	A F Wilding/	
	Mrs D R Larcombe	Miss M Broquedis	4-6, 6-4, 6-2
1915–18	*No Competition*		
1919	**R Lycett/**	A D Prebble/	
	Miss E Ryan	Mrs Lambert Chambers	6-0, 6-0
1920	**G L Patterson/**	R Lycett/	
	Miss S Lenglen	Miss E Ryan	7-5, 6-3
1921	**R Lycett/**	M Woosnam/	
	Miss E Ryan	Miss P L Howkins	6-3, 6-1
1922	**P O'Hara Wood/**	R Lycett/	
	Miss S Lenglen	Miss E Ryan	6-4, 6-3
1923	**R Lycett/**	L S Deane/	
	Miss E Ryan	Mrs D C Shepherd-Barron	6-4, 7-5
1924	**J B Gilbert/**	L A Godfree/	
	Miss K McKane	Mrs D C Shepherd-Barron	6-3, 3-6, 6-3
1925	**J Borotra/**	H L de Morpurgo/	
	Miss S Lenglen	Miss E Ryan	6-3, 6-3
1926	**L A Godfree/**	H O Kinsey/	
	Mrs L A Godfree	Miss M K Browne	6-3, 6-4
1927	**F T Hunter/**	L A Godfree/	
	Miss E Ryan	Mrs L A Godfree	8-6, 6-0
1928	**P D B Spence/**	J H Crawford/	
	Miss E Ryan	Miss D Akhurst	7-5, 6-4
1929	**F T Hunter/**	I G Collins/	
	Miss H Wills	Miss J Fry	6-1, 6-4
1930	**J H Crawford/**	D Prenn/	
	Miss E Ryan	Miss H Krahwinkel	6-1, 6-3
1931	**G M Lott/**	I G Collins/	
	Mrs L A Harper	Miss J C Ridley	6-3, 1-6, 6-1
1932	**E Maier/**	H C Hopman/	
	Miss E Ryan	Miss J Sigart	7-5, 6-2
1933	**G von Cramm/**	N G Farquharson/	
	Miss H Krahwinkel	Miss M Heeley	7-5, 8-6
1934	**R Miki/**	H W Austin/	
	Miss D E Round	Mrs D C Shepherd-Barron	3-6, 6-4, 6-0
1935	**F J Perry/**	H C Hopman/	
	Miss D E Round	Mrs H C Hopman	7-5, 4-6, 6-2
1936	**F J Perry/**	J D Budge/	
	Miss D E Round	Mrs S P Fabyan	7-9, 7-5, 6-4
1937	**J D Budge/**	Y Petra/	
	Miss A Marble	Mrs R Mathieu	6-4, 6-1
1938	**J D Budge/**	H Henkel/	
	Miss A Marble	Mrs S P Fabyan	6-1, 6-4
1939	**R L Riggs/**	F H D Wilde/	
	Miss A Marble	Miss N B Brown	7-9, 6-1
1940–45	*No Competition*		
1946	**T Brown/**	G E Brown/	
	Miss A L Brough	Miss D Bundy	6-4, 6-4
1947	**J E Bromwich/**	C F Long/	
	Miss A L Brough	Mrs N M Bolton	1-6, 6-4, 6-2
1948	**J E Bromwich/**	F A Sedgman/	
	Miss A L Brough	Miss D J Hart	6-2, 3-6, 6-3
1949	**E W Sturgess/**	J E Bromwich/	
	Mrs S P Summers	Miss A L Brough	9-7, 9-11, 7-5
1950	**E W Sturgess/**	G E Brown/	
	Miss A L Brough	Mrs P C Todd	11-9, 1-6, 6-4
1951	**F A Sedgman/**	M G Rose/	
	Miss D J Hart	Mrs N M Bolton	7-5, 6-2
1952	**F A Sedgman/**	E Morea/	
	Miss D J Hart	Mrs T D Long	4-6, 6-3, 6-4
1953	**E V Seixas/**	E Morea/	
	Miss D J Hart	Miss S J Fry	9-7, 7-5
1954	**E V Seixas/**	K R Rosewall/	
	Miss D J Hart	Mrs W duPont	5-7, 6-4, 6-3
1955	**E V Seixas/**	E Morea/	
	Miss D J Hart	Miss A L Brough	8-6, 2-6, 6-3
1956	**E V Seixas/**	G Mulloy/	
	Miss S J Fry	Miss A Gibson	2-6, 6-2, 7-5
1957	**M G Rose/**	N A Fraser/	
	Miss D R Hard	Miss A Gibson	6-4, 7-5
1958	**R N Howe/**	K Neilson/	
	Miss L Coghlan	Miss A Gibson	6-3, 13-11
1959	**R G Laver/**	N A Fraser/	
	Miss D R Hard	Miss M E Bueno	6-4, 6-3
1960	**R G Laver/**	R N Howe/	
	Miss D R Hard	Miss M E Bueno	13-11, 3-6, 8-6
1961	**F S Stolle/**	R N Howe/	
	Miss L R Turner	Miss E Buding	11-9, 6-2
1962	**N A Fraser/**	R D Ralston/	
	Mrs W duPont	Miss A S Haydon	2-6, 6-3, 13-11
1963	**K N Fletcher/**	R A J Hewitt/	
	Miss M Smith	Miss D R Hard	11-9, 6-4
1964	**F S Stolle/**	K N Fletcher/	
	Miss L R Turner	Miss M Smith	6-4, 6-4
1965	**K N Fletcher/**	A D Roche/	
	Miss M Smith	Miss J A M Tegart	12-10, 6-3
1966	**K N Fletcher/**	R D Ralston/	
	Miss M Smith	Mrs L W King	4-6, 6-3, 6-3

Date	Winners	Runners-up	Score
1967	**O K Davidson/**	K N Fletcher/	
	Mrs L W King	Miss M Bueno	7-5, 6-2

Open Championships began

1968	**K N Fletcher/**	A Metreveli/	
	Mrs B M Court	Miss O Morozova	6-1, 14-12
1969	**F S Stolle/**	A D Roche/	
	Mrs P F Jones	Miss J A M Tegart	6-2, 6-3
1970	**I Năstase/**	A Metreveli/	
	Miss R Casals	Miss O Morozova	6-3, 4-6, 9-7
1971	**O K Davidson/**	M C Riessen/	
	Mrs L W King	Mrs B M Court	3-6, 6-2, 15-13
1972	**I Năstase/**	K G Warwick/	
	Miss R Casals	Miss E F Goolagong	6-4, 6-4
1973	**O K Davidson/**	R Ramirez/	
	Mrs L W King	Miss J S Newberry	6-3, 6-2
1974	**O Davidson/**	M Farrell/	
	Mrs L W King	Miss L Charles	6-3, 9-7
1975	**M Riessen/**	A Stone/	
	Mrs M Court	Miss B Stöve	6-4, 7-5
1976	**A Roche/**	R Stockton/	
	Miss F Durr	Miss R Casals	6-3, 2-6, 7-5
1977	**R Hewitt/**	F McMillan/	
	Miss G Stevens	Miss B Stöve	3-6, 7-5, 6-4
1978	**F D McMillan/**	R O Ruffels/	
	Miss B F Stöve	Mrs L W King	6-2, 6-2

ABBREVIATIONS

ATA	American Tennis Association
ATP	Association of Tennis Professionals
FFLT	Fédération Française de Lawn Tennis
GP	Grand Prix
ILTF	International Lawn Tennis Federation
ITPA	International Tennis Players' Association
LTA	Lawn Tennis Association
LTC	Lawn Tennis Club
NTL	National Tennis League
USNLTA	United States National Lawn Tennis Association
USLTA	United States Lawn Tennis Association
USPTA	United States Professional Tennis Association
VITA	Veteran International Tennis Association
VS	Virginia Slims
WCT	World Championship Tennis
WITF	Women's International Tennis Federation
WTT	World Team Tennis
q/f	quarter-finals
r/u	runner-up
s/f	semi-finals
wo	walk over

BIBLIOGRAPHY AND ACKNOWLEDGEMENTS

The Encyclopaedia of Tennis, edited by Max Robertson (George Allen & Unwin)

100 Years of Tennis, by Lance Tingay (Guinness Superlatives Ltd)

Tennis – Its History, People and Events, by Will Grimsley (Prentice-Hall Inc, NJ)

Lawn Tennis Encyclopaedia, by Maurice Brady (David & Charles)

Wimbledon 1877–1977, by Max Robertson (Arthur Barker Ltd)

Tennis, Game of Motion, by Eugene Scott (Rutledge Books Inc, NY)

Tennis for Women (Rutledge Books Inc, NY)

Dunlop Lawn Tennis Annual series (J Burrow & Co)

Dawson's International Lawn Tennis Almanac series (Dawson's of Pall Mall)

World of Tennis series, BP Year Books (Macdonald and Jane's Ltd)

USLTA Year Book and Guide (H O Zimman Inc, Lynn, Mass)

Oxford Companion to Sports and Games, edited by John Arlitt (Oxford University Press)

The Concise Dictionary of Tennis was designed by Roy Williams and Charlton-Szyszkowski. The line drawings were compiled by Mr Peter Sedden.

All photographs in this volume were supplied by Le Roye Productions Limited of Kent England except for the following:

John Adams: 18, 36, 46, 63 (top right), 71 (top right), 72, 117 (top right), 125, 158, 159, 189 (top), 191, 225, 235

Roy Williams: 49, 54/55 (both), 106/107, 132/133, 134, 169, 170/171, 209, 210/211 (both), 250

Tennis World: 126, 142 (top right), 234 (top)

Peter Sedden: 51, 253, 255, 258

Author's collection: 80, 149 (top left), 161 (top right)

Thanks for assistance in the preparation of this book to the International Lawn Tennis Federation; Mr David Talbot, Tennis Correspondent of *The Birmingham Post*; Mr John Adams, Colourviews Ltd; Arthur Cole, Le Roye Productions; Miss Ann Wilson; Mrs Ellen Walker; and Mrs Pamela Hedges.